The Cervantes Encyclopedia

The Cervantes Encyclopedia

Volume I
A–K

Howard Mancing

GREENWOOD PRESS
Westport, Connecticut • London

Library of Congress Cataloging-in-Publication Data

Mancing, Howard, 1941–
    The Cervantes encyclopedia / Howard Mancing.
        p.   cm.
    Includes bibliographical references and index.
    Contents: v. 1. A–K—v. 2. L–Z.
    ISBN 0–313–30695–8 (set : alk. paper)—ISBN 0–313–32890–0 (v. 1 : alk. paper)—ISBN 0–313–32891–9
(v. 2 : alk. paper)
    1. Cervantes Saavedra, Miguel de, 1547–1616—Encyclopedias.   I. Title.
PQ6337.A2   2004
863'.3—dc21   2003054725

British Library Cataloguing in Publication Data is available.

Library of Congress Catalog Card Number: 2003054725
ISBN: 0–313–30695–8 (set)
        0–313–32890–0 (v.1)
        0–313–32891–9 (v.2)

First published in 2004

Greenwood Press, 88 Post Road West, Westport, CT 06881
An imprint of Greenwood Publishing Group, Inc.
www.greenwood.com

Printed in the United States of America

The paper used in this book complies with the
Permanent Paper Standard issued by the National
Information Standards Organization (Z39.48–1984).

10 9 8 7 6 5 4 3 2 1

❯❯• For Nancy, with love •❮❮

❧ Contents ❧

✈ Introduction ✦
Cervantes in Context

The goal of *The Cervantes Encyclopedia* is to place Miguel de Cervantes and his works in context—actually, in a series of contexts: historical, cultural, personal, literary, critical, textual, and intertextual. This work is intended for all readers of the works of Cervantes, whether they read in Spanish or in English. It is the first such work designed to be totally accessible to readers of English. In it, the reader will find entries of the following types:

- brief commentary on all known works written by Cervantes and a fairly detailed plot summary of each;

- virtually all the characters in Cervantes's works;

- historical personages of importance in the life and times of Cervantes;

- places and items of interest in Cervantes's life and works;

- names from history, myth, and literary works cited or alluded to in Cervantes's works;

- concepts and terms important to understanding the life, times, and works of Cervantes;

- most of the important episodes in *Don Quixote* and selected episodes from Cervantes's other works;

- authors and works of literature cited or alluded to in the works of Cervantes;

- important theories and theorists of the novel;

- many modern novelists and other writers inspired or influenced by Cervantes, especially by *Don Quixote*;

- some artists and musicians similarly inspired or influenced by Cervantes, especially by *Don Quixote*; and

- several of the more salient aspects of contemporary Cervantes scholarship and criticism.

My aim has been for comprehensiveness, but it is not possible to include everything that might conceivably be of interest to all readers. No attempt has been made, for example, to note every reference to the pantheon of the Christian hierarchy: God, Jesus, the Virgin Mary, and so forth. Similarly, no attempt has been made to cite all references to Nature, Love, Heaven, Fortune, or other commonplace personifications and/or allusions. Some common names or epithets are identified only in very brief form.

The coordination of English and Spanish has provided an interesting challenge. Since my own reading of all of Cervantes's works has been in Spanish, it is the Spanish version of names, geographical locations, concepts, titles, and terms that seems most natural to me. But since many readers of this work will not know Spanish, and for them many of these names or terms would be incomprehensible or unclear, it has been necessary to settle on a method of citation that both maintains the Spanish and is accessible to English speakers. After trying out several models, the one I have chosen is the following:

- All personal names that are Spanish in origin are kept in Spanish (with English versions provided in brackets when needed). Thus, for example, I cite Miguel, not Michael; Carlos, not Charles;

and Juan de la Cruz, not John of the Cross.

- Place names are cited in the form used in English (with Spanish versions provided in brackets when needed). Thus, I cite Algiers, not Argel; Castile, not Castilla; and Lisbon, not Lisboa.
- Fictional characters are listed under their first names but historical characters are listed under their last names, a frequent practice in works of this kind. Thus, I cite Sancho Panza (not Panza, Sancho) but Alemán, Mateo (not Mateo Alemán). A few characters are listed by their title when it is an inseparable part of their identity: Don Quixote, Cide Hamete Benengeli, Maese Pedro.
- Titles of works that are original in Spanish are cited in Spanish (with English translations in parentheses), whereas works from other languages are cited in their original (with English versions in parentheses when needed). Therefore, all the works of Cervantes are listed under their original Spanish title; for example, *Novelas ejemplares*, not *Exemplary Novels*. In every case, the English title is also listed separately, with a cross-reference to the Spanish original. The abbreviations I use throughout are also derived from the Spanish originals: *Fuerza* (*La fuerza de la sangre*), not *Power* (*The Power of Blood*).
- Common nouns and phrases are listed in English (with the Spanish provided in brackets and/or cross-referenced as necessary). So I have entries for honor, purity of blood, and romances of chivalry, with the Spanish terms (*honra*, *limpieza de sangre*, and *libros de caballerías*) cross-referenced.

Because English translations vary in the way they treat names, titles, terms, and concepts, I have made no attempt to include every possible English version for a Spanish title, name, or term. The title of *Don Quixote* alone can be—and has been—rendered in various ways in English. It would have been folly to attempt to include every known version of titles, names, places, terms, and concepts that have appeared in English. Therefore, I have arbitrarily chosen one translation for each of Cervantes's works (see final bibliography) to use as a reference for English versions:

- the Ormsby, Jones, and Douglas translation of *Don Quixote*;
- the Ife et al. translation of *Novelas ejemplares*;
- the Weller and Colahan translation of *Los trabajos de Persiles y Sigismunda*;
- the Smith translation of the *Entremeses*; and
- for the most part, my own translations for *La Galatea* and Cervantes's theater and poetry, which tend not to be available in recent translations in English.

Note, however, that passages of text from Cervantes's works cited in English are not taken from these translations. No single translation always captures the precise nuances I want to stress, so all translations throughout this encyclopedia are my own and enclosed in single quotation marks, although I have also consulted various translations at various times. (Translations from English or published translations are enclosed in double quotation marks.)

Spelling variants can also be a problem. Since there was no official standard for spelling in Renaissance Spain, names and terms often appeared in multiple variations: Mexía-Mejía, José-Josef-Iosef, Valdivielso-Valdivieso; and *dijo-dixo, tasa-tassa, viaje-viage*. The name *Cervantes* is documented in the following forms: Cerbantes, Cervante, Cervantes, Serbantes, Servantes, Zervantes. Since certain forms of writing were regularized after Cervantes's day, I have attempted consistently to use the modern form. Thus, for example, Cervantes wrote *Quixote*, pronounced kee-*sho*-tay—which is why the French spelling is *Quichotte* and the Italian is *Chisciotte*, both closer in pronunciation (as is, for that matter, the English *Quixote*: Quick-sot). But in the eighteenth century, the Royal Spanish Academy (founded in 1714) determined that after the sibilant shift of the seventeenth century, in which the pronunciation of words with an *x* shifted to a harder *j* sound, all words with *x* would henceforth be written with a *j*. So, today in Spanish the correct form of the name is *Quijote*, pronounced kee-*ho*-tay. (This is also why many Spaniards write *Méjico*, whereas Mexicans, proudly asserting their independence by retaining the original spelling, insist on *México*, even though the pronunciation is the same.)

Titles and important concepts have also proven vexing. Titles such as *don* or *cadí* mean things in Spanish that no single equivalent word in English could convey; therefore, they have been maintained throughout, and each has a separate entry in which they are described and/or defined in ways that I think will be helpful to non-Spanish readers. Similarly, there are terms used throughout the works of Cervantes that have no simple, direct English equivalent. Examples are *pícaro*, *hidalgo*, and *dueña*. Spanish terms such as these are used throughout the body of the encyclopedia and also described in separate entries.

Likewise, bibliographies have provided special challenges. I have included at the end of many entries a minimal bibliography of one or more (depending on the length of the entry and the quantity and quality of bibliography available) critical books and/or essays. Such a selection is, by definition, arbitrary (but not capricious), and I can only hope to give the reader an orientation in a search for more information about the entry. The same is true of the bibliography at the end of the encyclopedia; the works included there are but a selection of what is available. Over 100 scholarly studies are published each year on Cervantes and his works, and no attempt has been made to be inclusive. I have chosen to place emphasis on more recent works (sometimes at the expense of classic essays) and on works in English and Spanish (sometimes at the expense of important works in other languages). Because the production of Cervantes scholarship is so great, important new studies will have appeared while this work is in the process of being printed. Within a few years, the bibliographies included

here will begin to appear deficient. Certainly within a decade or so, they will be dated and of limited use.

One reason for the emphasis on English is that I assume that many users of this reference work will not know Spanish, and I have wanted to make the fruits of scholarship available to them. Anyone who speaks and reads Spanish and is consulting this work obviously also reads English, and thus has an advantage over the monolingual English speaker who needs more help. For this reason, I have attempted to provide both Spanish and English equivalents whenever possible, or to explain and/or translate important Spanish terms.

Furthermore, there already exists an excellent *Enciclopedia cervantina* in Spanish, by Juan Bautista Avalle-Arce. The present work was conceived and begun about the time Avalle-Arce's encyclopedia was published (1997), but I was not aware of his work until 2000, well after my project was underway. I have profited immensely from the availability of Avalle-Arce's encyclopedia, consulting it on innumerable occasions to verify my own work and answer questions that had arisen. These two compilations are similar in several ways, but are also radically different in others. Avalle-Arce, for example, does not have to deal with problems of English translations; he cites far more frequently and extensively than I do from the texts of Cervantes's works; he devotes more attention to detailed facets of Cervantes scholarship, especially the historical and textual, than I do, but he does not include bibliographies; he includes more information on works attributed to Cervantes than I do; he dedicates less space than I do to theorists of the novel and modern writers who have been influenced by Cervantes; he does not need to devote as much space to explanations of commonly known aspects of Spanish culture of the Renaissance—such as *desengaño*, *hidalgo*, and *honra*—as I do; he identifies and comments on all original poems and foreign phrases included within the prose works, whereas I do not; and he does not include entries for members of Cervantes's family, friends, and associates, but I do. Other important reference works on Cervantes have also proven valuable to me, none more than César Vidal's *Enciclopedia del Quijote* (1999). Overall, the three encyclopedias complement each other, I believe, and provide readers with options not available just a short time ago. (After this encyclopedia had been completed and was in the early stages of production, I learned of the projected 2005 publication of a 10-volume *Gran enciclopedia cervantina [Great Cervantes Encyclopedia]*, a collaborative effort sponsored by the Centro de Estudios Cervantinos and directed by Carlos Alvar. This enormous work will undoubtedly enrich the resources available to both scholars and other interested readers of the works of Cervantes.)

In addition to these specific Cervantes reference tools and others of a similar nature, I have drawn extensively from a large number of encyclopedias, dictionaries, and other reference works; annotated editions of Cervantes's works; critical and interpretive books and essays on Cervantes; biographies of Cervantes; dictionaries and histories of literature; historical studies; and even maps and tourist guides. I have made no attempt to cite all of these works in the bibliography.

It is important to call attention to a major theoretical assumption that I have employed in this work. I do not conceive of the elements of literature—authors, characters, and historical and geographical references—as mere signs and/or manifestations of language, nor do I treat the writings of Cervantes as self-referential, free-floating, decontextualized texts. In other words, I do not deal with Cervantes's works as would most structuralists, semioticians, or poststructuralists. I believe that it is legitimate (even necessary) to consider authorial intentions (as best we can infer them) as being of interest and often helpful, but never as absolutely authoritative. I assume that texts often refer to versions of historical and social reality. Most importantly, I treat characters as versions of people rather than as sign systems.

Throughout, I employ what in cognitive psychology is known as *Theory of Mind* (ToM): the folk-psychology assumption that other people have minds that function much as mine does; that people (including fictional versions of people) are motivated (they want, hope, remember, need, feel, and so forth) much as I would be in most situations; that authors (who have their own intentions and ToM) attribute a ToM to their characters and that readers must have such a theory in order to understand characters and plots. (For an introduction to the subject, see Sanjida O'Connell, *Mindreading: An Investigation into How We Learn to Love and Lie* [New York: Doubleday, 1998].)

Finally, I have gone to considerable length in including entries for writers subsequent to Cervantes who have been influenced by, or found inspiration in, his work, or who have written works comparable in important ways to *Don Quixote* and other works by Cervantes. Such entries make up, I believe, the most original and innovative contribution of this encyclopedia. Thus, there are hundreds of entries for what I call *quixotic novels*—imitations of and sequels to *Don Quixote*, and novels with quixotic characters, themes, and techniques—along with a variety of recastings, versions, and adaptations of *Don Quixote* and other works by Cervantes. I have done this because I believe that this very large body of creative work is one of the most important testimonies to the continuing presence (often unrecognized or unappreciated, when not denied) of Cervantes in the world today. Although I hope that this is the most extensive compilation ever made of such works, it is very far from complete. Emphasis throughout has been placed on works written in Spanish and English, and on works of fiction (novels and short stories), as opposed to dramatic works and poetry (and with very few works written primarily for children, a subject that deserves separate study). Entries are of necessity brief and schematic, often pointing out only the obvious. I have also included entries for some artists and musicians who have made graphic and musical interpretations of Don Quixote and other Cervantes characters, but have only scratched the surface in these domains, where much work remains to be done. In many ways, the real beginning of this encyclopedia project was in the spring of 1974, when I first began to read extensively works of fiction from all times and places with the explicit aim of noting any possible similarities to *Don Quixote*. My notes from nearly three decades of such reading have proven invaluable in the current project.

If readers of the works of Cervantes find this encyclopedia useful, it will have fulfilled its purpose. Certainly the labor of compiling it has proven of immense value to me, as I now appreciate Cervantes's subtlety in ways that had previously escaped me.

Finally, I want to thank the scholars, colleagues, students, and friends who have kindly and perceptively read parts of this encyclopedia and/or responded to my inquiries about specific details. Their generous assistance has been invaluable and has saved me from a number of embarrassing mistakes, inconsistencies, and ambiguities. Not all of them have agreed with some of my understandings of the works or my treatment of some of the material, and most often I have followed their suggestions, but occasionally have (at my own peril) ignored their comments and continued in my own way. All errors or inconsistencies, as well as dubious interpretations, that remain are entirely my own.

Special thanks goes first of all to Charles Ganelin, who has accompanied me throughout this project, reading, commenting, correcting, advising, and encouraging. Charles is the sort of colleague and friend who makes life much richer. I am indebted to some students and colleagues who have given assistance on certain specific matters: Rachel Bauer, Heidi Herron, Richard King, Paula Levinger, and Dan Eisenberg. Kristyn Kapetanovic, a Dean's Freshman Scholar, has worked with me on cataloguing

hundreds of works written in the wake of Cervantes. Several of my Purdue colleagues have given me advice in areas of their special linguistic and cultural expertise: Zena Breschinsky, John Kirby, Herb Rowland, and Allen Wood. A number of Cervantes and Golden Age specialists read and commented on sections of an early version of the manuscript, and their corrections, comments, suggestions, questions, and recommendations have proven invaluable: David Castillo, Catherine Connor, Dominick Finello, Dian Fox, Bob Fiore, Ed Friedman, Charles Ganelin, Fred Jehle, Carolyn Nadeau, Theresa Rosenhagen, George Shipley, and Marcia Welles. Diana de Armas Wilson, as consultant reader for Greenwood Press, was the first person to read the entire manuscript; her corrections, comments, suggestions, and advice have also proven invaluable. Paul Dixon, head of the Department of Foreign Languages and Literatures at Purdue University, went out of his way to help with the printing and copying of this very long and complicated manuscript. A very special word of thanks goes to Suzanne Ward, head of Access Services, and other members of the Interlibrary Loan staff of the libraries of Purdue University. They managed to secure for me a surprisingly large number of the several hundred interlibrary loan requests I flooded them with; this encyclopedia would have been very different without their dedicated efforts. And, above all, thanks to Nancy—for her occasional help with reference and in proofreading, of course, but mostly for her loving support, infinite patience, and good humor throughout the long gestation of this book.

Abbreviations

Adjunta	Adjunta al Parnaso		**Española**	La española inglesa
Amante	El amante liberal		**Fregona**	La ilustre fregona
Baños	Los baños de Argel		**Fuerza**	La fuerza de la sangre
ca.	Circa; about		**Galatea**	La Galatea
Capitán	El capitán cautivo; the autobiographical narrative of Ruy Pérez de Viedma in DQ I, 39–41		**Gallardo**	El gallardo español
			Gitanilla	La gitanilla
			Guarda	La guarda cuidadosa
Cardenio	The complex story of Cardenio, Dorotea, Fernando, and Luscinda that occupies parts of DQ I, 23–36		**Juez**	El juez de los divorcios
			Laberinto	El laberinto de amor
Casa	La casa de los celos y selvas de Ardenia		**MC**	Miguel de Cervantes
			Novelas	Novelas ejemplares
Casamiento	El casamiento engañoso		**Numancia**	La Numancia
Celoso	El celoso extremeño		**Parnaso**	El viaje del Parnaso
CHB	Cide Hamete Benengeli		**Pedro**	Pedro de Urdemalas
Coloquio	El coloquio de los perros		**Persiles**	Los trabajos de Persiles y Sigismunda
Comedias	Ocho comedias y ocho entremeses		**Poesías**	Poesías sueltas: 1–35
Cornelia	La señora Cornelia		**Retablo**	El retablo de las maravillas
Cueva	La cueva de Salamanca		**Rinconete**	Rinconete y Cortadillo
Curioso	El curioso impertinente (in DQ I, 33–35)		**Rufián**	El rufián dichoso
			Semanas	Semanas del jardín
Doncellas	Las dos doncellas		**SP**	Sancho Panza, the character from DQ
DQ	Don Quijote, the character in DQ		**SPA**	Sancho Panza, the character from DQA
DQ	Don Quijote (Partes I + II)			
DQ I	Don Quijote Parte I (1605)		**Sultana**	La gran sultana
DQ II	Don Quijote Parte II (1615)		**Tía**	La tía fingida
DQA	Don Quijote, the character in DQA		**Tratos**	Los tratos de Argel
DQA	Don Quijote, Avellaneda's sequel to MC's DQ I		**Vidriera**	El licenciado vidriera
			Viejo	El viejo celoso
DT	Dulcinea del Toboso		**Viudo**	El rufián viudo
Elección	La elección de los alcaldes de Daganzo		**Vizcaíno**	El vizcaíno fingido
Entretenida	La entretenida			

⚘ Chronology ⚘

1547   Sept. 29 (probable); Saint Michael's day. MC, son of Rodrigo de Cervantes, a surgeon, and his wife Leonor de Cortinas, is born in Alcalá de Henares.

Oct. 9. MC is baptized in the church of Santa María la Mayor in Alcalá.

1551   March or April. MC's family moves to Valladolid.

1553   MC's family, destitute, returns to Alcalá for a while before moving to Córdoba, home of MC's grandfather Juan de Cervantes.

1564   MC's family moves to Seville.

1566   MC's family moves to Madrid.

1568   MC is a student in the school directed by Juan López de Hoyos.

1569   MC's first published works, four poems, appear in a volume of poetry edited by López de Hoyos on the occasion of the death of Queen Isabel de Valois.

September 15. A royal order is issued for the arrest of MC, last known to be in Seville, for having wounded one Antonio de Sigura in a clash of arms. MC is to be returned to Madrid and have his right hand severed; if he survives this punishment, he is to be banished from the kingdom for ten years.

MC arrives in Rome late in the year.

1570   MC enters the personal service of Cardinal Giulio Acquaviva in Rome.

1570 or 71   MC enlists in the Spanish army in Naples.

1571   Oct. 7. MC participates in the battle of Lepanto, where, in spite of being ill and having a high fever, he fights valiantly and receives three wounds, two in the chest and one that results in the loss (or crippling) of his left hand.

1572   MC participates in expeditions against the Turks in Navarinon and Modon.

1573   MC participates in a military expedition to Tunis and La Goleta.

1575   Sept. 26. Returning to Spain on the galley *Sol*, MC and his brother Rodrigo are taken prisoner by Barbary pirates and held for ransom in Algiers.

1576   MC makes his first unsuccessful attempt to escape captivity.

1577   Rodrigo is ransomed and returns to Spain.

MC makes his second unsuccessful escape attempt.

1578   MC makes his third unsuccessful escape attempt.

1579   MC makes his fourth unsuccessful escape attempt.

1580   September 19. As MC is about to be taken to Constantinople, he is ransomed by Trinitarian friars for the sum of 500 *escudos*.

October 10. MC has sworn statements taken from 12 witnesses about his conduct during his years in captivity.

October 24. MC departs for Spain. He lives for a month in Valencia before going to the Court in Madrid to look for work.

1581	MC is briefly in Lisbon and then carries out a diplomatic mission to Oran.
	MC initiates his career as a dramatist in Madrid.
1582	February 17. MC applies for a position in New Spain (Mexico), but his application is denied.
1584	MC's love affair with Ana Franca de Rojas results in the birth of his only child, Isabel de Saavedra.
	MC receives some 1336 *reales* from book merchant Blas de Robles for the right to print *Galatea*.
	December 12. MC marries Catalina de Palacios in her home town of Esquivias.
1585	The first (and only) part of *Galatea* is published.
	MC signs a contract with Gaspar de Porres to write two plays.
	June. MC's father dies.
1586	MC joins the Imitative Academy, the first literary salon in Madrid.
1587	MC receives an appointment as a royal commissary in Andalusia requisitioning oil and grain for the upcoming expedition of the Armada against England.
	MC is excommunicated twice, in Ecija and Castro del Río.
1588	MC writes his two poems on the subject of the Armada.
1590	May 21. MC again applies for a position in America, either in Colombia, Guatemala, or Bolivia.
	June 6. His petition is denied.
1592	MC is held under charges of fraud for his professional activities. He is jailed briefly in Castro del Río before being declared innocent and set free.
	September 15. MC signs a contract with Rodrigo Osorio to provide him with six plays.
1593	MC's mother dies.

1594	MC returns to Madrid and soon assumes the position as tax collector in Andalusia.
1595	MC deposits some tax monies with a businessman in Seville, but the man goes bankrupt and absconds with the funds; as a result, MC receives a legal citation and must exert considerable effort to clear his name.
1597	MC is jailed in Seville for debts.
1598	April. MC is released from jail.
	MC writes the sonnet to the tomb of Felipe II and recites it in the Cathedral of Seville, causing a scandal.
1600	MC's brother Rodrigo dies in battle in Flanders.
1604	MC moves to Valladolid, where the Court now resides, to live with his wife Catalina, his daughter Isabel, his sisters Magdalena and Andrea, and his niece Constanza.
	MC finishes *DQ* I and begins the process of publication.
1605	*DQ* I is published and receives wide recognition.
	June. Gaspar de Ezpeleta is murdered in the entryway of the building where MC and his family live. They are jailed for a day as part of the investigation of the murder. The records indicate that at least some of the women with whom MC is living have less than admirable reputations.
1606	MC moves to Madrid when the Court is relocated there.
1609	MC joins the Brotherhood of the Slaves of the Most Holy Sacrament, a religious order whose members also include Lope de Vega and Francisco de Quevedo.
	MC is not invited to accompany the newly appointed Count of Lemos and an illustrious group of writers to Naples.
	MC's sister Andrea dies.

1611	MC's sister Magdalena dies.	**1615**	October. *Comedias* is published.
1612	The first translation of *DQ*, Thomas Shelton's version in English, is published.		November. *DQ* II is published.
		1616	March. MC finishes *Persiles*.
1613	*Novelas* is published.		April 2. MC takes his final vows in the Third Order of Saint Francis.
	MC joins the Third Order of Saint Francis.		April 18. Last rites are administered to MC.
1614	*Parnaso* is published.		April 23. MC dies of dropsy (diabetes) and is buried in the Trinitarian Monastery in Madrid.
	DQA is published.		
	The first French translation of *DQ*, by César Oudin, is published.	**1617**	*Persiles* is published by MC's widow.

A

A lo divino [In a religious way]. An adaptation or imitation of a popular secular work for religious purposes, a common practice in the Spanish Renaissance. Thus one could, for example, read Jorge de *Montemayor's best-selling pastoral romance *La Diana*, a work predictably censured by moralists as being licentious and corrupting of the morals of young women, in the "new and improved" version of Fray Bartolomé Ponce entitled *Clara Diana a lo divino* (1599; *Illustrious Diana in the Religious Way*). Alonso de Soria's *Historia y milicia cristiana del caballero Peregrino* (1601; *History and Christian Campaign of the Pilgrim Knight*), a book MC probably knew and which may have exerted some influence on *DQ*, is perhaps the best-known romance of chivalry *a lo divino*; it is a kind of pre-Bunyan allegory. Even the lyric poetry of *Garcilaso de la Vega underwent this sort of spiritual sanitizing for the moral good of the faithful. This curious fundamentalist movement to divinize literature is a reflection of the traditional belief that good Christians should never read anything except uplifting moral and religious works.

Bibliography: Bruce W. Wardropper, *Historia de la poesía lírica a lo divino en la cristiandad occidental* (Madrid: Revista de Occidente, 1958).

Abacú; Abacuc. *Habacuc.

Abad de Santa Sofía. *Colonna, Ascanio.

Abarca, Don Diego. A Spanish nobleman and occasional poet praised in *Parnaso* 4.

Abaurre y Mesa, José. Spanish writer. Abaurre's *Historia de varios sucesos ocurridos en la aldea después de la muerte del ingenioso hidalgo Don Quijote de la Mancha* (two vols.,

1901; *History of Various Events that Took Place in the Village after the Death of the Ingenious Hidalgo Don Quixote de la Mancha*) is one of the more interesting sequels to *DQ*. In the first volume, Sansón Carrasco begins to feel remorse for his role in bringing about the death of DQ. He has long conversations about the matter with the priest, Pero Pérez, and begins to contemplate taking up arms in imitation of DQ, as a sort of homage to the great man. Meanwhile, word arrives that the duke and duchess have heard of the death of DQ and are planning to come to the village to pay their respects to the deceased. This worries Sansón all the more, as he fears that the duke might take revenge on him for what he has done. In the second volume, Sansón sallies forth as the Knight of the White Moon, accompanied by Pedro Alonso (from *DQ* I, 5), as his squire. He meets and talks with Alvaro Tarfe (from *DQ* II, 72) and two friends from *DQA* about the relative merits, reality, and authenticity of the two DQs. The duke and duchess arrive, and Alvaro Tarfe and his friends also go to the village. After the requisite conversations among all involved, including DQ's niece Antonia, SP, Teresa, and Sanchica, a memorial service for DQ is held in the local church. During the ceremony, Sansón arrives, sees a newly unveiled statue of DQ, and collapses from his horse and dies: he pays the ultimate price for having killed DQ. What is relatively attractive about this novel is that it avoids the magical resurrection of DQ, his generally silly adventures in modern times, the absurd world travels of the characters, and the heavy-handed political message that are characteristic of most *DQ* sequels.

Bibliography: José Abaurre y Mesa *Historia de varios sucesos ocurridos en la aldea después de la*

muerte del ingenioso hidalgo Don Quijote de la Mancha, 2 vols. (Madrid: Sucesores de Rivadeneyra, 1901).

Abbot of Santa Sofía. *Colonna, Ascanio.

ABC entero. *Alphabet.

Abd al-Malik (1541–78). Sultan of Morocco. He married *Zahara, the daughter of *Hadji Murad and model for *Zoraida in *Capitán*, had one child by her, and died in the battle of Alcazarquivir. He was the model for the character *Muley Maluco in *Baños*.

Abencerraje y la hermosa Jarifa, El (The Abencerraje and the Beautiful Jarifa). Perhaps the most important piece of original short fiction written in Spain before MC's *Novelas*. Of uncertain authorship, it appeared several times in the mid-sixteenth century, most notably in the 1561 edition of Jorge de *Montemayor's *La Diana* and in Antonio de *Villegas's *Inventario* (finished by 1551 but not published until 1556; *Inventory*). It is the first example of the minor genre of the *Moorish novel, a romantic idealization of Muslim life and customs in medieval Spain. Betrothed to the beautiful Jarifa, the valiant Abindarráez, of the Abercerraje clan, is defeated in combat by the brave and virtuous Christian knight Rodrigo de Narváez. When Narváez learns that his noble rival is to be married, he releases him for three days on his word to return after the consummation of his marriage. Abindarráez does return at the appointed time, but with his beloved Jarifa, whose beauty and grace help convince Narváez to give both of the noble Muslims their freedom. The beautifully written story presents a positive, idealized vision of the nobility of the long-time religious enemies of the Spanish Christians, and represents an important step in the rewriting of Spanish cultural history. Traditional medieval and Renaissance themes of fortune, nobility, beauty, honor, and duty combine in a harmonious tale of valor and romance. The story was quite popular both in Spain and throughout Europe into the nineteenth century. In *DQ* I, 5, after his beating by the Toledan merchants, DQ is encountered by a neighbor,

Pedro Alonso, who takes him home to rest. The delirious DQ insists to Alonso that he is Abindarráez (and other heroes of the ballad tradition), ironically insisting 'I know who I am' at the only time in the novel when he claims multiple identities. See also *Celoso*.

Bibliography: María Soledad Carrasco Urgoiti, *The Moorish Novel:"El Abencerraje" and Pérez de Hita* (Boston: Twayne, 1976); Francisco López Estrada, ed., *"El Abencerraje": Novela y romancero* (Madrid: Cátedra, 1987); George A. Shipley, "La obra literaria como monumento histórico: El caso de *El Abencerraje*," *Journal of Hispanic Philology* 2 (1978): 103–20; and Begona Souviron López, "*El Abencerraje* en el templo de Diana," *Revista de Literatura* 61 (1999): 5–17.

Abila. *Djebel Musa.

Abindarráez. *Abencerraje y la hermosa Jarifa, El*.

Abiram [Abirón]. In the Old Testament, a Reubenite who, with his brother Dathan, conspired against Moses. See *Baños* 2.

Abispones. *Hornets.

Abiud. In *Persiles* IV, 3, one of the Jews who greets Periandro and the other pilgrims upon their arrival in Rome.

Abraham [Abrahán]. In the Old Testament, the first patriarch and ancestor of the Hebrews. He was especially known for his unswerving loyalty to God, even to the extent of being willing to sacrifice his son Isaac on command, and his longevity (he supposedly lived for some 175 years). See *Persiles* III, 5; *Poesías* 20.

Abramovitsh, Sholem Yankev (1835–1917). Yiddish novelist and short-story writer. His short novel *Kitser masoes Binyomin hashlishi* (1878; translated as *The Brief Travels of Benjamin the Third*) is a Yiddish version of *DQ*. In the story, the relationship between the quixotic Benjamin and his SP-like companion, Sendrel, is that of a homosexual marriage. Their travels and adventures in eastern Europe bring them into constant contact with anti-Semitic and homophobic realities. Abramovitsh's tale is a satire of the (quixotic) shtetl Jews, whose obsession with story-telling based on tales from the Bible hampered, in the author's opinion, their ability to deal with reality. The rustic Benjamin and Sendrel are the incarnation of this literary obsession, and they determine to travel to Israel in order to locate the living descendants of the mythical lost tribes. The narrative structure of the novella features Mendele, a sarcastic and ironic CHB-like author/narrator who is found in most of Abramovitsh's fictions.

Bibliography: S. Y. Abramovitsh, *Tales of Mendele the Book Peddler: Fishke the Lame and Benjamin the Third*, ed. Dan Miron and Ken Frieden (New York: Schocken Books, 1996); and Leah Garrett, "The Jewish *Don Quixote*," *Cervantes* 17, no. 2 (1997): 94–105.

Abravanel (or Abarbanel), Judas. *Hebreo, Léon.

Absalom [Absalón]. In the Old Testament, the son of King David, famous for his physical beauty. While fleeing the servants of David, he got his hair caught in a tree and died hanging there. See *Celoso*; *Pedro* 1.

Academia de Atenas. *Academy of Athens.

Academia de los Entronados. *Academy of the Enthroned.

Academia de los Imitadores; Academia Imitatoria. *Imitative Academy.

Academia de los Nocturnos. *Academy of the Night Revelers.

Academia de los Ociosos. *Academy of the Idle.

Academia del Parnaso (Academia Selvaje). *Academy of Parnassus (Savage Academy).

Academia Ochoa. *Ochoa Academy.

Academias literarias. *Literary Academies.

Academicians of Argamasilla [Académicos de la Argamasilla]. *DQ* I, 52, ends with six burlesque poems supposedly written by the members of a literary academy in the small town of *Argamasilla. This is a parody of the *literary academies popular in MC's Spain. In such academies, the members and participants often took burlesque names for themselves. MC parodies this custom by naming his academicians Monicongo (inhabitant of the Congo in Africa), Paniaguado (Protégé; literally, one whose bread [*pan*] and water [*agua*] are provided by someone else), Caprichoso (Capricious), Burlador (Trickster), Cachidiablo (Hobgoblin; but also the name of an Algerian pirate in the sixteenth century), and Tiquitoc (Tick-Tock).

Bibliography: Francisco Márquez Villanueva, "El mundo literario de los académicos de la Argamasilla," in *Trabajos y días cervantinos* (Alcalá de Henares, Spain: Centro de Estudios Cervantinos, 1995), 115–55.

Academy of Athens [Academia de Atenas]. The school founded in a sylvan grove around 380 BCE by Plato, which has become the model and forerunner of the modern university. The Academy was destroyed by the Roman general Sulla in his sack of Athens in 86 BCE, although the site remained as a school until the sixth century CE, when it was shut down permanently by Justinian, the Christian emperor of Rome. See *DQ* II, 18.

Academy of Parnassus (Savage Academy) [Academia del Parnaso (Academia Selvaje)]. *Literary academy established by Don Francisco de Silva y Mendoza in Madrid in 1612, which included MC among its members. In a letter dated in March of that year, Lope de *Vega relates the anecdote that at one meeting of the academy he borrowed MC's reading glasses (which, he writes, made his eyes look "like badly fried eggs") in order to see well enough to read one of his poems.

Academy of the Enthroned [Academia de los Entronados]: Academia degli Intronati. The first of the great Italian *literary academies established in Siena in 1525; it lasted until 1751. See *Persiles* III, 19.

Academy of the Idle [Academia de los Ociosos]. *Literary academy set up by the Count of Lemos in Naples for the retinue of Spanish writers who accompanied him when he became viceroy of that Spanish possession in 1611. The leading figures were the *Argensola brothers. When MC was denied a spot in the retinue, he lost an opportunity to form part of the membership of this academy. His resentment is made apparent in his comments in *Parnaso* 3.

Academy of the Night Revelers [Academia de los Nocturnos]. *Literary academy established in Valencia in the 1590s. This was one of the most active and famous of the Spanish academies of the Renaissance, especially outside of Madrid, with such illustrious participants as Guillén de *Castro, Andrés *Rey de Artieda, Francisco de *Tárrega, and others.

Bibliography: José María Ferri Coll, *La poesía de la Academia de los Nocturnos* (Alicante, Spain: Universidad de Alicante, 2001).

Aceca Ferry [Barca de Aceca]. A crossing place over the Tagus River east of Toledo. See *Fregona*.

Acevedo, Doctor Alonso de (ca. 1550–ca. 1620). Spanish priest and poet. He is the author of the epic poem *La creación del mundo* (1615; *The Creation of the World*) and other lyrics published in Italy. Acevedo is cited by Cervantes in *Parnaso* 8 as the first person he meets, and who greets him in Italian, upon his return to Madrid after the trip to Parnassus.

Acheron [Aqueronte]. In Greek myth, one of the four rivers of the underworld. Whoever crossed over could never cross back; in other words, once dead one could never return to life. See *Casa* 1.

Achilles [Aquiles]. In Greek myth, the greatest soldier in the Greek army of Agamemnon during the Trojan war. His mother, Thetis, dressed him as a woman so that he would not have to take part in the battle. But the wily Odysseus discovered the trick when he placed arms in front of the youth and Achilles instinc-

tively reached for them, thus revealing his masculine nature. His greatest accomplishment was to kill the Trojan hero Hector. See *Amante*; *DQ* I, 32, 47, 49; *Entretenida* 3.

Achilles Tatius (second century CE). Greek rhetorician and romance writer. His popular romance *Leucippe and Cleitophon* is a typical adventure story with impossible escapes and brushes with death. It was translated into Spanish in 1617, the same year in which MC's adventure tale *Persiles* was published.

Achish [Aquís]. In the Old Testament, the king of Geth, who took in the fleeing King David. See *Parnaso* 8.

Acker, Kathy (1948–97). American punk novelist. Acker, a student of the classics, consistently selected canonical works and authors as pretexts and intertexts for her own irreverent, obscene, and outrageously satirical fictions. In no case is this more true than in her novel *Don Quixote* (1986). The first of the three sections of the novel is a sustained paraphrasing, adaptation, recontextualization, and playful reproduction of the opening chapters of *DQ* I (with a few allusions to *DQ* II). The protagonist's equation of abortion with quixotic madness, the self-referential word play (catheter / Kathy; hack / Acker), the vision of men as evil giants, a speaking dog as squire, the reference to Amandia of Gaul, and much more make this part of the novel one of the most outlandish of all quixotic fictions.

Bibliography: Sylvia Söderlind, "Love and Reproduction: Plagiarism, Pornography, and Don Quixote's Abortions," in *Signs of Change*, ed. Stephen Baker (Albany: State University of New York Press, 1996), 247–59; and Richard Walsh, "The Quest for Love and the Writing of Female Desire in Kathy Acker's *Don Quixote*," *Critique* 32 (1991): 149–68.

Acorns [Bellotas]. After DQ and SP are hosted by the goatherds in I, 11, the knight picks up a handful of acorns (mentioned in Ovid's evocation of the Golden Age in the *Metamorphoses*) and uses them as a reminder of the past when nature generously provided for all of people's needs. Rather than what we tend to think of as acorns, the seeds of oak trees, which are usually eaten only by pigs, the *bellotas* served by the goatherds may have been ilex nuts, the fruit of the evergreen (or holm) oak.

Acosta, José María de (1882–1936). Spanish novelist. Acosta's novel *Amor loco y amor cuerdo* (1920; *Crazy Love and Wise Love*) is a literary satire that features Don Perfecto Pérez y Pérez, called Don Persiles for his studies of *Persiles* and other works by or attributed to MC. He has written a book called *Las diversas letras del abecedario en el "Quijote"* (*The Various Letters of the Alphabet in "Don Quixote"*), a monumental eight-volume work that cost him over a dozen years of continual and indefatigable labor. At the age of 40, Don Perfecto falls in love with a farm woman and compares himself with DQ in love with DT. The entire book is filled with references to, citations from, and other evocations of *DQ*, *Persiles*, and other works by MC.

Bibliography: José María de Acosta, *Amor loco y amor cuerdo* (Madrid: Pueyo, 1920).

Acquaviva y Aragón, Giulio (1546–74). Monsignor (soon cardinal) into whose service MC entered as chamberlain in Rome in 1569. Acquaviva had made a visit to Madrid in 1568 as a papal envoy, and it is speculated that MC might have met him then. MC mentions him in the prologue to *Galatea*.

Acroceraunian Rocks [Riscos de Acroceraunos]. A rocky promontory near Corfu where the Acroceraunian mountains descend into the sea. This area was dangerous because of its sudden storms, inaccessible coasts, and shallow waters. See *Amante*; *Parnaso* 3.

Actaeon [Acteón, Anteón]. In Greek myth, a great hunter. When he came across Artemis (Diana in Roman myth) bathing nude, she changed him into a stag and he was torn to pieces by his own hunting dogs. In Spain, Acteón was frequently confused with *Antaeus, the giant son of Neptune and Gaia, and their names were fused into the hybrid *Anteón*. See *DQ* II, 32, 58.

Actor(s) [Comediante(s), Farsante(s)]. 1. In *Coloquio*, a friend of the poet who is writing a play and who has a role in its production. **2.** In *Pedro* 3, the two men who help convince Pedro de Urdemalas to become an actor.

Actor theory. An interesting strand of *DQ* criticism, best exemplified by Mark Van Doren, in which it is maintained that DQ is not truly crazy but is consciously acting the role of a knight-errant, literally taking the world as his stage. Like Van Doren, Harold Bloom also maintains that DQ is only acting—playing at—the role of knight-errant. A variant of this view is that DQ is not mad but simply playing, as does a child (e.g., Serrano Poncela and Torrente Ballester). The proponents of such views cite DQ's 'I know who I am' (I, 5), his playful conversation with SP about the squire's supposed visit to DT (I, 32), and the statement that only when he is sumptuously received as a knight by the duke and duchess does he truly believe himself to be a knight (II, 31). The main problem with these positions, fascinating and suggestive as they are, is the overwhelming majority of the textual evidence to the contrary.

Bibliography: Gonzalo Torrente Ballester, *El "Quijote" como juego* (Madrid: Guadarrama, 1975); and Mark Van Doren, *Don Quixote's Profession* (New York: Columbia University Press, 1958).

Acuña, Don Hernando (Fernando) de (1520–80). Spanish poet and soldier. Acuña was both a distinguished soldier and one of the better-known Petrarchan sonneteers and lyric poets of the sixteenth century. His sonnet that begins 'There already approaches, sire, or has already arrived,' with its famous line 'one monarch, one empire, one sword,' captures much of the spirit of Spanish hegemony of the time. See *Galatea* 6.

Bibliography: W. Holzinger, "Acuña's Sonnet 'Al Rey Nuestro Señor' and the Tradition of European Millennial Prophecy," *Philological Quarterly* 55 (1976): 149–65.

Acuña, Duarte de. Spanish civil servant. As assistant magistrate in Madrid in 1569, Acuña took certified statements from MC's father Rodrigo that MC was a legitimate Christian, with no ancestors who were Muslim, Jewish, *converso*, or reconciled by the Inquisition (*Cervantes family). Witnesses to the document were Alonso *Getino de Guzmán, then a bailiff in Madrid, and two Italian businessmen named Pirro Bocchi and Francesco Musacchi.

Adam [Adán]. In the Old Testament, the first man created by God. See *Adjunta*; *DQ* I, 33; *DQ* II, 22; *Persiles* III, 4; *Rufián* 3; *Sultana* 1.

Adam of poets [Adán de los poetas]. In *Parnaso* 1, the phrase by which Mercury addresses MC.

Adjunta al Parnaso (Adjunta); Appendix to the Parnassus. **Viaje del Parnaso, El.*

Adlante. *Atlas.

Admiration (Admiratio) [Admiración]. An aesthetic principle of major importance to MC (*literary theory in Cervantes). The Aristotelian idea is that a text should arouse astonishment and wonder in its readers in order to keep them reading. Certainly in the romance tradition, marvelous events—shipwrecks, brushes with death, separations, disguises— were plot devices for inspiring *admiratio*. The frequency with which the words *admirar* and *admiración* appear in the works of MC make it clear that he, too, was conscious of the device.

Adonis. In Greek myth, the extremely beautiful young man who represents the object of female desire in ancient mythology. He was, for example, the object of the rivalry between Persephone and Aphrodite. See *Casa* 2; *Entretenida* 1; *Gallardo* 3; *Parnaso* 5; *Persiles* III, 21.

Adornos. An Andalusian family whose origins were in Genoa. See *Doncellas*.

Adriano. *Hadrian.

Aduana, Puerta de la. *Gate of the Aduana.

Adulation [Adulación]. With Lie, one of two nymphs who attend Vainglory in MC's dream in *Parnaso* 6.

Adúltero guerrero; Adulterous warrior. *Mars.

Adventure (Greek or Byzantine) romance. The type of romance whose prototype is the Greek adventure tale by *Heliodorus, *Achilles Tatius, and others. Whereas the chivalric romances tend to take their titles from the names of their masculine heroes (Amadís, Belianís), and pastoral romances are more likely to take theirs from the names of their feminine heroines (Diana, Galatea), adventure romances tend to identify the male-female pair in their titles (Theogenes and Chariclea, Daphnis and Chloe). In Spain, translations of Heliodorus's *History of Theogenes and Chariclea* were made in 1554 (reprinted in 1581) and 1587 (reprinted in 1614, 1615, and 1616), and Achilles Tatius's *Leucippe and Cleitophon* in 1617. In Spanish literature, the genre is represented by *Núñez de Reinoso's *Historia de Clareo y Florisea* (1552), Jerónimo de *Contreras's *Selva de aventuras* (1565), Lope de *Vega's *El peregrino en su patria* (1604), and MC's *Persiles*.

Advice to Sancho. *Don Quixote's advice to Sancho.

Aegisthus [Egisto]. In Greek myth, the son of Pelops, who was killed by Orestes because of his illicit love affair with Orestes's mother Clytemnestra. See *Galatea* 4.

Aeneas [Eneas]. In Greek and Roman myth, the son of Anchises and the goddess Aphrodite (Venus in Roman myth), and one of the Trojan leaders in the Trojan war. After the war, his mother helped him escape the destroyed city (which he supposedly fled carrying his aged father on his shoulders) and go to Italy. Aeneas is the protagonist of Virgil's great Latin epic poem the *Aeneid*, dealing with the legendary founding of Rome and making the Romans the direct descendants of the greatness of Greece. In the *Aeneid*, on his way from Troy to Rome, Aeneas visited Dido, the founder of Carthage. There the queen fell in love with him and committed suicide after he abandoned her (in *DQ* II, 44, Altisidora refers to this incident when she calls DQ a new Aeneas for rejecting her love). Aeneas was reputed to be obedient to the will of the gods, a responsible and strong leader, and an exemplary father and son. See also *Baños* 1; *Doncellas*; *DQ* I, 25; *DQ* II, 3, 47–48, 57, 71; *Galatea* 4; *Parnaso* 3, 8; *Persiles* II, 17; IV, 3.

Aeolus [Eolo]. In Greek myth, the god of the winds. See *Galatea* 6.

Aesop [Isopo, Esopo] (sixth century BCE). Legendary Greek author of fables. See *Casamiento*; *Coloquio*.

Aetolia [Oeta]. A mountain in Greece where Heracles is said to have died. See *Parnaso* 1.

Africa. Except for Algiers and the north coast, Africa was for MC, as for Europeans in general during the Renaissance, a dark, unknown, mysterious place inhabited by primitive black men. See *Casa* 3; *DQ* I, 39, 48; *DQ* II, 17, 54, 58.

Aganippe [Aganipe]. A spring on Mount Helicon in Boeotia that was sacred to the Muses. See *Parnaso* 1–3; *Persiles* III, 2; *Poesías* 13; *Sultana* 3.

Age of Gold. *Golden Age.

Agi Morato; Agimorato. *Hadji Murad.

Aglante. The dominion of the epic hero Roland in *Casa*, where he is often referred to as the Lord of Aglante.

Agoni Molina, Luis (1941–). Chilean literary critic and short-story writer. In Agoni's *El hombre que asesinó a Don Quijote y otras historias* (1997; *The Man Who Killed Don Quixote and Other Stories*), the title story is the last one in the book. It consists of a series of explanations given by an apparent madman named Roberto Donoso Fuentes to a (presumably psychiatric) doctor about some events that took place some six years earlier. Donoso, a professor and literary critic, tells of taking part in a debate between the author of *Amadís de Gaula* and MC over who gave the world the greater literary hero. Somehow, DQ intervenes in the debate and then begins to appear every night to talk with Donoso. It seems that a local resident, El Flaco Zúñiga, has been convinced to dress as DQ and meet Donoso each evening. But when the latter realizes that he is the object of a practical joke, he takes a gun and shoots the man—only to find out that it is an empty suit of tin armor with bullet holes in it. And El Flaco Zúñiga disappears and is never seen again.

Bibliography: Luis Agoni Molina, *El hombre que asesinó a Don Quijote y otras historias* (Rancagua, Chile: Ediciones del Círculo Literario Fénix, 1997).

Agostos. *Augusts.

Agrajes. A character from *Amadís de Gaula* whose reputed frequent use of the phrase "Agora lo veredes" ["Now we'll see about that"] became proverbially associated with his name. The phrase is not found in *Montalvo's Renaissance rewriting of the primitive *Amadís*, so it is assumed that it entered Spanish as a commonplace on the basis of the medieval manuscript version of the story. See *DQ* I, 8; *Elección*; *Guarda*; *Rufián* 1.

Agramante. A Saracen king from Ariosto's *Orlando Furioso* (*Agramante's Camp). In *DQ* I, 26, DQ confuses Agramante with Medoro.

Agramante's Camp [Campo de Agramante]. In *DQ* I, 45, a brawl breaks out in the inn of Juan Palomeque, and almost everyone is involved in attacking others and/or defending their interests. DQ puts a stop to the mayhem by comparing the fight to a famous battle in *Orlando Furioso*: the Muslim King Agramante lays siege to the city of Paris, and Charlemagne manages to sow the seeds of discord among the men in Agramante's camp. DQ reminds everyone about how in the camp of Agramante some were fighting for Roland's sword Durendal, others for the horse Frontino, and still others for a shield that had the figure of an eagle painted on it; and to this, he adds Mambrino's helmet as part of the dispute. The battle of Agramante's camp was finally ended by the good deeds and words of King Sobrino and King Agramante. Agramante's camp has be-

7

come synonymous with confusion. See also *Casa* 3; *DQ* I, 26, 46; *DQ* II, 1; *Laberinto* 3.

Agreda y Vargas, Don Diego de. Spanish short-story writer. Agreda y Vargas is the author of *Novelas morales, útiles por sus documentos* (1620; *Moral Novels, Useful for Their Documents*); like *Novelas*, its obvious model, it is a collection of 12 exemplary stories.

Aguas del olvido. *Lethe.

Aguas, Nuestra Señora de las. *Our Lady of the Waters.

Aguayo, Juan (de Castilla) (ca. 1533–?). Spanish poet praised in Calliope's song in *Galatea* 6. It has been suggested that Aguayo's *El perfecto regidor* (1586; *The Perfect Prince*) might have provided at least part of the inspiration for DQ's advice to SP in II, 42–43.

Aguayo, Miguel. Mexican writer. In Aguayo's *Cuentos* (1964; *Stories*), there is one story entitled "Dulcinea en la ventana" ("Dulcinea at the Window"), in which Aldonza, a serving lass at an inn, has taken to reading romances of chivalry, books that had been given to her by her uncle, a priest. She calls herself Dulcinea and talks with her imaginary friend Esperanza (Hope) about the knight who will come to take her away. Her mother, meanwhile, insists that she marry Lope Tocho (from *DQ* II, 5), a peasant like her. One day, DQ arrives at the inn and speaks to her as he did to the serving women there in I, 2, but Aldonza laughs at the ridiculous figure, does not ask the name of the woman he loves, and feels sorry for him as he rides off. At the end of the story she is still sitting at the window, waiting for her knight to arrive.
Bibliography: Miguel Aguayo, *Cuentos* (Mexico City: Jus, 1964).

Aguedilla. In *Entretenida* 3, the tailor's wife, who is just mentioned once.

Agüela de Don Quijote. *Don Quixote's grandmother.

Aguilar, Don Pedro de. Spanish soldier cited in the narration of Ruy Pérez de Viedma as the author of a pair of sonnets (which are recited from memory) on the theme of the fall of Tunis and La Goleta to the Turks in 1574, in *DQ* I, 39–40. There is some doubt as to whether this is a purely fictional character or a historical person, although the latter is more likely, as the name appears in a passage with other historical personages and in fact there was a soldier by that name who fought in North Africa. But surely the poetry ascribed to him was actually written by MC as part of his fictional tale. One of the characters present in the scene (a friend of Don *Fernando) announces that Don Pedro is his brother.

Aguilar, Gaspar (Pedro) de (1561–1623). Spanish dramatist and poet. An important member of the Valencian school of dramatists and one of the more significant precursors of Lope de *Vega. He was a charter member of the *Academy of the Night Revelers. In *DQ* I, 48, the Canon of Toledo praises his play *El mercader amante* [*The Merchant Lover*] as an example of a well-written play. In the prologue to *Comedias*, he is again praised as a dramatist, as he is in *Parnaso* 3 (where he is mistakenly cited as Pedro de Aguilar).
Bibliography: John G. Weiger, *The Valencian Dramatists of Spain's Golden Age* (Boston: Twayne, 1976).

Aguilar (y Córdoba), Don Diego de (ca. 1550–ca. 1613). Spanish soldier and poet. Aguilar took part in the exploration and colonization of Peru and wrote an unpublished epic poem entitled *El Marañón* (presumably about exploits that took place near the river of that name, a tributary of the Amazon). He is praised in Calliope's song in *Galatea* 6.

Aguirre, Nataniel (1843–88). Bolivian soldier, statesman, and novelist. Aguirre projected a four-volume autobiographical fiction but published only the first part, *Juan de la Rosa, Memorias del último soldado de la Independencia* (1885; *Juan de la Rosa, Memoirs of the Last Soldier of Independence*), dealing with his youth. (More accurately, the novel was published first by a newspaper as *Memorias . . . by Juan de la Rosa*; in the second edition, 1909, it was published as *Juan de la Rosa, Memorias . . .*, with Aguirre identified as the author.) An important part of the protagonist's education is reading Spanish literature, particularly dramatists such as Calderón and Moreto, and, of course, *DQ*. In the very first chapter, young Juan's mentor, a priest named Fray Justo (one of the didactic spokespersons for the author), teaches the boy to read using MC's novel as his preferred text. Fray Justo speaks of 'the fantastic and unequaled adventure' of the two main characters, and he takes SP's island of Barataria as a symbol of worlds governed for the benefit of their absent and distant masters, clearly a reference to Spain's absentee colonial rule in America. *DQ* becomes Juan's most frequently read book for many years (and later it and other books of his are burned in a scene reminiscent of *DQ* I, 6). In an interesting note, Juan's old, blind grandmother tells him tales of the lay sister Quintañona, a much admired mythic yet pragmatic character, and there is a reference to the unfair criticism of *Quintañona in works by MC and other Spanish writers. Apparently, this minor figure from the Spanish version of Arthurian legend became a part of Spanish American folklore.

Bibliography: Nataniel Aguirre, *Juan de la Rosa, memorias del último soldado de la independencia* (Cochabamba, Bolivia: El Heraldo, 1885).

Aguja de San Pedro. *Saint Peter's Needle.

Airón. There are various wells of this name in the provinces of Granada and Cuenca. See *Adjunta*.

Ajá. A Muslim woman in *Amante*.

Alá. *Allah.

Alabez. In *Gallardo* 3, a character who represents the Sidi Bel Abbès, the Muslim king of Algiers. He is wounded by Fernando de Saavedra in the Muslim assault on Oran.

Alaejos. A town located northeast of Salamanca and east of Medina del Campo. It was noted for its wines. See *Vidriera*.

Alagones. An Aragonese family name mentioned in *DQ* I, 13.

Alamillo. A well-known gathering place on the banks of the Guadalquivir River in Seville. See *Rufián* 1.

Alamos. The family name of the *hidalgo* in SP's anecdote in *DQ* II, 31.

Alanís. A small town located north and slightly east of Seville and west and slightly north of Córdoba that was well-known for the white wine produced there. See *Elección*; *Entretenida* 3; *Rufián* 1; *Vidriera*.

Alárabe. *Muslim woman.

Alarcón, Jerónima de. A woman living in Seville in the late 1580s when MC spent time there. At one point he acted as a guarantor for Alarcón and was living in the section of the city where she owned a house, so it has been speculated that they were lovers. There is, however, no documented support for such a claim, and it is entirely possible to see the relationship as entirely innocent, for example, that MC rented a room from her.

Alarcón, Juan Ruiz de. *Ruiz de Alarcón, Juan.

Alas, Leopoldo. *Clarín.

Alastrajarea. The wife of Prince Falanges de Astra in the romance of chivalry *Florisel de Niquea* by Feliciano de *Silva. See *DQ* II, 32.

Alba (de Tormes). A town located southeast of Salamanca and east and north of Avila. It is the place where *Saint Teresa de Jesús died and is buried. See *Poesías* 33.

Alba, Duke of; Albano. *Alvarez de Toledo y Pimentel, Fernando.

Al-Batha (La Pata). A fortress located very near the North African city of Oran. See *DQ* I, 40.

Alberdi, Juan Bautista (1810–84). Argentine social critic. Alberdi's *Peregrinación de Luz del Día, o viajes y aventuras de la verdad en el Nuevo Mundo* (1871; *Pilgrimage of Light of Day, or the Voyages and Adventures of Truth in the New World*) is a social satire in the form of an allegorical fiction. The work is divided into three parts. In the first part, Truth, bored and disgusted with the lies of Europe, decides to emigrate to South America; so she takes the form of a woman and the name of Luz del Día (Light of Day). Also making the trip are three literary figures: Molière's Tartuffe, Beaumarchais's Bazile, and Lesage's Gil Blas, and she has important discussions with each of them. In the second part, Luz del Día meets Beaumarchais's Figaro and some Spanish historical and literary figures, including El Cid, Pelayo, Don Juan Tenorio, and DQ. The latter has undertaken the task of colonizing Patagonia, in Argentina, and setting up a socialist republic of sheep. The third part takes place after the failure of DQ's republic, named Quijotanía (Quixotania), when Luz del Día delivers a long speech on the subject of freedom in Spanish American nations. For Alberdi, Spanish America is rife with scoundrels (like Tartuffe) and idiots (like DQ) and would be better off without either.
Bibliography: Juan Bautista Alberdi, *Peregrinación de Luz del Día, o viajes y aventuras de la verdad en el Nuevo Mundo* (Buenos Aires: C. Casavalle, 1871).

Alberti, Rafael (1902–99). Spanish poet, dramatist, and painter. During the dark days of the siege of Madrid in the Spanish Civil War, in 1937, the troops were inspired by a production of *Numancia*, a revision/adaptation of *Numancia* done by Alberti that was the first staging of a version of *Numancia* in the twentieth century. This version eliminates most of the magical and supernatural elements in order to stress the militaristic and heroic aspects of the play. The four acts are reduced to three, a couple of comic characters are added, some of the dialogue is modified, and the Duero River updates her prophesy about Spain's future. In 1943 the work was further modified and produced in Montevideo. Alberti specifically stresses the propagandistic value of the work, which he sees as unique in Spanish literature in this respect.
Bibliography: Rafael Alberti, *Numancia* (Madrid: Turner, 1975).

Alberto. In *Sultana* 3, a name used once for *Lamberto, perhaps an error.

Alberto de Sosa Coitiño. In *Persiles* III, 1, the man who has had a tomb built to his deceased brother Manuel. After showing the tomb to Periandro and the other travelers, he bids them farewell.

Albraca. King Galafrone's castle in China, where, as described in Boiardo's *Orlando Innamorato*, he held his daughter Angelica la Bella captive. Agricane assembled an army of 2,200,000 men, covering four leagues, to lay siege to the castle. See *DQ* I, 10; *DQ* II, 4, 27.

Alcaide de la fortaleza. *Warden of the fortress.

Alcalá de Henares. A Spanish city, formerly the site of an Arabic fortress—thus the name *Al-calá* (the Castle)—on the banks of the Henares River (a tributary of the Tagus), located east and very slightly north of Madrid; it is the birthplace of MC (a fact not rediscovered until the eighteenth century). The city's population at the time of MC's birth was perhaps 13,000, including some 3,000 students at its university, which was founded in 1508 by Cardinal Jiménez de *Cisneros, Archbishop of Toledo and Chancellor of Castile, and was second only to that of *Salamanca in power and prestige. The single most important achievement of the (mostly *converso*) scholars at Alcalá was the publication of the monumental Polyglot Bible (1514–17), with its parallel Hebrew, Chaldean, Greek, and Latin Vulgate texts of the Old and New Testaments. The Greek Testament had never been printed before, and the Polyglot version precedes by two years the much-praised but far inferior one prepared by Erasmus. The Casa de Cervantes (Cervantes's Home) that is one of the city's main modern tourist attractions is located on the site of the building where MC was born. It is a twentieth-century reconstruction of what a home in MC's time might have looked like, but it is far more elegant than anything his modest family could have actually afforded. The city was also referred to at times by the Roman name of *Complutum. See *Coloquio*; *Fregona*; *Parnaso* 4.

Alcalde. *Inn of the Alcalde; *mayor.

Alcaná. In MC's day, a commercial street in the Jewish quarter of Toledo; it no longer exists today. In *DQ* I, 9, it is where the author buys CHB's manuscript of *DQ* I.
    Bibliography: E. C. Graf, "When an Arab Laughs in Toledo: Cervantes's Interpellation of Early Modern Spanish Orientalism," *Diacritics* 29, no. 3 (1999): 68–85.

Alcañices, Marqués de. *Enríquez de Almansa, Don Alvaro Antonio.

Alcántara. *Order of Alcántara.

Alcántara Bridge [Puente de Alcántara]. A bridge over the Tagus River in Toledo. See *Fregona*.

Alcarria. A region of Spain located east and south of Madrid in the modern provinces of Cuenca, Guadalajara, and Madrid. Along with Extremadura, it is compared to La Mancha by one of the merchants DQ encounters in I, 4.

Alcázar (Reales Alcázares). The Christian royal palace in Seville. After the reconquest of Seville in the thirteenth century, King Pedro I ordered the construction of a royal residence where the Muslim palace had stood. Later royalty expanded the buildings and grounds until the present complex was completed in the sixteenth century. It is one of the landmarks of the city. See *Rinconete*.

Alcázar, Baltasar del (1530–1606). Spanish poet known as the 'Sevillian Martial' for his epigrams. His burlesque and jocose verse makes him the best and most famous comic poet of the Spanish Renaissance. He is praised in Calliope's song in *Galatea* 6.

Alcazarquivir [Alcázarquibir]. A city in Morocco, located south of Tangiers. It was the site of the defeat and death of King *Sebastião of Portugal in 1578. See *Persiles* III, 18.

Alchemist [Alquimista]. In *Coloquio*, in the Hospital of the Resurrection, a man who thinks he is on the verge of discovering the *philosopher's stone.

Alcides. In Greek myth, *Hercules, so called because he descended from Alcaeus. See *Casa* 2; *Galatea* 4.

Alcinous [Alcinoo]. The king of the Phoenicians, whose gardens were praised in the *Odyssey*. See *Parnaso* 3.

Alcoba. A garden in the Alcázar of Seville. See *Rufián* 1.

Alcobendas. A small city north of Madrid, today virtually a suburb of the city. See *DQ* I, 19.

Alcorán. *Qu'ran.

Alcudia, campo de. *Fields of Alcudia.

Aldana, Francisco de (1537–78). Spanish soldier and poet, called *el Divino* (the Divine One). Much admired in his time, he was often compared to *Garcilaso de la Vega, Fernando de *Herrera, and others who are much more highly esteemed today. He is praised in Calliope's song in *Galatea* 6 and called *Divine* in *Adjunta*.

Aldonza de Minijaca. In *Juez*, the wife who says that she has 400 reasons to divorce her surgeon husband.

Aldonza Lorenzo. In *DQ* I, 1, it is stated that DQ loved a peasant woman who lived nearby and had this name. Aldonza, a name of Arabic origin, was particularly common among the lower classes. In some instances, it was considered by antonomasia as the name of a woman of easy virtue, as suggested by the proverbial 'If there's no woman around, Aldonza will do.' DQ's transformation of the reality of Aldonza into the ideal of DT is a prototypical act in his systematic transformation of reality into fantasy. In I, 25, when DQ reveals to SP the name of the real woman behind the imaginary DT, SP claims that he knows her well and describes her as lusty, athletic, and with a powerful voice. This revelation is a major tactical mistake on DQ's part, as it takes away one of the major mysteries in his self-presentation to SP. Presumably, it is to Aldonza that the *Morisco* translator refers in I, 9, when he says that DT 'had the best hand of any woman of La Mancha for salting pork.' It is on Aldonza that SP bases his description of DT in the report of his supposed interview with DT in I, 31. And the figure of Aldonza is probably what inspires SP to deceive DQ in II, 10, by convincing him that three peasant women from El Toboso are DT and two ladies-in-waiting. See also *DQ* II, 14; 36.

Bibliography: Augustin Redondo, "Del personaje de Aldonza Lorenzo al de Dulcinea del Toboso: Algunos aspectos de la invención cervantina," *Anales Cervantinos* 21 (1983): 1–22; and Charlotte Stern, "Dulcinea, Aldonza, and the Theory of Speech Acts," *Hispania* 67 (1984): 61–73.

Aldonza Nogales. In DQ I, 25, the name of the mother of Aldonza Lorenzo.

Alecto. *Furies.

Alegre dios de la risa. *Bacchus.

Alejandra. *Argensola, Lupercio Leonardo de.

Alejandría. *Alexandria.

Alejandría de la Palla. *Alessandria della Paglia.

Alejandro; Alejandro Magno. *Alexander the Great.

Alejandro Castrucho, Señor. In *Persiles* III, 19, the uncle of Isabel Castrucho who is taking her to Italy to be married. In III, 21, when his niece's marriage to Andrea Marulo is recognized, he falls dead and is buried two days later.

Alemán Bolaños, Gustavo (1884–?). Nicaraguan writer. Writing as *El Pobrecito Hablador* [The Poor Chatterer, a pseudonym previously used by the Spanish romantic writer Mariano José de *Larra], Alemán Bolaños published a short novel entitled *Don Quijote de la Mancha en Managua* (1940). DQ and SP arrive in Nicaragua and proceed to the capital city where they have a series of "adventures," which consist of little more than being treated like VIP tourists. At one point, DQ interrupts a magic show by an Englishman (posing as a Chinese and going by the name of Fu Manchú) in order to save a woman from being cut in half (an obvious imitation of DQ's interruption of *Maese Pedro's puppet show). But then DQ takes a turn at show business and presents his own magic show in the same theater. This is by all standards one of the worst sequels to *DQ*.

Bibliography: Gustavo Alemán Bolaños, *Don Quijote de la Mancha en Managua* (Managua, Nicaragua: Atlántida, 1940).

Alemán, Mateo (1547–ca. 1616). Spanish novelist and prose writer. Son of the physician to the Royal Prison of Seville, Alemán studied medicine, worked for years in civil service, was once jailed in the prison in which his father worked, and wrote a report on the conditions of prisoners condemned to row in the Spanish galleys, as well as a biography of St. Antonio of Padua (1604) and a treatise on orthography (1609). In 1582 Alemán attempted to emigrate to the New World but his application was turned down, presumably on the basis of his *converso* status, but in 1607 he did receive permission (perhaps after a bribe) to emigrate to Mexico, where he died. Alemán's place in literature is due to *Guzmán de Alfarache* (1599, 1604), the first important picaresque novel after *Lazarillo de Tormes* (1554). More than ten times longer than its precursor, *Guzmán* has a complicated narrative structure. The story is an autobiography written by the mature protagonist from the galleys where he has been condemned for his crimes. Young Guzmán, the spawn of an adulterous affair of a con man of Jewish ancestry and a licentious woman, leaves home at the age of 12 and is immediately introduced into the world of materialism and deceit where he is lied to, served nearly hatched eggs and mule meat, robbed, and falsely accused. He takes naturally to criminal life, becoming a *pícaro*, beggar, thief, student, cutpurse, and more. He continues his adventures in Italy, both with members of his family, who renounce him and whom he robs, and as part of the household staff of a cardinal, where he continues his theft. In the second part of the novel, which carries the subtitle *Atalaya de la vida humana* (*Watchtower of Human Life*), Guzmán is a student, marries, prostitutes his wife, and is finally condemned to the galleys, where he self-servingly informs the authorities about a planned mutiny, undergoes a religious conversion, and writes his life story, alternating between his sinful adventures and a large amount of commentary. This digressive discursive commentary—on social, religious, narrative, moral, and other subjects—is an integral part of the work, in spite of the fact that much of it is sometimes edited out and/or skipped by readers more interested in the narrative action. Including five long embedded narratives and scores of shorter anecdotes, the digressive and unrelated narrative elements actually occupy more than half the text. Even so, Alemán's novel was extraordinarily popular in the seventeenth century, going through some twenty editions within a decade and sparking the vogue of the *picaresque novel, the genre that was dominant in the first half of the seventeenth century in Spain. The book was so frequently read and talked about that it was known simply as *El Pícaro*. *Guzmán* was translated into all major European languages, beginning with James Mabbe's translation into English (1622–23), and it inspired a number of versions, sequels, and imitations in English, French, Dutch, and German. Readers of the novel are divided by two kinds of critical concerns. Some praise the work's complicated but coherent structure and theme, whereas others condemn the lack of cohesion and consistency in the miscellany. On the other hand, some from each of the previous two orientations consider the work an optimistic Christian tale of sin and redemption, whereas others from the same two groups read the work as a pessimistic satire, a condemnation of superficial and always subverted religious piety. A consensus position might see the work as not quite consistent in aim or execution, with the author's own conflictive experiences and values reflected in those of his protagonist. Although he does not mention the book by name, MC was very aware of Alemán's accomplishment and implicitly wrote under his influence; *DQ* would not have been what it is without Alemán's novel. MC clearly has *Guzmán* in mind in the satiric scene in *DQ* I, 22, when the *pícaro* and galley slave (an allusion to Guzmán the narrator) *Ginés de Pasamonte discusses life-writing in the vein of *Lazarillo de Tormes*. In the opening passage of *Fregona*, the young Diego de Carriazo is described as so dedicated to the picaresque life, and so good at it, that he could give lessons to the famous Guzmán de Alfarache. Although in the prologue to his *Novelas* MC claims to have been the first to write original short stories in Spain, Alemán may also share some claim to that honor, as there are two original stories embedded in the first part of *Guzmán*—"Ozmín y Daraja" and "Dorido y Clorinia"—and three more in the second part—"Don Luis de Castro," "Bonifacio y Dorotea," and the first-person autobiographical narrative of Sayavedra that is largely integrated into the primary narrative. Alemán brilliantly anticipated MC in dealing with a pseudonymous rival who wrote an unauthorized sequel to his own unfinished work, when he personified Juan *Martí in his own second part of *Guzmán* and made him commit suicide. Surely Alemán's strategy in dealing with literary piracy was an important model for the way in which MC deals with *Avellaneda's sequel to *DQ* I in his own *DQ* II. One final detail: when Alemán arrived in Mexico in 1608, he had in his possession a book that because of its profane nature was forbidden in the Spanish possessions in America and consequently was confiscated by the authorities. The book was *DQ* I.

Bibliography: Joan Arias, *Guzmán de Alfarache: The Unrepentant Narrator* (London: Tamesis, 1977); Benito Brancaforte, *Guzmán de Alfarache: ¿conversión o proceso de degradación?* (Madison, WI: Hispanic Seminary of Medieval Studies, 1980); Michel Cavillac, *Pícaros y mercaderes en el "Guzmán de Alfarache"* (Granada, Spain: Universidad de Granada, 1995); Carroll B. Johnson, *Inside Guzmán de Alfarache* (Berkeley: University of California Press, 1979); Monique Joly, "Cervantes y la picaresca de Mateo Alemán: hacia una revisión del problema," in *La invención de la novela: Seminario hispano-francés organizado por la Casa de Velázquez (noviembre 1992–junio 1993)*, ed. Jean Canavaggio (Madrid: Casa de Velázquez, 1999), 269–76; C. A. Longhurst, "The Problems of Conversion and Repentance in *Guzmán de Alfarache*," in *A Face Not Turned to the Wall: Essays on Hispanic Themes for Gareth Alban Davies*, ed. C. A. Longhurst (Leeds, UK: Department of Spanish and Portuguese, University of Leeds, 1987), 85–110; Howard Mancing, "Embedded Narration in *Guzmán de Alfarache*," in *"Ingeniosa Invención": Essays on Golden Age Spanish Literature for Geoffrey L. Stagg in Honor of His Eightieth Birthday*, ed. Ellen M. Anderson and Amy R. Williamsen (Newark, DE: Juan de la Cuesta, 1999), 69–99; Donald McGrady, *Mateo Alemán* (New York: Twayne, 1968); and Joseph V. Ricapito, "Cervantes y Mateo Alemán, de nuevo," *Anales Cervantinos* 23 (1985): 89–95.

Alemania. *Germany.

Alemparte Robles, Julio (1904–?). Chilean writer. He is the author of "Un capítulo inédito de Cervantes que trata de una aventura amorosa de Don Quijote" ("An Unedited Chapter of Cervantes which Deals with an Amorous Adventure of Don Quijote"), a text that is presented as a discovery in an archive in Toledo, and that consists of a chapter that belongs in *DQ* II, between 42 and 43. DQ is pursued by a certain Doña Elvira, who lives in the home of the duke and duchess, and who employs a magic potion in order to make DQ love her. Apparently the story was never published.

Alencastros. A Portuguese family name mentioned in *DQ* I, 13.

Alessandria della Paglia [Alejandría de la Palla]. A fortress-city located between Milan and Genoa. See *DQ* I, 39.

Alexander the Great [Alejandro, Alejandro Magno, Magno Alejandro] (356 BCE–323 BCE). King of Macedonia and the greatest general of antiquity. Tutored by Aristotle in his youth, Alexander distinguished himself as a military leader in his teenage years. He succeeded to the throne at the age of 20 and quickly consolidated his rule. A series of successful military campaigns greatly expanded his empire as far east as India. Widely considered divine even in his own lifetime, Alexander was a brilliant strategist, a bold and daring general who led by example; he also had a well-deserved reputation as an honest and generous man. In MC's day, to call someone an Alexander was, above all, to praise that person's generosity. See *Baños* 3; *Casa* 2; *DQ* I, prologue, preliminary poetry, 6, 39, 47, 49, 52; *DQ* II, 2, 40, 59, 60; *Gallardo* 2; *Laberinto* 2; *Parnaso* 8; *Pedro* 2; *Vizcaíno*.

Alexandria [Alejandría]. A city in Egypt on the Mediterranean Sea. In the Hellenistic era, it was the capital of Egypt, founded by Alexander the Great. See *Amante*; *Parnaso* 6.

Alfalfa. A plaza in Seville. See *Rinconete*.

Alfeñiquén del Algarbe. In *DQ* I, 18, one of the participants in the battle (of sheep) as described by DQ. The Algarve is the southern coastal region of Portugal that had once been Muslim territory.

Alfeo. *Alpheus.

Alfonso de Este, Duke of Ferrara. In *Cornelia*, the lover and eventual husband of Cornelia Bentibolli (*Este family).

Alfonso, Gaspar. A Spanish poet praised in Calliope's song in *Galatea* 6.

Alfonso II (791–842). King of Asturias, known as *el Casto* (the Chaste) and *el Magno* (the Great). His sister Jimena, married to Sancho, Count of Saldaña, was the mother of *Bernardo del Carpio. See *Casa* 3.

Algarbe; Algarve. *Alfeñiquén del Algarbe.

Algarrobillas, Las. In *Retablo*, the town where Chanfalla and Chirinos stage the show of wonders. It has been identified as a town in the province of Cáceres, known in the Golden Age for the hams produced there, but there seems to be no such place in modern Spain. There is, however, a town named Garrovillas north and slightly west of Cáceres and south of Ciudad Rodrigo, which is probably the location in question. Apparently, its natives were known for their ignorance and gullibility.

Algerian pirates. *Pirate(s).

Algiers [Argel]. City in Algeria on the North African Mediterranean coast, located directly south of Barcelona. This strategic port city, with a good, well-defended harbor, was taken by the Turks in 1529 and remained in their hands throughout MC's lifetime. It was virtually a single-industry town, thriving on privateering and dealing in ransomed captives; in the late sixteenth century it had as many as 150,000 inhabitants, more than any city in Spain. The number of slaves held in the city in the final decades of the sixteenth century was estimated at 25,000; overall, between about 1520 and 1660, over a half a million Christians spent some time as slaves in Algiers. The city was probably the locus of the most multicultural population in the world at the time, with (at least temporary) inhabitants from as many as 40 different nationalities. Algiers was in many ways an exemplary egalitarian society, where ability and wealth mattered more than birth, and many of the major administrative officers were converts (renegades) rather than native Muslims. In 1541 an expedition (which included Hernán Cortés) sent by Carlos V failed to retake the city; 12,000 men and 150 ships were lost in a terrible storm off the North African coast. The disaster was a major setback for the imperial forces, and it left the western Mediterranean largely in control of the Turks until the battle of *Lepanto in 1571, an event recalled in both *Tratos* 1 and *Baños* 3. It was in Algiers that MC spent five years in captivity, 1575–80. Algiers is the setting for both *Tratos* and *Baños*, and it is from Algiers that *Poesías* 8 is supposedly written. See *Amante*; *DQ* I, 37, 39–42; *DQ* II, 54, 63, 65; *Española*; *Galatea* 5; *Gallardo* 2; *Pedro* 1, 3; *Persiles* III, 10; *Sultana* 3.

Bibliography: William Spencer, *Algiers in the Age of the Corsairs* (Norman: University of Oklahoma Press, 1976).

Alguacil. *Constable.

Alhama (de Granada). A town located northeast of Málaga and southwest of Granada. In *Persiles* II, 8, it is identified as the home of the witch Cenotia.

Alí. In *Baños* 3, a Muslim with a minor role.

Alí Bajá. In *Amante*, the outgoing viceroy of Cyprus, replaced by Hazán Bajá. He is one of three Muslims who fall in love with the incomparably beautiful Leonisa and is killed in the attempt to capture and possess her. Perhaps this fictional character is based on (or, at least, his name is taken from) the historical figure of the same name (*Ali Pasha), but there is no similarity between them.

Alí Izquierdo. In *Sultana* 3, he is mentioned by Madrigal as the person who bought Doña Catalina in Tetuán.

Ali Pasha [Alí Bajá]. Born in Calabria, he converted to Islam and rose to become governor of Algiers in 1570 and admiral in the Turkish navy. He was the commander of the fleet defeated in the battle of *Lepanto. Ali Pasha was killed during the battle and, according to some accounts, his head was presented to the victorious Christian general, Don Juan of Austria.

Alicante. An important Mediterranean port city located northeast of Málaga and directly south of Valencia. In modern Spain, it is known as a major tourist center more than anything else. See *DQ* I, 39; *Persiles* III, 10.

Alida. *Pastoral names.

Alifanfarón, señor de la grande isla de Trapobana [Lord of the Great Island of Trebizond]. In *DQ* I, 18, an emperor and the leader of the pagan army in the battle (of sheep) as described by DQ. Trapobana is a common corruption of Taprobana, an old name for the island of Ceylon, now Sri Lanka.

Alimuzel. In *Gallardo*, the brave Muslim and lover of Arlaxa, whom she marries in the end.

Aljafería. A very large Muslim palace built in the eleventh century just outside of Zaragoza. It was made into a palace for the Aragonese royalty and, later, for the *Catholic Monarchs. Then it was appropriated by the Inquisition and, later still, was converted into a military barracks. See *DQ* II, 26.

All Saints' Day [(Día de) Todos (los) Santos]. The Christian festival held annually on November 1 in honor of all the saints. See *Rinconete*.

Allah [Alá]. Arabic for God. See *Baños* 1–3; *DQ* I, 41; *Sultana* 1, 3.

Allecto. *Furies.

Allen, Woody (1935–). American film director, actor, writer, and musician. Among Allen's films is one that particularly reminds viewers of the metafictional aspects of *DQ*: *The Purple Rose of Cairo* (1985). Frustrated housewife Cecilia (Mia Farrow) escapes reality by watching movies, especially one entitled *The Purple Rose of Cairo*, which she sees repeatedly. On one occasion, the film's leading male character, Tom Baxter (Jeff Daniels), who has noticed Cecilia in the audience, turns and speaks to her and then walks out of the film to join her. This causes chaos in the theater, in Cecilia's life, in the film, and in the film industry. The brilliant blurring of the lines between reality and fiction does indeed replicate in film much of the metafictional effect of *DQ* (*self-conscious narration/ metafiction). Allen also directed and starred in the weak film *Bananas* (1971), which was very loosely based on Richard *Powell's *Don Quixote, U.S.A.*

Bibliography: Marie Barbieri, "Metafiction in *Don Quijote* and *The Purple Rose of Cairo*: Three Characters in Search of Their Freedom," *RLA: Romance Languages Annual* 5 (1993): 356–59.

Allende, Juan Rafael (1850–1909). Chilean writer. Allende wrote a short satiric picaresque novel entitled *Memorias de un perro escritas por su propia pata* (1893; *Memoirs of a Dog Written by His Own Paw*), whose adventures recall those of MC's Berganza (as well as those of the famous Cuatro Remos, a historical dog who also became a literary hero in the fiction of Daniel *Barros Grez). The hero is named Rompecadenas (Chainbreaker) but, like Berganza, acquires new names with several of the masters he serves: Chorrillos, Garibaldi, Campino (Can Pino). He even has a canine DT, called Musidora (and, later, Pati-Coja). After Rompecadenas makes his will and dies, his son Torquemada describes his father's death and the effect this event had on domestic and world events. Overall, Allende's *Memorias* is one of the better picaresque fictions in Spanish American literature.

Bibliography: Juan Rafael Allende, *Memorias de un perro escritas por su propia pata* (Santiago, Chile: Nascimiento, 1972).

Almadrabas de Zahara. *Zahara (de los Atunes).

Almar, George. English dramatist. Almar is the author of a two-act musical drama entitled *Don Quixote; or, The Knight of the Woeful Countenance* (1833). The play opens with a discussion (and burning) of DQ's books, as the barber, here named Sampson Carasco, also reveals his love for DQ's niece, Juey. The barber strikes a deal: he will make DQ and SP return if Juey agrees to marry him; she accepts. The action shifts to DQ and SP and their adventures in the inn, the puppet show, and a few other episodes from the novel. Sampson arrives with SP's friend Tommy Cecil as his squire and challenges DQ—who defeats him. The second act takes place at the palace of the duke and duchess and mostly involves SP's adventures as governor. A return by Sampson is more successful, and DQ admits to reality and blesses the marriage between the barber and his niece. Some of the dialogue, especially that involving SP, is really quite witty and genuinely funny, a rarity in plays of this type from the period.

Bibliography: George Almar, *Don Quixote; or, The Knight of the Woeful Countenance* (London: Richardson and Clarke, 1833).

Almarza. A fortress near Mazalquivir mentioned in *Gallardo* 3 as the place where Don Martín de Córdoba, brother of Alonso *Fernández de Córdoba, general in charge of Oran, is in command.

Almas de purgatorio. *Souls from purgatory.

Almedina. *Medina.

Almendárez (Almendáriz), Julián de (?– 1614). Spanish poet. He is the author of *Patrón Salmantino* (1603; *The Patron Saint of Salamanca*) and is praised in *Parnaso* 7.

Almete de Malandrino. In *DQ* I, 19, SP's corruption of *yelmo de Mambrino* (*Mambrino's helmet), combining the real name with the word *malandrín* (evil-doer).

Almodóvar del Campo. A town located southwest of Ciudad Real and just west of Puertollano. In the late Middle Ages it acquired considerable importance as a commercial center, but after the expulsion of the Jews in 1492 it went into decline. *Pedro Recio de Agüero uses it as a point of reference when identifying the location of his home town of Tirteafuera. See *DQ* I, 23; *DQ* II, 47.

Almohadas. In *DQ* II, 5, SP's mispronunciation (it means 'cushions,' as he says it) for Almohades, a powerful Moroccan dynasty who began their incursions in the Iberian Peninsula in the early twelfth century.

Almqvist, Carl Jonas Love (1793–1866). Swedish poet, novelist, and dramatist. Almqvist's youthful *Amorina, eller, Historien om de fyra* (1829; *Amorina, or the Disturbed Young Woman*) is a feverishly romantic 'poetic fugue.' The heroine, Amorina, is considered mad and deranged by everyone but, at heart, she retains saintly qualities. As such, Amorina is a kind of female DQ, accompanied by her stepfather Doctor Libius, who is explicitly compared to SP.

Almudena, Our Lady of. *Our Lady of Almudena.

Alone Pearls, The [Las Solas]. Pearls mentioned by Altisidora in her song to DQ in II, 44. This may be an allusion to a well-known set of pearls, perhaps part of the royal treasure, that for their size, beauty, and/or value stood alone, apart from all other pearls. It has also been suggested that it is a reference to a specific famous pearl called *La Peregrina* (The Perfect One) or *La Huérfana* (The Orphan) from the royal collection that was lost in a fire in 1734.

Alonso. In *Persiles* III, 6, the lover of Luisa before she meets and marries Ortel Banedre and with whom she runs off soon after her marriage. The couple is exiled, and Alonso eventually dies in jail.

Alonso, Agustín. Spanish poet. He was the author of *Historia de las hazañas y hechos del invencible caballero Bernardo del Carpio* (1585; *History of the Exploits and Deeds of the Invincible Knight Bernardo del Carpio*), a long heroic poem in octaves, a book not found in the examination of DQ's library in I, 6, but that, according to the inquisitorial priest, would be condemned to the flames if it were to be located.

Alonso Algarroba. In *Elección*, one of the two aldermen who interview candidates for magistrate.

Alonso de Córdoba, Don. *Fernández de Córdoba, Alonso de.

Alonso, Eduardo (1944–). Spanish novelist and short-story writer. In Alonso's collection of short stories *El amor en invierno (y otros percances)* (1999; *Love in Winter [and Other Mis-*

fortunes]), there is one story entitled "Así murió don Quijote" ("How Don Quixote Died"). It tells of how DQ, after his return from his adventures and recovery from his life-threatening illness, is visited one day by CHB, from 'Benengeli Publishing Associated.' The Muslim chronicler attempts to get DQ ('Ex DQ,' the now sane *hidalgo* insists) to sign a contract naming CHB as his agent. There is a lot of money to be made in franchising and merchandizing; Avellaneda is already cashing in on his best-selling book, even endorsing a new Rocinante car model with 120-Babieca power and preparing a television reality show entitled *Quijotadas* [Quixotic Deeds]. The former knight-errant refuses to get involved in commercial efforts, insisting that he no longer wants anything to do with his DQ phase. CHB tells him that everyone else is taking advantage of their notoriety: Maritornes is making pornographic films, the housekeeper is endorsing a laundry detergent, Maese Nicolás is promoting a new cologne for men entitled Eau de Fierabrás, and SP is promoting 'Pizzas Panza' for McDonald's. It is only when CHB suggests that even DT is now promoting bathing suits, underwear, and sanitary napkins that DQ gets angry and vows to defend DT against such vile accusations. He falls ill from this excitement and, within a short time, dies.

Bibliography: Eduardo Alonso, *El amor en invierno (y otros percances)* (Madrid: Acento Editorial, 1999).

Alonso Hurtado. In *Gitanilla*, the name first given by *Clemente when he meets up with the gypsy band.

Alonso López. In *DQ* I, 19, the bachelor from *Alcobendas whose leg is broken by DQ and who explains the circumstances of the death of the man whose body is being transported to Segovia. He also excommunicates DQ for having attacked a representative of the church. The name of this character is suggestive, as a man with such a name lived in Ubeda, a city MC visited in his capacity of commissary in 1592, the year after the death of Saint *Juan de la Cruz. Another man of the same name was also

a captive in Algiers during the time MC was there.

Alonso Moclín. *Moclín, Alonso.

Alonso Quijano the Good [el Bueno]. The surname of DQ is problematic throughout the novel, as Quijada, Quesada, and Quejana were all suggested and speculated upon from the very beginning in I, 1 (*name of Don Quixote). *Quijano* appears for the first time in II, 74, and is repeated several times, presumably making it the definitive version of his name. The epithet 'the Good' is used (by the narrator, other characters, and DQ himself) to describe DQ in II, 74, and is said to be how he was referred to by those who knew him. This stands in contrast to Don Quixote the Bad (*el Malo*), as the protagonist of *DQA* was referred to in II, 72, and draws attention to the moral stature of Alonso Quijano even before he transformed himself into DQ. Some have read the name *Quijano*, pronounced kee-*sha*-no, as an evocation of the phrase *quizá no* (perhaps not) and thus as an ironic undercutting of the character's supposed goodness.

Bibliography: Robert L. Hathaway, "Hypothesizing an Ancestry for Alonso Quixano," in *Not Necessarily Cervantes: Readings of the* Quixote (Newark, DE: Juan de la Cuesta, 1995), 1–11.

Alphabet [ABC entero]. In *DQ* I, 34, after reviewing the *four S's that all lovers should have, Leonela humorously describes an entire alphabet of qualities possessed by Camila's lover Lotario.

Alpheus [Alfeo]. One of the largest rivers in Greece; it rises in Arcadia and flows to the Ionian Sea. See *Galatea* 6.

Alpujarras. A mountain range that was the site of a revolt by *Moriscos in 1568. See *Gitanilla*.

Alquife. Enchanter from *Amadís de Grecia*, where he is the husband of *Urganda la Desconocida. In *DQ* II, 34, he is second in the procession of enchanters who precede the appearance of Merlin. See also *DQ* I, 43.

Alquimista. *Alchemist.

Altagumea, Hilarión de (Antonio José de Irisarri, 1786–1868). Guatemalan poet and prose writer. Irisarri's *Historia del perínclito Epaminodas del Cauca, El cristiano errante* (two vols., 1847; *History of the Renowned Epaminodas del Cauca, the Christian-Errant*) is a partly autobiographical novel, with a pseudo-Cervantine tone and manner, written with the main purpose of denouncing liberal politics in Ecuador. The protagonist, son of a poor Indian, reads and is influenced by contemporary political journalism, as well as by Enlightenment political theorists. His friend, the priest Don Prudencio, attempts to dissuade him from undertaking his quixotic deeds. His DT is one Perla de Popayán. Combining both the quixotic qualities of DQ and some of the more picaresque aspects of SP, Epaminodas engages in theft and deceit as he serves various masters and finally meets Simón Rodríguez, the mentor of Simón Bolívar, who is also unable to dissuade him from his obsession. Irisarri's rightwing, reactionary political stance is evident throughout the book.

Bibliography: Hilarión de Altagumea, *Historia del perínclito Epaminodas del Cauca, El cristiano errante*, 2 vols (Guatemala City: Ministerio de Educación Pública, 1951).

Alter, Robert. Theorist of the novel. Reacting more to F. R. Leavis's concept of a "great tradition" of the realist novel than to Watt's "rise of the novel" thesis, but, in effect, in opposition to both, Alter starts with the following premise: "The novel begins out of an erosion of belief in the authority of the written word and it begins with Cervantes. It fittingly takes as the initial target of its literary critique the first genre to have enjoyed popular success because of the printing press—the Renaissance chivalric romance. Although novelists were by no means the first writers to recognize clearly the fictional status of fictions, I think they were the first—and Cervantes of course the first among them—to see in the mere fictionality of fictions the key to the predicament of a whole culture, and to use this awareness centrally in creating new fictions of their own." Alter distinguishes two basic traditions in the novel, the realists and those who self-consciously subvert realism, and notes that MC "is the initiator of both traditions of the novel." Alter's recognition of the role of the printing press in the establishment of the genre of the novel, together with the related notion that the novel must therefore begin in the Renaissance, positions him close to *Bakhtin in the general approach to the *theory and history of the novel.

Bibliography: Robert Alter, *Partial Magic: The Novel as a Self-Conscious Genre* (Berkeley: University of California Press, 1975).

Altisidora (Altisidorilla). A young lady-in-waiting to the duchess, who plays an important role in DQ's visits to the duke's country palace in *DQ* II. First, she sings a love song to DQ (II, 44), then she accompanies the duchess to spy on DQ and Doña Rodríguez and punish the two (II, 48), and then she accuses DQ of stealing some of her personal belongings as he prepares to leave the duke's palace (II, 57). Later, DQ and SP are brought back to the palace, where it is claimed that Altisidora has died of love for DQ and descended into hell (II, 69–70). After SP is made to 'disenchant' her and restore her to life, she describes her experience in the underworld, where she saw devils playing tennis with a book—*DQA*. When DQ again spurns her, she loses her temper, calling him vile names and telling him that the whole death and revival scene was a lie. Altisidora is (we presume) first convinced to pretend that she is in love with DQ so that everyone can enjoy his antics. The trouble is that she seems to take genuine offense when he rejects her overture, suggesting that she may have become too involved in the game. Again later, after her return from the underworld, it seems as though her real feelings burst through the role she is playing and threaten to destroy the trick. The way in which Altisidora, like Sansón Carrasco and Doña Rodríguez, gets caught up in DQ's fantasies is one of the more interesting aspects of *DQ* II. See also *DQ* II, 46, 50, 58, 67, 71, 73.

Bibliography: Carroll B. Johnson, *Madness and Lust: A Psychoanalytical Approach to "Don Quix-*

ote" (Berkeley: University of California Press, 1983); and Rafael Osuna, "Una parodia cervantina de un romance de Lope de Vega," *Hispanic Review* 49 (1981): 87–105.

Altisidorilla. Diminutive of the name of *Altisidora used by Doña Rodríguez in *DQ* II, 48.

Altolaguirre, Manuel (1905–59). Spanish poet, printer, filmmaker, and dramatist. An important member of the Generation of 1927, during the Spanish Civil War Altolaguirre wrote an adaptation of *Retablo* entitled *El triunfo de las germanías* (1937, but never published; *The Triumph of the Thieves' Jargon*). The title may also refer to the Valencia *Germanías* of 1519–22, an uprising against the nobles.
   Bibliography: John Crispin, *Quest for Wholeness: The Personality and Works of Manuel Altolaguirre* (Valencia, Spain: Albatros Hispanófila, 1983).

Alvarado, Don Pedro de. Spanish poet praised in Calliope's song in *Galatea* 6.

Alvarez de Soria, Alonso (1573–1603). Spanish poet. Alvarez de Soria was considered a master of the satiric sonnet and is credited with the invention of the device of *cabo roto in burlesque poetry, which MC uses in some of the preliminary poems to *DQ* I.

Alvarez de Toledo y Pimentel, Fernando, Duke of Alba (Albano) (1507–82). Spanish nobleman and soldier, governor of the Netherlands 1567–73. The Duke of Alba entered the Netherlands with a force of some 10,000 men to quell the Protestant and nationalist rebellion there. His execution of the Counts of Horn and Egmont for treason in 1568 is recalled by Ruy Pérez de Viedma in *Capitán* (*DQ* I, 39). Having fallen from royal favor and exiled, in 1580 he was called from retirement to put down the rebellion in Portugal and secure that country for the Spanish crown. He is referred to as *Albano* in *Numancia* 1. See also *DQ* II, 25.

Alvarez, Julia (1951–). Dominican American novelist and poet. Born and raised in the Dominican Republic, Alvarez has lived in the United States since 1961, and she writes in English. Her first novel was *How the García Girls Lost Their Accents* (1991), the partly autobiographical story of the coming of age of four sisters. One of them, Sandra, or Sandi, is quixotic in her obsessive reading while in graduate school; in her mother's words, "Sandi was a toothpick. And that's not the least of it, she wouldn't put a book down, read, read, read. That's all she did." Sandi's problem is that she believes that she is turning into a monkey, and it is her goal to read as many great books as possible before the transformation is complete, in hopes that something of her human past will remain from her in her new form. In a later novel, entitled *¡Yo!* (1997), Yolanda, the oldest sister (and author surrogate) from the family, basks in literary celebrity brought about by a book she had written about her family and friends (presumably *García Girls*). But in a metafictional rebellion that recalls both MC and *Pirandello, various characters from the previous novel, cognizant of their fictional status and upset at the way they were presented, turn the tables and present a joint exposé of Yolanda.
   Bibliography: Julia Alvarez, *How the García Girls Lost Their Accents* (Chapel Hill, NC: Algonquin Books, 1991); and Julia Alvarez, *¡Yo!* (Chapel Hill, NC: Algonquin Books, 1997).

Alvarez Quintero, Serafín (1871–1938) and Joaquín (1873–1944). Spanish dramatists. The Alvarez Quintero brothers were lifelong collaborators in the production of a large and varied popular theatrical production. One of their more successful efforts is *Los galeotes* (1900; *The Galley Slaves*), an adaptation of *DQ* I, 22. In 1926, as funds were being raised for the construction of the monument to MC in the Plaza de España (*Madrid), the Alvarez Quintero brothers wrote a brief one-act fundraising *loa* (short dramatic panegyric) entitled *Los grandes hombres, o el monumento a Cervantes* (*Great Men, or The Monument to Cervantes*). In it, a modest printer in Seville explains to a young boy named Frasquillo why he is sending a small amount of money for the project and why everyone in Spain should do the same. At the end, a *dama* (lady) suddenly appears and makes the same appeal to the entire audience. In spite of an occasional nice comic turn, this is simply a forerunner of the charity telethon or public service fundraising drive.

Bibliography: Serafín Alvarez Quintero and Joaquín Alvarez Quintero, *Los grandes hombres, o el monumento a Cervantes* (Madrid: Imprenta Clásica Española, 1926); and Serafín Alvarez Quintero and Joaquín Alvarez Quintero, *Los galeotes* (Madrid: R. Velasco, 1900).

Alvaro Tarfe, Don. A major character in *DQA*. He accompanies DQA to Zaragoza, has a number of adventures with him, and at the end of the novel commits him to the madhouse in Toledo. DQ and SP meet Tarfe on the way home in II, 72, and convince him that they are the real characters by those names. Tarfe even signs an affidavit to that effect. This scene is probably the most brilliant episode in MC's metafictional criticism of his rival (*Avellaneda, Alonso Fernández de). At the same time that he ridicules his rival, however, MC concedes him a certain ontological status equal to that of his own protagonist: there really was another DQ in DQ's world, he was not just a fictional character, and Alvaro Tarfe swears to the fact.

Bibliography: María Soledad Carrasco Urgoiti, "Don Alvaro Tarfe: El personaje morisco de Avellaneda y su variante cervantina," *Revista de Filología Española* 74 (1993): 275–93; and Thomas Lathrop, "Cervantes' Treatment of the False *Quijote*," *Kentucky Romance Quarterly* 32 (1985): 213–17.

Ama; Ama de Satanás. *Housekeeper.

Amadís cycle. The best, longest, most popular, and most influential series of chivalric romances in the European Renaissance. Beginning with the 1508 version of Garci Rodríguez de *Montalvo's four books of *Amadís de Gaula*, an adaptation of a primitive, lost original, there were 12 books overall in the series. The remainder are Book 5, *Las sergas de Esplandián* (1510), also by Montalvo; Book 6, *Florisando* (1510), by Páez de Ribera; Book 7, *Lisuarte de Grecia* (1514), by Feliciano de *Silva; Book 8, *Lisuarte de Grecia* (1526), by Juan Díaz; Book 9, *Amadís de Grecia* (1530), by Silva; Book 10, *Florisel de Niquea* (1532), by Silva; Book 11, *Rogel de Grecia* (1535 and

1551), by Silva; and Book 12, *Silves de la Selva* (1546), by Pedro de *Luján. Among them, these romances were published some 66 times in sixteenth-century Spain. The Amadís family constituted a veritable dynasty that entertained a nation for over a century.

Bibliography: Daniel Eisenberg and Mari Carmen Marín Pina, *Bibliografía de los libros de caballerías castellanos* (Zaragoza, Spain: Prensas Universitarias de Zaragoza, 2000).

Amadís de Gaula. Protagonist of the romance of chivalry by Garci Rodríguez de *Montalvo that bears his name. Amadís is the author of a sonnet dedicated to DQ as one of the preliminary poems to *DQ* I. He and the romance in which he is the protagonist are the most frequently cited chivalric hero and book in *DQ*. DQ calls him the greatest of all knights-errant in I, 25, and says that the one who most closely imitates him comes closest to knightly perfection. Amadís then, more than Orlando, is the person imitated by DQ in his *penance in Sierra Morena. In *Pedro* 1, he is cited by Pedro de Urdemalas as a chaste lover, in comparison with his brother Galaor, a lover who enjoys women's sexual favors. See also *DQ* I, 1, 6, 13, 15, 18, 20, 24–27, 43, 49, 50, 52; *DQ* II, 1–2, 6, 32, 34, 38, 44, 49, 52, 74.

Amadís de Gaula. *Montalvo, Garci Rodríguez de.

Amadís de Grecia. *Silva, Feliciano de.

Amadís's squire. *Gandalín.

Amado discípulo. *Beloved disciple.

Amante liberal, El (Amante); The Generous Lover. The second story in *Novelas*. This is one of MC's most romantic, stylized, and idealistic stories, with a prototypical romance plot. Much of the action is based on MC's own experiences as a captive in Algiers and reflects his general familiarity with the ongoing Christian-Muslim conflicts in the Mediterranean area. In contrast to most other MC stories and plays about captivity, this one takes place in Cyprus, rather than Algiers, and the main characters are Sicilians (Sicily was a Spanish possession in MC's day), although Ricardo has all the typical characteristics of a Spaniard.

The story opens *in medias res* with a dramatic lament by a Christian captive, Ricardo, standing before the ruined walls of the city of Nicosia. He is joined by a handsome young Turk, named Mahamut, who is a good friend of his. The two were born and raised in the same town and had spent their childhood together. Though Mahamut has renounced Christianity, he plans to convert back if and when they ever manage to return to Christian lands. Ricardo tells his friend that his great sorrow is not, as one might expect, the result of his loss of freedom, but rather the loss of the woman he loves. He tells his story: in their native Trapani (a city on the island of Sicily) he loved Leonisa Florencio, the most perfectly beautiful woman imaginable. She, however, preferred the younger and more effeminate Cornelio Rótulo. One day, when he confronted the two and criticized Cornelio, swords were drawn, but Cornelio fled. At that very moment, a band of Turkish pirates raided the shore and took both Leonisa and Ricardo prisoner, but not before Ricardo killed four of the attackers and received multiple wounds himself. After long and complicated negotiations for their release, the two were separated in different ships and headed off to sea. Leonisa became the property of a Greek renegade named Yzuf, and Ricardo was sold to Fetala, captain of the second ship. The ships headed for Africa, but before arriving Ricardo watched as the other ship was destroyed in a storm, and he assumed that his beloved had perished. Soon his master Fetala died of a heart attack, and Ricardo passed to the possession of Hazán Bajá, the newly named viceroy of Cyprus, and this is how he has come to be in this place at this time. Mahamut offers to help Ricardo in any way possible and informs him that he is highly esteemed by and enjoys the confidence of his master, the cadí (civil magistrate) of the island. The two men form part of the crowd witnessing the transfer of power to the new viceroy and thus are present when an extraordinary event takes place. A Jewish merchant arrives and offers for sale a beautiful Christian woman, elegantly attired in Muslim dress. She is none other than Leonisa. Ricardo is amazed to see that she still lives, but can do nothing at this time. When Leonisa's beautiful face is revealed, both the outgoing viceroy, Alí Bajá, and the incoming official, Hazán Bajá (Ricardo's master), fall immediately in love with her and wish to possess her. They both offer to purchase her, ostensibly to make of her a gift to the Great Turk, Selim. As they are about to come to blows over the right to become her purchaser, the cadí intervenes and suggests a compromise: they should split the price and let him, the cadí, take the woman and present her to Selim in the names of both of them. This pleases no one, but both men acquiesce to the suggestion. The cadí has Mahamut take the woman to his home and present her to his wife Halima. Mahamut uses his influence and gets the cadí to purchase Ricardo for himself. In order not to warn Leonisa of his presence, Ricardo takes the name of Mario under his new master. When Halima sees the newcomer in the house, she is taken by his handsome looks and falls in love with him. Within a short time Halima convinces Leonisa to try to convince Mario to acquiesce to her mistress's interests, and at the same time the cadí enlists Mario to help convince Leonisa to give in to his amorous interests. Mario and Leonisa finally have a chance to be alone, and Leonisa recounts her story from the point where they were separated: when her ship was about to wreck on the rocks of the island of Pantelleria, Yzuf secured her in a barrel, to which he also tied himself, in hopes of surviving the shipwreck. Leonisa fainted as they entered the sea, and when she recovered she was on shore beside the dead body of Yzuf. Her rescuers sold her to the Jewish merchant, who first tried to seduce her, then decided to dress her up to sell to the Turks. They agree to deceive their masters and improvise a plan as they go along. Ricardo and Mahamut devise the following scheme: they will convince the cadí to embark for Constantinople, ostensibly to deliver Leonisa to the Great Turk, but in the meantime purchase another Christian woman; then, during the voyage, they will feign that Leonisa is ill and that she dies, casting the body of the other woman into the sea and claiming that it was Leonisa who died, thus securing Leonisa for the cadí. The cadí likes the plan except for one detail: he suggests using his wife Halima instead of the Christian substitute. Within three weeks, everything is ready for the trip. Halima is also anxious for the voyage to get underway, for she, too, has a plan: escape along the way with Ricardo, convert to Christianity, and marry him. But others also have plans: Hazán Bajá sends a ship of 50 soldiers to follow that of cadí, with orders to attack and kill everyone but Leonisa; the soldiers will receive all the booty the cadí's ship carries, and he will receive Leonisa. Six days out to sea, after already feigning an illness for Leonisa, the cadí gives the order to kill Halima. But just then Hazán Bajá's ship closes in and, at the same time, another ship, this one apparently Christian, also draws near. It turns out that this third ship is commanded by none other than Alí Bajá, who also has the idea of killing the cadí and keeping Leonisa for himself. Amidst a great deal of confusion, Alí wounds the cadí and a general fight breaks out, during which nearly all the Turks, including Alí, are killed or badly wounded. Leonisa and Mahamut, with the help of enslaved Christian oarsmen, take control of everything. They offer Halima safe passage to any port, but she chooses to go with them, still in hopes of converting to Christianity and possessing Ricardo. The cadí, recovered from his wound, chooses to go on to Constantinople to complain to the Great Turk about the betrayal of Hazán and Alí. The Christian group proceeds to Trapani in Sicily, and upon arrival, with everyone elegantly dressed in Turkish garb, makes a spectacular entry into the city. To the assembled masses, including the families of Leonisa, Ricardo, and Cornelio, Ricardo makes a speech in which he offers all he has to Leonisa and generously gives Leonisa to Cornelio. But then he realizes that Leonisa is not his to give away, for she has her own freedom of choice. Leonisa then speaks and offers her hand in marriage to Ricardo. They are married amidst great celebration. Mahamut and Halima

both convert to Christianity and also marry. Ricardo's fame as the *generous lover* extends throughout Italy; he has many children by Leonisa, who gives a rare example of discretion, honesty, modesty, and beauty.

Bibliography: Nina Cox Davis, "The Tyranny of Love in *El amante liberal*," *Cervantes* 13, no. 2 (1993): 105–24; Gonzalo Díaz Migoyo, "La ficción cordial de *El amante liberal*," *Nueva Revista de Filología Hispánica* 35 (1987): 129–50; Eleodoro J. Febres, "Forma y sentido de *El amante liberal*," *Anales Cervantinos* 19 (1981): 93–103; Thomas R. Hart, "La ejemplaridad de *El amante liberal*," *Nueva Revista de Filología Hispánica* 36 (1988): 303–18; Ottmar Hegyi, *Cervantes and the Turks: Historical Reality versus Literary Fiction in "La Gran Sultana" and "El amante liberal"* (Newark, DE: Juan de la Cuesta, 1992); Thomas A. Pabón, "Courtship and Marriage in *El amante liberal*: The Symbolic Quest for Self-Perfectibility," *Hispanófila* 76 (1982): 47–52; Thomas A. Pabón, "Viajes de peregrinos: la búsqueda de la perfección en *El amante liberal*," in *Cervantes, su obra y su mundo: Actas del I Congreso Internacional sobre Cervantes*, ed. Manuel Criado de Val (Madrid: Edi-6, 1981), 371–75; Sandi Thomson-Weightman, "The Representation of Woman in *El amante liberal*: Goddess, Chattel and Peer," *Mester* 21 (1992): 61–71; and Miguel Angel Vázquez, "Mahamut, el buen salvaje: Nacionalismo y maurofilia en *El amante liberal* de Cervantes," *RLA: Romance Languages Annual* 7 (1995): 642–46.

Amaranta o La del mayo, La (Amaranta or The Woman of May). One of MC's early plays from the 1580s that has been lost. It is included in the list of his plays in MC's conversation with Pancracio de Roncesvalles in *Adjunta*.

Amargura, Calle de. *Calle de Amargura.

Amarili (Amarilis). 1. In *Galatea* 2, 4, the shepherdess loved by Damón; she never appears in the text. **2**. *Pastoral names.

Amarili (La constante Amarilis). *Suárez de Figueroa, Doctor Cristóbal.

Ambassador [Embajador]. In *Laberinto* 1, the man sent by the Duke of Dorlán, who informs Manfredo that he is suspected of having abducted the Duke's missing daughter and niece, Julia and Porcia.

Amberes. *Antwerp.

Ambrosia Agustina. In *Persiles* III, 9, the woman, dressed as a man, who gets involved in the death of a local count in Quintanar de la Orden (who then marries Constanza on his deathbed). For her role in this affair, Ambrosia is sentenced to two years as a galley slave. Later (III, 11), still dressed as a man, she is shown a great kindness by Constanza as she is being taken away to serve her sentence, and, a short while after that (III, 12) in Barcelona, after being freed and reunited with her lover/husband, repays the kindness to Constanza and the other pilgrims.

Ambrosio. 1. In *DQ* I, 12–13, a friend of Grisóstomo's who makes a funeral speech in praise of the deceased. See also *DQ* I, 25. **2**. In *Baños* 2, a Christian captive (*Catalina). **3**. In *Entretenida*, a second suitor for Marcela who bribes the maid Cristina to deliver a love note on his behalf.

Ambrosio, Santi (?–ca. 1605). A Florentine businessman about whom nothing is known except that he was married to MC's sister Andrea in the 1590s.

America [América]. The most frequently used term in Spain for the lands encountered by Columbus and his successors was *Indias* (the Indies). MC follows this general usage, but uses the term *América* on two occasions when referring to the new continent. See *DQ* I, 48; *Vidriera*.

Amet. A commander of the janissaries mentioned in *Tratos* 2.

Amezqueta, Juan de. Spanish civil servant who signed the approval for the king for *DQ* I.

***Amicable Quixote; or, The Enthusiasm of Friendship, The* (four vols., 1788).** An anonymous English fiction; in the preface, the author cites (and implicitly places his own work in the company of) *DQ*, *Gil Blas*, and the nov-

els of Henry Fielding. The plot is straightforward: the amicable and gallant George Bruce amicably courts and eventually marries the beautiful Emily Bryant. Bruce is called 'a true Quixote' once in the first volume, but there is no further intertextual reference of this sort in the remainder of this justly forgotten fiction. What is surprising, however, is that the work was not forgotten. It was translated into French by P. Chanin, and then that translation was used by *D. F. E. C. y C for his greatly modified version in Spanish.
   Bibliography: Anonymous, *The Amicable Quixote; or, The Enthusiasm of Friendship*, 4 vols. (London: J. Walter, 1788).

Amiga de la mujer de don Antonio. *Friend of Don Antonio's wife.

Amigo de Anselmo. *Friend of Anselmo.

Amigo de Cervantes. *Friend of Cervantes.

Amigos (camaradas) del cautivo. *Friends of the captive.

Amigos de Basilio. *Friends of Basilio.

Amigos de Don Antonio Moreno. *Friends of Don Antonio Moreno.

Amigos de Rodolfo. *Friends of Rodolfo.

Aminta. *Tasso, Torquato.

Amnon [Amón]. In the Old Testament, the oldest son of King David, who raped his half-sister Tamar and was killed by his half-brother Absalom. See *Entretenida* 1; *Galatea* 4.

Amor. *Love.

Amor cortés. *Courtly love.

***Amor medico, o sia, Don Chisciotte/Die Liebe ein Arzt, oder, Don Quixote* (1739; *Love the Physician, or, Don Quixote*).** An anonymous bilingual libretto in Italian and German based in part on *DQ* and in part on the *DQ* opera of *Conti. It is not known if the work was ever performed. *Amor medico* consists of two parallel and completely unrelated plots (except for two brief moments when they come into contact), one involving the romantic adventures of two sisters, and the other the comic adventures of DQ and SP, and involving primarily DQ's penance, SP's encounters with several people as he goes to deliver his master's letter to DT, and aspects of the inn of Juan Palomeque.

Amos de Cristina. *Cristina's master and mistress.

Amphion (Other great musician) [Anfión (Otro gran músico)]. A great musician of legend. He was a consummate harp player whose beautiful strains caused the very stones to build themselves into the city of Thebes. See *Galatea* 1; *Rinconete*.

Amurates. In *Sultana*, name of the great turk, or sultan, of the Turkish empire, who falls in love with and marries Doña Catalina de Oviedo; his name is not mentioned until Act 3. Presumably, he is a fictional version of the historical figure *Murad III.

Ana. *Pastoral names.

Ana de Briones, Doña. In *Entretenida* 1, the name Torrente gives for the mother of Don Silvestre de Almendárez. The reference to a Doña Ana in *Entretenida* 2 may also be to her.

Ana de Treviño, Doña. *Treviño, Doña Ana de.

Ana Díaz. A name used in the proverbial expression "Allá darás rayo en casa de Ana Díaz" ("Go, lightning, hit Ana Díaz's house"), used to comment on the departure of an unwanted person; it is something like "Good riddance to bad rubbish." See *Cueva*.

Ana Félix (Ricota). A *Morisca*, daughter of *Ricote, friend and neighbor of SP. She is first mentioned in *DQ* II, 54, when Ricote tells SP that, following the edict of expulsion of the *Moriscos* (1609) that forced her family to separate, she went with her mother, Francisca Ricota, to Algiers. She was also followed to Africa by her Christian lover, Don *Gaspar Gregorio. Later,

she dresses as a man, commands a pirate ship, and returns to Spain, hoping to retrieve her family's wealth. But her ship is captured and she is taken prisoner, only to be recognized by her father and SP, who by chance happen to be on the ship where she is brought as a captive. Her life is spared and she is eventually reunited with Don Gaspar. Whether or not she and her father are permitted to stay in Spain or whether she and Don Gaspar get married is left unresolved. See *DQ* II, 63–65.

Ana, Santa. *Saint Anne.

Anales Cervantinos. The first modern scholarly journal devoted to MC and his works. It was published, under the auspices of the MC section of the Consejo Superior de Investigaciones Científicas, from 1951 to 1959, when publication was suspended. Restarted in 1971, it continued publication through Volume 35 until 1999, when it was again suspended. In spite of its sometimes very uneven quality, the journal remains a valuable source for much excellent scholarship in the field.

Anales de la Mancha. *Archives of La Mancha.

Anarda. *Pastoral names.

Anastasio. In *Laberinto*, son of the duke of Dorlán who dresses as a peasant, hears the charges against Rosamira, goes to verify the case, and eventually marries Julia.

Anatolia [Natolia]. The eastern part of Turkey. See *Amante*.

Anciano morisco. *Elderly *Morisco*.

Anciano venerable. *Montesinos.

Ancient (language) of the Greeks [Antigua (lengua) de los griegos]. Ancient Greek is one of the languages described by Madrigal in *Sultana* 2.

Ancient novel. *Theory and history of the novel.

Ancona. City in central Italy on the Adriatic Sea. See *Vidriera*.

Andalod. *Hermit.

Andalusia [Andalucía]. The large region that includes most of southern Spain, including the cities Seville, Granada, Córdoba, and Málaga. Originally a Vandal stronghold (*Vandalia), this was the area of Spain where the Muslims retained control for the longest period of time, finally ceding completely to the Christians after the fall of Granada in 1492. This is also the region where most of the stereotypes about Spain are to be found in abundance: bullfighting, flamenco, guitar, tourist beaches, elaborate fiestas, religious processions and celebrations, and sherry. MC knew the region well, and spent years traveling to many of its cities in his capacities as commissary and tax collector. See *Casa* 3; *Coloquio*; *Doncellas*; *DQ* I, 2, 24, 28, 36, 39, 45, 49; *DQ* II, 14; *Fregona*; *Gitanilla*; *Parnaso* 1, 7; *Rinconete*; *Vidriera*.

Andalusian knights. *Spanish knights.

Andandona. In *Amadís de Gaula*, a large, unattractive, masculine giantess, the sister of the giant Madarque. See *DQ* II, 25.

Andantes caballeros. *Knights-errant.

Anderson Imbert, Enrique (1910–2000). Argentine novelist, short-story writer, and literary critic. Anderson Imbert specialized in the short-short story, often writing enigmatic little works inspired in literature and philosophy. In *El gato de Cheshire* (1965; *The Cheshire Cat*), there is one short fiction inspired in *DQ*: "La cueva de Montesinos." In Anderson's version, DQ goes to sleep and dreams that he is descending into the famous cave and is met by the enchanted Montesinos. But just as Montesinos opens his mouth to say something, DQ wakes up. He has the same dream three nights in a row. But, finally, he is greeted at the door of the castle by Montesinos and asks 'May I enter?' To which Montesinos responds that of course he may, but that he has the habit of disappearing every time he is invited in.
Bibliography: Enrique Anderson Imbert, *El gato de Cheshire* (Buenos Aires: Losada, 1965).

Anderson, Poul (1926–2001). American science fiction writer. One of Anderson's earliest short stories is entitled "Quixote and the Windmill" (1950), included in his collection *Strangers from Earth* (1961). In it, two men, a manual laborer and a technician, who have been replaced by machines are getting drunk and complaining about their fate. As they talk, the first and only robot—a general-purpose, manlike machine—passes by. For the men, the robot represents the future in which the human race will be replaced by such machines. They try to take out their aggression on the robot, throwing stones at it and kicking it; one of the men says, "We can't hurt you. We're Don Quixote, tilting at windmills. But you wouldn't know about that. You wouldn't know about any of man's old dreams." But the robot surprises the men by telling them that there are machines for very many specialized tasks, but there is no role for a general-purpose machine. Ever since its creation the robot simply wanders around, with nothing to do, and will continue to do so until it wears out—in about 500 years. Human beings have one great advantage, the robot says: at least they can get drunk.

Andradilla. Presumably a well-known thief or card-shark, as the name (just Andrada) is also cited by Vicente Espinel. See *DQ* II, 49.

Andrea. In *Sultana*, the spy who arranges for the freedom of many of the characters at the end of the play. He is apparently based on the historical figure of Andrea *Gasparo Corso, a spy or secret agent for Felipe II in Algiers.

Andrea de Oria, Juan. *Doria, Giovanni Andrea.

Andrea, Juan. *Doria, Giovanni Andrea.

Andrea Marulo. In *Persiles* III, 20–21, the student who rushes to Lucca where his beloved Isabela Castrucha is pretending to be possessed in order to buy time until he can arrive and the two can be married.

Andrés. 1. In *DQ* I, 4, the youth whipped by *Juan Haldudo the Rich, from Quintanar, for having been inattentive in his job as a shepherd, as a sheep is lost every day (a shortcoming the boy admits when he promises not to do it again). DQ, passing by, hears the boy's cries and immediately assumes that they signal someone in distress. When he confronts Haldudo and makes him promise to free the boy and pay him his back salary, he proudly believes that he has righted a wrong. (A problem is DQ's miscalculation: $9 \times 7 = 63$, not 73 as DQ says; editors have often either corrected the mathematics as if it were a typographical error or pointed out that MC was notoriously bad with numbers and errs here, but clearly the mistake is DQ's and written this way on purpose by MC.) After DQ's departure, Haldudo whips Andrés even harder. It is in the context of this episode that DQ makes his famous statement, 'Each of us is the son of his works'; that is, we determine our own fate and character, a sentiment repeated more significantly in II, 66, after DQ's defeat in Barcelona. In I, 31, Andrés again shows up and reveals to the priest, Dorotea, and others then with DQ what had happened, much to DQ's embarrassment. **2**. In *Guarda*, the beggar who is bought off by the soldier so that he will not call at the house of Cristina.

Bibliography: Catherine E. Bourque and Ronald J. Quirk, "Andrés in *Don Quijote*: A Cervantine *Pícaro*," *Cervantes* 5, no. 1 (1985): 19–25; and Augustin Redondo, "Nuevas consideraciones sobre el episodio de Andrés en el *Quijote* (I, 4 y I, 31)," *Nueva Revista de Filología Hispánica* 38 (1990): 857–73.

Andrés Caballero. In *Gitanilla*, the young nobleman, whose real name is Don Juan de Cárcamo, so smitten by the beauty of Preciosa that he offers to marry her. In order to prove his worthiness, he accepts the challenge to become a gypsy for a period of two years. When it is revealed at the end of the story that Preciosa also is of noble blood, the two lovers marry at once.

Andrés Perlerino. The wealthy father of Clara Perlerina, mentioned by the peasant who requests dowry money of SP in *DQ* II, 47.

Andronio. In *Laberinto*, a comic student who speaks in an affected language difficult for others to understand.

Andújar. City in Andalusia located to the east of Córdoba and south of Ciudad Real. Nearby, in the Sierra Morena, the festival of Nuestra Señora de la Cabeza is celebrated. See *Persiles* III, 6.

Anfión. *Amphion.

Anfriso. 1. River in Thessaly. See *Galatea* 6. **2**. Shepherd from Lope de *Vega's pastoral romance *La Arcadia*. See *Coloquio*. **3**. *Apollo.

Angel. 1. In *DQ* II, 11, a character in the cast of *Las *Cortes de la Muerte*. **2**. In *Casa* 3, the one who comes to Charlemagne and exhorts him to turn his attention to his Muslim enemies. **3**. In *Rufián* 1, the messenger who announces that all of heaven rejoices when a sinner repents and takes religion seriously, as does the ruffian Cristóbal de Lugo.

Angel de la Madalena. *Angel of the Magdalena.

Angel, Fray. In *Rufián* 2–3, a priest in Fray Cristóbal's monastery who comments on his good deeds and miracles.

Angel of light . . . angel of darkness [Angel de luz . . . el de tinieblas]. Lucifer, whose name means 'light bearer' and who, after his failed celestial rebellion, was cast out of heaven and became Satan, the Prince of Darkness. For the Duke of Nemurs, when Auristela is poisoned and loses all her beauty (in *Persiles* IV, 9), it is as if she has turned from his angel of light into one of darkness, making it evident that he loved her for her heavenly physical beauty alone.

Angel of the Magdalena [Angel de la Madalena]. A weathervane in the form of an angel that formerly was atop the Church of Magdalena in Salamanca. It is an object of study by the humanist scholar who accompanies DQ and SP to the Cave of Montesinos. See *DQ* II, 22.

Angelica [Angélica]. Character from the chivalric poems of Boiardo and Ariosto, known as *la Bella* (the Beautiful), who was extraordinarily popular, both with cultured writers and the general public, in the Spanish Renaissance. She is the daughter of Emperor Galafron of Cathay and is sent to the court of Charlemagne to make the knights there fall in love with her and cause dissent. She becomes the beloved of Orlando and is the cause of his madness when he discovers that she has been unfaithful to him with the handsome young Muslim Medoro. The most famous Spanish version of the story is Góngora's ballad *Angélica y Medoro* (1602), which is alluded to in *DQ* I, 1. She is also one of the major characters in *Casa*. See also *DQ* I, preliminary poems, 10, 25–26; *DQ* II, 1, 26.

Anglante. The title of Orlando, lord of Anglante. See *Parnaso* 8.

Angulo. In *Coloquio*, not *Angulo el Malo but an actor by this name.

Angulo el Malo. A theatrical manager, or *autor*, probably named Andrés, who was well-known in MC's time. The actors whom DQ and SP meet riding in the cart in II, 11, are from the company of Angulo el Malo. See also *Coloquio*.

Angulo, Gregorio de. A doctor of law who held administrative positions in Toledo and Naples, and who was also a poet. He was a good friend of Lope de *Vega's, and Lope praised him on more than one occasion. He is included among the valiant defenders of Mount Parnassus in the battle with the bad poets in *Parnaso* 7.

Aníbal. *Hannibal.

Animas del Purgatorio. *Souls from purgatory.

Año Santo. *Holy Year.

Anselmo. 1. Principal character in *Curioso*: *DQ* I, 33–35. His obsessive need to test the virtue of his wife Camila by convincing his friend Lotario to seduce her sets into motion the events that will lead to the death of all involved. **2.** Eugenio's rival for the hand of Leandra in *DQ* I, 51.

Ansó, Carlos (1953–). Spanish dramatist. Ansó wrote *Don Quijote, o, el sueño de Cervantes* (*Don Quixote, or, Cervantes's Dream*), which he calls a 'farcical elegy in two acts,' in Italian in 1995, and then translated it into Spanish in 1998. The play, the two acts of which correspond roughly to the two parts of *DQ*, takes place primarily in and around the home of MC, where he lives with his wife Catalina and his illegitimate daughter Isabel. As MC agonizes over the writing of *DQ*, he is visited by DQ and SP, and a series of incongruous—sometimes funny and surprising in their originality, and sometimes silly and pedestrian—conversations take place. Characters slip into and out of roles from MC's novel: Catalina and Isabel want to burn MC's books; DQ ponders which of these two women to take as his lady; Catalina advises MC on how to puff up the rhetoric of his prologue; MC dons Muslim garb and spies on DQ and SP, taking notes for his book; Catalina and Isabel stage the puppet show of Melisendra; DQ dies in MC's home, surrounded by MC and his family; and so forth. Overall, this is one of the more original and interesting theatrical adaptations inspired by *DQ*.

Bibliography: Carlos Ansó, *Don Quijote, o, el sueño de Cervantes* (Pamplona, Spain: Pamiela, 1998); and Alberto Rodríguez Rípodas, "Reminiscencias cervantinas a las puertas del siglo XXI: *Don Quijote o el sueño de Cervantes* de Carlos Ansó," *Anales Cervantinos* 35 (1999): 439–57.

Antaeus [Anteo]. In Greek myth, a giant, son of the gods Poseidon (Sea) and Gaia (Earth). Whenever he was thrown to the ground, he drew strength from his mother and came back stronger than before. In order to kill him, Heracles lifted him into the air and crushed him. See *Casa* 3; *DQ* I, 1; *DQ* II, 32.

Antarctica [Antártico, Región anártica]. The frozen region around the South Pole, or the south in general. See *Galatea* 6; *Numancia* 1.

Anteo. *Antaeus.

Anteón. *Actaeon.

Antequera. City in Andalusia, located north of Málaga and west of Granada. See *Coloquio*; *DQ* I, 3, 5; *Rufián* 1; *Vidriera*.

Antich, Fray Jerónimo. A member of the expedition to Algiers in 1577 when MC's brother Rodrigo was ransomed.

Antigua (lengua) de los griegos. *Ancient (language) of the Greeks.

Antipodes [Antípodas]. According to pre-Copernican belief, the people living on the side of the earth opposite Europe and therefore a strange race that lived upside down. See *Persiles* III, 11.

Antón. *Pastoral names.

Antón Castrado. In *Retablo*, the name of the father of Juan Castrado.

Antón Clemente. In *Pedro* 1, a friend of Pedro de Urdemalas who helps him win the hand of Clemencia Crespo.

Antón del Olmet, Luis (1886–1922). Spanish journalist and novelist. Antón de Olmet's *La postrera salida de Don Quijote* (1910; *Don Quixote's Last Sally*) is nothing more than one long practical joke in which Don Rodrigo Meléndez, quixotic only in the sense of gullible, is tricked into getting involved in a romance by way of correspondence, only to find at the last moment that his beloved Efigenia does not exist. The same author's *El hidalgo don Tirso de Guimaraes, . . .* (1912; *The Hidalgo Don Tirso de Guimaraes, . . .*), set in Galicia, is clearly an attempt to evoke MC and Quevedo, but does not succeed in any meaningful way; the closest it comes is in the series of prefatory burlesque poems, reminiscent of those in *DQ* I, by a pedant, a miser, a glutton, and others.

Bibliography: Luis Antón del Olmet, *La postrera salida de Don Quijote* (Madrid: Los Contemporáneos, 1910).

Antona, Antoño. In *Retablo*, Benito Repollo's mistake in pronunciation for the Latin *ante omnia* (especially), a phrase used earlier by Chirinos.

Antonia. In *Rufián* 1, a prostitute who loves Cristóbal de Lugo but is rejected by him.

Antonia Quijana. In *DQ*, the protagonist's teenage niece (*sobrina*) who is unnamed throughout the novel until II, 74. Like the housekeeper, with whom she is usually paired, she worries about her uncle's well-being, blames his madness on the evil influence of the books he reads and gladly burns them, and cares for him when he is at home. See *DQ* I, 1, 6, 25, 52; *DQ* II, 1–2, 4, 6, 73.

Antonio. 1. The goatherd who sings a simple shepherd's song about his beloved Olalla for DQ in *DQ* I, 11. **2.** *Veneziani, Antonio.

Antonio. The popular name of *Introductiones latinae* (1481; *Introduction to Latin*), a standard textbook by Antonio de *Nebrija. See *Coloquio*.

Antonio de Almendárez, Don. In *Entretenida*, the nobleman who loves a woman named Marcela, the same name as that of his sister, which leads his sister to believe that perhaps she is the object of her brother's incestuous desires.

Antonio de Isunza, Don. In *Cornelia*, the Spanish student who takes Cornelia Bentibolli into his home when she is in distress and helps her resolve her honor conflict.

Antonio de Villaseñor. In *Persiles* III, 9, this is revealed as the original full name of *Antonio the Barbarian and also the name of his son *Antonio the younger.

Antonio, Fray. In *Rufián* 2, the name adopted by the boy Lagartija when he accompanies Cristóbal de Lugo to Mexico and takes holy orders.

Antonio, Marco. *Antony, Mark.

Antonio Moreno, Don. DQ's host in Barcelona. He has the marvelous talking head, takes the visiting knight on trips through the city, and is disappointed when Sansón Carrasco defeats DQ and deprives the world of the enjoyment of his madness. See *DQ* II, 62–65, 67.

Antonio the Barbarian (Antonio de Villaseñor, Sr.). In *Persiles*, the Spaniard who has lived for years on the island of barbarians, where he meets and gives shelter to Periandro and Auristela and tells (I, 5–6) how his exaggerated sense of honor led to a series of adventures, including one with a talking wolf, and eventually led to his presence on the island of the barbarians. There he met the barbarian woman Ricla, to whom he taught the basics of Catholicism, and with whom he had two children. He and his family accompany Periandro and Auristela throughout the northern adventures and the trip through Europe, only separating from them in Quintanar de la Orden, Spain, where he is reunited with his aging parents (III, 9), and where he and Ricla remain, while his children, Antonio the younger and Constanza, continue the journey to Rome. There was a Villaseñor family living in Quintanar de la Orden in the sixteenth century, and it is possible that MC used this name as a basis for his character of Antonio. But there is no reason to assume that MC's character is intended to represent a historical person.

Antonio the younger (Antonio de Villaseñor, Jr.). In *Persiles*, the brave son of Antonio the Barbarian and Ricla, who meets Periandro and Auristela on the barbarians' island (I, 4) and accompanies them on the remainder of their journey. Along the way he acquires fame for his loyalty, strength, chastity, and skill as an archer. In I, 19, he resists the lascivious advances of Rosamunda. In II, 8, he similarly rejects the advances of the enchantress Cenotia, and even attempts to kill her, but misses and accidentally kills the slanderer Clodio. In II, 9–11, Cenotia casts a spell on Antonio and he falls ill, but recovers quickly when his father makes the enchantress lift the spell. In III, 1, Antonio becomes a spokesperson for the group as the one who narrates their adventures as painted on a canvas by a Portuguese artist; he functions in this role from time to time throughout the novel. In III, 9, when his parents decide to remain home in Quintanar, Antonio and his sister Constanza choose to continue the pilgrimage with Auristela and Periandro to Rome. In III, 14–15, he rescues the beautiful and wealthy French woman Féliz Flora, but is badly wounded in the fight; during the month of his recovery, Féliz Flora never leaves his side; at the end of the novel (IV, 14) the two of them are married.

Antoño. *Antona.

Antonomasia. The enchanted princess named after a trope (the use of a proper name to represent a person or type of person) in the story told by the Countess *Trifaldi. See *DQ* II, 38–39, 41.

Antony, Mark [Marco Antonio]: Marcus Antonius (ca. 80–30 BCE). Ruler of the eastern part of the Roman empire, most famous for his political alliance and love affair with Queen Cleopatra of Egypt. See *Galatea* 4.

Antropófagos. *Cannibals.

Antwerp [Amberes]. Capital city of a province by the same name in northern Belgium, and an important commercial center. See *Cornelia*; *Vidriera*.

Anunciada. *Church of la Anunciada.

Anzarena, Cristóbal (Donato de Arenzana or Fernando Díaz de Valderrama?). Spanish novelist. Anzarena's *Vida y empresas literarias del ingeniosísimo caballero don Quixote de la Manchuela. Parte primera* (1767; *Life and Literary Undertakings of the Very Ingenious Gentleman Don Quixote de la Manchuela: First Part*) is dedicated to *Necedad* (Stupidity). The protagonist's name is Cirilo Panarra but one day, when he was very young, he yawned and dislocated his lower jaw (*quijada*; one of the surnames proposed for DQ in I, 1), and from that day forth was known as

DQ. Since he was from the (fictional) small town of La Manchuela (perhaps so named by someone from La Mancha, the author speculates), near Jaén, the name was extended to DQ de La Manchuela. But here is where any relation to DQ ends, as the remainder of the novel deals with the education of the young man.

Bibliography: Cristóbal Anzarena, *Vida y empresas literarias del ingeniosísimo caballero don Quixote de la Manchuela: Parte primera* (Seville: Imprenta del Dr. Don Gerónymo de Castilla, 1767); and Dámaso Chicharro, *Don Quijote de la Manchuela, novela del siglo XVIII: Estudio crítico y antología* (Jaen, Spain: Centro Asociado de la UNED "Andrés de Vandelvira," 1997).

Anzoátegui, Ignacio B. (1905–ca. 1975).

Argentine historian and poet. Anzoátegui's collection of poems entitled *Dulcinea y otros poemas* (1965; *Dulcinea and Other Poems*) begins with a brief romantic poem entitled "Dulcinea," but there is nothing else in the volume that refers to, is inspired in, or otherwise particularly reminds the reader of *DQ*.

Bibliography: Ignacio B. Anzoátegui, *Dulcinea y otros poemas* (Madrid: Ediciones Cultura Hispánica, 1965).

Aparicio's oil [Aceite de Aparicio]. A

popular (but expensive) medicinal oil invented by Aparicio de Zubia in the first part of the sixteenth century. In *DQ* II, 46, it is used to treat DQ's nose after he is bitten and clawed by a cat.

Apelles [Apeles] (fourth century BCE).

Greek painter, none of whose works survives, but still considered to have been the greatest artist of his time. See *DQ* II, 32, 59; *Parnaso* 7; *Persiles* IV, 7.

Apenine [Apenino]. The mountain range that runs the length of Italy. See *DQ* I, 18.

Apes [Jimios]. Symbols of lust. In *Persiles* II, 15, 12 apes pull the vehicle of Sensuality.

Apia, Vía. *Appian Way.

Apollo (the Delian, Delos, Delphic Apollo, Follower of the fleeing nymph,

Great lord of Delos, Lucid Apollo, Man from Delos, Phoebus, Shepherd of Anfriso, Son of Leto, Thymbraeus) [Apolo (el Delio, Delo, Apolo delfíco, Seguidor de la fugitiva ninfa, Gran señor de Delo, Apolo Lúcido, Señor de Delo, Febo, Pastor de Anfriso, Hijo de Latona, Timbreo, Timbrio)]. In Greek myth, the son of Zeus and Leto. More than any other Greek god, Apollo embodied perfection: he was physically beautiful, morally excellent, and associated with the beneficial aspects of civilization. He was the god of intelligence and understanding, of healing and archery, and of poetry and music. Often he was called Phoebus (Febo) or Lucid and identified with the sun. Since he was supposed to have been born on the island of Delos (he was called the Delian or the Lord of Delos), that island was a center of worship. He was also worshiped at Delphi (and sometimes called Delphic Apollo), which he adopted as his home. Another temple at Thymbra (Timbra) earned him the name of Thymbraeus (Timbreo). Because at one time he kept flocks of sheep belonging to King Admetus by the banks of the Anfriso River, he was known as the Shepherd from Anfriso. Among the many epithets for Apollo (as listed in the opening paragraph of *DQ* II, 45) are discoverer of the antipodes, torch of the world, eye of heaven, archer, physician, father of poetry, and inventor of music. Throughout *Parnaso*, Apollo, or the Delian, serves MC as guide and mentor; sometimes he comes across more as a comic figure than a divine one, and in *Adjunta* he sends MC a letter about poets and poetry. See also *Casa* 2; *Coloquio*; *DQ* I, preliminary poems, 2, 6, 20, 43, 46; *DQ* II, 18, 20, 38; 47; 71; *Entretenida* 1; *Galatea* 1, 6; *Pedro* 1; *Persiles* I, 15, 19, 21; IV, 1; *Poesías* 5, 10, 16, 19, 28, 29, 34; *Rufián* 1; *Sultana* 1, 3.

Apollonius of Tyana [Apolonio Tianeo] (ca. 4 BCE—?). A wandering Pythagorean

mystic and philosopher who became famous as a miracle worker. In *Sultana* 2, Madrigal cites him as a famous scientist who understood the language of birds.

Aponte. There are at least three possibilities for this name; of them, the most likely is Marcelo de Aponte y Avalos, a Jesuit priest and Latin teacher in Toledo. See *Parnaso* 1.

Appendix to the Parnassus. **Viaje del Parnaso, El.*

Appian Way [Vía Apia]: Via Appia. The major Roman road south from Rome to Naples and then to Capua.

Approval; Aprobación. *Preliminaries.

Apuleius (ca. 124–ca. 170). Roman rhetorician and author. Apuleius's fame is due primarily to *The Golden Ass*, the episodic and satiric adventures of a young man named Lucius who is transformed into an ass, a story that was translated into Spanish as *Metamorfosis o el Asno de oro* (1525; *Metamorphosis, or The Golden Ass*) by Diego López de Cartegana. *The Golden Ass* story is cited in *Coloquio* and so must have been known by MC. A scene in which Lucius stabs some *wineskins may have been the source for a similar one in *DQ* I, 35.
  Bibliography: Diana de Armas Wilson, "Homage to Apuleius: Cervantes' Avenging Psycho," in *The Search for the Ancient Novel*, ed. James Tatum (Baltimore: Johns Hopkins University Press, 1994), 88–100.

Aquapendente. A small Italian city near Rome; its name comes from a large waterfall located there. In *Española*, it is the city where Count Arnesto attempts to have Ricaredo killed. Periandro and his group of pilgrims pass through the city in *Persiles* IV, 1.

Aquel abad. In *DQ* I, 25, SP corrupts the name of Elisabat, a surgeon from *Amadís de Gaula* mentioned in the previous chapter, into "that abbot."

Aquelindo. Apparently a dance cited in *Rufián* 1, but perhaps simply a misprint.

Aqueronte. *Acheron.

Aquila, Serafino dell' (1466–1500). Italian poet. Aquila was one of the most popular and influential foreign poets in the Spanish Renaissance. MC cites one of his lines in a poem by Damón in *Galatea* 5.

Aquiles. *Achilles.

Aquís. *Achish.

Arabia. The peninsula in southwestern Asia, largely a desert, where Saudi Arabia is today the dominant country. Arabia was considered a source of the finest gold, especially before the discovery of new sources of the precious metal in America. Similarly, highly valued aromas and perfumes came from Arabia. See *Baños* 1; *DQ* I, 16; *DQ* II, 44; *Gitanilla*; *Persiles* III, 6; *Sultana* 2.

Arabia Felix [Felice Arabia]. The fertile region of southwestern *Arabia that today is basically the country of Yemen. See *DQ* I, 18.

Arabians, Arabs [Arabes]. Natives or inhabitants of Arabia. For MC, the term was sometimes synonymous with Moor, or Muslim.

Aragon (Kingdom of Aragon) [Aragón (Reino de Aragón)]. Medieval kingdom in northeastern Spain that included modern Aragon, together with Catalonia, Valencia, the Balearic Islands, Sicily, and Naples. This was the kingdom ruled by Fernando of Aragon when he married Isabel of Castile in 1479. See *DQ* I, 13, 41, 43; *DQ* II, 4, 27, 48; *Galatea* 5; *Gitanilla*; *Persiles* I, 5; *Sultana* 3; *Tratos* 2.

Aragón, Doña María de, Duchess of Luna and Villahermosa. *Duke.

Aragonés, Alonso. **Información de Argel.*

Aragonese [Aragonés]. 1. A resident or inhabitant of Aragon. **2.** One of the terms MC often uses specifically with reference to the author of *DQA*, who claimed to be Aragonese (*Avellaneda, Alonso Fernández de).

Aranda, Fray Miguel de. Spanish priest. He was stoned and burned to death by the Turks during the time MC was in Algiers. This is probably the incident alluded to in *Baños* 1.

Aranjuez. The southernmost city in the province of Madrid, located directly south of the capital at the place where the Jarama River flows into the Tagus. Some of the best produce in Spain comes from Aranjuez; an annual strawberry festival celebrates the city's most famous crop. In the sixteenth century Felipe II had a sumptuous palace, sometimes called the 'Versailles of Spain,' and gardens built there, with a set of magnificent fountains. Today's palace is an eighteenth-century structure built after the previous one was destroyed in a fire. In *Viudo*, the running sores on the legs and arms of the prostitute Pericona are by analogy compared to Aranjuez. Similarly, in *DQ* II, 50, Doña Rodríguez compares the *running sores of the duchess to the magnificent fountains at Aranjuez. See also *Casamiento; DQ* I, 52; *Persiles* III, 8; *Vidriera*.

Araucanian [Arauco]. A member of the native Americans of Chile and the Argentine Pampa. The conquest of the Araucanians by the Spanish is the subject of two important Spanish Renaissance epic poems by Alonso de *Ercilla and Pedro de *Oña. See *Parnaso* 4; *Poesías* 27.
Bibliography: Diana de Armas Wilson, "Jewels in the Crown: The Colonial War Epic," in *Cervantes, the Novel, and the New World* (Oxford: Oxford University Press, 2000), 161–82.

Araujo, Joaquim (1858–1917). Portuguese poet. Araujo wrote at least three poems about DQ: a sonnet in his book *Occidentais* (1888; *Occidentals*); "Carta à Mulher de Luto" ("Letter to the Grieving Woman") in *A Mulher de Luto* (1902; *The Grieving Woman*); and *Visões do "Quixote"* (1909; *Visions of Don Quixote*). In the latter, DQ and a very articulate and philosophical SP engage in an extended discussion about idealism and related subjects.
Bibliography: Joaquim de Arajuo, *Visões do "Quixote"* (Genoa, Italy: Pietro Pellas, 1909).

Arauz. In *Rinconete*, Maniferro's mistake for the name Eurídice.

Arbitrista. Schemer, problem solver, amateur political theorist, promoter, or projector. Persons of all sorts came forth with schemes or solutions (*arbitrios*) to aid king and country in the sixteenth and seventeenth centuries. The *arbitrista* became one of the stock comic types in the satiric writings of Quevedo and others. In *Coloquio*, one resident of the hospital is an *arbitrista* whose scheme is for all Spaniards to fast one day a month and contribute the money they would have spent on food to the royal coffers. See also *DQ* II, 1.

Arbolanche (Arbolanches, Arbolánchez), Jerónimo. The author of a chivalric romance in verse entitled *Los nueve libros de las Habidas* (*1566; The Nine Books of Las Habidas*); he is the general of the band of bad poets who attack Parnassus in *Parnaso* 7.

Arcabuceros. *Harquebusiers.

Arcabuz. *Harquebus.

Arcadia. The central region of Peloponnesus, the southernmost part of Greece, connected with the main part of the country by the Isthmus of Corinth. In Roman myth, and subsequently in Renaissance literature and culture, Arcadia came to represent the ideal setting for bucolic life. Jacoppo *Sannazaro entitled his famous pastoral romance *Arcadia* (1504) as did both Philip Sidney (1590) and Lope de *Vega (1598). In *DQ* II, 58, DQ and SP come across a setting in which several young men and women have set up a feigned (or mock) pastoral Arcadia in order to imitate the pastoral life and celebrate the poetry of Garcilaso de la Vega and Luis de Camões. See *Coloquio; DQ* I, 51; *DQ* II, 67.
Bibliography: Herrero, Javier. "Arcadia's Inferno: Cervantes' Attack on Pastoral." *Bulletin of Hispanic Studies* 55 (1978): 289–99.

Arcaláus. Enchanter and moral enemy of Amadís de Gaula. In *DQ* II, 34, he is the third in the procession of enchanters who precede the appearance of Merlin. See also *DQ* I, 15.

Arce, Fray Rodrigo de. Commander of the Order of Merced in Toledo and, like Fray Jorge de *Olivar, active in the ransoming of Christian captives in North Africa. In *Baños* 3, he is mentioned as one who has often come to Algiers to ransom captive Christians.

Archimedes [Arquímedes] (ca. 287–212 BCE). The great Greek mathematician, astronomer, physicist, and inventor. He is mentioned in *Parnaso* 8 as being (anachronistically) impressed by the structures erected for the celebration of the marriage of Louis XIII of France and the princess Doña Ana of Austria, in Naples in 1612.

Archipiela. In *DQ* II, 38, the deceased King of Candaya in the story told by the Countess *Trifaldi.

Archives of La Mancha [Archivos de la Mancha, Anales de la Mancha, Archivos manchegos]. In *DQ* I, the supposed location of some of the sources for the history of DQ. MC carries the convention of the discovered manuscript, a common feature of the romances of chivalry, that he begins in the prologue into the text itself, where there are further references to these archival sources until I, 9, when the definitive manuscript of CHB is located. There is further reference to a search for archival information in I, 52, in the discussion of a supposed third sally by DQ and the poems written by the *Academicians of Argamasilla. See *DQ* I, 2, 8, 52.

Arco de Portugal. *Portugal, Arch of.

Ardennes [Ardenia]. The name of a forest in Belgium and the setting for the action of *Casa*.

Arenal, Puerta del. *Gate of the Arenal.

Arequipa. A city in southern Peru. See *Galatea* 6.

Aretino, Pietro (1492–1557). Italian poet and dramatist known especially for his vicious satires. See the dedication to *Novelas*.

Arévalo. A small town located directly north of Avila and south of Valladolid. It is mentioned in *DQ* I, 16, as the home of the muleteer, a relative of CHB, with whom DQ fights.

Argales. A fountain in the province of Valladolid. See *Fregona*.

Argalia. In *Casa*, the brother of Angelica, who hopes to use an enchanted lance to defeat the Twelve Peers, but who is thrown into a river and killed by Ferraguto.

Argamasilla del Alba. A small agricultural town in La Mancha, located southeast of Toledo and east of Ciudad Real; it is not far from El Toboso. It is often assumed to be the unnamed 'village in La Mancha' mentioned in the first line of *DQ* I. (There is a second Argamasilla in La Mancha, Argamasilla de Calatrava, but this village has never been able to stake a claim as the home of DQ.) Two strong pieces of evidence in support of this thesis are the burlesque poems of I, 52, which are supposedly written by the (nonexistent) *Academicians of Argamasilla, and the fact that in *DQA* the home of DQ is specifically identified as Argamasilla. The modern village has done as much as possible to claim the honor of being the home of DQ by erecting statues to MC, DQ, SP, and DT in a small park in the town's center. It has also promoted the legend of the Cueva de Medrano (Medrano's Dungeon) as the jail in which MC conceived and started to write his novel during his supposed stay there in 1601–3. There is no documentary evidence for this claim. In 1863, the romantic dramatist Juan Eugenio Hartzenbusch (1806–80) moved the entire printing apparatus of the prestigious Rivadeneyra publishing house to Argamasilla in order to print a luxury (but textually not very good) four-volume edition of *DQ* in the jail of that city where MC supposedly conceived of the novel. It was a quixotic, if pointless and expensive, gesture.

Argel. *Algiers.

Argensola, Bartolomé Leonardo de (1562–1631). Spanish poet. Younger brother of Lupercio (MC refers to the two of them as *los Lupercios*), Bartolomé was a priest and poet of importance and esteem. One of the most restrained and 'classical' poets of the baroque era, Argensola was admired by MC, Lope de

*Vega, and many others. He is praised in Calliope's song in *Galatea* 6. He and his brother are mentioned resentfully in *Parnaso* 3 and cited again in *Parnaso* 7.

Argensola, Lupercio Leonardo de (1559–1613). Spanish poet and dramatist. Older brother of Bartolomé (MC refers to the two of them as *los Lupercios*), Lupercio was very much a classicist whose Senecan tragedies are today ignored, and his poetry is read less than that of his brother. In *DQ* I, 48, the Canon of Toledo lists several modern plays he considers exemplary. Among them are three by Argensola: *Isabela, Filis,* and *Alejandra.* Popular and respected as they might have been in their day, the first and third of these plays were not published until late in the eighteenth century, and the *Filis* has been lost. Lupercio is praised in Calliope's song in *Galatea* 6. He was also the secretary to the Count of *Lemos, famous patron of the arts, and in this capacity seems to have promised MC a place in the retinue of the count when the latter established a Spanish literary colony in Naples (a city where MC had spent time when he was in the military and that he loved) in 1608, but MC was not among those actually chosen. Both brothers were prominent members of the Academy of the Idle in Naples. MC mentions the brothers and his antagonism toward them in *Parnaso* 3 and again mentions Lupercio as being absent from the battle for Mount Parnassus in *Parnaso* 7. Lupercio died in Naples about the time MC was writing *Parnaso.*

Argos. 1. The ship of Jason and his sailors on their quest for the Golden Fleece. See *Parnaso* 1. **2**. *Argus.

Argote y de Gamboa, Don Juan de. An unknown poet mentioned in *Parnaso* 4.

Argüello, La. In *Fregona*, the employee at the inn who loves and propositions Tomás Pedro.

Arguijo. In *Sultana* 1, a Christian captive freed by the spy Andrea.

Arguijo, Don Juan de (1560–1623). A well-known Sevillian poet who hosted a literary academy during the time that MC was in that city. A poet and patron of the arts, Arguijo's best sonnets are carefully crafted, if sometimes stilted. He is one of the poets cordially greeted by Apollo upon arrival at Parnassus in *Parnaso* 3.

Argus [Argos]. In Greek myth, the herdsman who had eyes all over his body. He was sent by Hera to keep watch over Io, who had been converted by Hera into a heifer to protect her from the lascivious desires of Zeus. After he was killed by Hermes at Zeus's request, Hera took the monster's eyes and put them onto the feathers of the peacock's tail. The ever-watchful Argus is a symbol of eternal vigilance. See *Celoso; Cornelia; DQ* II, 65; *Entretenida* 2; *Galatea* 4; *Gallardo* 1; *Gitanilla; Parnaso* 1, 7; *Persiles* I, 21; II, 5; *Rinconete; Viejo.*

Ariadne [Aridiana]. In Greek myth, the daughter of King Minos of Crete. She fell in love with Theseus and gave him the thread that he used to find his way out of the labyrinth after killing the Minotaur. She fled with Theseus, then later was abandoned by him; but she then married Dionysus and became immortal. The crown of Ariadne is a constellation of stars. See *DQ* II, 38.

Arias de Bobadilla, Don Francisco, Conde de Puñonrostro. Court officer in Seville well-known both for his integrity and his ruthless treatment of criminals. In *Fregona* the Count of Puñonrostro is credited with executing the famous criminals Alonso *Genís and *Ribera, but this act of justice was actually carried out by the Count of Priego.

Arias de León, Luis. Spanish satirist. His *Historia del valeroso caballero Don Rodrigo de Peñadura: Tomo primero* (1823; *History of the Valorous Knight Don Rodrigo de Peñadura: Volume One*) presents some bibliographical problems. It is very likely that the author's name is a pseudonym, but if so, there is no way of knowing who the actual author is. The title page indicates that the book was published in

Marseilles, which was a refuge for liberal exiles at that time—but the book is an antiliberal, absolutist satire, which makes publication there unlikely. And, finally, there is the matter of a continuation to this "first part": was such a sequel intended? If so, it appears not to have been written. Whatever the answers to these questions, the novel itself is one more example of how *DQ* was used for the aims of social satire more than for aesthetic purposes. The protagonist, Don Rodrigo, has been influenced by his extensive readings in eighteenth-century neoclassical political theorists (Voltaire, Rousseau, and the like) and attempts to convince the world to accept his vision of things. He is accompanied by his SP-like servant Roque Zambullo. There is no DT figure in the novel; the protagonist's political philosophy is his obsession. In a series of intellectual encounters with others who expose the folly of his thought as they travel from León to Astorga and back, particularly noteworthy is Bachiller Cigarra, the Sansón Carrasco figure in the novel, who critiques Don Rodrigo's rhetoric more effectively than anyone else. By far the best part of the book is the final chapter, which recalls the events in the inn of Juan Palomeque in *DQ* I, 16–17.

Bibliography: Luis Arias de León, *Historia del valeroso caballero Don Rodrigo de Peñadura: Tomo primero*, ed. Nicolás Miñambres Sánchez (León, Spain: Ediciones Leonesas, D. L., 1988).

Arias Girón, Don Félix (?–1630). The son of Don Francisco, Count of Puñonrostro, he was a Spanish soldier in Flanders who also wrote some verse, at least some laudatory poems for writers such as Lope de *Vega and Vicente Espinel. He is praised among the good poets in *Parnaso* 2.

Aridiana. *Ariadne.

Arion [Arión] (seventh century BCE). Famous Greek lyric poet and musician, none of whose work survives. See *Galatea* 6.

Arioste, Ludovico (1474–1533). Italian poet and dramatist. Ariosto's fame rests primarily with his epic chivalric poem *Orlando Furioso* (first edition 1516, complete edition

1532; *The Madness of Orlando*), a sequel to *Boiardo's *Orlando Innamorato*. There are three primary centers of interest in the poem: 1) Orlando's love for the beautiful Angelica, 2) the war between the French (Franks) and the Muslims (Saracens), and 3) the love of the Saracen Ruggiero for the Christian warrior woman Bradamante. But at the same time, there is a plethora of subplots and digressions, magic intermingles with realistic scenes, and chivalric nobility is undercut by irony and humor. The narrative framework is one of self-conscious, self-deprecating metafiction. Extremely popular throughout Europe in the Renaissance, this Italian adaptation of the story of the French epic hero Roland was translated three times into Spanish by Jerónimo Jiménez de *Urrea (1549), Hernando de Alcocer (1550), and Diego Vázquez de Contreras (1585), any or all of which MC could have known; it is more likely that he read the work in Italian. Overall, Ariosto's work is one of major importance for MC in the writing of *DQ*, not far behind *Amadís de Gaula* itself, and allusions to, paraphrasings of, and quotations from *Orlando Furioso*, and references to its major characters (Orlando, Angelica, Mambrino, Reinaldos, Brunelo, Sacripante, and others) are found throughout MC's novel. Ariosto is referred to as 'the Christian poet' in *DQ* I, 6. In *Curioso*, the Florentine Lotario calls Ariosto 'our poet' (*DQ* I, 33). See also *DQ* II, 1, 62; *Galatea* 6.

Bibliography: Marina S. Brownlee, "Cervantes as Reader of Ariosto," in *Romance: Generic Transformation from Chrétien de Troyes to Cervantes*, ed. Kevin Brownlee and Marina S. Brownlee (Hanover, MA: University Press of New England, 1985), 220–37; Thomas R. Hart, *Cervantes and Ariosto: Renewing Fiction* (Princeton, NJ: Princeton University Press, 1989); and David Quint, "Narrative Interlace and Narrative Genres in *Don Quijote* and the *Orlando Furioso*," *Modern Language Quarterly* 58, no. 3 (1979): 241–68.

Aristotelianism. Spanish Muslim and Jewish scholars were among the most active and important in keeping works by and about Aristotle in existence during the centuries when the Iberian Peninsula was dominated by the Muslims, and intellectual activity was valued and supported in Córdoba, Toledo, and other centers. Aristotelian thought—especially in ethics, rhetoric, and poetics—was prominent in the Spanish Renaissance from the beginning and in many ways exerted greater influence than did Platonic thought. Aristotelianism included the doctrines of verisimilitude, the distinction between poetic truth and historical truth, and the legitimized marvelous, among others. The influence of Aristotelian thought on MC, especially in poetics and theory (*literary theory in Cervantes), has been shown to be substantial.

Bibliography: Alban K. Forcione, *Cervantes, Aristotle and the "Persiles"* (Princeton, NJ: Princeton University Press, 1970).

Aristotle [Aristóteles] (384 BCE–322 BCE).

The greatest of Plato's students; Greek philosopher, scientist, and literary theoretician, whose *Poetics* had a great influence on Renaissance writers, including MC (*Aristotelianism). See *DQ* I, prologue, 1, 25; *Rufián* 1.

Arlanza.

A Spanish river that rises in the mountains of north-central Spain, flows southwesterly, and empties into the Pisuerga east of Palencia. See *DQ* II, 44.

Arlaxa.

In *Gallardo*, the beautiful Muslim whose curiosity about Fernando de Saavedra sets in motion the action of the play.

Armada, The Invincible.

The Spanish naval force defeated by the English in 1588. Felipe II decided to eliminate the Protestant heresy in England once and for all with a combined army-navy attack. The plan was to send an overwhelming flotilla that would both destroy English naval power and facilitate the transportation of the 24,000 crack, experienced Spanish troops (the finest military force in the world at the time) in the Netherlands, under the able command of Alejandro *Farnesio, Duke of Parma, to England in order to overwhelm the entire country. But although the plan was sound, the execution was poor. After the death of the greatest Spanish naval captain of the age, Alvaro de *Bazán, Marqués de Santa Cruz, in January 1588, Felipe named the young, inexperienced, and mediocre Alonso *Pérez de Guzmán, duke of Medina Sidonia, to head the expedition. The armada consisted of some 200 fighting ships, over 350 supply vessels, and about 20,000 soldiers. In Spain, confidence was high and credit for the forthcoming victory was already accorded to the Virgin, who would guarantee success, just as she had done in the battle of Lepanto. Delays, bad weather, superior English leadership (by Lord Howard of Effingham and Sir Francis Drake) and equipment, the inability of Farnesio's troops to mobilize and move on time, and poor leadership by Medina Sidonia, however, combined to turn a probable victory into a complete rout, with a large part of the naval forces being lost in bad weather along the Scottish and Irish coasts in their desperate attempt to return home by circling north around the British Isles. Only about 50 of the large fighting vessels made it back to Spain; some 9,000 men perished. More than any other single event, the defeat of the Invincible Armada marked the end of unchallenged Spanish hegemony and the beginning of Spain's decline into mediocrity.

Bibliography: John Francis Gillmartin, *Gunpowder and Galleys: Changing Technology and Mediterranean Warfare at Sea in the Sixteenth Century* (Cambridge: Cambridge University Press, 1974); David Howarth, *Voyage of the Armada: The Spanish Story* (New York: Viking Press, 1981); Colin Martin and Geoffrey Parker, *The Spanish Armada* (New York: W. W. Norton, 1988); and M. J. Rodríguez-Salgado and Simon Adams, ed., *England, Spain, and the Gran Armada 1585–1604: Essays from the Anglo-Spanish Conferences, London and Madrid, 1988* (Savage, MD: Barnes and Noble Books, 1991).

Armenia [Armeña].

A country in southwest Asia that lies south of Russia, west of Iran, north of Turkey, and east of the Black Sea. See *DQ* I, 31; *Tratos* 4.

Arminda.

In *Galatea* 3, the shepherdess who may be the love interest of Lauso; she never appears in the text.

Arms and Letters [Armas y letras].

The arms versus letters debate has its roots in antiquity, where it is best illustrated in the comparison between Achilles and Ulysses. In medieval Christendom, the debate was often formulated in terms of *fortitudo* (strength) and *sapientia* (wisdom). A typical medieval expression of the theme is the thirteenth-century debate poem entitled *Disputa de Elena and María* (*Debate between Helen and Mary*) in which the former defends her lover, a knight, and the latter speaks for hers, a cleric; MC burlesques this genre in his *Guarda*, in which Cristina must choose between a poor soldier and a subsacristan. One of the most frequent themes of the Renaissance was that the ideal courtier should be equally accomplished at arms, the practice of knighthood and warfare, and letters, which can refer either to law or to creative writing. The prototype of this ideal in Spain was the poet *Garcilaso de la Vega, who died in battle. MC's life also illustrates the pattern, as his career as a soldier in the 1570s led to a certain glory before he turned to writing in the 1580s. DQ also endorses the ideal, especially in the speech, considered by many to reflect MC's own views, that he gives to an illustrious company at the *inn of Juan Palomeque in I, 37–38, in which he argues most strongly for arms over letters. It is probably no accident that DQ's speech comes between *Curioso* (I, 33–35), representing letters, and *Capitán* (I, 39–41), representing arms; or that Ruy Pérez de Viedma (arms) is reunited with his brother Juan (letters) in I, 42. In DQ's discussion with the page who is going off to join the army in *DQ* II, 24, he again extolls the virtues of arms over letters and describes the life of the soldier in terms that seem to recall aspects of MC's own military experiences. Several characters throughout MC's works also explicitly represent the fusion of arms and letters: the protagonist of *Vidriera* is almost the personification of arms and letters; in *Persiles*, Antonio the Barbarian (I, 5), Mauricio (I, 12), and Policarpo (I, 22) all studied both; and *Parnaso*, a military defense of the realm of poetry, is MC's most extended, if allegorical, version of the topic. See *DQ* II, 6; *Persiles* IV, 1.

Bibliography: Michel Moner, *Cervantes: Deux Thèmes Majeurs (L'amour—les armes et les lettres)* (Toulouse, France: France-Ibérie Recherche, 1986); and Peter E. Russell, "Arms versus Letters: Towards a Definition of Spanish Fifteenth-Century Humanism," in *Aspects of the Renaissance: A Symposium*, ed. Archibald R. Lewis (Austin: University of Texas Press, 1967), 47–58.

Army, Spanish [Ejército español]. The Spanish army was the best trained and most disciplined in Europe during the sixteenth and seventeenth centuries. It had the reputation of being invincible until the battle of Rocroi in 1643. Soldiers dressed in ostentatious, brightly colored clothing when not in battle; MC calls them *papagayos* [parrots] in *Vidriera*, where there is a description of the free and easy life of the soldier when not in combat. But in his *arms and letters speech in I, 37–38, DQ stresses the hardships of military service.

Arnaldo. In *Persiles*, the Prince of Denmark. In I, 1–3, he rescues the drowning Periandro and takes him, dressed as a woman, to the barbarian's island in order to see if Auristela is there. Later, in I, 15–17, they are reunited and Arnaldo tells Periandro how he had hosted Auristela in Denmark for two years and had fallen in love with her, even though ignorant of her true identity. The whole group sets sail in Arnaldo's ship (I, 18–19), but a mutiny sinks the ship and Auristela is separated from Arnaldo and Periandro. They are reunited in II, 2, on the island of Scinta, and after a lengthy stay there, the group departs and arrives at the Island of the Hermits (II, 18). In II, 21, Arnaldo returns to his homeland to take care of matters there, vowing to catch up with Auristela in Rome. In IV, 2, the pilgrims find Arnaldo just outside of Rome, badly wounded after his fight with the Duke of Nemurs over the right to love Auristela. He is nursed back to health and remains with the group throughout their stay in Rome. When Auristela reveals her identity as Sigismunda and marries Persiles, in IV, 14, Arnaldo receives the consolation prize of Eusebia, Sigismunda's younger sister, as his wife.

Arnao, Antonio (1828–89). Spanish poet and dramatist. In his book *Un ramo de pensamientos* (1878; *A Bouquet of Thoughts*), there is a section entitled "Galería histórica" ("Historical Gallery"), which consists of 33 sonnets dedicated to great historical figures and events (e.g., Mozart, Isabel the Catholic, and Lepanto). The first poem in this section is "A Cervantes" ("To Cervantes"), a poem in praise of a man who overcame great difficulties in order to give his name to his language (Spanish is often referred to as 'the language of MC').

Bibliography: Antonio Arnao, *Un ramo de pensamientos* (Madrid: M. Tello, 1878).

Arnarda. *Pastoral names.

Arnaut Mamí. The Albanian renegade pirate who captured MC and his brother Rodrigo when they were returning on the galley *Sol to Spain from Naples in 1575 and took them to Algiers, where they began their captivity. In 1592, he retired to Constantinople. In *Galatea* 5, he is the Turkish pirate leader who takes the ship in which Timbrio, Nísida, and Blanca are traveling. See also *DQ* I, 41; *Española*.

Arnaute. In *Sultana* 3, the name, mentioned once, of one of the three boys who serve the Sultan Amurates.

Arne, Thomas Augustine (1710–78). English composer. Arne wrote a musical farce entitled *The Sot* (1775), an adaptation of the Barataria episodes from *DQ* II, 45–53, by way of Henry *Fielding's *Don Quixote in England* (1754).

Arnesto, Count. In *Española*, a young Englishman who challenges Ricaredo for the hand of Isabela and later tries to have him murdered.

Arno. A river in Tuscany, Italy, that flows into the Ligurian Sea. See *Galatea* 6.

Arnold, Samuel. *Colman, George.

Aroba. A name mentioned in one of the songs in *Fregona*.

Aroute, François-Marie. *Voltaire.

Arquímedes. *Archimedes.

Arrabal, Fernando (1932–). Spanish dramatist, novelist, and filmmaker. Arrabal's 'psy-

chobiography' of MC, entitled *Un esclavo llamado Cervantes* (1996; *A Slave Named Cervantes*), reads more like a novel about MC than it does as a serious attempt at biography. Arrabal claims to reveal the truth about the 1569 document that contains an order remanding MC to Madrid to have his right hand severed and to face ten years of exile for having wounded one Antonio de *Sigura. Arrabal presents this document as "proof" of MC's homosexuality, which, together with MC's unquestioned *converso* status, explains the constant persecution he suffered throughout his life. Although specifics of MC's sexuality are not known in detail, there is no evidence whatsoever for Arrabal's thesis (which, in its basic form, had been presented years before by others). No serious scholar of MC's life and work gives credence to Arrabal's claims. Arrabal also has his own quixotic novel, which he wrote first in French under the title of *La fille de King Kong* (1988) but also wrote and published in Spanish as *La hija de King Kong* (1988; *King Kong's Daughter*). It is an erotic-picaresque first-person narrative of a nameless woman who fantasizes that she is the daughter of King Kong and Eloise. She is obsessed with MC and his works, carrying on imaginary dialogues with him and traveling mentally back in time to be with him on board the galley during the battle of Lepanto, during his captivity in Algiers, and as he writes *DQ*. In almost every one of the 100 short chapters, MC is evoked, addressed, and commented upon. She escapes from her asylum in Spain, goes to Paris and gets involved in a sordid world of prostitution, kills two of the men who are using her, and escapes to New York City. There she participates in the making of a film about DQ, with an international cast, among the skyscrapers (evoking at the same time the film adventures of her putative father). At the end of the novel, the protagonist rides off on a horse named Rocinante II, accompanied by her SP, Misha, on his ass. Few novels are as saturated with the presence of MC, the real "father" of the protagonist, as is this one.

Bibliography: Fernando Arrabal, *Un esclavo llamado Cervantes* (Madrid: Espasa Calpe, 1996); Fernando Arrabal, *La hija de King Kong* (Barcelona: Seix Barral, 1988); and Eduardo Urbina, "Historias verdaderas y la verdad de la historia: Fernando Arrabal vs. Stephen Marlowe," *Cervantes* 18, no. 2 (1998): 158–69.

Arráez. In *Amante*, the official, more or less the equivalent of a captain, who punishes Ricardo.

Arras [Ras]. French city, capital of the department of Pas-de-Calais. See *DQ* I, 49.

Arreola, Juan José (1918–2001). Mexican short-story writer. Included in his *Bestiario* (1958; *Bestiary*) are two short fictions entitled "La lengua de Cervantes" ("The Language of Cervantes") and "Teoría de Dulcinea" ("Theory of Dulcinea"). The former is a brief paragraph in which an artist realizes that a friend has a belly like that of SP. The latter, one of Arreola's better-known pieces, is about a man who avoids all contact with real women, preferring to read romances of chivalric adventure. But a certain peasant woman insists on interrupting him, entering his room, and leaving there her aroma. This causes the man to lose his mind; sally forth as a knight; have adventures with windmills, sheep, and so forth; return home; and die. But there is one peasant woman who sheds tears over his grave.
Bibliography: Juan José Arreola, *Bestiario* (Mexico City: J. Moritz, 1972).

Arriaza, Eugenio. Cuban writer. His *Don Quijote de la Mancha en Octavas* (1849; *Don Quixote de La Mancha in Octaves*) is a strained attempt at rewriting *DQ* in verse form.
Bibliography: Manuel Pérez Beato, *Cervantes en Cuba; estudio bibliográfico con la reproducción del "Quijote" en verso* (Havana: F. Ferdugo, 1929).

Arriero(s). *Muleteer(s).

Arroyo de las Palmas. *Brook of the Palm Trees.

Arsildo. The name first used for *Artidoro in *Galatea* 1.

Arsindo. In *Galatea* 3–6, an elderly shepherd who falls in love with the teenage Maurisa.

Artandro. In *Galatea* 4–5, the man who falls in love with Rosaura and then abducts her.

Arte mayor. A poetic term that refers, in general, to any line of poetry nine or more syllables in length; as such, it stands in opposition to *arte menor*, lines of eight or fewer syllables. The rhyme of the former is usually indicated with capital letters (ABBA), and that of the latter with lowercase letters (abba). More specifically, it is used to refer to the typically medieval poetic line, most frequently of 12 syllables, which is divided into two equal hemistiches. The form was perfected and was most popular in the fifteenth century in a stanza with a rhyme scheme of ABBAACCA; it fell almost completely out of favor in the sixteenth century. Its appearance in a poem sung by Orompo in *Galatea* 3 is an anachronism, the only known use of the form in the second half of the sixteenth century.

Artemisia (Beautiful widow) [Artemisa (Viuda bella)] (fourth century BCE). Sister and wife of Mausolus (*Mausolo*) of Caria (in southwestern Asia Minor). When her husband died, Artemisia had constructed for him a great tomb called the Mausoleum, one of the Seven Wonders of the Ancient World. See *DQ* II, 8; *Parnaso* 6.

Arthur [Artús, Arturo]. Legendary king of England, who ascended to the throne with the assistance of the arch-magician Merlin and presided over the knights of the Round Table at Camelot. In *DQ* I, 13, DQ relates the legend that King Arthur never died but, by means of enchantment, was cured of the wounds received in his battle with Mordred and turned into a crow. Someday the crow will return and rule again, which is why no Englishman ever kills a crow. See also *Coloquio*; *DQ* I, 49; *Persiles* I, 18.

Arthurian romance. The tales of King Arthur were popular in medieval Spain in the form of ballads and various prose and verse romances translated from various English or French sources. Arthurian themes and characters continued to infuse popular and high culture through both oral and printed versions of these stories throughout the Renaissance. Also popular in Spain were some medieval romances that were printed, widely circulated, and read in the sixteenth century: *El balardo del sabio Merlín* (1498; *The Cry of Wise Merlin*), *Demanda del Sancto Grial* (1515; *The Quest for the Holy Grail*), and *Lanzarote del Lago* (1515; *Lancelot of the Lake*). Except for a brief mention of the **Demanda del Santo Brial* (which subtly sexualizes the grail quest) in *Coloquio*, MC never cites any of these romances directly, but Arthur, Merlin, Lancelot, Guinevere, **Quintañona, and other characters from the Arthurian tradition are of crucial importance in *DQ*. And the fact that *Amadís de Gaula* is conceived and carried out within the general ambiance of the Arthurian cycle gives even greater importance to this literary tradition for MC.

Bibliography: Carlos Alvar, *El rey Arturo y su mundo: Diccionario de mitología artúrica* (Madrid: Alianza Editorial, 1991); and Edwin Williamson, *The Half-Way House of Fiction: "Don Quixote" and Arthurian Romance* (Oxford: Clarendon Press, 1984).

Artidoro (Arsildo). In *Galatea* 1–2, 4–6, the shepherd whose brother, Galercio, looks so much like him (is virtually his twin brother) that other people confuse their identities. He falls in love with Teolinda but winds up marrying her sister Leonarda, who resembles Teolinda so much (is virtually her twin sister) that other people confuse their identities also.

Artieda, Micer. **Rey de Artieda, Andrés.

Arturo; Artús. **Arthur.

Ascanio Rótulo. In *Amante*, the father of Cornelio.

Ascanio's garden. In *Amante*, the place where Leonisa, Cornelio, and their families are celebrating when they are surprised first by Ricardo, who expresses his love for Leonisa and his disdain for Cornelio, and then by Turkish pirates, who take Leonisa and Ricardo prisoner.

Asclepius [Esculapio]. In Greek myth, the god of healing, son of Apollo. See *Parnaso* 4.

Aseo. In *Poesías* 27, it is unclear what this might refer to; some editors modify the line to read Egeo, which does not help much.

Asia. The largest continent in the world. See *DQ* I, 48; *Galatea* 4.

Asirios. **Assyrians.

Asno de Oro, El. **Apuleius.

Asociación de Cervantistas [Association of Cervantes Scholars]. An international professional organization, located in Alcalá de Henares, Spain, and founded in 1988 by José María Casasayas. A meeting is held annually in a different city that is related in some significant way to MC and his work, and the proceedings of those meetings are a valuable source of current scholarship relating to MC.

Asperino. An Italian wine mentioned in *Vidriera*.

Ass-colts or fillies [Pollinos]. In *DQ* I, 25, DQ writes to his niece that he is granting three of his five ass-colts to SP in reward for his services. But this order, together with a letter to DT, is left behind by SP when he goes to deliver them.

Assistant priest [Teniente cura]. In *Gitanilla*, he is asked to marry Don Juan de Cárcamo and Doña Constanza de Azevedo y de Meneses.

Assyrians [Asirios]. Natives or inhabitants of Assyria, an ancient empire in western Asia in an area that in the seventh century BCE extended from India to Egypt; its capital was Nineveh. See *DQ* I, 6.

Asti [Aste]. City in Italy. See *Vidriera*.

Astolfo. An English hero, cousin of Orlando, and rider of the **hippogriff in Ariosto's *Orlando Furioso*. See *DQ* I, 25.

Astor. In *Galatea* 2, the name taken by Silenio when he adopts the guise of a traveling minstrel in order to gain entrance to the home of Nísida in Naples.

Astraliano. In *Galatea* 5, a 'famous shepherd,' often assumed to be the poetic name for Don *Juan of Austria.

Astrology [Astrología judiciaria]. Belief in astrology, firmly embedded in a Ptolemean cosmos in which the earth was the center of the universe, was widespread in the Renaissance. In *Persiles* I, 13, the astrologer Mauricio makes an important distinction: astrology as a science is certain, but individual astrologers often misunderstand the signs and make erroneous prophecies. Also noteworthy is the astrologer Padre Soldino in *Persiles* III, 18. See also *DQ* II, 8; *Entretenida* 1; *Parnaso* 4; *Persiles* II, 7; III, 11, 19.

Asturias. A region in northwestern Spain corresponding to the modern province of Oviedo. See *DQ* I, 16.

Asturias de Oviedo. Asturias was often described as being divided into two sections: an eastern section, Asturias de Santander, and a western section, Asturias de Oviedo. See *DQ* II, 48.

Asturias, Miguel Angel (1899–1974). Guatemalan novelist, poet, dramatist, and winner of the Nobel Prize. In a revised version of Asturias's play *La Audiencia de los confines* (1957; *The Audience of the Limits*), DQ and SP appear in a dream sequence.
   Bibliography: Marco Cipolloni, "Don Quijote soñado por Las Casas (En dos inéditos de M. A. Asturias)," *Anales Cervantinos* 35 (1999): 103–10.

Asurbanipal [Sardanapalo] (seventh century BCE). The legendary king of Assyria, who, according to the Greeks, was an effeminate and refined man. He is supposed to have had himself burned alive following a final celebration. See *Baños* 1.

Ataide, Don Antonio de, Conde de Castro Dairo (ca. 1560–1647). A Portuguese diplomat, soldier, and poet. He is mentioned in *Parnaso* 7.

Atalanta [Atlante]. In Greek myth, the daughter of Zeus and Clymene, a huntress who refused to marry any man who could not defeat her in a race. Hippomenes accepted the challenge and, as advised by Aphrodite, took with him some golden apples, which he dropped from time to time during the race. Whenever he did so, Atalanta stopped to pick up the apples, and Hippomenes won the race and married her. See *Casa* 2; *Galatea* 4.

Atalante. A generic term used for a drummer. See *Coloquio*; *Persiles* III, 12.

Atambor(es). *Drummer(s).

Athens [Atenas]. The capital city of Greece. In ancient times, it was the center of Greek culture and civilization. See *Adjunta*; *DQ* II, 18; *Galatea* 4, 6; *Parnaso* 4; *Pedro* 1; *Persiles* III, 10.

Atila. *Attila.

Atlas [Adlante, Atlante]. In Greek myth, the Titan who was condemned by Zeus to spend eternity holding the celestial sphere on his shoulders, as punishment for having taken part in the war of the Titans. He is mentioned in *Adjunta*, where the young poet Pancracio is described as wearing a ruffled collar so large that it would take the broad shoulders of Atlas to support it. See also *Galatea* 4; *Gallardo* 1; *Parnaso* 6; *Pedro* 3; *Persiles* I, 19; *Sultana* 2.

Atocha. *Monastery of Atocha.

Atrevido huésped. *Paris.

Atrevido mozo. *Phaethon.

Atterbom, Per Daniel Amadeus (1790–1855). Swedish poet and literary historian. Atterbom greatly admired the German romantics, and their influence is apparent throughout his work. His finest achievement is the two-volume dramatic poem entitled *Lycksalighetens ö* (1824–27; *The Isle of the Blessed*), a fairy tale about an island that floats above the earth and is the abode of poetry. In the first part, King Astolf talks with Zephyr, the west wind, about his discontent with his grim Nordic world. The latter becomes his guide to the magical island, where the romantically quixotic king meets and falls in love with Felicia, queen of the Isle of the Blessed. The lovers themselves compare their relationship to that between Amadís and his lady, the peerless Oriana. As the journey to the island is presented, it is clear that for Atterbom, the Astolf-Zephyr relationship is comparable to the one between DQ and SP (even though one of the last images the ethereal Zephyr would normally evoke is that of a rustic and pragmatic peasant). Between the two volumes, Atterbom also wrote a poem, "Befrierskan" ("The Liberator"), which was to serve as an introduction to his masterpiece but was not ultimately used for this purpose. The fairy of the title goes to an old castle, where he encounters valiant chivalric heroes from the past: King Arthur, Roland, Amadís, Tristan, and others. Standing off by himself is a romantic DQ.

Attila (the Hun) [Atila] (ca. 406–453). King of the Huns, sometimes called the Scourge of God, and known for his cruelty. See *Numancia* 1.

Attorney [Procurador]. In *Juez*, a lawyer for the accused party in the divorce proceedings.

Attributed works. The desire to identify anonymous or otherwise unattributed works to MC has been a constant in MC scholarship. The case made for some is interesting and will be examined individually: See *La *tía fingida, El *Buscapié, Las *Semanas del Jardín, La *Conquista de Jerusalén*, the **Relación de lo sucedido en la ciudad de Valladolid*, and Diego de *Haedo's *Topografía e historia de Argel*. Among the works that have been attributed throughout the ages, the following seem either to be clearly not by MC or to have only the most dubious claim on his authorship: 1) the prose report *Tercera parte de las cosas de la Cárcel de Sevilla, añadida a la que hizo Cris-

tóbal de Chaves (Third Part of Things Relating to the Seville Prison, Added to the One Written by Cristóbal de Chaves)*; several interludes: 2) *Doña Justina y Calahorra*, 3) *Durandarte y Belerma*, 4) *Ginetilla ladrón (The Thieving Little Weasel)*, 5) *Los habladores (The Talkers)*, 6) *Melisendra*, 7) *Los mirones (The Lookers-On)*, and 8) *Los refranes (Proverbs)*; 9) *La cárcel de Sevilla (The Seville Prison)*; two *comedias*: 10) *María la de Esquivias (Mary from Esquivias)* and 11) *La toledana (The Woman from Toledo)*; one *auto sacramental*: 12) *La soberana virgen de Guadalupe (The Sovereign Virgin of Guadalupe)*; several letters; and some three dozen poems, titles and descriptions of which can be found in the lists compiled by Avalle-Arce, Eisenberg, and Montero Reguera, and in the edition of Gaos.

Bibliography: Juan Bautista Avalle-Arce, "Atribuciones y supercherías," in *Suma cervantina*, ed. Juan Bautista Avalle-Arce and Edward C. Riley (London: Tamesis Books, 1973), 399–408; Daniel Eisenberg, "Repaso crítico a las atribuciones cervantinas," *Nueva Revista de Filología Hispánica* 38 (1990): 477–92; and José Montero Reguera, "La obra literaria de Miguel de Cervantes (Ensayo de un catálogo)," in *Cervantes* (Alcalá de Henares, Spain: Centro de Estudios Cervantinos, 1995), 43–74.

Audiencia. A tribunal, or high court. In *Fregona*, the reference is to the tribunal of Seville. In *DQ* I 42, it is to the tribunal of Mexico.

Augsburg [Augusta]. A Bavarian city located northwest of Munich, where the powerful *Fuggar banking family had their headquarters. The Peace of Augsburg, 1555, stipulated a degree of religious freedom in the region. In *DQ* II, 54, *Ricote says that he found there a climate of intellectual freedom suitable for his *Morisco* family, who was expelled from their homeland.

Augusts [Agostos]. In *DQ* II, 8, SP takes DQ's reference to Augustus Caesar to be a reference to the month named after him.

Augustus Caesar [Augusto César] (63 BCE–CE 14). Roman emperor. After the assassination of Julius *Caesar in 44 BCE, his adopted son, Octavian, returned from Greece to form, with Mark *Antony and Pompey, a ruling triumvirate. Within 13 years, Octavian was the sole ruler of the Roman Empire. In 27 BCE he took the titles *Augustus* (revered) and *Imperator* (general, in the sense of emperor). His pragmatism and ambition did not obscure his virtue and dedication to his people. See *DQ* I, 13.

Aurelio. 1. In *Tratos*, the protagonist, a Christian captive in Algiers who is in love with the beautiful Silvia. **2**. In *Galatea*, the 'venerable' father of Galatea. His decision to marry his daughter to a Portuguese shepherd sets into motion the plot complications that are left unresolved at the end of the novel.

Auristela. *Sigismunda.

Aurora. 1. In Roman myth, the goddess of the dawn (the equivalent of Eos in Greek myth), and the wife (or lover) of Tithonus. As such, she is often associated with Apollo. See *Baños* 1; *Coloquio*; *DQ* I, 2; *DQ* II, 20; *Galatea* 1; *Parnaso* 1, 5, 6, 8. **2**. An allusion to Doña Ana of Austria, daughter of Felipe III and future queen of France, born in 1601 in Valladolid, in a ballad sung by Preciosa in *Gitanilla*.

Austen, Jane (1775–1817). English novelist. Austen's posthumous novel *Northanger Abbey* (1818), her least characteristic and probably earliest (in the final years of the eighteenth century) work, is her only thoroughly quixotic work. It is also likely that Charlotte *Lennox's *Female Quixote* (1752), extremely popular in the second half of the eighteenth century, bears some intertextual relationship to Austen's novel. The heroine, Catherine Morland, is very much a female DQ (and simultaneously somewhat of a DT, although she is "almost pretty" rather than a peerless beauty) who sees the world in terms of her preferred literary texts, in this case, gothic romances (especially those of Anne Radcliffe). As she reads these books as a teenager, she is "in training for a heroine; she read all such works as heroines must read." The delightful, satiric way in which she complicates her own life and those of others by reading certain ordinary events as extraordinary adventures

from a gothic plot is the essence of the quixotic premise. At the end of the novel, as at the end of *DQ*, the heroine overcomes her book-inspired vision of the world and is reconciled with reality: "The visions of romance were over. Catherine was completely awakened." In her other, better known and more admired novels Austen shows relatively little of the spirit or values of MC, but at the beginning of her writing career, Austen wrote a beautiful retelling of the DQ story.

Bibliography: John G. Ardila, "Cervantes y la *Quixotic fiction*: La parodia de géneros," *Anales Cervantinos* 34 (1998): 145–68.

Auster, Paul (1947–). American novelist. Auster's novel *City of Glass* (1985), first in his New York Trilogy (which includes *Ghosts*, 1986, and *The Locked Room*, 1986), is a brilliant metafictional exploration of identity, authorship, and madness. Daniel Quinn writes mysteries under the name William Wilson about a detective named Max Work, sometimes seeming to exist more as his pseudonym and sometimes more as his character. But he begins to receive phone calls asking for Paul Auster, private detective. Quinn takes the identity of Auster and gets involved in a bizarre case involving a mentally deficient "wild child," the product of child abuse by a brilliant but mad philosopher and the boy's passionate mother. Complications develop as Quinn/Auster trails and gets to know the philosopher, but matters become even more complicated when Quinn goes to visit the "real" Paul Auster, who is a writer and not a detective. In a central chapter, Quinn and Auster discuss *DQ* and its multiple authors, MC, CHB, and so on. (Earlier hints of an MC connection come in references to a woman named Mrs. Saavedra and her husband, Michael.) Auster proposes an ingenious and complicated theory according to which CHB's text was dictated by SP to the priest and barber, who had Sansón Carrasco write it in Arabic; this manuscript was then found by MC, who had it translated back into Spanish; but, in fact, the whole set-up was conceived by DQ himself, who took the disguise of a *Morisco* and became the man MC hired to translate the Arabic manuscript. Thus, in *City of Glass*, a character with the initials DQ is alternately himself, his pseudonym, his character, and his author, and then he takes a number of identities when dealing with a madman. This sets up a discussion with his author of the question of authorship. At the end of the novel, after Quinn descends into madness and his entire world and identity crumble around him, an unnamed CHB-like first-person narrator intervenes, discussing his sources, criticizing Auster for his role in the whole affair, and documenting as best he can what little is known of Quinn's disappearance. Overall, Auster's novel is an extraordinary quixotic achievement.

Bibliography: Steven E. Alford, "Mirrors of Madness: Paul Auster's *The New York Trilogy*," *Critique* 37, no. 1 (1995): 17–33.

Austria. Country in central Europe, of which Vienna is the capital. It was made a Spanish possession by Carlos V in 1519. See *Poesías* 20.

Austria, Don Juan of (1545–78). Illegitimate son of Carlos V and Barbara of Blomberg. Felipe II recognized him as his brother in 1559. A proud and daring man, he was an accomplished military leader, leading the forces against the rebellious *Moriscos* of Granada in 1569–70 and engineering the *Holy League's rout of the Turks at the battle of *Lepanto in 1571. He was named governor of the Netherlands in 1576. In 1575, when MC left military service in order to return to Spain, Don Juan wrote a letter of recommendation for him in recognition of his bravery at Lepanto. This letter, along with one from the Duke of Sessa, convinced his Turkish captors that MC was a valuable prize, so they set his ransom at a figure considerably higher than was normal, which is the primary reason why he remained in captivity for five years while others, like his brother Rodrigo, were often ransomed much sooner. See *Baños* 2; *DQ* I, 39; *Parnaso* 1; *Tratos* 3.

Austria, Duke of (?–1439). Albert II, king of Hungary and Bohemia, and emperor of Germany, a knight mentioned by DQ in I, 49 (*Crónica de Juan II*).

Austria, House of [Casa de Austria]. The name by which the royal Hapsburg line was known. MC lived his entire life under the rule of a Hapsburg king. In Spain, the House of Austria consisted of Carlos I King of Spain and Carlos V of the Holy Roman Empire, 1517–56; Felipe II, 1556–98; Felipe III, 1598–1621; Felipe IV, 1621–65; and Carlos II 1665–1700. When Carlos II died childless, the Spanish crown went to the Bourbons and has remained with that family ever since. See *Persiles* III, 11; *Poesías* 20.

Bibliography: John Lynch, *Spain under the Habsburgs*, 2nd ed., 2 vols. (New York: New York University Press, 1981).

Austríada, La. *Rufo (Gutiérrez), Juan.

Austrian Sun [Sol de Austria]. An allusion to the Hapsburg dynasty in general (*Austria, House of) and Felipe III in particular in a ballad sung by Preciosa in *Gitanilla*.

Author of the story [Autor de la historia]. In *Persiles*, the author of the original work, for what we read is a translation; in some places (e.g., the first chapter of Book II), editorial changes are made during the translation. (See *narrative structure of *Los trabajos de Persiles y Sigismunda*.)

Author of this history. *Narrative structure of *Don Quixote*.

Authors [Autores]. The supposed sources, from the *Archives of La Mancha, for the information about DQ in I, 1–9. See also *DQ* I, 2.

Auto sacramental [Sacramental play]. A one-act religious drama, normally an allegorical reenactment of the sacrament of communion, generally performed annually at the Corpus Cristi feast. Although the popularity of mystery and morality plays waned toward the end of the medieval period throughout the rest of Europe, they became increasingly popular in sixteenth-century Spain and reached their height of popularity and influence in the period of the *Counter-Reformation. The greatest writer of *autos sacramentales* was Pedro *Calderón de la Barca, who considered the genre a kind of mimetic sermon. The didactic and often heavy-handed *autos* were directly aimed at the uneducated *vulgo*, a fact made evident by their traditional staging outdoors on carts or flatbed wagons that served as portable stages. There is no evidence that MC ever tried his hand at this theatrical genre, although one *auto* has been attributed to him (*attributed works). In II, 11, DQ has an encounter with a group of actors travelling from one city to another in costume, as the characters in the *auto* entitled "Las Cortes de la Muerte" ("Parliament of Death"). See also *DQ* I, 12.

Bibliography: Ricardo Arias, *The Spanish Sacramental Play* (Boston: Twayne, 1980); and Bruce W. Wardropper, *Introducción al teatro religioso del Siglo de Oro (La evolución del "auto sacramental" 1500–1648)* (Madrid: Revista de Occidente, 1953).

Autobiographical elements in *Don Quixote*. It has proven irresistible to see (or imagine) aspects of MC in DQ. DQ is about the same age as MC was when he wrote *DQ* I. MC's self-description in the prologue to *Novelas* is not far from that of DQ that emerges from the novel. The military career of the captive Ruy Pérez de Viedma, who tells his story in *DQ* I, 39–41, is very similar to that of MC, and his age and appearance upon release from captivity are very similar to those of MC at the same point in his life. Various opinions that DQ expresses are consistent in every way with what MC is known to have believed: wounds received in battle confer honor (*DQ* I, 15; *DQ* II, prologue), liberty is a precious gift from heaven (II, 58), and so forth. DQ is not MC, but they do share certain characteristics. Certainly the prologues to his works provide some sense of how MC perceived himself, and his explicitly autobiographical passages—when he talks about himself and his works in *Parnaso* 4 (and, to an extent, in *Adjunta*)—confirm aspects of our impression of MC the man and the writer (*Cervantes as author).

Bibliography: Jean Canavaggio, "Cervantes en primera persona," *Journal of Hispanic Philology* 2 (1977): 35–44; Ruth El Saffar, "The Woman at the Border: Some Thoughts on Cervantes and Autobi-

ography," in *Autobiography in Early Modern Spain,* ed. Nicholas Spadaccini and Jenaro Talens (Minneapolis, MN: Prisma, 1988. 191–214); and Mary Gaylord Randel, "Cervantes' Portraits and Literary Theory," *Cervantes* 6, no. 1 (1986): 57–80.

Auto-da-fé (Act of Faith) [Auto de fe]. A public ceremony of humiliation, punishment, and/or execution of those judged by the Inquisition to have committed acts against the Church or to have failed to live the life of a good Christian. The ceremony was staged to represent the divine Judgment Day in order to inspire fear among those who watched as much as to punish the guilty. Contrary to popular opinion, an auto-da-fé did not necessarily involve a burning at the stake. When the death sentence was imposed, those so sentenced were remanded to the secular authorities and burned elsewhere. The cruelty and bloodshed of autos-da-fé witnessed by large crowds was designed to inspire righteous horror and effectively kept the authoritarian, dogmatic presence of the Church at the forefront of Renaissance thought.

Autor [Theatrical director, manager, adapter, producer]. In the classic Spanish *comedia* the writer of the playscript was not called, as today, the *author*, but the *poet*. Normally, the poet sold all rights to production, printing, and royalties to the *autor*, an all-round impresario. The *autor* was the person who put together—*authored*, in this sense—the production. This person's duties included not only most of what would today be considered the *director*, but also a good deal of what we now attribute to the *producer*; the job also generally involved acting, personnel management, marketing, and bookkeeping.

Bibliography: N. D. Shergold, *History of the Spanish Stage: From Medieval Times until the End of the Seventeenth Century* (Oxford: Clarendon Press, 1967).

Autor desta historia. *Narrative structure of Don Quixote.

Avalos (y Ribera), Don Juan de (1553–1622). Peruvian poet, born in Lima, who is praised in Calliope's song in *Galatea* 6. Avalos spent some 15 years in Spain, where he was awarded the Order of Calatrava, before returning to his native country.

Ave fénix. *Phoenix.

Ave María [el Avemaría]. The first words of the Latin version of the prayer to the Virgin Mary, one of the *four prayers of most importance in the Roman Catholic Church. See *Baños* 2; *Rufián* 1; *Tratos* 2.

Aveleyra A(rroyo de Anda), Teresa. Mexican critic and writer. Aveleyra has written some traditional literary criticism, but in her book *Autobiografía sentimental de Alonso Quijano* (1970; *Sentimental Autobiography of Alonso Quijano*), she attempts something different. The book begins with a brief prologue in which the author describes her attempt to evoke the reality behind the novel in a way that traditional scholarship cannot grasp, but without ever contradicting anything in the text. This she does by writing a narrative that draws on MC's text (but sometimes recontextualizing specific passages, statements, or events) and simultaneously filling in gaps in that text with her own fictional imaginings. The prologue is followed by two fictional chapters entitled "De Aldonza a Dulcinea" ("From Aldonza to Dulcinea") and "Andanzas rumbo a la cordura" ("Happenings on the Way to Sanity") and a long set of notes. The first chapter—by far the better of the two—consists of a kind of interior monologue, combined with fragments of description and dialogue, in which Alonso Quijano recalls, reenacts, and thinks about his love for Aldonza: how he first met her, his attempts to marry her, how he realized that she would never actually be his, and how he transformed her into DT. In the second chapter, Aveleyra employs the same technique while rapidly passing over and summarizing some of the action in the two parts of the novel. The notes both identify passages from *DQ* on which parts of the fictional chapters are based and add some commentary.

Bibliography: Teresa Aveleyra A., *Autobiografía sentimental de Alonso Quijano* (Monterrey, Mexico: Instituto Tecnológico y de Estudios Superiores de Monterrey, 1970).

Avellaneda, Alonso Fernández de. The pseudonym of the author, who claims to be Aragonese, of the *Segunda parte del ingenioso hidalgo Don Quijote de la Mancha* (1614; *Second Part of the Ingenious Gentleman Don Quixote de la Mancha*), a sequel to *DQ* I. The last printed words in *DQ* I, after it was stated that there was a belief that DQ had a third sally but that no documentary evidence had yet been found (I, 52), are a near-quote from Ariosto: "Forsi altro canterà con miglior plectio" ("Perhaps another will sing with a better pick"). This certainly seems to be a clear invitation for another writer to take up the pen and write a continuation, a common practice at the time in chivalric, pastoral, sentimental, and other kinds of fiction (*sequels). But when someone did precisely this, using the pseudonym Avellaneda, MC reacted (as had Mateo *Alemán before him) with anger, resentment, and satire, especially in the prologue and final chapters of *DQ* II. DQ first learns of the book from Don *Jerónimo and Don Juan in II, 59; he recalls it when he is about to enter Barcelona in II, 61; he sees it being reprinted in the *print shop in Barcelona in II, 62; *Altisidora describes it being batted around by devils in hell in II, 70; *Alvaro Tarfe swears in II, 72, that his adventures with DQA were apocryphal; and CHB warns against another sequel when DQ dies in II, 74 (see also the dedication to *Comedias*). In his prologue, Avellaneda criticizes MC for his supposed satire directed toward Lope de *Vega and mocks MC's crippled left hand, his poverty, and his age. DQA leaves home in the company of Alvaro Tarfe, travels to Zaragoza in order to participate in the jousts celebrated in that city (as MC had suggested in I, 52), and is finally committed to the Casa del Nuncio, the famous madhouse in Toledo. DQA of the sequel is a far less interesting character than he had been in MC's hands. He proclaims that he is no longer in love with DT and should be called *El Caballero Desenamorado* (The Disenamored Knight), and acts like a second-rate mechanical imitation of his old self. Meanwhile,

SPA displays little of the crafty pragmatism that typifies MC's character, and is a crudely comic glutton (especially fond of *albondiguillas*, a kind of meatball) and stupid dupe. Still, *DQA* is not badly written and has some very comic moments, such as the one in which DQA interrupts a theatrical performance in order to save the heroine (perhaps either derived from—or a source for—the *Maese Pedro scene in *DQ* II, 26), and those involving the earthy Bárbara whom DQ takes to be Cenobia, queen of the Amazons. Had MC not responded with his own sequel that is in every way a superior work of art, Avellaneda would have a place as an important novelist in the seventeenth century. And it is possible that it was the appearance of Avellaneda's sequel that moved MC to finish his own part-two-in-progress more rapidly—a good thing, since MC died within a year and it is quite conceivable that his continuation might never have been published without the stimulus provided by *DQA*. Sometimes adversity is a spur to accomplishment. As it is, however, Avellaneda was so successfully bested by a superior competitor that for many he is but a footnote to Spanish literature. Unlike *DQ*, which was translated and published dozens of times throughout Europe throughout the seventeenth century, *DQA* was never reprinted in Spanish or translated into any other language during the same period of time. The real author behind the pseudonym has never been identified—not even by MC, apparently—though there has been no shortage of suggestions, as over two dozen names have been proposed for the honor. Candidates include Lope de *Vega, in an attempt anonymously to respond to the criticism of him and his theory of drama that MC included in his novel; a friend and/or defender of Lope such as *Tirso de Molina, for the same reason; Fray Luis de Aliaga, a supposed enemy of Cervantes; Juan *Martí, who, as the author of the unauthorized continuation of *Guzmán de Afarache*, also published under a pseudonym in 1602 and thus had the experience; the physician Juan *Blanco de Paz, a personal enemy of MC's since his days in Algerian captivity; Francisco de *Quevedo; Cristóbal *Suárez de Figueroa, a known critic of MC; and even MC

himself, in yet another brilliant metafictional ploy, or perhaps as a publicity stunt to hype his own work; and others. The most compelling recent theory is one proposed by Martín de Riquer: Jerónimo de *Pasamonte, a contemporary soldier and autobiographer who may have seen himself satirized in the figure of *Ginés de Pasamonte (introduced in *DQ* I, 22).

Bibliography: Edward T. Aylward, *Towards a Revaluation of Avellaneda's False "Quijote"* (Newark, DE: Juan de la Cuesta, 1989): Edward H. Friedman, "Insincere Flattery: Imitation and the Growth of the Novel," *Cervantes* 20, no. 1 (2000): 99–114; Stephen Gilman, *Cervantes y Avellaneda, estudio de una imitación*, trans. Margit Frenk Alatorre (Mexico City: Colegio de México, 1951); James Iffland, *De fiestas y aguafiestas: risa, locura e ideología en Cervantes y Avellaneda* (Madrid: Iberoamericana, 1999); James Iffland, "Do We Really Need to Read Avellaneda?" *Cervantes* 21, no. 1 (2001): 67–83; Thomas A. Lathrop, "Cervantes' Treatment of the False *Quijote*," *Kentucky Romance Quarterly* 32 (1985): 213–17; Marcela Ochoa Penroz, "En torno al *Quijote Apócrifo* de Avellaneda," in *Reescrituras del "Quijote"* (Santiago, Chile: LOM Ediciones, 1997), 15–45; and Ludovik Osterc, "Cervantes y Avellaneda," *Anales Cervantinos* 21 (1983): 91–102.

Avemaría. *Four prayers.

Avidas (Las Habidas). *Arbloanche, Jerónimo.

Avila. Spanish city located northwest of Madrid and southeast of Salamanca. It is particularly famous for its intact medieval walls and as the birthplace of *Saint Teresa de Jesús. See *Poesías* 33.

Avila, Francisco de. Spanish dramatist. Avila wrote an *Entremés famoso de los invencibles hechos de Don Quijote de la Mancha* (1617; *Famous Interlude of the Invincible Deeds of Don Quixote de la Mancha*). The farce takes advantage of the comic figure and madness of DQ, depicting scenes where he takes an inn for a castle and has encounters with *pícaros* who make fun of him, presenting a serving maid as DT—probably the first fusion of Maritornes-Aldonza-DT that becomes a staple in many subsequent versions of *DQ*.

Bibliography: Francisco de Avila, *Entremés famoso de los invencibles hechos de Don Quijote de la Mancha (1637)*, ed. Luciano García Lorenzo, *Anales Cervantinos* 17 (1978): 259–73.

Avila, Gaspar de. A calligrapher and secretary to the Marquesa del Valle, as well as a dramatist. MC mentions him in the prologue to *Comedias* and again in *Parnaso 7*.

Avila (y Zúñiga), Don Luis de (?–ca. 1572). Historian, author of *Comentario . . . de la guerra de Alemaña de Carlo V* (1548; *Commentary . . . on the War in Germany by Carlos V*), which is apparently what was intended by the title that appears in *DQ* I, 7, as *Los Hechos del Emperador* (*The Deeds of the Emperor*). But since that would be the only work of nonfictional prose included in *DQ*'s library that seems otherwise made up entirely of romances and poetry, it has also been suggested that MC may really have been referring to Luis *Zapata's *Carlo famoso* (1566; *The Renowned Carlos*), a long narrative poem more like the last works discussed in *DQ* I, 6. The specific mention of the author's name makes the former possibility seem more likely.

Avilés, René. Mexican writer. Avilés is the author of *"El Profesor Vidriera," precedido de "El Retablo de Maese Pedro"* (1942; *"Professor Vidriera," Preceded by "Maese Pedro's Puppet Show"*), two curious and interesting fictions. In *Maese Pedro*, Avilés tells of how, after hearing a performance of Manuel de *Falla's famous musical interpretation of the puppet show scene from *DQ* II, 26, he goes to the Biblioteca Iberoamericana (Interamerican Library), directed by his father, to read and ponder that episode from MC's novel. He falls asleep over the book and awakens to find the library dark and deserted after closing hours. Descending a staircase he never knew existed, he comes to a hall where there is a large crowd that includes his father, DQ and SP, and various other people, who are assembled to watch a performance of the puppet show staged by Maese Pedro and his young assistant from the novel. The show is presented, it is discussed at some length, and the author intervenes to talk about the role of the young assistant-narrator. Then he awakens to find that it was all a dream. The sequel, *Professor Vidriera*, begins when a descendant of Tomás Rueda from *Vidriera* comes to the author's house, stating that he has read a manuscript copy of *Maese Pedro* and he wanted to introduce himself to the person who wrote it. After some discussion about how a man of flesh and blood can be descended from a fictional character, Avilés admits that he has never read *Vidriera* or *Azorín's version of the story, but promises to do so. The remainder of the work consists of a series of conversations between the author and Professor Vidriera about MC's story, Azorín's rewrite, and life and literature in general. Appended is a series of musings and imagined dialogues by the author about his (until-then) unpublished fictions and other matters. *Maese Pedro*, especially, is an original dream-fiction that merits attention from readers of *DQ*. Avilés has written an interesting critical commentary within a (meta)fictional context.

Bibliography: René Avilés, *"El Profesor Vidriera," precedido de "El Retablo de Maese Pedro"* (México City: Artes Gráficas Comerciales, 1942).

Ayala, Francisco (1906–). Spanish jurist, essayist, literary critic, novelist, and short-story writer. Among his many critical writings are two books dedicated to MC: *La invención del "Quijote"* (1950; *The Invention of "Don Quixote"*) and *Cervantes y Quevedo* (1984), both of which display a sensitive and nuanced understanding of MC's work. From his earliest fictions to his latest, Ayala's work abounds in echoes of the themes, characters, and techniques of MC. But nowhere is this more evident than in his rewriting of the story told by the goatherd Eugenio in *DQ* I, 51, in Ayala's *El rapto* (1965; *The Kidnapping*). In Ayala's version, Vicente de la Roca (he keeps the name from MC) is not a braggart soldier, but a young man who rides into town on a motorcycle and wins the affections of the heroine. The outcome of the tale is the same: Vicente abducts and robs, but does not sexually violate, the heroine. But throughout the story, Ayala also incorporates passages from other parts of DQ and simultaneously interweaves aspects of *Curioso*, all the while suggesting an underlying homoerotic motive.

Bibliography: Carmen Escudero Martínez, *Cervantes en la narrativa de Francisco Ayala* (Murcia, Spain: Universidad de Murcia, 1989); and Estelle Irizarry, *Francisco Ayala* (Boston: Twayne, 1977).

Ayala, Isabel de. A resident of the building in which MC and his family lived in Valladolid. She seems to have had a reputation as a gossip and played a prominent role in the investigation of the *Ezpeleta affair in Valladolid in 1605. She accused the women living with MC of receiving male guests at all hours of the day and night and specifically accused MC's daughter Isabel of being the lover of Simón *Méndez.

Aydar. A soldier who appears briefly in *Tratos* 2, 4.

Ayres, James. English dramatist. Ayres is the author of *Sancho at Court: or, the Mock Governor* (1742), an adaptation of the Barataria episodes from *DQ* II, 45–53.

Ayuntamiento, plaza of the. A plaza in Toledo mentioned in *Fuerza*.

Azán. A Muslim name mentioned in *Baños* 2.

Azán; Azán Agá; Azán Bajá. *Hassan Pasha.

Azcaray. In *Vizcaíno*, the name used once by Solórzano to refer to *Quiñones in his role as a Basque.

Azcona, Rafael (1926–). Spanish film director and dramatist. Azcona formed part of a team of eight writers and critics assembled by Maurizio Scaparro to prepare a theatrical version of *DQ* for the Seville World's Fair in 1992. Scaparro had taken an interest in *DQ* a decade earlier (1983), when he prepared a multimedia presentation on the theme. This was followed by a film, in collaboration with Azcona and Tullio Kezich, entitled *Don Quijote: frammenti di un discorso teatrale* (1984; *Don Quixote: Fragments of a Theatrical Discourse*), which was then the basis for the play *Don Quijote: Fragmentos de un discurso teatral* by Azcona

and Scaparro. The intent is not to present a new version of *DQ* or a takeoff on the novel, but to put on stage very many of the scenes from the novel, sacrificing embedded stories and techniques of narration. The work's unique feature is that all the scenes are acted out by members of the theatrical company of Angulo el Malo (from *DQ* II, 11).

Bibliography: Rafael Azcona and Maurizio Scaparro, *Don Quijote: Fragmentos de un discurso teatral* (Madrid: Asociación de Directores de Escena de España, 1992).

Azevedo. *Acevedo, Alonso de.

Azoguejo de Segovia. The plaza in the heart of Segovia crossed by the Roman aqueduct (*picaresque geography).

Azores [Terceras]. Portuguese islands in the Atlantic Ocean southwest of Lisbon. See *Española*.

Azorín (José Martínez Ruiz, 1873–1967). Spanish critic, journalist, novelist, and dramatist. The book that made Azorín famous as a student of MC was a collection of his short articles originally published in a newspaper in celebration of the three-hundredth anniversary of the publication of *DQ* in 1905. Azorín made a trip through La Mancha, visiting places like Argamasilla del Alba, the supposed hometown of DQ and SP; Campo de Criptana, with its windmills; the Cave of Montesinos; and so forth. The book that resulted, *La ruta de don Quijote* (1905; *The Route of Don Quixote*), is a nostalgic evocation of the region and its roads, villages, and inhabitants. Azorín's technique was to mix travelogue, fiction, literary criticism (or, at least, commentary), and personal reflection. It was a technique, presented in an affected, slightly archaic style, that became the author's trademark as he wrote book after book evoking the eternal Spain of ordinary people, insignificant events, and small towns. The same romantic, elegiac, folkloric tone characterizes a series of themes that were characteristic of the prolific Azorín's work throughout his life, both when *DQ* is an explicit concern and when the subject is quite different. It can be seen in later essays/fictions, scattered through various books, such as "El buen juez" (1905; "The Good Judge"), about a judge who closely resembles Alonso Quijano; "La fragancia del vaso" (1912; "The Fragrance of the Glass"), a sequel to *Fregona*; "El Caballero del Verde Gabán" (1912; "The Knight of the Green Overcoat"), based on *DQ* II, 18; "Cajal y el *Quijote*" (1914; "Cajal and *Don Quixote*"), a comparison of Spain's great neuroscientist Santiago Ramón y Cajal and DQ, which brings Azorín close to *Unamuno's religious-patriotic concept of MC's novel and hero; "Al margen del *Quijote*" (1915; "On the Margin of *Don Quixote*"), which places Azorín even closer to the Unamuno position; "Al margen del *Persiles*" (1915; "On the Margin of *Persiles*"), one of the rare essays in which Azorín looks closely at a work other than *DQ*, and in which he comments on frustrated desire in *Persiles*; "Sancho, encantado" (1939; "Sancho Enchanted"), in which Azorín imagines a scene involving SP, his neighbor and friend Tomé Cecial, the duke, and Doctor Pedro Recio; "Cervantes nació en Esquivias" (1940; "Cervantes Was Born in Esquivias"), an imaginary scene in which one Miguel de Cortinas, distant relative of MC's maternal grandmother Leonor de Cortinas, shows Azorín proof that MC was born in Esquivias; "Aventuras de Miguel de Cervantes" (1940; "Adventures of Miguel de Cervantes"), about a man named Miguel de Cervantes López, a native of Alcázar de San Juan; "Claro como la luz" (1940; "As Clear as Light"), in which Alonso Fernández de Avellaneda discusses with his wife his authorship of *DQA*; "El pintor de España" (1940; "Spain's Painter"), in which Azorín talks with his close friend, Ignacio *Zuloaga, 'Spain's painter,' encouraging him to paint a portrait of MC; "Su mejor amigo" (1940; "His Best Friend"), about the close personal friendship between MC and Don Juan of Austria; "La vida en peligro" (1942; "Life in Danger"), about MC in captivity in Algiers; "Caramanchel" (1942), about a man named Caramanchel who contributes to the ransom of MC; "La familia de Cervantes" (1942; "Cervantes's Family"), about a supposed relative of MC's named Elías Cervantes; "Don Quijote, vencido" (1943; "Don Quixote, Vanquished"), in which, after his defeat in Barcelona, DQ returns home and explains to everyone that, without ever leaving his home, he has had a dream about being a knight-errant; "El tiempo pasado" (1943; "Past time"), in which SP argues that illusion is more important than truth; "La vida" (1947; "Life"), in which SP again meets Doctor Pedro Recio; "Quijotismo" (1948; "Quixotism"), a particularly characteristic manifesto for the restoration of what Azorín sees as DQ's moral dignity; and others too numerous to detail in this context. In many of these essays—some of which are collected in *Con Cervantes* (1947; *With Cervantes*)—Azorín differs with Unamuno on one major point: whereas the latter consistently sees DQ as superior to his creator MC, Azorín defends MC as having always been fully conscious and in control of his creations. Even so, just a year later, in the 108 short essays that comprise his book *Con permiso de los cervantistas* (1948; *Begging the Leave of Cervantes Scholars*), Azorín approaches MC more as an artist than a scholar and expresses the Unamuno-like opinion that writer and book co-create each other. Azorín's primary venture into a Cervantine fiction is *El Licenciado Vidriera visto por Azorín* (1915; *The Glass Graduate, as Seen by Azorín*), a title later changed in a slightly revised version to *Tomás Rueda* (1941). In his typical lyrical, nostalgic style, Azorín uses *Vidriera* as a pretext (as much as an intertext) to evoke characters, contexts, situations, and ideas; the term he accurately uses to describe his work is 'novelistic essay.' Azorín tells the story of Tomás Rueda's youth, his years as a student in Salamanca, his madness, and his final residence in a peaceful Flanders. None of MC's sharp-edged satire remains; the witch who poisons the protagonist becomes a woman with whom he falls in love; his death while a soldier in Flanders is eliminated.

Among Azorín's works for theater, two are related to MC. The first is *La fuerza del amor* (1901; *The Power of Love*), in which a character pretends to be mad, believing that he is Amadís de Gaula, in order eventually to win the woman he loves; reproduced or paraphrased are passages from *DQ*, including the Golden Age speech, and other well-known works from that period; the author includes careful documentation of all his literary sources. The second play is the metatheatrical *Cervantes, o la casa encantada* (1931; *Cervantes, or The Enchanted House*), in which the poet Víctor Brenes is writing a poem entitled "La casa encantada" about the house in which MC lived in Valladolid in 1605. Brenes drinks an enchanted liquid and finds himself in the very place he was writing about. He and MC discuss each other's work and, at the end of the play, go off to talk with a neighbor who was the model for DQ. In an epilogue that takes place after Brenes returns to the present, he discusses with a playwright friend the composition of a play to be entitled *Cervantes, o la casa encantada.*

Bibliography: Azorín, *La ruta de Don Quijote,* ed. José María Martínez Cachero (Madrid: Cátedra, 1984); Azorín, *Tomás Rueda*, ed. Miguel Angel Lozano Marco (Alicante, Spain: Instituto de Cultura Juan Gil-Albert, 1994); Elena Catena, "Azorín, cervantista y cervantino." *Anales Cervantinos* 12 (1973): 73–113; Edward Inman Fox, *Azorín as a Literary Critic* (New York: Hispanic Institute, 1962); Kathleen M. Glenn, *Azorín (José Martínez Ruiz)* (Boston: Twayne, 1981); José María Martínez Cachero, "*Con permiso de los cervantistas* (Azorín, 1948): Examen de un 'libro de melancolía'," *Anales Cervantinos* 25–26 (1987–88): 305–14; and Marguerite C. Rand, "El licenciado Vidriera, Created by Cervantes, Recreated by Azorín," *Hispania* 37 (1954): 141–51.

Azote, Don. *Don Whip or Don Chopped Meat.

Azotes. *Lashes.

Azpetia. *Sancho de Azpetia, Don.

✠ B ✠

Bab Azún (Bab-Azur) [Babazón]. One of the nine gates of Algiers, located opposite that of *Bab-al-wad. See *DQ* I, 40.

Bab-al-wad [Babalbete]. One of the nine gates of Algiers, located opposite that of *Bab Azún. See *Baños* 2.

Babieca. The famous horse of El Cid. Rocinante is compared to Babieca in the poem written by El Donoso as a preliminary to *DQ* I. The last of these prefatory verses consists of a comic dialogue between these two horses. See also *DQ* I, 1; 49.

Babieca's saddle [Silla de Babieca]. The saddle of the famous horse of El Cid, supposedly preserved as a historical artifact. See *DQ* I, 49.

Babylonia [Babilonia]. Ancient empire located in southwestern Asia, centered in the valley of the Tigris and Euphrates Rivers (*Hanging gardens). See *Galatea* 4.

Baca. *Vaca, Doctor.

Baca y de Quiñones, Jerónimo. *Vaca y Quiñones, Jerónimo.

Bacchus (the merry god of laughter) [Baco (el alegre dios de la risa)]. The Roman name for the Greek Dionysus, the god of wine and ecstasy. He was associated with poetry, music, laughter, and celebration; he brought joy and soothed cares. See *DQ* I, 15; *Elección*; *Entretenida* 3; *Fregona*; *Juez*; *Numancia* 1; *Parnaso* 4; *Persiles* I, 5; II, 5, 14; *Vidriera*.

Bachelor [Bachiller]. An academic degree that corresponds roughly to a modern high school diploma, rather than to a modern bachelor's degree. A bachelor is eligible for or is engaged in university study toward a degree of *licentiate.

Bacía de barbero. *Barber's basin.

Baciyelmo. *Basin-helmet.

Backscheider, Paula R. Theorist of the novel. Backscheider opens her book *A Being More Intense* (1984) by expressing her concern with critical approaches to the eighteenth century: "none of us, I believe, is yet satisfied with our understanding of the development of the form we call 'novel.' We cannot explain without some uneasiness the historical and cultural forces which spawned the modern novel. We cannot explain the remarkable variety of the 'new' form. How could Defoe, Richardson, Fielding, Sterne, and Smollett write such different 'novels' in a form so young? How could they include elements of the modern anti-novel before the shape of the genre was determined? What made them group their efforts and identify themselves as engaged in a similar enterprise? What made them precociously, technically self-conscious?" Backscheider's contribution is to study in some detail the works of three writers from the late seventeenth century and early eighteenth century—Bunyan, Swift, and Defoe—who wrote important fictions that helped shape the new form of the novel. Like her other conservative colleagues who assume uncritically that the novel is an English invention of the eighteenth century, however, Backscheider never even pauses to consider the possibility that the so-called "historical and cultural forces which spawned the modern novel" were all worked out in Renaissance Spain, with MC at the forefront of the development of the genre.

Bibliography: Paula R. Backscheider, *A Being More Intense: A Study of the Prose Works of Bunyan, Swift, and Defoe* (New York: AMS Press, 1984).

Baco. *Bacchus.

Bactria [Batria]. An ancient country in the northeastern part of what is now Afghanistan. See *Numancia* 4.

Bactro [Batro]. A river in *Bactria. See *Galatea* 4.

Bad Fame [Mala Fama]. In *Casa* 2, allegorical figure conjured up by Malgesí.

Badajoz. The major city in Extremadura, in western Spain, located southwest of Madrid and east of Lisbon, near the Portuguese border. See *Persiles* III, 2; *Tratos* 1.

Baeza. A city in Andalusia, located north of Granada and east of Córdoba. In *DQ* I, 19, it is the point of origin of the procession accompanying the dead body.

Bagatelle, Le [Trifles]. In *DQ* II, 62, an Italian book being translated into Spanish in the printshop in Barcelona. No book with this title is known to exist.

Bagnio [Baño]. The Spanish word *baño* means *bath,* but in the context of captivity in Constantinople and North Africa, the word—derived from the Latin *balneum* (bathhouse) and/or the Turkish *banyol* (royal prison)—refers to a building or prison consisting of a patio surrounded by small rooms where the prisoners were housed. The equivalent in English, *bagnio,* can mean both prison and bathhouse. In Algiers during the time when MC was captive there, there were cramped and squalid bagnios for common slaves who were used for forced labor and more comfortable (though by no means lavish) bagnios for prisoners, like MC,

being held for ransom. His repeated attempts to escape captivity, however, also meant that MC spent large periods of time in chains and shackles. See *DQ* I, 40.

Bagnios of Algiers, The. *Baños de Argel, Los.*

Bahama. The Bahama Islands, located southeast of Florida and north of Cuba. See *Entretenida* 3.

Baile del rey Perico. *Perico.

Bajá(s). *Pasha(s).

Bajá de Chío. *Pasha of Chius.

Bajá de Rodas. *Pasha of Rhodes.

Bakhtin, Mikhail M. (1895–1975). Russian philosopher, linguist, and literary theorist. Essential to Bakhtin's understanding of genre is the distinction between *romance (although he does not use this term) and novel. The former, which he calls the *First Stylistic Line* of the novel, has its origins in antiquity and is best seen in the sophistic, or adventure, romance of ancient Greece. The prototype of this genre is *Heliodorus's *Ethiopian History*, with its noble and beautiful lovers and their trials and tribulations. The romance is, according to Bakhtin, a characteristically authoritarian and monologic genre, one in which there is a single voice and a single consciousness. Like other traditional genres (epic, lyric, and dramatic), it originated in an ancient oral culture and over the centuries developed relatively rigid generic characteristics. The novel, Bakhtin's *Second Stylistic Line*, is something else entirely. Above all, the novel is characterized by heteroglossia and dialogism, multiple languages and multiple consciousnesses in open-ended dialogue. Novelistic discourse existed in ancient and medieval times, especially in such 'serio-comical' genres as the Socratic dialogue and the Menippean satire. In addition to, or alongside and informing, the serio-comical genres was *carnival: the pageant without footlights, the 'second life' of the people in opposition to official culture, the laughing, ambivalent, parodying celebration of the body and of birth and death. Particularly important is the role of laughter. It is the irreverent laughter of carnival and literary parody that counter the authoritarian seriousness, sentimentality, pathos, and monologism of high or official culture and literary genres, and that make inevitable the novel's oppositional stance. Greatness without laughter is, for Bakhtin, inconceivable: "Everything that is truly great must include an element of laughter. Otherwise it becomes threatening, terrible, or pompous; in any case, it is limited. Laughter lifts the barrier and clears the path." But if elements crucial to the novel have always existed, the novel has not, and it could not come into being until a number of specific historical developments took place. The conditions that in the Bakhtinian view make the novel possible all come together for the first time in the once-occurrent milestone in human history that we call the Renaissance: philosophy (complete worldview, horizontal orientation in space and time, and open-ended present), language (speech diversity, Galilean world of languages, and polyglossia), and culture (laughter and carnival). Add to this the fact that the printing press made the book in the modern sense possible for the first time, and the appearance of the novel becomes almost inevitable: "And there arrived on the scene, at last, the great Renaissance novel—the novels of Rabelais and Cervantes. It is precisely in these two works that the novelistic word . . . revealed its full potential and began to play such a titanic role in the formulation of a new literary and linguistic consciousness." Thus the novel is unique among literary genres: it is the one genre that comes into being "before our very eyes: the birth and development of the [modern, heteroglot] novel as a genre takes place in the full light of the historical day"; it is the only genre that is "younger than writing and the book: it alone is organically receptive to new forms of mute perception, that is, to reading." It is by definition the genre of modernity: modern world = dialogism = novel. So it is that Bakhtin writes of the 'novelization' of other genres; he might just as well have written of the 'modernization' or

'dialogization' of genres: "The novel emerged and matured when intense activization of external and internal polyglossia was at the peak of its activity; this is its native element. The novel could therefore assume leadership in the process of developing and renewing literature in its linguistic and stylistic dimension." Crucial here is the concept of *emergence*, the sudden coming into being of something that is greater than its component parts (like water is greater than its component parts, hydrogen and oxygen; therefore, water is an emergent property). The novel does not 'develop' out of another genre (e.g., the epic or the romance), nor does it 'rise' in the eighteenth century; it *emerges* in the Renaissance. And, for Bakhtin, the crucial text is *DQ*: "The classic and purest model of the novel as genre [is] Cervantes' *Don Quixote*, which realizes in itself, in extraordinary depth and breadth, all the artistic possibilities of heteroglot and internally dialogized novelistic discourse." In sum, for Bakhtin, the First Stylistic Line (essentially the romance) begins in antiquity with the Greek adventure novel and remains the primary, almost the only, type of lengthy fiction practiced for centuries. In the Renaissance, because of the convergence of the factors described above, the heteroglot novel of the Second Stylistic Line (essentially the modern European novel) emerges with Rabelais, the Spanish picaresque, and Cervantes. This Second Line becomes dominant, as the First Line becomes ever less significant, so that in our era the novel as a genre is, in effect, the novel of the Second Line. Although Bakhtin devoted books to Rabelais and Dostoevsky, *DQ* is the work he most frequently cites as exemplary of the genre of the novel. By definition, for Bakhtin, a novel cannot consist of a work in which there is a single voice, tone, point of view, ideology, or consciousness. What distinguishes the novel from all other genres is heteroglossia, the interanimation of different languages, the representation of multiple consciousnesses—in a word, dialogism. No set of formal or stylistic characteristics can ever be sufficient to define— to shackle or limit—the novel; its discourse is infinitely flexible, protean. But one thing is necessary: "The fundamental condition, that which makes a novel a novel, that which is responsible for its stylistic uniqueness, is the *speaking person and his discourse.*" In the nineteenth century, Dostoevsky perfects the *polyphonic novel*, a novel in which the author's word has no privilege and where each character's voice, worldview, and consciousness receive equal representation in their own terms. Early evidence of such novelistic polyphony already existed in *DQ*. Equally valuable for understanding *DQ* and MC's other works are Bakhtin's concepts of *carnival, *great time, dialogism and polyphony (*dialogue in *DQ*), speech genres (*language and style in Cervantes), and theoreticism (*narrative structure of *DQ*).

Bibliography: M. M. Bakhtin, *The Dialogic Imagination: Four Essays*, ed. by Michael Holquist, trans. by Caryl Emerson and Michael Holquist (Austin: University of Texas Press, 1981); M. M. Bakhtin, *Problems of Dostoevsky's Poetics*, ed. and trans. Caryl Emerson, intro. Wayne C. Booth (Minneapolis: University of Minnesota Press, 1984); M. M. Bakhtin, *Rabelais and His World*, trans. Hélène Iswolsky (Bloomington: Indiana University Press, 1984); M. M. Bakhtin, *Speech Genres and Other Late Essays*, ed. Caryl Emerson and Michael Holquist, trans. Vern W. McGee (Austin: University of Texas Press, 1986); Gary Saul Morson and Caryl Emerson, *Mikhail Bakhtin: Creation of a Prosaics* (Stanford, CA: Stanford University Press, 1990); and Walter L. Reed, "The Problem of Cervantes in Bakhtin's Poetics," *Cervantes* 7, no. 2 (1987): 29–37.

Balanchine, George. *Nabokov, Nicolas.

Balbastro. In *DQ* II, 31, a blacksmith and a resident of the village in La Mancha where DQ and SP live.

Balbuena, Doctor Bernardo de (1568–1627). A bishop who spent much of his life in Mexico and Puerto Rico. His best known work is *Grandeza mexicana* (1604; *Mexican Grandeur*); MC cites him as the author of the pastoral romance *Siglo de oro en la selvas de Erífile* (1608; *Golden Age in the Forests of Erífile*) in the list of good poets in *Parnaso* 2.

Balcázar, Juan de. *Información de Argel.

Balconies of the Orient [Balcones del Oriente]. The eastern sky, where the morning sun first shines (*Orient). See *DQ* I, 13.

Ballad [Romance]. The Spanish term *romance*—a ballad, or narrative (and sometimes lyrical) poem of indeterminate length in which there is assonance in the even-numbered lines, whereas the odd-numbered lines are free—should not be confused with the English term *romance, which refers to a kind of prose fiction. Ballad lines are traditionally octosyllabic (in medieval times, they were usually written as monorhymed 16-syllable lines divided into two hemistiches), but they may be of other lengths, such as the six-syllable *romancillo*. The popularity of ballads was never as strong as in the Renaissance, when they were published in cheap *pliegos sueltos* (broadsides) and larger collections called *romanceros* (ballad collections). The genre never faded from interest, and it certainly remains popular today; one of the best examples of modern ballad poetry is the famous *Romancero gitano* (1928; *Gypsy Ballads*) of Federico García Lorca. MC, like all of his contemporaries, was particularly fond of the rich Spanish ballad tradition. There is an anecdote that someone, upon hearing a recently composed ballad, stated that it could only have been written by one of three people, one of whom was MC. This suggests that MC had a ballad style that was in some way unique and recognizable. Like other writers of his age, MC included ballads in his works, as well as writing individual poems in the genre. None of the many ballads scattered throughout his works calls attention to itself as particularly distinguishable as his work. It is very possible, however, that a considerable number of the ballads included in the *Romancero general* (*General Ballad Collection*) of 1600, 1604, and 1605 are by MC. Probably his most famous ballad is the allegorical "Los celos" ("Jealousy," *Poesías* 22), which he mentions proudly in *Parnaso* 4, where he states that he wrote an 'infinite' number of ballads.

Bibliography: Daniel Eisenberg, "The *Romance* as Seen by Cervantes," *El Crotalón, Anuario de Filología Española* 1 (1984): 177–92; and Ruth H.

Webber, *Hispanic Balladry Today* (New York: Garland, 1989).

Ballad collection. **Romancero.*

Ballad of the priest who warned the king [Romance del cura que avisó al rey]. A popular medieval ballad about a priest who warns the king of a robber during a sermon. It is cited by name in *DQ* II, 1.

Ballads of the Cid. **Díaz de Vivar, Rodrigo.

Ballet de Don Quichot, Le (ca. 1614; *The Ballet of Don Quixote*). An anonymous French work, probably the first dance version of MC's novel.

Balm of Fierabrás [Bálsamo de Fierabrás]. A magical healing balm that has its origins in French chivalric legend and reaches its best-known expression in the Italian chivalric literature. Fierabrás is a giant Saracen who sacked Rome with his father Balán and then stole two containers of the remains of the fluid in which Christ was embalmed, which was reputed to be able to cure any wound. Fierabrás was in turn defeated by Oliveros, who turned the magic balm over to Charlemagne so that it could be returned to Rome. This legend was known in Spain both through Ariosto and the **Historia del emperador Carlomagno y de los doce pares de Francia, e de la cruel batalla que hubo Oliveros con Fierabrás* (1525; *History of the Emperor Charlemagne and the Twelve Peers of France, and of the Cruel Battle that Oliveros Had with Fierabrás*). In *DQ* I, 10, the balm is first mentioned when DQ tells SP about it and claims that he knows the recipe for it by heart. SP, ever the enterprising materialist, immediately offers to trade the *ínsula* (island) he is eventually to receive for that recipe. After the beating he receives in the inn (I, 17), DQ requests some rosemary, olive oil, salt, and wine (ingredients that recall the very effective mixture used by the goatherd to cure DQ's ear in I, 11: rosemary, saliva, and salt) to mix the magical balm, drinks it, vomits, sleeps, and feels better. The effect on SP, however, is not so positive, as he immediately begins to 'discharge at both ends' as soon as he drinks some. Similar scatological results occur after the second use of the balm in I, 18. See also *DQ* I, 15, 25.

Balmaseda, Andrés Carlos de. A minor poet who sometimes contributed prefatory verses to the books of others; he is counted among the good poets in *Parnaso* 2.

Balvastro. The father of **Leonora. See *DQ* II, 60.

Balzac, Honoré de (1799–1850). French novelist. His *Comédie humaine* (*Human Comedy*) consists of many novels he wrote and placed in contemporary French society, especially Paris, which form a single, coherent world with recurring characters and themes. Balzac, who once compared himself to DQ, is the author of several novels populated with characters who look, act, and/or talk like DQ. Examples include Balthasar Claes of *La Recherche de l'absolu* (1834; *The Quest of the Absolute*); Feragus in the first volume of the trilogy entitled *Histoire des treize* (1834; *History of the Thirteen*); Vautrin, who specifically calls himself a DQ, in *Le père Goriot* (1834; *Father Goriot*); Lucien de Rubempré, a role-player and imitator of Napoleon (like Julien Sorel, in **Stendhal's The Red and the Black*) in *Ilusions perdus* (1837–43; *Lost Illusions*); and the protagonist Sylvain Pons from *Le cousin Pons* (1847; *Cousin Pons*). The latter, in fact, is one of Balzac's most quixotic creations: "The realities of life always fell short of the ideals which Pons created for himself; the world was not in tune with the soul within, but Pons had made up his mind to the dissonance."

Bamba (Wamba) (seventh century CE). Legendary Visigothic king whose name is a symbol of a time long ago. See *DQ* I, 27; *DQ* II, 33.

Banana tree. **Man who adored a banana tree.

Bancos, Calle de. **Calle de Bancos.

Bancos de Flandes. *Flemish banks/shores/ pinewood.

Bandello, Matteo (ca. 1485–ca. 1561). Italian short-story writer. Bandello's *Novelle* (some 214 stories in all, published in two parts in 1554 and 1573) were translated into Spanish and published in 1589. Bandello's tales do not have the narrative framework of *Boccaccio's *Decameron*, but each work stands alone. The fact that Bandello's work appeared shortly before MC began to write his own short stories probably makes his work at least as important as that of Boccaccio for MC's *Novelas*.

Bandits [Bandoleros (catalanes)]. **1**. In *DQ* II, 60, the 40 men led by the famous Catalan bandit *Roque Guinart. The bandits of Catalonia were a serious social problem and were frequently cited and/or depicted in the fiction and theater of the time. **2**. The group that robs Leocadia and the others in her traveling party in *Doncellas*.

Baño. *Bagnio.

Baños de Argel, Los (Baños); The Bagnios of Algiers. The third play in *Comedias*. For some, this is MC's best treatment of the theme of captivity in all of his work, but it still suffers from strong elements of chauvinism, racism, and anti-Semitism. Clearly an improvement over the more primitive *Tratos*, *Baños* shares much in the way of plot with *Capitán* in *DQ* I, 39–41. A version of *Baños* by Francisco *Nieva was staged with great success in 1980.

Act I: The play begins with a Muslim raid on the coast of Spain. The Muslim corsairs are led by Cauralí, an Algerian captain, and guided by the renegade (convert to Islam) Yzuf, who knows the lay of the land in the area where he was born and raised. A fair amount of booty is taken, along with about 120 captives, including an old man and his two young sons, the sacristan Tristán, and the lovely Costanza de la Bastida. The latter's lover, Don Fernando de Andrada, when he sees his beloved carried away, jumps into the sea in order to be captured and taken with her. The scene switches to Algiers, where, among brief scenes of Muslim

cruelty and Christian suffering, two captives, Don Lope and Vivanco, are talking. As they do, a small package wrapped in a cloth is let down from the window of a house. Vivanco goes to get it, but it is pulled back up, then Don Lope is allowed to take it. It contains some 11 gold coins. The two are joined by Hazén, a Spanish renegade who wants to return to his native land and reconvert to Christianity. Hazén is able to inform them that the house from which the money was lowered is owned by an honest Muslim with an extremely beautiful daughter. He also recalls that in this house lived the Christian slave named Juana de Rentería before her death. When Don Lope and Vivanco are alone again, a second message is lowered, this one containing over 100 gold coins and a note from the young woman who lives in the house. She writes that she learned from Christians about Lela Marién (the Virgin Mary) and she has chosen Don Lope to help her escape to Christian lands and, if possible, marry her. She is very beautiful and very rich, and her name is Zahara. At this point Azán Bajá, King of Algiers, and the cadí of the city head the group that receives the victorious Cauralí upon his return. Various captives have brief scenes before being taken off; notably, the sacristan Tristán demonstrates his comic qualities. The cadí is especially interested in any young boys who might have been captured, for those from Spain are often very attractive, and when taken young can relatively easily be converted to the Muslim faith. Hazén, furious at the actions of Yzuf who betrayed his own people in the raid, attacks and stabs Yzuf to death. Before being taken off to be impaled, Hazén publicly affirms his Christianity.

Act II: Costanza and Fernando become slaves of Cauralí and his wife Halima. Predictably, each of the Muslim slave owners falls in love with the Christian slave of the opposite gender, and each enlists the assistance of the slave of the same gender to help win over the one desired. Zahara stops by to visit her friend Halima, and while there questions the new captives about love and the ways of life among the Christians. After a comic scene in which Tristán makes fun of a Jew, some Muslim boys come along and tease the Christian captives with the refrain, "Don Juan not come, you die here." In a series of brief scenes involving two young brothers named Juanito and Francisquito, the boys long to be reunited with their father, promise him that they will remain loyal to their faith, and defy the cadí when he expresses an interest in them. Don Lope and Vivanco have by now received more than 3,000 *escudos* from Zahara, and with much of the money have purchased their freedom. Zahara and Halima, accompanied by Costanza and another Christian named Señora Catalina, come by, and Zahara takes advantage of the opportunity to pretend that she has been stung by a wasp and remove her headdress, ostensibly in search of the wasp, so that Don Lope can see her beauty. He conveys to her that he hopes to take her soon to Spain. After another scene between the sacristan and the Jew, Fernando and Costanza have some time alone and profess their love for each other and promise to try to deceive their masters. As they embrace, Caural í and Halima see them and are furious, but the Christian lovers convince their Muslim masters that the embrace was to celebrate the fact that they have agreed to give in to their masters' desires. In the final scene, the two Spanish boys again defy the cadí and reaffirm their strong belief.

Act III: The Christian captives of Algiers prepare to present a play in honor of Easter, and Caurali also comes to watch, but he is offended by the sarcastic comments made by Tristán. The performance is interrupted by a Muslim, who announces that a Spanish armada is approaching the city. But as Guardián explains what has happened, it turns out to have been nothing but a convincing mirage (and a bit of hysteria on the part of the Muslims). One of the Christians describes how the cadí, furious because the boy Francisquito has continued to resist his advances and has refused to renounce his religion, has had him crucified. Halima has difficulty understanding why Zahara is not anxious to marry a man as fine and as important as Mulay Maluco. Zahara, meanwhile, reveals to Costanza that she is secretly a Christian. In a series of brief encounters, King Azán Bajá

and the cadí discuss and see examples of the unique and indomitable Spanish spirit of pride and resistance. Then, in an emotional scene, Francisquito's father consoles his son as the boy dies. This is followed by a Muslim wedding procession, and when Don Lope asks who is getting married, the Christian captive Ossorio says that it is Zahara marrying Mulay Maluco (in fact it is Halima, wearing a veil, who goes in Zahara's place). Don Lope expresses surprise, but Ossorio explains that the bride is the most beautiful and richest young woman in North Africa, and the groom speaks several languages; is a brave soldier, liberal, wise and gracious in every way; and is in line to become the king of Fez. Costanza talks with Don Lope and assures him that she loves only him, and they make plans for their escape, Don Lope promising to leave (now that he is a free man), secure a ship, and return within a week. Two Muslims talk about the fact that the wedding that was in progress was halted by the groom so that he could go to Morocco to take over his kingdom, planning to marry Zahara after that. Then Tristán informs others that the Jews have bought him his freedom so that he would leave them alone. News arrives that a ransom ship with the Trinitarian Fray Jorge de Olivar has arrived. In a brief scene, Zahara accidentally drops a rosary, which Halima picks up, accusing Zahara of being a secret Christian. But Costanza saves the day by claiming it is hers and that she loaned it to Zahara. Fernando tells Halima that he will be hers in just three more days, which makes her very happy. Finally, on the appointed night, Don Lope arrives with his ship and takes with him Zahara, Vivanco, Costanza, Fernando, Tristán, Ossorio, the father of the martyred boy, and as many other Christians as can come on stage. Don Lope's final words are that though this story can be brought to an end, there is no end to the suffering in Algiers.

Bibliography: Ellen M. Anderson, "Playing at Moslem and Christian: The Construction of Gender and the Representation of Faith in Cervantes' Captivity Plays," *Cervantes* 13, no. 2 (1993): 37–59; Jean Canavaggio, "La estilización del judío en *Los baños de Argel*," *Primer Acto* 270 (1997): 129–37; Edward H. Friedman, "Cervantes' Dramatic Development: From *Los tratos de Argel* to *Los baños de Argel*." *Revista de Estudios Hispánicos* 10 (1976): 31–55; María Antonia Garcés, *Cervantes in Algiers: A Captive's Tale* (Nashville, TN: Vanderbilt University Press, 2002); Nicolas Kanellos, "The Anti-Semitism of Cervantes' *Los Baños de Argel* and *La gran sultana*: A Reappraisal," *Bulletin of the Comediantes* 27 (1975): 48–53; Adrienne L. Martín, "Images of Deviance in Cervantes's Algiers," *Cervantes* 15, no. 2 (1995): 5–15; Franco Meregalli, "De *Los tratos de Argel* a *Los baños de Argel*," in *Homenaje a Casalduero: Crítica y poesía. Ofrecido por sus amigos y discípulos*, ed. Rizel Pincus Sigele, Gonzalo Sobejano, and Max Aub (Madrid: Gredos, 1972), 395–409; Alfredo Rodríguez López-Vázquez, "*Los baños de Argel* y su estructura en cuatro actos," *Hispania* 77 (1994): 207–14; and Kenneth A. Stackhouse, "Beyond Performance: Cervantes's Algerian Plays, *El trato de Argel* and *Los baños de Argel*," *Bulletin of the Comediantes* 52, no. 2 (2000): 7–30.

Barahona de Soto, Luis (1548–95). Spanish humanist, physician, and poet. Barahona was one of the best-known and most respected poets of the second half of the sixteenth century. His major work is a long epic poem entitled *Primera parte de la Angélica* (1586; *The First Part of the Angelica*) but commonly referred to as *Las lágrimas de Angélica* (*The Tears of Angelica*), on the theme of the love between Medoro and Angelica from Ariosto's *Orlando Furioso*. He is highly praised in Calliope's song in *Galatea* 6, and is cited as a famous Andalusian poet by DQ in II, 1. See also *DQ* I, 6.

Barahona, Don Luis de. A poet greeted by Apollo in *Parnaso* 3, and perhaps a reference to Luis *Barahona de Soto, but since this poet was dead by the time MC wrote *Parnaso*, where all the poets named are supposed to be living, it may be a reference to someone else with a similar name.

Barataria. The name of the "island" (*ínsula*) SP governs during his stay at the palace of the duke and duchess (*DQ* II, 45–53). The name is derived from the word *barato* (cheap) and the phrase *dar barato* ("give a tip"), and suggests deceit. It is also associated with the verb *baratar* (to change one thing for another), related

to the general theme in this episode of the 'world upside-down.' The duke and duchess, together with their retinue, expect to enjoy great laughs at SP's expense during his governorship, but he astonishes everyone by being a wise, fair, and intelligent ruler. The scenes set up to be comic—the physician who refuses to let SP eat the sumptuous food set before him, the impertinent peasant who asks for money, and the 'attack' on the island—all fail, and SP's moral superiority is evident to everyone. Few readers expect SP to be such a success at his governorship, but when he governs so well, it seems like a natural, even inevitable, consequence of his previous experiences and personality. One of the greatest ironies of *DQ* is that this supposed buffoon who is set up for laughs actually turns out to be an exemplary governor, certainly a far more humane and democratic ruler than the duke himself. The contrast in these chapters between the surprisingly successful SP and the dejected, impotent, and humiliated DQ, who is scratched by cats, pinched by *dueñas*, and generally laughed at, makes this section of the novel the one that best illustrates the continued rise of SP and decline of DQ. Interestingly, although there is no such place as Barataria in Spain, there are three in the Americas: 1) in Louisiana (where local lore has it that the name comes from the French pirate Jean Lafitte), a large area of the Gulf coast; 2) in Bermuda; and 3) in Trinidad. See also *DQ* II, 54–55, 62.

Bibliography: John J. Allen, "The Governorship of Sancho and Don Quijote's Chivalric Career," *Revista Hispánica Moderna* 38 (1974–75): 141–52; Joseph R. Jones, "The Baratarian Archipelago: Cheap Isle, Pourboire Isle, Chicanery Isle, Joker's Isle," in *"Ingeniosa Invención": Essays on Golden Age Spanish Literature for Geoffrey L. Stagg in Honor of His Eighty-fifth Birthday*, ed. Ellen M. Anderson and Amy R. Williamsen (Newark, DE: Juan de la Cuesta, 1999), 137–47; Augustin Redondo, "Tradición carnavalesca y creación literaria. Del personaje de Sancho Panza al episodio de la ínsula Barataria en el *Quijote*," *Bulletin Hispanique* 80 (1978): 39–70; and Diana de Armas Wilson, "Rethinking Cervantine Utopias: Some No (Good) Places in Renaissance England and Spain," in *Echoes and Inscriptions: Comparative Approaches to Early Modern Spanish Literatures*, ed. Barbara A. Simerka and Christopher

B. Weimer (Lewisburg, PA: Bucknell University Press, 2000), 191–209.

Baratario. In *DQ* II, 45, perhaps the original name of the village where SP reigns over the 'island' of Barataria.

Barato. A place described as an 'infernal abyss' in *Galatea* 4.

Barba, Pedro. A Spanish knight mentioned by DQ in *DQ* I, 49 (*Crónica de Juan II*).

Barba Roja. *Barbarossa, Khair ed-Din.

Barbacanas de Sevilla. *Picaresque geography.

Bárbara egipcia. *Barbarous Egyptian.

Barbarian(s) [Bárbaro(s)]. 1. A catchall term for anyone who was not of one's national, cultural, or religious group. Greeks considered any non-Greek a barbarian; the Romans thought of all those who lived outside the boundaries of the Roman Empire as barbarians; Christians called non-Christians barbarians; Spaniards and other conquerors and explorers called Native Americans barbarians. The term was also used to refer to any people considered primitive or not civilized. See *DQ* I, 6; *Persiles* I–II. **2.** In *DQ* II, 68, one of the insulting terms used by the men who take DQ and SP back to the palace of the duke and duchess. **3.** In *Persiles* I, 1–6, the inhabitants of the *Island of the Barbarians of the northern regions where the action of the story begins. **4.** In *Persiles* I, 1, four men who remove Periandro from the cave-prison and accompany him in a small boat, which is destroyed by a storm. One of the barbarians notches an arrow and is about to kill Periandro, but the latter's beauty makes him put down his bow. **5.** In *Persiles* I, 3, the governor of the barbarians' island who buys Periandro from Arnaldo and is killed by the son of Corsicurvo, which starts the conflagration that destroys the barbarian island. **6.** In *Persiles* I, 6, the unnamed man who asks Periandro and company to take with them the generous barbarian (Rutilio) who freed the prisoners.

Bárbaros, isla de los. *Island of the Barbarians.

Barbarossa [Barbarroja or Barba Roja]: Khair ed–Din (?–1556). Renegade Greek Christian turned Muslim. He was made admiral of the Ottoman fleet and terrorized the Spanish coast with his frequent raids. He and his brother founded the modern state of Algiers and thus played a decisive role in establishing the circumstances in which MC would spend five crucial years of his life (1575–80). In 1534 he captured the independent Islamic state of Tunis from the Spanish-controlled Muslims who ruled the city. In 1544, he retired as a wealthy man to live his final years in Constantinople. See *Gallardo* 2.

Barbarous Egyptian [Bárbara egipcia]. In the Old Testament, the wife of the Egyptian officer Potiphar, who attempted without success to seduce her husband's Hebrew slave Joseph. She is a symbol of lasciviousness, and as such is compared to Rosamunda in *Persiles* I, 19.

Barbary. *North Africa.

Barbas de Casildea. *Dulcinea's shoe and Casildea's beard.

Barber [Barbero]. 1. In *DQ* I, 21, an unnamed man who serves as barber-surgeon for two small communities. One day, when riding from one village to the other, it begins to rain, so he places on his head his *barber's basin, the identifying tool that is most essential to his profession. DQ sees the basin shining like gold, and believes it to be *Mambrino's helmet. The barber shows up again later in the inn of Juan Palomeque and gets into a fight over his basin (I, 44–45). **2.** In *Entretenida* 3, an accomplished dancer who takes part in the interlude put on by the servants in the household of Don Antonio. **3.** *Maese Nicolás. **4.** *Toledan apothecary.

Barber kitchen-boy [Pícaro barbero]. In *DQ* II, 32, the servant who tries to lather SP's beard with dirty water.

Barber's basin [Bacía de barbero]. In the Renaissance, barbers were more than mere hair-cutters; they also performed minor medical procedures, such as bloodlettings. The symbol of the profession was the distinctive basin, a bowl with a wide, flat brim, with one semicircular section cut out. This made the instrument useful in shaving, as it fit against the client's neck and acted as a receptacle of the lather. During a bloodletting, the basin also served to collect the blood. Because a *barber is wearing the shiny metal basin on his head as protection from the rain in *DQ* I, 21, DQ thinks it is *Mambrino's helmet.

Barbuda. A small island in the Leeward group of the West Indies. In *Entretenida* 3, it is mentioned along with Bermuda, and the comic servant Torrente confuses the two names (*Inn of la Barbuda).

Barca de Aceca. *Aceca Ferry.

Barcelona. The capital of Catalonia, located east and north of Madrid, on the Mediterranean coast, not far from the border with France. It is the second largest city in Spain and the most cosmopolitan of Spanish cities. But in MC's day, Barcelona may not have had more than about 30,000 inhabitants; it was far less important than several other Spanish cities. Barcelona is the scene of action in *Doncellas; DQ* II, 61–66; and *Persiles* III, 12. It is likely that MC had at least some degree of familiarity with the city. See also *DQ* II, 59–60, 66, 72; *Fuerza; Galatea* 2, 5; *Tratos* 1.
   Bibliography: Martín de Riquer, *Cervantes en Barcelona* (Barcelona: Sirmio, 1989).

Barcino. 1. In *Coloquio*, the name by which Berganza is known when he works with the shepherds. **2.** In *DQ* II, 74, along with Butrón, one of the two dogs that Sansón Carrasco plans to purchase from a herdsman from Quintanar so that he, DQ, and the others can take up the life of shepherds.

Barco encantado. *Enchanted boat.

Baretti, Giuseppe (1719–89). Italian dramatist. He is the author of *Don Chisciotte in Venezia* (ca. 1752; *Don Quixote in Venice*), a play based on *DQ* II, 25–26. In this version, both Melisendra and DT are held captive not in Sansueña in Spain, but in Venice.
   Bibliography: Giuseppe Carlo Rossi, "Un *Don Chisciotte in Venezia* de Giuseppe Baretti," *Anales Cervantinos* 18 (1979–80): 211–17.

Bariato. In *Numancia* 4, the young boy, last survivor of the city of Numantia, who commits suicide rather than be taken prisoner by Scipio in the final scene of the play.

Barleta: Barletta. A city in Italy. See *Guarda.*

Barnacle goose [Barnacla]. A European goose that feeds primarily on the barnacle (thus its name) and breeds in the Arctic. In *Persiles* I, 12, Periandro and company, along with Mauricio and company, are served barnacle goose at dinner in the inn on an island. According to legend, these birds are born of sticks placed in the ground along the shore. The part of the stick buried in the ground turns to stone, while that which is exposed begins to decay, and from this decaying part the bird is born.

Baroja, Pío (1872–1965). Spanish novelist. In Baroja's *El árbol de la ciencia* (1911; *The Tree of Knowledge*), Don Blas Carreño, from La Mancha, looks and talks like DQ. He constantly reads Spanish classics and virtually lives in the past, to the point of speaking in an archaic language just as DQ does when he most wants to sound like the heroes of his chivalric romances. The quest that characterizes the plots of many of Baroja's novels—*Camino de perfección* (1902; *The Way of Perfection*), *La busca* (1904; *The Quest*), *Paradox, rey* (1906; *Paradox, the King*), *Zalacaín el aventurero* (1909; *Zalacaín the Adventurer*), and *César o nada* (1910; *Caesar or Nothing*—always carries at least slight elements of quixotism.
   Bibliography: Carlos Orlando Nállim, "Baroja y la narrativa cervantina: Algunas reflexiones," *Revista de Literaturas Modernas* 20 (1987): 504–509.

Baronies of Utrique [Baronías de Utrique]. *Pierres Papín.

Baroque. A difficult term to define, it is best applied to the more elaborate and ornate style of the seventeenth century as opposed to the simpler and more refined style of the sixteenth.

Bibliography: John R. Beverley, "On the Concept of Spanish Literary Baroque," in *Culture and Control in Counter-Reformation Spain*, eds. Anne J. Cruz y Mary Elizabeth Perry (Minneapolis: University of Minnesota Press, 1992), 216–30.

Barrabas [Barrabás]. 1. In the New Testament, the name of the prisoner released in place of Jesus Christ before the crucifixion. It is also the name of one of Satan's lieutenants in Hell. See *DQ* I, 5; *DQ* II, 57; *Entretenida* 3; *Rufián* 1; *Vidriera* **2**. In *Fregona*, a mule driver who participates in the night of song and dance at the inn.

Barrett, Eaton Stannard (1786–1820). English novelist. Barrett is an almost completely forgotten writer, but his novel *The Heroine, or Adventures of Cherubina* (1809 and revised twice by the third edition of 1815) once enjoyed considerable popularity. The protagonist is Cherry Wilkinson, daughter of a comfortable squire. Inspired by her incessant reading of sentimental and Gothic romances, however, Cherry changes her name to the more poetic Cherubina, believes that she is actually the daughter of a nobleman, renounces her father (who burns her favorite books, a repeat of the scene in *DQ* I, 6), and sets out to lead the life of a heroine and ultimately assume her natural role. No similar work of fiction from the eighteenth or nineteenth centuries (e.g., the comparable novels of *Lennox, *Tenney, and *Austen) is as playfully self-conscious and metafictional as this, as Cherubina sallies forth to have a heroine's adventures, meet her hero, and marry him. She constantly practices for her role, acts in conscious imitation of her models, and comments on how what she is doing compares with her favorite books. She is, of course, easy prey for scoundrels who take advantage of her; foremost among them is the actor who convinces her that he is Lord Altamont Mortimer

Montmorenci. In the end Cherubina must face reality, admit her error, and marry properly. It is only after all this that she reads *DQ* and recognizes it as the prototype of her life. What is almost as interesting as this undeservedly neglected work itself is the metafictional prologue entitled "The Heroine to the Reader," written from the moon and dated May 1, 1813 (and thus presumably not included in the first edition). In it, the heroine, now "a corporeal being, and an inhabitant of the Moon," informs the reader that after a work is written, the characters described in it take form on the moon (an anachronistic anticipation of the same science-fiction device as used by writers such as Philip José Farmer, John Myers *Myers, and Clifford *Simak). These Lunarians, or Moonites, continue to live until they are completely forgotten on Earth. The first figure whom the lunar Cherubina meets is DQ, who becomes her guide to the new world.

Bibliography: Eaton Stannard Barrett, *The Heroine, or Adventures of Cherubina*, 3rd ed. (London: Henry Colburn, 1815); Jessamyn Jackson, "Why Novels Make Bad Mothers," *Novel* 27 (1994): 161–74; and Paul Lewis, "Gothic and Mock Gothic: The Repudiation of Fantasy in Barrett's *Heroine*," *English Language Notes* 21, no. 1 (1983): 45–52.

Barriobero y Herrán, Eduardo (1876–1939). Spanish writer. Barriobero is the author of a number of works of interest related to MC. The first of these is *Cervantes de levita: Nuestros libros de caballería* (1905; *A Middle-Class Cervantes: Our Books of Chivalry*), which consists of two separate hybrid works combining critical essay and fiction. In the first, Barriobero imagines MC leaving the jail of Argamasilla del Alba and arriving in Madrid in the early twentieth century. He attempts to sell the manuscript of *DQ* for publication, but has no success. In Barcelona he meets with similar failure, as it is suggested that he greatly abridge the work and change the title. He cannot even publish the work in installments in a magazine, and so, dejected, he gives up on getting his work published at all. Adapting to new circumstances, MC becomes a successful picaresque manipulator and operator in bourgeois society. Finally, he falls ill and dies, leaving the manuscript of *DQ* among his possessions; the book is never published. The second essay is the story of a young man whose readings in political philosophy and the social sciences lead him quixotically to attempt to spread the doctrine of socialism. After repeated failures, he returns home and renounces his political ideal, becoming a middle-class lawyer. The majority of the story consists of a scrutiny of his library (based on I, 6), and a discussion of some of the works therein.

Barriobero also wrote three theatrical works: a four-act lyrical comedy entitled *Don Quijote de la Mancha* (1905) that was written explicitly as a way of popularizing *DQ* on the three-hundredth anniversary of its publication, in which moving images are projected on stage, allowing DQ to fight with animated monsters; a comic opera entitled *Don Quijote y Sancho Panza* (1905); and another lyrical comedy, *Argumento y cantables de Don Quijote de la Mancha* (1916; *Plot and Music from Don Quixote de La Mancha*), all three works with music by Teodoro San José. Barriobero's novel *Vocación* (1909; *Vocation*) includes several references to MC and DQ, a beloved woman who is more an ideal than a person, and a scene based on the wineskins-giants from *DQ* I, 35. Finally, Barriobero wrote an original story entitled "Dos capítulos del *Don Quijote* suprimidos por la censura" (1915; "Two Chapters of *Don Quixote* Suppressed by Censorship"), a fiction (originally published in a literary magazine but also printed separately) presented as a manuscript found and purchased in Toledo (shades of *DQ* I, 9) that was addressed to Cardinal Bernardo Sandoval y Rojas and signed by MC. In the introduction, MC informs his mentor that he was advised by Doctor Gutierre de Cetina (who signed one of the approvals of *DQ* II) to pull two chapters, originally 11–12 of *DQ* II, because their publication would not be permitted by the censor, the Licentiate Márquez Torres (who signed another of the approvals for *DQ* II). He then includes the text of the two censored chapters. In them, there is some material that could be interpreted as critical of the king's *privado*, the Duke of Lerma, and presumably this is the reason for their suppression.

Interestingly, the second of the two chapters deals with the recovery of the bells of the cathedral of Paris, with direct reference to Rabelais's *Gargantua and Pantagruel*, a work MC could not have known, as it was not translated into Spanish until 1905—by Barriobero y Herrán himself.

Bibliography: Eduardo Barriobero y Herrán, *Cervantes de levita; Nuestros libros de caballería: dos ensayos de crítica* (Madrid: Imprenta de Ricardo Rojas, 1905); Eduardo Barriobero y Herrán, *Dos capítulos del "Don Quijote" suprimidos por la censura* (Madrid: Imp. Blas y Cía, 1915); Julián Bravo Vega, "Eduardo Barriobero y Herrán: otra perspectiva cervantina," in *Desviaciones lúdicas en la crítica cervantina: Primer convivio Internacional de "Locos Amenos,"* ed. Antonio Bernat Vistarini and José María Casasayas (Salamanca, Spain: Ediciones Universidad de Salamanca, 2000), 149–60; and Julián Bravo Vega, "Un Don Quijote regeneracionista: el caso de Eduardo Barriobero y Herrán," in *Actas del VIII Coloquio Internacional de la Asociación de Cervantistas*, ed. José Ramón Fernández de Cano y Martín (El Toboso, Spain: Exmo. Ayuntamiento de El Toboso, 1999), 55–68.

Barrionuevo, Gabriel de. Spanish dramatist. Little is known of this writer beyond the fact that he authored an interlude entitled *Triunfo de los coches* (*Triumph of the Coaches*), a satire on Madrid customs after the 1611 law limiting the use of *coaches—also the subject of MC's interlude *Vizcaíno*. What is curious about the work, however, is the presence of a character named 'Cervantes' who seeks to marry a wife who will provide him with a good, steady income, that is, from prostitution. (One possible etymology of the name *Cerv*antes involves the word *ciervo* (deer or stag), with its image of antlers, or horns, which suggests being cuckolded; that is, having 'horns' placed on you by your wife.) The temptation to see this as a topical reference to a man known to have had a difficult marriage and to have been associated with family members whose chastity had previously been called into question (See *Ezpeleta, Gaspar de) is strong. A similar imputation was made by Lope de *Vega in a sonnet about MC, and there is also a suggestion in an episode in *DQA*, in which there is a reference to the Castle of San Cervantes that could be interpreted in these terms.

Bibliography: Martín de Riquer, *Cervantes, Passamonte y Avellaneda* (Barcelona: Sirmio, 1988).

Barrionuevo, Gaspar de (?–ca. 1628). A minor poet and friend of Lope de *Vega's. He is praised in *Parnaso* 3.

Barrios, Eduardo (1884–1964). Chilean novelist. Barrios's best known novel, *El hermano asno* (1922; *Brother Ass*), is a superb retelling of the DQ-SP story—in a Chilean monastery. Fray Lázaro is quixotic in his passion and intellectual ruminations, whereas Fray Rufino is very sanchesque in his literal attempts to live in imitation of Saint Francis. The influence each has on the other as the story progresses is similar to that between DQ and SP. There is also some Cervantine metafiction in the novel as Fray Lázaro, in his earlier life as the secular Mario, had given the woman he loved, María, a copy of Barrios's own earlier novel *El niño que enloqueció de amor* (1915; *The Boy Who Went Mad Out of Love*). In *El niño*, the quixotic protagonist is carried away by books, loves his own DT in Angélica, and is accompanied by an SP figure in Don Carlos Romeral.

Bibliography: Eduardo Barrios, *El hermano asno* (Santiago, Chile: Librería Nascimiento, 1922); and Eduardo Barrios, *El niño que enloqueció de amor* (Santiago, Chile: C. J. Nascimiento, 1920).

Barros, Alonso de (1552–1604). A member of the court of Felipe II, he dedicated his *Filosofía cortesana moralizada* (1587; *Courtly Philosophy Moralized*) to Mateo *Vázquez. MC wrote a prefatory sonnet (*Poesías* 17) for the book.

Barros Grez, Daniel (1834–1904). Chilean novelist, dramatist, and poet. His six-volume novel *El huérfano* (1881; *The Orphan*) is a political satire. It is the story of Don Simpliniano Tragaderas, who believes that the nation should be governed in Latin, and who has sometimes been compared to DQ. But the similarity is superficial at best. Where it is most apparent is in the section where Simpliniano becomes a governor and includes episodes that recall SP at Barataria. Barros Grez's novel *La Academia Político-Literaria* (1890; *The Political-Literary Academy*) features Doña Nicolasa, a female SP who speaks constantly in clichés and popular proverbs. Two of his poetic *Fábulas originales* (1888; *Original Fables*) are about DQ. It has also been suggested that the canine hero (based on a real-life dog) of *Primeras aventuras del maravilloso perro "Cuatro Remos" en Santiago* (1888; *First Adventures of the Marvelous Dog "For Legs" in Santiago*) owes something to Berganza in *Coloquio*.

Bibliography: Daniel Barros Grez, *El huérfano* (Santiago, Chile: Imprenta Gutenberg, 1881).

Barros, Juan. Chilean writer. Barros's novel *El zapato chino* (1913; *The Chinese Shoe*), among other things a satire on the teaching of literature, includes a scene in which MC returns from the afterlife to visit a Jesuit school. The schoolmaster severely limits what the illustrious visitor can say (no mention of his captivity or characters such as Maritornes), and so MC makes a brief statement about censorship and 'puts on his hat, rattles his sword, looks out the corner of his eye, and leaves,' a quote from the famous last lines of MC's satiric sonnet to the tomb of Felipe II (*Poesías* 26).

Bibliography: Juan Barros, *El zapato chino* (Santiago, Chile: Impr. Barcelona, 1913).

Barth, Gaspar (?–1658). German humanist scholar and translator. Barth translated *La Celestina* into Latin with the title of *Pornoboscodidascadalus* (1624). He has sometimes been considered as the historical model for the protagonist of *Vidriera*.

Barth, John (1930–). American novelist. In Barth's literary essays, he frequently mentions MC, "the real inventor of postmodern fiction" (see *postmodernism), and his importance to the sort of novel that Barth himself has written. Several of those novels are peppered with references and allusions to *DQ*, a novel he rereads about every ten years, whose protagonist provides, for him, one of four "cardinal images" from all of literature (the other three are Odysseus, Scheherazade, and Huckleberry Finn). An example of Barth's use of MC is found in his consciously quixotic novel *The Sot-Weed Factor* (1960), whose protagonist, Ebenezer Cooke, boasts, "I shall be a splendid fool, a Don Quixote tilting for his ignorant Dulcinea." Even more Cervantine is *Giles Goat-Boy* (1966), with its elaborate prefatory materials (publisher's disclaimer, editor's cover letter, and author's commentary) and postscript and footnotes, all of which recall MC's comparably elaborate play on authorship centered around the figure of CHB. The academic world of the novel is filled with deans-errant, nannies in distress, dons-errant, wandering researchers, and so forth. The protagonist "was suspicious of adventuring heroes . . . because like that gentlest of dons, Quijote, they were wont at the very least to damage useful windmills in the name of dragonmachy." Barth's *Tidewater Tales* (1987) is a long novel in which a husband and wife go sailing on their boat *Story* on the Chesapeake Bay. Along the way they tell (and retell and elaborate on and spin off from) a large number of stories. Much of the final third of the novel involves another sailor, "a cross between Uncle Sam and the Ancient Mariner" named Don Quicksoat, usually called Capn Don. This DQ sails in a boat named *Rocinante IV* and has a certain air of mystery about him; some think he may be a drug runner, others say he is "a famous writer living incognito, gathering material for his next bestseller" (perhaps rather like John Barth himself). A discussion of *DQ* and the episode of the Cave of Montesinos leads to a purchase of MC's novel and a reading and commentary on *DQ* II, 23, where DQ's experience in the cave is related. The protagonist, Peter, then begins to write a story that is a continuation of DQ's adventure in the cave. In the dreamlike story, DQ sails down the river on a skiff named *Rocinante II* to the island of Barataria, where he spends time with the duke and duchess and Governor Panza. Then he continues on to Lisbon and, in *Rocinante III*, sails to America. Throughout the novel, the four storytelling anchors for the characters are the ones mentioned above as Barth's own favorites: DQ, Odysseus, Scheherazade, and Huckleberry Finn. *Tidewater Tales* is in many ways the cul-

mination of Barth's fascination with storytelling and the great storytellers of all time.

Bibliography: John Barth, *Further Fridays: Essays, Lectures, and Other Nonfiction 1984–1994* (Boston: Little, Brown, 1995).

Bartolomé (Bartolomé [el] Manchego). In *Persiles* III, 9, the servant sent by the father of Antonio the Barbarian to accompany the group of pilgrims on their journey to Rome (his name is not mentioned until III, 11). In III, 18, he and Luisa steal much of the pilgrims' belongings and run off together (although Bartolomé returns most of the stolen goods in III, 19). Later (IV, 5), Bartolomé and Luisa show up in Rome, where they are jailed for the killings of Luisa's former husband and one of her lovers. Bartolomé sends a letter to Periandro and the pilgrims and, with the intervention of Ruperta and Croriano, the two are set free; they marry in IV, 8. In IV, 14, it is reported that the two of them go to Naples, where they die as badly as they had lived.

Bartolomé (Tomé) Carrasco. A resident of the village in La Mancha where DQ lives. His son Sansón has been away as a student at the University of Salamanca and has just returned with the news that a book about DQ's adventures has recently been published. SP once worked for him in the past. In *DQ* II, 2, he is called Bartolomé, but in II, 28, SP refers to him as Tomé.

Bártulo. By metonymy, a law book, so called for the famous and widely used book by Bartolo de *Sassoferrato. See *Elección*.

Basel [Basilea]. City in northern Switzerland, situated on the Rhine River. See *DQ* I, 49.

Basilica of Saint Paul [Templo de San Pablo; San Pablo Extramuros]. One of the famous *seven churches of Rome. It is before this church, located outside the city proper, that Maximino catches up with his brother Persiles, blesses the marriage between Persiles and Sigismunda, and dies. See *Persiles* IV, 14.

Basilio. The clever peasant who fakes suicide in *DQ* II, 21, in order to marry the woman he loves (*Camacho's wedding).

Basilisk [Basilisco]. A mythological beast capable of killing with its gaze. See *DQ* I, 14; *Pedro* 1; *Sultana* 2.

Basin-helmet [Baciyelmo]. SP's brilliant neologism in *DQ* I, 44, in which he combines both *bacía* (basin), such as that used by a *barber, and *yelmo* (helmet), thus producing a hybrid word that acknowledges both realities at the same time (*perspectivism).

Basque [Vizcaíno]. In the Golden Age, Basques were considered to be men of little intelligence; they were often called burros, donkeys, or asses. Because they tended to speak Spanish with a typical accent and syntax, they were frequently ridiculed on stage and in works of fiction, characterized with a comic, broken Spanish speech, a language similar to that spoken both by *Indios* [Native Americans] in Renaissance America and by "Indians" in old western movies. For examples, see the Basque squires in *Casa* 1 (*Blas) and *DQ* I, 8–9.

Basque lady [Señora vizcaína]. The woman traveling in a coach whom DQ assumes is a princess stolen by evildoers, the *Benedictine friars. After routing the friars, DQ identifies himself to her and requests that she go to pay homage to DT. At this point, the lady's squire, also a *Basque, interrupts and challenges DQ.

Basque squire [Vizcaíno]. In *DQ* I, 8, after driving off the two *Benedictine friars, DQ approaches the coach in which a Basque lady is traveling and announces that he has freed her (a princess, he presumes) from her oppressors. The woman's squire, also a Basque, intervenes (in the broken Spanish that was standard for the conventional comic figure of a *Basque in MC's day) and gets into a swordfight with DQ. Just as the two adversaries are about to deliver furious blows, with their swords raised on high, the manuscript breaks off and the adventure is left unfinished. This leads to the search for further archival material in I, 9, and the discovery of the history of DQ written in Arabic by *CHB. When the story resumes, the Basque strikes first and slices away half of *DQ's left ear. DQ recovers, however, and delivers a strong blow, knocking the squire to the ground unconscious. The frightened lady in the coach promises to go to El Toboso and tell DT about DQ's great victory and how he undid a wrong, and DQ rides off proud of his accomplishments. The comedy of the episode resides in the funny language spoken by the Basque, the social satire of Basque presumption of nobility, the parody of the convention of the cliff-hanger commonly used in chivalric and other fiction and in epic poetry (e.g., by Ercilla), and the metafictional search for further manuscript material. See also *DQ* I, 25, 31; *DQ* II, 3.

Bibliography: Carmen R. Rabell, "Perspectivismo dialógico en el episodio de don Quijote con el vizcaíno: El estado de la cuestión," *Boletín de la Biblioteca de Menéndez y Pelayo* 69 (1993): 87–101.

Batalla naval, La (The Naval Battle). One of MC's early plays from the 1580s that has been lost. It is included in the list of his plays in MC's conversation with Pancracio de Roncesvalles in *Adjunta* and is mentioned again in the prologue to *Comedias*.

Batanes. *Fulling mill.

Bates. A river in North Africa, west of Algiers; it was also known as the Río del Azafrán [Saffron River]. Today its name is the Uad el Chelif. See *Tratos* 3.

Bath, Sir John [Juan Bateo]. Irish soldier and poet. He contributed preliminary verses in Latin to at least two Spanish books. He is mentioned in *Parnaso* 4.

Báthory, Zsigmond (1572–1613). Prince of Transylvania. In 1599 he renounced his throne to take religious vows, but then he immediately changed his mind and spent the remainder of his life attempting to regain the throne. See *Doncellas*; *Persiles* III, 21.

Batria. *Bactria.

Batro. *Bactro.

Baty, Gaston (1892–1952). French dramatist. Baty's theater tends to blur the lines between reality and make-believe, and this is
precisely the main feature of his *Dulcinée*
(1938), arguably the best—and certainly the
most influential—play ever written about DQ's
beloved DT. In preparation for the work, Baty
traveled to Spain and took up residence for a
while in El Toboso. The author read *DQ*
closely, and the work is filled with allusions to,
paraphrasings of, and quotations from MC's
novel. Characters from picaresque novels, such
as Lazarillo and the blind man from *Lazarillo
de Tormes*, and others from the novels of Mateo
Alemán and Francisco de Quevedo also appear.
An unnamed crippled soldier, veteran of the
battle of Lepanto, also puts in an appearance.
In the first part of the play, SP arrives at an inn,
sent by his master to look for DT. The servant/
prostitute Aldonza is presented as this figure,
and a thoroughly quixotic SP believes that the
beautiful DT has been converted by an enchanter into the woman with whom he talks.
The interview has a transformational effect on
Aldonza, and she begins to believe in the knight
who loves DT. DQ (who never fully appears in
the play, except by voice) is taken home in a
cage of wooden bars, and soon Aldonza follows. As DQ lies dying, he is forced by the
notary making out his will to admit that there
is no DT, and his last words are 'Dulcinea does
not exist.' Aldonza arrives just as he dies, and
identifies herself as DT. In the second part of
the play, Aldonza-DT is told by SP, now more
realistic and cynical, that DQ's last words were
'Dulcinea . . . exists.' She goes out to continue
the work of DQ and soon finds herself pursued
by law enforcement officers and involved with
a group of *pícaros*. She is even convinced to
kiss the open sore on the face of a leper (a false
sore on the face of a false *pícaro*) and is tricked
into believing that she has miraculously cured
the man. She is taken prisoner and put on trial,
during the course of which the truth about the
scene at the inn, DQ's last words, and the false
miracle all come out, and she has to confront
reality. But she is more determined than ever
that she is DT, and in the final scene goes out
to face an angry mob calling for her death. Echoes of this concept of DT can be seen in many
subsequent works, including Dale *Wasserman's *Man of La Mancha*.

Bibliography: Gaston Baty, *Dulcinea*, trans. Hub-
erto Pérez de la Ossa (Madrid: Gredos, 1944); and
Marcela Ochoa Penroz, "El teatro en el *Quijote* y el
Quijote en el teatro," in *Reescrituras del "Quijote"*
(Santiago, Chile: LOM Ediciones, 1997), 87–132.

Bautista, Fray Juan. *Capataz, Fray Juan
Bautista.

Bavaria [Baviera]. A division of southern
Germany, formerly an independent duchy,
kingdom, and republic. At the end of *Casa* 3,
Charlemagne orders Angelica to be held by the
Duke of Baviera while Roldán and Reinaldos
go off to war, with the promise that the one
who best acquits himself in battle will win her
hand.

Bayardo (Bayarte). The horse of Reinaldos
de Montalbán in Ariosto's *Orlando Furioso*.
See *DQ* I, 52; *DQ* II, 40.

Bayle, Henri. *Stendhal.

Bayrán. 1. In *Gallardo* 2, the character who
confirms the approach of the Turkish fleet. **2**.
In *Baños* 1, a Muslim who participates in the
raid on Spain. **3**. In *Baños* 2, the name given
to the boy Francisquito by his master, the cadí.
The name is also that of the Turkish *pascua*, a
holiday that is the approximate equivalent of
Easter, which makes it even more offensive to
the Christian youth. **4**. In *Sultana* 3, the name,
mentioned once, of one of the three boys who
serve the Sultan Amurates.

**Bazán, Don Alvaro de, Marqués de
Santa Cruz (1526–88).** Spanish admiral. In
the 1550s and 1560s, Bazán fought successfully
against Turkish forces and pirates from a variety of nations in the Mediterranean. In the battle of Lepanto, under the leadership of Don
Juan of Austria, he captained the reserve forces.
After further successes against the Portuguese,
Bazán was in charge of preparing the Invincible
Armada, which he was to lead against the English. Had he not died early in 1588, and had
command of the great naval force not been

handed to the inept Alonso *Pérez de Guzmán, Duke of Medina Sidonia, history might have taken a very different turn. MC, who dedicated *Poesías* 24 to Bazán, might have met him in Lisbon in 1581. See *DQ* I, 39; *Gallardo* 3.

Beaufremont, Pierre de, Sieur de Charny [Mosén Pierres de Charní]. A French knight mentioned by DQ in *DQ* I, 49 (**Crónica de Juan II*).

Beaulieu, Victor-Lévy (1945–). French-Canadian novelist. Beaulieu's *Don Quichotte de la démanche* (1974; *Don Quixote in Nighttown*) is a frantic novel about the life, health, loves, cats, and unpublished works of the novelist Abel Beauchemin. The final chapters of the novel consist of a long surrealistic dream in which Beauchemin meets DQ, who brings a woman about to give birth (both an analogue of the writer's failure to give birth to his literary creations and a personal reenactment of an episode of stillbirth with his former lover), and there ensues a long and incongruous conversation about life, birth, death, literature, creativity, and more. At one point, DQ tells Beauchemin, "I would like you to have a hero who would be for you what I, in my time, was for Spain. All the signs are there. People dream about me a great deal; you aren't the only one. People invoke me; you aren't the only one. A secret sect uses me as a symbol." Rocinante, SP, and a strange midwife are also involved in the powerful dream sequence.

Bibliography: Victor-Lévy Beaulieu, *Don Quixote in Nighttown*, trans. Sheila Fischman (Erin, ON, Canada: Press Porcépic, 1977).

Beaumont, Francis (1584–1616). English dramatist. Beaumont is either the sole author of *The Knight of the Burning Pestle* (ca. 1611) or, more likely, he wrote it in collaboration with John *Fletcher. The play presents a young grocer who dreams of being a knight-errant and comically attempts to live out his dreams. Although some English critics have denied any relationship to *DQ*, it is clear that the play is a conscious and direct imitation/adaptation of MC's novel. Beaumont and Fletcher also collaborated on *The Coxcomb* (written ca. 1609,

performed 1612), clearly based on *Curioso*; and *Love's Pilgrimage* (ca. 1615), based on *Doncellas*.

Bibliography: Lee Bliss, "*Don Quixote* in England: The Case for *The Knight of the Burning Pestle*," *Viator* 18 (1987): 361–80; and Ruth Sánchez Imizcoz, "La influencia de *Don Quijote* en *El caballero del pistadero ardiente*," *Cervantes* 15, no. 2 (1995): 75–82.

Becerra. The Spanish captain who avoided coming to the rescue of Cádiz when it was attacked and sacked by the English in 1596. See *Poesías* 25.

Becerra, Doctor Domingo de. Spanish soldier and poet praised in Calliope's song in *Galatea* 6. Becerra was a captive with MC in Algiers and was among the group ransomed with him in 1580.

Becerril. A prostitute mentioned in *Pedro* 1.

Beckett, Samuel (1906–89). Irish/French dramatist and novelist. Beckett's most famous play, *En attendant Godot* (1953; *Waiting for Godot*) centers on two tramps, Vladimir and Estragon, who have been compared to DQ and SP. In his novels, Beckett's figures of Molloy, Moran, Mahood, and Worm are all variants of DQ in the limited sense of a kind of clownish quixotic invention.

Bibliography: Frederick A. Busi, "*Waiting for Godot*: A Modern *Don Quixote*?" *Hispania* 57 (1974): 876–85.

Bécquer, Gustavo Adolfo (Gustavo Adolfo Domínguez Bastida, 1836–70). Spanish poet and prose writer. The late romantic Bécquer was the finest lyric poet of nineteenth-century Spain. His brief posthumous collection of *Rimas* (1871; *Rhymes*) was his life's work and consists of short lyrics that are among the most popular ever written in Spanish. His poetic *Leyendas* (1871; *Legends*) are romantic and mysterious evocations of medieval tales. Writing under the name of Don Adolfo García, Bécquer wrote a three-act *zarzuela* entitled *La venta encantada* (1850; *The Enchanted Inn*), with music by Antonio Reparaz. Act I takes place in Sierra Morena and involves the priest and barber, SP, Cardenio, and Dorotea. In Act II, they arrive at the inn, where they are joined first by some law officers and then by Fernando, with his friends and Luscinda. Act III presents the resolution of the *Cardenio* affair and ends with DQ being enchanted so that he can be taken home. The play really is just an adaptation of *Cardenio*, with DQ and SP in purely incidental roles.

    Bibliography: Adolfo García, *La venta encantada* (Madrid: Imprenta de José Rodríguez, 1850); and Juan Antonio Tamayo, "Una obra cervantina de Bécquer," *Anales Cervantinos* 1 (1951): 295–324.

Bedregal, Juan Francisco (1883–1945). Bolivian poet, novelist, and folklorist. Bedregal's "Don Quijote en la Ciudad de La Paz" ("Don Quixote in the City of La Paz"), first published in his book *Figuras animadas* (1935; *Animated Figures*), has DQ and SP arrive at the Bolivian capital, where they have a brief encounter with a train (perceived as a dragon) and then with some Native Americans, who flee when DQ offers to defend them but is misunderstood as having threatened them. In La Paz, after a series of incongruous episodes, including DQ's defense of the virtue of some prostitutes (who throw him out of the brothel when they learn that he has no money), SP becomes a politician, Rocinante is confiscated to pay a lodging bill, and DQ leaves the city, never to return again.

    Bibliography: Juan Francisco Bedregal, *Figuras animadas* (La Paz, Bolivia: Editorial "América," 1935).

Beelzebub [Belcebú, Bercebú]. The prince of devils and one of Satan's major lieutenants. The name is derived from *Baal Zebub* (Lord of the Flies), the Philistine god mentioned in the Old Testament. See *Baños* 2; *Casa* 3; *Fregona*; *Gallardo* 2; *Viejo* (used in the plural *Bercebuyes*).

Beerbohm, Max (1872–1956). British wit, essayist, cartoonist, novelist, and dandy, known as "the incomparable Max." Near the beginning of Beerbohm's most famous novel, *Zuleika Dobson* (1911), the protagonist is definitively described in a passage (replete with a meta-

fictional dialogue, very Cervantine in spirit, between reader and writer) based explicitly on MC's Marcela (*DQ* I, 12–14). Zuleika, writes the narrator, "was as pure as that young shepherdess Marcella, who, all unguarded, roved the mountains and was by all the shepherds adored. Like Marcella, she had given her heart to no man, had preferred none. Youths were reputed to have died of love for her, as Chrysostom dies for the love of his shepherdess; and she, like the shepherdess, had shed no tear. When Chrysostom was lying on his bier in the valley, and Marcella looked down from the high rock, Ambrosio, the dead man's comrade cried out on her, upbraiding her with bitter words—'Oh basilisk of our mountains!' Nor do I think Ambrosio spoke too strongly. Marcella cared nothing for men's admiration, and yet, instead of retiring to one of those nunneries which are founded for her kind, she chose to rove the mountains, causing despair to all the shepherds. Zuleika, with her peculiar temperament, would have gone mad in a nunnery. 'But,' you may argue, 'ought not she to have taken the veil, even at the cost of her reason, rather than cause so much despair in the world? If Marcella was a basilisk, as you seem to think, how about Miss Dobson?' Ah, but Marcella knew quite well, boasted even, that she never would or could love any man. Zuleika, on the other hand, was a woman of really passionate fiber." The Marcela-Zuleika comparison is explicitly recalled again near the end of the novel, suggesting that it may well have formed much of the original inspiration for Beerbohm's most memorable literary creation.

Behn, Aphra (1640–89). English dramatist and novelist. The subplot of Behn's first play, *The Amorous Prince, or the Curious Husband* (1671), is based on *Curioso*.

Bejaia [Bugía]. A cape located east of Algiers. See *Baños* 3.

Béjar, Duke of. *López de Zúñiga y Sotomayor, Don Alonso Diego.

Belarmina. In *Persiles* III, 13, one of the three candidates for the position of wife of the

Duke of Nemurs. With Deleasir and Féliz Flora, she accompanies the pilgrims to Rome, but returns to France with the Duke of Nemurs in IV, 9 (which we only learn in IV, 14).

Belcebú. *Beelzebub.

Belén. *Bethlehem.

Belén, monasterio de. *Monastery of Belem.

Belerma. A well-known character, from the Carolingian cycle (but not in French legend itself, where she does not appear) in the Spanish ballad tradition. She is the beloved lady of Durandarte, to whom he has his heart sent after his death. She appears in DQ's dream vision in the Cave of Montesinos, leading a mourning procession, carrying Durandarte's heart, wearing an outsized Turkish turban, and with an unattractive, yellowish face (not due, she insists, to menses, which apparently would be the logical reason for her off-color complexion). Her appearance is one of the significant aspects of DQ's grotesque, prosaic, unchivalric account of the events of the cave. See *DQ* II, 22–23.
Bibliography: Helena Percas de Ponseti, "¿Quién era Belerma?" *Revista Hispánica Moderna* 49 (1996): 375–92.

Belerofonte. *Bellerophon.

Belianís de Grecia. Protagonist of the romance of chivalry that bears his name (*Fernández, Jerónimo). Belianís is the author of a sonnet dedicated to DQ as one of the preliminary poems to *DQ* I.

Belianís de Grecia. *Fernández, Jerónimo.

Belica (Belilla). In *Pedro* 1, a young gypsy woman who is chosen by Maldonado to be Pedro de Urdemalas's wife, and who turns out to be the queen's niece.

Belisa. In *Galatea* 3, 6, the shepherdess loved by Marsilio who does not love him in return; she never appears in the text.

Belisarda. **1**. Shepherdess from Lope de *Vega's pastoral romance *La Arcadia*. See *Coloquio*. **2**. *Pastoral names.

Bellerophon [Belorofonte, Belerofonte]. In Greek myth, the hero who was able (with divine assistance) to capture the winged horse Pegasus, which he rode in order to kill the Chimera. Bellerophon died when he attempted to fly to heaven on Pegasus and was thrown by the horse. See *DQ* II, 40; *Parnaso* 3.

Bellona [Belona]. In Roman myth, the goddess of war, sometimes considered to be either the wife or the sister of Mars. See *DQ* I, 52; *Tratos* 1.

Bellotas. *Acorns.

Bellow, Saul (1915–). American novelist, winner of the 1976 Nobel Prize for literature. Bellow's work falls into three periods: 1) his early novels, 2) the three great novels published between 1953 and 1964 that established his place in modern literature, and 3) his later works. It is precisely the three works that won him the much-deserved reputation of mid-twentieth-century America's most important novelist that most specifically recall MC: *The Adventures of Augie March* (1953), *Henderson the Rain King* (1959), and *Herzog* (1964). In his breakthrough *Augie March*, a freewheeling "picaresque" romp, the protagonist makes a quixotic trip to Mexico in search of a better version of reality: "There must be something better than what people call reality." There, after a serious fall on a clumsy Rocinante-like nag called Old Bizcocho, Augie does a DQ-like penance (*DQ* I, 25) in order to work out his philosophy of life: "Everyone tries to create a world he can live in, and what he can't use he often can't see." Finally, Augie decides that the struggle of humanity is "to recruit others to your version" of reality.

Bellow himself has said that Eugene Henderson is an "absurd seeker of high qualities." This is what leads him to abandon his comfortable life in America and search for himself in Africa, where he has a symbolic encounter with a lion (recalling DQ's lion adventure in II,

17) that changes his life and his name—to Leo E. Henderson, reminiscent of DQ's name change to the Knight of the Lions. Henderson's native guide, Romilayu, is his SP-like reality instructor and their old jeep is a sort of mechanical Rocinante. Henderson admits his madness, describes his mission as a quest, and attempts to rescue maidens-in-distress and right wrongs, sometimes making the situation even worse.

In *Herzog*, Moses Herzog, a Jewish, intellectual DQ, writes absurd letters (that he never sends) to everyone from Spinoza to God, and worries that he is out of his mind and has fallen under some sort of spell. As his life seems to be disintegrating and he is incapable of taking action (with an old family pistol, reminiscent of DQ's family armor), he has a (once more, Rocinante-like) car accident and muses that he should not have brought the gun with him, that "then and there he might have stopped being quixotic. For he was not a quixote, was he? A quixote imitated great models. What models did he imitate? A quixote was a Christian, and Moses E. Herzog was no Christian. This was the post-quixotic, post-Copernican U.S.A. where a mind freely poised in space might discover relationships utterly unsuspected by a seventeenth-century man sealed in his smaller universe. There lay his twentieth-century advantage. Only . . . in nine-tenths of his existence he was exactly what others were before him." Herzog is in fact one of the greatest of all modern DQs. Though there are occasional allusions or references to MC or DQ in other Bellow novels and stories—especially the questing Joseph in *Dangling Man* (1944) and the old philosopher Sammler, who muses on madness and the imitation of models in *Mr. Sammler's Planet* (1970)—it is primarily in these three, and especially the last two, that Harry Levin's Quixotic Principle fully applies to Bellow, who at his best is also at his most Cervantine.

Bibliography: Howard Mancing, "Cervantes y Saul Bellow," *Anales Cervantinos* 16 (1977): 125–37; and Barbara Probst Solomon, "The Spanish Journey of Saul Bellow's Fiction," *Salmagundi* 106–7 (1995): 94–99.

Belmonte. A city in Cuenca Province, located southeast of Madrid and west of Valencia. The city was ruled by the famous Marqués de Villena, who was notorious for fleecing foreigners. In *Gitanilla*, there is a reference to this practice with respect to the *gabachos*—originally a term used to refer to some natives of the Pyrenees Mountains and later extended as a disdainful word for Frenchmen in general; it is still popularly used in this sense in modern Spain.

Belmonte Bermúdez, Luis de (ca. 1587–1650). Spanish dramatist, poet, and biographer. The first story in Belmonte's collection entitled *Doce novelas* (*Twelve Stories*) was "La vida de Cipión" ("The Life of Cipión"), but, unfortunately, this entire work has been lost.

Belona. *Bellona.

Belorofonte. *Bellerophon.

Beloved Disciple [Amado discípulo]. Saint John, disciple of Christ, who cared for Mary after the crucifixion and was assumed to be the author of the Gospel of John. See *Persiles* II, 18.

Beltenebros. The name taken by Amadís de Gaula when he does his famous tearful penance in *Peña Pobre. The name is derived from *Bel* + *tenebroso* (Beautiful + gloomy). This episode is cited and discussed by DQ during his own *penance in Sierra Morena in I, 25. See also *DQ* I, 15.

Beltrán. **1**. In *Rinconete*, a name mentioned by Chiquiznaque in the proverb, "Quien quiere a Beltrán quiere a su can" "Who loves Beltrán loves his dog: Love me, love my dog"; he also invents the corollary, "Quien mal quiere a Beltrán, mal quiere a su can" ("Hate me, hate my dog"). **2**. In *Rufián* 3, a priest who is mentioned but does not appear in the play.

Beltrán y Colón, Juan. Spanish writer. Beltrán published *La acción de gracias de doña Paludesia, obra póstuma del Bachiller Sansón Carrasco* (1780; *Doña Paludesia's Thanksgiving, a Posthumous Work by Bachelor Sansón*

Carrasco), another of those works sometimes classified as an imitation of *DQ* because it is presented as a posthumous work of Sansón Carrasco, but in fact a text that cannot sustain even the minimal fictional thread.

Bibliography: Juan Beltrán y Colón, *La acción de gracias de doña Paludesia, obra póstuma del Bachiller Sansón Carrasco* (Madrid: Joaquín Ibarra, 1780).

Bembo, Pietro (1470–1547). Italian poet and prose writer. Bembo is never mentioned by MC, but his *Gli asolani* (1505), a disquisition on Platonic love, is clearly alluded to and/or paraphrased in *Galatea* IV and *DQ* II, 67.

Benavente, Jacinto (1866–1954). Spanish dramatist, winner of the Nobel Prize for literature in 1922. Benavente was the most popular and respected Spanish dramatist in the first quarter of the twentieth century. His best-known work, *Los intereses creados* (1907; *The Bonds of Interest*) draws upon two classical theatrical traditions, the Italian *commedia dell'arte* and the Spanish *comedia*. The protagonists of this play, Leandro and Crispín, have much of DQ and SP to them. In addition, Benavente is the author of a play called *Nuevo coloquio de los perros* (1908; *New Dialogue of the Dogs*), an obvious reworking of *Coloquio*. Additionally, Benavente wrote but never published a one-act play about the last days of DQ entitled *La muerte de don Quijote* (written before 1928; *The Death of Don Quixote*). The play begins with DQ in bed, surrounded by his friends and family, just as in the novel. Much of the dialogue is lifted verbatim or closely paraphrased from *DQ* II, 74. What is original and interesting about the piece is the final scene in which SP casts doubt on the exemplary Christian death of his master. Whereas the priest insists that DQ died with his thoughts firmly fixed on eternity, SP insists that he heard DQ's last words: 'Ah, my lady Dulcinea!' This final note of romantic ambiguity completely rewrites the last scene of the novel in an original and interesting way.

Bibliography: José A. Díaz, *Jacinto Benavente and His Theater* (New York: Las Américas, 1972); and Lola Montero Reguera, "Jacinto Benavente: *La muerte de Don Quijote*," *Anales Cervantinos* 34 (1998): 279–87.

Benavides, Diego de. *Información de Argel.*

Benedictine friars [Frailes de la Orden de San Benito]. After the adventure of the windmills (I, 8), DQ and SP head toward Puerto Lápice, and as they arrive DQ sees two evil figures riding on dromedaries (*dromedarios*) escorting a princess they have abducted; they are actually two Benedictine friars riding on mules and followed by a woman traveling in a coach. DQ challenges the friars, rejects their reasonable explanation of who they are ('No bland words with me, for I know you, you lying rabble'), calls them devils, and attacks, driving them off. Some readers see this as a metaphorical attack on religion, or at least an example of anticlericalism, but there is never an easy interpretation of matters of *religion with MC. Immediately after this encounter, a victory, DQ has his battle with the *Basque squire and the manuscript is broken off, the action left suspended before the discovery of the history of CHB in I, 9. See also *DQ* II, 10.

Benedictine giants [Gigantes benitos]. Sansón Carrasco's way of referring, in *DQ* II, 3, to DQ's adventure with the *Benedictine friars of I, 8.

Beneficiado de aquel pueblo. *Priest of the town.

Benengeli. *Cide Hamete Benengeli.

Benita. In *Pedro* 1, a friend of Clemencia.

Benito, Nicolás. MC's assistant commissary in the 1590s.

Benito Repollo. In *Retablo*, the mayor of the town where the marvelous show is produced.

Bentivoglio family. A powerful family in Bologna, Italy, in the fifteenth and sixteenth centuries. In *Cornelia*, the fictional Bentibolli characters, including the protagonist Cornelia and her brother Lorenzo, are linked to this historical family.

Berbería. *North Africa.

Bercebú. *Beelzebub.

Bergamasca. An Italian dialect. See *Casa* 2; *Sultana* 2.

Berganza. In *Casamiento*, one of the two dogs whom Campuzano hears talking one night. Berganza is the one who tells the story of his life in *Coloquio*, while the other, Cipión, listens and comments.

Bergman, Hjalmar (1883–1931). Swedish novelist, short-story writer, and dramatist. Bergman's first popular novel, *Hans nads testamente* (1910; *The Baron's Will*), evokes *DQ* in tone and spirit, in details down to the comic chapter titles.

Bibliography: Hjalmar Bergman, *The Baron's Will*, trans. Henry Person with Robert Lindquist (Stockholm: n.p., 1961).

Berkeley, August (Rev. S. A. Gardner) American writer. Gardner's novel *A Modern Quixote, or, My Wife's Fool of a Husband* (1884) is the first-person narrative of the forgetful, impulsive, generous, naïve, gullible, clumsy, thoughtless, exaggerating, and lying—in a word, supposedly quixotic—August Berkeley and his long-suffering wife Augusta. If being a stumblebum and as dumb as a stump is quixotic, then Berkeley is that in spades. Sometimes his escapades are a little funny, and there is one comic narrative moment in the novel: he begins a "most momentous" chapter on his mother-in-law, only to truncate it in mid-sentence within less than a page, and then explain in the following chapter how his wife saw what he was writing, which led to "a quiet little talk, of two days' and one night's duration," with the result that he prefers not to write of his wife's "respected mother." The final third of the novel, labeled Part II, descends into a dreary mystery investigation. Outside of the title, there is no reference anywhere in the novel to DQ.

Bibliography: August Berkeley, *A Modern Quixote* (Hartford, CT: American Publishing Company, 1884).

Bermuda. A group of islands in the Atlantic Ocean east of South Carolina, discovered in 1527 by Juan Bermúdez and taken over by the English in 1612. The region was considered one of dangerous navigation. See *Entretenida* 3; *Pedro* 1; *Rufián* 2.

Bermúdez de Carvajal, Fernando. Servant to the Duke of Sesa and a minor poet; he contributed one of the prefatory poems to MC's *Novelas*. He is praised as one of the good poets in *Parnaso* 2.

Bermúdez, María Elvira (1916–88). Mexican novelist and short-story writer. Bermúdez is perhaps the best-known and most popular author of mystery stories in Mexico. One of her best stories is entitled "La clave literaria" ("The Literary Clue"). In it, the murder of a thoroughly unlikable Hispanophile (and Franco sympathizer) is investigated by Armando H. Zozaya, a Mexico City journalist and amateur private investigator on vacation and staying in the deceased man's hotel. The victim was always particularly fond of MC, and a broken plaster bust of the author provides the clue that enables the journalist to solve the case. In the end, justice—more poetic than legal—is done.

Bibliography: María Elvira Bermúdez, ed., *Los mejores cuentos policiacos mexicanos* (Mexico City: Libro-Mex, 1955).

Bernardinas. Meaningless talk; gibberish. See *Laberinto* 1.

Bernardo Agustín, Don. In *Persiles* III, 12, the brother of Ambrosia Agustina. There was a historical Agustín family in Aragon, of whom the most noteworthy was Jerónimo Agustín, a soldier and friend of the poet Juan *Boscán. A later descendant, also named Jerónimo, was a contemporary of MC; he was a soldier and sea captain at the time of the expulsion of the *Moriscos* in 1609. There may or may not be some intended evocation of the historical figures in this character and his sister.

Bernardo del Carpio. Legendary Spanish hero, invented about the twelfth century, who seems to have come into being in reaction to the French heroes of the *Carolingian cycle. Bernardo does not exist in the French legends, but he is very prominent in Spanish versions of the Roland story. Supposedly the nephew of the ninth-century Castilian King Alfonso II, Bernardo successfully schemed to align his king with the Muslims against Charlemagne's forces led by Roland in the battle of Roncesvalles. Bernardo thus is an important early symbol of Spanish pride and nationhood. His great claim to fame was to have killed Roland at Roncesvalles, crushing him in his arms. In MC's day, it was universally believed that Bernardo was a historical figure (see DQ's reference to his historicity in I, 49), even to the extent that Lope de *Vega is supposed to have claimed to be a direct descendant of his. In *Casa,* Bernardo del Carpio is the Spanish knight involved in the adventures in the enchanted forest of Ardenia. See also *DQ* I, 1, 26; *DQ* II, 10, 32; *Gallardo* 1.

Bernardo del Carpio. *Alonso, Agustín.

Bernardo (Famoso Bernardo). A title MC mentions as a forthcoming book in the dedication to *Persiles,* presumably a work about the legendary *Bernardo del Carpio. Nothing is known about what sort of book it might have been—poetry, drama, or fiction—but Daniel Eisenberg has made the intriguing suggestion that MC's *Bernardo* would have been his romance of chivalry, a more measured and verisimilar alternative to the fantastic adventures of Amadís, Belianís, and the rest.
   Bibliography: Daniel Eisenberg, "El *Bernardo* de Cervantes fue su libro de caballerías," *Anales Cervantinos* 21 (1983): 103–17.

Berni, Francesco (Bernia) (ca. 1497–1535). Italian poet best known for his burlesque verse. See the dedication to *Novelas,* where he is called Bernia.

Berrío, Gonzalo Mateo de (?–ca. 1609). Spanish jurist and occasional poet praised in Calliope's song in *Galatea* 6.

Berrueca. A resident of the village in which SP lives; she and her daughter are mentioned by Teresa Panza in the letter to her husband in *DQ* II, 52.

Best part of Spain [Parte que es mejor de España]. In *Poesías* 28, MC uses this phrase together with a play on the name *Vega* (plain) to praise (ironically?) Lope de *Vega on the occasion of his new book of poetry.

Bestsellers. Although the term is a modern one, the phenomenon of the bestseller began in the Renaissance as a result of the invention of the printing press. The Bible, various religious works, and other types of nonfiction clearly achieved bestseller status throughout the sixteenth and seventeenth centuries. In fiction, the first bestsellers in Europe were all from Spain. First and foremost are three works first published in the final decade of the fifteenth century: Diego de *San Pedro's *Cárcel de Amor* (1492), Garci Rodríguez de *Montalvo's version of *Amadís de Gaula* (generally considered to have been published about the 1490s, although the first known edition is from 1508), and Fernando de *Rojas's *La Celestina* (1499). In the sixteenth and seventeenth centuries, some of the primary examples are Jorge de *Montemayor's *La Diana* (1559), Mateo *Alemán's *Guzmán de Alfarache* (1559), and MC's *DQ, Novelas,* and *Persiles.* Urfé's *L'Astrée* (1607–27) was arguably the first non-Spanish fictional bestseller of the age. Bestselling Renaissance fiction was exclusively a Spanish phenomenon (*printing in Spain).
   Bibliography: Keith Whinom, "The Problem of the Best-seller in Spanish Golden-Age Literature," *Bulletin of Hispanic Studies* 57 (1980): 189–98.

Bethlehem [Belén]. An ancient town in Judea, the birthplace of Jesus Christ. See *Rufián* 2.

Betis. The Roman name for the *Guadalquivir River that flows through Seville to the Atlantic

Ocean. The name is still sometimes used with a poetic connotation in modern Spain. See *DQ* I, 14, 18; *Galatea* 1, 6.

Bible (Sacred Scripture, Divine Scripture) [Biblia (Sacra Escritura, Divina Escritura)]. The Bible is never mentioned by name in any of MC's works, but it is referred to as the Holy Scripture. Nevertheless, there are well over 100 biblical references, allusions, citations, paraphrasings, and evocations of the Bible in *DQ* and many more throughout his other works. See *DQ* I, prologue, 33; *DQ* II, 1.
Bibliography: Juan Antonio Monroy, *La Biblia en el "Quijote"* (Madrid: V. Suárez, 1963).

Bibliographies of Cervantes and his works. Because of the very large amount of critical material published annually on MC (over 100 articles and books per year), bibliographies tend to become dated soon after publication. Of recent efforts, the monumental *DQ* bibliography of Jaime Fernández is the most complete; it has the advantage of a meticulous thematic taxonomy. The very extensive bibliography included in the second volume of the Rico et al. edition of *DQ* is also excellent. Also very useful are the annual Cervantes bibliographies by Eduardo Urbina, first published by *Cervantes: Bulletin of the Cervantes Society of America*, and more recently by the *Centro de Estudios Cervantinos in Alcalá de Henares. Urbina also directs the increasingly valuable *Cervantes International Bibliography Online* (*Cervantes on the Internet). The best way to keep up with the most recent bibliography related to MC is to check the annual MLA bibliography published in *PMLA,* the MLA bibliography on CD-Rom (available at most research libraries).
Bibliography: C.I.B.O.: Cervantes International Bibliography Online, http://www.csdl.tamu.edu/cervantes/; and Jaime Fernández, *Bibliografía del "Quijote" por unidades narrativas y materiales de la novela* (Alcalá de Henares, Spain: Centro de Estudios Cervantinos, 1995).

Bickerstaffe, Isaac (1735–1812). Irish dramatist. Bickerstaffe's comic opera *The Padlock* (1768) is based on *Celoso.* The elderly Don Diego is both guardian and fiancé of young Leonora. He keeps her in a house with an ostentatious padlock on the door to protect her from other men. But, during an absence by Don Diego, the young Leander manages to cajole the black servant Mungo to help him gain admission to the house. Don Diego returns to find the young lovers together, recognizes that they are well suited for each other, and generously endows their marriage. The music for the play was written by Charles Dibden (1745–1814), who also played the role of Mungo in blackface, supposedly the first such performance on an English stage.

Biedma. *Ruiz de Biedma, Fernán.

Biendonado. In *Poesías* 16, wordplay on the name of Gabriel *López Maldonado.

Billiards table [Mesa de trucos]. A early version of billiards was introduced into Spain by the Italians in the sixteenth century. In the prologue to *Novelas,* MC states that with this book he metaphorically intends to set up a billiards table in the public square where people can entertain themselves as they please. Like the comparable statements in the prologue to *DQ* I, this comment makes it clear that MC recognizes that interpretive power resides with the reader and not the author or the text itself.

Biographies of Cervantes. The first biography of MC was that of Gregorio Mayáns y Síscar in 1738. Also important are those by Vicente de los Ríos (1780) and Martín Fernández de Navarrete (1819), both published by the *Royal Spanish Academy. Since then, there have been dozens of biographies, far too many to mention here. The monumental biography of Luis Astrana Marín remains indispensable (7 vols.; 1948–58). Of the recent serious biographies, the best is Jean Canavaggio's *Cervantes* (1986). Some other recent biographies in English that are basically reliable and readable are those of Richard Predmore (1973), William Byron (1978), Melveena McKendrick (1980), and Donald P. McCrory (2002). In addition, there have been others that are somewhat fictionalized (Francisco Navarra y Ledesma, 1905), or very creative and imaginative (Fernando Arrabal, 1996), whereas others are outright novels based on the life of MC (Bruno Frank, 1934; Federico Jeanmaire, 1990; Stephen Marlowe, 1991; Juan Eslava Galán, 1994). For a bibliography, see *Cervantes Saavedra, Miguel de.

Bireno [Vireno]. A character from Ariosto's *Orlando Furioso.* He fell in love with Olimpia, daughter of the Count of Holland, but then abandoned her for the daughter of the king of Frisia. See *Doncellas; DQ* II, 57.

Birthmarks and beauty marks. Birthmarks, beauty marks, and blemishes play a role in several of MC's works. In *Gitanilla*, Preciosa is identified as Doña Constanza de Azevedo y de Meneses by means of two birthmarks: a mole in the shape of a white moon under her left breast and a small section of skin that binds together the two smallest toes on her right foot. In *Española,* Isabel is identified by her mother by a mole behind her right ear. MC parodies this convention on two occasions. The first is in *DQ* I, 30, when Dorotea, as Princess Micomicona, says that the brave knight who is to kill the evil giant, restore her throne, and marry her is supposed to have a mole on his back—on the right side, just below the left shoulder. DQ wants to disrobe and check to see if he has such a mark, but SP, anxious to get on with the adventure and not tempt fate, assures everyone that DQ does indeed have such a mole in the middle of his back. The second time is in II, 10, when SP describes in detail the grotesque mole he says he saw on DT's left lip (*Dulcinea's mole).

Biserta. A Mediterranean port city on the north coast of Tunis, not far from Carthage. See *Amante*; *Tratos* 1.

Bituania. In *Persiles* II, 14, the kingdom ruled by Cratilo; presumably it is Lithuania. See also *Persiles* II, 1.

Bivar, Juan Bautista de. *Vivar, Juan Bautista de.

Bizarra Arsinda, La (Bizarre Arsinda). One of MC's early plays from the 1580s that

has been lost. It is included in the list of his plays in MC's conversation with Pancracio de Roncesvalles in *Adjunta.*

Black Legend [Leyenda negra]. A quintessential example of political myth-making, the Black Legend was the widespread and exaggerated European myth of Spanish excess, cruelty, and stupidity. Like most versions of the "Evil Empire" approach to diplomacy, the aim was to deprecate and demean the enemy in order to make one's own policies and history look enlightened by comparison. Since Spain was arguably the most powerful and feared empire in European history, attempted to spread Spanish hegemony literally throughout the world, and was the most successful colonizer of all time, her enemies fomented exaggerated tales of Spanish arrogance (by far the most frequent complaint, and certainly not without foundation), pride, presumption, fanaticism, intolerance, cruelty, and excess. The Spanish had supposedly humiliated the refined Italians and viciously crushed Dutch nationalism during the periods of occupation of these countries. Through their bloody Inquisition, they had supposedly murdered countless thousands of innocent Protestants and Jews. And all the while they were a primitive people, whose typical activities were the cruel bullfight, the simple guitar, and the frenzied dancing of the flamenco. Over the years, it became an article of faith that Spain failed as a political power because of inherent weaknesses in the Spanish character. To at least some degree this was a racist attitude, since Spain was the only nation in Europe with a substantial Muslim "racial" component. That the Spanish had in fact been haughty, fanatical, excessive, cruel, and genocidal (though overall probably no more than the English or the French) gave the necessary degree of truth that informed the legend. The Spanish had themselves to blame for at least part of the Black Legend. The single most important indictment of Spanish practices in the New World colonies was that of Fray Bartolomé de *Las Casas in his book *Brevísima relación de la destrucción de las Indias* (1552; *Very Brief Relation of the Destruction of the Indies*; translated as *The*

Tears of the Indians). Las Casas, a true human-itarian in the best sense of the word, documented (and exaggerated) the extermination, enslavement, and general mistreatment of the natives by the Spanish conquerors and colonists. It is worth noting that in Spanish America today there is a far greater percentage of native Americans in the general population than there is in the United States and Canada (which suggests that they were not exterminated as efficiently as they were in the English American colonies), and there has never existed any concept of a "reservation" where they should be confined. The enormous popularity of Las Casas's book, which had over 50 editions in at least six languages by the eighteenth century, helped "prove" that the Spanish were the worst of all possible imperialists. By the eighteenth century, Spain was less a powerful enemy than a pathetic backwater, but the Black Legend continued, now with increased emphasis on the elements of stupidity and cultural barrenness. When Nicholas Masson de Morvilliers wrote the article on Spain for the great French *Encyclopédie* (1751–65), under the general editorship of Denis *Diderot, he asked, "What has Spain ever contributed to the world?" and answered his own question: "Nothing." The Spanish response to this attack on national pride inevitably featured MC and *DQ*. Bathed in emotional and rhetorical excess, these books, essays, and newspaper articles regularly trotted out the story of the idealistic knight, practical squire, skinny nag, and idealized lady as one of mankind's greatest achievements. Today the remnants of the Black Legend persist in ignorance and neglect more than fear or disdain. Modern historians often treat Europe as though it ended at the Pyrenees; literary critics and historians blithely assume that the novel is an invention of eighteenth-century England; Spain is lumped together with Spanish America, especially Mexico, in an imperialistic and Anglo-centric view of culture and history; and "Latin America" includes those regions of the Americas where Spanish and Portuguese are spoken but not those where French is the language (i.e., French Caribbean countries and Quebec), all clearly an elitist (and racist) exercise in cultural

power. Old legends never die; sometimes they don't even fade very much.

Bibliography: Ricardo García Cárcel, *La leyenda negra: historia y opinión* (Madrid: Alianza, 1992); Charles Gibson, ed., *The Black Legend: Anti-Spanish Attitudes in the Old World and the New* (New York: Knopf, 1971); A. Gordon Kinder, *Creation of the Black Legend: Literary Contributions of Spanish Protestant Exiles* (Valletta, Malta: Midsea Books, 1996); William S. Malby, *The Black Legend in England* (Durham, NC: Duke University Press, 1971); and Rafael Núñez Florencio, *Sol y sangre: la imagen de España en el mundo* (Madrid: Espasa, 2001).

Black slaves. *Slave(s).

Black vassals [Vasallos negros]. When the Princess *Micomicona explains her story, and plans are made for DQ to slay her enemy Pandafilando and restore her kingdom, SP assumes that DQ will marry the princess and inherit her kingdom. That is when he is supposed to reward SP with an island to govern. But, reasons SP, in that part of the world the natives, and therefore his future subjects or vassals, are black. At first, that seems to worry him, but he soon decides that it will be no problem, as he can always convert them to gold or silver (i.e., by selling them as slaves). Does this make SP a racist? Probably so. See *DQ* I, 31.

Bibliography: Baltasar Fra-Molinero, "Sancho Panza y la esclavización de los negros," *Afro-Hispanic Review* 13, no. 2 (1994): 25–31; and Augustin Redondo, "Burlas y veras: La Princesa Micomicona y Sancho negrero (*Don Quijote*, I, 29)," *Edad de Oro* 15 (1996): 125–40.

Blair, Erich. *Orwell, George.

Blanca. In *Galatea,* the younger sister of Nísida. She winds up loving and being loved by Silerio.

Blanca paloma. *White dove.

Blanco de Paz, Juan. Spanish ex-Dominican priest (he was expelled from that order). He was captured by pirates and taken to Algiers in 1577. There, Blanco de Paz betrayed MC by denouncing his fourth escape attempt to *Hassan Pasha in 1579. Apparently he was jealous that he was not among those chosen by MC to make the escape attempt and, out of spite, exposed him (see *Cervantes, escape attempts of). Not content to denounce MC, Blanco de Paz began to spread rumors about his rival. He was described by several witnesses to the events as a liar and cheat.

Blas. In *Casa* 1, the Basque squire of Bernardo del Carpio, who speaks in the comic, affected language typical of the literary stereotype of the *Basque.

Blind archer; Blind child; Blind god; Blind one; Blindfolded blind one. *Cupid.

Blind man [Ciego]. In *Pedro* 2, a beggar who talks briefly with Pedro, also dressed as a blind man, about the prayers they know.

Blind men's jargon [Jerigonza de ciegos]. The typical speech of blind beggars, listed among the languages described by Madrigal in *Sultana* 2.

Bloodthirsty lions [Leones carniceros]. In *DQ* II, 68, one of the insulting terms used by the men who take DQ and SP back to the palace of the duke and duchess.

Boatswain [Cómitre]. In *DQ* II, 63, the officer on a galley who is in charge of the rowers and who uses a whistle to give orders to the crew.

Bobadilla, Emilio. *Fray Candil.

Boccaccio, Giovanni (1313–75). Italian story writer and poet. Boccaccio's *Decameron* (written around 1350), a collection of 100 courtly, satiric, licentious, and ribald tales, was first translated into Spanish as *Las cien novelas* (1496; *The Hundred Short Stories*). The work was widely read throughout the sixteenth century in Spain (there was a copy in the personal library of Queen Isabel la Católica), even after it was placed on the *Index of Forbidden Books* in 1559, by which time it had already had four editions. Given Boccaccio's fame, MC had to be familiar with his work, which he may well have read in Italian during his years in Italy, and various attempts have been made to identify specific Boccaccian influences in *DQ* and other works. Boccaccio's first work to become popular in Spain was his *De Casibus*; the Spanish translation was begun by Pero López de Ayala, finished by Alonso García, and published with the title of *Caída de príncipes* (1495; *The Fall of Princes*). MC never mentions this work but seems to allude to it in *Persiles* III, 4.

Bibliography: Edward C. Dudley, "Boccaccio and Cervantes: *Novella* as Novella," *Hispano-Italic Studies* 2 (1979): 23–40; and Donald McGrady, "Cervantes and the *Decameron*: A Note on the Source and Meaning of Don Quijote's Prototypical Chivalric Adventure Story," *Cervantes* 5, no. 2 (1985): 141–47.

Boccherini, Giovanne Gastone. Italian dramatist. He wrote *Don Chisciotto alle nozze di Gamace* (1771; *Don Quixote at Camacho's Wedding*), with music by Antonio Salieri (1750–1825).

Bocina. *Little Dipper.

Bodas de Camacho. *Camacho's wedding.

Bodies of bandits [Cuerpos de bandoleros]. In *DQ* II, 60, the bandits who have been hanged in some trees outside of Barcelona. DQ and SP discover their bodies there and then are immediately taken captive by the band led by *Roque Guinart.

Boiardo, Matteo Maria (1441–94). Italian poet. Boiardo's major work is *Orlando Innamorato* (1483; *Orlando in Love*), a long and uneven poem about the legendary French hero Roland. The unfinished work (only two of a projected three volumes were written) never achieved much popularity, but it is important as providing the point of departure for *Ariosto's superior sequel, *Orlando Furioso*. It also provided the material for the Spanish prose version of Pedro de *Reinoso, a book ambiguously saved from destruction in the examination of DQ's library in I, 6. The combined influence of Boiardo and Ariosto on MC can hardly be overestimated.

Bojiganga [Acting troupe; jester commonly included in such a troupe]. A name for a kind of small theatrical company and a member of such a company dressed as a clown. DQ encounters the acting troupe of *Angulo el Malo in II, 11, and while confronting the actors, a *bojiganga* shakes a clown-stick with jingle bells in front of *Rocinante, causing him to throw his master and make the situation worse.

Bold guest. *Paris.

Bolívar Sevilla, Carlos. Ecuadorian novelist. Bolívar Sevilla's *Don Quijote en la gloria: Cuento fantástico* (1928; *Don Quixote in Glory: A Fantastic Story*) begins when DQ dies and ascends to heaven. God the Father wants to receive him directly in the seventh and highest level of paradise, but is convinced to let those who occupy the sixth realm enjoy his company first. DQ (mad as ever) is soon joined by SP (still spouting proverbs and mispronouncing words), and the two discuss their situation in the company of a divine lieutenant named Akiriel. DQ, SP, and the heavenly hosts watch a movie that is an accurate reproduction of the scenes from DQ, and both knight and squire discuss their adventures and the marvelous invention that makes it possible for them to see themselves. Meanwhile, the assembled heavenly multitude laughs heartily at the film. After being blessed by Jesus himself, DQ is elevated to the highest realm of glory.

Bibliography: Carlos Bolívar Sevilla, *Don Quijote en la gloria* (Ambato, Ecuador: Imprenta de L. A. Miño T., 1928).

Bolívar, Simón (1783–1830). Venezuelan general and revolutionary leader, the greatest liberator of Spain's South American colonies. According to Peruvian writer Ricardo Palma, on his deathbed Bolívar stated, "The three greatest fools of History have been Jesus Christ, Don Quixote, . . . and me!" (*real-life Don Quixotes).

Bologna [Bolonia]. Important commercial and industrial city in northern Italy. In the Middle Ages and Renaissance, it was the site of one of the greatest universities in Europe. Prominent there was the Spanish College, founded in the fourteenth century, where Spaniards stud-

ied; it still functions today. After restrictions imposed on foreign study by Felipe II in 1559, the Spanish College at Bologna was the only university outside of Spain at which Spaniards were permitted to study (a law that remained in force until the nineteenth century). Bologna is the setting for the adventures of the two young Spaniards in *Cornelia*. See also *DQ* II, 18.

Bona. City in Algiers. See *Gallardo* 2.

Bonanza. In *Parnaso* 2, the personification of calm weather and a tranquil sea.

Book of Liveries [El (libro) de las libreas]. One of the books written by the humanist scholar who accompanies DQ and SP to the Cave of Montesinos. Liveries are the outfits, decorations, and ornamentations alluding to their loves worn by knights and ladies during tournaments. See *DQ* II, 22.

Bootes. The constellation of the northern sky known as the Plowman. It is not, as stated by the Countess Trifaldi in *DQ* II, 40, the name of one of the *horses of the Sun; she was probably thinking of the celestial horse named Eous (*Eoo* in Spanish).

Booth, Wayne C. Theorist of the novel. In his monumental *The Rhetoric of Fiction* (1961) Booth takes issue with Ian *Watt's thesis that *formal realism* is the defining characteristic of the novel, but not with the related thesis that it was during the eighteenth century in England when the novel arose as a genre. If Watt privileges Defoe, Booth is the staunch defender of Laurence Sterne as an alternative prototype. Booth's brilliant study of voice in fictional narrative may never explicitly attribute the invention of the novel to England, but it is clear that in this work, all fictions before the eighteenth century comes across as being precursors, embryonic examples, and/or failed early efforts at the kind of sophistication that is best exemplified in a writer such as Sterne. MC is mentioned only occasionally and, even when commented on perceptively or approvingly, merely as an important early pre-Sternean writer. Booth's unquestioning acceptance of CHB as the unproblematic voice that speaks for the norms of the novel reveals an inadequate understanding of *DQ* (although, in Booth's defense, it must be acknowledged that in the 1960s even Hispanists tended to accept too uncritically the narrative authority of the narrative voices of *DQ*). This and his complete lack of knowledge of the Spanish picaresque tradition of *Lazarillo de Tormes*, Alemán, López de Ubeda, *Estebanillo González*, and other self-conscious, unreliable, and/or playful narrators, are perhaps the weakest points in an otherwise extraordinary achievement.

Bibliography: Wayne C. Booth, *The Rhetoric of Fiction* (Chicago: University of Chicago Press, 1961).

Borbón: Carlos de Borbón, Duke of Milan (1490–1527). Head of the Bourbon dynasty who fought on both the French and the Imperial Hapsburg sides. He led the Imperial troops that sacked the city of Rome in 1527, dying during the attack. See *DQ* II, 41.

Bordelon, Laurent (1653–1730). French writer. Bordelon's novel entitled *L'Histoire des imaginations extravagantes de Monsieur Oufle, causées par la lecture des livres que traitent de la magique, du grimoire, des démoniaques . . .* (1710; *The History of the Extravagant Imaginations of Monsieur Oufle, Caused by the Reading of Books that Deal with Magic, Spells, and Demons . . .*) is a minor example of the influence of MC (specifically cited in the work's preface) in the early French novel, and an illustration of the tendency to see in *DQ* nothing more than superficial social satire. In this case, the protagonist reads books of magic, charms, apparitions, divinations, and related subjects, and is influenced by them much as DQ is by his romances of chivalry.

Bibliography: Cristina Sánchez Tallafigo, "Un ejemplo francés de imitación cervantina: *L'Histoire des imaginations extravagantes de Monsieur Oufle (1710)*," *Anales Cervantinos* 35 (1999): 489–99.

Boreas [Bóreas]. In Greek myth, the god of the north wind. See *Parnaso* 5.

Borges, Jorge Luis (1899–1986). Argentine short-story writer, poet, and essayist. Bor-

ges is often considered the greatest and most influential of all Spanish American writers; he certainly is one of the undisputed major figures of twentieth-century literature. Borges first read *DQ* in English in 1907 or 1908 and maintained (facetiously, one hopes) that he always preferred the English version to the original Spanish. The works of MC, especially *DQ*, are crucial to an understanding of the writings of Borges, which are filled with references to them; in fact, except for several admiring references to Quevedo (and a statement once in praise of Fray Luis de León and Saint Juan de la Cruz), MC appears to be the only Spanish writer for whom Borges had much respect. And of the works of MC, whom he referred to as 'a mediocre writer,' *DQ* is the only one he ever praised, although Borges also criticized the novel as boring, repetitious, and poorly written, offering the opinion that numerous writers of less talent often wrote better Spanish. One of the most celebrated pieces Borges ever wrote is the fascinating "Pierre Menard, autor del *Quijote* ("Pierre Menard, Author of *Don Quixote*"), originally included in his *Ficciones* (1941; *Fictions*). It is the paradoxical tale of a minor French poet who undertook to write, not copy, *DQ* word for word. The brief segments he actually produced, parts of I, 9, are indeed the very words MC originally wrote, but are radically different in their meaning and effect on the reader because of the different context in which they were written (e.g., an archaic foreign language by a Frenchman, rather than contemporary native language by a Spaniard) and read. "Pierre Menard" is one of the key texts for theorists and critics of *postmodernism and *metafiction. Another important Borges text is "Magias parciales del *Quijote*" ("Partial Magic in *Don Quixote*") from *Otras inquisiciones* (1952; *Other Inquisitions*). Here Borges considers the effect of the realization by DQ and SP, in II, 2–4, that they are characters in a book. This scene by MC is one of the earliest metafictional texts, and is therefore crucial in the history of modern fiction, and Borges's commentary on it calls attention to its foundational status. In *El Hacedor* (1960; *The Maker*), Borges returns again to *DQ* with "Párabola de Cervantes y de Don Quijote" (written in 1955; "Parable of Cervantes and Don Quixote"), again dealing with the relationship between author and work and the romantic understanding of the novel. In "Un problema" ("A Problem"), Borges contemplates what the effect would have been had it been revealed that in one of his combats with others in the novel, DQ had actually killed someone. Borges's other essays on MC are "Nota sobre el *Quijote*" ("Note on *Don Quixote*"), "La conducta novelística de Cervantes" ("A Note on Cervantes's Novelistic Practice"), and "Análisis del último capítulo del *Quijote*" (1956; "Analysis of the Last Chapter of *Don Quixote*"). Although these prose texts have been frequently discussed and analyzed, what is less often noticed is the importance of DQ in Borges's poetry. Several beautiful poems by Borges evoke MC, DQ, and La Mancha: "Lectores" ("Readers") and "Un soldado de Urbina" ("A Soldier from Urbina") from *El otro, el mismo* (1964; *The Other, the Same*), Borges's own favorite book of his poetry; "Miguel de Cervantes," "Sueña Alonso Quijano" ("Alonso Quijano Dreams"), and "El testigo" ("The Witness") from *La rosa profunda* (1972; *The Profound Rose*); and "Ni siquiera soy polvo" ("I'm Not Even Dust") from *Historia de la noche* (1977; *History of Night*). The gentle, poetic, melancholic Borges of these poems only faintly resembles the cerebral, ambiguous, scholarly Borges of his prose, and completes the picture of one great writer's appreciation of another.

Bibliography: Jesús Aguilar, "Can Pierre Menard Be the Author of *Don Quixote?*" *Variaciones Borges* 8 (1999): 166–67; Arthur Efron, "Perspectivism and the Nature of Fiction: Don Quijote and Borges," *Thought* 50 (1975): 148–75; Lelia Madrid, *Cervantes y Borges: la inversión de los signos*, (Madrid: Pliegos, 1987); Steven Matthews, "Jorge Luis Borges: Fiction and Reading," *Ariel* 6 (1989): 62–67; Carlos Orlando Nállim, "Cervantes a la velada luz de un soneto de Borges," "Cervantes y don Quijote en una parábola de Borges," and "Borges y Cervantes, don Quijote y Alonso Quijano," in *Cervantes en las letras argentinas* (Buenos Aires: Academia Argentina de Letras, 1998), 25–80; Rafael Olea Franco, "La lección de Cervantes en Borges," *Inti* 45 (1997): 99–103; and Julio Rodríguez-Luis, "El *Quijote* según

Borges," *Nueva Revista de Filología Hispánica* 36 (1988): 477–500.

Borgoña. *Burgundy.

Borgoña, Guy de. *Guy de Borgoña.

Borja, Don Carlos de, and Doña María Luisa de Aragón; Duke and Duchess of Villahermosa. The historical figures frequently mentioned as the models for the duke and duchess of *DQ* II, 30–52. As usual, there is no reason to assume that MC had to base his fictional characters on real people.

Borja, Don Francisco de, Príncipe de Esquilache (1582–1658). A very respected poet who also was viceroy of Peru. He is praised as one of the good poets in *Parnaso* 2.

Borja-Moncayo, Luis Alberto de. Argentine writer. Borja-Moncayo's *Reencarnación de D. Quijote y Cyrano de Bergerac: Andanzas por América* (1920; *Reincarnation of Don Quixote and Cyrano de Bergerac: Events for America*) literally brings DQ and Cyrano back to life to have conversations, tell stories, make speeches, spout aphorisms, and so forth. They discuss a wide range of subjects: crass Yanquilandia and the evil Theodore Roosevelt, a Spanish American utopia of 1995, prostitution, and much more. The thin guise of fiction cannot make palatable a sociopolitical diatribe.

Bibliography: Luis Alberto de Borja-Moncayo, *Reencarnación de D. Quijote y Cyrano de Bergerac* (Buenos Aires: Maucci, 1920).

Borrás, Tomás (1891–?). Spanish novelist, short-story writer, and dramatist. In Borrás's *El Anti-Quijote* (1940), which takes place a year after the death of DQ, SP rides out with the barber Maese Nicolás. SP is now the one who sees a castle, enchanted princess, and magician, whereas the barber sees an inn, serving woman, and innkeeper. On their way back home, the figure of DQ appears and chastises the barber.

Borrero Echevarría, Esteban (1849–1906). Cuban poet and prose writer. In his *Alrededor del "Quijote"* (1905; *About "Don Quixote"*), after two rather straightforward literary studies, there is a story entitled "Don Quijote, poeta: Narración cervantesca" ("Don Quixote, Poet: A Cervantesque Narration"). The story is presented as a sequel to chapter 41 of *DQ* II, and consists of a second version of what happened during the ride on Clavileño. The introductory paragraphs explain how CHB's manuscript of this chapter was omitted from the original novel because the *Morisco* translator did not believe that it was consistent with the rest of the work and that it was probably apocryphal. The editor then goes on to comment on how MC's book is mistreated by scholars, who often concentrate on counting minutiae rather than on actually understanding the book. The text of Chapter 41 (bis) then commences, as DQ and SP discuss their ride on the wooden horse. During his trip through the heavens, DQ begins to feel more like a poet than a knight-errant. At one point he dismounts and meets Homer, Dante, Shakespeare (!), and other great writers, who gather to crown one among them who is not named but is described in detail using the words from MC's self-portrait in the prologue to *Novelas*.

Bibliography: Esteban Borrero Echevarría, *Alrededor del "Quijote"* (Havana: Lib. e Imp. La Moderna Poesía, 1905).

Boscán, Juan (ca. 1487–1542). Spanish poet whose greatest claim to fame is that he successfully urged his good friend *Garcilaso de la Vega to try writing lyric poetry in the Italianate way, thus launching the most profound revolution in the history of Spanish poetry. Boscán is also noted for his excellent translation of Castiglione's *Book of the Courtier* (1534; *El Cortesano*). MC, like many of his contemporaries, occasionally mentions Boscán in passing together with the beloved Garcilaso. See *DQ* II, 67; *Galatea* 6; *Rufián* 1.

Bibliography: David H. Darst, *Juan Boscán* (Boston: Twayne, 1978).

Bosio. *Bozio, Tomasso.

Bosque amoroso, El (The Forest of Love). One of MC's early plays from the 1580s that has been lost. It is included in the list of his plays in MC's conversation with Pancracio de Roncesvalles in *Adjunta*. Perhaps *Casa* is a reworking of this early play.

Bosque, Carlos. Argentine writer. His *Don Quijote en Sudamérica* (1926; *Don Quixote in South America*) is a fictional story of how the first copy of *DQ* arrives in Argentina in 1612. The book winds up in the hands of a cousin of MC, named Doña Leonor de Cervantes. Her reading of the work has the same effect on her as the reading of romances of chivalry has on DQ.

Boticario toledano. *Toledan apothecary.

Bougeant, Guillaume Hyacînthe (1690–1749). French novelist. His *Le voyage merveilleux de Prince Fan-Férédin* (1735; *The Wonderful Travels of Prince Fan-Férédin*) is a satire in imitation of the technique of *DQ*.

Bovarysm. A term first used by Jules de Gaultier in 1902, inspired by Flaubert's heroine Emma Bovary, to refer to the self-delusional capacity to conceive of yourself in terms other than what you actually are. Clearly, however, the origins of the fictional exploration of this universal human capacity are found in *DQ*, a good two and a half centuries before Flaubert. Bovarysm is nothing but a modern version of one aspect of *quixotism.

Bibliography: Carol Rifelj, "Bovarysme," in *A Gustave Flaubert Encyclopedia* (Westport, CT: Greenwood Press, 2001), 42.

Boy(s) [Muchacho(s), garzon(es)]. **1**. In *Numancia* 1, figures who accompany that of the Duero River and represent three tributaries that join that river near Numantia. **2**. In *DQ* I, 3, the youth who assists the innkeeper when he dubs DQ a knight-errant. **3**. In *DQ* I, 9, the youngster who sells the manuscript of *DQ* I by CHB to MC. **4**. In *Rinconete*, the sentinel who warns Monipodio and company of the approach of the constable. **5**. In *Fregona*, the youths who tease Lope Asturiano about the time he used the tail of an ass to win at cards. **6**. In *Sultana*, the three assistants who accompany and serve the Sultan Amurates at times when he is on stage. **7**. In *DQ* II, 25, the residents of a nearby town who make fun of the *braying aldermen, braying at them whenever they see them. **8**. In *DQ* II, 25–27, the assistant to *Maese Pedro, who narrates the puppet show. **9**. In *DQ* II, 61, the youngsters who place furze, a thorny branch, under the tails of Rocinante and SP's ass in Barcelona so that they will buck and cause their riders to fall, providing laughs for everyone watching. **10**. In *DQ* II, 73, the two children who are playing as DQ and SP enter their village and whose words DQ takes as a prophecy that he will never see DT again.

Boyero. *Carter.

Bozal. A term used for recently arrived black slaves who did not speak Spanish; most often they spoke Portuguese, if they spoke any European language at all. *Guiomar and the other black slave purchased by Felipo de Carrizales to serve his wife Leonora are *bozales*.

Brackenridge, Hugh Henry (1748–1816). American poet and novelist. In his novel *Modern Chivalry: Containing the Adventures of Captain John Farrago and Teague O'Regan, His Servant* (published in installments, 1792–1815), Brackenridge presents a classic DQ-SP pair in Farrago and O'Regan, explicitly making the comparison with MC's characters in the novel. A classic quixotic figure, Farrago has a "greater knowledge of books than of the world."

Bibliography: Sally C. Hoople, "The Spanish, English, and American Quixotes," *Anales Cervantinos* 22 (1984): 119–42.

Bracmanes de la India. *Brahmans from India.

Bradamante. A woman warrior who is also the sister of Reinaldos and the lover of Ruggiero in Boiardo's *Orlando Innamorato* and Ariosto's *Orlando Furioso*. See *Doncellas*; *DQ* I, 25.

Bradamiro. In *Persiles* I, 4, the arrogant barbarian who claims Periandro (dressed as a woman) for his own and who is killed by the barbarian governor.

Braga. City in Portugal, located north of Oporto and south of Santiago de Compostela.

In *Persiles* III, 1, the archbishop of Braga is also the governor of Lisbon, and in this capacity he welcomes Periandro and the pilgrims.

Braga, Teófilo (1843–1924). Portuguese poet. There are two DQ poems in Braga's *Visão dos Tempos* (1864; *Vision of Time*): "O riso de Cervantes" ("The Laughter of Cervantes") and "A Batalha de Lepanto" ("The Battle of Lepanto"). The former consists of a scene involving MC and his wife Catalina, and the latter sets up a contrast between the battle of Lepanto and DQ's battle with the windmills.

Bibliography: José Ares Montes, "Evocaciones cervantinas en poetas portugueses del siglo XIX," *Anales Cervantinos* 31 (1993): 231–38.

Braggart [Valentón]. The swaggering speaker of the final lines of *Poesías* 26, who seconds the statements in praise of the king's tomb made by the previous speaker, and then puts on his hat with a flourish and departs.

Brahmans from India [Bracmanes de la India]. Hindu priests or philosophers who supposedly wore no clothing. See *DQ* I, 47.

Braín. In *Sultana* 2, the name of one of the four pashas who talk with the Ambassador of Persia.

Brandabarbarán de Boliche, señor de las tres Arabias [Lord of the Three Arabies]. In *DQ* I, 18, one of the participants in the battle (of sheep) as described by DQ. Arabia was divided into three sections: Pétrea, Feliz, and Desierta.

Bras. In *Galatea* 1, a rustic shepherd from the banks of the Henares River whose only role is to take part in the pastoral games.

Brass ape [Jimia de bronce]. In *DQ* II, 39, the form of the enchanted Antonomasia in the story told by the Countess *Trifaldi. The ape is often a symbol of sexual lasciviousness.

Bravos. *Thugs.

Braying aldermen [Regidores rebuznadores]. The men who, while searching for a missing donkey, bray in an attempt to attract the animal but only succeed in deceiving each other. When the people from another town begin to make fun of them and everyone from their village, a battle between the inhabitants of the two towns is arranged. The story is told by a resident of the town of the brayers in *DQ* II, 25; and in II, 27, DQ and SP come across some 200 men from the village as they await their opponents from the rival town. DQ delivers a lecture on the concept of a just war and persuades them not to fight over a frivolous subject. But then SP displays his own braying ability and evokes an angry response from the townspeople, who knock him to the ground. DQ turns and flees, abandoning SP and fearing at each step that he will be shot in the back.

The folkloric braying aldermen story is comic in its own right, but it becomes more significant in the context of the previous events in the inn and for the effect it has on the DQ-SP relationship (and it also reprises the *theft of SP's ass in *DQ* I). In the inn there was an ape who spoke like a human being, and here there are men (including SP) who bray like asses. Nothing is as clear-cut as it should be and the human-animal boundary is blurred. In the next chapter (II, 28), SP is angry and disappointed with his master and proposes returning home. DQ responds by offering SP the salary he has frequently requested, but when the squire overstates his demand, DQ becomes angry and humiliates him, calling him an ass; SP tearfully responds that he agrees and the only thing he lacks to be a complete ass is a tail.

Bibliography: Alberto Sánchez, "Fábula quijotil del asno perdido (*Don Quijote* I, 23 y 30; II, 3, 4 y 27)," in *Don Chisciotte a Padova*, ed. Donatella Pini Moro (Padua, Italy: Programma, 1992), 13–29.

Brecht, Bertolt (1898–1956). German poet and dramatist. Although Brecht wrote a considerable amount of prose and, especially, poetry, he is best known for his plays and dramatic theory. In addition to his great full-length plays, Brecht wrote a series of *Einakter* (1919; *One-act Plays*), which he specifically relates to MC's interludes.

Bibliography: Mercedes García Ramírez, "Cervantes-Brecht: modernidad o vejez (Sobre el *Re-*

tablo de las Maravillas)," in *Instituto de Bachillerato Cervantes—Miscelánea en su cincuentenario, 1931–1981* (Madrid: Servicio de Publicaciones del Ministerio de Educación y Ciencia, 1982), 131–39.

Brécourt, Guillaume Marcoureau de (1638–85). French dramatist. Brécourt's play *Le Jaloux invisible* (1666; *The Invisible Jealous Man*) was, the author claims, taken verbatim from a Spanish *novela* entitled *El celoso engañado* (*The Jealous Man Deceived*), which he found in an old book. That claim is probably no more than a ploy, for the work, the protagonist of which is named Carizel (recall Carrizales), is derived, albeit very loosely, from *Celoso*.

Bretaña. *Brittany; *Great Britain.

Breton [Bretón]. 1. A man from Brittany, a province in France; also sometimes used in the sense of a foreigner in general. See *DQ* I, 41. **2.** In *Coloquio*, the man entrapped and bilked by the dishonest constable and La Colindres is a Breton.

Bretón de los Herreros, Manuel (1796–1873). Spanish dramatist and poet. Bretón's best-known play, *Marcela, o ¿cuál de los tres?* (1831; *Marcela, or Which of the Three?*), bears an interesting resemblance to *DQ*. In addition to the names, the parallels between Bretón's Marcela and the Marcela of *DQ* I, 13–14, are several: each is an independent woman who refuses to marry the man who loves her, makes an impassioned speech explaining her reasons, and is called cruel and ungrateful by the men involved.

Briareos [Briareo]. In Greek myth, one of three giants with 100 arms, the sons of Uranus (Heaven) and Gaia (Earth). The four-armed windmill-giants in *DQ* I, 8, are compared with Briareos. See also *DQ* II, 3.

Brígida, Doña. In *Vizcaíno*, the prostitute friend of Cristina who is jealous of her friend's good luck.

Brilladoro. Orlando's horse in *Orlando Furioso* of *Ariosto. See *DQ* I, 52; *DQ* II, 40; *Parnaso* 8.

Briseno. In *Galatea* 4, the father of Artidoro and Galercio; he never appears in the text.

Brittany [Bretaña]. A province on the northwest coast of France. See *Numancia* 1.

Brocabruno de la Gran Fuerza [Brocabruno of Mighty Strength]. Name of an imaginary giant mentioned by DQ in his summary of the career of a knight-errant in *DQ* I, 21.

Brocades from Milan. *Milan.

Brocense, El. *Sánchez de las Brozas, Francisco.

Broken end. *Cabo roto.

Broken foot. *Pie quebrado.

Bronze head. *Enchanted head.

Brook of the Palm Trees [Arroyo de las Palmas]. A fictional location where some of the action in *Galatea* takes place. See *Galatea* 1, 6.

Brooke, Henry (1703–83). English poet, novelist, and dramatist. Brooke's novel *The Fool of Quality; or, The History of Henry Earl of Moreland* (five vols., 1765–70) is explicitly inspired by and in imitation of *DQ*: "In a fragment of the Spanish history, bequeathed to the world by one Signior Cervantes. . . . How greatly, how gloriously, how divinely superior was our hero of the Mancha, who went about righting of wrongs, and redressing of injuries, lifting up the fallen, and pulling down those whom iniquity had exalted!" In addition to an ongoing "conversation" between Friend and Author (reminiscent of MC's prologue to *DQ* I), the embedded narratives also recall MC's technique.

Brother of the daughter of Diego de la Llana. *Daughter of Diego de la Llana.

Brothers of la Capacha [Hermanos de la Capacha]. Popular name for the order known as the Sagrada Religión de San Juan de Dios (Sacred Religion of Saint John of God), taken from the name of the baskets (*capachas*) in which they collected alms. This is the religious organization that administered the Hospital of the Resurrection in Valladolid in MC's day. See *Casamiento*.

Browning, Robert (1812–98). English poet. Browning is best known for his dramatic monologues, one of the earliest of which is "My Last Duchess" (1842), a poem that derives at least part of its inspiration from *Cornelia*.

Brunelo. Famous thief in the Italian chivalric epic tradition of Boiardo and Ariosto. Among other things, Brunelo stole Angelica's ring, Sacripante's horse, and the swords of Marfisa and Orlando. See *DQ* II, 4, 27; *Pedro* 2.

Brushtein, Aleksandra I. (1884–1968). Russian dramatist. Brushtein directed an experimental theater in Moscow; the initial work presented there was her comedy entitled *Don Quixote* (1926).

Brussels [Bruselas]. The capital of Belgium. See *Fregona*; *Vidriera*.

Bucephalus [Bucéfalo]. The favorite horse of Alexander the Great, who rode him for some 20 years. See *DQ* I, 1; *DQ* II, 40.

Buchan, John (1875–1940). English novelist. Buchan's *Sir Quixote of the Moors: Being Some Account of an Episode in the Life of the Sieur de Rohaine* (1896) is a romanticized historical novel that relates less to *DQ* than the title would suggest. It is the story of the Scottish adventures of a French nobleman and ends with a choice of honor over love, presumably a quixotic action.

Buen linaje. *Good lineage.

Buena Fama. *Good Fame.

Buena Fortuna. *Good Fortune.

Buenavía. *Duke.

Buero Vallejo, Antonio (1916–2000). Spanish dramatist. Imprisoned for six years after the Spanish Civil War, Buero burst onto the theatrical scene in Spain with *Historia de una escalera* (1949; *The Story of a Stairway*), probably still his most popular and admired play. Buero was perhaps the most respected dramatist in Spain in the second half of the twentieth century. In his acceptance speech when he was awarded the Cervantes Prize in 1986, as well as on other occasions, Buero has acknowledged MC as an important inspiration for much of his own writing. Not surprisingly, many of his plays include references to DQ and feature characters who are, in one way or another, at least slightly quixotic (as dreamers, mad or obsessed individuals, idealists, questers, or altruists). Buero's never-performed *Mito (libro para una ópera)* (1967; *Myth [Book for an Opera]*) is his only overtly quixotic drama (as well as his only play in verse rather than prose). It is the story of an aging (fiftyish) former opera star named Eloy, now only an extra in the opera company. The role he once had of DQ is sung by the younger, more arrogant Rodolfo. Eloy is considered mad by everyone because he hears communications from visitors from outer space. Early in the play he explains to Simón, who plays SP in the opera and is, in effect, Eloy's SP, that the prop of Mambrino's helmet (itself shaped like a flying saucer) is really a special receiver for messages sent by extraterrestrials. Eloy also idealizes and loves the wardrobe worker named Marta (whose name, Eloy notes, evokes Mars, the planet of origin of the visitors). The plot becomes very involved and deals with government manipulation, possibly real nuclear destruction, and not one but two sets of possibly real extraterrestrials. At one point Rodolfo and others deceive Eloy and Simón, blindfold them, and make them believe they are being taken on a space voyage, while they are merely sitting on chairs on stage as a crowd laughs at them—obviously a recreation of the ride on Clavileño.

Bibliography: Antonio Buero Vallejo, *Mito (libro para una ópera)* (Madrid: Alfil, 1968); Carmen Caro Dugo, *The Importance of the Don Quixote Myth in the Works of Antonio Buero Vallejo* (Lewiston, ME: Mellen University Press, 1995); and Martha T. Halsey, *Antonio Buero Vallejo* (New York: Twayne, 1973).

Buitrago. In *Gallardo*, the always hungry and comic—but genuinely brave—soldier, who kills Nacor.

Bujía. *Bejaia.

Buldero. *Seller of Papal bulls.

Bulgakov, Mikhail (1891–1940). Russian dramatist and novelist. Bulgakov was particularly fond of *DQ*, and even wrote some letters to his wife in Spanish as a kind of homage to MC. Bulgakov's great novel, *La Majstro Kaj Margarita* (1966; *The Master and Margarita*), is characterized by a self-conscious, self-deprecating narrator reminiscent of the narrative structure of *DQ*. Truth is frequently asserted, and just as frequently undercut and called into question. There is no explicit reference to *DQ*, but the Cervantine spirit of the novel is evident throughout. One of Bulgakov's last projects, at the height of the Stalinist purges, was a play about DQ, but the work was never staged. The author considered it not an adaptation of MC's novel, but rather a text derived from some aspects of it. In the play there is an interesting assortment of episodes from MC's novel, and DQ is hardly different from other characters until near the end, when his more traditionally romantic side begins to be more apparent.

Bibliography: Vsevolod Bagno, "El quijotesco catálogo de desgracias de Mijaíl Bulgákov," *Turia* 21–22 (1992): 29–33; and Mijail A. Bulgakov, *Don Quijote*, trans. Jorge Saura (Madrid: Publicaciones de la Asociación de Directores de Escena de España, 1992).

Bull that killed the porter of Salamanca [Toro que mató al ganapán de Salamanca]. In *Retablo*, either a reference to an actual event or to the scene in the first chapter of *Lazarillo de Tormes*, when the blind beggar smashes Lazarillo's head against a stone figure of a bull.

Bullock, Christopher (ca. 1690–1724). English dramatist. Bullock's farce *The One-Eyed Cobler of Preston* (1716) contains one scene based on SP's judgments as governor of Barataria.

Bullón, Godofre de. *Godfrey of Bouilon.

Bulls [Toros]. The herd of animals who trample DQ and SP in II, 58. They were bred on the banks of the Jarama River, reputed in the Golden Age to be the home of the fiercest of all fighting bulls. See also *DQ* II, 67.

Bulls of Guisando [Toros de Guisando]. Four (five in MC's day) crudely carved granite figures of bulls standing in an open field near San Martín de Valdeiglesias, southeast of Avila. The origin of the ancient bulls is unknown, and they remain an enigma. In *DQ* II, 14, when Sansón Carrasco is boasting of his achievements as the Knight of the Mirrors, he tells DQ that one of his victories was over the bulls of Guisando. See also *DQ* II, 22.

Buñuel, Miguel (1924–). Spanish novelist, short-story writer, and author of books for children. Buñuel's *Rocinante de la Mancha* (1963) is a charming children's book about the adventures of Rocinante and his companion Rucio. The tale is populated by such characters as a canary called Carrascón (Sansón Carrasco); the cat Curiambro and the dog Niculoso, based on the priest and barber, respectively, from *DQ*; Blanca del Toboso, the mule who is adored by Rocinante; and others. Important to the story are the romance of chivalry entitled *Amadís de Unicornia*, Mambrino's enchanted (unicorn-like) horn, the windmill-elephants, and Rocinante's speech on the Golden Age that he delivers to a group of actual goats, not mere goatherds, as in *DQ* I, 11.

Bibliography: Miguel Buñuel, *Rocinante de la Mancha* (Madrid: Editora Nacional, 1963).

Burgas, José. *Valbuena, Padre.

Burgess, Anthony (1917–93). English novelist, critic, and man of letters. Much of Burgess's fame rests on the novel *A Clockwork Orange* (1962) and the sensational film subsequently made from the novel. Among his other novels is one entitled *Nothing like the Sun* (1964), a fictional version of the life of William Shakespeare (the title is from a famous line of one of Shakespeare's sonnets). His short story entitled "A Meeting in Valladolid" (1989; original version in Spanish, "Encuentro en Valladolid," 1987) takes place during the English state visit to the Spanish court in Valladolid in the year 1605, while MC was living in that city. In the story, part of the English delegation is the acting troupe The King's Men, including Shakespeare, in order to stage some examples of English theater for the Spanish hosts (there are also presentations of works by Lope de *Vega and others for the English guests). The meeting of the title is one that takes place between Shakespeare and MC in the latter's home. Matters of religion, politics, the theater, and MC's recent novel *DQ* are discussed. It has been speculated that in actual historical fact, MC and Shakespeare might have met on this occasion, but there is no documented evidence of the English acting troupe's actual participation in the state visit. Still, it is nice to imagine, as Burgess does here (and as have others, such as Stephen *Marlowe), a meeting between the two writers. Alas, we must be content with the fact that *Shakespeare read *DQ* I and wrote a play based on it. Sadly, MC probably never heard of Shakespeare.

Burgos. Important city in Spain, located directly north of Madrid and south of the Bay of Biscay. In the Middle Ages, it was the capital of the united kingdoms of Castile and León and an important stop in the Camino de Santiago (Way of Saint James). The gothic cathedral of Burgos is the third-largest in Spain. Spain's national hero, El Cid, was born just north of the city. In the Spanish Civil War, it was the capital of the Nationalist forces of Francisco Franco. See *Fregona*; *Gitanilla*.

Burgos, Juan de. Spanish writer. Burgos wrote the first known ballad on the theme of DQ: "Gracioso romance, en que se queja Sancho Panza a su amo Don Quixote, de que no le da de comer; por cuya causa se despide de la caballería andante. Y respuesta que Don Quixote le da en unas agudas quintillas" (1657; "Amusing Ballad in which Sancho Panza Complains to His Master Don Quixote that He Does not Give Him Enough to Eat; and Because of This He Resigns from Knight-Errantry. And the Answer Don Quixote Gives Him in Some Sharp *Quintillas*"). The title adequately summarizes the 21-line poem.

Burgundy [Borgoña]. Former kingdom and current province in eastern France, on the border with Italy. See *DQ* I, 49.

Burla. A joke, hoax, practical jest, or trick played on someone. *Burlas* are common in the picaresque and courtly fiction, interludes, and satiric, pornographic, and scatological poetry of the time, and often include the infliction of pain, personal humiliation, ridicule, fraud, excrement, and bawdy humor. MC's *burlas* tend to be more along the line of practical jokes, sometimes a little embarrassing, pointless, or silly from a more modern point of view (typical examples include the priest's reconciliation of the Pérez de Viedma Brothers in *DQ* I, 42; Estefanía's introduction of Leocadia to her son Rodolfo in *Fuerza;* and the Duke of Ferrara's little ploy about why he cannot marry Cornelia in *Cornelia*). Sometimes, however, MC's *burlas* reach some of the more extreme levels; probably the best examples are some of those perpetuated against SP when he is governor of *Barataria.

Bibliography: Anthony J. Close, "Seemly Pranks: The Palace Episodes in *Don Quixote* Part II," in *Art and Literature in Spain: 1600–1800. Studies in Honour of Nigel Glendinning*, ed. Charles Davis and Paul Julian Smith (London: Tamesis, 1993), 69–87; and Kimberly Contag, *Mockery in Spanish Golden Age Literature: Analysis of Burlesque Representation* (Lanham, MD: University Press of America, 1996).

Burlador. *Academicians of Argamasilla.

Burns, Wayne. Theorist of the novel. Burns, somewhat of a maverick English professor, was extraordinarily popular with his students and created a following for his approach to literary criticism. His major theoretical statement is his short publication entitled *The Panzaic Principle* (1962), in which he criticizes what he perceives to be the prevailing tendency toward the ideal and the abstract when dealing with literature. Taking his cue from D. H. Lawrence, in *Lady Chatterley's Lover*, Burns concludes that "the guts are always right; it is an axiom or principle of the novel that they are always right, that the senses of even a fool can give the lie to even the most profound abstractions of the noblest thinker. And it is this principle I have designated the Panzaic principle, after Sancho Panza." Burns wrote before the work of *Bakhtin became known in America, but his approach to literature is quite compatible in many ways with Bakhtin's concept of *carnival.

Bibliography: Wayne Burns, *The Panzaic Principle, Parts I and II*, critical afterword by Gerald Butler, scientific afterword by R. A. Brown (Vancouver, BC, Canada: Pendejo Press, nd; and *Paunch* 46–47, Wayne Burns Issue (1977).

Burton, Mrs. H. S. (María Amparo Ruiz de Burton, 1832–95). American novelist and dramatist. Burton wrote an adaptation of *DQ* entitled *Don Quixote de la Mancha: A Comedy, in Five Acts, Taken from Cervantes' Novel of that Name* (1876). The play jams as many scenes and episodes from *DQ* into as little space as possible, sacrificing everything to action. Act I alone includes the naming scene; the recruitment of SP; the niece, housekeeper, and priest discussing DQ's madness; arrival at the inn/castle; the windmills; the armies of sheep; Maritornes; SP's blanketing; and DQ tied by his hand. Act II continues with more unrelated episodes from both parts of the novel; Act III takes place at the palace of the duke and duchess; Act IV is devoted to SP as governor of Barataria; and Act V involves both Barcelona and a return to the duke's palace, where DQ and SP are mocked and DQ is placed in a cage to be taken home. The hodgepodge of unconnected scenes often includes detailed translations and/or paraphrases of the original novel. What is noticeably absent is all the action involving Cardenio and company, one of the traditional staples of dramatic adaptations of *DQ*.

Buscapié, El (1848; The Explanation)

It is quite possible that the author based her version on a careful reading of the Spanish original, since many names, quotations, and paraphrasings seem original with Burton and are not necessarily derived from any translation.

Bibliography: Mrs. H. S. Burton, *Don Quixote de la Mancha* (San Francisco: J. H. Carmany, 1876).

***Buscapié, El* (1848; *The Explanation*).** The generic term *buscapié* means something like a 'key' or set of explanations that unlocks the interpretation of a work of literature, such as a roman à clef. In the nineteenth century, Adolfo de Castro made the stunning revelation that he had discovered the manuscript of a short work by MC, entitled *El Buscapié*, that revealed the allegorical meaning behind the characters and events of *DQ*. The text was exposed as a fraud by Cayetano Alberto de la Barrera and today represents nothing more than a curious detail in the history of the *esoteric readings of Cervantes's novel.

Bibliography: Manuel Fernández Nieto, *En torno a un apócrifo cervantino: el "Buscapié" de Adolfo de Castro* (Madrid: Gráficas Alocén, 1976); and Manuel Morales Borrero, ed., *El Buscapié: estudio y edición del apócrifo cervantino* (Madrid: Funcación Universitaria Española, 1995).

Busiris. 1. In Greek myth, an Egyptian king who sacrificed all strangers to Zeus. He was killed by Heracles. See *Persiles* III, 10. **2**. *Osiris.

Butler, Samuel (1612–80). English poet and satirist. Butler's long mock-heroic poem *Hudibras* (published in three parts in 1663, 1664, and 1678) is a satirical miscellany in which fun is poked at the Puritans, chivalry, poetic imagination, church doctrines, and the idea of progress. Sir Hudibras is a grotesque knight: a pedantic Presbyterian whose physical appearance, Rocinante-like horse, and blindness to reality all make his relationship to DQ obvious. His Independent squire named Ralpho is clearly based on SP, but is far less original or interesting a character.

Bibliography: Annalisa Argelli, "Cervantes y Butler en la cultura inglesa del seiscientos," *Symposium* 53 (1999): 123–35.

Butrón. In *DQ* II, 74, along with Barcino, one of the two dogs Sansón Carrasco plans to purchase from a herdsman from Quintanar so that he, DQ, and the others can take up the life of shepherds.

Buxton, George. American writer. He wrote *The Political Quixote, or, The Adventures of the Renowned Don Blackibo Dwarfino, and His Trusty "Squire," Seditonio* (1820), a heavy-handed diatribe against liberal reformers in which the author sets out "to ridicule the glaring follies, and inconsistencies of seditious and infidel writers, and to excite a good-humored laugh at their expense."

Bibliography: George Buxton, *The Political Quixote, or, The Adventures of the Renowned Don Blackibo Dwarfino, and his Trusty "Squire," Seditonio* (London: C. Chapple, 1820).

Byron, George Gordon, Lord (1788–1824). English Romantic poet. In his long poem *Don Juan* (1819–24), Byron makes one of the most often cited statements about MC, "Cervantes smiled Spain's chivalry away," reducing to a simple phrase both the hard reading of *DQ* as a comic satire and, by implication, the soft reading that such gaiety is ultimately sad.

Byzantine romance. *Adventure romance.

C

Caballero. *Knight.

Caballero de [Spanish phrase]. *Knight of [equivalent English phrase].

Caballero de la Ardiente Espada. *Knight of the Burning Sword.

Caballero de la Blanca Luna. *Sansón Carrasco.

Caballero de la Cruz. *Salazar, Alonso de.

Caballero de la cruz bermeja. *Saint James the Great.

Caballero de San Juan. *Order of Malta.

Caballero del Febo. *Ordóñez de Calahorra, Diego de.

Caballero Platir, El. An anonymous romance of chivalry published in 1533. It is the fourth volume in the *Palmerín* cycle and is condemned to the flames in the scrutiny of DQ's library in *DQ* I, 6. In I, 9, there is a reference (but not by name) to Galtenor, the wizard who was the author of the book.

Caballeros castellanos; Caballeros de la Mancha; Caballeros de Navarra; Caballeros leoneses; Caballeros tartesios. *Spanish knights.

Caballeros cortesanos y caballeros andantes; Caballeros que en la corte andan. *Courtly knights and knights-errant.

Caballo de Cratilo. *Cratilo's horse.

Caballos del Sol. *Horses of the Sun.

Cabell, James Branch (1879–1958). American novelist. Cabell's offbeat fantasies are unique in American literature. Interestingly, although he called DQ one of the greatest of all fictional characters, he claimed not to have particularly liked *DQ* and to have believed that it was overrated. Yet in reviews and criticism of Cabell's works, the connection with DQ is almost inevitably brought up; in fact, Cabell made constant use of the imaginative quixotic hero, the power of fantasy, and the contrast between reality and appearance. Like his fellow Southern writers William *Faulkner and Walker *Percy, Cabell saw the American South's obsession with codes of honor and chivalry as comparable to DQ's chivalric obsession. The novel in which this concern is first apparent is *The Rivet in Grandfather's Neck: A Comedy of Limitations* (1915). Rudolph Musgrave is quixotic in his adherence to the code of chivalry and in his choice to lead his life by this code, at least partly as a way of avoiding reality. His first DT is the common Patricia Stapylton, for in her "there was much of his own invention," and later Anne Willoughby "was of his own creation, his masterpiece." *Jurgen: A Comedy of Justice* (1919) and *Figures of Earth: A Comedy of Appearances* (1921) are probably Cabell's most representative dark fantasies. The two protagonists, Jurgen and Manuel, have much in common as parodies of the chivalric standard. Both have chivalric dreams, but at the same time both are cynics, lacking any shred of faith or idealism. In Cabell's hands, in these two novels it is fantasy that encroaches on reality, rather than the reverse as in *DQ*. The women of these stories tend to be more earthy and physical than the heroes would prefer; they are more Aldonza than DT. Jurgen, for example, kills a rival (by stabbing him in the back) and then returns to his beloved Dorothy, only to see clearly her reality: "And she was leering at him, and he was touching her everywhere, this horrible lascivious woman, who was certainly quite old enough to know better than to permit such liberties. And her breath was sour and nauseous. Jurgen drew away from her, with a shiver of loathing, and he closed his eyes, to shut away that sensual face." The contrast between Jurgen's actions and thoughts and those of DQ in the scene with Maritornes, for example, in I, 16, could not be greater.

Bibliography: Montserrat Ginés, "James Branch Cabell: Quixotic Love—The Exercise of Self-Deception," in *The Southern Inheritors of Don Quixote* (Baton Rouge: Louisiana State University Press, 2000), 45–71.

Cabeza de bronce; Cabeza encantada. *Enchanted head.

Cabezo, El. *Sagrario.

Cabin boy [Grumete]. In *Persiles* 1, the crew member who announces the arrival of a ship to the island of Golandia.

Cabinet [Cámara]. The Apostolic Cabinet of the Pope in Rome. See *Persiles* IV, 6.

Cabo roto [Broken end]. A poetic term that refers to the practice of omitting the final syllable of a line of verse, literally "breaking off" the line just short of its end. The technique is said to have been invented by the minor Sevillian poet Alonso *Alvarez de Soria specifically for comic purposes. MC uses this technique in several of the prefatory poems to *DQ* I, which help establish a lighthearted, jocular tone as the reader begins the text of the novel proper, and also make fun of pretentious prologues and their inflated sense of importance with poems of praise. He also uses *cabo roto* in a sonnet in *Entretenida* 2.

Cabra. A small city in Córdoba Province, located southeast of Córdoba and northwest of Granada. MC's uncle Andrés lived there for many years and for some years was mayor of the city, and it is very likely that MC visited Cabra, or perhaps even lived there for a while, in the mid-1560s. Its population was no more than about 3,000. The city's most famous landmark is a great *chasm just outside the city that is mentioned in *DQ* II, 14.

Cabral, Manuel del (1907–). Dominican writer. Cabral's *Antología del caballo* (1998; *Anthology of the Horse*) is a collection of poems and short prose pieces, both his own and from a variety of other writers, on the subject of horses (included is MC's description of the ride on Clavileño from *DQ* II, 41). The book opens with Cabral's own poem entitled "Una carta a Rocinante que empieza con su jinete" ("A Letter to Rocinante Who Sets Out with His Rider"), using DQ's horse as a kind of emblem of horses in general.

Bibliography: Manuel del Cabral, *Antología del caballo* (Santo Domingo, Dominican Republic: Editora de Colores, 1998).

Cabrera, Catalina de. MC's great-grandmother, wife of Rodrigo Díaz de Cervantes, of whom nothing is known.

Cabrera (de Córdoba), Luis (1559–1623). Spanish historian. Cabrera de Córdoba's best-known work is his *Historia de Felipe II* (1619; *The History of Felipe II*). He is praised as a poet in *Parnaso* 2.

Cabrero(s). *Goatherd(s).

Cabrillas. In *Rinconete*, mentioned as Repolido's servant.

Cabrón. *Goat.

Cáceres. A city in Extremadura, in western Spain, located southwest of Madrid and northeast of Badajoz. In *Persiles* III, 4, Periandro and the other pilgrims are taken to Cáceres when they are suspected of having killed Don Diego de Parraces.

Cachidiablo. 1. The name by which an Algerian pirate who served under Barbarossa was known. He made some raids on the Spanish coasts in the region near Valencia in the sixteenth century. **2**. *Academicians of Argamasilla.

Cachopines de Laredo. A venerable family from northern Spain; Laredo is a small port city on the Cantabrian Sea, located east of Santander and west and slightly north of Bilbao. See *DQ* I, 13.

Cacus [Caco]. In Roman myth, the fire-breathing son of Vulcan and a famous thief and cattle rustler. His name is proverbial for *thief* in Spanish. See *Adjunta; DQ* I, prologue, 2, 6; *DQ* II, 49; *Gitanilla; Pedro* 3; *Rufián* 1.

Cadells. *Nyerros and Cadells.

Cadí. 1. A title used by both Turks and Arabs for civil magistrates; thus it is similar to the Spanish term *alcalde* (magistrate or mayor). Sometimes, at least in MC's works, the term also suggests ecclesiastical power. **2**. In *Amante*, the high-ranking judge who plots to possess the beautiful Leonisa. **3**. In *Baños*, the ecclesiastical head of the Muslim community in Algiers who lusts after the boy Francisquito, whom he later has crucified. **4**. In *Sultana* 2, the judge who sentences Madrigal to death but is tricked into letting him live so that he can tell him what the birds are saying and so that he can train an elephant to talk.

Cádiz. An important seaport, founded by the Phoenicians, on the Atlantic coast, located south of Seville and northwest of Gibraltar. At first, Cádiz was the port city granted the exclusive rights to exercise trade with the New World, but in 1503 this license was transferred to Seville (presumably largely because it was less exposed to attack by sea than Cádiz; witness the 1596 raid), which then became the commercial center of the Spanish empire. Cádiz remained, however, an important and prosperous port city throughout the Golden Age. When Cádiz was sacked by the English, led by the Earl of *Essex, in July 1596, Spanish military authorities did nothing to defend or rescue the city until the enemy had departed. MC's satiric sonnet on the subject, *Poesías* 25, is one of his best poems. In *Española*, the English raid on

the city provides the starting point for the plot. See also *Celoso*; *Coloquio* (where it is called Cáliz); *DQ* II, 29; *Galatea* 2 (where it is called the Island [*Isla*] of Cádiz); *Rufián* 2.

Cadmus [Cadmo]. In Greek myth, the legendary founder of the city of Thebes. See *Adjunta*.

Caesar, Gaius Julius [Julio César] (ca. 100 BCE–44 BCE). Celebrated Roman general, statesman, and dictator. Caesar was the most famous of all Roman leaders; his *Commentaries* on the war in Gaul, his affair with Cleopatra, his famous phrase "I came, I saw, I conquered," and his assassination by Brutus and others in the Roman Senate are all the stuff of legend. See *Casa* 2; *DQ* I, prologue, 47, 49; *DQ* II, 2, 6, 8, 24, 43.

Caesars of Rome [Césares de Roma]. *Caesar*, from the name of the great Julius Caesar, was used as the title of the emperor of Rome from *Augustus to Hadrian (27 BCE–CE 138). See *DQ* II, 6.

Cafalud. In *Laberinto* 3, the innkeeper swears on the life of Cafalud, an invented name presumably meant as that of a saint.

Cage of wooden bars [Jaula de palos enrejados]. In *DQ* I, 46, the cage in which DQ is taken back home at the end of the novel.

Caieta. In Virgil's *Aeneid*, the wet nurse of Aeneas. See *Parnaso* III.

Cain, Henri (1857–1937). French dramatist. Cain adapted Jacques *Le Lorrain's play about DQ as an opera entitled *Don Quichotte* (1910) with music by Jules Massenet (1842–1912). Massenet's music was composed, at least in part, for the great Russian singer Fyodor Chaliapin, who starred in the title role and then translated the work into Russian. The plot is minimal: DQ, more a hapless lover than a madman, retrieves a necklace from bandits who have stolen it and returns it to DT (there is, of course, a windmill scene), but she rejects him and he withdraws to the mountains to die after he sees one more vision of DT. This work has become perhaps the most popular and most admired of all musical adaptations of MC's novel.

Bibliography: Jules Massenet and Henri Cain, *Don Quichotte: Opera in Five Acts in French*, French and English in parallel columns, trans. Avril Bardoni (Chicago: Lyric Opera of Chicago, 1993).

Cairasco (de Figueroa, Bartolomé) (1538–1610). Spanish poet known as the 'prince of the Canary Islands poets' in his day, he was the author of an extensive body of poetry, religious writings, and theater. He is praised in Calliope's song in *Galatea* 6.

Cairo. The capital of Egypt, located on the banks of the Nile River. See *Amante*; *Rufián* 1.

Cairoli, Irma. Argentine writer. Cairoli's novel *Teresa Panza en Buenos Aires* (1967) is the story of the life, loves, and political activities of Teresa and her husband Pancho. Along the way, there are characters with the quixotic names of Dulzina, Dr. Alonso Quesada, and Mari Tormes.

Bibliography: Irma Cairoli, *Teresa Panza en Buenos Aires* (Buenos Aires: Falbo, 1967).

Caístro. *Kaüstrios.

Caja de plomo. *Old physician.

Calaínos. A Muslim from the Spanish cycle of medieval ballads based on Carolingian legend. He had to defeat and kill three of the Twelve Peers of France in order to win the hand of Sevilla, daughter of King Almanzor. Calaínos defeated Valdovinos, but later was killed by Roland. See *DQ* II, 9.

Calatayud, Don Francisco de. An official in the House of Trade in Seville and, later, in Madrid, secretary to Felipe IV. Calatayud was a well-known poet whose verse appeared in various anthologies compiled in the seventeenth century. He is praised in *Parnaso* 2.

Calatrava. *Order of Calatrava.

Caldeos. *Chaldeans.

Caldera, Benito de. A Portuguese poet praised in Calliope's song in *Galatea* 6. Caldera translated Luis de Camões's epic poem of the Portuguese people, *Os Lusíadas* (1580), into Spanish. He may have been a personal friend of MC.

Calderón de la Barca, Pedro (1600–81). Spanish dramatist. Calderón was the leading figure of the second cycle of Spanish classic drama, and the major rival to Lope de *Vega for the honorific title of premier playwright in Spanish literary history. His philosophical masterpiece, *La vida es sueño* (1636; *Life Is a Dream*), bloody honor plays, extravagant court operatic productions, and *autos sacramentales* are brilliant theatrical pieces. Too young to have had any meaningful contact with MC, Calderón clearly read the work of his elder contemporary and wrote a play, now lost, entitled *Don Quijote de la Mancha* (sometimes referred to as *Los disparates de don Quijote* [*Don Quixote's Nonsense*]), which was staged in the royal palace in 1637. Given the image of DQ at the time, and considering the nature of DQ figures in other plays by Calderón and other seventeenth-century dramatists, it was probably a farcical presentation of MC's character. One of Calderón's best plays, *El alcalde de Zalamea* (ca. 1642; *The Mayor of Zalamea*) features a character named Don Mendo, who is specifically called a DQ, accompanied by an SP-like squire named Nuño. Although Mendo is not central to the primary action of the play, he appears in each act and provides much of the work's humor. In addition, over a dozen of Calderón's other plays and *autos* contain direct and/or indirect references to *DQ* and other works by MC. Calderón's *Entremés del dragoncillo* (*Interlude of the Little Dragon*) is based on *Cueva*.

Bibliography: Ignacio Arrellano, "Cervantes en Calderón," *Anales Cervantinos* 35 (1999): 9–35; Franco Meregalli, "Cervantes en Calderón," in *Atti delle Giornate cervantine*, ed. Carlos Romero Muñoz, Donatella Pini Moro, and Antonella Cancellier (Padua, Italy: Unipress, 1995), 129–35; and Ana Suárez Miramón, "Cervantes en los autos sacramentales de Calderón," *Anales Cervantinos* 35 (1999): 511–37.

Calderón, Luis Francisco. Spanish priest and poet about whom nothing is known. He wrote a dedicatory sonnet for *Persiles*.

Calicut. A city (not to be confused with Calcutta) on the western coast of the state of Madras, in southern India. See *Parnaso* 4.

Calidonia. *Calydonian.

Calíope. *Calliope.

Calipso. *Calypso.

Calisto. *Callisto.

Cáliz. *Cádiz.

Calle de Amargura [Street of Bitterness]. A place name used metaphorically by the father in *Baños* 3, whose son has been crucified by the cadí.

Calle de Bancos [Street of Banks]: Via dei Banchi. A street in Rome near the Tiber River. See *Persiles* IV, 6.

Calle de Cantarranas. *Calle de Cervantes.

Calle de Cervantes [Cervantes Street]. Formerly the Calle de Francos [Street of the Franks], but renamed for MC in the nineteenth century. MC never actually lived on the Madrid street named after him, but he did live in the building on the corner of that street and the *Calle de León, the entrance to which was on León, not Francos. The result is that today the memorial stone on the building that now occupies the site where he lived (the building in which MC actually lived is long gone) implies that he lived on the street named after him, but such is not the case. Ironically, Lope de *Vega did live on the Calle de Francos until his death. The site of Lope's home is now occupied by the very nice Casa de Lope de Vega, a museum that includes some of Lope's actual furniture. A further irony is that MC is buried in the Trinitarian Monastery on what was then the Calle de Cantarranas (Street of the Singing Frogs) and is now known as the Calle de Lope de Vega (Lope de Vega Street). So Lope lived on Cervantes and MC is buried on Lope de Vega.

Calle de Francos. *Calle de Cervantes.

Calle de Huertas [Street of the Gardens]. An important street in the Madrid of MC's day; in *Adjunta*, Pancracio de Roncesvalles delivers a letter to MC at the address across the street from the home once occupied by *Muley Xeque, the former prince of Morocco, on this street.

Calle de la Caza [Street of the Hunt]. There were two streets in Seville with this name. The larger one (*grande*) led to the Plaza de la Alfalfa, while the smaller one (*chica*) led to the Plaza of San Isidoro. See *Coloquio*.

Calle de la Sierpe [Street of the Serpent]. A busy commercial street in Seville and also the location of the main prison of the city. MC was jailed for debts in this prison on at least one occasion, in 1597–98. See *Rufián* 1.

Calle de León [Street of the Lion]. The Madrid street on which MC and his family lived from 1610 to 1612 and again from 1615 to 1616, on the corner of the Calle de Francos (today *Calle de Cervantes). The site of the building in which he lived and died is marked by a plaque, but the building itself no longer stands, nor is there any sort of museum on the site.

Calle de Lope de Vega. *Calle de Cervantes.

Calle de San Francisco [Street of Saint Francis]. A street in Valladolid. See *Vidriera*.

Calle de Santiago [Street of Saint James]. A street in the heart of Madrid, near the Plaza Mayor. See *DQ* II, 48.

Calle de Tintores [Street of Dyers]. A street in Seville mentioned in *Rinconete*.

Calle de Toledo [Street of Toledo]. A street in Madrid that runs south from the Plaza

Mayor to the Manzanares River. See *Gitanilla*; *Guarda*.

Calle Mayor [Main Street]. An important street in Madrid that runs from the Puerta del Sol in the heart of town, past the Plaza Mayor, and west to the Royal Palace. In *Guarda*, it is where the shoemaker has his shop.

Callejas. The phrase *se verá quién fue* (or *es*) *Callejas* (you'll see who Callejas was [or is]) is a way of proclaiming your prowess. It is used in *Gallardo 2*; *Guarda*; *Parnaso 3*; *Pedro 1*; *Rinconete*.

Calliope [Calíope]. In myth, one of the nine *Muses. She was specifically the muse of epic poetry, and was often depicted with a writing tablet and stylus. In *Galatea 6* she appears—as the muse of poetry in general—to the shepherds at the site of the dead poet Meliso and sings a long narrative poem in 111 octaves in praise of over 100 living Spanish poets. The list begins with several poet-soldiers and then is organized by rivers: poets of the Tagus, the Ebro, the Guadalquivir (Betis), and the Duero. After a list of the poets of New Spain and one poet from the Canary Islands, the listing by rivers continues: poets of the Tormes, the Pisuerga, the Ebro again, and the Turia. Finally, special mention is made of Francisco de Figueroa and Pedro Laínez, MC's good friends. The great majority of those named are of little or no interest today. The list of poets praised throughout *Parnaso* is similar in spirit and function to Calliope's song. See also *Parnaso 2*.

Callisto [Calisto]. In Greek myth, the nymph seduced by Jupiter and then converted by Juno into a bear, along with her son Arcas, who became the constellations known as the *Osa mayor* (Ursa Major or Big Dipper) and *Osa menor* (Ursa Minor or Little Dipper). Because these constellations are seen in the northern sky, Callisto can be a reference to the north pole. See *Numancia 1*; *Parnaso 2*.

Calpe. Former name of Gibraltar. Together Calpe and Abyla, in North Africa, formed the *pillars (or columns) of Hercules, the symbol of the end of the known world, the Strait of Gibraltar. See *Española*.

Calvario, Monte de. *Mount Calvary.

Calvete. In *Doncellas,* the servant of Rafael who faithfully accompanies his master throughout his adventures.

Calvo. *Nieva Calvo, Sebastián.

Calydonian [Calidonia]. A resident or inhabitant of the ancient Greek city of Calydonia. See *Casa 2*.

Calypso [Calipso]. In Greek myth, a nymph, sometimes known as the goddess of silence, who detained *Odysseus for some seven years on the island of Ogygia where he had shipwrecked. She offered him immortality if he agreed to stay there as her husband, but he still wanted to return home. Finally Zeus intervened and made Calypso send Odysseus back home to Ithaca. See *DQ* I, prologue; *Parnaso 3*; *Vidriera*.

Camacha de Montilla. There was a line of famous witches with this name from Córdoba, at least one of whom was known during the years when MC traveled in Andalusia. In *Coloquio*, she is the witch who may have been responsible for turning Montiela's twin sons into dogs.

Camacho Guizado, Eduardo (1937–). Colombian novelist and literary critic. Camacho Guizado's *Sobre la raya* (1985; *Above the Line*) is the story of a frustrated writer named Luis Carlos Ybarra who, among other things, is supposed to be writing an article on *DQ*. He carefully chooses the edition of the novel he will read (that of Martín de Riquer) and explains the reasons for his choice. Fragments of *DQ*—words, phrases, longer passages—permeate his thoughts as well as his conversations with other characters. Other writers and texts (classical writers, Neruda, Quevedo) also function this way, but evocations of DQ outnumber all the rest combined. He even begins to conceive of the woman he loves, Lía, as a sort of DT, and recalls (and reproduces) DQ's entire love letter to DT from I, 25. Ultimately, he is meta-fictionally obsessed with the question of the writer who calls his own work into question.

Bibliography: Eduardo Camacho Guizado, *Sobre la raya* (Bogotá, Colombia: Oveja Negra, 1985).

Camacho the Rich [Camacho el rico]. In *DQ* II, 19–22, the wealthy shepherd who is supposed to marry Quiteria the Beautiful but who is cheated out of his bride by the clever Basilio (*Camacho's wedding).

Camacho's wedding [Bodas de Camacho]. According to the story DQ and SP first hear from some travelers in *DQ* II, 19, a peasant woman known as Quiteria the Beautiful loved the handsome and talented Basilio, but her father arranged for her to marry Camacho the Rich. In II, 20, DQ and SP attend the great wedding celebration, where SP especially enjoys the abundant good food and DQ takes particular pleasure in the allegorical dance and song. But in II, 21, Basilio surprises everyone by showing up and interrupting the marriage ceremony. He proclaims his love for Quiteria and then stabs himself, apparently committing suicide. He asks with his dying breath to be wedded to Quiteria, who will then become a virgin widow and can marry Camacho. She consents, as does Camacho, and the two are married. Basilio then jumps up and reveals that his suicide was a trick. DQ helps avert a violent confrontation, and it is decided that the marriage should be respected. Camacho generously agrees to let the feast take place as planned, but now in honor of the newly married couple. Afterwards, in II, 22, DQ and SP accompany the newlyweds to their home and spend three days with them. The wedding celebration in *Galatea* 3 is MC's first version of this sort of occasion. The elaborate fisherfolk's wedding in *Persiles* II, 10, is comparable in its elegant song and dance, but has no rich-poor conflict. See also *DQ* II, 24, 28, 31, 62, 67.

Bibliography: John J. Allen, "Don Quixote and the Origins of the Novel," in *Cervantes and the Renaissance*, ed. Michael D. McGaha (Easton, PA: Juan de la Cuesta, 1980), 125–40; Kathleen Bulgin, "*Las bodas de Camacho*: The Case for *el Interés*," *Cervantes* 3, no. 1 (1983): 51–64; and Francisco Vivar, "Las bodas de Camacho y la sociedad del espectáculo," *Cervantes* 22, no. 1 (2002): 83–109.

Cámara. *Cabinet.

Camaradas de don Fernando. *Friends of Don Fernando.

Camarera mayor de la reina. *Chambermaid of Elizabeth I.

Cambray linen. *Holland.

Camila. The female protagonist of *Curioso*: *DQ* I, 33–35. Camila is silent and is the object of the male characters' discourse and desire in the first half of the story as her husband Anselmo convinces his friend Lotario to test her virtue by attempting to seduce her (the events that will lead to the death of all involved). But in the second half she speaks more often than the men, controls the action, and masterfully stages the climactic scene when she feigns suicide for the benefit of her voyeuristic husband and stunned lover.

Bibliography: Georgina Dopico Black, "La herida de Camila: la anatomía de la evidencia en 'El curioso impertinente,'" in *En un lugar de La Mancha: Estudios cervantinos en honor de Manuel Durán*, ed. Georgina Dopico Black and Robert González Echevarría (Salamanca, Spain: Ediciones Almar, 1999), 91–107.

Camila's parents [Padres de Camila]. They are mentioned in *DQ* I, 34.

Camilo. *Julia.

Camões, Luis Vaz de (1524–80). Portuguese poet. As a soldier, Camões lost an eye during one of the ill-fated Portuguese military campaigns against the Muslims in Africa. In addition to his fine body of sonnets and other lyric poems, Camões's masterpiece is *Os Lusiadas* (1572; *The Lusiads*), considered by many to be the best heroic poem of the European Renaissance. It sings in Homeric tones of the coming into existence of Portugal as a nation and the glorious conquests and exploits of the Portuguese explorers, particularly Vasco da Gama and his discovery of the maritime route to India. MC is believed to have read and admired the poem in the 1580s, but the only reference to Camões in any of his works is when he is cited as a pastoral poet in *DQ* II, 58.

Bibliography: Thomas R. Hart, "History, Epic, Novel: Camões and Cervantes," *Kentucky Romance Quarterly* 34 (1987): 95–101; and Osvaldo Orico, *Camoens y Cervantes* (Madrid: Editora Nacional, 1948).

Camón Aznar, José (1898–1979). Spanish poet, dramatist, novelist, art critic, art historian, and art theorist. Camón Aznar wrote both a book on *DQ* in the history of aesthetics and a literal sequel to *DQ*. The latter is *El pastor Quijótiz* (1969; *The Shepherd Quijótiz*), which in the prologue he describes as *DQ* III, the 'true story' of DQ's last years. In the novel, the decision by DQ and SP to become shepherds (II, 73) once their chivalric career had ended is realized. Interestingly, the novel features a second character who calls himself DQ and acts quixotically (rescuing DQ from commitment to a madhouse). The best pages of the novel also bring to life DT as a (romantic) shepherd woman. Two-thirds of the way through the novel, SP dies in defense of DQ, who later has the satisfaction of defeating the duke in combat before he also dies. This is not exactly an inspired work, but one that illustrates how a preoccupation with MC and his characters can have a quixotic effect itself.

Bibliography: José Camón Aznar, *El pastor Quijótiz* (Madrid: Espasa-Calpe, 1969).

Camp, Jean (1891–?). French novelist. Camp's novel *Sancho* (1933), much indebted to Unamuno's understanding of *DQ*, is divided into two parts. In the first part, "The Squire," SP follows a very Christlike DQ through episodes brought over from MC's novel. The second, and by far most interesting, part of the novel, "The Epopee," consists of SP's life after the death of DQ. Here SP becomes the village storyteller and his fame spreads. He is approached by a Franciscan friar named Serapio who recruits a prophetlike SP in his crusade to rescue DT, who is held by Muslims in Africa. The crusade turns to pillage and rape, and even-

tually only a handful of Christians reach Africa. In the end, SP dies alone on a North African desert, his carcass eaten by a hyena. The DQ-Christ and SP-apostle/prophet figures are among the most extreme examples of the romantic tendency to sanctify DQ (*Don Quixote and Christ).

Bibliography: Jean Camp, *Sancho* (Paris: Editions des Portiques, 1933).

Campo de Agramante. *Agramante's Camp.

Campo de Alcudia. *Fields of Alcudia.

Campo de Montiel. *Fields of Montiel.

Campo, Estanislao del (1834–80). Argentine poet. Campo's gaucho poem *Fausto: impresiones del gaucho Anastasio el Pollo en la representación de esta ópera* (1866; *Faust: Impressions of the Gaucho Anastasio el Pollo of the Performance of this Opera*) involves a scene in which the protagonist becomes caught up in the theatrical illusion and interrupts the performance in the same way that DQ does the performance of the puppet theater in *DQ* II, 26, and DQA does the performance of a Lope de *Vega play (*Maese Pedro's puppet show).

Campo, Puerta del. *Gate of el Campo.

Campos de Santa Bárbara. *Fields of Santa Bárbara.

Campos Elíseos. *Elysian Fields.

Campuzano. In *Casamiento*, the soldier deceived by Doña Estefanía in their marriage and who, while taking a sweating cure for the case of syphilis she gave him, hears two dogs talking and transcribes their conversation.

Campuzano, Doctor (Francisco de) (?–ca. 1583). Spanish poet praised in Calliope's song in *Galatea* 6.

Camus, Jean Pierre (1582–1653). French priest and author. His story "La Bonne Femme" ("The Good Woman") is based on *Celoso*, and

"La Chastité courageuse" ("Brave Chastity") is based on *Fuerza*.

Caña mágica. *Magic wand.

Canario. The name of a dance from the Canary Islands. See *Viudo*.

Cañas del rey Midas. *Midas.

Canastel. A cape near the Spanish possession of Oran, in North Africa. See *Gallardo* 1, 3.

Canción de Grisóstomo; Canción desesperada. *Song of Despair.

Cancionero. *Ballad.

Cancionero, El. *López Maldonado, Gabriel.

Cancionero general. *Castillo, Hernando del.

Candaya. The kingdom from which the Countess *Trifaldi comes in search of DQ. See *DQ* II, 38–41, 44.

Candia. An alternate name (pronounced *Candía* after the seventeenth century) for Crete, which was, among other things, famous for its good wines. See *Persiles* I, 1, 5; *Vidriera*.

Cangas, Fernando de (ca. 1540–?). Spanish poet praised in Calliope's song in *Galatea* 6.

Cañizares. 1. In *Coloquio*, the witch who tells Berganza the fantastic story of his origins as one of two twins of Montiela, colleague of Cañizares's and fellow disciple of the famous witch Camacha, who were transformed into dogs by Camacha out of envy and revenge. This is supposedly the reason why the two dogs have acquired the gift of speech. After hearing this tale and watching Cañizares go into a trance, Berganza drags her grotesque nude body out into public, where it is discovered by the people of the city. **2**. In *Viejo*, the jealous old husband who is deceived by his young wife.

Bibliography: María Antonia Garcés, "Berganza and the Abject: The Desecration of the Mother," in *Quixotic Desire: Psychoanalytic Perspectives on Cervantes*, ed. Ruth Anthony El Saffar and Diana de Armas Wilson (Ithaca, NY: Cornell University Press, 1993), 292–314.

Cañizares, José de (1676–1750). Spanish dramatist and poet. Cañizares continued the baroque tradition of the seventeenth-century *comedia* into the neoclassic eighteenth century. He was probably the most popular Spanish dramatist of his age. His *La más ilustre fregona* (*The Most Illustrious Kitchen Maid*) is derived from *Fregona* by way of Lope de *Vega's *La ilustre fregona y amante al uso* (*The Illustrious Kitchen Maid and Contemporary Lover*). The earlier cape and sword comedy becomes a slapstick comedy, and the conventionally noble Don Pedro becomes the burlesque figure of Policarpo in Cañizares's version.

Bibliography: Kim L. Johns, *José de Cañizares, Traditionalist and Innovation* (Valencia, Spain: Albatros Hispanófila, 1980).

Cannibals [Antropófagos]. In *DQ* II, 68, one of the insulting terms used by the men who take DQ and SP back to the palace of the duke and duchess.

Caño de Vecinguerra de Córdoba. *Sewer of Vicenguerra in Córdoba.

Caño Dorado. A fountain in Madrid, located on the Prado de San Jerónimo. See *DQ* II, 22; *Fregona*.

Canon of Toledo [Canónigo de Toledo]. A staff priest from the Cathedral of Toledo. In *DQ* I, 47, he joins the company of those who are escorting DQ home. In I, 47–50, he engages in conversations with Pero Pérez and DQ about literature. The canon tends to express very traditional Aristotelian aesthetic principles, and has often been taken as a spokesperson for MC himself. More reasonable judgment, however, points out that he is a literary character who speaks for himself, and MC's own views appear to be quite different in some respects (see also the commentary on theater in *Persiles* III, 2). In I, 52, he and members of his retinue help prolong the fight between DQ and the goatherd

Eugenio, and the canon laughs heartily at the scene.

Bibliography: Alban K. Forcione, "The Dialogue between the Canon and Don Quixote," in *Cervantes, Aristotle, and the Persiles* (Princeton, NJ: Princeton University Press, 1970), 91–130.

Cantar (or Poema) de mío Cid [Song (or Poem) of the Cid]. *Díaz de Vivar, Rodrigo, el Cid.

Cantarranas, Calle de. *Calle de Cervantes.

Cantillana. The name of two villages, one called *la Nueva* and the other *la Vieja*, located directly west of Cáceres, about a third of the way to the Portuguese border. The name often appears in the phrase *El diablo está en Cantillana*, meaning that the devil, or trouble, can be found everywhere. See *DQ* II, 49.

Cantimpalos. A town located directly north of Segovia. In a popular folkloric tale, a woman called *Gansa* (Goose) from Cantimpalos went out to rendezvous with a priest called *Lobo* (Wolf), giving rise to a saying about a goose who went out to meet the wolf. See *Vizcaíno*.

Canto de Calíope. *Calliope.

Cantor de Tracia. *Orpheus.

Cantor y poeta. *Young musician.

Cantoral, (Jerónimo de Lomas) (ca. 1542–ca. 1600). Spanish poet praised in Calliope's song in *Galatea* 6.

Canvas depicting Periandro's adventures [Lienzo de las aventuras de Periandro]. Upon arrival in Lisbon in *Persiles* III, 1, Periandro has a famous *painter prepare a canvas on which are depicted all of his (and the group's) adventures in the northern lands from Books 1 and 2. This canvas is then used as a visual aid when Antonio the younger narrates the group's trials in the far north.

Bibliography: Carlos Brito Díaz, " 'Porque lo pide así la pintura': La escritura peregrina en el lienzo del *Persiles*," *Cervantes* 17, no. 1 (1997): 45–64.

Capacha, Hermanos de la. *Brothers of la Capacha.

Capacho. In *Sultana* 3, mentioned once as the name of one of two musicians.

Capataz, Fray Juan Bautista. A Trinitarian friar and a book censor who wrote one of the approvals for *Novelas*. He is included as one of six religious poets on Parnassus in *Parnaso* 4.

Capillán. *Chaplain.

Capitán. *Captain.

Capitán cautivo, El (Capitán); The Captive's Tale. An embedded narrative that occupies *DQ* I, 39–41. With its theme of arms, *Capitán* stands in contrast to *Curioso* (33–35) with its theme of letters. After he tells his heroic love story, the protagonist, Ruy Pérez de Viedma (whose full name is not mentioned until I, 42), and his beloved renegade Zoraida become characters in the events that take place in the *inn of Juan Palomeque in I, 42–46. The military career of Pérez de Viedma closely parallels that of MC himself and the story overall is strongly autobiographical, until the romance plot becomes dominant when Zoraida first lowers a note to the Christian captives in I, 40. The description of captive life in Algiers is based on MC's own experiences and is related to the comparable settings and events in *Tratos, Amante, Baños, Sultana, Gallardo, Persiles* III, 10–11, and *Poesías* 8. Although the captain's narrative is presented as being on the same ontological plane as other events in DQ's life, in II, 44, it is referred to by CHB as an embedded narrative, a fiction like *Curioso*.

Bibliography: John J. Allen, "Autobiografía y ficción: El relato del Capitán cautivo (*Don Quijote* I, 39–41)," *Anales Cervantinos* 15 (1976): 149–55; George Camamis, "El hondo simbolismo de la hija de Agi Morato," *Cuadernos Hispanoamericanos* 319 (1977): 71–102; María Antonia Garcés, "An Erotics of Creation: *La historia del cautivo*," in *Cervantes in Algiers: A Captive's Tale* (Nashville, TN: Vanderbilt University Press, 2002), 182–229; E. Michael Gerli, "Rewriting Myth and History: Discourses of Race, Marginality, and Resistance in the Captive's

Tale (*Don Quijote*, I, 37–42)," *Refiguring Authority: Reading, Writing, and Rewriting in Cervantes* (Lexington: University Press of Kentucky, 1995), 40–60; Juergen Hahn, "*El capitán cautivo*: The Soldier's Truth and Literary Precept in *Don Quijote*, Part I," *Journal of Hispanic Philology* 3 (1979): 269–303; Carroll B. Johnson, "Organic Unity in Unlikely Places: *Don Quijote* I, 39–41." *Cervantes* 2, no. 2 (1982): 133–54; Michael McGaha, "Hacia la verdadera historia del cautivo de Cervantes," *Revista Canadiense de Estudios Hispánicos* 20 (1996): 540–46; Diane E. Sieber, "Mapping Identity in the Captive's Tale: Cervantes and Ethnographic Narrative," *Cervantes* 18, no. 1 (1998): 115–33; Paul Julian Smith, " 'The Captive's Tale': Race, Text, Gender," in *Quixotic Desire: Psychoanalytic Perspectives on Cervantes*, ed. Ruth Anthony El Saffar and Diana de Armas Wilson (Ithaca, NY: Cornell University Press, 1993), 227–35; and Stanislav Zimic, "Un sueño romántico de Cervantes: *El cuento del cautivo* (*Don Quijote* I, 37–42)," *Angélica* 6 (1994): 37–66.

Capitanes de infantería española. *Captains in the Spanish infantry.

Capoches de Oviedo. In *Entretenida* 1, the lineage from which the maid Cristina suggests she descends.

Caporali, Cesare [César Caporal] (1531–1601). Italian poet born in Perugia. He wrote the *Viaggio in Parnaso* (1582; *Voyage to Parnassus*), the most immediate source for MC's *Parnaso*. Although Caporali and MC were contemporaries, there is no indication that they knew each other personally (although Caporali, like MC, served at one time in the Acquaviva household). In *Parnaso* 1, in the opening lines, MC cites Caporali's trip as the model for his own voyage.

Capri. An Italian island in the Bay of Naples. See *Parnaso* 3.

Caprichoso. *Academicians of Argamasilla.

Capricious god. *Cupid.

Captain [Capitán]. In *Baños* 1, the brother of the protagonist Don Fernando.

Captains in the Spanish infantry [Capitanes de infantería española]. Two Spanish noblemen on their way to Italy who are captured by *Roque Guinart's men. Roque takes only a small amount of money from them and then sends them on their way. See *DQ* II, 60.

Captive [Cautivo]. In *Baños* 1, one of those taken in the raid on Spain.

Captive's Tale, The. *Capitán cautivo, El.

Captivity [Cautiverio]. The practice of taking Christian captives (usually by capturing their ship on the high seas, but also often by conducting brief raids on the mainland) and holding them as slaves in North Africa while negotiating for their ransom via intermediaries was common in the Mediterranean area in the sixteenth century. The city of *Algiers was the center for this activity, and its economy was based primarily on privateering and ransom. The ransom price varied according to numerous circumstances, but especially the perceived social status and wealth of the individual. The *Order of Merced made it a specialty to raise funds for enslaved Christians and were recognized intermediaries in the negotiations. In general, Christian slaves held for ransom were treated more as prisoners of war than as jailed criminals or laborers, but those deemed to be of little or no ransom value were often assigned to menial tasks or sent to row in the galleys. When MC and his brother *Rodrigo were taken from the galley *Sol in 1575, their ransom prices were very different. Rodrigo's was quite standard for an average soldier of no particular status, but MC's was set considerably higher because of the impressive letters of commendation (from Don Juan de Austria and the Duke of Sessa) he was carrying after his brave performance during the battle of *Lepanto. Rodrigo was ransomed within just two years, but MC spent five long years in captivity before the money for his release could be raised. Much of what we know about MC's experiences in Algiers is from the *Información de Argel that he had prepared upon his release. By all accounts, MC's conduct was both heroic and exemplary. He was a legend in his own time; according to one contemporary anecdote, Algerian king (and owner of MC) Hassan Pasha was supposed to have said that 'as long as Cervantes is under lock and key my ships and the city itself are safe.' MC constantly recalled his experience in captivity and drew upon it in works written throughout his life: *Tratos*, *Amante*, *Baños*, *Sultana*, *Gallardo*, *Capitán*, *Persiles* III, 10–11, and *Poesías* 8.

Bibliography: Ahmed Abi-Ayad, "El cautiverio argelino de Miguel de Cervantes," *Notas y Estudios Filológicos* 9 (1994): 9–17; Juan Bautista Avalle-Arce, "La captura: Cervantes y la autobiografía," in *Nuevos deslindes cervantinos* (Barcelona: Ariel, 1975), 277–333; George Camamis, *Estudios sobre el cautiverio en el Siglo de Oro* (Madrid: Gredos, 1977); and María Antonia Garcés, *Cervantes in Algiers: A Captive's Tale* (Nashville, TN: Vanderbilt University Press, 2002).

Capua. City in Italy, near Naples. In *Persiles* III, 19–20, it is the home of *Isabel Castrucho.

Carácciolo, Don Troiano. A nobleman mentioned in *Parnaso* 8 as a contributor to the celebration of the marriage of Louis XIII of France and Doña Ana of Austria, in Naples in 1612. This flesh-and-blood 'Trojan' is compared to the literary Trojan Eneas.

Caracuel (de Calatrava). A village located southwest of Ciudad Real and north of Puertollano. According to *Pedro Recio de Agüero, his home town of Tirteafuera is located between Caracuel and Almodóvar del Campo, but in fact it is located between Cabezarados and Almódovar; Caracuel is nearby, but not where the doctor says it is. See *DQ* II, 47.

Caraculiambro. In *DQ* I, 1, the giant whom DQ imagines defeating and sending to pay homage to DT. The name is derived from *cara* (face) and *culo* (anus or ass) and thus is slightly obscene. At the same time, this name illustrates Bakhtin's theory of *carnival in which parodic reversals are common and the face and buttocks both complement and stand in opposition to each other.

Caraffa, Francesco. *Nocera, Duke of.

Carahoja. In *Baños* 1, a Muslim who punishes a Christian who tried to escape from captivity in Algiers.

Caravino. In *Numancia* 3, a prominent member of the city leaders in Numantia who proposes a combat between one Roman and one Numantian to decide the fate of the city.

Carcajona. *Timonel de Carcajona, príncipe de la Nueva Vizcaya (Prince of New Biscay).

Cárcamo, Alonso de. *Francisco de Cárcamo, Don.

Cárcamo, Don Juan de. *Juan de Cárcamo, Don.

Cárcamo, Fernando de. A hero of the defense of the fortress of San Salvador in Oran. He was apparently modeled on the historical Don Fernando de Cárcamo, the captain of the Spanish fortress of Mers-el-Kebir during the siege of Oran in 1563. See *Gallardo* 3.

Cárcel de Sevilla. *Seville Prison.

Carcelero. *Jailer.

Cardenales, Colegio de los. *College of Cardinals.

Cardenio. 1. The madman doing penance in the Sierra Morena whom DQ and SP meet in I, 23, and who becomes an important character in DQ's story as well as in *Cardenio*. His name, Cardenio, from *cardo* (thistle), is suggestive of both his personality and the setting in which he is introduced. When first seen, Cardenio is dressed in rags, bounding about in the mountains. The narrator refers to him as the Ragged Knight of the Disreputable Countenance (Roto de la Mala Figura) and the Knight of the Forest (Caballero del Bosque) in contrast to DQ, the Knight of the Mournful Countenance (Caballero de la Triste Figura). When DQ interrupts Cardenio's story, Cardenio goes berserk and thrashes DQ, SP, and the innocent goatherd who is with them (I, 24). Later he teams up

with the priest and barber to help Dorotea (I, 27), plays the role of the squire to Dorotea in her guise as Princess Micomicona (I, 28–30), and participates in the events in Juan Palomeque's inn (I, 32–45). Cardenio is important for more than his role in the complicated story involving Dorotea, Fernando, and Luscinda. In I, 25, DQ cites only the literary models of Amadís and Orlando for their famous penances, while in fact the real model is Cardenio (*Don Quixote's penance). **2.** In *Entretenida,* the student who poses as Don Silvestre de Almendárez in order to have a chance of marrying Marcela.

Bibliography: Edward Dudley, "The Wild Man Goes Baroque," in *The Wild Man Within: An Image in Western Thought from Renaissance to Romanticism*, ed. Edward Dudley and Maximilian E. Novak (Pittsburgh, PA: University of Pittsburgh Press, 1972), 115–39; Stephen Gilman, "Cardenio furioso," in *Studia in honorem prof. M. de Riquer* (Barcelona: Quaderns Crema, 1988), III, 343–49; and Charles Oriel, "Narrative Levels and the Fictionality of *Don Quijote,* I: Cardenio's Story," *Cervantes* 10, no. 2 (1990): 55–73.

Cardenio, Dorotea, Fernando, and Luscinda (Cardenio).

This tale is perhaps the single most interesting experiment in narrative embedding in all of Golden Age prose fiction. The story is told by no fewer than three different narrators over a space of 14 chapters and is seamlessly integrated into the primary narrative of the adventures of DQ and SP. The tale begins in I, 23, when DQ and SP enter the Sierra Morena and find the decaying corpse of a mule. As they investigate the contents of the animal's saddlebags, they discover bits of amorous correspondence and poetry, and they also see a ragged figure jumping from rock to rock in the distance. A goatherd informs them that the madman is a nobleman who rode the mule to death here in the hills some six months previously and then over time has alternated between lucid states and periods of madness when he would steal food and engage in violent acts. In his more lucid moments, he explained that he was in this remote place in order to do a penance for his many sins and alluded cryptically to betrayal by a certain Fernando. Then DQ has

a face-to-face encounter with the man, who graciously offers to tell his story. In I, 24, the man, named Cardenio, tells how the wealthy and powerful Fernando, supposedly in love with a rich peasant woman, deceived Cardenio and began to court Cardenio's beloved Luscinda. But when in passing Cardenio mentions *Amadís de Gaula*, DQ interrupts the story to talk about romances of chivalry. Cardenio lapses back into madness; beats DQ, SP, and the goatherd; and flees. In I, 27, the priest and barber run into Cardenio, and he tells them his story beyond the point where DQ had interrupted him. Barely has he finished, when, in I, 28, the three men hear a voice that turns out to be that of the rich peasant woman, Dorotea, who, at their behest, tells them the story from her point of view, placing emphasis on Fernando's reneging on his promise of marriage after he had had sex with her. Cardenio and Dorotea both agree to help with DQ, and are present in the inn when Fernando and Luscinda arrive there in I, 36, and Dorotea convinces Fernando to honor his word to her. All four characters continue to be factors in DQ's life through I, 46, when he is taken away in a cage, supposedly under enchantment. One traditional understanding of this story is that it is based on a historical incident and that the characters involved can all be identified: Don Fernando is Don Pedro Girón, second son of the Duke of Osuna; Cardenio is of the Cárdenas family of Córdoba; and Dorotea is Doña María de Torres, who was seduced by Don Pedro. Such historical connections are always tenuous at best, and the story is normally considered to be, and is usually read as, nothing more than a fiction.

Bibliography: Javier Herrero, "Sierra Morena as Labyrinth: From Wilderness to Christian Knighthood," *Forum for Modern Language Studies* 17 (1981): 55–67; Jean M. Hindson, "The Fernando-Dorotea-Cardenio-Luscinda Story: Cervantes's Deconstruction of Marriage," *RLA: Romance Languages Annual* 5 (1992): 483–86; Myriam Yvonne Jehenson, "The Dorotea-Fernando/Lucinda-Cardenio Episode in *Don Quijote*: A Postmodernist Play," *MLN* 107 (1992): 205–9; Helena Percas de Ponseti, "Luscinda y Cardenio: Autenticidad psíquica frente a inverosimilitud novelística," in *"Ingeniosa Invención": Essays on Golden Age Spanish*

Cardenio's father [Padre de Cardenio]

Literature for Geoffrey L. Stagg in Honor of His Eighty-fifth Birthday, ed. Ellen M. Anderson and Amy R. Williamsen (Newark, DE: Juan de la Cuesta, 1999), 193–205; and Victoriano Ugalde, "*Quijote*, I, 36: Hacia su revalorización," *Anales Cervantinos* 13–14 (1974–75): 79–91.

Cardenio's father [Padre de Cardenio]. In *DQ* I, 24, he is mentioned during Cardenio's narrative.

Cardillo de Villalpando, Gaspar (1527–82). Spanish theologian at the University of Alcalá. Cardillo de Villalpando's *Summa summulurum* (1557), commonly called the *Súmulas*, was a required textbook. He and his text are mentioned in *DQ* I, 47.

Cardinals, College of. *College of Cardinals.

Cardonas. A well-known and respected Catalan family name. See *Doncellas*.

Cardoso Pires, José (1925–). Portuguese novelist and short-story writer. Cardoso Pires's book of stories entitled *Jogos do Azar* (1960; *Games of Chance*) includes the story "Dom Quixote, as velhas viuvas e a rapariga dos fósforos" ("Don Quixote, the Old Widows and the Little Match Girl"). A central image in the tale of young Esmeralda's descent into a life of prostitution is that of Rocinante as an automobile in our unheroic modern society.
Bibliography: Nicholas G. Round, "Towards a Typology of Quixotisms," in *Cervantes and the Modernists: The Question of Influence*, ed. Edwin Williamson (London: Tamesis, 1994), 9–28.

Caribdis. *Charybdis.

Carino. 1. In *Galatea* 1, the friend of Crisalvo, relative of Silvia, who plots Leonida's murder by Crisalvo, and who in turn is stabbed to death by Lisandro. **2.** In *Persiles* II, 10–20, the handsome fisherman who loves the ugly Leoncia and who joins Periandro's group of fisherman pirates in order to go in search of their stolen women.

Carlo Magno; Carlomagno. *Charlemagne.

Carlos, Don (1545–68). The first son of Felipe II, whose early death is alluded to in *Poesías* 5.

Carlos V (Carlos I, Carlo, Carlo Quinto, Gran pastor del ancho suelo hispano) [Charles V (Charles I, Charles, Charles Fifth, Great shepherd of the spacious Spanish land)] (1500–58). Carlos I King of Spain and Carlos V of the Holy Roman Empire. Son of Archduke Felipe el Hermoso (the Handsome) and Queen Juana la Loca (the Mad), Carlos was raised and educated in the Netherlands and arrived in Spain for the first time at the age of 17, with no knowledge of Spanish, to take the crown. Increasingly Hispanized, Carlos became the most beloved and the most capable of all Spanish kings. He was also the most powerful ruler in the history of the world to that point. He carried on lifelong struggles for power with Francis I and the French, Henry VIII and the English, Suleiman the Magnificent and the Turks, and Martin Luther and the Protestants. His empire, which consisted of Spain, Flanders (the Netherlands), much of Italy, and the vast Spanish possessions in the New World, was the greatest history had ever seen. After his abdication and retirement in the Monastery of Yuste in 1556, his son Felipe II inherited and largely continued his father's work. His was, indeed, a *Golden Age. See *Amante*; *DQ* I, 39; *DQ* II, 8; *Novelas* prologue; *Numancia* 4; *Persiles* I, 5; II, 19, 21; III, 18; *Poesías* 8; *Tratos* 1.
Bibliography: William Maltby, *The Reign of Charles V* (London: Palgrave, 2002); and Alberto del Río Nogueras, "Semblanzas caballerescas del Emperador Carlos V," in *La imagen triunfal del Emperador: La jornada de la coronación imperial de Carlos V en Bolonia y el friso del Ayuntamiento de Tarazona*, ed. Gonzalo M. Borrás and Jesús Criado (Madrid: Sociedad Estatal para la conmemoración de los centenarios de Felipe II y Carlos V, 2000), 63–85.

Carloto. A popular character from the medieval Spanish ballad tradition, originally from the French chivalric tradition, where he is the son of Charlemagne. Carloto kills *Valdovinos and is in turn killed by the Marqués de Mantua. See *DQ* I, 5.

Carmelo, Monte. *Mount Carmel.

Carmen, Hill of. *Hill of Carmen.

Carmen, Nuestra Señora del. *Our Lady of Carmen.

Carne, Puerta de la. *Gate of la Carne (Meat).

Carnicería. *Slaughterhouse.

Carnival. According to M. M. *Bakhtin, carnival is the pageant without footlights, the "second life" of the people in opposition to official culture; it is the laughing, ambivalent, parodying celebration of the body and of birth and death. The spirit of carnival—a popular-festive, grotesque-realistic, spirit—formed the foundations of medieval folk culture. Carnival is ambivalent, antihierarchic, parodic, and laughing; it frees the people from the oppression of the serious, dogmatic, authoritarian realities of official culture. Although most prominently manifest during periods of official carnival celebrations, this folk culture was a fundamental characteristic of everyday life in the Middle Ages. Its primary base was the marketplace, where people mingled and spoke freely in a language not sanctioned by the church, where the material bodily principle (and especially the bodily lower stratum) had its most elaborate expression. Carnival sustained the masses for centuries and reached a high point in the Renaissance, when Rabelais gave it definitive expression in *Gargantua and Pantagruel*: for Bakhtin, only MC approached Rabelais in celebrating carnival in his writings; he considered *DQ* as "one of the greatest and at the same time most carnivalistic novels of world literature." Bakhtin sees the presence of carnival in MC's novel primarily in two ways: first, of course, there is SP, whose "fat belly (*panza*), his appetite and thirst still convey a powerful carnivalesque spirit"; SP is the laughing, parodic

alternative to the "abstract and deadened idealism" of DQ. Many of the adventures, especially those from the first half of *DQ* I (windmills, inns, balm of Fierabrás, sheep, and so on), represent the "gay principle of regeneration" and "form a typical grotesque carnival," and this is what "creates the grand style of Cervantes' realism, his universal nature, and his deep popular utopianism."

Bibliography: M. M. Bakhtin, *Rabelais and His World*, trans. Hélène Iswolsky (Bloomington: Indiana University Press, 1984); James Iffland, *De fiestas y aguafiestas: risa, locura e ideología en Cervantes y Avellaneda* (Madrid: Iberoamericana, 1999); and Augustin Redondo, *Otra manera de leer el "Quijote": historia, tradiciones culturales y literatura* (Madrid: Castalia, 1997).

Carolea, La. *Sempere, Jerónimo.

Carolingian cycle. Tales of *Charlemagne and the *Twelve Peers of France, which were very popular in medieval Spain in the form of ballads and various prose and verse romances translated from the French. Carolingian themes and characters continued to infuse popular culture through oral and printed versions throughout the Renaissance, especially in the versions translated from the Italian works of *Boiardo and *Ariosto. Often as popular as the original French characters are the uniquely Spanish characters—Belerma, Bernardo del Carpio, Calaínos, Durandarte, Gaiferos, Melisendra, Montesinos, and others—who prominently populate the Carolingian stories in Spain. Also popular were two medieval romances that were printed and widely circulated and read in the sixteenth century: *Paris e Viana* (ca. 1494; *Paris and Viana*) and *Enrique fi de Oliva* (1498; *Enrique, Son of Oliva*). MC never mentions either of these romances, and it is possible that he did not know them, even though his overall familiarity with the Carolingian tradition was profound and the themes and characters from it had a large influence on the creation of *DQ*.

Carón. *Charon.

Carpentier, Alejo (1904–). Cuban novelist. Carpentier's *Los pasos perdidos* (1953; *The*

Lost Steps) is his most obviously quixotic novel. The narrator-protagonist, a music composer, recites the opening lines of *DQ* I and specifically refers to himself as a kind of DQ in his romance-inspired quest for an idealized world that is superior to mere reality and a DT-like ideal woman to love. This DT, however, is not the traditional Petrarchan European ideal of a blue-eyed, blonde, noble lady, but an American hybrid of Indian and black heritage. Although the composer seems for a while to find the pure and genuinely American idyll of his quest, relentless reality imposes itself again in the end.

Bibliography: Frederick A. de Armas, "Metamorphosis as Revolt: Cervantes' *Persiles and Sigismunda* and Carpentier's *El reino de este mundo*," *Hispanic Review* 49 (1981): 297–316; and Edwin Williamson, "The Quixotic Roots of Magic Realism: History and Fiction from Alejo Carpentier to Gabriel García Márquez," in *Cervantes and the Modernists: The Question of Influence*, ed. Edwin Williamson (London: Tamesis, 1994), 103–20.

Carpio, Bernardo del. *Bernardo del Carpio.

Carpio, Roberto. Spanish dramatist. His version of *Las bodas de Camacho* (1971; *Camacho's Wedding*) was staged at the Almagro theater festival and filmed for television.

Carranza, (Jerónimo Sánchez de). Spanish nobleman and poet who also wrote a treatise on fencing. He is praised in Calliope's song in *Galatea* 6.

Carraolano. In *Cueva*, apparently the name of the student who pretends to have learned magic in the Cave of Salamanca and who conjures up two devils who have the appearance of the local sacristan and barber. It has also been suggested, however, that this word—documented nowhere else as either a proper name or an adjective—may be a misprint.

Carrasco, bachiller. *Sansón Carrasco.

Carrascón. An alternative pastoral name DQ suggests for Sansón Carrasco. See *DQ* II, 67, 73.

Carrascosa. In *Rufián* 1, the *padre*, or master, of the house of prostitution, who is saved from being taken to jail by the protagonist Lugo.

Carrascosas de Antequera. The lineage claimed by Carrascosa, the man who runs a house of prostitution in *Rufián* 1.

Carretero; Carretero de bueyes. *Carter.

Carriego, Evaristo (1883–1912). Argentine poet. In his book of poetry entitled *Misas herejes, La Cancíon del Barrio* (1925; *Heretical Masses, The Song of the Neighborhood*), there are two poems inspired by DQ. The first is entitled "Por el alma de Don Quijote" ("For the Soul of Don Quixote") and the second is "La apostasía de Andresillo" ("The Apostasy of Young Andrés"). Of the two, the second is more interesting; in it, Andrés (of *DQ* I, 4, 31), who becomes a knight-errant like DQ, muses on how in the modern age the spirit of chivalry has given way to a universal materialism, and there are no more figures like DQ or Christ.

Bibliography: Evaristo Carriego, *Misas herejes, La Cancíon del Barrio* (Buenos Aires: Tor, 1925).

Carrier [Esportillero]. In *Rinconete*, basket carriers, or small-item delivery persons; a profession that Rinconete and Cortadillo practice briefly in Seville before they are taken to Monipodio's house.

Carrillo Cerón, Ginés. Spanish novelist. Carrillo wrote a sequel to *Coloquio* entitled *Segunda parte de los perros de Maúdes* (*Second Part of the Dogs of Mahudes*), which has been lost.

Carrillo de Mendoza, Don Pedro, Conde de Priego. Court officer in Seville who executed the famous criminals Alonso *Genís and *Ribera. In *Fregona*, it is mistakenly stated that it was the Count of Puñonrostro who carried out this act of justice.

Carro de bueyes. *Ox-cart.

Carro de la Muerte. *Cart of Death.

Carro del Sol. *Chariot of the Sun.

Carro tirado de leones. *Chariot drawn by lions.

Carro triunfal. *Triumphal car.

Carroll, Lewis (Lewis Dodgson, 1832–1898). English mathematician and writer. His great creation, Alice, from *Alice in Wonderland* (1865) and its sequel *Through the Looking-Glass* (1872), is a sort of obverse DQ: she is the only sane person in a mad world. In the sequel, Lewis Carroll creates his most personal and pathetic figure in the image of DQ: the White Knight. The knight's absurd armor and impractical inventions, his special ability to fall headfirst off his horse, and his determination to rescue Alice and see her through to the end of the chessboard, are balanced by his kind, gentle, and earnest demeanor. Certainly the figure of the White Knight as depicted by John Tenniel in his famous illustrations of the *Alice* books would appear to be directly inspired in the iconography of DQ. It has been suggested that among other things the White Knight represents Carroll himself: kindly, absurd, and devoted to Alice, as he sees his beloved little girl through to womanhood (going from pawn to queen in the allegorical chess game of the book) and seeing her go out of his life forever.

Bibliography: Mary Fuertes Boynton, "An Oxford Don Quixote," *Hispania* 47 (1964): 738–50; and John Hinz, "Alice Meets the Don," *South Atlantic Quarterly* 52 (1953): 253–66.

Cart of Death [Carro de la Muerte]. In *DQ* II, 15, a reference to the cart carrying the actors in *DQ* II, 11, which included a figure of Death.

Carta a Dulcinea. *Letter to Dulcinea.

Carta escrita por D. Quixote de la Mancha a un pariente suyo, en que le hace saber varias cosas necesarias para la perfecta inteligencia de su historia (1790; *Letter Written by Don Quixote de la Mancha to a Relative of His, in which He Informs Him of Various Things Essential for the Perfect Understanding of His History*). An anonymous letter in which DQ, who

did not die in II, 74, but was enchanted by Merlin, writes from the Cave of Montesinos in order to clear up some doubts concerning the understanding of the book written about him.

Cartagena. 1. Spanish Mediterranean seaport located southwest of Alicante and directly south of Mérida. It was an important possession of the Carthaginians (thus the name of the city) and then of the Romans. In the Golden Age, its major traffic and commerce were with Italy. See *Coloquio*; *DQ* I, 29; *DQ* II, 24; *Gitanilla*; *Parnaso* 1; *Persiles* III, 11–12; *Vidriera*. **2.** An important port city in the Spanish colony Nueva Granada (today the nation of Colombia). See *Celoso*.

Cartel de desafío, y protestación cavalleresca de Don Quixote de la Mancha Cavallero de la Triste Figura en defensión de sus Castellanos (1642; *Written Challenge, and Chivalric Protest of Don Quixote de La Mancha, Knight of the Mournful Countenance in Defense of Spaniards*). An anonymous text published in Lisbon shortly after Portugal regained complete political freedom from Spain in 1640. In it, DQ offers a comic challenge, as the Knight of the Lions, defending true Castilian chivalry and not the shameful conduct of the Duke of *Medina Sidonia.

Bibliography: María Cruz García de Enterría, "Marginalia cervantina, 2: Relectura de un texto marginal: Cartel de desafío de Don Quijote," in *Actas del II Congreso Internacional de la Asociación de Cervantistas*, ed. Giuseppe Grilli (Naples: Instituto Universitario Orientale, 1995), 419–28.

Carter [Boyero, carretero (de bueyes)]. **1.** The owner of the *ox cart used to take the 'enchanted' DQ home at the end of *DQ* I. See *DQ* I, 46–47, 52. **2.** In *DQ* II, 17, the man who rides alongside the cart carrying the lion.

Cartero. *Messenger.

Carthage [Cartago]. A powerful colony of Tyre on the coast of North Africa, directly south of Rome, in what is today Tunis. Carthage, particularly under the leadership of

*Hannibal, was the principal rival to imperial Rome. The city was finally destroyed by Scipio Africanus in 146 BCE. Carthage, or its ruins, is often evoked as a symbol of the passage of time and the inevitability of death and oblivion. See *DQ* I, prologue, 49; *DQ* II, 71; *Galatea* 4; *Parnaso* 1.

Carthusian friars [Frailes cartujos]. The Carthusian Order was founded in France in the eleventh century. The monks of this order live in complete silence, devoting their life to study, prayer, and tilling the soil. See *DQ* I, 13.

Carvajal, Gutierre. A little-known poet praised in Calliope's song in *Galatea* 6.

Carvajal (Caravajal), Juan de. Most probably he was a professor of medicine in Seville. See *Parnaso* 5.

Casa de Austria. *Austria, House of.

Casa de Contratación (La Lonja). *House of Trade.

Casa de la Moneda. *Mint.

Casa de los celos y selva de Ardenia, La (Casa); The House of Jealousy and Forest of Ardenia. Second play in *Comedias*. According to many readers, *Casa* is the least successful of MC's dramatic works. Quite clearly this is a (fairly crude) reworking of an earlier text, probably from the period of the 1580s, perhaps *El bosque amoroso* (*The Forest of Love*). One obvious indication that it is a rewrite is found in the second act, where there is a moment when it is announced that the act is over, but the action continues. Ostensibly a tale of marvelous chivalric deeds, the play is characterized by absurdities, inconsistencies, and a comic tone that one suspects is not always intended. In fact, the main difficulty this work presents is that of determining when or if the action is serious and when or if it is an intentional parody. It is clear, however, that the French heroes are consistently ridiculed: Reinaldos and Roldán in their frivolity, Galalón in his manifest cowardice, and Charlemagne in his

powerlessness and indecision. In contrast, the Spaniard Bernardo del Carpio and even the warrior woman Marfisa come off relatively positively. Two sonnets from the play also appear with few changes in *DQ* I, 23 (by Cardenio) and I, 34 (Lotario's sonnet to Clori).

Act I: As the play opens, Reinaldos is complaining to the magician Malgesí that he has seen his cousin Roldán and the traitor Galalón laughing at him, and so he needs to avenge this slight. Roldán and Galalón arrive, but Galalón immediately leaves in order to avoid Reinaldos. Just as Reinaldos and Roldán are about to duel, the Emperor Charlemagne stops them. At this moment Angélica la Bella makes her appearance, richly dressed and riding a palfrey guided by two savages dressed in ivy. Angélica is followed by a *dueña* riding a mule and carrying a small coffer and a lapdog. Angélica announces that she will marry the person who defeats in singular combat (but only with lances, not using swords) her little brother Argalia, who awaits them in the Forest of Ardenia. Both Reinaldos and Roldán are anxious to undertake this adventure, but Malgesí warns them that it is a trick: Argalia's lance is enchanted and cannot be defeated; the plan is to capture all of Charlemagne's Twelve Peers, one by one. But Charlemagne is not convinced that Malgesí's tale is true and will not stop his knights from undertaking the adventure; it will be up to Malgesí to avoid disaster. In a change of scene, Bernardo del Carpio comes on stage with his squire, a Basque named Blas, a stock theatrical figure who, as here, talks in a comic ungrammatical dialect. Bernardo takes a rest beside Merlin's column. The figure of the spirit of Merlin arises out of the column, awakening Bernardo, promising him his assistance, and instructing him to enter into the column without saying a word, which Bernardo does. First Reinaldos and then Roldán come along in search of Angélica, and again begin to squabble about the matter. As the two draw swords and begin to fight, a fire separates them and the voice of Merlin orders Bernardo del Carpio to appear. Bernardo tries to separate the two, but the two French knights then gang up on the Spaniard. But Roldán is removed from the scene by Merlin's magic. Bernardo del Carpio and Reinaldos follow him over the mountain where he has disappeared, and at this time the warrior woman Marfisa comes on the scene. Marfisa follows the men over the mountain, and Roldán, Reinaldos, and Bernardo del Carpio come back on stage, fighting, although Roldán cannot move his sword because he is enchanted. Angélica arrives crying, along with the Basque, who informs the rest that Ferraguto has thrown Argalia into the river.

Act II: This act opens with a pastoral interlude. Lauso and Corinto are both in love with Clori, but she prefers the shepherd Rústico. The two more cultured shepherds try to play a joke on Rústico in an attempt to change Clori's attentions, but it does not work. Angélica arrives, fleeing the French knights, and asks for shelter among the shepherds. Reinaldos arrives on the scene and Malgesí emerges from the mouth of a serpent, calls himself Horror, and brings forth a series of allegorical figures: Fear, Suspicion, Curiosity, Desperation, and Jealousy. He then evokes the figures of Venus and Cupid (Love). He informs Lauso and Corinto that Clori will never love them, that she will remain faithful to Rústico, and then announces the end of the act. As the action continues, Bernardo del Carpio, Roldán, and Marfisa all talk, and the figures of Good Fame and Bad Fame come forth. As the act ends, Bernardo del Carpio and Marfisa decide to return to Paris.

Act III: Corinto plays another practical joke on Rústico. Reinaldos arrives and Angélica flees, but soon calls to him for help. Two satyrs drag Angélica across the stage, pulling her by a rope tied around her neck, but Reinaldos is powerless to move to rescue her. The satyrs leave her for dead and Reinaldos laments his fate, pulling out a dagger with which to commit suicide. But Malgesí appears and stops him, explaining that what he saw was an illusion and Angélica is fine. Back in Paris, Charlemagne receives Bernardo del Carpio and Marfisa, the latter claiming to follow Mars rather than Venus (and to care little for Christ and nothing for Mohammed), and challenging the Twelve Peers to singular combat. Charlemagne laments that Angélica is the reason why his finest knights

are not available to him at a time like this. Galalón catches up with Bernardo del Carpio and Marfisa and proves his cowardice by avoiding a fight with either of them. When he asks for Marfisa's hand, she extends hers and almost crushes his with her strength. The satyrs carry Galalón off, and Malgesí helps Bernardo del Carpio and Marfisa write of Galalón's cowardice on a shield. The figure of Castile, with the symbols of a lion and castle, appears to Bernardo del Carpio and admonishes him to look after the interests of Spain. Corinto, boasting of his bravery, helps Angélica flee, but when Reinaldos arrives Corinto turns and runs. Roldán also arrives, and he and Reinaldos again squabble over Angélica until a cloud descends upon them and suspends the action. Again back in Paris, Galalón is boasting of his victories over Marfisa and Bernardo del Carpio, until Malgesí arrives with the shield that proves his ignominy, and Galalón quickly departs. As Charlemagne again laments the absence of Roldán and Reinaldos, an angel flies by on a cloud and urges Charlemagne to direct his forces against the Muslim enemy. Charlemagne orders Angélica held by the Duke of Baviera while his knights sally forth in defense of religion and country, promising Angélica as a prize to the one who best acquits himself. Both Reinaldos and Roldán agree to these conditions, and the play is brought to a conclusion.

Bibliography: John J. Allen, "*La casa de los celos* and the 1605 *Quijote*," in *Cervantes for the 21st Century/Cervantes para el siglo XXI: Studies in Honor of Edward Dudley*, ed. Francisco La Rubia Prado (Newark, DE: Juan de la Cuesta, 2000), 1–9; Iluminada Amat, " 'And These Be the Fruits of Plays': Sexuality in *La casa de los celos y selvas de Ardenia*," *Bulletin of the Comediantes* 52, no. 2 (2000): 31–51; Edward H. Friedman, "Double Vision: Self and Society in *El laberinto de amor* and *La entretenida*," in *Cervantes and the Renaissance*, ed. Michael D. McGaha (Easton, PA: Juan de la Cuesta, 1980), 157–66; Edward H. Friedman, "*La casa de los celos*: Cervantes' Dramatic Anomaly," in *Cervantes, su obra y su mundo: Actas del I Congreso Internacional sobre Cervantes*, ed. Manuel Criado de Val (Madrid: Edi-6, 1981), 281–89; Paul Lewis-Smith, "Cervantes and Inversimilar Fiction: Reconsidering *La casa de los celos y selvas de Ar-*

denia," in *Studies in Honour of John Varey by His Colleagues and Pupils*, ed. Charles Davis and Alan Deyermond (London: Westfield College, 1991), 127–36; Paul Lewis-Smith, "Cervantes on Human Absurdity: The Unifying Theme of *La casa de los celos y selvas de Ardenia*," *Cervantes* 12, no. 1 (1992): 93–103; Francisco López Estrada, "Las canciones populares en *La casa de los celos*," *Anales Cervantinos* 25–26 (1987–88): 211–19. Morley Hawk Marks, "Deformación de la tradición pastoril en *La casa de los celos* de Miguel de Cervantes," in *Cervantes and the Pastoral*, ed. José J. Labrador Herráiz and Juan Fernández Jiménez (Cleveland, OH: Cleveland State University, 1986), 129–138; Alma Leticia Mejía González, "*Fama quiero y honra busco: La casa de los celos y selvas de Ardenia* de Miguel de Cervantes," in *Palabra crítica: Estudios en homenaje a José Amezcua*, ed. Serafín González (Mexico City: Universidad Autónoma Metropolitana, Unidad Iztapalapa, Fondo de Cultura Económica, 1997), 218–29; and Stanislav Zimic, "Algunas observaciones sobre *La casa de los celos* de Cervantes," *Hispanófila* 49 (1973): 51–58.

Casa de los locos de Sevilla. *Madhouse of Seville.

Casa de placer. *Country house.

Casa del Nuncio. *Nuncio's Asylum.

Casa del Rey. The royal building in Cartagena where munitions were stored; it is mentioned by Ambrosia Agustina in the story of her adventures in *Persiles* III, 12.

Casa Otomana. *Ottoman or Turkish Empire.

Casa Santa. *Heraclius.

Casamiento engañoso, El (*Casamiento*); *The Deceitful Marriage.* The eleventh story in *Novelas* and one of those with a very clear exemplary message: cheaters should not complain when they themselves are cheated. The shortest of the stories in the collection, it is both a clever picaresque narrative and the frame for the twelfth and final story, which is, in effect, an episode within it.

One day, as an ensign named Campuzano walks out of the Hospital of the Resurrection in Valladolid, he meets an old friend, Licenciado Peralta. Campuzano explains to Peralta that he has just taken a sweating cure for syphilis and then accepts an invitation to go to Peralta's house and tell him the story behind it. After a pleasant meal, he tells his story: not long ago he met an attractive young woman named Estefanía and, after several days of conversation, Estefanía made it clear that she was in search of a husband. What she had to bring to the marriage was primarily the house in which she was living. Campuzano's contribution was to be a gold chain he wore and some other jewels. The marriage was arranged and within a few days it took place, with two of Campuzano's friends and a cousin of Estefanía's as witnesses. Campuzano moved his goods into the house and for a week they lived a happily married life. Then one day some people came to the house and treated it as their own. Estefanía explained to Campuzano that the woman, Doña Clementa Bueso, wanted to pretend that the house was hers in order to play a trick on the man, Don López Meléndez de Almedráez. So Campuzano and Estefanía packed up and moved to the home of a friend of Estefanía's. After a week, when Campuzano complained about the cramped situation, the friend told him that the house really did belong to Doña Clementa and that Estefanía had presented it as hers in order to trick Campuzano into marrying her. Angry, Campuzano went out to look for Estefanía, but did not find her and returned to learn that Estefanía had taken all of his possessions and disappeared. As Peralta consoles his friend, Campuzano admits that there was also some deceit on his part: the gold chain and all his other goods were cheap imitations and not worth what he had claimed. But Campuzano did take one more thing from the marriage: a case of syphilis. While he was in the hospital, however, a strange thing happened. There are two dogs, trained to carry lanterns, that accompany the brothers of the Capacha Order as they go through the streets begging for alms, and also serve as guard dogs for the hospital. Well, one night, the next to last of his stay there for his cure, Campuzano heard the dogs, named Berganza and Cipión, talking. Peralta refuses to believe that dogs can talk, but Campuzano insists that he listened to their conversation all night and he wrote down their dialogue, which deals with the life of one of the dogs. Furthermore, he says, on the following night the second dog also told the story of his life, and, if the first dialogue is well received he will also write the second one. Campuzano offers the manuscript of the dialogue to Peralta to read while he takes a nap. Peralta opens the manuscript and sees that it is entitled "Colloquy that took place between 'Cipión' and 'Berganza,' dogs of the Hospital of la Resurrection, which is in the city of Valladolid, outside the Campo Gate, and the dogs are commonly called the Mahudes' Dogs."

(Next follows the text of the dogs' conversation, *Coloquio*, the twelfth and last story in *Novelas*.)

Peralta finishes reading the manuscript just as Campuzano awakens from his nap. Peralta says that even though it is a fiction, it is well written, and Campuzano promises to write the second installment. They agree not to discuss the matter of fiction and reality, and go out to take a walk along the Espolón.

Bibliography: Galen Brokaw, "Holistic Fiction: Cervantes's *El casamiento engañoso* and *El coloquio de los perros*," *RLA: Romance Languages Annual* 10 (1998): 460–66; J. A. Drinkwater, "The Return of the Body in *El casamiento engañoso* and *El coloquio de los perros*," in *After Cervantes: A Celebration of 75 Years of Iberian Studies at Leeds*, ed. John Macklin (Leeds: Trinity and All Saints, 1993), 29–41; Peter N. Dunn, "Framing the Story, Framing the Reader: Two Spanish Masters," *Modern Language Review* 91 (1996): 94–106; Alban K. Forcione, *Cervantes and the Mystery of Lawlessness: A Study of "El casamiento engañoso y El coloquio de los perros"* (Princeton, NJ: Princeton University Press, 1984); Steven Hutchinson, "Sexo y economía: *El casamiento engañoso*," in *Actas del VIII Coloquio Internacional de la Asociación de Cervantistas*, ed. José Ramón Fernández de Cano y Martín (El Toboso, Spain: Exmo. Ayuntamiento de El Toboso, 1999), 215–22. Cecile Mazzucco, "The Doorways to the Maelstrom of Discourse in Cervantes's *El casamiento engañoso* and *El coloquio de los perros*," *RLA: Romance Languages Annual* 4 (1992): 16–20; and Stephen Rupp, "Cervantes and the Soldier's Tale: Genre and Disorder in *El Casamiento Enga-*

ñoso," *Modern Language Review* 96 (2001): 370–84.

Casanate de Rojas, Don Agustín de. A minor poet of MC's day who wrote a sonnet in Latin as one of the preliminary verses to *Parnaso*.

Casante, Juan Luis de. Probably refers to Mosén Luis de Casante, a lawyer and poet, perhaps related to Don Agustín de Casante Rojas, who wrote one of the epigrams for *Parnaso*. He is praised in *Parnaso* 3.

Cascajo. The name of Teresa Panza's father, cited by her in *DQ* II, 5.

Case, Alexander T. American writer. Case was the primary author of *Sancho Panza: A Grove Play* (1965), with music by Leigh Harline. This was the sixtieth Grove Play of the Bohemian Club of San Francisco. A light entertainment, the most original part of the play takes place when Ginés de Pasamonte kidnaps the duke and Governor SP and holds them for ransom. But SP engineers an escape, just as DQ and some dragoons come to the rescue. Earlier, Case also collaborated on the fiftieth Grove Play: *Don Quijote: An Adventure of that Ingenious Gentleman of La Mancha* (1955).

Casella, Mario (1886–1956). Italian literary critic. In addition to his scholarly work relating to MC, he wrote the libretto for the opera *Don Chisciotte* (1951), with music by Vito Frazzi.

Casilda, Doña. In *DQ* II, 48, a lady for whom Doña Rodríguez worked at one time in Madrid.

Casildea de Vandalia (Casilda). In *DQ* II, 12–14, the name invented by Sansón Carrasco for the lady he says he loves while he assumes the role of the Knight of the Mirrors. Casildea (compare DT) is a poetic derivation from the common name Casilda, and *Vandalia is an archaic and poetic version of Andalusia.

Casildea's beard. *Dulcinea's shoe and Casildea's beard.

Casona, Alejandro (Alejandro Rodrí-guez Alvarez, 1903–1965). Spanish dramatist. One of the most popular and successful dramatists of the twentieth century in Spain, Casona specialized in plays on traditional and literary themes set in the Middle Ages and Golden Age. One of these is *Sancho Panza en su ínsula* (1947; *Sancho Panza on His Island*), which dramatizes some of the events from *DQ* II, 45–53: his arrival at Barataria, some of his judgments, his encounter with Pedro Recio de Agüero, and an episode from his rounds of the island.

Bibliography: Alejandro Casona, *Retablo jovial: cinco farsas en un acto* (Buenos Aires: El Ateneo, 1949).

Castalia. Originally, in Greek myth, a nymph who, when she was chased by Apollo, jumped into the spring on Mount Parnassus that was held to be sacred by Apollo and the Muses. After that, anyone who wanted to consult the oracle at Delphi was required to purify him- or herself in the waters of that spring. For the Romans, to drink of the waters of Castalia was to receive poetic inspiration. In *Parnaso* 8, MC cites it as the fountain that was created by a blow of the hoof of the winged horse Pegasus, but in fact it was the fountain Hippocrene that was supposedly so created. This provides a small-scale example of the difficulty in interpreting MC: was this MC's mistake, or is it an example of his burlesque sense of humor? See also *Parnaso* 3; *Persiles* III, 2.

Castellana. A fountain in Madrid. See *Fregona*.

Castellani, Leonardo (1899–1979). Argentine priest, social critic, and novelist. Castellani wrote a trilogy of satiric fictions loosely but explicitly derived from *DQ*. First is *El nuevo gobierno de Sancho; traducción directa del arábigo por Jerónimo del Rey* (1942, revised and expanded in 1944 and 1965; *Sancho's New Governorship; A Direct Translation from the Arabic by Jerónimo del Rey*), which transplants the squire away from Barataria to Agatháurica (i.e., Argentina), where he has many evils to combat; most of the work consists of SP's judg-ments concerning a variety of social and political ills. The second work, which 'happened tomorrow,' is entitled *Su Majestad Dulcinea* (1946, 1955; *Her Majesty Dulcinea*), and the final work is *Juan XXIII (XXIV); o sea, La resurrección de Don Quijote* (1964; *John XXIII [XXIV]; or, The Resurrection of Don Quixote*), enigmatically described by the author as a 'fantastic symphony à la Berlioz in three movements and with a coda; for use by underdeveloped countries.' Both works continue the author's examination of and personal commentary on social and political problems in Argentina.

Bibliography: Carlos Orlando Nállim, "El *Quijote* en *El nuevo gobierno de Sancho*, de Leonardo Castellani," *Anales Cervantinos* 35 (1999): 337–46.

Castellano. *Castilian.

Castellano, Diego. *Información de Argel.*

Castellanos, Agustín. An illiterate peasant known as the 'tailor poet' or the 'tailor from Toledo' who devoted himself to the composing of poetry and theater and was a protégé of Lope de *Vega. MC never mentions him by name but does appear to allude to him twice: in *Parnaso* 2 and *Persiles* I, 18.

Castellar, Conde de. A reference to Don Juan Arias de Saavedra, Count of Castellar. See *Rufián* 1.

Castelo Branco, Camilo (1825–95). Portuguese novelist and short-story writer. His most famous novel is the sensational and partly autobiographical *Amor de Perdição* (1852; *Love and Damnation*). In *No Bom Jesus do Monte* (1864; *On the Good Jesus of the Mountain*), Castelo evokes and identifies with 'his maestro' DQ and his love for (not DT but) Aldonza Lorenzo. Castelo's novel *A Sereia* (1865; *Mermaid*) is based in part on *Gitanilla*. And, finally, his novel *A Queda dum Anjo* (1865; *The Fall of an Angel*) features both a quixotic protagonist, Calisto Elói, and a Cervantine, playful narrator.

Bibliography: Maria Fernanda de Abreu, "Camilo Castelo Branco: Cervantes, 'camarada' e 'mestre,' " in *Cervantes no romantismo português: Cavaleiros andantes, manuscritos encontrados e gargalhadas moralíssimas* (Lisbon: Estampa, 1997), 261–326.

Castidad. *Chastity.

Castilblanco (de los Arroyos). A small town located directly north of Seville and west and slightly south of Córdoba. In *Doncellas*, it is the scene for the events in the inn that unite brother and sister Rafael and Teodosia.

Castile [Castilla]. The former medieval kingdom that was ruled by Isabel when she married Fernando of Aragon in 1474. The old kingdom included the modern regions of Castilla-León—formerly Castilla la Vieja (Old Castile)—and Castilla-La Mancha—formerly Castilla la Nueva (New Castile). It occupied the majority of the central part of the Iberian Peninsula. Castile was for centuries a focal point of the conflict between Christians and Muslims. In the early sixteenth century, Castile had some 5 million inhabitants, whereas Aragon had just over a million. In *Casa* 3, Castile appears as an allegorical figure that addresses Bernardo del Carpio in his sleep. See *Baños* 1; *Casa* 3; *DQ* I, 2, 13, 31, 49; *DQ* II, 12, 66; *Fregona*; *Gitanilla*; *Numancia* 1; *Parnaso* 1; *Pedro* 1; *Persiles* III, 1, 16, 19; *Rinconete*; *Vidriera*.

Castilian [Castellano]. 1. Spanish. Castilian was the dialect of central Spain, both Old and New Castile, which became the official language of the country and the primary language of its literature. **2.** In *DQ* II, 62, the man in Barcelona who angrily tells DQ he should go home, tend to his family, and stop providing laughter for others. **3.** In *Persiles*, I, 4, Periandro understands Castilian very well but does not speak it as well; in III, 2, Auristela does not understand the language.

Castilian knights. *Spanish knights.

Castilla; Castilla la Nueva; Castilla la Vieja. *Castile.

Castilla la Vieja. *Old Castile.

Castilla y de Aguayo, Juan de. *Aguayo, Juan de Castilla y de Aguayo.

Castillejo, Cristóbal de (ca. 1492–1550). Spanish poet. Castillejo is best known as the champion of traditional, or national, poetic meter and themes during the period when *Garcilaso de la Vega and others cultivated primarily the new Italianate meter. He is praised in Calliope's song in *Galatea* 6.

Castillo. In *Sultana* 1, a Christian captive freed by the spy Andrea.

Castillo de la Fama. *Castle of Fame.

Castillo del buen recato. *Castle of Caution.

Castillo, Julia (1956–). Spanish poet. Castillo's *Poemas de la imaginación barroca* (1980; *Poems of Baroque Imagination*) includes a series of three poems on the subject of Marcela (from *DQ* I, 12–14): "Recordando a la pastora Marcela; habla de sí misma" ("Remembering the Shepherdess Marcela; She [the poet] Speaks of Herself"), "A la pastora Marcela; Poema que contiene un verso de Lezama Lima" ("To the Shepherdess Marcela; A Poem that Contains a Line from Lezama Lima"), and "Otro a la pastora" ("Another Poem to the Shepherdess"). Castillo evokes one of MC's most outstanding literary creations as an inspiration and model for herself.
  Bibliography: Julia Castillo, *Poemas de la imaginación barroca* (Santander, Spain: La Isla de los Ratones, 1980).

Castle of Caution [Castillo del buen recato]. In *DQ* II, 20, a prop used as a part of the celebration of *Camacho's wedding.

Castle of Fame [Castillo de la Fama]. The name of a castle in London in the 1579 continuation of the romance *Belianís de Grecia* (*Fernández, Jerónimo), mentioned in *DQ* I, 6. It was a huge and elaborate structure (large enough for some 2,000 knights) on silver wheels that was pulled by a team of 40 elephants.

Castor and Pollux [Cástor y Polux]. The mythological brothers who founded Rome and were transformed into the constellation Gemini. They are also considered a model of friendship. See *DQ* I, 23.

Castrador de puercos. *Pig gelder.

Castro del Río. Small town of about 1,500 inhabitants in Andalusia located north of Málaga and southeast of Córdoba, where in 1592 MC was briefly detained and jailed (probably for less than a week) before clearing his name. There is a commemorative plaque in the town, but the actual location of the jail is not known.

Castro, Licenciado (Licentiate) Jerónimo de. A poet and musician cited on Parnassus in *Parnaso* 3.

Castro, Pedro. *Mantuano, Pedro.

Castro y Bellvis, Guillén de (1569–1631). Spanish dramatist; probably the best of the group who began their career in Valencia, rather than in Madrid. A knight in the Order of Santiago, he was a member of the *Academy of the Night Revelers in Valencia, where his name was *Secreto* (Secret). A friend and follower of Lope de *Vega, Castro was one of the most important theatrical writers of his generation. His best-known play is *Las mocedades del Cid* (*The Youthful Deeds of the Cid*); it was the model for Corneille's *Le Cid*. Castro wrote three plays based on the works of MC: *Don Quijote de la Mancha*, *La fuerza de la sangre* (*The Power of Blood*), and *El curioso impertinente* (*Foolish Curiosity*). The *DQ* play may have been written within a year of the publication of *DQ* I; it is almost certainly the first theatrical work based on any of MC's works. Most of the plot is from the *Cardenio* episode, with an important name change: Fernando is called simply El Marqués. In the end, the crossed love relationships are resolved when Cardenio turns out to be the son of the duke, and therefore the social equal of Luscinda, whereas El Marqués is revealed to be of lower social status and therefore more the equal of Dorotea. Traditional social order is restored with a marriage of equals, whereas in MC's original story the final Dorotea-Fernando marriage is more subversive. For the most part, DQ and SP are the object of derision in their brief stage appearances and with their funny lines (DQ often speaks in *fabla). Only in the third act does DQ take on some degree of interest when the priest, the barber, Dorotea, and Cardenio all recall their roles in *DQ* I, 23–29. The plays based on *Fuerza* and *Curioso* are conventional cape and sword comedies with little of the originality or profundity of MC's stories. Castro is cited by MC for his contributions to the theater in the prologue to *Comedias* and is praised in *Parnaso* 3.

Bibliography: Ignacio Arellano, "Del relato al teatro: La reescritura de *El curioso impertinente* cervantino por Guillén de Castro," *Criticón* 72 (1998): 73–92; Christiane Faliu-Lacourt, "Formas variantes de un tema recurrente: *El curioso impertinente*: Cervantes y Guillén de Castro," *Criticón* 30 (1985): 169–81; Luciano García Lorenzo, *El teatro de Guillén de Castro* (Barcelona: Planeta, 1976); and William E. Wilson, *Guillén de Castro* (New York: Twayne, 1973).

Catalan [Lengua catalana]. The language of Catalonia, the region of Spain around Barcelona. Catalan is not a dialect of Spanish, but a separate Romance language, actually more closely related to Provençal than to Spanish. Dialects of Catalan (or separate languages related more closely to Catalan than to Spanish) are spoken in the area around Valencia and in the Balearic Islands. In *DQ* II, 60, Catalan is spoken by the bandits headed by *Roque Guinart.

Catalan bandits [Bandoleros catalanes]. *Bandits.

Catalan gentleman. *Gentleman, gentlemen.

Catalina. 1. In *Española*, the wife of Clotaldo, who raises Isabel in London. Just as Isabel (Elizabeth) is a significant name in the story, Catalina, a secret Catholic, also recalls Catherine of Aragon, Spanish Catholic wife of Henry VIII, who provided, involuntarily, the pretext for the English break with the Catholic Church.

2. In *Baños* 2, Señora Catalina is designated as the person who plays the role of Ambrosio, who has a singing part. Later in the same act, she appears dressed in Muslim garb and says a few words. Because the stage directions are so specific, it seems that MC wrote this role especially for the actress Catalina Hernández Verdeseca, the wife of theatrical impresario Gaspar de Porres, and that Porres produced the play (or that MC hoped that Porres would produce it, for the subtitle of *Comedias* indicates that the plays in that volume were never staged). **3.** *Catalina de Oviedo.

Catalina de Oviedo, Doña. In *Sultana*, the protagonist, a noble Spanish woman, who marries the Sultan Amurates.

Catalina la Otomana. In *Sultana* 2, a name Amurates proposes using for Doña Catalina de Oviedo, which she rejects.

Catalina Micaela (1567–97). The second daughter of Felipe II and Isabel de Valois. She is addressed at the end of *Poesías* 4.

Catalonia [Cataluña]. The region of northeastern Spain, whose capital is Barcelona, and whose language is Catalan. In the Middle Ages, it was part of the kingdom of Aragon, but has always maintained a separate identity because of its unique language and culture. See *Cueva*; *DQ* I, 13; *Galatea* 2, 5.

Caterer [Dispensero]. In *Celoso*, the man who provides food and other supplies for the home of Carrizales.

Cathay [Catay]. Former name for a large part of China. According to the Italian chivalric tradition, Angelica was from Cathay. See *Casa* 3; *DQ* I, 1, 52; *DQ* II, 1; *Rufián* 1.

Catholic Monarchs [Reyes Católicos]. The title given to *Fernando of Aragon and *Isabel of Castilla in 1496 by Pope Alexander VI, recognizing them as staunch defenders of the faith. Their joint reign saw the completion of the conquest of the Muslims in the Iberian peninsula, political unification, the establishment of the Inquisition, the discovery of the New World, and the creation of the modern era's first superpower. See *Numancia* 1.

Bibliography: John Edwards, *The Spain of the Catholic Monarchs 1474–1520* (Oxford: Blackwell, 2000).

Catiline [Catilina]: Lucius Sergius Catilina (?–62 BCE). Roman politician of disreputable character, generally known for his cruelty and as an archetypal traitor. See *Baños* 1; *DQ* I, 27.

Cato the Censor [Catón Censorino] (first century BCE). Roman poet and grammarian. He was known to posterity as "the censor" for the maxims and sayings attributed to him. See *DQ* I, prologue, 42, 47; *DQ* II, 42; *Elección*; *Entretenida* 1; *Parnaso* 3; *Pedro* 1; *Viudo*.

Catón Zonzorino. SP's corruption of the name of Catón Censorino (*Cato the Censor) in *DQ* I, 20. In popular culture, Cato was frequently cited as a source of maxims and proverbs, so it is not in any way inappropriate for SP to cite this classical figure.

Catonian sentences [Sentencias catonianas]. Maxims attributed to Dionysius Cato, the supposed author of *Dicta Catonis* (*The Sayings of Cato*), a collection of moral maxims in prose and verse that was translated into several European languages and was very popular as a school text in the Middle Ages. Beginning in the sixteenth century, the attribution to the fictitious Dionysius Cato became universal. See *DQ* II, 33.

Cats [Gatos]. The animals involved in a trick played on DQ by the duke and duchess. A sack containing cats with bells tied to their tails is lowered to DQ's window after he finishes his song to Altisidora in *DQ* II, 46. The trick goes awry when some of the cats escape and enter DQ's room, where one of them badly bites and claws his nose. There is a certain irony in the fact that the ferocious lion in II, 16, is harmless, whereas a mere house cat inflicts one of the most serious wounds the knight-errant ever receives.

Catullus, Gaius Valerius [Catulo] (ca. 84–54 BCE). Roman poet. Catullus wrote a wide variety of poetry, but is best known for his very personal love lyrics. See *Galatea* 6.

Caucasus [Cáucaso]. A mountain range in southeastern Europe between the Black Sea and the Caspian Sea. See *Poesías* 17.

Cauralí. In *Baños*, the Muslim captain who leads the raid on Spain and takes several captives. He falls in love with the Christian Costanza.

Cautiverio. *Captivity.

Cautivo. *Captive.

Cava, La (Mala mujer cristiana). The name given by the Arabs to Florinda, the daughter of Count Julián of Spain. In 711 she was seduced, or raped, by Rodrigo, the last king of the Visigoths, and in anger and revenge, Julián called in the Muslims of North Africa, who defeated Rodrigo. The invaders then proceeded to overrun almost the entire Iberian Peninsula, initiating the seven-century Muslim presence in Spain and Portugal. In 718 the Christian Reconquest began with the victory over the Muslims at Covadonga, and the war lasted until the capture of Granada in 1492. See *DQ* I, 41; *DQ* II, 32.

Cava Rumía. A small promontory or cape on the northern coast of Algiers named after La *Cava, who was supposed to have been buried there. See *DQ* I, 41.

Cave of Montesinos [Cueva de Montesinos]. Cave in La Mancha, in the province of Ciudad Real, near the town of Osa de Montiel and the *Lagoons of Ruidera. Although DQ describes the cave as a vertical shaft, in fact it consists of a number of chambers, connected by a gently sloping path. The name is evidently derived from the legend of *Durandarte and his cousin *Montesinos. DQ's descent into the cave was probably suggested by two earlier episodes: DQ's description of the underwater adventure of the Knight of the Lake in I, 50, and

the Knight of the Mirrors (Sansón Carrasco) when he described his descent into the Chasm of Cabra in II, 14. DQ's dream vision in this cave in *DQ* II, 22–23, which consists of elements from both Carolingian and Arthurian legends (as filtered through the Spanish ballad tradition), is perhaps the most studied and discussed episode of the entire novel. The absurd and prosaic, when not grotesque, details of the dream that DQ recounts—the weight of Durandarte's heart, the salt used to keep the heart from smelling bad, Durandarte's inane comment 'Patience and shuffle the cards,' Belerma's large turban and yellowish complexion, DT's attendant asking DQ for money, and so forth—all spoil what could have been a perfectly elegant literary fantasy not disturbed by crude reality, which is suggestively revealing of DQ's state of mind. Scholars have proposed a variety of sources for the elements of the dream, primarily from the romances of chivalry (especially *Las sergas de Esplandián* and *Espejo de príncipes y caballeros*). The dream itself has provided rich material for analysis according to Freudian and Lacanian psychoanalytic theory. CHB's comment on the events of the cave in II, 24, lends ambiguity and absurdity to the episode. DQ is plagued by the experience (which he insists was not a dream, but reality) when he asks Maese Pedro's divining ape if what happened there was true (II, 25) and repeats the question to the enchanted head in Barcelona (II, 62). After SP tells of his adventures among the stars after the ride on Clavileño (II, 41), DQ takes his squire aside and rather pathetically proposes a bargain: he will believe SP's lie if SP believes his version of his own experiences in the cave. See also *DQ* II, 18, 29, 33–36, 55, 59, 60.

Bibliography: Peter N. Dunn, "La Cueva de Montesinos, por fuera y por dentro. Dos claves: estructura épica y fisonomía," *MLN* 88 (1973): 190–202; Harry Sieber, "Literary Time in the 'Cueva de Montesinos,' " *MLN* 86 (1971): 268–73; Henry Sullivan, *Grotesque Purgatory: A Study of Cervantes's "Don Quixote," Part II* (University Park: Pennsylvania State University Press, 1996); and Diana de Armas Wilson, "Cervantes and the Night Visitors: Dream Work in the Cave of Montesinos," in *Quix-*

otic Desire: Psychoanalytic Perspectives on Cervantes, ed. Ruth Anthony El Saffar and Diana de Armas Wilson (Ithaca, NY: Cornell University Press, 1993), 59–80.

Cave of Salamanca [Cueva de Salamanca]. The University of Salamanca. Because of the aura of mystery and magic that sometimes surrounded higher education, and because of a tradition of exaggerating the marvels studied at the university, the institution came to be represented as a mysterious cave in which the magical arts were studied. Also, according to legend, there was a cave near the city in which the devil himself taught magical arts to university students. Juan *Ruiz de Alarcón also wrote a play entitled *La cueva de Salamanca* about the legend. See *Cueva*.

Caybán. A renegade used by Juan *Blanco de Paz to inform *Hassan Pasha that MC was again attempting to escape from Algiers (for the fourth time) in 1579.

Cayo Mario. In *Numancia*, a Roman officer under Scipio. He is based on the historical figure of Gaius *Marius.

Caza, Calle de la. *Calle de la Caza.

Cazadores. *Hunters.

Cazalla (de la Sierra). A town located northeast of Seville and west of Córdoba, well-known for its wines. See *Doncellas*; *Elección*; *Entretenida* 3; *Rufián* 1; *Vidriera*.

Ceballos, María de. The servant who lived with MC and his family in Valladolid in 1604–6.

Ceballos Quintana, Enrique. Spanish writer. Ceballos's novel *El Quijote de los siglos* (1876; *The Quixote of Centuries*) uses *DQ* to express politically progressive ideas, particularly in favor of the working class and women. A starving schoolteacher, Calleja, loses his mind and is sent to a madhouse, where he conceives of the nineteenth century as the DQ of centuries and himself as the century's SP. The idea is that the nineteenth century quixotically tilts at major social problems but is ineffective in solving them. As poor Callejas loses his mind, his daughter, the beautiful Ernestina, is seduced and left to turn to prostitution. Prostitution, in fact, is a major preoccupation of the author's, and several pages are devoted specifically to a diatribe against this problem.

Bibliography: Enrique Ceballos Quintana, *El Quijote de los siglos* (Madrid: M. Minuesa, 1876).

Cebrián. In *Gallardo* 1, the Muslim servant of Alimuzel.

Ceca. The name of the mosque in Córdoba; it is used in the phrase "de Ceca en Meca" in the sense of 'from one place to another,' as it is by SP in *DQ* I, 18.

Ceceo. A kind of lisp. It consists in misusing the *ce-* sound in cases where *se-* would be more appropriate. It is often used by gypsies in speaking with nongypsies. See *Gitanilla*; *Pedro* 1.

Céfalo y Pocris. *Cephalus and Procris.

Céfiro. *Zephyr.

Cejudo, Doctor Miguel. Spanish poet. He was the cousin of Bernardo de Balbuena, a knight in the Order of Calatrava, a humanist, and a minor poet. He is cited among the list of good poets in *Parnaso* 2.

Celaya, Gabriel (Rafael Gabriel Múgica Celaya, 1911–). Spanish poet and novelist. Celaya's best-known poem relating to the works of MC is "A Sancho Panza" ("To Sancho Panza") from his book *Cantos iberos* (1955; *Iberian Songs*), perhaps his most important social statement. In a striking series of images, the fairly long poem sings the praise of SP as a symbol of the Spanish people. In Celaya's *Lázaro calla* (1949; *Lazarus Becomes Quiet*), the protagonist Lázaro is dissatisfied enough with his routine life that he quits his job, inspired by thoughts of liberty and heroism. Somewhat like Saul *Bellow's Henderson, however, Lázaro wants, but does not know quite what it is that he wants. The frustration and anguish he feels is reminiscent of the condition of Alonso Quixano in I, 1.

Bibliography: Gabriel Celaya, *Cantos iberos* (Alicante, Spain: Verbo, 1955); and Gabriel Celaya, *Lázaro calla* (San Sebastián, Spain: Escelicer, 1949).

Celestina, La. *Rojas, Fernando de.

Celia. 1. In *Laberinto* 1, a character who is mentioned once as the intended bride of Anastasio. **2**. The woman to whom MC's friend Antonio *Veneziani wrote a series of love poems. MC contributed a prefatory poem (*Poesías* 9) for the (unpublished) work.

Celia. *Veneziani, Antonio.

Celio. One of the hills of Rome. See *Vidriera*.

Celos. *Jealousy.

Celoso extremeño, El (Celoso); The Jealous Old Man from Extremadura. The seventh story in *Novelas*. One of the most interesting novelas in the collection, *Celoso* exists in two forms. In addition to the one published, there exists an earlier version discovered in the eighteenth century in the *Porras de la Cámara collection. There are three substantial differences between the two versions. First, in the Porras version the young wife's name is Isabela, whereas in the *Novelas* version it is Leonora, a change made, perhaps, in order to avoid any possible suggestion of a reference to King Felipe II and his young wife Isabel de Valois. Second, in the Porras version Leonora and Loaysa engage in sex, whereas in the *Novelas* version they do not. The second version is less plausible, and it has been conjectured that MC might have made the important change after the reaction of the cardinal who read the original version or because of a fear of censorship. Third, in the Porras version Loaysa joins the army and is killed, whereas in the *Novelas* version he goes to the New World, as Carrizales had done in his own youth. Thus, the cycle of profligate youth and jealous old man may be beginning all over again. The story is a remarkable psychological study of an old man obsessed with jealousy. His extraordinary ef-

forts to keep his innocent young wife secluded from and ignorant of the world are doomed to failure. The house in the story is simultaneously a convent, a jail, a harem, and a fortress; binary oppositions are set up for in/out, young/old, confinement/freedom, and the usual appearance/reality. The portraits of the black slave Luis (although tinged with blatant racism), the frivolous but wily youth Loaysa, and the innocent Leonora are among MC's best.

Felipo de Carrizales, son of an *hidalgo* from Extremadura, spent his youth and fortune frivolously, and at the age of 48 set out for the Indies to gain a fortune. Successful after 20 years, he returns home and settles in Seville, where he finds that all of his old friends have died. Desirous of having someone to whom he can leave his fortune, he decides to marry. One day, while walking along a street, he sees a beautiful young woman at a window and thinks that she might be a likely candidate for marriage. He negotiates with the woman's poor but noble parents, who are impressed by his wealth and generosity, and give their assent to the marriage, even though their daughter Leonora is just over 13 years old, some 55 years his junior. As the marriage is arranged Carrizales, an obsessively jealous man, cannot consent to anyone's touching his wife-to-be, so he finds a substitute with her exact build to act as a model for the many dresses he commissions for her. Then he buys and prepares a house with a large interior patio with several orange trees for his new bride. He modifies an entry into the house with enough room for a hayloft, but separated from the rest of the house by a locked door. In this space he places an elderly black slave named Luis, a eunuch, who lives in this small area between two locked doors. Carrizales elevates the walls of the house so that those inside can see nothing but the sky, and he installs a turnaround between the entryway and the house for the transfer of goods. He furnishes the house very lavishly, but permanently boards up all windows that have a view of the outside world. He employs four white and two black slaves, an experienced *dueña*, and two other young girls about Leonora's age. He arranges for supplies to be delivered in bulk from time to time. Into this context, he introduces his innocent bride. He lectures everyone on the iron-clad rule that no one, under any circumstance, is to be allowed into the house beyond the second locked door. He promises the women that they can regularly attend mass, but only at the very earliest hours of the day when the streets are nearly deserted. Carrizales is so insistent on maintaining the innocence of his wife that even the cats and dogs allowed into the house must be female; he insists that no story be told that has any lascivious content. For a year, the household lives under these circumstances.

There is in Seville a group of people, called *gente de barrio* (neighborhood folk), who live a frivolous and carefree life. One of these, a *virote* named Loaysa, becomes curious about the inhabitants of the closed house. With the help of a couple of friends, Loaysa devises a plan: he dresses poorly, trims his beard, covers one eye, feigns a limp and walks with crutches, and carries a guitar. Stationing himself outside Carrizales's house, he begins to play and sing, primarily for the benefit of Luis, who, like blacks in general, is very fond of music. They begin to talk through the locked door and Loaysa offers to give Luis music lessons, but Luis explains that he is locked in and cannot have direct contact with anyone. Since Luis will do anything to become a better musician, he agrees to the suggestion that they remove the door from its hinges in order to let Loaysa in to the loft area. Within a couple of days, and with the help of his friends, Loaysa enters into Luis's area of the house and begins to give him guitar lessons at night. The next day, when Carrizales leaves the house, Luis begins to strum the guitar and this awakens the curiosity of the women inside. That night he has Loaysa play for all the slaves and servants (Leonora is in bed with her husband), and they all enjoy the music. The next night Leonora joins the group, and they are all allowed to take turns looking through a hole in order to see the charming musician (now well dressed, and no longer in his rags). Loaysa has his friends bring him an unguent that can cause a deep and prolonged sleep, and Leonora applies it to the sleeping Carrizales. Then she retrieves the key from un-

der the mattress and lets Loaysa enter, but only after he swears to do nothing inappropriate. Before Loaysa is permitted into the house, the *dueña*, whose name is Marialonso, informs him that everyone (except Leonora) is a virgin, and that he must respect their purity. Loaysa swears, in an elaborate oath, that he will do so. Leonora joins the group, leaving the black slave Guiomar as a guardian, in case Carrizales should awaken. All the women look Loaysa over carefully and praise every aspect of his appearance. Then he sings a currently popular song, to everyone's enjoyment. Just then Guiomar arrives, warning them that Carrizales is awake. Everyone hides, and Marialonso places Loaysa in her own room. Luis takes the guitar and hides in the hayloft, covered with a blanket and trembling with fear, but still lightly strumming the guitar. Once it is determined that this is a false alarm, Marialonso tries, unsuccessfully, to proposition Loaysa. Then, rather than resume the festivities, Marialonso sends all the slaves and servants to their quarters and persuades Leonora to spend the night with Loaysa in her room. Leonora agrees, but manages to resist Loaysa's amorous advances, and the two fall asleep in each other's arms. After a while, Carrizales does wake up and, not finding his wife in his bed or the key under the mattress, goes in search of Leonora, finding her sleeping with Loaysa in Marialonso's room. He returns to his bedroom for a dagger with which to avenge his honor, but collapses on the bed in a faint. Leonora and the rest think that the unguent is still having its effect, and that they have not been discovered. Upon awakening, however, Carrizales asks Leonora to summon her parents, and when they arrive, he explains that he is near death. He tells them that he has discovered the two young lovers in bed together (at this point, Leonora faints). But then he admits that everything is his fault rather than hers; he constructed the house of his own dishonor, and he takes all responsibility. Leonora, he states, should, upon his death, marry the young man with whom she spent the night. He remakes his will, doubling Leonora's inheritance, assuring her parents that they will have sufficient funds for the rest of their lives, rewarding

generously all the servants (except the pernicious Marialonso), and granting the slaves their
freedom. Leonora tells him that although she
was tempted by Loaysa, she offended her husband only in thought and not in deed. But
within a few days, Carrizales dies. Leonora, a
rich widow, chooses not to marry Loaysa, but
to enter a convent. Loaysa, disappointed, departs for the Indies. The narrator brings the
story to a close, citing it as an example of how
little one can trust in keys and prisons when
one's will remains free, but he cannot understand why Leonora did not insist more on her
innocence.

Bibliography: Shifra Armon, "The Paper Key:
Money as Text in Cervantes's *El celoso extremeño*
and José de Camerino's *El pícaro amante*," *Cervantes* 18, no. 1 (1998): 96–114; Nina Cox Davis, "Marriage and Investment in *El celoso extremeño*,"
Romanic Review 86 (1995): 639–55; Myriam
Yvonne Jehenson, "Quixotic Desires or Stark Reality?" *Cervantes* 15, no. 2 (1995): 26–42; Paul Lewis-
Smith, "The Two Versions of *El Celoso Extremeño*:
On the Questions of Authorship and Intent," *Neo-
philologus* 76 (1992): 559–68; Maurice Molho,
"Aproximación al *Celoso Extremeño*," *Nueva Revista de Filología Hispánica* 38 (1990): 743–92; Emilia Navarro, "To Read the Bride: Silence and Elision
in Cervantes' *The Jealous Extremaduran*," *Novel: A
Forum on Fiction* 22 (1989): 326–37; Helena Percas
de Ponseti, "El 'misterio escondido' en *El celoso extremeño*," *Cervantes* 14; no. 2 (1994): 137–53;
Mario Ritter, "Perspective and Frames: The Exem-
plarity of *El celoso extremeño*," *RLA: Romance Languages Annual* 10 (1998): 807–14; Alison Weber,
"Tragic Reparation in Cervantes' *El celoso extremeño*," *Cervantes* 4, no. 1 (1984): 35–51; and Edwin
Williamson, "El 'misterio escondido' en *El celoso
extremeño*: una aproximación al arte de Cervantes,"
Nueva Revista de Filología Hispánica 38 (1990):
793–815.

Cenotia (Zenotia). In *Persiles* II, 8–9, a
Morisca sorceress or enchanter who has been
driven out of Spain by the Inquisition and who
is an advisor to King Policarpo of Scinta. She
offers herself to Antonio the younger, who rejects her advances and tries to shoot her, but
his arrow misses and kills Clodio instead. Cenotia vows revenge and places a spell on Antonio, who falls very ill. In II, 11, Antonio the

Barbarian threatens and intimidates Cenotia,
making her lift the spell on his son. Cenotia
then lobbies Policarpo to punish Antonio the
younger and not permit the travelers to leave
the island. Finally, in II, 17, she helps Policarpo
(who is in love with Auristela), devise a plot to
fake an emergency, set the palace on fire, and
steal their loved ones. The plot fails, Periandro
and the others all escape, and the people of
Scinta revolt and depose Policarpo—and hang
Cenotia.

Censorship. Governments, churches, and
other organizations censor speech and literature
because they fear that the spoken and/or written
word can empower the masses to think for
themselves instead of automatically receiving
and endorsing the entrenched ideology. In
Spain, the establishment of the Inquisition in
1478 put into place one of the most powerful
censoring structures in history. The number of
conversos who suffered persecution and punishment because of what they did or said, or
were reputed to have done or said, was quite
large. The occasional *autos-da-fé*, which rarely
featured the public burning of heretics, were the
most dramatic manifestations of this facet of
life under censorship and repression. Nothing
enables the solitary individual to think for him-
or herself as much as does a book; it was the
invention and dissemination of printing, as
much as anything, that made possible the Protestant Reformation that so shook Spain and the
rest of Europe in the sixteenth century. It was
natural that the desire to control what can be
read led to measures to censor writing. The Inquisition issued lists of banned books in 1551,
1558, and 1559 (*Index of Forbidden Books*).
The earliest lists did not include any works of
Spanish literature, but by 1559 works such as
Lazarillo de Tormes and some of the writings
of figures as prominent as *Erasmus, the *Valdés brothers, and Fray Luis de *Granada were
included. In 1558 an edict made the importation
of foreign books illegal. Sometimes works of
literature were not prohibited but merely ex-
purgated or sanitized in subsequent printings;
the title of the 1574 censored edition of *Lazarillo*, for example, was *Lazarillo castigado* (*La-

zarillo Chastised). By the late-sixteenth century, a complicated governmental machinery was in place to regulate publication of new material (*Preliminaries). Censorship must have had the effect of making writers of the time wary of official intervention and reluctant to deal with certain topics. Yet the age that produced the greatest poetry, drama, and prose fiction of all times in the Spanish language can hardly be characterized as one severely inhibited by (at least the threat of) censorship. One could even argue that censorship made a positive contribution, in the sense that, as Leo Strauss has proposed, it encouraged a kind of 'writing between the lines' in such a way that the censors found no objection to the literal content but those in the know understood an unstated (or ambiguous) textual meaning. MC appears never to have had any difficulty in receiving printing permission for any of his books, and in one case, the approval written by the Licentiate *Márquez Torres for *DQ* II, contains special extended praise. But MC did have some minor brushes with censorship. In some editions of *DQ*, beginning in 1616, the passage from I, 26, in which the penitent knight fashions a makeshift rosary from his shirttail and recites 'a million' prayers, and the statement by the duchess in II, 36, 'works of charity done weakly and in a lukewarm fashion have no merit and are not worth anything,' were both censored; they were officially suppressed by the Inquisition in 1632. In 1624 the Portuguese Inquisition censored several passages: *DQ*'s Petrarchan description of DT in *DQ* I, 13, in which he refers to 'those parts of her body hidden from human eyes'; a long passage in I, 16, when DQ talks with and then gets involved in the fight over *Maritornes in the inn; a brief passage in I, 20, when DQ commends himself to DT; a sentence in II, 17, when DQ says 'hundreds' of prayers over the concoction he calls the balm de Fierabrás, together with the words 'most holy' a little later on in the same chapter; and a long passage in I, 28, where Dorotea describes her seduction by Fernando. MC—or, at least, some of his characters—seem to approve of censorship, however. The culmination of DQ's first sally is the scrutiny of his library in I, 6, by the priest and barber, which results in the burning of many of his books. The illiterate niece and housekeeper are particularly fearful of the power of the printed word, as the former refers to the books as 'heretics' that deserve to be burned in an auto-da-fé. In *DQ* I, 47–48, the Canon of Toledo and Pero Pérez engage in an extended discussion of literature in general and theater in particular. The canon offers the opinion that there should be a censor for the theater and perhaps a second one for the romances of chivalry. In fact, in 1615, the Council of Castile did rule that works of theater be submitted to censor. Overall, the most regulative and prescriptive characters in MC novel are the representatives of the Church—the priest, the canon, and the household priest of II, 31–32.

Bibliography: Angel Alcalá, ed., *The Spanish Inquisition and the Inquisitorial Mind* (Boulder, CO: Social Science Monographs, 1987); Américo Castro, "Cervantes y la Inquisición," in *Hacia Cervantes* (Madrid: Taurus, 1957), 159–66; José García Oro, *Los reyes y los libros: la política libraria de la Corona en el Siglo de Oro, 1475–1598* (Madrid: Cisneros, 1995); Henry Kamen, *The Spanish Inquisition: A Historical Revision* (New Haven, CT: Yale University Press, 1998); José López Navío, "Sobre la frase de la duquesa: 'Las obras de caridad hechas floja y tíbiamente' (*Don Quijote*, 2, 36)," *Anales Cervantinos* 9 (1961–62): 97–112; Virgilio Pinto Crespo, *Inquisición y control ideológico en la España del siglo XVI* (Madrid: Taurus, 1983); and Leo Strauss, *Persecution and the Art of Writing* (Glencoe, IL: Free Press, 1952).

Centeno, Pedro (1730–1803). Spanish Augustinian priest and writer. Centeno wrote a stinging attack on Jacinto María *Delgado's *Adiciones . . .* and then, writing under the pseudonym of Eugenio Habela Patiño, he published *El Teniente del Apologista universal*, no. 1 (1788; *Lieutenant to the Universal Apologist*), which contains the "Primera salida de D. Quixote el Segundo, alias el Escolástico" ("First Sally of Don Quixote the Second, alias the Scholar"), an attack on Juan Pablo Forner in the guise of a Cervantine imitation. A year later, using the same pseudonym, Centeno published a sequel: *Apéndice á la primera salida de Don Quixote el Escolástico* (1789; *Appendix to the First Sally of Don Quixote the Scholar*).

Bibliography: Eugenio Habela Patiño, *El Teniente del Apologista Universal* (Madrid: D. Antonio Espinosa, 1789).

Centinelas. *Sentinels.

Centopiés. In *Rinconete*, a character who is mentioned by la Pipota but does not appear in the work.

Centro Cervantino. *Toboso, El.

Centro de Estudios Cervantinos. Begun in 1990, with its center of operations in Alcalá de Henares, this very active organization under the direction of Manuel Alvar has sponsored international conferences, exhibitions, and concerts, as well as established an active publishing program. The Centro publishes not only important scholarly works on MC and his works, but has also initiated a superb series of texts of the romances of chivalry (the series is entitled "Los libros de Rocinante") and a parallel series of introductory studies of those romances ("Guías de lectura caballeresca"), and has sponsored the publication of the complete works of MC, edited by Antonio Rey Hazas and Florencio Sevilla Arroyo, consisting of both text and CD-Rom.

Cepeda, Baltasar de (?–1560). A minor poet and dramatist mentioned in *Parnaso* 7.

Cepeda y Ahumada, Teresa. *Saint Teresa de Jesús.

Cephalus and Procris [Céfalo y Pocris]. In Greek myth, husband and wife. She, thinking her husband is unfaithful to her, hides in the bush, and he, thinking she is an animal he is hunting, accidentally kills her with a spear. See *Persiles* III, 2.

Cerberus (Infernal Three-Headed Guardian of the Gate) [Cerbero (Portero infernal de los tres rostros)]. In Greek myth, the three-headed dog whose duty it was to guard the entrance to the underworld, both in order to keep the dead from leaving and the living from entering. See *DQ* I, 14; *Numancia* 2.

Cerco de Numancia, El. *Numancia, La.

Cerdas. A Castilian family name mentioned in *DQ* I, 13. In *Parnaso* 5, the same family name is again cited, but in this context it is intended as a humorous way of avoiding use of the word *cerdo* (pig).

Cerdeña. *Sardinia.

Ceres (Goddess of the crops [Diosa de las mieses]). In Roman myth, a divinity who represented the regenerative power of nature (more or less the equivalent of Demeter in Greek myth). She was identified with fertility, abundance, and the harvest and was the goddess of wheat and grain. MC alludes to the myth that her daughter Persephone was raped by Hades, god of the Underworld. Ceres (Demeter) searched throughout the world for her daughter, neglecting her duties, with the result that the earth became barren. In order to appease her, Hades agreed to release Persephone for part of each year, clearly an allegory of the cycle of planting, growth, and harvest. See *Entretenida* 2; *Numancia* 2; *Persiles* I, 5.

Cerlone, Francesco (1730–1817). Italian writer. Cerlone is the author of a play entitled *Lo zingaro per amore* (1775; *The Gypsy for Loving*), based on *Gitanilla*.

Cernícalo. A law officer mentioned in *Rinconete*.

Cerro Gordo. A hill in Algeria, located near the city of Mostaganem. See *Tratos* 3.

Cervantes and America. MC twice applied for positions in the Spanish colonies of the New World, in 1582 and 1590, but was denied permission to emigrate on both occasions. We can only imagine how the literatures of Spain and Spanish America might have been changed had his requests been granted. The only work of MC's that takes place in any of Spain's possessions in the New World is *Rufián*, in which the first act takes place in Seville, but the last two in Mexico, where the protagonist, previously a sinner, has become an exemplary Christian saint and martyr. In *Celoso*, the protagonist Carrizales is an **Indiano* who returns wealthy to Spain and sets up his house in Seville; at the end of the story, the young seducer Loaysa also departs for the New World. Occasional brief references to aspects of America are scattered throughout MC's works, however, and there is a surprising number of American words that appear in his works. MC clearly read one of the major works on the Spanish in the conquest of the Araucanian Indians, Alonso de **Ercilla's* epic poem, *La Araucana*, which is spared from the flames in the examination of DQ's library in I, 6. Furthermore, it has recently been suggested that a deep concern with America is a constant subtext that informs almost everything MC wrote, especially *DQ* and *Persiles*.

Bibliography: James D. Fernández, "The Bonds of Patrimony: Cervantes and the New World," *PMLA* 109 (1994): 969–81; Barry W. Ife, "The Literary Impact of the New World: Columbus to Carrizales," *Journal of the Institute of Romance Studies* 3 (1994): 65–85; and Diana de Armas Wilson, *Cervantes, the Novel, and the New World* (Oxford: Oxford University Press, 2000).

Cervantes and the canon.

Is *DQ* the greatest work of literature of all time? It is according to the results of a spring 2002 poll of 100 writers worldwide conducted by the Norwegian Book Club. Each of the writers was asked to list the ten works of imaginative literature that he or she thought were the best of all time. *DQ* came out as the clear first choice, outdistancing the runner-up (**Proust's Recherche du temps perdu*) by over 50 percent. This informal and unofficial writers' poll thus places *DQ* at the core of the canon, a very disputed concept. Popularity polls, however, even those of a prestigious group of writers, hardly provide a meaningful way to assess quality (consider the example of political polls), and perhaps little stock should be placed in this one.

The canon wars of recent decades—the effort by some to dislodge the Great White Males from their privileged place in the patriarchal and arbitrary power structure known as the canon—have often been carried out in the name of gender, ethnic equality, and multiculturalism. Sometimes this is done under the rubric of dubious theories about power and language; not infrequently, however, the supposedly altruistic canon-busting efforts mask an insidious presentism, an ahistorical effort to level the playing ground by eliminating the past and reading virtually nothing but works from the twentieth century (**great time*). In fact, much good has come from opening up reading lists and literary anthologies to previously little-read women and minorities. As in society itself, inclusion in the study of literature is always preferable to exclusion. But if the canon has been opened up and expanded, there are certain writers from the past who remain well entrenched in their positions as "classics." First and foremost among these is Shakespeare, for canon enthusiasts like Harold Bloom, the writer who stands alone at the heart of the Western canon. Following behind the Bard, according to Bloom, we find Dante, Chaucer, MC, and Milton (along with the ancient Torah, the Gospels, and Homer); and then come others with varying degrees of centrality, importance, and universality. Bloom's list, heavily weighted toward English writers, might be balanced by a look at a frequency count for authors included in the annual bibliography published by the Modern Language Society of America (note that this bibliography does not include the literature of antiquity, so the roles of Homer, Virgil, or the Bible are not be included). It turns out that among active literary scholars, Shakespeare is in fact in a class by himself as the subject of over 600 scholarly studies per year in the final decade of the twentieth century. A second group, made up of those (non-English) writers who are the subject of over 100 studies annually, consists of Dante, MC, and Goethe. These four writers—one Englishman, one Italian, one Spaniard, and one German—arguably form the essential minimal core of the Western canon, the authors who are the defining figures of the Western tradition. But one can make a special case for MC in this group, a case that his position is at least as unique as that of his contemporary, Shakespeare. If one takes a Bakhtinian approach to the **theory* and history of the novel, the novel emerges as the dominant genre of modern times, the genre that redefines all other genres, and the genre that best expresses the modern sentiment. In that view, MC stands virtually alone (Rabelais is there too, to an extent) as the prototypical exemplar of the new genre: the first and also the best. Since, as Bakhtin maintains, all traditional genres, most explicitly including lyric and epic poetry and the theater, have their origins in the distant past, writers like Dante, Milton, or Shakespeare cannot in any way be considered the first poet or dramatist in the way that MC is considered the first novelist. If the best practitioners of all kinds of novels—comic, realist, and postmodern—trace their roots back to MC, then the author of *DQ* is the central figure in the tradition of the novel in all times and all places. Today the novel is the hegemonic genre in literature in general; epic poetry is moribund, lyric poetry is increasingly a minority (and, too often, an elitist) enterprise, and theater (more a multimedia performance activity than a literary one) is dwarfed by film and television. To no small extent, whether we like it or not, literature *is* the novel. If all this is true, then, as Bakhtin would implicitly suggest, no writer anywhere can be more central to the canon, to literature, than MC. Maybe the writers polled by the Norwegian Book Clubs were right after all.

Bibliography: Harold Bloom, *The Western Canon: The Books and School of the Ages* (New York: Harcourt Brace, 1994); and "*Don Quixote* Gets Authors' Votes," Reuters, May 7, 2002.

Cervantes, Andrea de (1544–1609). Older sister of MC. In Seville, Andrea became the lover of Nicolás de Ovando, and her daughter of this union, Constanza de *Ovando, was MC's favorite niece and a member of his household in later years. In 1569 Andrea received an extravagant gift (clothing, jewels, cash, and so on) from an Italian banker named Gian Francesco Locadelo. It is generally assumed that the gift was for (sexual) services rendered. Later she worked as a dressmaker or seamstress in order to support her daughter. In the 1590s she married an Italian businessman named Santi *Ambrosio. With her sister Magdalena, she moved to Valladolid, then the site of the royal court, in 1603; the next year they

were joined by MC. In 1606 she moved back to Madrid with MC and the rest of the family. In 1609 she (along with MC's wife Catalina de *Palacios, and following shortly after her sister Magdalena) took the habit of the Third Order of Saint Francis; on that occasion, she claimed to be the widow of one General Alvaro Mendaño, a complete fabrication. Shortly thereafter, in the same year, Andrea suddenly died of a fever.

Cervantes, Andrés de (?–ca. 1587). Oldest son of Juan de *Cervantes, and uncle of MC. He married well and settled in the town of Cabra, in Andalusia, where he remained for the rest of his life and where, for some years, he served as mayor.

Cervantes, Andrés de (1543). Older brother of MC who died in his infancy.

Cervantes as author. The author is dead, or, at best, merely a function of the text; and besides, the very concept of an "author" is an eighteenth-century invention. Such, at least, are some of the fashionable positions taken by some contemporary literary theorists and critics (*poststructuralist and postmodernist readings of *Don Quixote*). But it is difficult to imagine a writer more conscious of his role as author than MC, who played self-conscious games with the concept of author so that we would realize that the author is anything but dead. In the prologue to *DQ* I (1605), for example, he uses the metaphors AUTHOR IS PARENT and BOOK IS CHILD, and then playfully calls himself not the father but stepfather of *DQ*. In the prologue to *Novelas* (1613), MC paints his verbal portrait and dubs it that of the face of the author of *Galatea, DQ* I, and *Parnaso*; and he states with pride that he is the first to have written *novelas* in Spanish. In *Parnaso* 4 (1614), MC makes a partial inventory of his literary works and stresses his originality and inventiveness. In *Comedias* (1615), he calls attention to his role as author of theatrical works in the 1580s. In the prologue to *DQ* II (1615), he takes offense at the ad hominem criticism leveled at him by the author of *DQA*, relates two short anecdotes about what it takes to write a book, and insists that only his is the true continuation of *DQ* I because it was 'cut from the same cloth and by the same artisan' as was the first volume. In the prologue to *Persiles* (1617), MC relates an anecdote of a student who recognizes him and praises his fame as an author. MC was an author in all meaningful senses of the word, and he was very much aware of the fact.

Bibliography: Asun Bernárdez, *Don Quijote, el lector por excelencia* (*Lectores y lectura como estrategias de comunicación*) (Madrid: Huerga y Fierro, 2000).

Cervantes, Calle de. *Calle de Cervantes.

Cervantes de Gaete, Feliciana. A relative of MC's who may be the model for *Feliciana de la Voz in *Persiles*.

Cervantes, escape attempts of. During his captivity in Algiers in 1575–80, MC organized and led no fewer than four attempts to escape. The first was early in 1576 when he and a small group of colleagues simply attempted to walk through the desert to the Spanish possession of Oran (somewhat over 200 miles from Algiers). They were guided by a Muslim who knew the route but who simply abandoned them a few days into the trip; the prisoners had no recourse but to turn back to Algiers. MC was chained and beaten but not killed, as was often the custom with those who attempted to run away from captivity; it is generally assumed that his high ransom price convinced his owner, Dalí Mamí, to spare his life. This episode is dramatically represented in the figure of *Pedro Alvarez in *Tratos*. The second attempt to escape came a year later, in 1577, and involved the participation of MC's recently ransomed brother Rodrigo. This time MC and 14 others enlisted the aid of a Christian gardener to hide out (for about five months) in a cave just outside the city until Rodrigo could arrange for a ship to be sent for them. The fugitives were to meet the ship on September 28 (the eve of MC's birthday), but they waited in vain for two nights. At this point a Spanish renegade named El *Dorador, who had been providing MC and his companions with supplies, feared detection

and betrayed the plot to *Hassan Pasha, the newly appointed king of Algiers. (It turned out that the rescue sailors had been spotted by sentinels and had to weigh anchor and depart without the captives.) MC appeared before Hassan Pasha and took sole responsibility for the incident. Again, astonishingly, MC was not executed, but merely confined to chains for some five months. The only person who paid with his life was the Christian gardener. MC's third attempt to escape took place in 1578. This time he secretly sent a Muslim envoy to Oran with a letter addressed to Don Martín de *Córdoba, general of the Spanish garrison there, with an appeal for help. But the envoy was captured at the gates of Oran and returned to Algiers, where he was executed. Hassan ordered that MC be given 2,000 blows (traditionally administered to the belly and soles of the feet), virtually a death sentence. But, for reasons unknown, the order was never carried out. There has been a great deal of unfounded speculation about the reason why MC might have been treated so leniently (for example, his ransom value, a love affair with the daughter of an influential resident of the city, and his homosexual relationship with his master). The fourth and final escape attempt took place in September 1579. MC arranged for a Spanish renegade to conspire with a Valencian merchant named Onofre *Exarque to purchase an armed vessel to take him and a number of other prisoners to safety. This effort might have been successful if it had not been denounced by Juan *Blanco de Paz, a Spanish Dominican priest who apparently was resentful that he had not been included in the escape party. Blanco de Paz sent word to Hassan Pasha via a renegade known as Caybán. This time Hassan Pasha sentenced MC to death by hanging and had him led to the scaffold with a rope around his neck and his hands tied behind his back. But once again he was spared (apparently the intervention of an influential renegade known as *Maltrapillo was an important factor) and spent the next five months in chains and under heavy guard. By all accounts, MC repeatedly demonstrated extraordinary courage, generosity, and bravery during all of these failed escape attempts; the statements to this effect by witnesses and participants in the events ring true. MC was respected by friend and foe alike; Antonio de *Sosa remarks at one point that Hassan Pasha once remarked that 'as long as the maimed Spaniard was under guard, all his Christian slaves, his ships, and the city itself were safe.' The reason why so much is known about these escape attempts is that extensive documentation exists in the historical account written by Sosa and the notarized depositions contained in *Información de Argel*.

Bibliography: María Antonia Garcés, *Cervantes in Algiers: A Captive's Tale* (Nashville, TN: Vanderbilt University Press, 2002); and Emilio Sola, and José F. de la Peña, *Cervantes y la Berbería: Cervantes, mundo turco-berberisco y servicios secretos en la época de Felipe II* (México City: Fondo de Cultura Económica, 1995).

Cervantes family. MC's ancestry may well have originated in Galicia (in northwest Spain; *Mena, Juan de) and migrated to Andalusia by the sixteenth century. MC's grandfather, Juan de Cervantes, was a cloth merchant in Córdoba, who resettled the family in Alcalá de Henares. Many scholars assume that the prominence of trades (draper and cloth merchant), jobs (tax collector), and professions (barber-surgeon) in the family are a clear indication of a *converso* lineage. The further fact that no evidence exists that might prove *hidalguía* (membership in the *hidalgo* class of *nobility) or Old Christian status in the Cervantes clan is in itself a strong indication that purity of blood was lacking, as most true aristocrats proudly displayed evidence of their status, whereas those with a past that was less than purely Christian often remained silent on the subject. In 1569, when MC requested from his father a statement of Old Christian status while in Rome (perhaps in order to secure employment), the document that was prepared was full of ambiguity, equivocation, and hearsay deposition; it was far short of the typical official documentation of *purity of blood common in the epoch. Again, later when he sought release from debtor's prison as an *hidalgo*, he provided only recent and minimal proof of that status, with some witnesses who affirmed that his father and grandfather had

'been thought to be' gentlemen. Most of the women in the family—MC's sisters Andrea and Magdalena, his niece Constanza, and his daughter Isabel—never married well, were involved in affairs with married and moneyed men, and lived more by their wits than by their status. The mere fact that none of them had a conventional marriage is in itself suggestive of a lack of social status and dowry. MC's literary texts deal frequently and ambiguously with the theme of purity of blood, but never in such a way as to provide definitive evidence one way or another. Thus, although there is no absolute proof that the Cervantes family was of *converso* origin, it seems more likely than not.

The family died out in the seventeenth century, as MC's brother Rodrigo died in 1600, his sister Andrea in 1609, Magdalena in 1611, MC himself in 1616, and Luisa in 1620. His only niece, Constanza (illegitimate daughter of Andrea), died childless in 1622. MC's own illegitimate daughter, Isabel, died childless (her only daughter, the illegitimate baby Isabel, died in 1609) in 1652, and with her the Cervantes line was extinguished.

Bibliography: Américo Castro, *Cervantes y los casticismos españoles* (Madrid: Alianza Editorial, 1966); Ellen Lokos, "The Politics of Identity and the Enigma of Cervantine Genealogy," in *Cervantes and His Postmodern Constituencies*, ed. Anne J. Cruz and Carroll B. Johnson (New York: Garland, 1999), 116–33; and Arsenio Lope Huerta, *Los Cervantes de Alcalá* (Alcalá de Henares, Spain: Centro de Estudios Cervantinos, 1998).

Cervantes in America. *DQ* was read in the English colonies in America, and the first American novels, by Hugh Henry Brackenridge, Tabitha Tenney, and so forth, are in large part imitations of *DQ*. By the nineteenth century, when American literature begins to take on substance, important writers such as Kate Chopin, Stephen Crane, Nathaniel Hawthorne, William Dean Howells, Washington Irving, Henry James, Herman Melville, and Mark Twain take no small part of their inspiration from MC. In the twentieth century, the list of MC-inspired/influenced novelists include writers as different as Kathy Acker, Paul Auster, John Barth, Saul Bellow, William Faulkner,

Bernard Malamud, Joyce Carol Oates, James Thurber, Kurt Vonnegut, and Eudora Welty. Interestingly, MC has had a particular importance for American science fiction writers such as Poul Anderson, Marcos Donnelly, Alexis Gilliland, Lee Hoffman, James McConkey, Emil Petaja, Robert Sheckley, Clifford D. Simak, and Chet Williamson.

Bibliography: Montserrat Ginés, *The Southern Inheritors of Don Quixote* (Baton Rouge: Louisiana State University Press, 2000).

Cervantes in England. *DQ* has arguably had more resonance in England than in any other country outside of Spain. The first translation of *DQ* I was Shelton's in 1612, the first allusions to *DQ* outside of Spain occur in England beginning in 1606, the first critical edition of *DQ* is the monumental edition sponsored by Lord Cateret and published in England in 1738 (it includes the first biography of MC [*biographies of Cervantes], by Gregorio Mayáns y Síscar; it is adorned with 67 illustrations by John Vanderbank; and it also includes the first graphic interpretation of MC, by Kent), and the first edition of the novel with scholarly annotation is John Bowles's in 1781. England is probably the country where there are more seventeenth-century allusions to, mentions of, and adaptations (mostly theatrical) of *DQ* and other works by MC. *DQ* saturates literary culture in eighteenth-century England; the first truly great quixotic English novels are those of Joseph Fielding and Laurence Sterne, but less famous writers such as Charlotte Lennox and Tobias Smollett were also very conscious of writing in the tradition of MC. Noteworthy nineteenth-century novelists, such as Jane Austen, Lewis Carroll, Charles Dickens, George Eliot, Walter Scott, Mary Shelley, and William Thackeray, were also profoundly influenced by *DQ*. In the twentieth century, the list of British and other English-language writers who draw inspiration from MC is also quite inclusive: Max Beerbohm, Anthony Burgess, Robin Chapman, G. K. Chesterton, Joseph Conrad, John Fowles, Graham Greene, Wyndham Lewis, Salman Rushdie, Muriel Spark, and Virginia Woolf, among others.

Bibliography: Edwin B. Knowles, "Cervantes and English Literature," in *Cervantes across the Centuries: A Quadricentennial Volume*, ed. Angel Flores and M. J. Benardete (New York: Gordian Press, 1947), 277–303; Ronald Paulson, *Don Quixote in England: The Aesthetics of Laughter* (Baltimore: Johns Hopkins University Press, 1998; and Robert ter Horst, "The Spanish Etymology of the English Novel," *Indiana Journal of Hispanic Literatures* 5 (1994): 291–307.

Cervantes in film. The first *DQ* film was a French silent movie entitled simply *Don Quichotte* (1902) by Ferdinand Zecca and Lucien Nonguet; the most recent, as of this writing, is the Spanish production for TVE (Television Español) entitled *El caballero Don Quijote* (2002; *The Knight Don Quixote*). Based on *DQ* II only, it is a sequel to its 1991 version of *DQ* I (see below), directed by Manuel Gutiérrez Aragón, with Juan Luis Galiardo as DQ, Carlos Iglesias as SP, and Marta Etura as DT. In between, there have been over 40 other attempts to bring the novel to the silver screen. Among the most noteworthy are the first *DQ* with sound (1933), in French, directed by Georg Wilhelm Pabst and starring the Russian tenor Feodor Chaliapin as DQ; the first Spanish sound film based on the novel (1947), directed by Rafael Gil, and with Rafael Rivelles as DQ and Juan Calvo as SP; the Russian *Don Kikhot* (1956; winner of the Cannes prize in 1957) directed by Grigori Kozinstev, and starring Nicolai Charkassov as DQ and Vladimir Tolubeyev as SP, considered by many to be the greatest film version of all time; the Mexican production of *Don Quijote cabalga de nuevo* (1973; *Don Quixote Rides Again*, also released as *Un Quijote sin mancha* [*A Spotless Quixote*]), directed by Roberto Gavaldón, and with the Spanish actor Fernando Fernán Gómez as DQ and the great Mexican comedian Cantinflas as SP; the film version of Dale Wasserman's musical comedy *Man of La Mancha* (1972), directed by Arthur Hiller and starring Peter O'Toole as DQ, James Coco as SP, and Sophia Loren as DT; the unfinished versions of Orson Welles and Terry Gilliam; the Spanish production for TVE of *DQ* I only (1991) directed by Manuel Gutiérrez Aragón, based on a script by

Nobel Prize–winning novelist Camilo José Cela, and starring Fernando Rey as DQ and Alfredo Landa as SP; and the TNT Original version of *DQ* directed by Peter Yates (2000), and with John Lithgow, Bob Hoskins, and Vanessa Williams as DQ, SP, and DT, respectively. In addition, there have been other films with quixotic themes and characters, such as *They Might Be Giants* (1971), Woody Allen's *The Purple Rose of Cairo* (1985), the film of Graham Greene's *Monsignor Quixote* (1988), *Toy Story* (1995), *Kissing a Fool* (1998), and *Shrek* (2001). Worth note also is the videorecording originally prepared by the British Broadcasting Company entitled *"Don Quixote": Legacy of a Classic* (1995), in which novelists such as A. S. Byatt, Carlos Fuentes, and Ben Okri, together with a variety of students and common people, reflect on the importance of *DQ* in their lives and in their own work. There are also scenes from DQ-related places in La Mancha and from several filmed versions of *DQ*.

Bibliography: *"Don Quixote": Legacy of a Classic*, videorecording (Princeton, NJ: Films for the Humanities, 1998); Robert Stam, *Reflexivity in Film and Literature: From "Don Quijote" to Jean-Luc Godard* (Ann Arbor, MI: UMI Research Press, 1985); Rafael Utrera, "*Don Quijote, Don Juan y La Celestina* vistos por el cine español," in *Actas del V Congreso de la Asociación Internacional Siglo de Oro*, ed. Christoph Strosetzki (Madrid: Iberoamericana, 2001), 1286–95; and Rafael Utrera, "El *Quijote* en cine y televisión," *Insula* (1993): 558–59.

Cervantes in France. France is only slightly behind England in its seventeenth-century adaptations of *DQ* and other works by MC. The first translation of *DQ* I into French was that of César Oudin (1614), although his translation of *Curioso* appeared six years earlier; the first translation of *DQ* II was by François Rosset (1618). But the most important and influential seventeenth-century translation was that of François Filleau de Saint-Martin, 1677–78. Filleau omitted *DQ* II, 74, the death of DQ, in order to continue the story himself, and published his sequel in 1695. This translation was not surpassed until that of Louis Viardot (1800–1883) in 1836, which is still regarded by many as the best French translation ever done. Span-

ish literature—often considered extravagant and exotic—was popular and influential in general in the seventeenth century, but no writer was more often cited, praised, imitated, and appropriated than MC, as numerous French writers made extensive use of his plots and characters, especially in the theater (Guérin de Bouscal, Hardy, Molière, and Pichou), but also in prose fiction (Lesage, Scarron, and Sorel). In the eighteenth century that influence declined somewhat, but can still be seen in the fictions of Robert Challe, Denis Diderot, Alain-René Lesage, Pierre Marivaux, and others, and in less original theatrical works of Charles-Simon Favart and Philidor. In the nineteenth century, many French novelists drew inspiration directly from *DQ*: Honoré de Balzac, Alphonse Daudet, Gustave Flaubert, Stendhal, and others. Important writers from the twentieth century whose work is quixotic to some degree include Gaston Baty, Andre Gide, Henri de Montherlant, Marcel Proust, Raymond de Queneau, and Jean-Paul Sartre.

Bibliography: Maurice Bardon, *"Don Quichotte" en France au XVIIe et au XVIIIe siècle, 1605–1815*, 2 vols. (Paris: Honoré Champion, 1931); J. J. A. Bertrand, "Génesis de la concepción romántica de Don Quijote en Francia," *Anales Cervantinos* 3 (1953): 1–41; 4 (1954): 41–76; 5 (1955–56): 79–142; and Esther J. Crooks, *The Influence of Cervantes in France in the Seventeenth Century* (Baltimore: Johns Hopkins University Press, 1931).

Cervantes in Germany. MC hardly made an appearance in Germany in the seventeenth century, and not much more in the eighteenth century until the rise of the Romantic writers and philosophers in the latter part of the century. Until then, *DQ* was known primarily through French translations, imitations, and adaptations; perhaps the most interesting work from this period is the opera by Daniel Schiebeler and Georg Philipp Telemann. But in the period of 1750–1800, MC and *DQ* rivaled Shakespeare as a source of inspiration for Johann Wolfgang von Goethe, Friedrich Schiller, August Wilhelm, Friedrich von Schlegel, Ludwig Tieck, Christoph Martin Wieland, and others. It would be difficult to overstate the importance of these writers in reinterpreting *DQ* as a positive, noble, even tragic figure and definitively reorienting our understanding of MC's novel (*reception history of *DQ*). In the nineteenth century, writers as different as Jean Paul and Hoffmann sought inspiration directly in the work of MC. Major twentieth-century writers of quixotic fictions include Hermann Hesse, Franz Kafka, Thomas Mann, and Paul Schallück.

Bibliography: Lienhard Bergel, "Cervantes in Germany," in *Cervantes across the Centuries: A Quadricentennial Volume*, ed. Angel Flores and M. J. Benardete (New York: Gordian Press, 1947), 315–22; and J. J. A. Bertrand, *Cervantes en el país de Fausto*, trans. José Perdomo García (Madrid: Ediciones Cultura Hispánica, 1950).

Cervantes in music.

The works of MC, especially *DQ*, have served as the point of departure for literally hundreds of musical compositions, from full-fledged grand operas to popular songs—more, it is said, than any other work of secular literature. A detailed study (or even list) of such works lies far outside the bounds of the current work. Worthy of note, however, are the following: Henry Purcell's music for Thomas D'Urfey's *The Comical History of Don Quixote* (1694); George Philipp Telemann's *Ouverture burlesque sur Don Quichotte* (1721) and his music for Daniel Schiebeler's *Basilio und Quiteria* (1761); António José da Silva's opera *Vida do Grande D. Quixote de La Mancha e do Gordo Sancho Pança* (1733); Henry Fielding's musical *Don Quixote in England* (1734); Philidor's opera bouffe *Sancho Pança dans son Isle* (1762); Antonio Salieri's opera *Don Chisciotte alle nozze di Gamace*, with libretto by Giovanne Gastone Boccherini (1771); Felix Mendelssohn's comic opera *Die Hochzeit des Camacho* (1827); Ludwig Minkus's ballet *Don Quichotte* (1869), written with Marius Petipa; Richard Strauss's symphonic poem *Don Quixote* (1898); Ruperto Chapí's zarzuela, *La venta de Don Quijote* (1902); Jules Massenet's opera *Don Quichotte* (1910), with libretto by Jacques Le Lorrain; Manuel de Falla's *El retablo de Maese Pedro* (1923); Oscar Esplá's symphonic poem *Don Quijote velando las armas* (1929); Maurice Ravel's three songs that make up his *Don Qui-chotte à Dulcinée* (1934); Rodolfo Halffter's *Tres epitafios* (1952); the music by Mitch Leigh for Dale Wasserman's play *Man of La Mancha* (1965); Gordon Lightfoot's popular folk-like song "Don Quixote" (1972); and Richard Carr's piano music for the album *An American Quixote* (1999).

Bibliography: Victor Espinós, *El "Quijote" en la música universal* (Barcelona: Instituto de Musicología, 1947); Bárbara Esquival-Heinemann, *Don Quijote's Sally into the World Opera: Libretti between 1680 and 1976* (New York: Lang, 1993); and Charles Haywood, "Musical Settings to Cervantes Texts," in *Cervantes across the Centuries: A Quadricentennial Volume*, ed. Angel Flores and M. J. Benardete (New York: Gordian Press, 1947), 264–73.

Cervantes in poetry.

The Spanish and Spanish-American poets who have written in honor of and/or about MC, his works, and his characters number in the hundreds if not the thousands. Some are particularly outstanding: Jorge Luis Borges, Rubén Darío, León Felipe, Ramón de Garciasol, Jorge Guillén, Antonio and Manuel Machado, Francisco de Quevedo, and others. There are several anthologies of Cervantine and quixotic poetry, all of which contain some poetry of interest, as well as much that is better forgotten. Outside of the Hispanic world, there are also some poets who have found inspiration in the works of MC; examples include the Brazilians Menotti del Picchia and Raul Pedrosa, the English William Wordsworth, the Greek Nikos Kazantzakis, the Russian Fyodor Sologub, the Rumanian Mihai Eminescu, the Sicilian Giovanni Meli, and the Swedish Carl Almqvist and Daniel Atterbom.

Bibliography: Francisco Sánchez-Castañer, ed., *Homenaje a Cervantes*, vol. 1 (Valencia, Spain: Mediterráneo, 1950); and Enrique Vázquez de Aldana, ed., *Cancionero cervantino* (Madrid: Ediciones Studium de Cultura, 1947).

Cervantes in Russia.

MC entered Russia relatively late, as the first translation of *DQ* was made in 1769 by N. Osipov, using the French translation of Filleau de Saint-Martin. Not until 1838 was the novel translated directly from Spanish by Konstantin Massal'skii. The early

DQ in Russia, as in most other European countries (with the exception of Fielding and Sterne in England), was an antihero, a figure of derision and satire. Overall, eighteenth-century Russian writers made modest use of *DQ* and other works by MC, with a travel book by Aleksandr Radischev perhaps the most interesting. But in the nineteenth century a significant number of major Russian writers—including Fyodor Dostoevsky, Nikolai Gogol, Nikolai Leskov, Aleksandr Pushkin, Ivan Turgenev, and Leo Tolstoy—sought inspiration in *DQ*. Turgenev's essay on DQ and Hamlet was especially important and became a point of departure for almost all subsequent Russian understandings of and writings inspired by *DQ*. Among twentieth-century writers, the work of MC was influential for Mihail Bulgakov, Maksim Gorky, Anatoliy Lunacharsky, Fyodor Sologub, Alexandr Solzhenitsyn, and others.

Bibliography: Vsevolod Bagno, *El "Quijote" vivido por los rusos* (Madrid: CSIC, 1995); and Ludmilla Buketoff Turkevich, *Cervantes in Russia.* (Princeton, NJ: Princeton University Press, 1950).

Cervantes in Spanish America.
Records show that, in spite of a prohibition of sending works of fiction to the colonies, within weeks of its publication, copies of *DQ* I were shipped to Colombia, Mexico, and Peru, and within a few years several hundred copies (maybe over 1,000) of the early printings of *DQ* I wound up in Spanish colonies in the Indies (none of these copies has ever been located). As early as 1607, figures from MC's novel began to appear in popular festivals and processions, just as they did in Spain. By the time of the growing movement for freedom from colonial status in the nineteenth century, MC and DQ were often evoked as symbols of the ideals of freedom at the center of the struggles. The earliest novels of Spanish America, those of José Joaquín Fernández de Lizardi, for example, were directly inspired in *DQ*. Juan Montalvo is the great nineteenth-century exemplar of Cervantine writing in Spanish America. In addition to the spate of bad sequels to *DQ* written for political and/or ideological purposes throughout the nineteenth and early twentieth centuries, Spanish American novelists of the earlier part of the twentieth century who wrote particularly Cervantine works include Eduardo Barrios, Jorge Ferretis, Heriberto Frías, and Alberto Gerchunoff. By the time of the so-called boom in the Spanish American novel in the 1960s, *DQ* was a major source of inspiration for writers such as Juan José Arreola, Jorge Luis Borges, Alejo Carpentier, Mario Denevi, Carlos Fuentes, Gabriel García Márquez, Angelina Muñiz-Huberman, and Agustín Yañez, among others.

Bibliography: Guillermo Díaz-Plaja, *Don Quijote en el país de Martín Fierro* (Madrid: Instituto de Cultura Hispánica, 1952); Juan Uribe-Echevarría, *Cervantes en las letras hispano-americanas (Antología y Crítica)* (Santiago, Chile: Ediciones de la Universidad de Chile, 1949); and Rafael Heliodoro Valle and Emilia Romero, *Bibliografía cervantina en la América Española* (Mexico City: Imprenta Universitaria, 1950).

Cervantes in the theater.
Characters from *DQ* begin to appear on stage in Spain immediately after the publication of *DQ* I with the works of Francisco de Avila, Guillén de Castro, and Pedro Calderón de la Barca, among others; throughout the seventeenth century, adaptations of scenes from *DQ* and/or versions of the *Novelas* are frequent. The earliest seventeenth- and eighteenth-century adaptations of *DQ* in both France and England are much more often in the theater than in the novel. In France, the work of Guyon Guérin de Bouscal, Alexandre Hardy, Molière, and Le Sieur Pichou illustrate this trend, whereas in England the most important theatrical versions of *DQ* are those of Henry Fielding, Shakespeare, Fletcher, and Thomas D'Urfey. When *DQ* is brought to the stage, the most frequent subjects are *Cardenio* and *Curioso* from *DQ* I, and Camacho's wedding and SP's governorship from *DQ* II. In Germany and Italy, also, whether in grand or comic opera or more straightforward dramatic presentations, these same scenes (often adapted from French versions) are the ones more frequently staged. In more modern times, Gaston Baty's romantic *Dulcinée* (1939) stands out as the most influential theatrical version of the play, as DQ, SP, and DT become the subject of a variety of stage versions of the novel. In Spain, works by Car-

los Ansó, Jacinto Benavente, Antonio Buero Vallejo, Benjamín Jarnés, Alfonso Paso, Alfonso Sastre, Narciso Serra, and José Carlos Somoza are among those most worthy of note. Elsewhere, there are interesting theatrical versions of *DQ* by the American Mrs. Burton (María Amparo Ruiz de Burton) and Tennessee Williams, the English G. E. Morrison, the Portuguese Carlos Selvagem and José Antonio da Silva, the Russian Mikhail Bulgakov, and the Swedish August Strindberg. The most successful of all theatrical versions is Dale Wasserman's *Man of La Mancha* with thousands of performances worldwide in some 40 languages. Overall, *DQ* (not to mention other works of MC) have been brought to the stage in one form or another well over 100 times.

Bibliography: *Cuadernos de Teatro Clásico* 7, special issue devoted to *Cervantes y el teatro*, (1992); Gregory Gough La Grone, *The Imitations of "Don Quixote" in the Spanish Drama* (Philadelphia: University of Pennsylvania, 1937); Felipe Pérez Capo, *El "Quijote" en el teatro: Repertorio cronológico de 290 producciones relacionadas con la inmortal obra de Cervantes* (Barcelona: Millá, 1947); and Gregorio Torres Nebrera, "Don Quijote en el teatro español del siglo XX," *Cuadernos de Teatro Clásico* 7 (1992): 93–140.

Cervantes, Juan de (?–ca. 1540). Uncle of MC. Little is known of this member of the family, who died prematurely.

Cervantes, Juan de (ca. 1554–ca. 1593). Younger brother of MC about whom virtually nothing is known.

Cervantes, Leonor de. *Cortinas, Leonor de.

Cervantes, Licenciado (Licentiate) Juan de (ca. 1470–1556). Grandfather of MC. Born in Córdoba, Juan was a lawyer and a graduate of the University of Salamanca. Beginning in 1500 he held various administrative positions in his native city. He and his wife Leonor Fernández de *Torreblanca (they were married in late 1503 or early 1504) had one daughter, María, and three sons, Juan, Rodrigo (MC's father), and Andrés. Juan then held a series of administrative positions in a number of different cities, including Alcalá de Henares (where Rodrigo was born). Beginning in 1527, Juan served as secretary and confidant to Diego Hurtado de Mendoza, duke of El Infantado (?–1531), in his final years, during which time the duke secretly married a commoner named María Maldonado. Juan had to deal with the heirs' anger upon learning about their stepmother. One of the duke's illegitimate sons, Don Martín de Mendoza, whose maternal line was gypsy and who was called *el Gitano* (the Gypsy), became the lover of Juan's daughter María. Mendoza reneged on the dowry for which he contracted and a lengthy series of lawsuits was begun. In the wake of all this, Juan was imprisoned in Valladolid (in the same jail where his son Rodrigo and grandson MC would also later be confined) before ultimately clearing his name. María de Cervantes was well compensated by her former lover and gave birth to a child who went by the name of Martina de Mendoza (who was later living with MC's family in Alcalá and helping run the family's finances). In 1551 Juan separated from his wife Leonor, left Alcalá, and returned to Córdoba, where he spent the remainder of his life, a wealthy and respected senior citizen.

Bibliography: Krzysztof Sliwa, *El licenciado Juan de Cervantes: Efemérides del licenciado Juan de Cervantes, documentos y datos para una biografía del abuelo paterno del autor del "Quijote"* (Kassel: Edition Reichenberger, 2001); and Krzysztof Sliwa and Daniel Eisenberg, "El licenciado Juan de Cervantes, abuelo de Miguel de Cervantes Saavedra." *Cervantes* 17, no. 2 (1997): 106–14.

Cervantes, Licenciado (Licentiate) Miguel de. Spanish writer. This Cervantes, no relation to MC, is the author of *Exemplos de Catón* (1609; *Examples from Cato*); nothing more is known of him than his name.

Cervantes, Luisa de (1546–ca. 1620). Older sister of MC. Known as *Santita* (Little Saint), in 1565 she became a Discalced Carmelite nun, with the name of Sor Luisa de Belén, at the convent of La Concepción in Alcalá at the age of 18. MC and his father were present at the ceremony. Luisa would live longer than any other member of her family and in many ways be the most successful: three times she was elected prioress of her convent.

Cervantes, Magdalena de (1553–1611). Fifth child of Rodrigo de *Cervantes, and MC's younger sister. Like her older sister Andrea, Magdalena had difficulties with men. She never married or had children, but in the late 1570s and early 1580s she was involved with Fernando de *Lodeña and a Basque named Juan *Pérez de Alcega, both of whom appear to have made certain promises that they did not keep. In order to provide a guise of respectability, she adopted the name of Doña Magdalena Pimentel de Sotomayor. With her sister Andrea she moved to Valladolid, new site of the royal court, in 1603. In 1606 she moved back to Madrid with MC and the rest of the family. In 1608 she took the habit of the Third Order of Saint Francis (to be followed the next year by her sister Andrea and MC's wife Catalina de *Palacios), adopted the name of Magdalena de Jesús, and died early in 1611.

Cervantes, María de. The only daughter of Juan de *Cervantes, and an aunt of MC. She had an affair with Martín de Mendoza, illegitimate son of the duke of El Infantado, which produced one child, a daughter named Martina de Mendoza.

Cervantes, Miguel de. *Cervantes Saavedra, Miguel de.

Cervantes, Miguel de. Author of *Galatea* and a good friend of the priest's in *DQ* I, 6. MC's presentation of a fictional version of himself in his novel—both here and in the reference by Ruy Pérez de Viedma about a captive soldier, a certain Saavedra, he knew in Algiers—along with his own role as editor/author of the novel (*narrative structure of *DQ*) is an important and innovative metafiction that is a distinctive characteristic of the work.

Cervantes, niece of [Sobrina de Cervantes]. A reference to *Constanza de Ovando, daughter of MC's sister Andrea, who lived with MC and other women in the family in Valla-

dolid in the years 1604–5. In *Adjunta*, MC recalls an occasion when his niece accepted a letter for him—only to find that the message consisted of a sonnet, probably by Lope de *Vega, in which *DQ* was severely criticized.

Cervantes on the Internet. There are dozens, if not hundreds, of web sites devoted to or substantially involving MC. Many of them are superficial, sometimes filled with errors and ephemera. Any list made just a couple of years ago would already contain sites that have gone defunct. By the time this work gets into print, others will have been created. Therefore, no effort to include a lengthy or detailed list or bibliography of such sites will be included here. But, since the amount of "information" received by means of the Internet is greater every day, a few of the more substantial sites with good probabilities of long-term availability are found at the following URLs:

1) *Biblioteca Virtual Miguel de Cervantes*: http://cervantesvirtual.com, which contains texts of many Spanish and Spanish American writers, including an extensive page on MC; this is supposedly the most-visited of all Spanish web sites;
2) *Cervantes: Bulletin of the Cervantes Society of America*: http://www2.h-net.msu.edu/ ~cervantes/bcsalist.htm, which contains the contents of all issues of the journal and the full text of most;
3) *H-Cervantes*: http://www2.h-net.msu.edu/ ~cervantes/, an online scholarly discussion about MC and his works;
4) *Instituto Cervantes*: http://www.cervantes .es/internet/indice.html, an organization that promotes Spain and things Spanish in general, as well as matters relating to MC;
5) *Miguel de Cervantes Saavedra*: http:// cervantes.uah.es/inicio.htm, which has a great deal on MC including his complete works (UAH stands for Universidad de Alcalá de Henares);
6) *The Cervantes Project; C.I.B.O: Cervantes International Bibliography Online*: http:// www.csdl.tamu.edu/cervantes/, a large site with the most complete MC biography on

the web, texts, bibliography, images, links, and more; and

7) *Works of Miguel de Cervantes*: http://users. ipfw.edu/jehle/cervante.htm/, which contains old- and modernized-spelling versions of ten volumes of the edition of MC's *Obras Completas* by Schevill and Bonilla.

Bibliography: Daniel Eisenberg, "Los textos digitales de las obras de Cervantes," in *Cervantes 1547–1997: Jornadas de investigación cervantina*, ed. Aurelio González (Mexico: Colegio de México, Fondo Eulalio Ferrer, 1999), 53–61; and Eduardo Urbina, "Cervantes en la red: últimos avatares y cautiverio feliz," in *Cervantes 1547–1997: Jornadas de investigación cervantina*, ed. Aurelio González (Mexico City: Colegio de México, Fondo Eulalio Ferrer, 1999), 63–72.

Cervantes Prize [Premio Cervantes]. The Premio de Literatura en Lengua Castellana Miguel de Cervantes (Miguel de Cervantes Prize for Literature in the Castilian Language) is the most prestigious and most remunerative literary award given to an author writing in the Spanish language (it is sometimes called the Nobel Prize of the Hispanic world). The prize is presented by the king of Spain each April 23 (anniversary of the death of MC) to a writer from Spain or Spanish America for his or her lifetime achievement in literature. It was inaugurated in 1976, the year after the death of Francisco Franco (such an award would have been impossible for political reasons during the years of the Franco dictatorship). The list of recipients of the prize reads like a who's who of Hispanic letters:

1976 Jorge *Guillén
1977 Alejo *Carpentier
1978 Dámaso Alonso
1979 Gerardo *Diego and Jorge Luis *Borges
1980 Juan Carlos *Onetti
1981 Octavio Paz
1982 Luis Rosales
1983 Rafael *Alberti
1984 Ernesto *Sábato
1985 Gonzalo *Torrente Ballester
1986 Antonio *Buero Vallejo
1987 Carlos *Fuentes
1988 María Zambrano

1989 Agusto Roa Bastos
1990 Adolfo Bioy Casares
1991 Francisco *Ayala
1992 Dulce María Loynez
1993 Miguel Delibes
1994 Mario *Vargas Llosa
1995 Camilo José Cela
1996 José García Nieto
1997 Guillermo *Cabrera Infante
1998 José Hierro
1999 Jorge Edwards
2000 Francisco Umbral
2001 Alvaro Mutis
2002 José Jiménez Lozano

Cervantes, Rodrigo de. A keeper of accounts at La Goleta in the sixteenth century; he is not related in any way to MC.

Cervantes, Rodrigo de (1509–85). Second son of Juan de *Cervantes, and the father of MC. Rodrigo was a surgeon, the lowest rung of the medical profession, whose primary activity was to set broken bones, let blood, cure open wounds, and prescribe remedies for common ailments. Although he was virtually deaf from infancy, Rodrigo was fond of music; he was less ambitious than his father, but comparably anxious to appear to be a nobleman. He married Leonor de Cortinas, perhaps in 1542, the daughter of a Castilian landowner living in Arganda, near Madrid. He seems to have had little ambition and never provided his family with the means to live in comfort. In 1551, after an incident with a noble patient that left Rodrigo with a reputation for medical incompetence, the family (including Rodrigo's sister María, who controlled the family's finances, and his mother) moved to Valladolid. There the family's finances continued to decline, and in 1552 Rodrigo landed in prison (the same one where his father before him had been jailed and where his son MC would also be briefly incarcerated); in 1553, the family returned, destitute, to Alcalá, and then moved to Córdoba in the same year. In Córdoba, under his father's patronage, he probably practiced his profession and perhaps held a minor bureaucratic position. In 1566 he moved the family to Madrid. Except for his activities in support of his son—the preparation in 1569 of a statement that MC was from an Old Christian family, and some activity in the late 1570s in support of the raising of funds to ransom MC from captivity—little more is known about Rodrigo's final two decades.

Cervantes, Rodrigo de (1550–1600). Younger brother of MC. Rodrigo enlisted in the Spanish army in the late 1560s or early 1570s and fought in the same regiment, probably on the same galley, as his brother Miguel, in the battle of Lepanto. He was taken captive along with his brother in 1575 and spent two years in Algiers before being ransomed in August 1577. Back in Spain, he arranged a rescue mission for his brother, sending a ship to pick up MC and other prisoners at a designated spot, but the plot was foiled by the betrayal of El *Dorador. Meanwhile, Rodrigo reenlisted in the army and died in the battle of the Dunes in Flanders. He never achieved a military rank higher than *alférez* (ensign or second lieutenant).

Cervantes, Rodrigo de. Son of Andrés de *Cervantes and MC's cousin. MC hired him briefly as an assistant commissary in 1588. He joined the army in 1602 and nothing else is known of him.

Cervantes, Ruy (or Rodrigo) Díaz de (ca. 1430–?). MC's great-grandfather. He was a well-to-do cloth manufacturer in the late fifteenth century in Córdoba.

Cervantes Saavedra, Gonzalo de. A distant relation of MC who fled Córdoba in 1568 after a duel, joined the army, and may have participated in the battle of *Lepanto. He is praised as a poet by MC in Calliope's song in *Galatea* 6, which suggests that MC knew him personally.

Cervantes *Saavedra, Miguel de (1547–1616). MC's life is outlined in the chronology preceding this encyclopedia and discussed in more detail in various entries herein. In brief, he was the third of five children of the surgeon Rodrigo de Cervantes and Leonor de Cortinas.

He was born (probably on September 29) and raised in Alcalá de Henares, but also lived in Valladolid, Córdoba, and Seville during his youth. He was 19 when the family moved to Madrid in 1566, and soon he was a favorite pupil in the school of Juan *López de Hoyos. Some sort of altercation involving honor led to his banishment from Spain in 1569, and late in that year he was in Rome, serving in the household of a cardinal. He soon enlisted in the army and in 1571 fought heroically during the battle of *Lepanto. He received multiple wounds during that event; he was shot twice in the chest, but the most serious wound was the maiming of his left hand (*manco de Lepanto). MC remained in military service in Italy, achieving the rank of *soldado aventajado* (elite trooper), until 1575 when he and his brother Rodrigo were captured by Turkish pirates during their return to Spain. He spent five years in captivity in Algiers, earning respect and praise from his companions for his bravery, especially during four unsuccessful attempts to escape (*Cervantes, escape attempts of). Finally ransomed in 1580, just as his owner *Hassan Pasha was about to depart for Constantinople, he returned to Spain, participated in a minor diplomatic mission to Oran, and then settled in Madrid. He became active in the theater, writing and staging some 20 to 30 plays (only two of which survive: *Tratos* and *Numancia*) in the 1580s. In 1582 he applied for an administrative position in the New World but was turned down. In 1584 his only child, the illegitimate Isabel de *Saavedra, was born. Later the same year he married Catalina de *Palacios, from the town of Esquivias, located outside of but close to La Mancha, and in 1585 he published his first book, the pastoral novel *Galatea*. In 1587 he accepted an appointment as royal commissary and spent the next several years traveling throughout southern Spain—to Ecija (where he was excommunicated for carrying out his orders in the face of local opposition), Castro del Río (where, for the same reason, he was excommunicated again), Espejo, Cabra (where his uncle Andrés lived), Jaén, Ubeda, Baeza, Estepa, Montilla, Andújar, and others—carrying out his duties, requisitioning grain and oil. In

1590 he wrote to the Council of the Indies, describing his exemplary record as a soldier and a commissary and requesting one of three administrative positions in America. The request was denied with the terse comment, 'Let him look for a job here.' His next position was that of tax collector, again in Andalusia. He was jailed at least twice, first very briefly in Castro del Río and then for over seven months in Seville (never in *Argamasilla del Alba, as local legend has it), and had many of the experiences that would later provide him with material for his novels and stories. During these years, MC rarely lived with his wife, who stayed on in Esquivias while he moved about, primarily among the cities of Seville, Toledo, and Madrid, but with occasional stays in Esquivias. Meanwhile, MC continued to write, working on *DQ* I and *Persiles*, writing poetry, and once signing a contract to write some plays. In 1604 he settled in Valladolid, then the site of the royal court, with his wife Catalina, his sisters Magdalena and Andrea, his daughter Isabel, his niece Constanza, and a maid. There he finished *DQ* I (published in 1605) and wrote some of his short stories. After the court returned to Madrid in 1606, MC made the same move. In the wake of the popular success of *DQ* I, MC became famous but not wealthy. He continued to write, but published nothing more until 1613 when his collection of short fictions, *Novelas*, appeared. This book was followed in rapid succession by *Parnaso* in 1614 and *Comedias* and *DQ* II in 1615. By this time, MC was very ill with dropsy (he probably had diabetes) and aware that he was dying. He managed to finish *Persiles*, literally on his deathbed, and died on April 23, 1616; no trace of a will has ever been found. He was buried in the Trinitarian Monastery, around the corner from where he lived, on the Calle de Cantarranas (now, ironically, the Calle de Lope de Vega). His widow published his last book the following year.

Bibliography: Fernando Arrabal, *Un esclavo llamado Cervantes* (Madrid: Espasa Calpe, 1996); Luis Astrana Marín, *Vida ejemplar y heroica de Miguel de Cervantes Saavedra*, 7 vols. (Madrid: Instituto Editorial Reus, 1948–58); William Byron, *Cervantes: A Biography* (Garden City, NY: Doubleday, 1978); Jean Canavaggio, *Cervantes*, trans. J. R. Jones (New York: W. W. Norton, 1990); Donald P. McCrory, *No Ordinary Man: The Life and Times of Miguel de Cervantes* (London: Peter Owen, 2002); Melveena McKendrick, *Cervantes* (Boston: Little, Brown, 1980); Alberto Sánchez, "Nuevas orientaciones en el planteamiento de la biografía de Cervantes," in *Cervantes* (Alcalá de Henares, Spain: Centro de Estudios Cervantinos, 1995), 19–40; and K. Sliwa, *Documentos de Miguel de Cervantes Saavedra* (Pamplona, Spain: Ediciones Universidad de Navarra, 1999).

Cervantes, San. *San Servando.

Cervantes scholarship [Cervantismo]. *Cervantismo* is a term used to refer to scholarly work concerning MC and his works (a *cervantófilo* is a fan of MC; a *cervantista* is an MC scholar). The scholarly study of MC really begins in England with the first critical edition of *DQ*, by Lord Carteret in 1738, which had as a preface the first biography of MC ever written, by Gregorio Mayáns y Síscar, and the first edition with extensive scholarly commentary by John Bowle in 1781. In the nineteenth century, as more works of MC were found in various libraries and private holdings, as scholarly editions of texts become more sophisticated, and as interpretive polemics raged, *cervantismo* reached a new level. One particular highlight is Diego Clemencín's monumental edition of *DQ* (1833–39), unsurpassed to this day in documenting the relationship between MC's novel and the romances of chivalry and other earlier works. Too often what passed for literary criticism in this period was really a series of *esoteric readings of the novel, often little more than deliberate attempts to use *DQ* to further a private agenda. In the twentieth century, another new standard is set for editing *DQ* with the Rodríguez Marín seven-volume edition, the 18-volume edition of the *Obras completas* [1914–41; *Complete Works*] of MC by Rodolfo Schevill and Adolfo Bonilla (still, alas, the most authoritative complete works edition ever done), and the seven-volume biography by Luis Astrana Marín, *Vida ejemplar y heroica de Miguel de Cervantes Saavedra* (1948–58; *The Exemplary and Heroic Life of Miguel de*

Cervantes Saavedra). Critical interpretations become more sophisticated, and two scholarly studies, still influential and often cited today, stand out: Américo Castro's *El pensamiento de Cervantes* (1925; *Cervantes's Thought*), arguably the most important and influential book ever written on MC, and Salvador de Madariaga's *Guía del lector del "Quijote"* (1926; translated by the author as *"Don Quixote": An Introductory Study in Psychology*). Contemporary *cervantismo* is initiated by E. C. Riley's monumental *Cervantes's Theory of the Novel* (1962), the work that might most rival Castro's book in the annals of MC scholarship. All of these books have been reprinted or reedited in recent years, an indication of their enduring importance. Since then there has been a steady stream of superb scholarship (as well as much that is far less than that) on the life, works, and sociocultural context of MC. It is far beyond the scope of this encyclopedia to attempt to identify specific modern scholars. Much of the best scholarship is found in the pages of the journals *Anales Cervantinos* (1951–59, 1979–99), and *Cervantes: Bulletin of the Cervantes Society of America* (1981–present), the single best source today for the latest in research relating to MC. Juan de la Cuesta Press, a publishing house (named after the printer of four of MC's books) run by Hispanist Thomas Lathrop, specializes in books relating to MC and his works. Furthermore, there are excellent *bibliographies of MC's works and much that is made available about *Cervantes on the Internet.

Bibliography: Ralph Merritt Cox, *The Rev. John Bowle: The Genesis of Cervantean Criticism* (Chapel Hill: University of North Carolina Press, 1971); Anne J. Cruz and Carroll B. Johnson, eds., *Cervantes and His Postmodern Constituencies* (New York: Garland, 1999); Dana B. Drake and Dominick L. Finello, *An Analytical and Bibliographical Guide to Criticism on "Don Quixote" (1790–1893)* Newark, DE: Juan de la Cuesta, 1987); José Montero Reguera, *El "Quijote" y la crítica contemporánea* (Alcalá de Henares, Spain: Centro de Estudios Cervantinos, 1997); and Ludovik Osterc, *Breve antología crítica del cervantismo* (Mexico City: UNAM, 1992).

Cervantes Society of America (CSA). A professional society dedicated to the study and promotion of the works of MC. The CSA was founded by a group of Hispanic scholars at a meeting at Fordham University in the winter of 1977. First president was Juan Bautista Avalle-Arce, one of the most distinguished Cervantes scholars of the twentieth century; he has been succeeded by some of the best and most influential scholars in the field. The first editor of the society's journal was the brilliant John Jay Allen, and he, too, has been succeeded by comparably outstanding and dedicated scholars. The primary activity of the CSA is to publish *Cervantes: Bulletin of the Cervantes Society of America*, the single most important source for the latest and best scholarship on MC. In addition, the CSA organizes annual meetings (both in conjunction with the annual meeting of the Modern Language Association and at a variety of other sites) for the presentation and discussion of research on MC and his works. The society originally planned to sponsor the preparation of an annual bibliography of MC and a "definitive" edition of his complete works, but the bibliography project has been inconsistently carried out, and an inability to agree on criteria for an edition has kept the complete works project from getting underway.

Bibliography: "Constitution: The Cervantes Society of America," *Cervantes* 6, no. 1 (1986): 91–96; and Patricia Kenworthy, "The Cervantes Society of America: A Brief History," *Cervantes* no. 1, 1–2 (1981): 7–8.

Cervantes Sotomayor, Alonso de. Poet and cousin of MC who also fought in the battle of Lepanto.

Cervantes Street. *Calle de Cervantes.

Cervantes the dramatist. When MC returned to Spain in 1580, after his five years of captivity in Algiers, he turned from arms to letters and attempted to gain recognition as a dramatist. He was an important figure in the Madrid theater scene in the early years of the decade of the 1580s, writing, he claims, between 20 and 30 plays, all of which he says were successfully produced. Only two plays—

Tratos and *Numancia*—remain from this period. We know of the names of several more from the list he provides in *Adjunta*. It is likely that at least a few of the later plays in *Comedias* (*Casa*, *Sultana*, and *Laberinto*) are reworkings of some of these earlier efforts. None of MC's full-length plays is fully convincing as theater. His strengths are a vivid imagination, ambitious plots, and original attempts to use personification, allegory, and symbolism; in theater, MC is a theoretician, an innovator, and an experimenter. But he tends to overcrowd the stage with characters, present too many plots and subplots at the same time, engage in propaganda and religious and cultural stereotyping (curiously, the great comic writer generally handles comedy poorly on stage), and make poor transitions from one scene to the next. All it takes is the reading of any two or three of MC's plays in comparison with a reading of a few by Lope de *Vega to see why the latter was a dramatic genius and the former was not. Lope's plays are simple, elegant, and moving; MC's are relatively complex, clumsy, and boring. Like his poetry, MC's theater is prosaic—in the sense that it would generally be more successful if written as prose fiction. But if his full-length plays are not very good, his interludes are for the most part brilliant; no other writer in this minor genre surpasses his work. Here we see MC's comic genius, keen observation of human psychology, sharp sense of satire, great sense of timing, ability to write lively and realistic dialogue (as he does in *DQ*), and ability to create great characters in a brief space. His interest in the theater also comes across in some of his novels. This can be seen best in *DQ*, in the long discussion about the theater involving the canon of Toledo in I, 49–50; in the puppet show staged in II, 26; and in all the scenes staged for the benefit of DQ and SP, particularly during the long stay in the palace of the duke and duchess in II, 31–57, and throughout both parts of the novel. In *Persiles* III, 2, a play is staged and the dramatist attempts to convince Auristela to become an actress. For bibliography, see *Ocho comedias y ocho entremeses*.

Cervantes the novelist. MC was a great experimenter with forms of long fiction. His first book was *Galatea*, written within the then-popular genre of the pastoral romance, but with aspects not generally seen in such works, such as scenes of physical violence and death, and embedded stories that are different in tone and subject matter from the earlier pastoral tales. His last book, *Persiles*, published posthumously, is an experiment in adventure fiction, but with strong metafictional elements not typical of the genre. And then there is *DQ*, the prototype of the modern novel in all of its manifestations (*quixotic novel).

Cervantes the poet. Poetry was MC's first love and he wrote poetry throughout his life. But on two occasions he admits that he was not a gifted poet: in the prologue to *Comedias* when he cites the opinion of a theatrical producer that from MC you could expect quality prose, but not good poetry; and in *Parnaso* 4, where he acknowledges that he does not have the poetic gift. MC's early poetic works are immature and slight in every way. The occasional verse he wrote as prefatory pieces for friends' works is far from distinguished. Most of the abundant poetry in *Galatea* is relatively pedestrian, with a few bright spots. The same can be said of nearly all of the verse in his theatrical works, with a few exceptions. Most of the verses included in his other prose fiction—*Novelas*, *DQ*, and *Persiles*—are average at best, but some of them are worthy of note. MC's only efforts at heroic poetry, the two odes addressed to the Invincible Armada (*Poesías* 21–22), are interesting for the way they reveal a shift from enthusiastic patriotism to cynicism and despair. His one long poetic work, *Parnaso,* is mostly undistinguished, but has some excellent satiric passages, and the section about himself and his own works in chapter 4 is a masterpiece of autobiographical writing and self-deprecating humor. Probably the two best poems MC ever wrote are satiric sonnets: the one on the occasion of the Spanish military reaction to the English sack of Cádiz in 1596 (*Poesías* 25), and the one he read in the cathedral of Seville in which he satirized the opulent tomb erected there for the recently deceased Felipe II (*Poesías* 26). MC claimed to have written an 'infinite' number of ballads (*Parnaso* 4), and he was reputed to be one of a very few Spanish poets with a recognizable style in that form. He probably wrote a number of (and perhaps many) ballads published in some of the *romanceros,* but his work there cannot be identified. A few other poems, such as the ballad on jealousy (*Poesías* 22) and the sonnet about Preciosa playing the tambourine in *Gitanilla,* are really quite good. The epistle to Mateo Vázquez (*Poesías* 8), traditionally attributed to MC, may not be (at least in its entirety) his, but the segment of the poem repeated in *Tratos* suggests that at least this section of it was written by him. Certainly the poem reflects MC's authentic sentiments about the plight of the Christian captives in Algiers. MC's talent lay more toward narrative than lyric, and even his best poetic passages are often more narrative than lyrical; only occasionally do we have the sensation that his lyrics reveal his innermost self, as we do when reading, for example, the poetry of his model, Garcilaso de la Vega, or that of his rival, Lope de Vega. Apparently MC was not considered a major poet by his contemporaries, as is made clear by his absence in the great anthology of contemporary poets compiled by Pedro *Espinosa. It is perhaps somewhat surprising that MC never pulled together and published a selection of his verse, a practice common at the time, even by many poets of far less quality than he. Perhaps his prose works so overshadow his poetry in the eyes of modern readers that the latter cannot be adequately appreciated. An overall assessment might be that MC was a better poet than very many of his age (when nearly everyone seemed to write poetry), but that his poetry is less distinguished than that of a number of his contemporaries.

Bibliography: Jean Canavaggio, "Garcilaso en Cervantes ('¡Oh dulces prendas por mi mal halladas')," in *Busquemos otros montes y otros ríos: Estudios de literatura española del Siglo de Oro dedicados a Elias L. Rivers,* ed. Brian Dutton and Victoriano Roncero López (Madrid: Castalia, 1992), 67–73; Dominick L. Finello, "Cervantes y su concepto de la fama del poeta," *La Torre* 1 (1987): 399–409; Mary M. Gaylord, "Los espacios de la poética cervantina," in *Actas del Primer Coloquio Internacional de la Asociación de Cervantistas, Alcalá de Henares 29/30 nov.–1/2 dic. 1988* (Barcelona: Anthropos, 1990), 357–68; Adrienne Laskier Martín, *Cervantes and the Burlesque Sonnet* (Berkeley: University of California Press, 1991); Elias L. Rivers, "Cervantes, poeta serio y burlesco," in *Cervantes*, ed. Anthony J. Close (Alcalá de Henares, Spain: Centro de Estudios Cervantinos, 1995), 211–24; Pedro Ruiz Pérez, "Contexto crítico de la poesía cervantina," *Cervantes* 17, no. 1 (1997): 62–86; and Jenaro Talens, "Poetry as Autobiography: Theory and Poetic Practice in Cervantes," in *Autobiography in Early Modern Spain*, ed. Nicholas Spadaccini and Jenaro Talens (Minneapolis, MN: Prisma, 1988), 215–46.

Cervantes the satirist. Satire, often graphic, vicious, and personal, was a constant in Spanish literature of the sixteenth and, especially, seventeenth centuries. Writers such as Góngora and Quevedo, probably the two most famous satirists of the age, often attacked specific individuals (frequently each other), women in general, sexuality (especially homosexuality), religion, and politics. Although *Avellaneda accused MC of unfair satire in *DQ* I, MC himself claimed never to have written satire. Perhaps this claim is a slight exaggeration, for the prologue to *DQ* I is largely satiric in intent, and certain scenes in *DQ* (e.g., the description of the absent hermit in II, 24), some of the *Novelas* (especially *Vidriera* and *Coloquio*), some of his interludes (especially *Retablo*), his two best sonnets (*Poesías* 25 and 26), and parts of *Parnaso* do contain clearly satiric passages. But, overall, the tone of MC's works is not as intensively satirical as much of the writings of his contemporaries.

Cervantes the storyteller. In the prologue to *Novelas,* MC claims to have been the first person to write *novelas*—original short fictions, not translations or adaptations of traditional or Italian stories—in Spain. The anomaly of the anonymous *El *Abencerraje* not withstanding, for all practical purposes, what he claims is true. Certainly no one before him conceived of the *novela* as an independent literary medium that could be written in multiple generic forms and published separately from a larger fictional context. Mateo *Alemán had included some independent fictions in *Guzmán de Alfarache,* and MC himself had embedded four independent narratives in *Galatea* (two of them are incomplete, awaiting the often-promised but never-written *Galatea* II), and two more (*Curioso* and *Capitán*) in his *DQ* I, but no one previously in Spain had ever considered publishing a number of autonomous short fictions. MC is the first writer to use the term *novela* in this sense (in the title of *Curioso, DQ* I, 33) in Golden Age Spain. The 12 stories in *Novelas* represent the most original and influential collection of short fiction published in Europe before the nineteenth century. They range across a generic spectrum from the very idealized or romantic tales of *Amante* and *Española* to the realistic or novelistic stories of *Rinconete* and *Casamiento,* with the hybrid fictions of *Gitanilla* and *Fregona* located at the midpoint of the spectrum. The brilliant metafictional beast fable in the dialogue of *Coloquio* is clearly the high point of the collection. Even if he had never written *DQ,* the fictions of *Novelas* would have earned MC a secure place as one of the great writers of fiction in European literature.

Bibliography: Agustín G. de Amezúa y Mayo, *Cervantes, creador de la novela corta española,* 2 vols. (Madrid: CSIC, 1956); Howard Mancing, "Prototypes of Genre in Cervantes' *Novelas ejemplares,*" *Cervantes* 20, no. 2 (2000): 127–50; and Walter Pabst, *La novela corta en la teoría y en la creación literaria: Notas para la historia de su antinomia en las literaturas románicas,* trans. Rafael de la Vega (Madrid: Gredos, 1972).

Cervantismo. *Cervantes scholarship.

Cervellón, Gabrio. Italian soldier and engineer named governor of Tunis by Don Juan of Austria. He constructed the defenses at La Goleta and then was captured in the loss of that fortress in 1574. See *DQ* I, 39.

Cervino. The son of the king of Scotland, rescued by Orlando in Ariosto's *Orlando Furioso.* See *DQ* I, 13.

Cervinus, C. *Diecke, Eugen.

César. *Caesar.

César, Julio. *Caesar, Julius.

Cetina, Agustín de. Spanish civil servant. In 1594 he hired MC as a tax collector.

Cetina, Doctor Gutierre de. Spanish religious civil servant and official censor, not to be confused with the well-known Sevillian poet of the same name who died in about 1557. Cetina signed one of the four approvals to print *Novelas,* one of the two licenses to print *Parnaso,* and one of the three approvals for the Royal Council for *DQ* II.

Chacón Rodríguez, Alfonso. Costa Rican writer. Chacón's collection of stories entitled *El reloj maldito; Cuentos de bolsillo* (1996; *The Damned Clock; Stories for Your Pocket*) includes "Donde se trata de la accidentada visita de Don Quijote y su escudero a una ciudad embrujada" ("Which Deals with the Accidental Visit of Don Quixote and His Squire to a Bewitched City"). The manuscript of the story supposedly consists of some pages preserved with CHB's original manuscript. The hand appears to be that of CHB, but the style is not; the editor suspects it may be apocryphal. Since the editor has translated other writings by CHB, he considers it his duty to publish these pages also, without affirming their authenticity. DQ and SP enter a cave behind a waterfall. They travel through the cave and emerge in an enchanted city of very tall buildings and carriages that travel on wheels without horses, puffing smoke out their rear ends. After almost causing a traffic accident, knight and squire find they cannot understand the language spoken by the strange inhabitants of the city. They attempt to take refuge in a church, but it is closed. After causing other problems and almost getting arrested, DQ decides that the city is enchanted by an evil enchanter, but SP believes that it is hell itself.

Bibliography: Alfonso Chacón Rodríguez, *El reloj maldito; Cuentos de bolsillo* (San José, Costa Rica: Jera, 1996).

Chacona. A popular dance that had its origins in Spanish America. In its European version, it is quite similar to the Portuguese *follia* (*folía* in Spanish as cited by MC in *Fregona*) and the Italian *passacaglia*. It is interesting to note that this sprightly, popular, reputedly lascivious dance was converted over time into the stately *chaconne*, a courtly musical form used, among many others, by J. S. Bach. See also *Coloquio*; *Retablo*; *Sultana* 3.

Chaeremus [Cremo] (fourth century BCE). Greek dramatist. See *Galatea* 4.

Chaldeans [Caldeos]. The ancient inhabitants of Mesopotamia, cited in the Old Testament. See *DQ* I, 10.

Chaliapin Fyodor. *Le Lorrain, Jacques.

Challe(s), Robert (1659–1711). French novelist. Challe wrote a sequel to *Filleau de Saint-Martin's sequel to *DQ* entitled *Continuation de l'histoire de l'admirable Don Quichotte de la Manche* (1711; *Continuation of the History of the Admirable Don Quixote of La Mancha*). Challe invents a historian-narrator called Ruy Gomez, who edits the account of Filleau's *Zulema*; his papers are purchased in Spain by a Frenchman and brought to France. Like most other eighteenth-century French imitations of MC's novel, it is a satire on topical themes. It does at least make DQ into a typical French *honnête homme* and give him somewhat more dignity than is usually seen.

Bibliography: English Showalter, Jr., "Robert Challe and *Don Quixote*," *French Review* 45 (1972): 1136–44; and English Showalter, Jr., "Did Robert Challe Write a Sequel to *Don Quixote*?" *Romanic Review* 61 (1971): 270–82.

Chambermaid of Elizabeth I [Camarera mayor de la reina]. In *Española*, the mother of Arnesto who promotes her son's case as Ricaredo's rival and, in a jealous rage, poisons Isabela.

Chambers, Whitman (1896–). American novelist. Of all the namesakes of *DQ*, the story of Don Lawrence, protagonist of Chambers's *Don Coyote* (1927), is one of the most camp and absurdly entertaining. Lawrence is a typical cowboy, handy in every practical way on the range, honest as the day is long, and shy and ill-at-ease around women. His character, as well as his name, are explained in a scene in which the heroine (Gayle Dorrington, whose father's mine Lawrence—gallantly, quixotically—saves at the end of the novel) begins to react romantically toward the handsome cowboy, calling him "sort of a Don Quixote." Lawrence admits that he was called that by another woman and adds, "Fact is, I'm known all over the southwest as Don Coyote. That's what the boys down there called this Quixote feller that used to ride his cayuse round the range takin' pot shots at windmills." Then he adds: "Funny feller, that Quixote person. He must have been loco, don't you reckon? I never could figure why he went around shootin' up windmills. But I've heard tell that was his favorite game. Liked it better'n poker. Maybe you could tell me, Miss Dorrington. You've read about him a lot, I guess." Dorrington admits that she has, and notes that "Don Quixote was quite a Lothario." The final reference in this exchange contains a specific irony that Chambers surely never realized: Lothario (Lotario in Spanish) is the name of the reluctant but successful seducer in MC's *Curioso*. The name of Lothario as a synonym for an irresistible lover in English (it does not have that connotation in Spanish) comes from the rake of that name in Nicholas *Rowe's once-popular melodrama entitled *The Fair Penitent* (1703). So the name of the character comes full circle: from the seventeenth-century text of *DQ*, to the eighteenth-century British stage, to the English language in general, to an application to a twentieth-century American cowboy named after DQ.

Bibliography: Whitman Chambers, *Don Coyote* (Cleveland, OH: International Fiction Library, 1927).

Chamisso, Adalbert von (1781–1838). German/French poet and prose writer. Chamisso's fame rests almost solely on *Peter Schlemihls wundersame Geschichte* (1814; *The*

Wondrous History of Peter Schlemihls), a satiric novella about a man who sells his shadow to the devil. The influence of MC's *Rinconete* and *Coloquio* have frequently been noted.

Chanfalla. In *Retablo*, the *pícaro* who organizes and stages the show of wonders that can only be seen by those who are of legitimate birth and of Old Christian blood.

Chaos theory and Cervantes. Theories of complexity and chaos have been an important factor in the understanding of modern mathematics and physics in the final decades of the twentieth century. Terms like *fractals*, the unexpected repetition of patterns by chance, or the *butterfly effect*, the long-term importance of minor initial events, have become popular even in nonscientific contexts. The use of these and related scientific terms in an attempt to understand better such literary techniques as self-reflexivity, metafiction, nonlinearity, and others has been made both in the study of literary theory in general and specific writers and works. Few would seem to lend themselves better than MC to such an approach.

Bibliography: Robert Flores, "A Portrait of Don Quijote from the Palette of Chaos Theory," *Cervantes* 22, no. 1 (2002): 43–70; and Amy R. Williamsen, *Co(s)mic Chaos: Exploring "Los trabajos de Persiles y Sigismunda"* (Newark, DE: Juan de la Cuesta, 1994).

Chapí, Ruperto (1851–1909). Spanish composer. Chapí was one of the finest composers of *zarzuelas* (light musical comedies). His *La venta de Don Quijote* (1902; *The Inn of Don Quixote*) is based on the events of the *inn of Juan Palomeque. He collaborated with Carlos *Fernández Shaw on *Las bodas de Camacho* (1902; *Camacho's Wedding*). Chapí also wrote a *zarzuela* based on *Gitanilla* and a symphonic poem entitled *Scherzo* based on *DQ*.

Chaplain [Capillán]. A character in the anecdote about the *madman of Seville told by the barber in *DQ* II, 1.

Chapman, Robin (1933–). English novelist. Chapman's *The Duchess's Diary* (1980) is one of the most extraordinary and moving of the many sequels to *DQ*. Chapman's premise is unique: the text is presented as the (slightly edited) personal diary of María Isabel (Maribel) de Caparroso who, with her husband Jerónimo, duke of Caparroso, had entertained MC at their luxurious home during the summer of 1608, after the 1605 publication and great popularity of *DQ* I. While MC was there, the duke and duchess, together with their retinue, staged several festive scenes featuring the main characters of the famous novel—the procession of enchanters and Dulcinea, the flight on Clavileño, and so on. There was a tense scene when MC was confronted by their household priest but defended himself brilliantly. These events became the grist for the parallel scenes when DQ and SP visit the palace of the duke and duchess in MC's *DQ* II. But when she reads *DQ* II after its publication in 1615, the duchess is gravely offended by the fact that MC also reveals in his sequel her own most intimate secret, the two *running sores she has on her inner thighs, where a physician draws from her body the "bad humors" that are the cause of her "melancholy." Reacting with anger, humiliation, and frustration upon perceiving MC's ignoble deed in exposing her to the world (even though he did not reveal her name in his novel), and also feeling the cumulative effects of the chronic oppression and humiliation she suffers at the hands of her cruel husband and the haughty priest, Maribel undertakes a desperate flight from her home and social position and travels alone to Madrid, arriving just in time to glimpse MC at a distance the day before his death in April 1616, and gaining admission to his quarters as his body lies in preparation for burial. The manuscript of the diary breaks off at this point; there is a note from the editor that there is some documented evidence that Maribel died in 1645 in Puerto Rico. The manner in which Chapman integrates the moving personal story of a misunderstood and abused woman with the events of the text of *DQ* and the life of MC is really quite admirable.

Bibliography: Robin Chapman, *The Duchess's Diary* (London: Boudicca Books of Battersea, 1980); and Edward H. Friedman, "Voices Within: Robin Chapman's *The Duchess' Diary* and the Intertextual Conundrum of *Don Quixote*," *RLA: Romance Languages Annual* 2 (1990): 400–05.

Charcas. Charcas de la Plata, also called Chuquisaca, in Bolivia, the location of the fabulous mine of *Potosí and thus an important source for much of the silver that went to Spain in the Golden Age. See *Entretenida* 2.

Chariot drawn by lions [Carro tirado de leones]. In *Casa* 2, the vehicle on which Venus comes on stage.

Chariot of the Sun [Carro del Sol]. In Greek myth, Helios, the sun god, drove his chariot across the heavens every day. According to a famous story told by Ovid in his *Metamorphoses*, Helios granted his son Phaethon his wish of driving the chariot for a day, but the youth lost control of the horses and the sun was about to crash into the earth when Zeus hurled a thunderbolt and Phaethon fell into a river and died. See *DQ* II, 41.

Charlemagne [Carlomagno, Carlo Magno] (742–814). Son of Pippin III, king of the Franks, and Holy Roman Emperor. He was of supreme importance in extending the Catholic Church throughout western Europe. He also became a legendary figure, the leader of the Twelve Peers of France, defender of the faith, and exemplary ruler (*Carolingian cycle). He is a major character in *Casa,* where he despairs at the antics of Roldán and Reinaldos; in the end, he makes them turn their attentions to war. See also *Celoso*; *DQ* I, 5 (where he is simply the Emperor), 48; *DQ* II, 24, 26.

Charles V. *Carlos V.

Charní, Mosén Pierres de. A French knight—his full name is Pierre de Beaufurmont, Sieur de Charny—mentioned by DQ in I, 49 (*Crónica de Juan II).

Charon [Carón]. In Greek myth, the oarsman who transported the dead in his boat across the river Styx to their final resting place in the underworld. See *DQ* II, 11; *Numancia* 2; *Poesías* 5; *Rufián* 1.

Charondas [Corondas]. According to legend, a Tyrian legislator who committed suicide when he broke his own law punishable by death. See *Coloquio*.

Charybdis [Caribdis]. In Greek legend, a whirlpool in a narrow channel of water, traditionally considered to be located in the Straits of Messina, between Sicily and Italy. It was most memorably described by Homer in the *Odyssey*. Sometimes it was depicted as a female monster who sucked in water and later spewed it out. Opposite it was *Scylla, equally dangerous. The problem for mariners was to navigate between the rock of Scylla and the whirlpools of Charybdis. Scylla and Charybdis have thus come to refer to two equally dangerous options and/or the need to run a straight and narrow course between two perils. See *DQ* I, 37; *Galatea* 5; *Parnaso* 3; *Persiles* I, 9; *Poesías* 21; *Tratos* 1.

Chasca, Juana la. *Juana la Chasca.

Chasm of Cabra [Sima de Cabra]. Just outside the city of *Cabra, there is a great chasm or cave. In *DQ* II, 14, when Sansón Carrasco is boasting of his achievements as the Knight of the Mirrors, he tells DQ that one of them, at the order of his beloved Casildea, was to descend into the chasm of Cabra and report to her what he saw there. This brief mention perhaps plants the seed of an idea in DQ, an idea that comes to fruition when he descends into the *Cave of Montesinos in II, 23. See also *Adjunta*; *Celoso*.

Chastity [Castidad]. In *Persiles* II, 15, in Periandro's dream, the figure that Auristela represents on the island of precious jewels.

Chaves, Cristóbal de. Spanish jurist and writer. He is the author of a two-part *Relación de la cárcel de Sevilla* (written about 1599 but not published until 1863; *Account of the Seville Prison*), a knowledgeable and detailed account of the conditions of the most famous prison in Spain in the Renaissance. Chaves may also be the author of the interlude entitled *La cárcel de Sevilla* (*The Seville Prison*), written around the turn of the seventeenth century and sometimes attributed to MC. It is a lively evocation of a setting MC knew very well, having been imprisoned there himself.

Chaves, Rodrigo de. *Información de Argel.*

Chávez Camacho, Armando. Mexican writer. Chávez, a self-described passionate admirer of MC, is the author of a brief book entitled *La última salida de Don Quijote* (1970; *Don Quixote's Last Sally*), in which DQ and SP ride out in the twentieth century, visiting various cities and towns in Spain, and commenting on what they see and hear: airplanes, modern music, television. They discuss historical, religious, and political developments since the seventeenth century, and find all of it very depressing as they fade off into the distance.
   Bibliography: Armando Chávez Camacho, *La última salida de Don Quijote* (Mexico City: Fondo de Cultura Económica, 1970).

Cheese from Flanders. *Flanders.

Chéntola. An Italian wine mentioned in *Vidriera*.

Cherwinski, Joseph (1914–). American poet. One of Cherwinski's books of poetry is entitled *Don Quixote with a Rake* (1964); it is divided into three sections, the last of which has the same title, as does the first poem in the section. The poem is a sonnet about raking leaves and ends "A Don Quixote tilting at the mill, / Fighting the winter, losing with a will!" In a *reductio ad absurdum*, raking leaves becomes a quixotic endeavor.
   Bibliography: Joseph Cherwinski, *Don Quixote with a Rake* (Boston: Bruce Humphries, 1964).

Chesterton, G(ilbert) K(eith) (1874– 1936). English novelist, poet, and essayist. Chesterton was a flamboyant figure and a pro-

lific writer whose Father Brown mysteries have proven to be his most popular works. His novel *The Return of Don Quixote* (1927) culminates when Herne, who is playing the role of a knight-errant on stage, walks out of the theater with his lance in hand, followed by a friend, Murrel, who offers to be his SP, mounts a horse pulling a handsome cab, and rides off to perform quixotic deeds. Herne describes the new quixotism of the twentieth century: "All your machinery has become so inhuman that it has become natural. In becoming a second nature, it has become as remote and indifferent and cruel as nature. The Knight is once more riding in the forest. Only he is lost in the wheels instead of in the woods. You have made your dead system on so large a scale that you do not yourselves know how or where it will be hit. That's the paradox! Things have grown incalculable by being calculated. You have tied men to tools so gigantic that they do not know on whom the strokes descend. You have justified the nightmare of Don Quixote. The mills really *are* giants."
   Bibliography: G. K. Chesterton, *The Return of Don Quixote* (London: Chatto & Windus, 1927).

Chief justice of the ecclesiastical court of Naples. *Guiomar de Quiñones, Doña.

Chifutí. The docks in the city of Constantinople. See *Sultana* 3.

Child [Niño]. In *Tratos* 2, an infant who appears as a prop.

Child of Feliciana de la Voz [Hijo de Feliciana de la Voz]. In *Persiles* III, 2, the pilgrims and a group of shepherds are given a newborn baby boy by a mysterious man on horseback and told to deliver the child to two men who live in Trujillo. When Feliciana examines the child in III, 4, she fails to recognize him as the baby to whom she gave birth two nights earlier, but when she is reunited with her lover Rosanio, the child's father and the mysterious horseman of II, 2, she takes the baby as hers.

Chimera [Quimera]. A fire-breathing, three-headed monster (with heads of a lion, a snake, and a goat). See *DQ* I, 47.

China. For MC and his contemporaries, a large, fabulous, and mysterious nation in eastern Asia. It was known largely through the stories about Marco *Polo and the *Historia del gran reino de la China* (1585; *History of the Great Kingdom of China*), published in Rome by Juan González de Mendoza, Spanish ambassador to the emperor of China. In the dedication to *DQ* II, MC claims that he received a letter from the emperor of China inviting him there to administer an academy in which *DQ* would be used as a text to teach Spanish. See also *Rufián* 1.

Chío. *Chius.

Chipre. *Cyprus.

Chiquiznaque. 1. In *Rinconete*, one of two thugs present at the home of Monipodio when Rinconete and Cortadillo are accepted into the thieves' brotherhood. **2**. In *Viudo*, a friend and fellow ruffian of the widowed Trampagos.

Chirinos. In *Retablo*, the co-conspirator with Chanfalla in the production of the magical show that can only be seen by those who are of legitimate birth and Old Christian blood.

Chito. In *Entretenida* 3, the phrase "voto a Chito" ("I swear to Chito") is used as a mock oath based on "Chito!" ["Hush!"].

Chius [Chío]. A Greek island in the Aegean Sea and the name of its capital city. See *Sultana* 3.

Chivalric themes in Cervantes. The entire premise of *DQ* I is that the protagonist goes mad from reading romances of chivalry, and as a result everything he does and says early in the novel is done and said in conscious imitation of these romances. *Amadís de Gaula*, others in that series, and other unrelated romances of chivalry were the most popular literature of the Renaissance and, as such, were a major factor in popular culture. The names DQ invents, his *fabla*, his invocation of DT, his transformation of prosaic reality according to the models in his favorite romances, and so forth are all in accord with his chivalric vision. DQ's concept of chivalry and his understanding of the romances of chivalry are the point of departure for everything else in the novel. Modern readers not familiar with the romances that DQ constantly imitates and cites probably miss at least part of the parody and humor of the novel. *DQ* I exists because of *Amadís de Gaula*, *Belianís de Grecia*, and others of the same genre. In *DQ* II, however, there is an important shift in emphasis, as the action is initiated not in the context of, or in response to, the romances of chivalry, but in the context of *DQ* I: *DQ* II exists because of *DQ* I.

Bibliography: Edward Dudley, *The Endless Text: "Don Quixote" and the Hermeneutics of Romance* (Albany: State University of New York Press, 2000); Howard Mancing, *The Chivalric World of "Don Quijote": Style, Structure and Narrative Technique* (Columbia: University of Missouri Press, 1982); and Edwin Williamson, *The Half-way House of Fiction; "Don Quixote" and Arthurian Romance* (Oxford: Clarendon Press, 1984).

Chopin, Kate (1851–1904). American novelist and short-story writer. Increasingly a part of the modern American canon, Chopin's novel *The Awakening* (1899) is in many ways another female version of the mythic DQ story. The protagonist Edna Pontellier has all the characteristics of a quixotic heroine: "At a very early period she had apprehended instinctively the dual life—that outward existence which conforms, the inward life which questions." Edna's inability to fit in with the reality prescribed by her husband (and by society in general) conflicts with her romantic imagination and her dreams; as one character comments, "She is not one of us; she is not like us."

Christ. *Jesus Christ.

Christian(s) [Cristiano(s)]. 1. In *Tratos* 4, an escapee spotted by a Muslim youth and beaten to death by order of King Azán. **2**. In *Baños* 1, a prisoner beaten by Guardián Bají. **3**. In *Baños* 3, the character who announces the arrival of the ransom ship. **4**. In *Española*, 300 men freed by Ricaredo in the skirmish near Gibraltar. Later one of them identifies him in Seville as the English corsair who set him free. **5**. *Father of Doña Catalina de Oviedo.

Christian Moses [Moisés cristiano]. Felipe II, leader of the Christian (i.e., Catholic) forces against the infidels (i.e., Protestants) of England. See *Poesías* 21.

Christian rowers. In *DQ* I, 41, men recruited by Ruy Pérez de Viedma to row in the ship in which he plans to make his escape.

Christmas [Pascua de Natal]. December 25, the annual *paschal festival of the birth of Jesus Christ. See *Baños* 3.

Christ's cross. *López de Zárate, Francisco.

Christus. 1. A cross printed at the beginning of alphabets and spelling manuals, and, by metonym, simply the alphabet. See *DQ* II, 42. **2**. *Order of Christus.

Chronicler [Sabio, coronista]. 1. All the Spanish romances of chivalry are presented as a translation of an ancient text written in an exotic language (Greek and Arabic are the two most common) by a sage historian (*sabio*), a wizard or enchanter who has used his great power and wisdom to write the fabulous story. *Belianís de Grecia*, for example, is supposed to have been translated from the Greek original written by Fristón (*Frestón). MC clearly parodies this convention and uses it to great comic advantage in his presentation of CHB and the *narrative structure of *DQ*. **2**. In *DQ* II, 45 a servant of the duke who writes a summary of SP's actions as governor so that they can be read and enjoyed by the duke and duchess.

Chronology in Cervantes's works. MC's four long prose fictions—*Galatea* (1585), *DQ* I (1605), *DQ* II (1615), and *Persiles* (1616)—take place over an extended period of time. Since *Galatea* is situated in a kind of idealized, extratemporal world, there is no problem with internal chronology in this romance, but the other three works all present problems for those who have attempted to trace a consistent temporal sequence of events in them. *DQ* I takes place 'not long ago,' yet much of the source material on which it is based consists of archived historical documents, some of which are old and crumbling (I, 52). When Ruy Pérez de Viedma narrates his life history (*Capitán*), he says that he first left home in 1567, some 22 years previously. Since one of his contemporaries in Algerian captivity was 'a certain Saavedra' (MC himself), Pérez must have been there some time between 1575 and 1580. Yet he and Zoraida have just escaped from Algiers and the year is 1589. Either it took them nine years to cross the Mediterranean and travel north from where they landed near Málaga to the inn in La Mancha where (still dressed in the clothing they wore when they left Algiers) they meet the other characters, or MC was making no attempt to present a consistent chronology. The latter is, of course, more likely. At any rate, it would seem logical to assume that the events of *DQ* I take place in the final decade of the sixteenth century: 'not long ago' in 1605 when the book is published. In *DQ* II the problems of chronology are even greater. *DQ* II, 1, takes place just one month after the end of *DQ* I— presumably, then, also in the late 1590s or around 1600. Yet when Sansón Carrasco arrives, he brings news that *DQ* I has been published (i.e., that it is after 1605). Furthermore, during the one month of DQ's recuperation after his first sallies, the book has been written, printed multiple times, and read all over Spain. The only possible "logical" explanation of how this could have been done is, as is suggested in the novel, by enchantment (which leads to the paradox that one of the few "real" things in the fiction that is *DQ* II is *DQ* I—but it is there only because of magic). Later, SP's letter to his wife written from the duke's palace (II, 36) is dated 1614, which makes clear that no consistent internal chronology for the two *DQ* novels is possible. There are other inconsistencies in *DQ* as well, but they need not be detailed here, as the point seems clear with this brief outline.

In *Persiles* the chronological dilemma is

even greater. Overall, the novel seems to take place during a two-year period, presumably about 1558–59. But (in addition to 'prophetic' allusions to events such as Lepanto, 1571; the death of Portuguese King Sebastião, 1578; and the expulsion of the *Moriscos*, 1609), there are several times when the time line makes no logical sense. For example, there are allusions to the dictates of the Council of Trent (1545–64) in I, 20, and II, 19, and references to the presence of the Spanish court of Felipe III in Madrid (after 1606) in III, 6; these and other anachronisms make any attempt at a coherent chronology impossible. MC is writing fiction, and there is no need to expect historical accuracy from him, but since scholars have devoted so much attention to matters such as these, it is important to state explicitly that internal chronology in these novels is not to be found.

Bibliography: Kenneth P. Allen, "Aspects of Time in *Los trabajos de Persiles y Sigismunda*," *Revista Hispánica Moderna* 36 (1971): 77–107; Luis Andrés Murillo, *The Golden Dial: Temporal Configuration in "Don Quijote"* (Oxford: Dolphin, 1975); and Rafael Osuna, "Vacilaciones y olvidos de Cervantes en el *Persiles*," *Anales Cervantinos* 11 (1972): 69–85.

Chronology of Cervantes's works. Determining when MC actually wrote his works is not always easy. It is clear that certain occasional poems were composed in conjunction with the events to which they refer. *Tratos, Numancia*, and the lost plays were written during the early 1580s when he was active in the theater. *Galatea* was obviously written in the first half of the 1580s. The final chapters of *DQ* I and the stories *Vidriera, Casamiento*, and *Coloquio* must have been written during MC's stay in Valladolid in the years 1604–6. *Adjunta*, the final section of *Parnaso*, was written in 1614, but it is possible that the poem itself was composed, in its entirety or in part, at least two years before that. The latter part of *DQ* II was probably written between 1614 (when Avellaneda's sequel was published) and 1615. The ending of *Persiles* was written in the final months before MC's death in the spring of 1616. Beyond this, however, little is certain. Many believe that *DQ* I was begun and largely

written in the 1590s and may have circulated in manuscript for some while before its publication in 1605. It is clear that the stories in *Novelas* were written over a long period of time, perhaps as much as two decades in some cases, before their publication in 1613. *Comedias* contains works that are probably revisions of plays from the 1580s as well as some more recent ones, and it is not possible to date any of them with certainty. Some have placed the writing of *Persiles* as early as the 1560s, whereas others argue for its entire composition in the final years of MC's life. Modern consensus is that the first two books were probably written relatively early, perhaps simultaneously with *DQ* I in the 1590s, and that the latter two were composed much later, probably along with and then following the publication of *DQ* II. For a long time, there was an assumption that MC began his career by writing more naïve, idealistic, romantic romances (rather than novels), and generally evolved toward more sophisticated, realistic, metafictional novels. This facile assumption was dramatically challenged by Ruth El Saffar in 1974, when she completely reversed the chronology and compellingly described a writer who began with the more realistic works and evolved toward the more traditional kinds of romance. Persuasive as this theory is, it fails to convince. There is no reason to believe that MC could not write a romance-oriented story like *Española* one day and a novel-like story such as *Rinconete* the next, that he could not alternate between *DQ* and *Persiles*, and that he could not write a realistic comic *entremés* and a relatively serious and conventional *comedia* at the same time. Besides, there is not a single work of MC's that is a pure example of any particular type: all the 'romances' contain realistic, comic, and/or metafictional elements; all the 'realistic' works contain some element(s) of romance.

Bibliography: Milton A. Buchanan, "The Works of Cervantes and Their Dates of Composition," *Transactions of the Royal Society of Canada* 32 (1938): 23–39; Ruth S. El Saffar, *Novel to Romance: A Study of Cervantes's "Novelas ejemplares"* (Baltimore: Johns Hopkins University Press, 1974); and E. C. Riley, "Cervantes: A Question of Genre," in *Mediaeval and Renaissance Studies on Spain and Portugal in Honour of P. E. Russell*, ed. F. W. Hodcroft et al. (Oxford: Society for the Study of Mediaeval Languages and Literatures, 1981), 69–85.

Church of la Anunciada: la Annunziata. A church in Naples to which the captive Madrigal promises to go after his release. See *Sultana* 1.

Church of Nuestra Señora de Atocha. *Our Lady of Atocha.

Church of Our Lord God. *Roman Catholic Church.

Church of San Ginés. A church in Madrid that was destroyed in the seventeenth century. See *Entretenida* 1.

Church of San Jerónimo. A church in Madrid, dating from the reign of the Catholic Monarchs, which was destroyed in the eighteenth-century War of Independence. See *Entretenida* 3; *Gitanilla*.

Church of San Román. A church in the *Feria district of Seville. See *Rufián* 1, 3.

Church of San Salvador. A major church in Seville. See *Rufián* 1.

Church of San Sebastián. 1. A church in Madrid. See *Entretenida* 3. **2**. An old and venerated church in Seville. See *Española*; *Rinconete*; *Rufián* 1.

Church of Santa María. *Our Lady of Almudena.

Church of Santa María la Mayor. The church in Alcalá de Henares where MC was baptized on October 9, 1547.

Church, sea, or royal service. *Pérez de Viedma family.

Chusma. *Crew.

Cicero, Marcus Tullius (Tully) [Cicerón, Tulio] (106–43 BCE). Roman statesman, rhetorician, and orator. See *DQ* I, prologue, 48; *DQ* II, 22, 32; *Elección*; *Galatea* 6; *Poesías* 31.

Ciceronianca. In *Retablo*, a pronunciation error for *Ciceroniana* (Ciceronian), made by Benito Repollo.

Cicilia. *Sicily.

Cid, El; Cid Campeador; Cid Ruy Díaz Campeador. *Díaz de Vivar, Rodrigo (or Ruy), el Cid Campeador.

Cid, Miguel. A poet of religious themes, whose son published a book of his verse after his death; he is praised in *Parnaso* 2.

Cide Hamete Benengeli. The Muslim who writes the manuscript that becomes the main source for the events in the life of DQ and SP, thus the primary historian of DQ's life. The use of the title *Cide* (Lord, as in El Cid) suggests the holy men (seers, wise magicians) of Algiers called *marabouts*, whom MC would have known during his years of captivity. CHB is a parody of ancient historians, such as Turpin, and of the supposed chroniclers of the romances of chivalry. According to the scene narrated in *DQ* I, 9, after the original historical sources from the *Archives of La Mancha come to an end, the narrator (i.e., MC) conducts a search for more information relating to DQ. In Toledo, he comes across a bit of manuscript being sold by a young boy and sees that it is written in Arabic. Intrigued by the manuscript he does not understand, he has a *Morisco aljamiado*, a bilingual Muslim convert, take a look at it for him and learns that it deals with characters called DT and SP. Sure that he now has an important historical document dealing with DQ, he purchases the entire manuscript and pays the *Morisco* to translate it for him. It turns out that the complete title is *Historia de don Quijote de la Mancha, escrita por Cide Hamete Benengeli, historiador arábigo* [*History of Don Quixote de la Mancha, Written by Cide Hamete Benengeli, Arabic Historian*], and this becomes the source for nearly everything recorded about DQ in both parts of the novel (*narrative structure of *Don Quixote*). CHB, then, is the "author" or original narrator of the story of DQ and SP. His work is translated by the *Morisco* and then edited and written in final form by MC (in his fictional role as editor).

Evidence of the editor's role is apparent at various points. For example, it is stated in I, 9, that the *name of SP is sometimes given in the Arabic text as Sancho Zancas, but this variant never appears in the version we read, presumably because the editor regularized the name. There are other occasions when what CHB wrote was not translated but was edited out. Examples are his comments on the friendship between Rocinante and SP's ass (II, 12) and the description of the house of Don Diego de Miranda (II, 18). In II, 5, the translator doubts the accuracy of CHB's text, believing that the discourse attributed to SP is actually beyond the squire's intellectual capabilities. And occasionally the editor lets his own voice override that of the original historian, as when he refers to the Christian ships skirmishing with a Turkish vessel in the Barcelona harbor (II, 63) as 'our' soldiers. None of these examples presents anything more than a minor problem for the reader, while foregrounding the narrative play of the text. Further evidence of the editor at work is seen in the fact that even the Arabic historian's title for his book is changed, as the one we read on the title page of the published book is *El ingenioso hidalgo don Quijote de la Mancha* (*The Ingenious Hidalgo Don Quixote of La Mancha*), rather than the one cited in I, 9. As the novel progresses, particularly in *DQ* II, there is an ongoing implicit dialogue between the narrator and the Arabic historian, with the former commenting on, criticizing, making fun of, and/or pointing out the inconsistencies of the latter. One of the greatest ironies in the figure of CHB is that we have a representative of a minority, marginalized, and heterodox figure as the model of a historian; textual authority in this case comes from Muslim sources, rather than orthodox Christian ones. MC, far more than the great majority of his contemporaries, knew firsthand and, perhaps, respected cultural and religious otherness. So, ultimately, the great tradition of the novel in the West has its fictional origins in the (Middle) East in the fig-

ure of CHB. Among CHB's most notable moments in the novel are I, 16, when he turns out to be a relative of the muleteer in the inn; II, 8, when he thrice praises Allah as DQ and SP set out anew; II, 10, where he questions DQ's acts in the scene of the enchantment of DT but assures the reader that he will recount what happened in scrupulous detail, down to the atoms of the story, only to be very confused about what kinds of animals the three women are riding; II, 24, where he calls into question DQ's account of what happened in the Cave of Montesinos; II, 27, where he swears like a Catholic Christian; II, 31, when he (confusingly, ambiguously; perhaps a lie) notes that upon arrival at the duke's palace, DQ felt like a real knight-errant for the first time in his life; II, 38, when he lies about the 'real' name of the Countess Trifaldi; II, 40, where the narrator ecstatically proclaims his greatness; II, 44, where he absurdly complains that his translator did not translate this chapter correctly and justifies the technique of including other narratives in his history; II, 48, where he says he would give his best cape to see Doña Rodríguez and DQ together; II, 53, where he gets the order of the seasons of the year mixed up; and II, 74, where he addresses his pen as he hangs it up. See also *DQ* I, 22, 27; *DQ* II, 1, 27, 34, 50, 52, 54–55, 60–61, 70, 73.

Bibliography: John J. Allen, "The Narrators, the Reader and Don Quijote," *MLN* 91 (1976): 201–12; Thomas E. Case, "Cide Hamete Benengeli y los *Libros plúmbeos*," *Cervantes* 22, no. 2 (2002): 9–24; R. M. Flores, "The Rôle of Cide Hamete in *Don Quixote*," *Bulletin of Hispanic Studies* 59 (1982): 3–14; Santiago Alfonso López Navia, *La ficción autorial en el "Quijote" y en sus continuaciones e imitaciones* (Madrid: Universidad Europea de Madrid-CEES, 1996); Jesús G. Maestro, "El sistema narrativo del *Quijote*: la construcción del personaje Cide Hamete Benengeli," *Cervantes* 15, no. 1 (1995): 111–41; Howard Mancing, "Cide Hamete Benengeli vs. Miguel de Cervantes: The Metafictional Dialectic of *Don Quijote*," *Cervantes* 1, no. 1–2 (1981): 63–81; José Manuel Martín Morán, *El "Quijote" en ciernes: Los descuidos de Cervantes y las fases de elaboración textual* (Torino, Italy: Edizioni dell'Orso, 1990); James A. Parr, "The Rôle of Cide Hamete Benengeli: Between Renaissance Paradox and Baroque Emblematics," *Indiana Journal of Hispanic Literatures* 1, no. 1 (1992): 101–14; C. A. Soons, "Cide Hamete Benengeli. His Significance for *Don Quijote*," *Modern Language Review* 54 (1959): 351–57; and Geoffrey Stagg, "El sabio Cide Hamete Venengeli," *Bulletin of Hispanic Studies* 33 (1956): 218–25.

Cide Hamete Berenjena. SP's mispronunciation (linguistically justified in a way that SP cannot realize) for the Muslim historian CHB, author of *DQ* I. *Berenjena*, DQ points out, means 'eggplant,' hardly a name for a historian, but SP observes that Muslims are known to be very fond of eggplants. See *DQ* II, 2.

Ciego. *Blind man.

Ciego; Ciego arquero; Ciego dios. *Cupid.

Cielo empíreo. *Empyrean heaven.

Cifar; *Cifar, Libro del caballero.* *Libro del caballero Cifar.*

Cila. *Scylla.

Cilenio. *Mercury.

Címbalo. *Zembra.

Cinco Viñas. An Italian wine described as 'great' in *Vidriera*.

Cínicos. *Cynics.

Ciniras. *Cinyras.

Cintia. *Cynthia.

Cipión. 1. In *Casamiento*, one of the two dogs whom Campuzano hears talking one night. Then in *Coloquio*, Cipión listens to and comments on Berganza's autobiographical narrative. **2**. *Scipio.

Cipiones. A Roman family name mentioned in *DQ* I, 13.

Cipre. *Cyprus.

Cipreses, valle de los. *Valley of the Cypress Trees.

Cipria diosa; Ciprinia. *Venus.

Circe. In the *Odyssey*, the goddess who used her powerful magic to turn Odysseus's men into swine, although Odysseus himself resisted her spell and spent over a year with her. See *Coloquio*; *DQ* I, prologue; *Galatea* 4.

Cirongilio de Tracia. *Vargas, Bernardo de.

Cirujano. *Doctor.

Cisneros, Cardinal Francisco Jiménez de (1436–1517). Confessor to Queen Isabel the Catholic, patron of education, founder of the University of *Alcalá in 1508, and inquisitor general. Cisneros was a person of enormous power and influence in the early Spanish Renaissance. Many of the faculty he hired at the university were *conversos*, and they played an important role in that institution's major achievement: the Polyglot Bible. Cisneros was also tolerant (and even supportive) of Erasmus and his followers in Spain.

   Bibliography: Erika Rummel, *Jiménez de Cisneros: On the Threshold of Spain's Golden Age* (Tempe: Arizona Center for Medieval and Renaissance Studies, 1999).

Cita (Citia). *Scythia.

Citizen of Florence [Ciudadano de Florencia]. In *Curioso* (*DQ* I, 35), the man who informs the distraught Anselmo that the talk in the city is all about the flight of Lotario and Camila, and Anselmo's own disappearance; it is the final confirmation that his wife and best friend have betrayed him.

Citizen of Tordesillas. *Avellaneda, Alonso Fernández de.

Citizens [Ciudadanos]. In *Rufián* 3, two men who recount the miracle performed by Fray Cristóbal de la Cruz (formerly Cristóbal de Lugo) and crowd into his cell and steal off with remnants of his clothing as relics when he dies.

Citizens of Novara [Ciudadanos de Novara]. In *Laberinto*, two men who discuss the Rosamira case with Anastasio.

City, castle, or fortress [Ciudad, castillo o fortaleza]. *Enchanted boat.

City of a hundred doors [Ciudad de las cien puertas]. In *DQ* I, 15, DQ refers to this city in connection with Bacchus, 'the merry god of laughter,' and his tutor Silenus. He may be somewhat in error, however, for the city Homer refers to as having 100 doors is the Thebes of Egypt, not the Thebes of Boeotia in Greece (a city of seven doors), which is where Bacchus is from and into which Silenus entered.

Ciudad Real. The capital of the province of that name in the region of La Mancha, located south of Madrid and northeast of Córdoba, about halfway between them. Like other locations in La Mancha, it was known for its wines. See *Coloquio*; *DQ* II, 13, 47; *Sultana* 3; *Vidriera*.

Ciudadano de Florencia. *Citizen of Florence.

Ciudadanos de Novara. *Citizens of Novara.

Ciudades libres de Alemania. *Free cities of Germany.

Civil Wars of Granada. *Pérez de Hita, Ginés.

Clara. 1. In *Gitanilla*, the wife of the lieutenant who invites Preciosa to his home to perform her song and dance. **2**. In *Sultana*, a Christian woman captured by the Turks, who winds up in Amurates's harem under the name of Zaida.

Clara de Viedma, Doña. The 16-year-old daughter of Juan Pérez de Viedma, who arrives with her father at the *inn of Juan Palomeque, where her love for Don Luis becomes a matter of interest. She appears in *DQ* I, 42–45.

Clara Perlerina. The intended bride of the son of the peasant who comes to SP for help in financing the marriage. In *DQ* II, 47, the man describes her in great detail as being just as lovely as a pearl, as her name suggests, except for her missing eye, pitted face, few teeth, hunched back, and so forth. This grotesque description is the equivalent in *DQ* II of the description of Maritornes in *DQ* I, 16.

Claraura. In *Galatea* 3, the absent shepherdess loved by Crisio; she never appears in the text.

Claricia. In *Persiles* III, 14–15, the wife of the deranged Domicio whom he attempts to kill by throwing her from a tower; however, her skirts form a sort of parachute and she lands unharmed. After her husband's death, she helps nurse Periandro back to health and explains how Domicio had been enchanted and driven to madness.

Claridiana. The peerless daughter of the Emperor of Trebizond and the lady loved by the protagonist in *Espejo de principes y caballeros* (*Ordóñez de Calahorra, Diego de). See the sonnet from the Caballero del Febo to DQ, one of the preliminary poems in *DQ* I.

Clarín (Leopoldo Alas, 1852–1901). Spanish novelist and critic. One of the great novels of the nineteenth century is Clarín's *La Regenta* (1884–85; *The Regent's Wife*), whose protagonist Ana Osores joins Emma Bovary, Isidora Rufete, Anna Karenina, and others in the pantheon of quixotic women who find that reality does not correspond to their romantic and literature-inspired vision of it. References and allusions to DQ and other characters and situations in *DQ* appear from time to time in both *La Regenta* and Clarín's other major novel, *Su único hijo* (1890; *His Only Son*).
   Bibliography: Stephanie Sieburth, "*La Regenta* as Quixotic Novel: Imitation and Intertextuality," *Romance Quarterly* 35 (1988): 319–37.

Clarísima estrella de María. *Mary's shining star.

Clark, Walter Van Tilburg (1909–71). American novelist, poet, and short-story writer.

Clark's *The Ox-Bow Incident* (1940) is one of the finest of all western novels. In it, the protagonist Art Dawes talks against the lynching that is the focal point of the story in a manner that could be a commentary on the premise of *DQ* I, 1: "And there's another thing I've always noticed, that arguments sound a lot different indoors and outdoors. There's a kind of insanity that comes from being between walls and under a roof. You're too cooped up, and don't get a chance to test ideas against the real size of things. That's true about day and night too; night's like a room; it makes the little things in your head too important. A man's not clear headed at night." Later, when Dawes repeats his arguments against the lynching, another character says to him, "It's them books, Art, them books. You better lay off them."

Claudia Jerónima. In *DQ* II, 60, the beautiful young woman dressed as a man who has shot and killed her lover because she mistakenly believed that he was about to marry another woman. She is assisted by *Roque Guinart and then decides to become a nun.
Bibliography: Robert L. Hathaway, "Claudia Jerónima (*DQ* II, 60)," *Nueva Revista de Filología Hispánica* 36 (1988): 319–32.

Claudino Rubicón. In *Persiles* III, 16–17, the killer of Count Lamberto de Escocia, husband of Ruperta, the woman he loves. After his death, Ruperta vows to avenge herself by killing his son Croriano, but she winds up marrying him.

Clauquel Torrellas. In *DQ* II, 60, an enemy of Simón Forte, who is father of *Claudia Jerónima, and the father of Vicente, Claudia's lover.

Claustro de la iglesia mayor. *Cloister of the cathedral.

Clavijo. 1. In *Entretenida* 3, the friend who arrives with Don Silvestre de Almendárez. **2.** In *DQ* II, 38–41, the lover of the Princess Antonomasia in the story told by the Countess *Trifaldi.

Clavileño the Swift [Clavileño el Alígero]. The wooden horse, guided by a peg on its forehead, which DQ and SP ride in order to undertake the adventure set up for them by the enchanter Malambruno (*Trifaldi, Countess); the original architect of this marvelous device is no less than Merlin himself. The name is derived from the materials from which the horse is made: *clavija* (peg) and *leño* (wood); *Alígero* is derived both from *ala* (wing) and *ligero* (light). The supposed flight on the wooden horse can hardly fail to evoke a parodic image of Ariosto's famous winged steed, the *hippogriff. See *DQ* II, 40–42, 44.
Bibliography: Augustin Redondo, "De don Clavijo a Clavileño: Algunos aspectos de la tradición carnavalesca y cazurra en el *Quijote*," *Edad de Oro* 3 (1984): 181–99.

Clemencia Crespo. In *Pedro* 1, the daughter of the mayor of Junquillos who marries Clemente.

Clemens, Samuel Langhorne. *Twain, Mark.

Clementa Bueso, Doña. In *Casamiento*, the real owner of the house Doña Estefanía passed off as hers.

Clementa (Mari) Cobeña. In *Persiles* III, 8, the daughter of the mayor who is pregnant by Tozuelo.

Clemente. 1. In *Gitanilla*, a page-poet who from time to time writes poetry for Preciosa to perform. Later (after introducing himself as Alonso Hurtado and then revealing his name as Don Sancho) he joins the gypsy band—where he is given the name of Clemente—in order to be near and sing the praises of Preciosa. He becomes the close friend of Andrés Caballero, and the two celebrate the beauty of Preciosa in poetry. **2.** *Antón Clemente.

Clenardo. In *DQ* I, 29, the father of *Dorotea who is merely mentioned in her account of her problems.

Cleopatra VII (69–30 BCE). Queen of Egypt, nominally married to her brother Ptolemy XIII, and lover of Julius Caesar and Mark Antony. According to legend, she committed suicide by permitting a poisonous asp to bite her. See *Casa* 2; *Galatea* 4.

Clergy. The Church dominated many facets of life in the Spanish Golden Age, and at times it seemed as though there were priests everywhere. In fact, the clergy only made about 2 or 3 percent of the entire population, but even this was a number higher than anywhere else in Europe at the time.

Clérigo. *Priest.

Clérigos o estudiantes. *Priests or students.

Clicia, Clicie. In Greek myth, a nymph who fell in love with Apollo, the sun, following him everywhere, and was turned into a heliotrope, or sunflower, which always faces toward (follows) the sun. See *Galatea* 4; *Laberinto* 3.

Clifet. An infernal deity (invented by MC) evoked by Fátima in *Tratos* 2.

Clifford, Rosamonde. *Rosamunda.

Clio; Clío. *Muses.

Clisterna. In *Española*, the beautiful Scottish woman (and a secret Catholic) chosen by Ricaredo's parents to be his bride before they get to know Isabel, and who is brought back near the end of the story when Isabel loses her beauty.

Cloanto. A shepherd mentioned in *Casa* 2.

Clodio. In *Persiles* I, 12, the man who arrives on Mauricio's ship, chained to Rosamunda. Just as Rosamunda is the personification of lust, Clodio personifies satire. In I, 14, he explains that he has been exiled from England for being a slander and gossip. In I, 16, Arnaldo sets him and Rosamunda free of their chains. He travels in the group with Periandro and, on the island of Scinta, begins to make others suspicious about the real relationship between Periandro and Auristela (II, 2–4). In II, 7–8, he writes a love letter to Auristela, who reacts furiously,

and then he is accidentally killed by Antonio the younger with an arrow through the tongue.

Cloelia. In *Persiles* I, 1, the woman who helps retrieve Periandro from the cave-prison. In I, 4–6, she arrives with Auristela at the barbarians' island, escapes the destruction of the island with Periandro and the others to the cave of Antonio the Barbarian, where she falls ill and dies after giving Auristela a valuable diamond cross and two precious pearls that she has been carrying for her. She is buried on the island. Later, in II, 10–12, Periandro tells how Cloelia, Auristela's servant, originally set out with him and his sister, fled with them from the pirates to the fisherman's island, and was taken captive with Auristela by other pirates. How and why she was on the barbarians' island, and in the capacity of jailer, is not at all clear.

Cloister of the cathedral (of Toledo) [Claustro de la iglesia mayor]. The place where MC contracts the *Morisco aljamiado* to translate into Spanish the Arabic text of the manuscript of CHB (*translator).

Clori. 1. In *DQ* I, 34, Lotario in *Curioso* uses this name (one frequently used as a poetic pseudonym in romantic poetry) for the woman he addresses in his sonnets. **2.** In *Casa*, the shepherdess who rejects Lauso and Corinto in favor of Rústico. **3.** *Pastoral names.

Clotaldo. In *Española*, the Englishman who takes a young Spanish girl, Isabel, during the raid on Cádiz and raises her in London.

Cnossus [Gnido, Nido]. An ancient city and former capital of Crete, the site of a temple of Venus, goddess of love. See *Parnaso* 5; *Persiles* I, 21.

Coaches, carriages [Coches]. In MC's day, the coach or carriage was an important symbol of wealth and nobility. So, naturally, coaches were frequently used for deception, especially by prostitutes. In 1611, a law was promulgated that allowed only women of a certain social standing to ride in coaches, with the proviso that they were not permitted to cover their faces

(Gabriel de *Barrionuevo for an interlude on this subject in which MC is implicated). Clearly, this proclamation was aimed at curbing rampant prostitution in which courtesans posed as respectable women. The new law provides the pretext for much of the humor in *Vizcaíno*.

Coachman [Cochero]. The man driving the coach carrying the *Basque lady in *DQ* I, 8.

Coca. A city located northwest of Madrid and south of Valladolid. It is the site of one of the most spectacular Muslim castles in all of Spain and was also noted for its wine. See *Vidriera*.

Coches. *Coaches, carriages.

Cocinero. *Cook.

Cocito. *Cocytus.

Cockaigne [Cucaña]. A legendary land of eternal pleasure and luxury. See *Entretenida* 2.

Cocles, Publius Horatius [Horacio] (sixth century CE). Not the famous poet Horace, but a great Roman hero and a member of the same clan. His most famous deed was to hold back the entire Etruscan army while his comrades destroyed a wooden bridge over the Tiber River into Rome. Then Cocles jumped into the river and swam back to the city. See *DQ* II, 8.

Cocodrilo de un metal no conocido. *Crocodile of an unknown metal.

Cocytus [Cocito]. In Greek myth, a tributary of the Acheron River in the underworld. See *Poesías* 30.

Coelho Rebello, Manoel. Portuguese dramatist. He is the author of an interlude entitled *El enredo más bizarro y historia verdadera* (1658; *The Most Bizarre Plot, and True History*) based on *Cueva*.

Coello y Ochoa, Antonio (1600–53). Spanish dramatist. One of his plays is *El celoso extremeño, o Los celos de Carrizales* (*The Jealous Old Man from Extremadura, or The Jeal-ous of Carrizales*), an adaptation of *Celoso*. The beautiful woman kept in a locked and guarded house, which must be penetrated by the young lover, remains, but the thematic and sexual tension of the original *novela* is sacrificed to a much more conventional romance plot in which the possibility of adultery is entirely absent.
  Bibliography: Manuel García Martín, "El celoso extremeño y su influencia en la comedia del siglo XVII," in *Cervantes, su obra y su mundo: Actas del I Congreso Internacional sobre Cervantes*, ed. Manuel Criado de Val (Madrid: Edi-6, 1981), 409–21.

Coello y Pacheco, Carlos (1850–88). Spanish dramatist. One of Coello's plays is *Roque Guinart* (1874), a drama in three acts and in verse. It is the story of sibling rivalry among noble Catalan bandits. The hero Don Jaime de Moncada, also known as Roque Guinart, escapes from jail, becomes a famous and generous bandit, and eventually is reunited with the woman he loves, even as he shows up his half-brother for the liar and traitor that he is. At the beginning of the third act, DQ and SP cross the stage in brief cameo roles; they play no part in the action.
  Bibliography: Carlos Coello y Pacheco, *Roque Guinart* (Madrid: Imprenta de la Biblioteca de Instrucción y Recreo, 1874).

Colada. The name of one of the swords of El Cid. See *Entretenida* 3.

Colegio de mase Rodrigo. *College of Maese Rodrigo.

Colegio trilingüe. *Trilingual College.

Coles, Elizabeth. *Taylor, Elizabeth.

Colindres. In *Coloquio*, the prostitute who works with the constable and the notary to entrap and bilk foreigners.

College of Cardinals [Colegio de los Cardenales]. The assembly of cardinals of the Roman Catholic Church in Rome. This body serves as a privy council to the pope, administers the Holy See when the pope is absent, and elects new popes. See *Vidriera*.

College of Maese Rodrigo [Colegio de mase Rodrigo]. Popular name of the University of Seville, which was founded by Maese Rodríguez Fernández de Santella (1444–1509) under the name of Colegio Mayor de Santa María. See *Coloquio*.

Colman, George (1732–94). English dramatist. Colman's first play, *Polly Honeycombe* (1760), is a satire on the prototypical quixotic theme of the excessive reading of romantic novels. Polly, a merchant's daughter, is led by her illusions to reject the wealthy suitor who has her father's support for a more poetic rival. Colman also wrote the libretto for the opera *The Mountaineers* (1795), with music by Samuel Arnold (1740–1802), based loosely on *Cardenio*.

Coloma, Juan, Conde de Elda. Spanish nobleman, viceroy of Sardinia. He is known primarily for his religious poem entitled *Década a la Pasión* (1576; *Decade of Passion*), which is praised in Calliope's song in *Galatea* 6.

Colón, Cristóbal. *Columbus, Christopher.

Colonas. A modern family name mentioned in *DQ* I, 13.

Colonna (Colona), Ascanio (ca. 1559–1608). Italian humanist and cardinal. Colonna was a friend of Giulio Acquaviva, in whose household MC served in Rome in 1569–70, and whom he must have known. In the 1580s Colonna, while holding the honorific title of Abbot of Santa Sofía, was residing in Alcalá de Henares (where he had studied at the university). MC's friend Luis *Gálvez de Montalvo was serving in Colonna's household during this period and may also have been influential in securing the prominent clergyman as patron for MC. In 1585, MC dedicated *Galatea* to Colonna and in the prologue mentions his father, Marco Antonio *Colonna, Duke of Pagliano, a general in the battle of Lepanto and whom MC probably also knew personally.

Colonna, Marco Antonio, Duke of Pagliano (1535–84). Italian sea captain. Colonna was one of the commanders of the Venetian forces during the battle of *Lepanto. He was the father of Cardinal Ascanio *Colonna, to whom MC dedicated *Galatea*.

Coloquio de los perros, El (Coloquio); The Dialogue of the Dogs. The final story in *Novelas*. By most standards, it is the most original and the best story in the collection. The two talking dogs are drawn from MC's personal experience when he lived in Valladolid in 1604–6 and undoubtedly saw the two well-known dogs of Mahudes, who carried lanterns for the alms collector in benefit of the Hospital of the Resurrection. The talking animals are drawn from the tradition of Aesop's fables, *Apuleius's *Golden Ass* (both of which are mentioned in the story), and the Renaissance dialogue tradition. The central metafictional episode of the witches known as las Camachas, which takes place in the town of Montilla, is also based on a historical incident from the mid-sixteenth century, which MC most likely heard when he was in that location in the early 1590s. The presence of this ambiguously fantastic episode in the midst of an otherwise realistic (given the premise of talking dogs, that is) narrative can be seen as a bold aesthetic move on MC's part. Among the noteworthy readers and fans of this story was Sigmund *Freud. A statement made by the dog Berganza early in the dialogue provides an important clue to MC's concept of prose genres. There are two kinds of stories, he says, one of which has its pleasure in the telling itself, whereas the other type is interesting for the way in which it is told. This has been seen by many MC scholars as a distinction between novel and *romance and a way of classifying MC's fictional works, not just in *Novelas*, but in general. Berganza's picaresque narrative of his life is made even more interesting by the running commentary provided by Cipión and the series of insightful exchanges between the two dogs on the subjects of gossip, backbiting, and satire. Cipión's injunctions against digressions have also been read as a criticism of *Guzmán de Alfarache*, whose picaresque narrator frequently digresses from his primary narrative.

(Ensign Campuzano, who is one of the main characters in *Casamiento*, spent some time in the Hospital of Resurrection taking a sweating cure for a case of syphilis. In his last two nights there, he had the extraordinary experience of overhearing a conversation between two dogs, named Berganza and Cipión. On the first night Berganza told his life story, and on the second night Cipión did the same. Campuzano wrote down the first night's dialogue and is prepared to write the second one if the first one is well received.)

As the two dogs break into conversation, they are amazed at their ability to use human speech and to reason like human beings. Even as they are speaking, they find it difficult to believe that they can actually talk intelligently. After checking to be sure that no one can hear them (they assume the soldier—Campuzano—in a nearby bed is asleep), they decide to spend the entire night in conversation. On the first night Berganza will tell the story of his life and adventures, and on the second night, if they still have the gift of speech, Cipión will tell his. Berganza remembers first seeing the light of day in Seville, and his first master is one Nicolás el Romo, who works in the slaughterhouse of that city. Romo gives the dog the name Gavilán and teaches him to carry a basket in his mouth. One day he is tricked by an attractive young woman who wants to get even with Romo for some unmentioned event. When he returns with an empty basket to his master, Berganza is beaten and decides to run away. He goes out into the country where he is taken in by a group of shepherds, who put a collar on him and call him Barcino. He enjoys the life of a sheepdog and notes that in real life shepherds do not lament unrequited love or spend the day composing and singing verses, as they do in pastoral romances. Neither do shepherds and shepherdesses have the poetic names—like Diana, Galatea, Lisardo, or Lauso—as they do in fiction, but common names like Antonio and Pablo. At this point in his narrative, Berganza remembers an important event that happened to him with a witch in Montilla and that might

explain their ability to speak. Cipión wants to hear this right away, but Berganza insists on following a chronological sequence. There seems to be a major problem with wolves, for from time to time the shepherds cry wolf and send the dogs off to fend off the intruder. But inevitably the wolf seems to outsmart the dogs, for when they return to the flock the wolf has killed and partially eaten a sheep. One night, instead of going off after the wolf, Berganza hides and watches the flock. To his dismay, he sees the shepherds kill a sheep, making it look like a wolf attack, and eat the best parts of the meat. Disillusioned, Berganza returns to Seville and enters into the service of a rich merchant. The merchant sends his sons to a Jesuit school, and one day one of them leaves his book behind. Berganza, on his own, takes the book in his mouth, carries it to the school, and gives it to his master. This is such a popular event that he begins to accompany the boys to school on a regular basis. There he gets to listen to the lessons they receive from the wise and accomplished Jesuit teacher and becomes a general mascot of the students, who frequently give him tasty snacks. Because the teachers see Berganza as too much of a distraction for the students, he is sent back home to his previous function as a guard dog. The merchant has in the house two black slaves, a man and a woman. Each night the woman goes to sleep with the man, giving Berganza a treat to keep him quiet. But the virtuous Berganza is troubled by the immoral life of the two slaves, so one night, in silence, he bites the woman, and some time later he mauls her with his claws. In order to get even, she prepares for him a sponge cooked in lard, but he does not eat it, for he recognizes that it would swell up in his stomach and cause his death. Unwilling to carry on his campaign against the wicked slaves, Berganza leaves the merchant's home. He joins up with a constable, an old friend of his first master, and forms part of a law enforcement team. His new master sets up a scheme with a notary and a prostitute named La Colindres to trap and bilk foreign visitors in Seville. One night, however, while they are apprehending La Colindres *in flagrante* with a mark, Berganza smells some meat in the pocket of the man's clothing, which he drags outside in order to be able to eat the meat. When the victim is told to pay up or be taken to jail, he finds his clothing with his money missing and accuses the law officers of robbing him. A major row develops, and Berganza goes outside to retrieve the clothing, only to realize that someone has come along and taken the garments (and the money). In the end, only the innocent innkeeper and the victim of the scam do some jail time. Soon after this, the constable has an encounter with six ruffians, whom he bests in a duel, and he gains fame as a brave law officer. But later Berganza accompanies him to a private home where it turns out that it was all staged, part of a plan of the master thief Monipodio to help the constable establish a reputation for bravery and honesty. Finally, after the constable himself is caught in a scam to acquire a horse named Piedrahierro, Berganza decides to take action to expose the dishonest law officer. That night, instead of attacking a thief, he turns on his master and, after mauling him, leaves town. In the nearby town of Mairena, about four leagues from Seville, Berganza comes across a company of soldiers, and the company's drummer takes a particular liking to him. Within a couple of weeks Berganza has learned to do several tricks, and the drummer puts on a profitable show with the Wise Dog, as he is known. Then during a show in Montilla, when the drummer makes a comment about a famous witch in the community, the show is interrupted by an old woman who shouts and carries on that she is not a witch. When the crowd breaks up, the old woman comes to Berganza, asks if he is 'Montiel,' and tells him to follow her. Berganza then tells Cipión the story that he thinks might explain how the two dogs have come to have the gift of speech. Berganza follows the woman to the small, dark room where she lives, and there listens to her story: the most famous witch in the world, named Camacha, lived in Montilla. She had many marvelous powers, including the ability to freeze clouds, transport people great distances, restore women's virginity, change people into animals, and make things appear different from what they were. She, whose

name was Cañizares, and Berganza's mother, whose name was Montiela, were disciples of Camacha. Montiela became pregnant, and when it was time for her to give birth, her twins were born in the form of dogs. Camacha took the pups away and they were not seen again. On her deathbed, Camacha admitted that she had changed the babies into dogs and said that they would resume their human form at some future time. Ever since then, Cañizares had always tried to find Montiela's children by calling dogs by a masculine variant of her name, Montiel, in hopes that that might identify them. Cañizares, 75 years old when she told this story, admitted that she was a witch, but not also a sorceress like Camacha. She then said that she was going to apply an unguent to herself that would put her in contact with the devil, whom she would ask about these events. She undressed, applied the unguent, and went into a deep trance. Berganza contemplates her grotesquely ugly body, and then drags her unconscious body out into the public plaza, where, the next morning, she is discovered and recognized for the witch that she is. Next, Berganza runs off and joins a gypsy camp near Granada.

Cipión interrupts the narration at this point to reject Berganza's hypothesis that this could explain the two dogs' ability to speak rationally. His opinion is that there is no such thing as witches' magical abilities and that what Cañizares told Berganza was all a fiction. Berganza seems to be convinced, and continues his story: in the nearly three weeks he spends with the gypsies, he has ample opportunity to see their evil and thieving ways. He describes aspects of their way of life, including the tale of how a noble page once joined their group out of love and was made their leader, whom they call Count and who always takes the name of Maldonado. After leaving the gypsies, Berganza is taken in by a *Morisco* in Granada. Again, Berganza describes the evil, money-grubbing, and irreligious way of life of this plague on Spanish society. Cipión concurs, reassuring Berganza that there are wise people in power who will take care of this nest of vipers in the nation (an allusion to the expulsion of the *Moriscos* in 1609). Berganza also gets to know a poet who is writing a play and who occasionally gives him something to eat. The play is a historical drama and the author insists that every aspect, down the color of cardinals' robes, be exactly as he describes it. When the play is finally produced, it is an abysmal failure. Berganza, however, joins the actors' troupe and within a short time is very successful on stage, especially in interludes. After a while, he also leaves this job and decides that he would like to join Christian Mahudes and Cipión, whom he had seen in Valladolid, in a simpler and honorable way of life. He is successful, and in the time he has been with them working for the hospital, the most interesting things he has seen have been four classic stereotypes: a bad poet who is writing a book about King Arthur and the Holy Grail, an alchemist who believes he is on the brink of discovering the philosophers' stone, a mathematician who believes he has discovered the fixed point and the way to square the circle, and an *arbitrista who has a tax plan to enrich the royal coffers. Berganza finishes his story with brief anecdotes about the local magistrate and a woman with a lapdog. As day dawns, the dogs end their conversation and agree to meet the next night so that Cipión can tell the story of his life. Throughout Berganza's narrative, Cipión interrupts to comment, criticize, and philosophize. The two dogs talk about the differences between philosophy and gossip, what the latter consists of, various social types and individuals, and more.

Bibliography: José Luis Alvarez Martínez, "Berganza y la moza ventanera," *Cervantes* 12, no. 2 (1992): 63–77; Jorge Checa, "Cervantes y la cuestión de los orígenes: Escepticismo y lenguaje en *El coloquio de los perros*," *Hispanic Review* 68 (2000): 295–317; Ruth El Saffar, *"El casamiento engañoso" and "El coloquio de los perros"* (London: Grant and Cutler, 1976); Alban K. Forcione, *Cervantes and the Mystery of Lawlessness: A Study of "El casamiento engañoso y El coloquio de los perros"* (Princeton, NJ: Princeton University Press, 1984); Roberto González Echevarría, "The Life and Adventures of Cipión: Cervantes and the Picaresque," *Diacritics* 10 (Fall 1980): 15–26; Thomas R. Hart, "Renaissance Dialogue into Novel: Cervantes's *Coloquio*," *MLN* 105 (1990): 191–202; Frank Pierce, *Two Cervantes Short Novels: "El casamiento engañoso" y "El col-*

oquio de los perros," rev. ed. (Oxford: Pergamon Press, 1976); Antonio Rey Hazas, "Género y estructura del *Coloquio de los perros*, o 'cómo se hace una novela,' " in *Lenguaje, ideología y organización teatral en las Novelas Ejemplares* (Madrid: Universidad Complutense, 1983), 119–43; Marcia Welles, "Cervantes's *Coloquio de los perros*: Why the Witch?" *RLA: Romance Languages Annual* 2 (1991): 591–95; and Edwin Williamson, "Cervantes as Moralist and Trickster: The Critique of Picaresque Autobiography in *El casamiento engañoso y El coloquio de los perros*," in *Essays on Hispanic Themes in Honour of E. C. Riley,* ed. Jennifer Lowe and Philip Swanson (Edinburgh: Department of Hispanic Studies, University of Edinburgh, 1989); 104–26.

Colossus of Rhodes [Coloso de Rodas]. A huge bronze statue of Helios (in Greek myth, the god of the sun) that stood at the entrance to the harbor of the city of Rhodes. It was one of the Seven Wonders of the Ancient World and was destroyed by an earthquake in 224 BCE. See *Parnaso* 6.

Columbus, Christopher [Cristóbal Colón] (ca. 1451–1506). Genoese-Spanish explorer and sea captain. Columbus is mentioned only once, in passing, by MC: in *Vidriera* when the protagonist of the story visits Columbus's birthplace in Venice during his travels. Mexican novelist Carlos *Fuentes makes an interesting comparison between the achievement of Columbus and that of MC in his important essay *Don Quixote: or, The Critique of Reading* and his related novel *Terra Nostra*.

Bibliography: Jennifer R. Goodman, " 'I Ought to Be Judged as a Captain': The Chivalry of Columbus," *Medievalia et Humanistica* 19 (1993): 47–68.

Columnas de Hércules. *Pillars of Hercules.

Comedia (Comedia nueva). 1. The general term for *play* in the Spanish Golden Age. The basic formula of the *comedia* was established by Lope de *Vega and consisted of the following: 1) three acts, 2) about 3,000 lines, and 3) polymetry. No subject was off-limits; any conceivable source might be used; and there was no attempt to follow the classical unities of time, place, and action. Unlike on the contemporary Elizabethan stage, women (as of about 1583) were permitted to perform. A love plot was essential in nearly every type of play; the theme of obsessive honor was rarely absent; and characters tended to be character types, rather than psychologically unique individuals. Plots were complicated; there was a great deal of fast-paced action; and a happy ending, often with multiple marriages, was the expected outcome, but there were notable exceptions. There were two phases to Spanish Golden Age *comedia*: a first cycle of writers, centered around Lope de Vega and featuring *Tirso de Molina, Guillén de *Castro, Juan *Ruiz de Alarcón, and others; and a second cycle, centered around Pedro *Calderón de la Barca and including primarily Agustín *Moreto and Francisco de *Rojas Zorilla. Among them, these and other dramatists wrote and staged literally thousands of plays in the century 1580–1680. Almost everyone, from the humblest of peasants to the royal court, enjoyed theatrical productions (*corral*). But the theater also had its critics and detractors. Moralists, primarily churchmen, believed that both the plays themselves and the world of theater in general contributed to the corruption of public morals: according to their many treatises, the theater's songs and dances were licentious, provocatively dressed actresses were little better than public whores, and the plots and actions of the characters were both frivolous and immoral. The death of Catalina, duchess of Savoy and daughter of Felipe II, in 1597, and the period of public mourning it brought about meant the closing of the theaters for a while. Theaters were again closed after the death of Felipe II in 1598, but they reopened four months later. In 1603 a royal decree by Felipe III forbade the performance of plays during Lent or at any time in monasteries and convents. The same decree established exactly eight companies of actors that were permitted to perform in major cities (other, smaller, traveling troupes were allowed); the number was increased to 12 in 1615. **2.** In *Rufián* 2, the allegorical figure who appears at the beginning of the second act to discuss with Curiosity why today's theater bears so little resemblance to the classic theater of the past. She explains how

and why the aesthetics of theater have changed over the years, and justifies the abrupt changes in place, time, and theme in the work in progress.

Bibliography: Ignacio Arellano, *Convención y recepción: Estudios sobre el teatro del Siglo de Oro* (Madrid: Gredos, 1999); Charles Ganelin and Howard Mancing, eds., *Text, Theory, and Performance: Golden Age Comedia Studies* (West Lafayette, IN: Purdue University Press, 1994); Melveena McKendrick, *Theatre in Spain 1490–1700* (Cambridge: Cambridge University Press, 1989); Barbara Simerka, ed., *El arte nuevo de estudiar comedias: Literary Theory and Spanish Golden Age Drama* (Lewisburg, PA: Bucknell University Press, 1996); John E. Varey, *Cosmovisión y escenografía: el teatro clásico español* (Madrid: Castalia, 1987); and Anthony N. Zahareas, ed., *Plays and Playhouses in Imperial Decadence* (Minneapolis, MN: Institute for Ideologies and Literature, 1985).

Comediante. *Actor.

Comendador Griego. *Núñez de Guzmán, Hernán.

Comentarios; Commentaries. *César, Julio.

Cómitre. *Boatswain.

Commandant (general, admiral) [Cuatralbo (general, almirante)]. In *DQ* II, 62–64, a Valencian nobleman and naval officer who is a friend of Don *Antonio Moreno in Barcelona; he commands a squadron of four ships. He hosts the visit of DQ and SP to the ships in the harbor, then gives chase to and captures the ship commanded by *Ana Félix.

Comorin [Comorín], Cape. The southernmost tip of the Indian subcontinent. See *DQ* II, 38.

Compadre. *Friend.

Compañeros de los heridos. *Friends of the wounded.

Compañía de Jesús. *Jesuits.

Compás (de Sevilla). An area of Seville frequented by *pícaros,* thieves, and other unsavory types, and perhaps the most celebrated location on the picaresque map of Spain (*picaresque geography). It was also the location of a famous brothel of the same name. See *DQ* I, 3; *Fregona*; *Parnaso* 4; *Rufián* 1–2.

Complete works of Cervantes [Obras completas de Cervantes]. There is no generally recognized and authoritative edition of the works of MC. The monumental edition of Rudolfo Schevill and Adolfo Bonilla (1914–41) remains the best overall edition we have. One of the stated goals of the *Cervantes Society of America at the time of its founding in 1977 was the preparation of a complete works, but profound theoretical and conceptual differences among scholars have paralyzed the project. The recent appearance of the magnificent edition of *DQ* by a team headed by Francisco Rico makes available what for a long time to come will probably be considered the definitive text of MC's greatest novel (*editions of *DQ*). But the complete works project remains to be done. More recently, under the auspices of the Centro de Estudios Cervantinos, Antonio Rey Hazas and Florencio Sevilla Arroyo have begun to publish a multiple-volume edition of MC's complete works, both in text and on CD-Rom.
Bibliography: José M. Casasayas, "La edición definitiva de las obras de Cervantes," *Cervantes* 6, no. 2 (1986): 141–90; and Florencio Sevilla Arroyo, "La edición de las obras de Miguel de Cervantes, I" and "La edición de las obras de Miguel de Cervantes, II," in *Cervantes* (Alcalá de Henares, Spain: Centro de Estudios Cervantinos, 1995), 43–135.

Complutum. The Roman name for *Alcalá de Henares. This name is used in *Galatea* 2 in order to identify the birthplace of the character Tirsi, usually assumed to represent MC's friend Francisco de *Figueroa, who was born in Alcalá.

Compo. A shepherd mentioned in *Casa* 2.

Concejo, Soto del. *Thicket of the Council.

Conceptismo. The poetic style that is characterized by clever and witty concepts, such as antithesis, oxymoron, original and surprising metaphor, and word play. Its main proponent in baroque Spain was Francisco de *Quevedo. *Conceptismo* stood in contrast to the technique of *culturanismo*, although in fact these are not clear binary opposites, but two (somewhat related and similar) tendencies that share many qualities.

Concilio de Trento. *Council of Trent.

Conde. *Count.

Conde de la Insula Firme. *Gandalín.

Conde de Lemos. *Fernández Ruiz de Castro y Osorio, Don Pedro.

Conde de Leste. *Devereux, Robert.

Conde de los gitanos. *Count of the gypsies.

Condesa de las Tres Faldas. *Trifaldi, Countess.

Confraternity (and Congregation of the Unworthy Slaves) of the Most Holy Sacrament [Hermandad (y Congregación de Indignos Esclavos) del Santísimo Sacramento]. A religious/literary congregation founded in Madrid in 1608 under the patronage of Cardinal Bernardo *Sandoval y Rojas and the Duke of *Lerma after the Court moved back to that city from Valladolid in 1606. MC joined in 1609, a year after its founding. Duties of members included daily attendance at mass, monthly communion, regular prayer and self-discipline, and visitations to the infirm. But for many of the members, it was the secular activities of the organization that provided most interest. The group met frequently as a literary academy, which included such illustrious names as Lope de Vega, Francisco de Quevedo, Vicente Espinel, Alonso de Salas Barbadillo, and Luis Vélez de Guevara. On the occasion of Corpus Christi, 1609, MC won first prize for a series of poetic compositions (no record of them remains) in honor of God. Later, however,

MC resigned from the organization when it became more secular than religious.

Confusa, La (*The Confusing Play*). One of MC's early plays from the 1580s, which has been lost (*Porres, Gaspar de). It is cited in *Parnaso* 4 as a justly famous theatrical work of his and is included in the list of his plays in MC's conversation with Pancracio de Roncesvalles in *Adjunta,* where MC calls it one of the best cape and sword plays ever written. Perhaps *Laberinto* is a reworking of this early play.

Bibliography: Vicenta Esquerdo Sivera, "Acerca de *La confusa* de Cervantes," in *Cervantes, su obra y su mundo: Actas del I Congreso Internacional sobre Cervantes,* ed. Manuel Criado de Val (Madrid: Edi-6, 1981), 243–47.

Conquest of Jerusalem. *Conquista de Jersualén, La.*

Conquest of the New World [Conquista del nuevo mundo]. In the space of just a few years, Spaniards turned their attention directly from the seven-century reconquest of the Iberian Peninsula to the discovery and conquest of the New World, even as they dreamed of the conquest of the Muslims and Turks in Africa and Middle East and the Protestants in England and Northern Europe. It is both interesting and significant that the Spanish explorers and soldiers saw much of the fabulous new islands and continents they were encountering in terms of the romances of chivalry. Even though the exportation of these romances to the Indies was banned by royal decrees in 1531 and 1543, they formed an important part of the conquistadors' literary and cultural background. Bernal Díaz del Castillo (1492–1582), in his *Verdadera historia de la conquista de la Nueva España* (not published until 1632; *The True History of the Conquest of New Spain*), refers to the Aztec capital of Tenochtitlán as resembling an enchanted city straight out of the pages of a chivalric romance. The region of Patagonia was named after a tribe of monsters in *Primaleón,* and California was named after a kingdom of Amazons led by Queen Califa in *Las sergas de Esplandián.*

Bibliography: Manuel Alvar, "Fantastic Tales and Chronicles of the Indies," in *Amerindian Images and the Legacy of Columbus,* ed. René Jara and Nicholas Spadaccini (Minneapolis: University of Minnesota Press, 1992), 163–82; James C. Murray, *Spanish Chronicles of the Indies: Sixteenth Century* (New York: Twayne, 1994); and Cora Polk, *The Island of California: A History of the Myth* Spokane, WA: Arthur H. Clark, 1991).

Conquista de Jerusalén, La [*The Conquest of Jerusalem*]. In *Adjunta,* MC lists the titles of ten plays he wrote in the 1580s. Among them is *La Jerusalén,* a work long assumed to have been lost. Recently, however, Stefano Arata located the manuscript of a play in the library of the Royal Palace in Madrid entitled *La conquista de Jerusalén por Godofre de Bullón* (*The Conquest of Jerusalem by Godfrey of Bouilon*), which he proposes is MC's lost work. It is an adaptation of Torquato Tasso's *Jerusalem Delivered* (MC mentions Tasso in *DQ* II, 62; *Parnaso* 2, 5; *Persiles* IV, 6), and must have been written about 1581–85. The versification, number of characters, and use of moral and allegorical figures all are similar to MC's practices in his early theater. The case is a strong one, and it is likely to be accepted by many.

Bibliography: Stefano Arata, "*La conquista de Jerusalén,* Cervantes y la generación teatral de 1580," *Criticón* 54 (1992): 9–112; and Stefano Arata, "Notas sobre *La conquista de Jerusalén* y la transmisión manuscrita del primer teatro cervantino," *Edad de Oro* 16 (1997): 53–66.

Conquista del nuevo mundo; Conquistadores. *Conquest of the New World.

Conrad, Joseph (Teodor Jozef Konrad Korzeniowski, 1857–1924). English/Polish novelist and short-story writer. In *Lord Jim* (1900), the sea itself is the source of quixotic illusion: "In no other kind of life is the illusion more wide of reality—in no other is the beginning *all* illusion—the disenchantment more swift—the subjugation more complete." The quixotic Jim, who wants to be a saint, a devil, a fine fellow, is not strong enough to bring his dreams to reality. In *The Secret Agent* (1907), the quixotic Mr. Verloc may actually believe that he is an important secret agent, but it is the assistant commissioner of police who is described in quixotic terms: "a long, meager face with the accentuated features of an energetic Don Quixote . . . looking like the vision of a cool, reflective Don Quixote, with the sunken eyes of a dark enthusiast and a very deliberate manner." The figure of Kurtz in the novella *Heart of Darkness* (1902) resembles DQ in a dark and foreboding manner. Both are frustrated idealists who become mad and wind up facing reality on their deathbeds. Kurtz's quest is the opposite of that of DQ in every way, yet structurally they are quite similar. There is a similar parallel between DT and Kurtz's ideal woman, the Intended.

Bibliography: Gustavo Pérez Firmat, "*Don Quixote* in *Heart of Darkness*: Two Notes," *Comparative Literature Studies* 12 (1972): 374–83.

Consejo Real. *Royal Council.

Consejos de Don Quijote a Sancho. *Don Quixote's advice to Sancho.

Constable [Alguacil]. **1**. In *Rinconete,* a police officer who is an accomplice of Monipodio and who does him favors. **2.** In *Doncellas,* a law officer who helps get Teodosia, dressed as a man, to open the door to her room in the inn and permit another man, who is her brother Rafael, to share the room for the night. **3.** In *Coloquio,* a dishonest law officer who is Berganza's master after he leaves the home of the rich merchant. **4.** In *Rufián* 1, the law officer who informs Tello de Sandoval of Lugo's wicked and illegal deeds and thus indirectly plays an important role in the decision to relocate the ruffian to Mexico. **5.** In *Pedro* 2–3, a town official who helps organize the festivities for the visit of the king and queen and later is in charge of the presentation of the play for the royal couple. **6.** In *Vizcaíno,* the officer who comes to investigate the row between Cristina and Solórzano when they argue over the authenticity of the gold chain. **7.** In *Viejo,* the officer who enters the house of Cañizares to investigate the shouting going on there, but is convinced it is nothing but a lovers' spat. **8.** In *DQ* II, 48, law enforcement officers mentioned

by Doña Rodríguez when she tells her story to DQ.

Constantino. *López de Zárate, Francisco.

Constantinople [Costantinopla]. The former name of Istanbul and the capital of the Ottoman Empire in MC's day. The action of *Sultana* takes place in Constantinople. See *Amante*; *DQ* I, 39–42.

Constanza. In *Persiles*, the daughter of Antonio the Barbarian and Ricla, who is second only to Auristela herself in physical beauty. She accompanies Periandro and Auristela throughout their adventures in the north and their trek across Europe to Rome. In Spain she marries a wealthy dying count (III, 9), and at the end of the novel marries the count's brother (IV, 14).

Constanza de Azevedo y de Meneses, Doña. In *Gitanilla*, the birth name of *Preciosa and the one she takes again at the end of the story when she is married to Don Juan de Cárcamo.

Constitutions of the Great Governor Sancho Panza [Constituciones del Gran Gobernador Sancho Panza]. The set of laws promulgated by SP during his reign as governor of Barataria, which are still respected and obeyed to this day by the people who live there. See *DQ* II, 51.

Contarino de Arbolánchez. In *Persiles* III, 12, the lover of Ambrosia Agustina who later becomes her husband.

Conti, Francesco. *Zeno, Apostolo.

Continencia. *Restraint.

Contrapás. A popular dance of Italian origin. See *Fregona*.

Contrarreforma. *Council of Trent.

Contratación, Casa de. *Casa de Contratación.

Contreras. In *Gitanilla*, the squire of Doña Clara who is present when Preciosa sings and dances.

Contreras, Jerónimo de (1520–85). Spanish romance writer. Contreras is best remembered for his adventure romance entitled *Selva de aventuras* (1565; *Forest of Adventures*), which recounts the adventures of the lovers Luzmán and Arbolea. It may have been at least a partial model for Lope de *Vega's *El peregrino en su patria* (1604; *The Pilgrim in His Own Homeland*) and MC's *Persiles*.

Bibliography: Alberto Navarro González, "La *Selva de aventuras* de Jerónimo de Contreras y *Los trabajos de Persiles y Sigismunda* de Cervantes," in *Actas del Primer Coloquio Internacional de la Asociación de Cervantistas, Alcalá de Henares 29/30 nov.–1/2 dic. 1988* (Barcelona: Anthropos, 1990), 63–82.

Contreras, Pedro de. Spanish civil servant. He signed the approval for the king for *DQ* II and the grant of royal privilege to print *Persiles*, in San Lorenzo del Escorial on September 24, 1616.

Converso, Cristiano nuevo [Convert, New Christian]. A Christian who converted from Judaism or a descendant of such a convert. Although medieval Spain, particularly during the seven centuries of Muslim rule during the Reconquest, was probably the most tolerant, multicultural nation in Europe, beginning with the reign of the Catholic Monarchs, Fernando and Isabel, and the establishment of the *Inquisition in 1478, Jews met with increasing hostility and persecution. Finally, after the conquest of Granada in 1492 and the unification of the peninsula under Christian rule, the Jews were given the option to convert to Christianity or leave the country. *Conversos* could be persecuted by the Inquisition whenever there was any reason whatsoever (e.g., an offhand comment by a rival) to suspect the purity and authenticity of their Christianity, yet they remained a major influence in Spanish society throughout the sixteenth and seventeenth centuries. Humanists Juan Luis Vives and the twin brothers Juan and Francisco de Vergara were of *converso* stock, as were architect Diego de Siloë, naturalist and physician Andrés *Laguna, mathematician Pedro Nuñes, poet and theologian Fray Luis de *León, the mystics Saint *Teresa de Jesús and Saint *Juan de la Cruz, and many others. The same is true of writers such as poet Juan del *Encina; Fernando de *Rojas, author of *La Celestina*; dramatist Bartolomé de *Torres Naharro; Mateo *Alemán, MC's contemporary and rival who wrote *Guzmán de Alfarache*; and probably the anonymous author of *Lazarillo de Tormes*. That MC was also a descendant of a *converso* family seems most likely, though specific confirming documentary evidence is lacking (*Cervantes family). In *DQ* I, 21, SP is proud of being an Old Christian, believing that that fact alone qualifies him to be a governor. All of *Retablo* is a brilliant satire on the theme of purity of blood and *converso* identity. See also *Elección*.

Bibliography: Antonio Domínguez Ortiz, *Los judeoconversos en la España moderna* (Madrid: Mapfre, 1992); Steven Gilman, *The Spain of Fernando de Rojas* (Princeton, NJ: Princeton University Press, 1972); David M. Gitlitz, *Secrecy and Deceit: The Religion of the Crypto-Jews* (Albuquerque: University of New Mexico Press, 2002); and Gregory B. Kaplan, *The Evolution of Converso Literature: The Writings of the Converted Jews of Medieval Spain* (Gainesville: University Presses of Florida, 2002).

Cook [Cocinero]. In *DQ* II, 20, the one who generously provides SP with food during the celebration of *Camacho's wedding.

Coomonte, Pilar. Spanish artist. Coomonte did the illustrations for John Jay Allen's Cátedra edition of *DQ* (1977), the first time a woman illustrated the text. Her strong, stark line drawings reveal a very personal style and make an important contribution to this edition.

Coover, Robert (1932–). American novelist and short-story writer. In the midst of his collection of "fictions" entitled *Pricksongs and Descants* (1969), Coover places a group of "seven exemplary fictions," headed by a prologue dedicated to MC in which he pays homage to the master fiction-writer: "You teach us, *Maestro*, by example, that great narratives remain meaningful through time as a language-medium between generations, as a weapon against the fringe-areas of our consciousness, and as a mythic reinforcement of our tenuous grip on reality. . . . And it is above all to the need for new modes of perception and fictional forms able to encompass them that I, barber's basin on my head, address these stories." Coover's novel *The Universal Baseball Association, Inc., J. Henry Waugh, Prop.* (1968) features a protagonist who creates an alternate, exciting fantasy game world of sport as his escape from his prosaic, boring reality: in the modern world, the romances of chivalry can take many forms.

Copla real. *Royal couplet.

Coplas de Mingo Revulgo, Las [Mingo Revulgo's Verses]. An anonymous fifteenth-century satiric poem written as a dialogue between two shepherds, Mingo Revulgo (from *vulgo*, 'vulgar') and a friend. See *DQ* II, prologue.

Corbato. A shepherd mentioned in *Casa* 2.

Córcega. *Corsica.

Corchetes. *Policemen.

Corchuelo. One of the group whom DQ and SP meet in *DQ* II, 19, and who tells them about the upcoming wedding of Camacho and Quiteria. He then argues that passion is worth more than science in fencing, but loses the match with the superior swordsman, the licentiate.

Cordero. *Lamb.

Córdoba. City in Andalusia, located south and west of Madrid and northeast of Seville, on the Guadalquivir River, near the border with La Mancha. Córdoba was an important city in Roman Spain; its greatest claim to fame from that period is to have been the birthplace of the famous dramatist and stoic philosopher *Seneca. In Muslim Spain, Córdoba rose to become the second most important city in Islam, after Mecca, and by the eleventh century it was the largest city in Europe, a vibrant intellectual and

cultural center with a population of nearly a million. The fabulous mosque (*mezquita*) in the city stands today (even after being partially destroyed by the Christians, who constructed a cathedral within its walls after the reconquest of the city in 1236) as the most significant Islamic monument outside of the Middle East. The city went into serious decline after the Christian reconquest, and many buildings were abandoned as the population (as well as commercial and religious activities) fell to a mere fraction of what it had been in the glorious days of the caliphate; by the mid-sixteenth century, Córdoba had only some 40,000 inhabitants. MC lived there from 1553 until he moved with his family to Madrid in 1557. See *Comedias*, prologue; *DQ* I, 6, 15; *DQ* II, prologue; *Pedro* 1.

Córdoba, Maestro. Probably Juan de Córdoba, a friend of Lope de Vega. He is praised in Calliope's song in *Galatea* 6.

Córdoba y de Velasco, Don Martín de (?–1604). Brother of Alonso *Fernández de Córdoba, with whom he served in Africa. Córdoba was taken prisoner in the battle of Mostaganem and ransomed by his brother in 1561. He was general of the Spanish fortress at Oran during the period of MC's captivity in nearby Algiers. In *Gallardo*, he is the brother of the Spanish general of Oran.

Cordovan poet. *Mena, Juan de.

Corellas. An Aragonese family name mentioned in *DQ* I, 13.

Corfu [Corfú]. One of the Ionian Islands, located to the west of Greece. See *Amante*; *Parnaso* 3.

Corinth [Corinto]. Ancient city in southern Greece, noted for its commerce, luxury, and arts. See *Galatea* 4.

Corinto. In *Casa*, a shepherd in love with Clori in the pastoral scenes.

Corneille, Thomas (1625–1709). French dramatist. He adapted Charles *Sorel's novel

Le Berger Extravagant, an imitation of *DQ*, as a play (1653; *The Extravagant Shepherd*).

Cornelia. 1. In *Cornelia*, Don Antonio, Don Juan, the Duke of Ferrara, and Lorenzo Bentibolli return to Bologna for Señora Cornelia—but she is not in the house where they left her. They are told, however, that a woman named Cornelia is in the room of the page Santisteban. They rush to that room, only to find that there is a woman named Cornelia there, but not the one they are looking for. **2**. In *Cornelia*, a second woman of the same name, also sleeping with another page. The duplication of names is supposedly mere coincidence for the characters, but it is an unexpected source of comedy, in a serious story, for readers.

Cornelia Bentibolli, Señora. In *Cornelia*, the beautiful heroine who, with the help of two Spanish students, resolves her conflict with her family and marries the man she loves and who has fathered her child.

Cornelio. In *Laberinto*, the servant to Anastasio.

Cornelio Rótulo. In *Amante*, the dandy antagonist who vies unsuccessfully for the hand of the beautiful Leonisa.

Corondas. *Charondas.

Coronista. *Chronicler.

Corpa. A fountain located near Alcalá de Henares. See *Fregona*.

Corpus Christi. The Christian celebration of the body of Jesus Christ in the act of communion; it is a relatively modern festival, beginning in Spain in the fourteenth century. Corpus takes place on the first Thursday following the first Sunday after Pentecost and usually falls in the months of May or June. Traditionally, in Golden Age Spain, it was the occasion for the presentation of *autos sacramenetales*, such as the one in *DQ* II, 11. See also *Elección*.

Corpus of ballads. *Romancero.

Corral. The name commonly given to the theater, or the place where plays were staged (*theatrical performances). In Madrid in MC's day, there were two important *corrales* where the plays of Lope de *Vega and other dramatists (including MC in the 1580s) were regularly staged: the Corral de la Cruz (which dates from 1579) and the Corral del Príncipe (1582); the latter was located on the spot where the Teatro Español is located today. There were also *corrales* at that time in Alcalá de Henares, Almagro, Granada, Seville, Toledo, Valladolid, Valencia, and Zaragoza. *Corrales* were rectangular enclosures, usually covered with a canvas to protect the audience from the sun, with a special balcony in the rear called a *cazuela* (cooking pot) for women spectators. In addition to the view from the windows of the houses that looked in upon the enclosure, another balcony (referred to as the *aposento*) was reserved for more important male viewers. Along the sides was a series of graduated seats (*gradas*), and near the stage, on ground floor, was a series of portable benches. Finally, standing behind those seated on the benches, were the standees, the infamous *mosqueteros* who were very able, and often willing, to boo a production off the stage. The stage itself was a rectangular platform backed by a two-story façade and flanked on each side by doors leading offstage. Plays were staged all year round, normally to full houses. Interestingly, the phrase used most often was "oír una comedia" ("hear a play") rather than "ver una comedia" ("see a play"). Apparently, the metrics and the poetic imagery were as important (and as well perceived) as the spectacle itself.

Bibliography: John J. Allen, *The Reconstruction of a Spanish Golden-Age Playhouse: El Corral del Príncipe 1583–1744* (Gainesville: University Presses of Florida, 1983); David Castillejo, *El corral de comedias: escenarios, sociedad, actores* (Madrid: Concejalia de Cultura del Ayuntamiento de Madrid, 1984); and Vern G. Williamsen, "A Commentary on 'The Uses of Polymetry' and the Editing of the Multi-Strophic Texts of the Spanish Comedia," *Michigan Romance Studies* 5 (1985): 126–145.

Correa de la Cerda, Fernando. A Portuguese poet and soldier who wrote some heroic verse in Spanish. See *Parnaso* 7.

Corrector's statement. *Preliminaries.

Corregidor. *Magistrate.

Correia da Rocha, Adolfo. *Torga, Miguel.

Correo. *Messenger.

Corridón. A shepherd mentioned in *Casa* 2.

Corsica [Córcega]. A French island in the Mediterranean Sea, north of Sardinia. See *Vidriera*.

Corsicurbo. In *Persiles* I, 1, the barbarian who takes Periandro from the cave-prison and then dies when the boat capsizes in a storm.

Cortadillo (Diego Cortado). In *Rinconete*, one of the protagonists, a *pícaro* whose specialty is that of cutpurse. He is given the name Cortadillo by the crime boss Monipodio, who then later modifies it to *Cortadillo el Bueno (the Good).

Cortes de la Muerte, Las [The Parliament of Death]. The *auto sacramental* performed by the actors whom DQ and SP encounter in II, 11. The play is probably one written by Lope de *Vega, but the cast of characters is not quite identical to what is called for in that play. The actors, who belong to the company of *Angulo el Malo, travel in costume because they are going from one town to another to present the same dramatic piece. This is what gives DQ the opportunity to encounter face-to-face the figure of Death, as well as those of a knight-errant, an angel, an emperor, a queen or empress, a soldier, a devil, and Cupid. These are figures not normally seen along these roads—the very stuff of chivalric adventure. Among the more interesting aspects of this episode are the way DQ listens carefully to the explanation given by the actors without changing any part of it to fit his chivalric vision (as he did constantly in the first part of the novel; e.g., in I, 8, with the Benedictine friars: 'No bland words with me, for I know you, you lying rabble'), the way he allows himself to be talked out of taking action by SP, and, most of all, the way he comments on the episode after it is over: 'And now I say it is necessary to touch appearances with your hand in order not to be deceived.' This attitude is the exact opposite of his stance in I, 8, when he says, 'What I say is the truth,' and it demonstrates clearly how different he is in *DQ* II right from the very start of the novel.

Cortés de Tolosa, Juan. *Lazarillo de Tormes*.

Cortés, Hernán (1485–1547). Spanish conquistador. After he landed at Vera Cruz, Mexico, with just some 600 soldiers, Cortés ordered his ships burned so that there could be no thought of retreat or desertion. He then went on to conquer the Aztec Empire and become governor of New Spain (Mexico). See *DQ* II, 8; *Vidriera*.

Cortinas, Leonor de (ca. 1520–93). Mother of MC. The Cortinas family was of a higher status than was the Cervantes family; there appears to have been little social contact between them. Though she married down, it must have appeared a good match at the time, as Rodrigo de Cervantes was the well-to-do son of a respected civil servant in Alcalá. She was probably the strong factor in MC's family, more decisive and controlling than her husband Rodrigo. She took the lead in attempting to raise funds to obtain the release of her sons when they were held for ransom in Algiers, selling some of the family's material goods and petitioning the Royal Council for subsidies.
  Bibliography: Krzysztof Sliwa, "La dualidad de Leonor de Cortinas, madre de Miguel de Cervantes Saavedra, genio de la literatura española," in *Actas del XIII Congreso de la Asociación Internacional de Hispanistas*, vol. 1, *Medieval, Siglos XVI–XVII* (Madrid: Castalia, 1998), 758–63.

Corzantes, Manuel de. *Madariaga, Salvador de.

Cosario(s)

Cosario(s). *Pirate(s).

Cosca Bayo, Estanislao (1804–64). Spanish historical novelist. One of Cosca Bayo's better known historical novels is *La conquista de Valencia por el Cid* (1831; *The Conquest of Valencia by El Cid*), which, in spite of taking place in the heroic-chivalric-fantastic twelfth century, often sounds more like a Cervantine novel, with echoes of DQ's *Golden Age speech and SP's proverbs.

Coscolina. In *Viudo*, a prostitute who is merely mentioned.

Cosmografía; *Cosmography*. *Turpin.

Costanilla, La. A small plaza on a slope located near the church of San Isidoro in Seville where the fish market was located. See *Coloquio*; *Rinconete*.

Costantinopla. *Constantinople; *Our Lady of Constantinople.

Costanza (Costancica). In *Fregona*, the title character, who turns out to be a noble woman raised at the inn by humble but honest parents.

Costanza de la Bastida, Doña. In *Baños*, the young Christian woman taken during the raid on Spain, who eventually escapes along with Don Lope and her beloved Don Fernando.

Council of Trent [Concilio de Trento]. A congress of the heads of the Catholic Church that took place in 1545–64 as a (somewhat belated) response to the Lutheran Reformation. At this prolonged assemblage, dominated by Spanish Jesuit theologians, traditional Church dogma was reaffirmed in the face of the Protestant heresy, and a new stern, conservative, even reactionary, tone—the Counter Reformation (*Contrarreforma*)—was set for the Spanish Church as the official champion of orthodoxy in Europe. The once-popular works of Erasmus were banned as censorship began to restrict the possession and reading of certain books; the Inquisition was strengthened to enforce conformity throughout all segments of the nation's population. The council's ban on duels is cited in connection with the battle between DQ and Tosilos (II, 56) and alluded to in *Persiles* I, 20, when two young men kill each other in a fight over Taurisa; and in II, 19, in Renato's description of the duel he lost.

Bibliography: Paul M. Descouzis, *Cervantes, a nueva luz: El "Quijote" y el Concilio de Trento* (Frankfurt: V. Klostermann, 1966); and Michael Mullett, *The Catholic Reformation* (London: Routledge, 1999).

Count [Conde]. 1. In *Persiles* III, 9, a descendant of the man with whom Antonio the Barbarian had his disagreement and who was the reason for Antonio's 16-year absence from home. On his deathbed he marries Antonio's daughter Constanza, leaving her wealthy and a countess. Later, in IV, 14, his younger brother, who inherits the title of count, also marries Constanza. **2.** In *Persiles* III, 9, the younger brother of the count who is killed in the skirmish with the soldiers. He arrives from Salamanca, where he has been a student, in time for his brother's burial. Then, in IV, 14, he marries his widowed sister-in-law Constanza.

Count of the gypsies [Conde de los gitanos]. The leader of a gypsy band was always referred to with the honorific title of count. See *Coloquio*.

Count of the Insula Firme. *Gandalín.

Counter Reformation. *Council of Trent.

Countess of the Three Skirts. *Trifaldi, Countess.

Country house [Casa de placer]. The residence, also sometimes called a castle, of the duke and duchess. It is the scene of most of the action in *DQ* II, 30–57.

Courtly knights and knights-errant [Caballeros cortesanos y caballeros andantes]. DQ makes a distinction between two types of *caballeros* (knights, but also courtiers or noblemen) in *DQ* II, 1, 6, 17, 46. Knights-errant go forth into the world to right wrongs and rescue maidens; they are strong, active, and manly; and theirs is a difficult and noble profession. Courtiers spend their time at the court, currying favor with the king and engaging in gossip; they are weak, passive, and feminine; and theirs is an easy and demeaning profession. In effect, this is the same sort of criticism that other social critics, such as Francisco de *Quevedo, made when they wrote satirically of the softness of the Spanish nobility and longed for a return to those traditional Spanish values that once made the nation strong. A related theme is that of *Disdain for the Court and Praise for the Village.

Courtly romance. *Sentimental romance.

Cousin [Primo]. In *Casamiento*, the supposed cousin of Doña Estefanía who acts as a witness to her marriage to Campuzano and who turns out to be her lover, with whom she runs away, taking all of her husband's possessions.

Cousin of the licentiate [Primo del licenciado]. The pedantic humanist scholar, cousin of the licentiate swordsman of *DQ* II, 19, who accompanies DQ and SP to the Cave of Montesinos. See also *DQ* II, 22–23, 25.

Couturier, Maurice. Theorist of the novel. Couturier's approach to the novel in his book *Textual Communication: A Print-Based Theory of the Novel* (1991) places him within the *emergence of the novel* camp of Bakhtin et al. (*theory and history of the novel). Like Bakhtin and Reed, he places emphasis on the role of the printing press in making possible the novel as we know it; like Reed and Wilson, he rejects the idea that the novel arose for the first and only time in eighteenth-century England, but holds that "the novel was not born once, as we will show, but many times and at various stages. . . . Fielding did not create a new genre, in that respect, he only perfected the Cervantic mode in *Joseph Andrews* and *Tom Jones*." Much more than Rabelais, MC "belongs unambiguously to the new typographic era." Couturier writes that *DQ* is "the first genuine novel. This book is truly a product of the printing age." Couturier's important work makes one of the strongest cases for the role of print culture in the emergence of the genre we call the novel.

Bibliography: Maurice Couturier, *Textual Communication: A Print-Based Theory of the Novel* (London: Routledge, 1991).

Covarrubias y Orozco, Sebastián de (1539–1613). Spanish lexicographer. Covarrubias was from an illustrious family that included his father, the poet Sebastián, and his brother, the religious writer Juan de *Orozco. Like his brother, he published a book of *Emblemas morales* (1610; *Moral Emblems*), but, most importantly, he is recognized for his work as a lexicographer. His *Tesoro de la lengua castellana o española* (1611; *Treasury of the Castilian or Spanish Language*) is the most important Spanish dictionary before the Royal Spanish Academy published its *Diccionario de autoridades* (1726–39; *Dictionary of Authorities*). The *Tesoro* is still invaluable for anyone studying sixteenth- or seventeenth-century literature. MC is likely to have known it, and it may have been the source for the list of animals with special abilities described by DQ in II, 12 (*Mexía, Pero).

Coypel, Charles-Antoine (1694–1752). French artist and dramatist. Coypel's series of 28 tapestries based on scenes from *DQ* are among the eighteenth century's most memorable graphic interpretations of MC's novel. In addition, Coypel wrote a ballet entitled *Les Folies de Cardénio*, (1720; *Cardenio's Madness*), which was performed in the Tuileries Chateau with the king himself dancing as part of the cast.

Crane, Stephen (1871–1900). American novelist, short-story writer, and poet. Crane's classic *The Red Badge of Courage* (1895) is the story of the youthful, optimistic, quixotic Henry Fleming, who has romantically imagined the glory of combat: "He had, of course, dreamed of battles all his life—of vague and bloody conflicts that had thrilled him with their sweep and fire. In visions he had seen himself in many struggles. . . . He had read of marches, sieges, conflicts, and he had longed to see it all. His busy mind had drawn for him large pictures extravagant in color, lurid with breathless deeds." But just as DQ finds out that in the real world combat is not as exciting as it is in books and the imagination, Henry becomes disillusioned when reality fails to conform to his dream. And just as DQ turns and flees, terrified that he will be shot in the back as he rides away, when confronted with overwhelming odds during the episode of the braying aldermen in *DQ* II, 27, Henry experiences the reality of fear instead of the ecstasy of glory: "Since he had turned his back upon the fight his fears had been wondrously magnified. Death about to thrust him between the shoulder blades was far more dreadful than death about to smite him between the eyes."

Crassus [Craso, Crasos]: Marcus Licinius Crassus (115–53 BCE). Roman leader and landowner; he formed the first Triumvirate with Caesar and Pompey. Crassus is best known for having put down the famous slave revolt led by Spartacus. In his lifetime, he became very wealthy and was sometimes cited along with Midas for his accumulation of riches. It is also possible that *Craso* could be an error or misprint for *Creso* (Croesus), king of Lydia, who was also proverbial for his great wealth. See *Coloquio*; *Galatea* 6; *Persiles* I, 19.

Cratilo. In *Persiles*, the king of Bituania. In II, 14, he is mentioned as the father of Sulpicia, and then in II, 18–20, he hosts Periandro and his crew for three months after they become trapped in the ice of the Frozen Sea. While in Bituania, Periandro tames Critilo's great white horse.

Cratilo's horse [Caballo de Cratilo]. In *Persiles* II, 20, Periandro tells how he tamed the previously untamable horse of King Cratilo of Bituania. He mounted the horse, rode him to a cliff, and forced him to jump into the sea. On the way down, however, he remembered that the sea was completely frozen, but neither he nor the horse was harmed in the fall. The incredulity of some of his listeners is greater here than in any other segment of his much-criticized account of his adventures (*Periandro's narrative).

Credo; Creed. *Four prayers.

Cremo. *Chaeremus.

Cresos. *Croesus.

Crespo. In *Persiles* III, 10, an alderman who is merely mentioned.

Crespo, Gonçalves (1846–83). Portuguese poet. In his *Nocturnos* (1882; *Nocturnes*), there is a poem entitled "A morte de Don Quixote" ("The Death of Don Quixote"), in which a sad and broken DQ, after being defeated and returning home, sits outside his house and watches life go on around him. He is told that DT has died, and his final hours are not as described by MC; rather, animated by the priest and Sansón Carrasco, he (romantically) calls to SP for his lance and sword before he dies.
  Bibliography: José Ares Montes, "Evocaciones cervantinas en poetas portugueses del siglo XIX," *Anales Cervantinos* 31 (1993): 231–38.

Crespo, Rafael. Spanish writer. Crespo's *Don Papís de Bobadilla, o sea defensa del cristianismo y crítica de la seudo-filosofía* (six vols., 1829; *Don Papís de Bobadilla, or Defense of Christianity and Critique of Pseudo-Philosophy*) is a ponderous and pedantic tale of one Don Papís who, like DQ, goes mad from reading the works of the philosophers of the Enlightenment. The work is a reactionary diatribe against progressive ideas.
  Bibliography: Rafael Crespo, *Don Papís de Bobadilla* (Zaragoza, Spain: Polo y Monge, 1829).

Crete [Creta]. Island in the Mediterranean Sea, located southeast of Greece and southwest of Asia Minor, a position of great strategic importance. It was the center of the pre-Greek Minoan civilization. In Greek myth, Crete was where Daedalus constructed a great labyrinth for King Minos. The Minotaur was kept in the labyrinth, and supposedly no one could escape from the structure's complicated maze (see *DQ* I, 11). When Zeus fell in love with Europa, the daughter of the king of Tyre, he adopted the form of a beautiful white bull and, when Europa mounted on his back, swam away with her to Crete, where she bore him three sons (see *Galatea* 4). In *DQ* I, 52, the poet Monicongo refers to the trophies Jason took to Crete, but in Greek myth Jason had nothing to do with the island.

Crew [Chusma]. In *DQ* II, 63, the sailors on board the ship visited by DQ and SP. They hoist SP into the air and pass him along from hand to hand as a practical joke during the visit.

Criado(s). *Servant(s).

Criado de Val, Manuel (1917–). Spanish literary critic. As part of the celebration of the Fourteenth Festival of Medieval Theater in Hita, Spain, in 1978, conference organizer Criado de Val staged an original one-act theatrical adaptation of his own entitled *Don Quijote no es caballero (Tragicomedia cervantina)* (*Don Quixote Is not a Knight [A Cervantine Tragicomedy]*). The play begins with the defeat of DQ by the Caballero de la Blanca Luna (from II, 64), and then the majority of the action consists of DQ's dream about various adventures he had during the course of his chivalric career (the enchanted DT, Andrés, the galley slaves, the duke and duchess, and others). He awakens, returns home, and, in the presence of SP and his family, dies.
Bibliography: Manuel Criado de Val, *Don Quijote no es caballero (Tragicomedia cervantina)*, in *Cervantes, su obra y su mundo: Actas del I Congreso Internacional sobre Cervantes*, ed. Manuel Criado de Val (Madrid: Edi-6, 1981), 1165–83.

Cribela. In *Cornelia,* the housekeeper (*Crivelli) who helps care for Señora Cornelia's baby and advises Cornelia to take refuge in the home of a priest she knows, which first causes confusion, but ultimately leads to the happy resolution of the matter.

Cricket cage [Jaula de grillos]. In *DQ* II, 73, the object of dispute between the two *boys playing as DQ and SP return home to their village. Because of the ambiguity of the direct object pronoun *la,* DQ believes they are referring to a woman (specifically, DT), rather than a feminine object, the cage.
Bibliography: Alan S. Trueblood, "La jaula de grillos (*Don Quijote*, II, 73)," in *Homenaje al Pro-*

fesor Antonio Vilanova, 2 vols., ed. Adolfo Sotelo Vázquez and Marta Cristina Carbonell (Barcelona: Universidad de Barcelona, 1989), vol. I, 699–708.

Crier [Pregonero]. In *Tratos* 2, the auctioneer who sells off the two Christian children.

Crisalvo. In *Galatea* 1, friend of Carino, brother of Leonida, and in love with Silvia. He mistakenly murders his sister and is killed by Lisandro.

Crisio. In *Galatea* 2, one of the shepherds who participate in the eclogue sung at the wedding of Daranio and Silveria. He represents absence because the beautiful Claraura has left him.

Cristiano(s). *Christian(s).

Cristiano nuevo; Cristiano viejo: *Converso.

Cristina (Cristinica, Cristinilla). 1. In *Gitanilla*, a gypsy friend of Preciosa who, early in the story, warns her not to go into a house where only several men are present. **2**. In *Entretenida*, the maid for whose hand Ocaña and Quiñones vie. **3**. In *Vizcaíno*, the prostitute who is deceived by Solórzano. **4**. In *Cueva*, the maid who has the barber Maese Nicolás as a lover. **5**. In *Viejo*, the niece and maid of Doña Lorenza, who encourages her to take a lover. **6**. In *DQ* II, 18, the wife of Don Diego de Miranda.

Cristina de Parrazes (Cristinica). In *Guarda*, the maid who is courted by a sacristan and a soldier.

Cristina's master and mistress [Amos de Cristina]. In *Guarda*, the employers of Cristina who help her decide whom to marry.

Cristinica; Cristinilla. *Cristina; *Cristina de Parrazes.

Cristóbal de la Cruz, Fray. In *Rufián* 2–3, the name adopted by the ruffian Cristóbal de Lugo when he turns from his life of sin to a religious vocation.

Cristóbal de Lugo. *Lugo, Cristóbal de.

Cristóbal del Pino. In *Gallardo* 2, the name used in the oath "Voto a Cristóbal del Pino" ("I swear to Cristóbal del Pino"), probably a euphemism for "Voto a Cristo divino" ("I swear to the Divine Christ") or something very similar.

Crivelli [Cribelos]. A distinguished family from Milan. In *Cornelia*, the housekeeper who serves Don Juan and Don Antonio in Bologna states that she is from this family.

Crocodile of an unknown metal [Cocodrilo de un metal no conocido]. In *DQ* II, 39, the form of the enchanted Don Clavijo in the story told by the Countess *Trifaldi.

Croesus [Creso]. *Crassus.

Crónica de Juan II (Chronicle of Juan II). An account—a collaborative effort, but largely by Alvar García de Santa María—of the reign of King Juan II of Castile in the fifteenth century. This chronicle appears to be the specific source of most of the information concerning the knights mentioned by DQ in his conversation with the canon of Toledo in I, 49: Juan de Merlo, Mosén Pierres de *Charní, Enrique de Remestán, Pedro Barba, Gutierre *Quijada, Count of San Polo, Fernando de Guevara, Micer Jorge, Duke of Austria, Suero de *Quiñones, Luis de Falces, and Gonzalo de Guzmán.

***Crónica del muy noble caballero Guarino Mezquino* (1512; *Chronicle of the Very Noble Knight Guarino Mezquino*).** The Spanish version of an Italian romance of chivalry by Andrea de Barberino entitled *Guerrin Meschino* (1473). It was well-known and popular in translation in Spain. Juan de *Valdés cites it in his *Diálogo de la lengua* as an example of a book that is badly written and filled with lies. See *DQ* I, 49.

Croriano Rubicón. In *Persiles* III, 16–17, the son of the man who killed Ruperta's husband, and the object of her desire for revenge; but when she sees how attractive he is, she falls in love and the two of them are immediately

married. They accompany the pilgrims to Rome and support them throughout the remainder of the novel, returning to France in IV, 14.

Cross. *Heraclius.

Crosses of Alexandria [Cruces de Alejandría]. Apparently, crosses located at the entrance to the Dardanelles. See *Amante.

Crowne, John (ca. 1640–ca. 1712). English dramatist. His play *The Married Beau, or The Curious Impertinent* (1694) is based on *Curioso.

Cruces de Alejandría. *Crosses of Alexandria.

Crucifijo de plata. *Silver cross.

Cruise, James. Theorist of the novel. Although the subtitle of Cruise's *Governing Consumption* (1999) suggests that he is writing specifically about the English novel in the eighteenth century, Cruise makes it clear from the beginning that he is a card-carrying member of Ian *Watt's "rise of the novel" club. After describing briefly the enormous influence of Watt's book, he states that "we have yet to demonstrate much of an inclination to challenge the foundational premise of his work: namely, that methodological imperium of the prehistory of the novel, that doggedly elusive 'before' which would determine, once and for all, the provenance, origin(s), and rise of the novel." Then, after briefly considering the possibility that the novel could have a history that stretches back to ancient times, Cruise settles on the following definition: the novel is "a form of prose fiction in its printed form; this way it continues as an amalgam of features, a way of telling a story, while also maturing into a writing practice that is authored, time-bound, and proprietary, if not in fact, then in principle." This would seem to invite a consideration of the emergence of the novel in the sixteenth century, the earliest period of print culture, but Cruise only dares to push the beginnings of the novel back to the late seventeenth century—with

Aphra Behn in England, of course. Spain, the picaresque novel, and MC are never mentioned.

Bibliography: James Cruise, *Governing Consumption: Needs and Wants, Suspended Characters, and the "Origins" of Eighteenth-Century English Novels* (Lewisburg, PA: Bucknell University Press, 1999).

Cruz. *Heraclius.

Cruz de Cristo; *Cruz y Constantino*. *López de Zárate, Francisco.

Cruz de diamantes. *Diamond cross.

Cruz, Ramón de la (1731–94). Spanish dramatist. Ramón de la Cruz was the most popular and most prolific dramatist of the second half of the eighteenth century, specializing in the *sainete* (one-act comic sketch, similar to and derived from the *paso and *entremés), of which he wrote some 400. *Sainetes*, with their comedy, light tone, music, folkloric characters, and uncomplicated plots were often condemned by more serious neoclassical writers, but were hugely successful with the public in general. Evocations of and references to MC and his works are common in Cruz's short plays, and in *Las bodas de Camacho el Rico* (1784; *The Wedding of Camacho el Rico*), he dramatized the events of *DQ* II, 20–21.

Bibliography: Gregorio Martín, "Cervantine Discretion in Ramón de la Cruz," *Estudios Ibero-Americanos* 4 (1978): 235–37; and John A. Moore, *Ramón de la Cruz* (Boston: Twayne, 1972).

Cruz y Gómez, Cesáreo de la. Spanish novelist. His *Vida de otro pícaro* (1971; *Life of Another Pícaro*) draws on both MC and the picaresque tradition in order to tell the story of the quixotic and picaresque Justo. There are frequent references to and citations of *DQ* in the novel, and in one comic scene Justo decides not to wait his turn in a crowded doctor's office, so he goes out, finds an old chamber pot, places it on his head (like, he says, Mambrino's helmet), returns to the office, and whirls his arms like a windmill. The trick is successful, as everyone lets him go first.

Bibliography: Cesáreo de la Cruz y Gómez, *Vida de otro pícaro* (Segovia, Spain: Imp. Ceyde, 1971).

Cuadrillero(s). *Officer(s).

Cuaresma. *Lent.

Cuarta esfera; Cuarto cielo. *Fourth sphere.

Cuatralbo (general, almirante). *Commandant.

Cuatro oraciones. *Four prayers.

Cuatro S. *Four S's.

Cubas. *Santa Cruz.

Cucaña. *Cockaigne.

Cuco, King of. In *Gallardo* 2–3, a Muslim killed by Fernando de Saavedra in the Muslim assault on Oran.

Cuenca. A city located east and slightly south of Madrid and northwest of Valencia. It is best known today for its "hanging houses," which are built on a precipice. In MC's day it was, among other things, the source for good-quality woolen cloth with a characteristic blue color (*palmilla*). See *DQ* II, 21, 33; *Persiles* III, 8.

Cuenca, Luis Alberto de (1950–). Spanish writer. Cuenca adapted MC's *Sultana*, and the play was performed for the first time in 1992 in Seville by the Compañía Nacional de Teatro Clásico, under the direction of Adolfo Marsillac. The production was then taken on the road and was acclaimed in Madrid, Barcelona, and Almagro, and then in London and Mexico City, with the run lasting until 1994.

Bibliography: Susana Hernández Araico, "Estreno de *La gran sultana*: Teatro de lo otro, amor y humor," *Cervantes* 14, no. 2 (1994): 155–65.

Cueros de vino. *Wineskins.

Cuerpo muerto. *Dead body.

Cuerpos de bandoleros. *Bodies of bandits.

Cuesta de Zambra. *Hill of Zambra.

Cuesta del Carmen. *Hill of Carmen.

Cuesta, Juan de la. Spanish printer whose shop was in Madrid and who printed and distributed many important works between 1604 and 1623. His emblem, which appears on the frontispiece of most of his books, depicts a hooded falcon and a sleeping lion, and the words *Post tenebras spero lucem.* Cuesta published four of MC's books: *DQ* I, *Novelas*, *DQ* II, and *Persiles*.

Bibliography: Richard W. Clement, "Juan de la Cuesta, the Hispanic Book Trade and a New Issue of the First Edition of Cervantes' *Persiles y Sigismunda*," *Journal of Hispanic Philology* 16 (1991): 23–41.

Cuesta Zulema. *Hill of Zulemz.

Cueva de Montesinos. *Cave of Montesinos.

Cueva de Salamanca. *Cave of Salamanca.

Cueva de Salamanca, La (Cueva); The Magic Cave of Salamanca. The seventh interlude in *Comedias*. One of the finest of the short pieces in the collection, it combines the Boccaccian theme of the deceived husband with that of the picaresque student. The treatment of conjugal fidelity, adultery, honor, and superstition makes this a high point in MC's comic and satiric accomplishments.

In the opening scene, Leonarda weeps uncontrollably as her husband Pancracio is about to leave for four days in order to attend his sister's wedding. Pancracio offers to forgo the trip if his absence is so difficult for his wife to bear, but she assures him that she can survive a short while without him. As soon as he is gone, however, Leonarda and her maid Cristina hurry to get ready for the arrival of their lovers, Reponce, the sacristan, and Maese Nicolás, the barber, who are bringing food and wine for the evening. But before the lovers arrive, a student (*Carraolano) calls at the house requesting a place to spend the night. He is admitted and joins in the party when Reponce and Nicolás arrive. In a brief change of scene, Pancracio and his friend Leoniso find that the coach that was to take them on their trip has a broken wheel and decide to postpone their departure until the

following day. Pancracio returns home just as the celebration there is getting underway. When he knocks at the door, Leonarda pretends not to believe it is him while the others hide. After Pancracio is admitted, the student comes out (Pancracio is assured by all that his presence in the house is a matter of charity) and, during the discussion, says that since he has studied magic at the Cave of Salamanca, he can conjure up (innocent) devils, in the form of the local sacristan and barber, and make them sing and dance. Curious, Pancracio wants to see this done, and so the student calls forth Reponce and Nicolás, and everyone joins in song, dance, food, and drink.

Bibliography: M. García Blanco, "El tema de la Cueva de Salamanca y el entremés de este mismo título," *Anales Cervantinos* 1 (1951): 73–109; and Stanislav Zimic, "*La cueva de Salamanca*: Parábola de la tontería," *Anales Cervantinos* 21 (1983): 135–52.

Cueva, Juan de la (ca. 1550–ca. 1610). Spanish dramatist and poet. A contemporary of MC in the early days of the Spanish theater in the 1580s, but writing and performing in Seville rather than in Madrid, Cueva is best known for his plays based on Spanish history and legend, especially *Los siete infantes de Lara* (*The Seven Princes of Lara*). His collected *Comedias y tragedias* (1584; *Comedies and Tragedies*) was published after he abandoned the theater for other pursuits. He is praised—as Juan de las Cuevas—in Calliope's song in *Galatea* 6.

Bibliography: Richard F. Glenn, *Juan de la Cueva* (New York: Twayne, 1973).

Cueva (y Silva), Francisco de la (1550–1628). Spanish lawyer, poet, and dramatist. He is included in the list of good poets in *Parnaso* 2 and praised again with the variant name of Francisco de las Cuevas in Calliope's song in *Galatea* 6.

Cuevas, las. *Monastery of Santa María de las Cuevas.

Culturanismo. The poetic style in which erudite references to history, mythology, Latin, and various other obscure matters, together with a special poetic vocabulary and an intricate syntax, make the poetry difficult to read for any reader without sufficient cultural background. Its main proponent in baroque Spain was Luis de *Góngora, and *gongorismo* is another term that amounts to virtually the same thing. In contrast was the technique of *conceptismo*, although in fact these are not clear binary opposites, but two (somewhat related and similar) tendencies that share many qualities.

Bibliography: Dámaso Alonso, *Poesía española, ensayo de métodos y límites estilísticos: Garcilaso, Fray Luis de León, San Juan de la Cruz, Góngora, Lope de Vega, Quevedo* (Madrid: Gredos, 1950).

Cunningham, John William (1780–1861).

The protagonist of Cunningham's *Sancho, or, the Proverbialist* (1816) is named after DQ's squire by a quixotic aunt who "had vowed, early in life, that should she ever be presented of a human being on whom she might be privileged to bestow a name he should be enriched by at least one half of the title of the illustrious squire of Don Quixote." Sancho affirms that if his aunt were "a knight-errant in the cause [i.e., of living according to proverbs and maxims], I might without presumption pretend to the dignity of squire."

Bibliography: John William Cunningham, *Sancho, or, the Proverbialist* (London: Cadell, 1816).

Cunqueiro, Alvaro (1911–81).

Galician essayist, journalist, and novelist. Cunqueiro has called himself an 'impassioned Cervantine' writer, and there are frequent references to MC and his works throughout his writings. The protagonist of Cunqueiro's novel *Cuando el viejo Simbad vuelva a las islas* (1961 in Galician, 1962 in Spanish; *When Old Sinbad Returns to the Islands*) resembles DQ more than he does the traditional Arabic hero. The similarity is even clearer when his servant Sari is seen as an SP figure and Alba is viewed as a kind of DT. Cunqueiro's last novel, *El año del cometa con la batalla de los cuatro reyes* (1974; *The Year of the Comet, with the Battle of the Four Kings*), is perhaps his most obviously quixotic. The protagonist Paulos has clear similarities to DQ in his imaginative quest for adventures, and he even has a horse that recalls Rocinante. The novel is narrated by one Al Faris Ibn Iaqim al Galizi (which can be understood as "Alvaro, son of Joaquín of the Galician nation," clearly a version of the author's self), who finds some of his material in Toledo and has it translated.

Bibliography: Alvaro Cunqueiro, *El año del cometa con la batalla de los cuatro reyes* (Barcelona: Destino, 1974); and J. González-Millán, "Cunqueiro y Cervantes: juegos de erudición," *Anales Cervantinos* 28 (1990): 125–42.

Cuntiloquios.

In *Laberinto* 1, an obscenity for *Coliloquios* (*Colloquies*) used by the student Tácito while talking with Julia, who immediately takes great offense.

Cupid (the blind archer, blind child, blind god, blind one, blindfolded blind one, capricious god, lewd son of Venus, little blind boy, little blind youth) [Cupido (el ciego arquero, niño ciego, ciego dios, ciego, vendado ciego, dios antojadizo, torpe hijo de Venus, niño ceguezuelo, rapaz ceguezeluo)].

1. In Roman myth, the boy god of love, son of Venus and Vulcan. He was based on the figure of Eros, the Greek childlike god with wings and a quiver filled with arrows made for him by his father. With golden arrows, Cupid wounds with love; when the arrow is made of lead, the person who is shot falls out of love. Therefore, along with his mother Venus, Cupid is the personification of love (and therefore often described as blind, for love is blind). Cupid's most comic appearance in any of MC's works is in *DQ* II, 56, when the little blind god takes advantage of an opportunity to triumph over the soul of a lackey and makes Tosilos fall in love with the daughter of Doña Rodríguez, shooting him through the heart with a golden arrow some two yards long. See also *Casa* 3; *Doncellas*; *Entretenida* 1–2; *Galatea* 2, 4; *Gallardo* 3; *Gitanilla*; *Laberinto* 2; *Pedro* 1; *Persiles* I, 18; *Poesías* 10; *Sultana* 1, 3; *Tratos* 2. **2.** In *Casa* 2, allegorical figure conjured up by Malgesí. **3.** In *DQ* II, 11–12, a character in the cast of *Las *Cortes de la Muerte*. **4.** In *DQ* II, 20, a person dressed as this god, complete with wings and bow and arrows, who participates in the celebration of *Camacho's wedding. **5**. In *Persiles* II, 10, one of the four boats in the fishermen's regatta.

Cura. *Pero Pérez; *Priest.

Cura de la parroquia. *Parish priest.

Curambro. A variant of *Curiambro, mentioned by DQ in II, 73.

Curcio. *Curtius, Marcus.

Curcios. A Roman family name mentioned in *DQ* I, 13.

Curiambro. In *DQ* II, 67, a pastoral name DQ suggests for the priest, Pero Pérez.

Curiosity [Curiosidad]. 1. In *Casa* 2, an allegorical figure conjured up by Malgesí. **2**. In *Rufián* 2, the allegorical figure who appears on stage to inquire of *Comedia* why she is so different as to be virtually unrecognizable these days.

Curioso impertinente, El (Curioso); The Story of Ill-Advised Curiosity. The anonymous story read (out of curiosity) by the priest to the assembled group in the inn of Juan Palomeque in *DQ* I, 33–35. The basics of the plot are derived from an episode in *Ariosto's *Orlando Furioso*. *Curioso* is an independent tale that is technically, stylistically, and structurally distinct from the primary narrative of *DQ*; unlike all other embedded narratives in the novel, it is simply and clearly an independent fiction, and none of its characters has any role in the primary action. Readers have disagreed about its relevance to the story of DQ. Some dismiss it completely as an unrelated, irrelevant, and inappropriate intrusion in the novel: an impertinent tale. It is sometimes suggested that MC ran out of inspiration and, desperate to continue his story, began to fill the pages with unrelated material he had previously written. Others point out that its theme of one man's obsession can be seen as a cautionary tale for DQ (ironically, the one person who sleeps through the reading and thus does not hear it). Still others note that its implicit theme of *letters* provides a contrast

to the story of *Capitán* (I, 39–41) which represents *arms*, while DQ delivers a speech on the subject of *arms and letters between the two tales in I, 37–38. *Curioso* and *Capitán* also bracket the conclusion of *Cardenio* that takes place in I, 36. Those who defend the work's inclusion also tend to take the position that MC felt the need to vary the tone, pace, and structure of his long novel and chose strategically to incorporate texts and characters that would provide variety and freshness in his story. Some readers have perceived a strong hint of homoeroticism in the relationship between the two male characters—the 'two friends'—while others see *Curioso* as a subtle psychological study in which the heroine, Camila, evolves from the silent object of desire to an active agent who controls both the discourse and the action of the plot. Some passages, such as Lotario's long argument as to why he should not undertake the project proposed by Anselmo (I, 33), are excellent examples of MC's best rhetorical style. One problem *Curioso* has caused translators is its title. The words *curioso* and *impertinente* function simultaneously as nouns and adjectives because of the great syntactic flexibility of the Spanish language: Anselmo is both a *curious* man who is *impertinent* and an *impertinent* man who is *curious*. How to capture this polysemy in an English translation? Here are some examples: Shelton, 'The History of the Curious-Impertinent'; Jarvis, 'The Novel of the Curious Impertinent'; Putnam, 'The Story of One Who Was Too Curious for His Own Good'; Ormsby, Douglas, and Jones, 'The Story of Ill-advised Curiosity'; Raffel, 'The Story of the Man Who Couldn't Keep from Prying'; and Rutherford, "The Tale of Inappropriate Curiosity." See also *DQ* I, 47; *DQ* II, 3, 44.

Bibliography: Iluminada Amat, "Doubling the Homoerotic: *El curioso impertinente* in *Don Quixote*," *Postscript* 14 (1997): 63–68. William H. Clamurro, "The *Quijote*, the 'Curioso' and the Diseases of Telling," *Revista de Estudios Hispánicos* 28 (1994): 379–93; Clorinda Donato, "Leonora and Camila: Female Characterization and Narrative Formula in the Cervantina Novela," *Mester* 15, no. 2 (1986): 13–24; Robert Richmond Ellis, "The Tale within the Tale: A Look into the World of the *Cu-*

rioso impertinente," *Anales Cervantinos* 22 (1984): 171–79; Gustavo Illades, "Tres miradas a la *Novela del Curioso impertinente*," *Medievalia* 12 (1992): 12–22; Yvonne Jehenson, "*Masochisma versus Machismo* or: Camila's Re-Writing of Gender Assignations in Cervantes's *Tale of Foolish Curiosity*," *Cervantes* 18, no. 2 (1998): 26–52; Hans Jörg Neuschäfer, "El curioso impertinente y la tradición de la novelística europea," *Nueva Revista de Filología Hispánica* 38 (1990): 605–20; Bruce W. Wardropper, "The Pertinence of 'El curioso impertinente,' " *PMLA* 72 (1957): 587–600; Nicolás Wey-Gómez, "The Jealous and the Curious: Freud, Paranoia and Homosexuality in Cervantine Poetics," in *Cervantes and His Postmodern Constituencies*, ed. Anne J. Cruz and Carroll B. Johnson (New York: Garland, 1999), 170–98; and Diana de Armas Wilson, " 'Passing the Love of Women': The Intertextuality of El curioso impertinente," *Cervantes* 7, no. 2 (1987): 9–28.

Curious man who took the care to have them [the papers of Cide Hamete Benengeli] translated [Curioso que tuvo cuidado de hacerlas traducir]. In *DQ* II, 3, while Sansón Carrasco is discussing CHB's book with DQ, he also praises the narrator-editor who paid the *Morisco* to translate the manuscript to Spanish. In effect, the person receiving this praise is MC himself (*narrative structure of *DQ*).

Currency. No attempt has been made throughout this encyclopedia to record prices sometimes mentioned with respect to MC or to estimate what those prices might equal in modern value. The basic units of currency at the time were the *escudo* (shield), the *real* (royal), and the *maravedí*. There were 34 *maravedís* to a *real* and 400 *maravedís* to an *escudo*. Older kinds of coins still in circulation were the *ducado* (ducat) and the *doblón* (doubloon). But with rampant inflation, caused largely by the enormous influx of silver from the New World, and the constantly changing value of currencies today, it is impossible to fix values with much certainty. In his 1990 biography of MC, Jean Canavaggio makes the following calculations: 1) the 500 *escudo* ransom paid for MC in 1580 was the equivalent of about $17,000, 2) MC's annual salary during his years as a commissary

was about $10,000, 3) the publication of *DQ* I brought MC about $1,500, and 4) the price of a copy of the first edition of *DQ* I was about $20.

Bibliography: Jean Canavaggio, *Cervantes*, trans. J. R. Jones (New York: W. W. Norton, 1990).

Curtius, Marcus [Curcio]. A legendary Roman soldier who in the fourth century CE is supposed to have ridden, fully armed, on a horse into a pit that had developed in the Roman Forum. After this deed, the cleft then closed up and Rome was saved. See *DQ* II, 8; *Parnaso* 6.

Custodio, Alvaro (1912–92). Spanish dramatist who was particularly successful as an author of adaptations or rewrites of classic plays. A good example of his work is *El patio de Monipodio* (1973; *Monipodio's Patio*), a two-act musical that features characters from *Rinconete*, *Celoso*, and *Pedro*, with some lines (but no characters) from *DQ*.

Bibliography: Alvaro Custodio, *El patio de Monipodio* (Mexico City: Ediciones Teatro Clásico de México, 1973).

Cuvelier de Trye, Jean Guillaume Antoine (1766–1824). French dramatist. His *pantomime bouffonne* (burlesque pantimime) *Sancho dans l'isle de Barataria* (1816; *Sancho on the Island of Barataria*) is another stage version of SP's adventures as a governor. He also wrote *L'Empire de la folie: ou La Mort et l'apothéose de Don Quichotte* (1799; *The Empire of Madness, or The Death and Apotheosis of Don Quixote*).

Cyllenian [Cilenio]. Someone from Mount Cyllene in Greece. It is used particularly with reference to *Mercury (in Greek myth, Hermes), who was supposed to have been born there. See *Parnaso* 1, 4, 7, 8; *Poesías* 28.

Cynics [Cínicos]. A group of Greek philosophers, of whom the most famous was Diogenes, who developed no particular school of beliefs, but believed that virtue itself was the only fundamental good; they stressed self-restraint and independence from all worldly needs and pleasures. See *Novelas*, dedication.

Cynthia [Cintia]. In Greek myth, a name derived from Mount Cynthus in the land of Delos. It was often used as an epithet for Artemis (in Roman myth, Diana). Because of the association of Diana with animals and the forest, Cynthia became a frequently used name for shepherdesses in the pastoral literature of the Renaissance.

Cyprian goddess. *Venus.

Cyprus [Chipre, Cipre]. Island in the eastern Mediterranean Sea south of Turkey, often a site of conflict between Christian and Muslim forces. Long a Venetian possession, in 1570 Cyprus was captured by the Turks. It was this event that sparked the creation of the *Holy League and prepared the way for the Christian victory in the battle of *Lepanto. There was a temple to Venus on the island. In *Amante*, it is the setting of the beginning of the story. See also *Amant*; *DQ* I, 39; *DQ* II, 18; *Persiles* I, 21.

Bibliography: Ronald C. Jennings, *Christians and Muslims in Ottoman Cyprus and the Mediterranean World, 1571–1640* (New York: New York University Press, 1993).

D. A. A. P. y G. *Gatell, Pedro.

D. E. R. H. Pseudonym of an unidentified early-nineteenth-century Spanish writer, author of the *Diálogo entre Don Quijote de la Mancha y Sancho Panza su escudero, escrito en lengua árabe por Cide Amete Benengeli, testigo presencial, y traducido al español por D. E. R. H.* (1811; *Dialogue between Don Quixote de la Mancha and Sancho Panza, His Squire, Written in the Arabic Language by Cide Hamete Benengeli, a Witness Who Was Present, and Translated to Spanish by D. E. R. H.*), a short work in defense of the clergy in the face of growing liberal social movements.

D. F. E. C. y C. Pseudonym of an unidentified early-nineteenth-century Spanish writer, author of the *Historia de Bruce y Emilia, o, El Quixote de la Amistad* (2 vols., 1808; *The History of Bruce and Emily, or, The Amicable Quixote*) is a translation/adaptation of the anonymous *Amicable Quixote.* In an introductory statement, the author says that he was not able to translate the work as it was originally written because the English society it depicts is so foreign to Spanish culture. As a result, he says, he had to make frequent modifications and abridgements, reducing the long four-volume work to two relatively short volumes. In the end he retained little but the names of the protagonists, and wrote an ending that is very different from that of the original. Interestingly, however, he did not work directly from the original English, but from the French translation of P. Chanin. It would be worthwhile to compare the three stages of the fiction—English, French, and Spanish—to trace its development. In the Spanish version, there is more intrigue, deception, manipulation, and humiliation of the main characters before it is revealed in the final chapter that both Jorge Bruce and Emilia are of higher social station than had been believed. Virtue is rewarded and evil is punished, as the young couple go off to enjoy the fruits of their marriage. Along the way, the author places strategic footnotes in which he censures the actions of the characters and urges Christian virtue on the reader.

Bibliography: D. F. E. C. y C., *Historia de Bruce y Emilia, o, El Quixote de la Amistad*, 2 vols. (Madrid: Imprenta de Repullés, 1808).

D. F. V. y C. P. Pseudonym of an unidentified eighteenth-century Spanish writer, author of *El tío Gil Mamuco* (1789, *That Guy Gil Mamuco*). This is one of the more interesting imitations of *DQ* in the eighteenth century. The protagonist is obsessed with writings about the search for the philosopher's stone (the substance that alchemists believed would turn base metals into gold). Accompanied by his servant, Mamuco sets out to preach the excellencies of a certain liquid that he believes can make anyone achieve his or her goal. Along the way he has such quixotic adventures as believing that a goat is a beautiful woman, and has a dream comparable to that of DQ in the *Cave of Montesinos. He even believes that he has his own enchanter, the evil Maluquín. The narrative is suddenly interrupted and brought to an end.

Dádiva. *Largess.

Dafne. *Daphne.

Daganzo (de Arriba). A small town located just northwest of Alcalá de Henares and northeast of Madrid. It is the setting for *Elección.*

Dagoberto, Duke of Utrino. In *Laberinto*, he accuses Rosamira of having illicit sexual relations and stands ready to defend this accusation against anyone who chooses to defend her. In fact, it was he himself who has had the intimate relationship with Rosamira, and at the end of the play the two marry.

Dalí Mamí. Renegade corsair. Known as *El Cojo* (The Cripple), he was lieutenant to Arnaut Mamí when MC was captured in 1575, and he became MC's first owner in Algiers. Misled by MC's impressive letters of recommendation from Don Juan of Austria and the Duke of Sessa, he set MC's ransom price at 500 gold *escudos*, considerably higher than what would normally have been asked for someone like MC. Later, probably in 1577, he sold MC to *Hassan Pasha, king of Algiers.

Dalí, Salvador (1904–89). Spanish artist. Dalí was the leading painter of the surrealist movement and an extravagant figure in his personal life. In addition to the extraordinarily brilliant and evocative figures of DQ, SP, and others he did for an edition of *DQ* first published in 1957, Dalí returned to the theme of DQ repeatedly during his life. He did a number of engravings and sketches of DQ, often composed simply of swirling lines and/or blocks, very much in the style of his illustrations for the edition of the text.

    Bibliography: Miguel de Cervantes, *El ingenioso hidalgo Don Quixote de la Mancha*, illus. Salvador Dalí, 3 vols. (Buenos Aires: Emecé, 1958).

Dalida. *Delilah.

Dalin, Olof von (1708–63). Swedish poet. Often considered the first modern Swedish writer, Dalin is best known for his allegorical sagas. He also published a weekly literary periodical entitled *Then Swänska Argus* (1732–34; *The Swedish Argus*). Dalin evokes a world in which Egoism and Ambition drive out Objectivity, Modesty, and Inner Peace, so that madness becomes universal. His figure for this madness is DQ, who has become a Swedish bourgeois, complete with an SP-figure in his servant Mats and a DT-like wife.

Dama(s). *Lady, Ladies.

Damasco de Milán; Damask from Milan. *Milan.

Damascos de Siria; Damasks from Syria. *Syria.

Damón. In *Galatea*, the shepherd from the banks of the Henares River, originally from León and raised in Alcalá de Henares, friend of Tirsi and Elicio, in love with Amarili. This is the figure who is taken by most critics to represent MC's friend Pedro *Laínez.

Damsel(s), maiden(s), young women [Doncella(s)]. **1.** The beautiful and virginal young women from (chivalric, pastoral, sentimental, and adventure) romances who spend years in the fields and mountains and manage to retain their virtue. In *DQ* I, 9, the narrator comments slyly on such characters who have been known to spend 80 years without ever sleeping under a roof and go to their graves as virginal as the mothers who bore them. **2.** In *DQ* I, 28, the servant to Dorotea who is the only other person present when Don Fernando gains entrance to Dorotea's room and then to her heart and body with a promise of marriage. **3.** In *Gitanilla*, a character who is present with her mistress Doña Clara when Preciosa sings and dances at their home; she asks to have her fortune told. **4.** In *Española*, the young woman who admires Ricaredo in his military garb. **5.** In *Celoso*, two employees of Felipo de Carrizales who serve his wife Leonora and who are about the same age as she. **6.** In *DQ* II, 20, participants, ranging in age from 14 to 18, and dressed in green, in the celebration of *Camacho's wedding. **7.** In *DQ* II, 23, two rows of attendants who accompany *Belerma in DQ's dream in the Cave of Montesinos. **8.** In *DQ* II, 31, two servants of the duke and duchess who place a scarlet cape around DQ's shoulders in imitation of the sort of greeting often given to a knight-errant upon arrival at a palace or castle in the romances of chivalry (and exactly as DQ had described to SP in I, 21). **9.** In *DQ* II, 31, six servants of the duke and duchess who attend to DQ and SP when they first arrive at the duke's country house. **10**. In *DQ* II, 32, four servants at the country home of the duke and duchess who lather and wash DQ's beard, and then also that of the duke. One, referred to as the barber damsel (*doncella barbera*), is the person who actually lathers DQ's beard. Presumably, at least some of these damsels at the duke's palace play multiple roles. **11**. In *DQ* II, 44, along with some *dueñas*, servants the duchess offers to accompany DQ after SP goes off to assume his governorship. DQ refuses the offer. Specifically, she suggests sending four maidens with him when he retires for the evening. **12**. In *DQ* II, 60, a maid who is part of the retinue of Doña Guiomar de Quiñones. **13**. In *Persiles* III, 8, one of the participants in a peasant dance who explains that Tozuelo and Clementa Cobeña have fallen in love and that he has dressed as a woman and taken her place in the dance because she is pregnant.

Danaë [Dánae]. In Greek myth, the woman about whom it was prophesied that her son would cause the death of her father and who was therefore imprisoned in a tower. Zeus (Jupiter) visited Danaë in the form of a shower of gold and made her pregnant. The son of that union was Perseus who did in fact cause the death of Danaë's father. See *DQ* I, 33.

Danaids. The 50 daughters of Danaus who were forced to marry the 50 sons of their uncle Aegyptus. After the marriages took place, all but one of the daughters followed their father's instructions and killed their husbands. After their death, the Danaids were punished in the underworld by having to spend eternity attempting to fill leaky jars with water. See *DQ* I, 14; *Galatea* 4.

Danaus [Dánao]. In Greek myth, the king of Egypt and father of 50 daughters known as the *Danaids. See *Galatea* 4.

Dancourt, Florent Carton (1661–1725). French actor and dramatist. Dancourt's one-act comedy *Le bon Soldat* (1691; *The Good Soldier*) is derived from *Cueva*. His play *Sancho Pança, Gouverneur* (1713; *Sancho Panza, Governor*) is taken both from *DQ* and Guyon

*Guérin de Bouscal's play about SP's governorship.

Danea (Dánea). In *Persiles* II, 13, the kingdom headed by Leopoldio. (Some editors accent the first syllable, whereas others the penultimate syllable.) In MC's day, Danea was another name for Denmark, but in *Persiles* there is a clear distinction between Dinamarca and Danea, with the latter apparently a fictional realm or, given MC's ambiguous and imaginative northern geography in the novel, perhaps Sweden. See also *Persiles* II, 21.

Danican, François André. *Philidor.

Dante Alighieri (1265–1321). Greatest of all Italian poets. Dante's *Divina commedia* (ca. 1310–14; *Divine Comedy*) was translated into Spanish in 1428 but had surprisingly little resonance in Spain during the Renaissance, where Dante was not nearly as well-known or as influential as other Italian writers, such as *Ariosto, *Boccaccio, Castiglione, *Petrarch, or *Tasso. The 1515 Spanish translation of the *Inferno* was probably somewhat more influential in Spain. Having traveled in Italy and with a general familiarity of the great Italian writers, MC must at least have heard of Dante and his work, but there is no direct evidence that he ever read the *Divine Comedy*, although he may well have done so in the original Italian. His only reference to Dante is a brief mention in *Galatea* 6, along with other famous Italian poets. There are some, however, who find a strong inferential link between the two. The most suggestive link might be made between Dante's Lucifer and MC's *windmills. In the lowest circle of hell, Lucifer is trapped in ice up to his waist, but he waves and flails his arms in a manner compared to a windmill. Since DQ perceives the innocent windmills on the plane of La Mancha as malevolent giants, it is an intriguing (but by no means necessary) possibility to think that MC may have had Dante in mind when writing this scene.

Bibliography: William T. Avery, "Elementos dantescos del *Quijote*," *Anales Cervantinos* 9 (1961–62): 1–28; and William T. Avery, "Elementos dantescos del *Quijote* (Segunda parte)," *Anales Cervantinos* 13–14 (1974–75): 1–28.

Daphne [Dafne]. In Greek myth, the daughter of the river god Peneus. She was a nymph who loved no one but who was pursued by Apollo and fled, praying to be delivered from him. Her wish was granted and she was changed into a laurel tree. See *Casa* 2; *Parnaso* 4–5; *Persiles* I, 15, 19.

Dapple. The name used for SP's ass in some English translations. It is derived from the term **rucio* (silvery gray, perhaps with dapples) often used by SP to refer to his unnamed mount. The use of *Dapple* as a proper name is an understandable liberty sometimes taken by translators, but it is not an accurate reflection of the way the animal is referred to in MC's text.

Daraida. A character in *Rogel de Grecia* (by Feliciano de *Silva) mentioned in *DQ* I, 24. It is the name assumed by Prince Agesilao, who dresses as a woman in order to gain access to the woman he loves.

Daranio. In *Galatea* 2–3, the rich shepherd who marries the beautiful Silveria. Daranio anticipates the figure of Camacho in *DQ* II, 20–21.

Dardinel. In *DQ* II, 1, he is referred to simply as the friend of Medoro who almost cost him his life. In Ariosto's *Orlando Furioso*, he is killed by Reinaldos de Montalbán and buried by Medoro and Angelica.

Darinel. A shepherd in two romances of chivalry by Feliciano de *Silva, *Amadís de Grecia* and *Rogel de Grecia*. Darinel is not a knight but, as DQ notes, a shepherd, which suggests that MC was specifically sensitive to the fact that Silva was the one writer of chivalric romances who also incorporated some pastoral elements into that genre. See *DQ* I, 6, 24.

Daring youth. *Phaethon.

Darinto. In *Galatea* 4–5, the courtly gentleman, friend of Timbrio and Nísida, who falls in love with Blanca.

Darío, Rubén (Félix Rubén García Sarmiento, 1867–1916). Nicaraguan poet, generally considered the greatest and most influential of all Spanish American poets. Darío is the author of two of the most frequently cited poems ever written about MC and DQ, which he published in *Cantos de vida y esperanza* (*Songs of Life and Hope*) on the three hundredth anniversary of the publication of *DQ* I (1905). The first is the gentle "Soneto a Cervantes" ("Sonnet to Cervantes"), an uncharacteristically pensive poem in which the poet reflects on hours of sadness and solitude, but 'Cervantes is a good friend.' The second is entitled "Letanías de Nuestro Señor don Quijote" ("Litany for Our Lord Don Quixote"), and in it the poet invokes the spirit of DQ, a sort of patron saint and liberator of the downtrodden, and asks him to pray for troubled modern mankind. In addition to these, several other poems by Darío contain passing references to MC and DQ, always in the same positive, enthusiastic, romantic sense. Darío's story "D. Q." (1899) is the first-person narrative of a Spanish soldier in Cuba at the time of the blockade of Santiago de Cuba in 1898 near the end of the Spanish-American War. The soldier's company is joined by an older man, reputed to be valiant and noble, as standard-bearer. The man's exact name is not known, but some of his possessions bear the initials "D. Q." Word comes of the final defeat of the Spanish army and the troops are ordered to surrender their arms. When it is time for the Spanish flag to be handed over, D. Q., 'with a centuries-old look in his eyes,' leaps with the flag into the abyss. Darío thus equates DQ and Spain with a certain nobility, even in well-deserved defeat.

Bibliography: Santiago Alfonso López Navia, "Dos Quijotes finiseculares: 'D.Q.' de Rubén Darío (1899) y *El alma de Don Quijote* de Jerónimo Montes (1904)," *Anales Cervantinos* 31 (1993): 99–111. and Graciela Palau de Nemes, " 'D. Q.': un cuento fantástico de Rubén Darío," in *Cervantes, su obra y su mundo: Actas del I Congreso Internacional sobre Cervantes*, ed. Manuel Criado de Val (Madrid: Edi-6, 1981), 943–47.

Darius [Darío] (521–486 BCE). King of Persia who invaded eastern Europe and met defeat in Greece. When Alexander the Great found a precious jeweled box that had belonged to Darius, he decided to store a copy of Homer's *Iliad* in it. See *DQ* I, 6.

Dark-skinned Indian girl [Indiana amulatada]. A reference to the *chacona, a dance that originated in America.

Dathan [Datán]. Together with Abiram, he rebelled against the authority of Moses and Aaron. Jehovah made the earth open and swallow them and their families and possessions. See *Baños* 2.

Daudet, Alphonse (1840–97). French novelist. The hero of Daudet's *Tartarin de Tarascon* (1872; *Tartarin of Tarascon*) and its two sequels—*Tartarin sur les Alpes* (1885; *Tartarin in the Alps*) and *Port Tarascon* (1890)—represents an attempt to combine both of MC's heroes in a single character: Tartarin "bore within him the soul of a Don Quixote; the same chivalric impulse, the same heroic ideal, the same passion for the romantic and the grandiose" but he also had "the short and pot-bellied body on paws of the immortal Sancho Panza." Then the narrator exclaims, "Don Quixote and Sancho Panza in the same man! you understand what a household that must have made! what struggles! what wrenchings!" Tartarin's amusing stories of his adventures plus his search for adventures themselves have not worn well over the years, but were in their time very popular.

Daughter of a rich nobleman [Hija de un caballero rico]. In *Persiles* I, 8, the Italian woman who takes dancing lessons from Rutilio, falls in love and elopes with him, but is captured and returned home by her parents.

Daughter of Diego de la Llana [Hija de Diego de la Llana]. The beautiful young woman dressed as a man whom SP and his retinue come across during their rounds of the island. She explains that she is so dressed in order to get out of the home in which she is confined and see a little bit of the world. Her brother, dressed as a woman, is also brought before SP. The governor lectures them and

sends them home. But the daughter is so attractive that the steward who accompanies SP decides to ask for her hand in marriage, and SP sees in the son a possible husband for his own daughter. See *DQ* II, 49, 51.

Daughter of Don Tomás de Avendaño [Hija de don Tomás de Avendaño]. At the end of *Fregona*, the woman who marries Don Juan, son of the magistrate of Toledo.

Daughter of Doña Rodríguez [Hija de Doña Rodríguez]. The young woman seduced and abandoned by the son of an influential neighbor of the duke, who refuses to use his power to right the wrong. When the young woman agrees to marry the duke's lackey *Tosilos, the duke intervenes to prevent the marriage. The family is broken up as the poor young woman enters a convent, her mother Doña *Rodríguez returns alone to Castile, and Tosilos is bought off. See *DQ* II, 52, 54–56, 66.

Daughter of la Berrueca. *Berrueca.

Daughter of Peneus. *Daphne.

Daughter of Pentapolín [Hija de Pentapolín]. In *DQ* I, 18, the daughter of the Christian king in the battle (of sheep) as described by DQ.

Daughter of the magistrate [Hija del corregidor]. At the end of *Fregona*, the woman who marries Don Diego de Carriazo.

Daughters, seven. *Ruidera.

Daughters of Danaus. *Danaids.

Daumier, Honoré (1808–79). French painter and caricaturist. DQ was one of the themes to which Daumier returned repeatedly throughout his career, although he never did a set of illustrations for an edition of the novel. Most of his works on the subject are impressionistic paintings in which DQ and SP ride along, sometimes with stress on the knight, other times on the squire, although he also has some more realistic, satiric interpretations (and one charcoal drawing of SP doing what no one can do for him in the scene from *DQ* I, 20). If Gustave *Doré was the greatest nineteenth-century illustrator of *DQ*, Daumier was perhaps the greatest graphic interpreter of DQ outside the context of the book itself.

Bibliography: Bruce Laughton, "Daumier's Drawings of Don Quixote," *Master Drawings* 34 (1996): 400–13; and Rachel Schmidt, "The Romancing of *Don Quixote*: Spatial Innovation and Visual Interpretation in the Imagery of Johannot, Doré and Daumier," *Word and Image* 14 (1998): 354–70.

Dauphiné [Delfinado]. A former province in southeastern France, north of Provence. See *Persiles* III, 19.

Dauro. Poetic variant, implying that the name is derived from *aurum* (gold), for the very small and short Darro River that flows into Granada, where it empties into the Genil River. See *Galatea* 6; *Parnaso* 2.

Davenant (or D'Avenant), William (1606–68). English poet and dramatist. Davenant's play *The Cruel Brother* (1630) is about a country gentleman named Lotario and his farmer servant, Borachio, who are obviously based on DQ and SP. Lotario becomes ever less quixotic as he engages in courtly schemes, while Borachio quotes proverbs, hopes to rise in the world, and sometimes acts as reality instructor for his master.

David. In the Old Testament, a great king of the Hebrews, slayer of the giant Goliath, and famous as wise, brave, prudent, and handsome. David is often represented with a harp, and many of the biblical psalms are attributed to him. He fell in love with the married Bathsheba, arranged for her husband to be killed in battle, and married her. Their son was another great king, *Solomon. See *DQ* I, prologue; *Galatea* 4; *Parnaso* 3; *Poesías* 20; *Rufián* 1.

Dávila, Gaspar. *Avila, Gaspar de.

Dávila Padilla, Fray Agustín (1562–1604). Dominican missionary and the author of a history of his order in Mexico entitled *Historia de la fundación y discurso de la Provincia de Santiago de México, de la Orden de Predicadores . . .* (1596; *History of the Foundation and Discourse of the Province of Santiago in Mexico, of the Order of Preachers . . .*). MC based *Rufián* on Davila Padilla's version of the saintly life of Fray Cristóbal de la Cruz, the reformed ruffian previously called Cristóbal de Lugo.

Davis, Lennard J. Theorist of the novel. In *Factual Fictions: The Origins of the English Novel* (1983), Davis argues that *DQ* "should not be considered a novel in the same sense as the novels of Defoe, Richardson, Fielding—perhaps should not even be considered a novel at all." Davis presents the thesis that the early novel's distinguishing characteristic was the reader's "uncertainty to the factual or fictional reality of the work," which for him "was one of the major components in the phenomenology of reading during the early eighteenth century and which was largely absent when Cervantes wrote." Although Davis accurately describes some of differences between Defoe's novels and those of MC, his understanding of *DQ* is far less than adequate. Equally important, if not more so, is Davis's failure to take into consideration the Spanish *picaresque tradition, which is never mentioned in his book. To an extent even greater than in the novels of Defoe and his contemporaries, the anonymous *Lazarillo de Tormes* (1554) was presented as a factual memoir and was indeed perceived by many of its contemporary readers as possibly being an authentic autobiography. The same is true, at least to some extent, of several other subsequent picaresque novels. Not only is it in error to assert that the uncertainty between fact and fiction was not as great a factor in MC's day as in Defoe's, but quite the opposite is true: it was a greater problem in the Spanish *Golden Age (*historia) than in the English eighteenth century.

Bibliography: Lennard J. Davis, *Factual Fictions: The Origins of the English Novel* (New York: Columbia University Press, 1983).

Davus [Davo]. A character from the plays of Terence. See *Parnaso* 2.

Dayamira. *Deianeira.

Daza, Licenciado. Poet praised in Calliope's song in *Galatea* 6; this is perhaps a reference to Dionisio Daza Chacón, physician to Felipe II.

De legibus. *Cicero.

Dead body [Cuerpo muerto, Muerto]. 1. In *Numancia* 2, the figure called forth from his grave by Marquino to predict the inevitable destruction of the city. **2.** In *DQ* I, 19, DQ and SP come across a nighttime procession of white-robed figures escorting a dead body. On the basis of similar scenes in some of the romances of chivalry (one in *Palmerín de Inglaterra* offers noteworthy similarities), DQ assumes there is a wrong to be righted and charges, wounding one of the men, who then explains that the deceased has died a natural death. Some of the details of the episode—the fever from which the man died, the removal of the body from its original grave in Baeza (near Úbeda), its transportation by night, its relocation to Segovia, and the prominence of the phrase *noche oscura* (dark night) so characteristic in the mystic poetry of *Saint Juan de la Cruz—all bear a strange resemblance to what happened to the body of Saint Juan: the revered monk died in 1591 and was buried in Úbeda (not in the nearby Baeza, as in the adventure), then in 1593 his body was disinterred and moved secretly by night to Segovia. The details could be mere coincidence, and none of those who have remarked on the similarity between the adventure and the reality of Saint Juan have convincingly speculated about what MC's motive might have been in evoking the historical episode.

Bibliography: Alberto Sánchez, "Posibles ecos de San Juan de la Cruz en el *Quijote* de 1605." *Anales Cervantinos* 28 (1990): 9–21.

Dead Sea [Lagos de Sodoma]. The Dead Sea is supposed to be the site of the city of *Sodom when it was destroyed. See *Baños* 1.

Dear reader [Lector amable]. In *DQ* II, 44, the term used by the narrator to refer to the reader of his version of the translation of CHB's text.

Dearmer, Mabel (1872–1915). English dramatist. Dearmer's life was cut short as she was beginning to develop her literary career. Her *Don Quixote: A Romantic Drama* was her first work and, apparently, was never staged. It reads better than many more famous dramatic adaptations of MC's novel, frequently making use of passages adapted directly from the novel, sometimes in very different (but appropriate) contexts. After an opening scene of book burning as DQ's madness is established, the general framework of the play is the *Cardenio* story, in which the intervention of DQ is crucial to the happy resolution. Meanwhile, the main action is interrupted by scenes involving DQ's adventures: the armies of sheep, the windmills, the enchanter. After the defeated DQ is taken home in a cage, Cardenio, Dorotea, Fernando, and Luscinda follow and testify to DQ's helpfulness and sanity, and to reanimate the dejected and dying knight to rekindle his chivalric spirit.

Bibliography: Mabel Dearmer, *Three Plays*, intro. Stephen Gwynn (London: Erskine Macdonald, 1941).

Death [Muerte]. One of the members of the cast of Las *Cortes de la Muerte* in *DQ* II, 11.

Death of Alonso Quijano. The final chapter of *DQ* II, in which Alonso Quijano falls ill, regains his sanity, repents of his life as DQ, makes his will, and dies, has been the subject of considerable critical discussion. It is clear, first of all, that MC kills off his character so that no one would write another sequel, as *Avellaneda had done (although even at the end of *DQ* I, it was already assumed that DQ had died, and epitaphs in his honor were composed by the *academicians of Argamasilla). This ploy was successful for the seventeenth century, but by the late eighteenth century, sequels began to appear, and ever since then there have been dozens of them (*quixotic novel). Many readers find great satisfaction in Alonso Quijano's reposed Christian death, and see the novel as having its thematic and conceptual culmination in this scene of *desengaño*. Others, however, have difficulty in reconciling the *hidalgo*'s renunciation of his more interesting life as DQ, and see it as an accommodation with the more prosaic, conformist, and repressive reality of the priest, barber, and Sansón Carrasco. It is ironic that the priest and Sansón, who strove throughout both parts of the novel to "help" DQ and encourage him to return to sanity, continue to call him DQ, rather than Alonso, and talk to him of assuming the guise of shepherds, even after he has completely rejected his romance-inspired life of madness and returned to his original sanity. Ironic, also, is the fact that the last person who cites the authority of the romances of chivalry is SP, whereas the last proverb of the novel comes from DQ: 'There are no birds this year in the nests of yesteryear.'

Bibliography: Juan Fernández Jiménez, "Anticipation and Meaning in Don Quixote's Death," *Indiana Journal of Hispanic Literatures* 5 (1994): 81–90; Edward H. Friedman, "Executing the Will: The End of the Road in *Don Quixote*," *Indiana Journal of Hispanic Literatures* 5 (1994): 105–25; and Rachel Schmidt, "The Performance and Hermeneutics of Death in the Last Chapter of *Don Quijote*," *Cervantes* 20, no. 2 (2000): 101–26.

Debají. A lieutenant in the corps of *janissaries. See *Baños* 2.

Debate about love [Disputa sobre el amor]. The debate, a set piece, between Lenio and Tirsi in *Galatea* 4. The topic was a popular one in the Renaissance and appears in several pastoral works, various works by MC, and several *comedias* of the epoch. The most influential treatise on the subject was León *Hebreo's *Dialogues of Love*. It is in the subtle distinctions made about the spirit of *Platonism that enliven such debates. In *Galatea* 4, Lenio begins and delivers a long speech critical of love: he defines love as a desire for physical beauty; cites all the evils committed in the name of love; recalls famous cases of ill-fated love from myth, the Bible, and history; and ends with a poem against the effects of love. Tirsi replies: he distinguishes between love and desire; enumerates the positive effects of three kinds of love: honest, useful, and enjoyable; praises the effects of corporal beauty, especially the beauty of a woman's face; notes that love makes everyone equal; and ends with a poem in praise of the effects of love.

Deceitful Marriage, The. *Casamiento engañoso, El.*

Décima. Also known as *espinela*, from the name of its supposed inventor Vicente *Espinel, the *décima* is a popular stanza form consisting of ten octosyllabic lines with a rhyme scheme of abbaaccddc. MC wrote a number of *décimas*, such as the burlesque poem by Urganda la Desconocida in the prefatory pages of *DQ* I.

Deconstructive readings of *Don Quixote*. *Poststructuralist and postmodernist readings of *Don Quixote*.

Defoe, Daniel (1660–1731). English journalist, pamphleteer, and novelist. Defoe did not appreciate another writer's remark about Robinson Crusoe's quixotism and, even while he recognized that *DQ* was a book that "thousands read with pleasure," resented the comparison of his work with that of MC. He considered *DQ* an allegory or satire on the Duke of *Medina Sidonia, commander of the Spanish Invincible Armada. But Defoe knew several languages, possibly Spanish among them, and clearly drew upon the Spanish picaresque tradition in order to write *Moll Flanders* (1722). It has also been suggested that Defoe may well have owed much of the conception of *Robinson Crusoe* (1719) to MC's *Persiles*, as well as *DQ* (especially *Capitán*).

Bibliography: Diana Armas de Wilson, "The Novel as 'Moletta': Cervantes and Defoe," in *Cervantes, the Novel, and the New World* (Oxford: Oxford University Press, 2000), 60–77.

Dehesa de Córdoba. *Pastures of Córdoba.

Deianeira [Deyanira]. In Greek myth, the wife of Heracles. She was abducted by Nessus, a centaur, which her husband managed to kill, but as he was dying Nessus advised Deianeira to preserve some of his blood in order to make Heracles love her again if he should ever stray. This she did, and after Heracles fell in love with Iole, Deianeira sent him a robe soaked in the centaur's blood. But the blood had been contaminated by that of the Hydra (which Heracles had used to poison his arrows), and it caused Heracles terrible suffering. Deianeira committed suicide after she saw the effect that her actions had on her husband, and Heracles also finally had to kill himself in a funeral pyre in order to escape the unbearable pain. See *Casa* 2; *Persiles* III, 15.

Dekker, Eduard Deuwes (1820–87). Dutch novelist. In Dekker's best-known novel, *Max Havelaar* (1860), the protagonist is explicitly based on DQ: "Full of the love of truth and justice, he often neglected his nearest and most obvious duty, in order to redress a wrong that lay higher, farther, or deeper, and that allured him by the probable need for greater effort in the struggle. He was chivalrous and brave, but often, like the other Don Quixote, wasted his valour on a windmill."

Del amor de Dios. *Fonseca, Cristóbal de.

Delaney, Juan José (1954–). Argentine writer. Delany's *La carcajada* (1974; *The Guffaw*) includes one short story entitled "Capítulo perdido del *Quijote*" ("A Lost Chapter of *Don Quixote*"). As DQ and SP ride along, they meet and talk with another traveler, who engages them in a discussion about their identity and activities. At the end of the story, it is revealed that the other traveler is none other than MC.

Bibliography: Juan José Delaney, *La carcajada* (Buenos Aires: Literamérica, 1974).

Deleasir. In *Persiles* III, 13, one of the three candidates for the position of wife of the Duke of Nemurs. With Belarmina and Féliz Flora, she accompanies the pilgrims to Rome, but returns to France with the Duke of Nemurs in IV, 9 (which we only learn in IV, 14).

Delfinado. *Dauphiné.

Delgado, Jacinto María. Spanish novelist and satirist. Delgado is the author of the most important sequel to *DQ* published in the eighteenth century: *Adiciones á la historia del ingenioso hidalgo Don Quixote de la Mancha, en que se prosiguen los sucesos ocurridos á su escudero el famoso Sancho Panza, escritas en arábigo por Cide-Hamete Benengeli, y traducidas al castellano con las memorias de la vida de este por don Jacinto María Delgado* (1786; *Additions to the History of the Ingenious Hidalgo Don Quixote de la Mancha, in which the Events that Happened to His Squire the Famous Sancho Panza Are Related, Written in Arabic by Cide Hamete Benengeli, and Translated to Spanish along with the Memoirs of the Life of the Latter by Jacinto María Delgado*). In the novel, SP is brought back to the palace of the duke and duchess of *DQ* II as an advisor, is named a baron, and dies after overeating. The thin plot is, above all, a pretext for some anti-French social satire. What is fascinating about the work, however, is the role of CHB, who is omnipresent throughout the text in ways that would have made MC proud: CHB comments on the text, addresses the characters, informs the reader of his editorial decisions, speculates on SP's intelligence, stumbles over the translation of some Arabic words, and more. But best of all is the brief appendix to the work entitled "Memorias del esclarecido Cide-Hamete Benengeli, autor celebérrimo de la historia del ingenioso Don Quixote de la Mancha. Recogidas por Melique Zulema, Autor igualmente verdadero, que Arabigo" ("Memoirs of the Illustrious Cide Hamete Benengeli, Most Celebrated Author of the History of the Ingenious Don Quixote de la Mancha. Prepared by Melique Zulema, an Author as Truthful as He Is Arabic"). The 16 numbered items of "fact" concerning CHB—his mother as janitress of the mosque, his smallpox, his recipe for *acelgas* (collard greens), his modification of the bagpipe, his role in organizing the jokes on DQ and SP at the duke's palace, his return to Africa and his death, and others—are whimsical and comically absurd. The story of SP may not be of much interest to modern readers, but the performance in this novel by CHB has rarely been matched by any realist, modern, or postmodern author. Overall, this may be the best Spanish novel of the eighteenth century.

Bibliography: Santiago Alfonso López Navia, *La ficción autorial en el "Quijote" y en sus continuaciones e imitaciones* (Madrid: Universidad Europea de Madrid-CEES Ediciones, 1996); Howard Mancing, "Jacinto María Delgado and Cide Hamete Benengeli: A Semi-Classic Recovered and a Bibliographical Labyrinth Explored," *Cervantes* 7, no. 1 (1987): 13–43; and Juana Toledano Molina, "Otra secuela cervantina del siglo XVIII: *Adiciones a la historia del ingenioso hidalgo Don Quijote de la Mancha, continuación de la vida de Sancho Panza*," in *Actas del III Coloquio Internacional de la Asociación de Cervantistas: Alcalá de Henares, noviembre de 1990* (Barcelona: Anthropos, 1993), 131–37.

Delgado, Sinesio (1859–1928). Spanish dramatist. Delgado wrote light, comical works, often musicals, and enjoyed considerable popularity in the late-nineteenth and early-twentieth centuries. In his play *El retablo de Maese Pedro* (1916; *The Puppet Show of Maese Pedro*), there is no puppet show, no Maese Pedro, and no DQ or SP. Rather, the play presents a version of the *Cardenio* episodes from *DQ* I, with the *pícaro* Ginés de Pasamonte working for Don Fernando in an attempt to win over Dorotea, who is served by Doña Rodríguez. In the second act, the *pícaros* Rinconete and Cortadillo along with the servant woman Maritornes are also involved in the action. Overall, this is a fairly original and interesting adaptation from MC's novel. Delgado also wrote a one-act *zarzuela* entitled *La ilustre fregona* (1906; *The Illustrious Kitchen-Maid*), with music by Rafael Calleja. It takes the concept of a woman servant in an inn who is more than she seems, but gives it a new twist. Manuela, the second cook at a nameless inn, is transported in time and becomes a Greek goddess, a noble Spanish lady courted by a Christian knight and a Muslim, and a noble Frenchwoman about to be executed during the French Revolution before being returned to the present. It is certainly not a retelling of MC's *Fregona*.

Bibliography: Sinesio Delgado, *El retablo de Maese Pedro* (Madrid: Imprenta de los Hijos de M. G. Hernández, 1916); and Sinesio Delgado, *La ilustre fregona* (Madrid: Hijos de M. G. Hernández, 1916).

Delian, the; Delio; Delo; Delos; Delphic Apollo. *Apollo.

Delilah [Dalida]. In the Old Testament, the woman who stripped Samson of his strength by cutting off his hair while he slept. She is a symbol of the seductress who brings her lovers to ruin. See *Galatea* 4.

Dello me pesa. A popular dance in MC's time. See *Cueva*.

Demanda del Sancto Grial con los maravillosos hechos de Lanzarote y de Galaz su hijo [Quest for the Holy Grail with the Marvelous Deeds of Lancelot and Galahad His Son]. An anonymous chivalric romance from Arthurian legend translated into Spanish in 1515 and very popular in the sixteenth century in Spain. See *DQ* I, 49.

Demon(s), Devil(s) [Demonio(s), Diablo(s)]. **1.** In *Tratos* 2, a figure conjured up by Fátima who states that he is powerless against Christian resolve. **2.** In *Numancia* 2, a figure that rises up and steals the ram being sacrificed by the priests. **3.** In *Rufián* 2, the identity of some figures who sing and dance. **4.** In *DQ* II, 11, one of the members of the cast of *Las *Cortes de la Muerte*. **5.** In *DQ* II, 34, the messenger (*postillón*), in the form of the devil, who announces the arrival of the enchanters who will reveal the means by which DT is to be disenchanted. **6.** In *DQ* II, 70, a dozen of the residents of hell whom Altisidora says she saw playing tennis with *DQA* instead of a ball. One of the devils asks if the book is really as bad as they say it is, and the other responds that it is so bad that even he could not write one worse.

Demosthenes [Demóstenes] (384–322 BCE). The greatest of all Greek orators. His eloquence was matched by his patriotism and pragmatism. Demosthenes's preserved speeches are of great value in understanding ancient society, especially in the areas of law, politics, and economics. See *DQ* II, 32; *Galatea* 6; *Pedro* 2; *Poesías* 31.

Denevi, Marco (1922–). Argentine novelist and short-story writer. Denevi's collection of very short fictions entitled *Falsificaciones* (1966; *Falsifications*) contains two excellent short stories relating to MC. The first is "El precursor de Cervantes" ("Cervantes's Precursor"), which describes the discovery of a manuscript dated 1563 in the archives of the University of Alcalá de Henares. The manuscript is described as being totally undistinguished and uninteresting except for one brief entry that describes how a young woman named Aldonza Lorenzo, living in El Toboso, read many romances of chivalry, lost her mind, called herself DT, had people treat her as a great lady, actually believed she was beautiful (she was not), invented a chivalric champion named DQ, and spent her days waiting for her prince to come for her. Meanwhile, an *hidalgo* in a nearby village, who was in love with Aldonza in spite of her looks, decided to become her DQ, took that name, and went out in search of chivalric deeds. When he believed that he had achieved sufficient fame to win his lady's hand, he returned to her—only to find that she had died while he was away. The second is a brief tale of one Don Román Móguez de la Sierra, a humorist who scandalized the serious academicians of the Academy of Argamasilla del Alba by proposing that the true cause of DQ's madness was that as a youth he had been in love with DT and had prepared to marry her. On the eve of their wedding, she showed him her dowry, which included a number of things she had monogrammed with her initials. When DQ saw her intimate clothing bearing the three 'atrocious initials' (evidently he means DDT, for Dulcinea del Toboso, but also the initials of the poisonous insecticide), he lost his mind. Denevi's *Los locos y los cuerdos* (1975; *The Mad and the Sane*) includes several short stories and some poems, as well as the one-act play that is used as the title for the volume. In the play, SP arrives in El Toboso, having been sent by DQ to find DT. He asks for information at a brothel and gets into a conversation with the madame, whose name Celesta recalls that of the famous bawd Celestina. Their dialogue is a highly original mixture of elements from MC's novel and a very informal, colloquial style, with amusing touches of absurdity. In the end, Celesta agrees to be DT, and a disarmingly prosaic and realistic DQ agrees, for a price, to take her as such. The piece is a real tour de force.

Bibliography: Marco Denevi, *Falsificaciones* (Buenos Aires Editorial Universitaria de Buenos Aires, 1966); Marco Denevi, *Los locos y los cuerdos* (Buenos Aires: Huemul, 1975); and Carlos Orlando Nállim, "Marco Denevi y la sin par Dulcinea," *Revista de Literaturas Modernas* 28 (1995–96): 171–83.

Denia. Spanish port city on the Mediterranean Sea, located southeast of Valencia and northeast of Alicante. It was here that MC first landed when he returned to Spain after his five years of captivity.

Denia, Marqués de. *Lerma, Duke of.

Denmark [Dinamarca]. For the Spaniards of the *Golden Age, Denmark was a nation tinged with exoticism. It was a northern country sometimes confused with Lithuania, and was probably best known as the origin of the Doncella de Dinamarca (Maiden from Denmark) from *Amadís de Gaula*. In *Persiles* it is the homeland of Prince *Arnaldo, loyal lover of Auristela and friend of Periandro who, when he is unable to marry Sigismunda at the end of the novel, gladly accepts her younger sister Eusebia as a consolation prize. See *DQ* I, 10; *Persiles* I, 2, 16; II 20–21; III, 9; IV, 9.

Depravada edad nuestra. *Our depraved age.

Descargamaría. A small town in western Spain, located southwest of Salamanca and north of Cáceres, near the border with Portugal. It was noted for its wine. See *Vidriera*.

Descendants of Hagar [Generación agarena]. Muslims. In the Old Testament, Hagar was the Egyptian servant of Sarah, wife of the patriarch Abraham. She was also Abraham's mistress and the mother of his oldest son Ishmael (Sarah's son Isaac was not born until many years later). Muslims have traditionally claimed to have descended from Ishmael and thus hold Hagar in special veneration, usually as the true wife of Abraham.

Descuido. *Forgetfulness.

Desengaño [Disillusionment]. The theme of *desengaño*, recognizing reality and coming to terms with God, yourself, and the world in general, was a popular one in Spanish *Golden Age literature. Perhaps the single most famous example is that of Segismundo in the final act of *Calderón's *La vida es sueño*. The ideal was to achieve a state of *desengaño* before death in order to pave the way to paradise in the afterlife. On his deathbed, DQ renounces the romances of chivalry, proclaims a state of *desengaño*, and wishes he had more time to read books that might be a *light to his soul. This act is seen as exemplary by some and as a sellout to convention by others (*death of Alonso Quijano).

Bibliography: Otis H. Green, "*Desengaño*," in *Spain and the Western Tradition: The Castilian Mind in Literature from "El Cid" to Calderón*, 4 vols. (Madison: University of Wisconsin Press; 1963–66), vol. 4, 43–76; and Pedro López Lara, "En torno al desengaño de Don Quijote," *Anales Cervantinos* 25–26 (1987–88): 239–54.

Desengaño(s) de celos. *López de Enciso, Bartolomé.

Deseo. *Desire.

Desesperación. *Desperation.

Désespoir amoreux, avec Les nouvelles visions de Don Quichotte, histoire espagnole, Le (1715; Amorous Desperation, with the New Visions of Don Quixote, a Spanish History). An anonymous French imitation/continuation of *DQ*.

Desire [Deseo]. The father of Vainglory in MC's dream in *Parnaso* 6.

Desmochado. In *Rinconete*, a thug in Monipodio's brotherhood who is just mentioned by name.

Desperation [Desesperación]. In *Casa* 2, an allegorical figure conjured up by Malgesí.

Desposorio. *Secret marriage.

Destiny [Destino]. The necessary and/or inevitable succession of events; what eventually becomes of someone. The concept of destiny is tied closely to those of *fortune, *fate, and divine providence, and, like them, is sometimes personified in MC's works. See *Fregona*; *Galatea* 3; *Pedro* 1–2.

Destouches, Philippe Néricault (1680–1754). French dramatist. Destouches's *Le curieux impertinent* (1710; *The Curious Impertinent One*) is an interesting adaptation of *Curioso* in which the emphasis is on testing the fidelity of a fiancée, rather than that of a wife. In this, he follows the priest's statement after reading the *novela* in *DQ* I, 35, that it would be more psychologically believable if the person whose fidelity was tested were a lover rather than a wife.

Destrucción de Numancia, La; Destruction of Numantia, The. *Numancia, La.

Devereux, Robert, Count of Essex [Conde de Leste] (ca. 1566–1601). The English leader of the raid on *Cádiz in 1596. When MC writes *Leste*, he appears to be confusing the count of Leicester (Robert Dudley, first count of Leicester, dead in 1588; or Robert Sidney, second count of Leicester, beginning in 1618) with the count of Essex. MC wrote a brilliant satire on the official Spanish military response to this raid in *Poesías* 25. The incident also provides the starting point for the action in *Española*.

Devil. *Courier.

Deyanira. *Deianeira.

Día de Santa Ana. *Saint Anne.

Día del Juicio. *Judgment Day.

Diablo(s). *Demon(s), Devil(s).

Diálogo de Cilena y Selanio; Dialogue between Cilena and Selanio. *Semanas del jardín, Las.*

Dialogue in *Don Quixote*. DQ and SP talk to each other—and with other characters—in a natural, conversational way. Before MC, no other fiction writer was able to convey such a sustained sense of realistic human dialogue in fiction. Characters in Italian short fiction and the lovers, knights, shepherds, and *pícaros* of sentimental, chivalric, pastoral, and picaresque fiction at best only rarely engaged in dialogue; they tended to speak in alternating monologues (a style MC was also capable of dominating, as in *Curioso*, for example). What is more, the narrator rarely interprets, overrides, or otherwise contextualizes what the characters say. In this sense, *DQ* truly is one of the first examples of what *Bakhtin calls the "polyphonic" novel: a novel in which the narrator's (or author's) voice has no privilege over those of the characters, all of whom speak from within their own personal consciousness and with their own point of view. (Not to exaggerate: MC at least approaches real polyphony in *DQ*, but, as Bakhtin conceives of the term, there is still some significant difference between MC's accomplishment and the fully polyphonic novels of Dostoevsky.) Perhaps the most significant role SP has to play in *DQ* is that of interlocutor with DQ. SP makes his master discuss everyday, mundane details of life; enables him to laugh at himself and others; and forces him to argue his position. In *DQ* II, there is even more dialogue and conversation than in *DQ* I, as the growing familiarity and degree of friendship of the two main characters come more to the fore, and as the plot becomes less action-oriented and consists more of conversations of all kinds.

Bibliography: M. M. Bakhtin, *Problems of Dostoevsky's Poetics*, ed. and trans. Caryl Emerson, intro. Wayne C. Booth (Minneapolis: University of Minnesota Press, 1984). Elias L. Rivers, "El principio dialógico en el *Quijote*," *La Torre*, nueva época, 2 (January-March, 1988): 1–21; and Alberto Rodrí-

guez, *La conversación en el "Quijote": subdiálogo, memoria y asimetría* (York, SC: Spanish Literature Publications, 1995).

Dialogue of the Dogs, The. *Coloquio de los perros, El.*

Diamante, Juan Bautista. *Matos Fragoso Juan de.

Diamond cross [Cruz de diamantes]. In *Persiles*, along with two fine pearls, it is the most valuable possession of Periandro and Auristela during their pilgrimage. The diamond and pearls are first mentioned in I, 9, when the dying Cloelia hands them to Auristela, who in turn gives them to Periandro for safekeeping. They are the first material signs of the nobility of the two central characters in the novel. In IV, 7, Periandro is wearing the cross when he visits the courtesan Hipólita and is accused by her of having stolen it, a matter quickly cleared up with the local authorities. In IV, 14, Sigismunda gives the cross to Constanza when the latter departs for Spain.

Diana. 1. The Roman name of the Greek virgin goddess Artemis, daughter of Zeus and Leto. She was a huntress who transformed Actaeon into a stag when he saw her bathing; he was then killed by his own dogs. She was also associated with Selene, the moon goddess, and as such is sometimes seen as the personification of the moon. More frequently, she is the patron of hunters and athletes. See *DQ* II, 8, 57–58, 68; *Galatea* 1; *Numancia* 4; *Persiles* I, 10. **2.** *Pastoral names.

Diana, La. *Montemayor, Jorge de.

Díaz de Benjumea, Nicolás (1829–84). Spanish poet and critic. Díaz de Benjumea was probably the central figure in nineteenth-century *esoteric (a term he applied to himself) readings of *DQ*. Benjumea insisted that MC's works, especially *DQ*, had secret meanings that he was able to discover. For example, he was convinced that DQ's antagonist in *DQ* II, Sansón Carrasco, was the incarnation of MC's own archenemy, Juan *Blanco de Paz, who was his nemesis in Algiers. Benjumea consistently found anagrams and secret hints in the text to support his idea about Blanco de Paz and, in what was probably his most consistent overall understanding of the novel, his conviction that MC wrote a political allegory criticizing the Inquisition. Benjumea's works, with their often outrageous titles as well as their highly controversial theses, were widely read, discussed, and criticized, with his critics and attackers far outnumbering his defenders.

Bibliography: Nicolás Díaz de Benjumea, *La estafeta de Urganda, o aviso de Cid Asam-Ouzad Benengeli, sobre el desencanto del "Quijote"* (London: J. Wertheimer, 1861); and Dominick Finello, "Notes on Nineteenth-Century *Quijote* Scholarship," *Cervantes* 7 no. 1 (1987): 59–69.

Díaz de Cervantes, Miguel de. Great-uncle of MC, perhaps for whom MC was named.

Díaz de Cervantes, Rodrigo (Ruy). MC's great-grandfather, a Cordovan draper.

Díaz de Torreblanca, Juan. *Torreblanca, Juan Díaz de.

Díaz de Vivar, Rodrigo (or Ruy), el Cid Campeador (ca. 1043–1099). The greatest heroic figure of medieval Spain, whose victorious career earned for him the epithet of *el Campeador* (the Champion) and made him the hero of works from medieval chronicles and epic poetry to the Charlton Heston–Sophia Loren film *El Cid*. The subject of both the epic poem *Cantar* (or *Poema*) *de mio Cid* (*Song* [or *Poem*] *of the Cid*) and the cycle of ballads known as the *Romancero del Cid*, Ruy Díaz de Vivar received the honorific title *Cid* (*Lord*, from the Arabic *Sidi*) out of the respect his enemies developed for his prowess and integrity. The *Cantar* is the oldest known work of literature written in Spanish; there exists a single copy dating from the twelfth century. One of the fabulous heroes of medieval European letters, El Cid accepts unjust exile from Castile by King Alfonso VI, establishes his own fiefdom in Valencia, wins great fame as a soldier in battles against the Muslims, leaves a rich legacy for his two daughters, and is eventually reconciled with the king. The poem's mixture of history and legend, its relative restraint and realism, and the austerity and nobility of the protagonist make it unique among European national epics. El Cid was best known for centuries in Spain as the hero of some 200 ballads, dating mostly from the fifteenth century. These ballads, together, related many of the events of his life and greatly elaborated his legend. Many of the ballads imaginatively fill in periods and events in the hero's life omitted or glossed over in the epic poem and in the historical record, especially some of the youthful events involving his courtship and marriage to his beautiful and faithful wife Ximena. Guillén de Castro's plays of 1618, *Las mocedades del Cid* (*Youthful Deeds of the Cid*) and *Las hazañas del Cid* (*Deeds of the Cid*), were drawn primarily from the ballad tradition and capture well the popular image of the great national hero. MC and his contemporaries did not know the epic poem but were well acquainted with the more romantic and legendary figure of El Cid through the ballad tradition. DQ refers to El Cid several times, considering him a good knight but not as good as the (fictional) Knight of the Flaming Sword (Amadís de Grecia) in I, 1. See also *DQ* I, 19, 49; *DQ* II, 22, 33; *Entretenida* 1; *Gallardo* 1; *Pedro* 1; *Poesías* 20; *Rufián* 1.

Bibliography: Edmund de Chasca, *The Poem of the Cid* (Boston: Twayne, 1976); Alan D. Deyermond, ed., *Epic Poetry and the Clergy: Studies on the Mocedades de Rodrigo* (London: Tamesis, 1969); Alan D. Deyermond, ed., *"Mio Cid" Studies* (London: Tamesis, 1968); Ramón Menéndez Pidal, *The Cid and His Spain*, trans. Harold Sunderland (London: Cass, 1971); and Colin Smith, *The Making of the "Poema de mio Cid"* (Cambridge: Cambridge University Press, 1983).

Díaz del Castillo, Bernal (1492–1582). Spanish soldier and historian. Díaz took part in the conquest of Mexico with Hernán *Cortés. Back in Spain, he wrote his *Verdadera historia de la conquista de la Nueva España* (1632; *True History of the Conquest of New Spain*), largely in response to *López de Gómara's history of the conquest. Whereas the latter places all the emphasis on Cortés himself, Bernal Díaz stresses the role of the common soldier, and especially his own contributions. In comparison with the more learned and traditional history of López de Gómara, Díaz writes from memory and employs a less formal style that at times reads more like fiction than history. His is the most frequently reprinted and read of all contemporary accounts of the conquest of Mexico. It has been suggested that MC saw in Díaz's technique of telling a "true" history, together with his interweaving of truth and fiction, a model, at least partial, for the technique used in *DQ*.

Bibliography: Anthony J. Cascardi, "Chronicle toward Novel: Bernal Díaz's *History of the Conquest of Mexico*," *Novel* 15 (1982): 197–212; and María E. Mayer, "El detalle de una 'historia verdadera': Don Quijote y Bernal Díaz," *Cervantes* 14, no. 2 (1994): 93–118.

Díaz, Doctor Francisco. Physician to Felipe II and the author of a treatise entitled *Tratado nuevamente impresa de todas las enfermedades de los riñones, y carnosidades de la verga y utrina . . .* (1588; *Newly Printed Treatise on All the Infirmities of the Kidneys, Gall Bladder, and Fleshy Parts of the Penis and Uterus . . .*), to which MC contributed a laudatory sonnet (*Poesías* 19). He is also praised in Calliope's song in *Galatea* 6.

Díaz, Juan. Spanish romance writer. Virtually nothing is known of the author of *Lisuarte de Grecia* (1526), the eighth book in the *Amadís* cycle and not to be confused with the romance of the same name (1514) by Feliciano de *Silva, the seventh book in the series.

Díaz Loyola, Carlos. *Rokha, Pablo de.

Díaz, María. Longtime mistress/housekeeper of MC's grandfather, Juan de Cervantes.

Dibden, Charles. *Bickerstaffe, Isaac.

Dice player [Jugador]. In *Persiles* III, 13, in the city of Perpignan the pilgrims witness a strange game of dice in which the loser is self-condemned to row in the galleys for six months. But after a plea by the man's wife and children, Constanza purchases his freedom.

Dichoso día. *Fortunate day.

Dickens, Charles (1812–70). English novelist. The Dickens-MC nexus is best seen in two novels written in part simultaneously: *The Posthumous Papers of the Pickwick Club* (1836–37) and *Oliver Twist* (1837–38). In the preface to *Oliver Twist*, Dickens cites the famous phrase by *Byron that in *DQ* MC "laughed Spain's chivalry away." But it was a very different Cervantine inspiration that informs this novel: *Rinconete*. Fagin is usually—and logically—assumed to be modeled on *Monipodio, the leader of a criminal ring in Seville that features cutpurses and capestealers. Surely Bill Sykes, Oliver himself, and other characters in the novel are very much within the literary tradition of the Spanish *pícaro*. *The Pickwick Papers*, on the other hand, is Dickens's overt attempt to rewrite *DQ* (and Oliver Goldsmith's *Vicar of Wakefield*) in a contemporary British context. The kindly, genial, optimistic, quintessentially quixotic Pickwick and his down-to-earth, folkloric, loyal sidekick Sam Weller make perhaps the most consciously created DQ-SP pair in nineteenth-century literature (even though, surprisingly, there is no direct allusion to DQ in the novel). Weller's difficulties with the English language explicitly recall SP's (although Sam's 'Wellerisms' are formally and thematically quite unlike SP's proverbs drawn from folk wisdom) and make the former one of the latter's most famous and loveable literary progeny.

Bibliography: Argus Easson, "Don Pickwick: Dickens and the Transformation of Cervantes," in *Rereading Victorian Fiction*, ed. Alice Jenkins, Juliet John, and John Sutherland (New York: Macmillan, 2000), 173–88; Pamela H. Long, "Fagin and Monipodio: The Source of *Oliver Twist* in Cervantes's *Rinconete y Cortadillo*," *Dickensian* 90 (1994): 117–24; and Mercedes Potau, "Notes on Parallels between *The Pickwick Papers* and *Don Quixote*," *Dickens Quarterly* 10, no. 2 (1993): 105–10.

Diderot, Denis (1713–84). French philosopher and novelist. The famous *Encyclopedia* author's best-known attempt at a comic novel *Jacques le fataliste et son maître* (1773, but not published until 1796; *Jacques the Fatalist and*

His Master) is a clear, if strained, direct imitation of the DQ-SP pair: "Jacques and his master are good only when they're together, and are worth no more separated than Don Quixote without Sancho." Owing as much to Mateo Alemán and Laurence Sterne, with its digressions and ongoing self-consciousness, as to MC, *Jacques* was very famous and influential during its time.

Dido. Legendary daughter of the king of Tyre. She was married to *Sychaeus, but after his murder she fled to Libya, founded the city of Carthage, and became its first queen. In Virgil's *Aeneid*, when Aeneas departed Troy after the city's destruction, he was made by Juno (who hated all Trojans) to fall in love with Dido. But Venus, with assistance from her son Cupid, made Dido fall in love with Aeneas. When Aeneas left Carthage to go to Italy, Dido committed suicide. See *DQ* II, 48, 71; *Persiles* II, 17; *Poesías* 8.

Diecke, Eugen. German dramatist. Diecke collaborated with C. Cervinus to write the libretto for the comic opera *Don Quichotte* (1897), with music by Georg Rauchenecker.

Diego Cortado. In *Rinconete*, the name of the of the protagonists, called *Cortadillo by Monipodio.

Diego de Bastida. In *Baños* 2, the father of Doña Constanza, who is merely mentioned.

Diego de Carriazo, Don. In *Fregona*, the youth who spends three years as a *pícaro* and convinces his friend Tomás to go off with him, thus setting in action the plot of the story.

Diego de la Llana. *Daughter of Diego de la Llana.

Diego de Miranda, Don, Knight of the Green Overcoat [Caballero del Verde Gabán]. The traveler who joins DQ and SP in II, 16; watches DQ's encounter with the *lion in II, 17; and then invites knight and squire to his home in II, 18. Don Diego is one of the more interesting secondary characters in *DQ* II,

as reader assessments of him run the gamut from saint to hypocrite. Those who take his self-description literally see him as a positive counterpart for DQ (the root for his surname is the Latin *mirandus*, 'wonderful'). The two men are of about the same age and social station; the main differences between them are that Don Diego is married, a father, and well-off economically. Those who take his self-praise as ironic see him as a parody of a good Christian. There are ambiguous textual hints that support both interpretations. Unlike many other characters in *DQ* II, Don Diego has not read *DQ* I, and so he has no familiarity with DQ before meeting him. He is amazed by DQ's madness in facing the lion but recognizes that in all matters not pertaining to chivalry he talks and acts quite normally. He is generous in opening his home to DQ and SP, and sets a standard of comfort that particularly impresses the squire. See also *DQ* II, 24, 28, 31, 67.

Bibliography: Darío Fernández-Morera, "Chivalry, Symbolism, and Psychology in Cervantes' Knight of the Green Cloak," *Hispanic Review* 61 (1993): 531–46; Gerald L. Gingras, "Diego de Miranda, 'Bufón' or Spanish Gentleman? The Social Background of His Attire," *Cervantes* 5, no. 2 (1985): 129–40; and Charles D. Presberg, " 'Yo sé quién soy': Don Quixote, Don Diego de Miranda and the Paradox of Self-Knowledge," *Cervantes* 14, no. 2 (1994): 41–69.

Diego de Parraces, Don. In *Persiles* III, 4, the man who is treacherously murdered by his relative Don Sebastián de Sorzano and dies in the company of Periandro and the other pilgrims.

Diego de Ratos. In *Persiles* IV, 1, the hunchbacked shoemaker from Tordesillas who has made a contribution to the book of sayings being compiled by a pilgrim. Because he is from Tordesillas, supposedly the home of the author of *DQA*, it has been suggested that this might represent in a satirical fashion that author who has never been identified, but there is really no clue here as to the identity of the author of *DQA*.

Diego de Valdivia, Don. In *Vidriera*, the infantry captain who takes Tomás Rodaja with him to Italy and Flanders. The character may be based on the historical Diego de *Valdivia, who hired MC as a commissary in 1587.

Diego de Valladolid. A name cited by SP in *DQ* I, 29, to illustrate the practice of taking one's surname from the place in which one lives.

Diego de Villaseñor and his wife. In *Persiles* III, 9, the parents of *Antonio the Barbarian, who welcome home their son and his family after 16 years of absence. The existence of a family of *hidalgos* with the surname Villaseñor in Quintanar de la Orden has been demonstrated, but the relationship, if any, between this historical family and the family in MC's novel is not clear at all.

Diego, Don, de la casa de Córdoba. *Fernández de Córdoba, Don Diego.

Diego, Fray. In *Vidriera*, along with Fray Jacinto and Fray Raimundo, this name is cited as typical of humble saints, in contrast with the rich and powerful who are less likely to achieve sainthood.

Diego, Gerardo (1896–1987). Spanish poet and critic. Diego's fame derives primarily from his leadership in avant-garde poetic movements of the 1920s. His achievement was recognized with the award of the Cervantes Prize in 1979. In the second part of the double volume entitled *"El Cordobés" dilucidado y Vuelta del peregrino* (1966; *"El Cordobés" Explained* and *The Return of the Traveler*), there are two Cervantine sonnets: "Soneto ingenuo de Don Quijote" ("Ingenuous Sonnet about Don Quixote") and "Después de Cervantes" ("After Cervantes"). In the first, DQ articulates his chivalric mission, whereas the second is a meditation on MC's accomplishment. Among his later poetry, mostly from the 1970s, there are two more poems worthy of note. One is "Soneto en fuga a Don Quijote" (1977; "Sonnet in Flight to Don Quixote"), a rewrite of his earlier "Soneto ingenuo." The second is his "Jinojepa del Cervantes" (1980; *jinojepa* is a nonsense word

used in the title of several poems), a whimsical evocation of MC's works.

Bibliography: Gerardo Diego, *"El Cordobés" dilucidado y Vuelta del peregrino* (Madrid: Ediciones de la Revista de Occidente, 1966).

Diego Mostrenco. In *Pedro* 2, a peasant who participates in the dance for the king and queen.

Diego Tarugo. In *Pedro* 1, one of the aldermen of Junquillos.

Dieste, Rafael (1899–1981). Spanish philosopher, short-story writer, and dramatist. Dieste's clever and satiric *Nuevo retablo de las maravillas* (1937; *The New Marvelous Puppet Show*), an updating of MC's *Retablo*, was performed and published during the Spanish Civil War, and the conflict between democracy and fascism is the work's theme. Three strolling players, Fantasio, Mónica, and the young musician Rabelín, arrive in a village controlled by the Nationalist forces. They stage a performance for local dignitaries, including military officers, a priest, and the local nobility. There is just one catch to their performance: no one who is tainted with communist, Marxist, socialist, or other leftist ideology can see the action. Of course, everyone in the audience pretends to see the figures described by the narrator, just as did the villagers afraid to reveal their own possible illegitimacy or tainted blood in MC's original interlude. This is an excellent example of an original and contextually relevant update of a classic work.

Bibliography: Rafael Dieste, *Teatro, II*, ed. Manuel Aznar Soler (Barcelona: Laia, 1981); and Estelle Irizarry, *Rafael Dieste* (Boston: Twayne, 1979).

Dieulafoy, Michel (1762–1823). French dramatist. Dieulafoy's three-act *Le portrait de Michel Cervantes* (1802; *Portrait of Michel Cervantes*) is a conventional play of love and intrigue. It is set in early-seventeenth-century Spain and involves a pair of schemers who attempt to cash in on the fame of the recently deceased MC with a bogus portrait. The popular play was translated/adapted to English by Charles Kemble (1775–1854) as *Plot and Counterplot* (1808).

Diez libros de Fortuna d'amor, Los. *Lofraso, Antonio de.

Digressions. In Mateo *Alemán's picaresque novel *Guzmán de Alfarache*, text that does not form part of the primary narrative (including digressive discourse, embedded tales, and anecdotes) actually occupies more space than does the main story itself. MC was aware of the problems that such a procedure creates and tended to avoid obvious and lengthy digressions in his own work. He even has DQ criticize the technique during the puppet show episode (II, 26). Similarly, he acknowledges in *DQ* II, 44, that the inclusion of embedded narratives such as *Curioso* and *Capitán* in *DQ* I may have been a mistake. Yet it could be argued that anything that breaks the thread of primary narrative—whether it be called digression, episode, tale, commentary, or something else—is in effect a digression from the story being told. With this broad concept in mind, it is clear that MC's works are full of digressions of all types.

Bibliography: Anthony Close, "The Truth of the History I: Relevance and Rhetorical Pitch," in *Cervantes and the Comic Mind of His Age* (Oxford: Oxford University Press, 2000), 117–50; and Howard Mancing, "Embedded Narration in *Guzmán de Alfarache*," in *"Ingeniosa Invención": Essays on Golden Age Spanish Literature for Geoffrey L. Stagg in Honor of His Eightieth Birthday*, ed. Ellen M. Anderson and Amy R. Williamsen (Newark, DE: Juan de la Cuesta, 1999), 69–99.

Diligence [Diligencia]. In *Persiles* II, 10, one of the four boats in the fishermen's regatta.

Diluvio de Sevilla. *Seville flood.

Dinamarca. *Denmark.

Dío. The pronunciation of *Dios* (God) by Jewish characters. See *Baños* 2; *Sultana* 1.

Dio de Lisboa. An extremely large cannon won from the Turks by the Portuguese in the siege of Diu, in India, about 1538. It was on display in the fortress of San Julián in Lisbon, where MC probably saw it when he was in that city in 1581. See *Guarda*.

Dionysius I [Dionisio] (430 BCE–367 BCE). The first tyrant of that name who ruled Syracuse; he is a symbol of cruelty. He is also known as the man who suspended the sword over the head of Damocles. See *Baños* 1.

Dios antojadizo. *Cupid.

Dios de las batallas. *Mars.

Dios de las herrerías; Dios de los herreros. *Vulcan.

Dios del alígero calzado; Dios parlero. *Mercury.

Dios del gesto horrendo. *Pluto.

Dios es Cristo. *God is Christ.

Diosa de las mieses. *Ceres.

Dioscorides, Pedanius [Dioscórides] (40–90 CE). Greek physician whose *De materia medica* was a standard botanical and pharmacological text for a millennium and a half (*Laguna, Andrés).

Director [Rector]. The top administrator of the madhouse of Seville in the story told by the barber in *DQ* II, 1.

Dirlos, Count. The brother of Durandarte and a popular character in the Spanish ballad tradition. See *DQ* II, 20.

Dis [Dite, Lite]. In Greek myth, Pluto, or Hades, god of the underworld. In Spanish, the name *Dite* is sometimes corrupted to *Lite*, as it is in *DQ* II, 69. See also *DQ* II, 35.

Disciplinantes. *Penitents; *Triumphal car.

Discreet king of Portugal [Discreto rey de Portugal]. It was long believed that *Palmerín de Inglaterra* (*Moraes, Francisco de) was originally written by a Portuguese king, most likely João II. See *DQ* I, 6.

Discretion [Discreción]. In *DQ* II, 20, one of the eight nymphs who participates in the celebration of *Camacho's wedding.

Disdain for the Court and Praise for the Village [Menosprecio de corte y alabanza de aldea]. A popular theme in the Renaissance, best expressed in Spain in the odes of Fray *Luis de León and the book of that title by Antonio de *Guevara. The contrast is made between the intrigue, luxury, and danger of the court in comparison with the honesty, simplicity, and security of the simple life of the village or countryside. The idea is found in the works of MC, particularly in a poem sung by Damón and the commentary by Darinto in *Galatea* 4. A related theme is that made by DQ between *courtly knights and knights-errant. See also *Poesías* 17.

Dispensero. *Caterer.

Disputa sobre el amor. *Debate about love.

Distressed Dueña; Distressed One; Distressed Lady. *Countess Trifaldi.

Dite. *Dis.

Divina Escritura. *Bible.

Divine chronicler [Divino coronista]. In *Rufián* 3, an allusion to the gospel of Matthew.

Divine Magician [Mágico divino]. In *Poesías* 33, the phrase MC uses for God in his sonnet in praise of *Saint Teresa de Jesús.

Divine Mantuan. *Virgil.

Divining ape [Mono adivino]. In *DQ* II, 25–27, the trained ape owned by *Maese Pedro who is capable of revealing facts about the past and present.

Divino coronista. *Divine chronicler.

Divorce Court Judge, The. *Juez de los divorcios, El.*

Djebel Musa [Aliba]. Mountain in North Africa, across from Gibraltar, or Calpe, as it was then known. Together, Abila and Calpe formed the *pillars of Hercules, the symbol of the end of the known world, the Strait of Gibraltar. See *Española*.

Doblón. *Currency.

Doce hijos de Jacob; Doce tribus de Israel. *Twelve tribes of Israel.

Doce Pares de Francia. *Twelve Peers of France.

Doctor [Cirujano]. In *Juez*, the husband who has four good, but not very clear, reasons for wanting to divorce his wife.

Doctors of the Church [Doctores de la Iglesia]. The highest authorities on matters of dogma. The Spanish *Saint Teresa de Jesús and *Saint Juan de la Cruz, for example, are both doctors of the Church, among the ultimate authorities on matters of mysticism. See *DQ* I, prologue.

Dodgson, Lewis. *Carroll, Lewis.

Dog from Alba [Perro de Alba]. A term for something of little value. The phrase supposedly had its origin in an incident in which a dog from the town of Alba de Tormes would constantly bark at and otherwise harass Jews, who brought suit against it. See *Elección*.

Dolfos, Vellido. Famous traitor. During the eleventh-century siege of the city of Zamora by King Sancho II of Castile and León, Dolfos secretly came out and killed the king and then returned to the haven of the city. His name has since then been synonymous with treachery. See *DQ* II, 27.

Dolorida, Dueña; La Dolorida; Señora Dolorida. *Countess Trifaldi.

Domicio. In *Persiles* III, 14–15, the man driven mad by enchantment who attempts to kill his wife Claricia by throwing her from a tower. Periandro races into the tower and struggles with the knife-wielding Domicio, and both of them fall to the ground. Domicio is dead of a knife wound and Periandro is badly injured by the fall, but is treated and regains his health.

Domingo [Sunday]. **1**. In *Vidriera*, a name used by the protagonist to refer to an Old Christian. **2**. *Pastoral names.

Domínguez Bastida, Gustavo Adolfo. *Bécquer, Gustavo Adolfo.

Don/doña. An honorific title that goes with the first name of a Spanish nobleman holding the rank of *caballero* or above, or a lady of equivalent status (*nobility). It was not appropriate for an *hidalgo* to use the title, and it is pointed out by SP in *DQ* II, 2, that locals have taken note of the fact that the village's *hidalgo*, Alonso Quijano, was out of line in calling himself *Don* Quixote. However, there are exceptions to this general rule; Don Diego de Miranda in *DQ* II, 16, uses the term, to which he might feel that he is entitled because of his wealth and social prominence, even though he says he is an *hidalgo*. Because *don* was such an obvious status symbol, there was much criticism of its misuse during MC's day, and there are many examples of satiric writings on the subject. Its application by DQ to the two prostitutes at the first inn in I, 3, is clearly satiric. Both Teresa Panza (II, 5) and SP (II, 45), acknowledging their peasant status, shun the use of the title for themselves. MC never used the term for himself, but some of the women in his family did so (as when his sister called herself Doña Magdalena Pimentel de Sotomayor). In modern Spanish, the title is used far less often, and without precise limits to its application, but it still suggests respect and tends to be associated with higher socioeconomic classes. It is, by the way, never correct to refer to someone as "the Don." The word should not be used as a noun (there is undoubtedly some confusion here with the English noun *don*, in the sense of a head or tutor at Oxford or Cambridge); such usage would be like calling someone in English "the Sir." The fact that many non-Hispanists (and some less sensitive Hispanic scholars) have long referred to DQ as "the Don" does not make it a proper or acceptable practice.

Don Azote o don Gigote. *Don Whip or Don Chopped Meat.

Don bacallao. *Don Codfish.

Don Belianís. *Fernández, Jerónimo.

Don Cirongilio de Tracia. *Vargas, Bernardo de.

Don Codfish [Don bacallao]. In *DQ* II, 70, an insulting name used by the angry and offended Altisidora when DQ again rejects her love and reiterates his devotion to DT.

Don Defeated and Don Beaten [Don vencido y don molido a palos]. In *DQ* II, 70, an insulting name used by the angry and offended Altisidora when DQ again rejects her love and reiterates his devotion to DT.

Don Demented [Don Tonto]. In *DQ* II, 31, the insulting name the grave *ecclesiastic calls DQ as he launches into his criticism of the knight.

Don Luis's father [Padre de don Luis]. He sends his servants after his runaway son and they catch up with him in *DQ* I, 44.

Don Olivante de Laura. *Torquemada, Antonio de.

Don Quijote (DQ): Don Quixote. *DQ* I and *DQ* II are treated throughout this encyclopedia as two separate works, but *DQ* (i.e., both parts combined) is normally read and discussed as a single work. As a result, most of the important bibliography is for *DQ*, rather than *DQ* I or *DQ* II.

Bibliography: John J. Allen, *Don Quixote: Hero or Fool: A Study in Narrative Technique*, 2 vols. (Gainesville: University Presses of Florida, 1969, 1979); Juan Bautista Avalle-Arce, *Don Quijote como forma de vida* (Madrid: Fundación Juan March/Castalia, 1976); Richard Bjornson, ed., *Approaches to Teaching Cervantes' "Don Quixote"* (New York: Modern Language Association of America, 1984); Anthony J. Close, *Miguel de Cervantes: "Don Quixote"* (Cambridge: Cambridge University Press, 1990); Anthony Close, *The Romantic Approach to "Don Quixote": A Critical History of the Romantic Tradition in "Quixote" Criticism* (New York: Cambridge University Press, 1977); Arthur Efron, *Don

Quixote and the Dulcineated World (Austin: University of Texas Press, 1971); Daniel Eisenberg, *Cervantes y "Don Quijote"* (Barcelona: Montesinos Editor, 1993); Daniel Eisenberg, *A Study of "Don Quixote"* (Newark, DE: Juan de la Cuesta, 1987); Jaime Fernández, *Bibliografía del "Quijote" por unidades narrativas y materiales de la novela* (Alcalá de Henares: Centro de Estudios Cervantinos, 1995); Laura J. Gorfkle, *Discovering the Comic in "Don Quixote"* (Chapel Hill: University of North Carolina Press, 1993); George Haley, ed., *El "Quijote" de Cervantes* (Madrid: Taurus, 1980); Carroll B. Johnson, *"Don Quixote": The Quest for Modern Fiction* (Boston: Twayne, 1990); Carroll B. Johnson, *Madness and Lust: A Psychoanalytical Approach to "Don Quixote"* (Berkeley: University of California Press, 1983); Howard Mancing, *The Chivalric World of "Don Quixote": Style, Structure and Narrative Technique* (Columbia: University of Missouri Press, 1982); José Antonio Maravall, *Utopia and Counterutopia in the "Quixote,"* trans. Robert W. Felkel (Detroit: Wayne State University Press, 1991); Francisco Márquez Villanueva, *Personajes y temas del "Quijote"* (Madrid: Taurus, 1975); Félix Martínez-Bonati, *"Don Quixote" and the Poetics of the Novel,* trans. Dian Fox in collaboration with the author (Ithaca, NY: Cornell University Press, 1992); José Montero Reguera, *El "Quijote" y la crítica contemporánea* (Alcalá de Henares, Spain: Centro de Estudios Cervantinos, 1997); Carolyn A. Nadeau, *Women of the Prologue: Imitation, Myth, and Magic in "Don Quixote I"* (Lewiston, PA: Bucknell University Press, 2002); James A. Parr, *"Don Quixote": An Anatomy of Subversive Discourse* (Newark, DE: Juan de la Cuesta, 1988); José María Paz Gago, *Semiótica del "Quijote": Teoría y práctica de la ficción narrativa* (Amsterdam: Rodopi, 1995); Helena Percas de Ponseti, *Cervantes the Writer and Painter of "Don Quijote"* (Columbia: University of Missouri Press, 1988); Helena Percas de Ponseti, *Cervantes y su concepto del arte: Estudio crítico de algunos aspectos del "Quijote,"* 2 vols. (Madrid: Gredos, 1975); Charles D. Presberg, *Adventures in Paradox: "Don Quixote" and the Western Tradition* (University Park: Pennsylvania State University Press, 2001); Augustin Redondo, *Otra manera de leer "El Quijote"* (Madrid: Castalia, 1997); E. C. Riley, *Don Quixote* (London: Allen and Unwin, 1986); Martín de Riquer, *Nueva aproximación al "Quijote"* (Barcelona: Teide, 1989); Javier Salazar Rincón, *El mundo social del "Quijote"* (Madrid: Gredos, 1986); César Vidal, *Enciclopedia del "Quijote"* (Barcelona:

Planeta, 1999); and Edwin Williamson, *The Halfway House of Fiction: "Don Quixote" and Arthurian Romance* (Oxford: Clarendon Press, 1984).

Don Quijote I: El ingenioso hidalgo don Quijote de la Mancha Madrid: Juan de la Cuesta, 1605 (*DQ* I); *The Imaginative Gentleman Don Quixote de la Mancha.*

The success of *DQ* I was great and immediate. It was printed six times in 1605, 11 times by 1617, and 13 more times together with *DQ* II in the seventeenth century in Spanish. The figures of DQ and SP (and even those of Rocinante and DT) immediately entered the popular imagination and became common points of reference, appearing in public festivals and parades right after the novel was published. Part of the first printing of the novel was shipped to Peru in 1605 and there is evidence of its influence in popular culture there also as early as 1607, when a DQ figure was on public display; similarly, in 1621, in a religious festival in Mexico DQ and SP figures were part of the public celebration. Figures of DQ, SP, DT, Rocinante, and various knights-errant (including Amadís, Palmerín, and Belianís) were also popular figures in various festivals and parades in Spain early in the seventeenth century. *DQ* I was translated into English (1612) and French (1614) during MC's lifetime, and into Italian (1622) shortly after he died (*first translations of *Don Quixote*). *DQ* I may have been written largely or even entirely in the 1590s and may have circulated to some extent in manuscript, a common practice at the time. One theory of its genesis is that MC first wrote a short *novela*, perhaps based on the anonymous *Entremés de los romances* (*Interlude of the Ballads*) and consisting of the first six to nine chapters of *DQ* I, and then expanded the work into the long novel that we now have (*Ur-Quixote). There has been much debate about MC's editorial revisions as he wrote and the errors and/or inconsistencies that remain in the text (*textual problems).

Preliminaries: The price is set by Juan Gallo de Andrada, in Valladolid, on December 20, 1604. The corrector's statement is signed by Licenciado Francisco Murcia de la Llana, in the Colegio de la Madre de Dios de los Teólogos of the University of Alcalá, on December 1, 1604. The king's permission to print is signed by Juan de Amezqueta, in Valladolid, on September 26, 1604. After the dedication and prologue, there are ten burlesque preliminary verses written by MC himself.

Dedication: To Don Alonso Diego López de Zúñiga, the sixth duke of Béjar. This dedication is partially plagiarized from the one Fernando de Herrera wrote for his edition of the poetry of Garcilaso de la Vega (1580). MC never dedicated another work to the duke of Béjar, and there is no evidence of his ever having received any support from him.

Prologue: Addressing the idle reader, MC writes that he wishes that his book were more beautiful, but that would be too much to ask of an imagination as sterile and dry as his, especially since the book was engendered in a jail. But although MC seems to be the father, he is really only the stepfather of the work, and so the reader, who is free to form his own opinions, can say whatever he or she wishes about it. MC would rather have published the book without any prologue, for it has proven harder to write than the story itself. One day, when he was sitting with blank paper in front of him, trying to come up with an idea for a prologue, a good friend of his, a clever man, came in. When MC explained his dilemma and stated that he was determined that DQ should remain in the Archives of La Mancha, his friend laughed at him and explained to him how to adorn his work with the necessary accoutrements: write the introductory sonnets and other poems yourself; fill the margins with annotations of common quotations, and do the same with your notes. All you really have to do is take advantage of imitation in what you write, because your aim is to satirize the atrocious romances of chivalry that vulgar readers enjoy so much. MC listened to his friend and decided to make his comments the substance of the prologue. The satiric comments about writers who adorn their books with elaborate and pedantic allusions and poetry seem clearly aimed at Lope de Vega, whose books—for example, his

El peregrino en su patria (1604; *The Pilgrim in His Own Country*), published just as MC was finishing *DQ* I—often display exactly these characteristics (the criticism of Lope is continued in the conversation between the priest and the canon of Toledo in I, 47). No small part of the inspiration of the person who wrote *DQA* was to avenge the satire directed at Lope.

Chapter 1: In a village of La Mancha there lives an *hidalgo*, one of those who has a lance hanging on the wall, an old shield, a skinny nag, and a fast greyhound. His household consists of a housekeeper who is in her forties, a niece in her teens, and a lad who helps in the field and in the marketplace. The *hidalgo* himself is nearing 50 years of age and is fond of hunting. Some say his surname is Quijada, or Quesada, but most likely he is called Quejana. In his spare hours, which is most of the time, he reads romances of chivalry; he particularly enjoys the complex style of the works of Feliciano de Silva, and has often felt the urge to complete the unfinished story of Belianís de Grecia. He often engages in debates with the local priest and barber about the relative merits of various chivalric heroes. Finally, from so much reading and so little sleep, he loses his mind and conceives the idea of actually becoming a knight-errant himself. His motives are two: to gain glory and fame and to do good deeds. He refurbishes some old armor, names his nag of a horse Rocinante, himself DQ, and selects as his lady-love a young peasant woman (named Aldonza Lorenzo) who lives nearby in El Toboso, giving her the name of DT.

Chapter 2: DQ leaves home before dawn one hot July day, imagining how an enchanter will some day write the true history of his adventures and invoking, in an archaic style reminiscent of the romances of chivalry, the support of his lady DT. Some authors say that his first adventure is that of Puerto Lápice, and others that it is that of the windmills, but as best the narrator can tell, and what is recorded in the Annals of La Mancha, nothing happens at all that day. As nightfall approaches, he arrives at an inn, which he perceives as a castle; sees two prostitutes (maidens in his version); and hears a pig herder sound his horn (a dwarf announcing his arrival at the castle). His odd figure startles the women and they start to enter the inn, but he addresses them, again in his archaic style, and offers his services. Because he cuts such a strange figure and because he speaks in such an odd way, the two women cannot but laugh at him. He gently chastises their frivolity, and dismounts, as he is received by the innkeeper (lord of the castle), with whom he has an exchange paraphrasing a well-known ballad about Lanzarote. DQ eats some stale codfish (fine trout to him) and is fed wine via a straw stuck through his visor, which he cannot remove.

Chapter 3: DQ falls to his knees and begs a boon of the lord of the castle, which, of course, is granted. The favor is that DQ be dubbed a knight the next morning after standing vigil over his arms in the chapel of the castle. The innkeeper grants the request, but states that his chapel is under repair and suggests that DQ perform his vigil in the courtyard (where everyone in the inn can watch him and enjoy a laugh). When he learns that DQ has no money with him (knights-errant never have to pay for anything), he recommends that DQ be better prepared with a certain quantity of money, a few clean shirts, and some ointments to cure wounds received in battle. DQ promises to take such precautions in the future. While DQ is standing there thinking of DT, a muleteer approaches and removes DQ's arms in order to get some water for his animals. DQ invokes DT's support and delivers a strong blow to the muleteer's head, knocking him unconscious. The same thing happens again when another muleteer arrives. By now, the onlookers are not amused and begin to throw stones at DQ, who shouts insults at them. The innkeeper intervenes, decides that there is no need to wait for the morning, and dubs DQ a knight in a burlesque ceremony. The two prostitutes, whose names are La Tolosa and La Molinera, participate in the ceremony, and DQ calls them Doña Tolosa and Doña Molinera.

Chapter 4: Departing early the next morning, DQ hears cries of help from a wooded area and assumes that this is the stuff of chivalric adventure. Investigating, he sees a man whipping a boy who is tied to a tree. The man, Juan Haldudo, explains that the boy is a shepherd in his employ who seems to lose about one sheep a week. DQ is not interested in details and demands that the boy be untied, paid, and set free. As soon as DQ leaves, puffed up with pride at the way he has undone a wrong and liberated an innocent victim, Haldudo, sarcastically parodying DQ's words, reties the boy to the tree and whips him even harder than before. Further along the road, DQ encounters a group of merchants from Toledo on their way to buy silk in Murcia, and challenges them, insisting that they swear that DT is the most beautiful woman in the world. They are reluctant to do so without seeing a picture of the lady—even if it is as small as a grain of wheat, and even if she is blind in one eye and the other is unhealthy—which infuriates DQ, who lowers his lance and charges. But Rocinante stumbles and falls, leaving DQ sprawled on the ground and badly shaken by the fall. One of the servants to the merchants breaks the knight's lance into several pieces and beats him badly with one of them. The merchants ride on, leaving DQ raving at them and considering himself fortunate to have had such an adventure and to be able to suffer for the woman he loves.

Chapter 5: As DQ lies on the ground in his madness and pain, comparing himself to Valdovinos from the Spanish chivalric ballad tradition, along comes a farmer by the name of Pedro Alonso, who recognizes his neighbor and comes to his aid. He helps DQ to the saddle of his own ass and leads him home. Along the way DQ identifies himself as Abindarráez, famous Muslim ballad hero, and Pedro as the Christian knight Rodrigo de Narváez, Abindarráez's respected enemy. When Pedro attempts to set him straight about identities, DQ responds, 'I know who I am,' ironically at the one moment in the novel when he assumes multiple identities. Upon arriving at their village, Pedro waits until dark before entering, in order not to embarrass DQ by parading him through town when people are about. When they reach his home, they find that the priest, Pero Pérez, and barber, Maese Nicolás, are there discussing with the niece and housekeeper

DQ's absence. The women blame everything on the heretical books DQ has been reading and propose burning them in an auto-da-fé. Pedro and DQ arrive, and the latter goes straight to bed, calling for the enchantress Urganda the Unknown to help cure him.

Chapter 6: While DQ sleeps, his friends go to his library in order to burn the books that had driven him mad; however, what they actually do is save many of the books for themselves. Of the romances of chivalry, five are spared the flames: 1) *Amadís de Gaula*, which the priest (correctly) calls the first and best of the genre; 2) the *Espejo de caballerías*, a Spanish prose version of Boiardo's *Orlando Innamorato*; 3) *Palmerín de Inglaterra*, supposedly originally written by a Portuguese king; 4) *Belianís de Grecia*, the most popular of the second wave of Spanish chivalric romances; and 5) *Tirante el Blanco* (originally written in Catalan, though MC may not have known that), the most comic, erotic, and realistic of the chivalric romances. At least eight other romances, however, are thrown out the window to be burned. The inquisitors then examine other types of books in the library, mostly pastoral romances and works of lyric and epic poetry, and keep the majority of them. At one point they come across *La Galatea* by Miguel de Cervantes. The priest claims to be a good friend of this writer, says that he is more versed in adversity than in verses and that his novel proposes much but concludes little, and saves it from the bonfire.

Chapter 7: DQ awakens and interrupts the inquisition, still raving about the wounds he received in battle. After he goes back to bed and sleeps, that evening the books are burned in a large bonfire in the corral. Meanwhile, DQ's friends and family also wall up his library, so that two days later when DQ is up and about he cannot find his beloved books. At the prompting of the priest and barber, the niece says that while her uncle slept an enchanter came in on a flying serpent and took away the library. Though she and the housekeeper comically mispronounce the enchanter's name, DQ realizes that it must be none other than Frestón, wicked enchanter and enemy of Belianís de Grecia, who is now envious of DQ's fame.

Thus is DQ provided with the evil enemy on whom he will often blame his misfortunes. DQ spends two weeks recuperating, often engaging in chats with his friends about knights-errant and chivalric literature. Though he appears content to stay at home, he is in fact gathering together the money, shirts, and items for a first-aid kit, as had been recommended by the innkeeper in II, 3, and enlisting the aid of a local peasant by the name of SP as his squire, promising him an island (*ínsula*) to govern as the reward for his loyal service. Then one night the two of them steal away, DQ on Rocinante and SP on his trusty ass, without telling anyone where they are going.

Chapter 8: As they ride along, DQ and SP see some 30 windmills on a hill. DQ immediately makes them into giants and, though SP warns him about what they really are, charges into battle. The spill he takes prompts SP to say 'I told you so,' and gives DQ the opportunity to employ the excuse that he will use repeatedly on subsequent occasions: the envious enchanter Frestón converted them into windmills in order to deprive him of a victory. Shortly afterward, they spot some friars of the order of Saint Benedict riding along, and closely behind them comes a coach in which a woman is traveling. DQ immediately makes this into the material of an adventure: evil enchanters are carrying away a princess in the coach. He challenges the priests, charges, chases them away, and announces to the surprised woman in the coach that he has freed her. The woman's servant, a Basque (who speaks a broken Spanish characteristic of stock comic Basque characters), challenges DQ and the two begin to engage in a sword battle. But just as they stand in the stirrups of their mounts with swords raised and are about to deliver a blow, the manuscript breaks off and the episode is interrupted.

Chapter 9: MC is concerned that further adventures of DQ may not be available, and he begins to search for information about his exploits. One day when he is in the Alcaná district of Toledo, he comes across a youth who wants to sell some papers written in Arabic. Curious, MC hires a *Morisco aljamiado* (Spanish-Arabic bilingual convert) to take a look at the material and tell him what it is about. The *Morisco* begins to laugh and comments on something comic written in the papers about one DT; there is also a drawing of SP and the Basque squire. MC realizes that this must be a manuscript of a historical account of DQ, buys the lot of papers, and hires the *Morisco* to translate them for him, which he does within a month and a half. As the manuscript, written by the Arabic historian CHB, takes up the story, the Basque strikes a strong blow and cuts away half of DQ's ear. DQ strikes back and knocks his opponent unconscious. He then threatens to behead him, but the woman in the coach intervenes and spares his life. DQ requests the two of them to go to El Toboso and inform DT about her beloved knight's exploits.

Chapter 10: SP wants his island won in this adventure, but DQ informs him that this is a minor crossroads adventure that only contributes to the fame of the knight; the island comes later. SP is worried about the blood lost from DQ's ear, but the latter informs his squire that knights-errant do not complain about wounds they receive in battle, but then twice recognizes that the ear hurts more than he would like and more than it should. DQ also promises SP that soon he will make up a batch of the miraculous *balm of Fierabrás, which can cure any wound. As night approaches, they come across a group of goatherds who invite the knight and squire to join them.

Chapter 11: A dinner is laid out for all to partake, and DQ invites SP to sit at his side, since chivalry, like love, is a great equalizer. When SP says that he prefers to eat alone rather than in polite company, DQ forces him to sit beside him and be his equal. After dinner, the goatherds bring out some acorns for dessert. DQ gathers up a handful of them and they inspire him to deliver a long rhetorical speech on the theme of the Golden Age, a time of plenty when there was peace and harmony. This he contrasts to the present age when the institution of chivalry has been created to defend innocent maidens. The simple goatherds, of course, have no idea what he is talking about. A shepherd named Antonio arrives and is invited to sing a song, which he does, accompanying himself

with a rebec as he sings a rustic love song to someone named Olalla. DQ enjoys the song very much and requests another, but SP insists that it is time for sleep rather than for poetry, and so there is no more. DQ complains once again that his ear hurts more than is necessary and asks SP for some help. But one of the shepherds takes care of the matter by picking some rosemary leaves, chewing them to mix them with saliva, and adding some salt. He applies this folk remedy and bandages the ear, assuring DQ that it will never hurt again, which turns out to be true.

Chapter 12: At that moment another shepherd, named Pedro, arrives and informs the group that the famous student-shepherd named Grisóstomo has died of love for the shepherdess Marcela and will be buried the next day at the foot of the cliff where he first met her. All the goatherds, except one who has an injured foot and who volunteers to stay behind with all the goats, plan to attend the funeral. DQ wants to hear the whole story and Pedro begins to tell him all about it, but DQ interrupts three times to correct his pronunciation. But as the story goes on, Pedro speaks more and more eloquently. The beautiful and wealthy Marcela, adored by many of the men in the village, felt affection for no one and took to solitude dressed as a shepherdess in order to avoid men. Grisóstomo, his friend Ambrosio, and several others also dressed as shepherds and went out to roam the hills lamenting their unrequited love. Now Grisóstomo has died because of Marcela's cruelty. Everyone finally retires for the night, DQ to pine for DT in imitation of Marcela's lovers and SP to sleep soundly.

Chapter 13: As the party sets out the next morning, they are joined by a group consisting of half a dozen shepherds, two gentlemen on horseback, and their three servants. As they ride along, one of the men, a playful fellow named Vivaldo, begins to ask DQ questions about knight-errantry. DQ states that chivalry was instituted in England by King Arthur and that all knights-errant have ladies whom they love and to whom they dedicate their deeds. Vivaldo presses hard on the issue of the traditional knightly invocation of his loved one as he enters into combat, suggesting that if anyone is invoked at such a perilous time it should be God. DQ defends the tradition and responds to further inquiries by describing DT in stock Petrarchan language (hair of gold, shining eyes, cheeks like roses, and so on) and rationalizing that her lineage, although not an illustrious one, will someday be famous. Of those listening, only SP believes what his master says about DT. Just then the group is joined by some other shepherds who bring the body of the defunct Grisóstomo, surrounded in his bier by flowers and pages of his writings. Ambrosio informs all that the deceased has ordered that his writings be burned. But Vivaldo objects and grabs a handful of loose sheets, including one that contains a poem entitled "Song of Despair," which he proceeds to read to the assembly.

Chapter 14: Vivaldo reads Grisóstomo's song, in which it is implied that his death was a suicide. As the men debate Marcela's guilt in the situation, a dramatic event occurs: Marcela herself appears high on the cliff at whose foot the burial is taking place and delivers a brilliant, long, rhetorical speech in self-defense. She recognizes that she is beautiful and that beauty inspires love, but this in no way obliges her to love in return; she was born free and in order to preserve her freedom, she chose the solitude of the forest; Grisóstomo's death is in no way her fault. After she finishes speaking, Marcela disappears in the forest and several men start to go after her, but DQ enacts his chivalric mission to defend maidens, and prevents them from going. The burial is completed and the group begins to break up. Vivaldo invites DQ to accompany him and his friend to Seville, where many adventures would await. But DQ refuses, declaring that he intends to clear the woods of the many bandits it hides. But in his heart, he proposes to find Marcela and offer her his services.

Chapter 15: After a fruitless two-hour search for Marcela, DQ and SP rest in a pleasant meadow, and SP sets Rocinante free to graze. But the old nag gets wind of some mares grazing nearby and goes off in a sprightly trot to communicate his sexual need to them. They, however, are more interested in grazing than

anything else and receive him with hooves and teeth. Their owners, some Galician herdsmen, come to their assistance, beating Rocinante with sticks. DQ, noting that these are not armed knights-errant and therefore not his equal, suggests that SP take revenge for the offense to Rocinante. But SP notes that there are 20 of them, to which DQ responds, 'I am worth a hundred,' and pulls his sword. SP joins him, but the two are badly beaten by the herdsmen, who gather up their mares and depart, leaving knight and squire lying inured on the ground. SP requests a sample of the magic balm of Fierabrás, and DQ promises to make it for him soon. DQ also tells him that it is typical for knights to receive blows and beatings, citing a case from the romance of Amadís in which the knight was whipped by his adversary, the magician Arcaláus. Besides, he adds, injuries received in combat confer honor more than misfortune. SP helps his master to rise, places him on the ass, and leads them and Rocinante to a nearby inn, which DQ sees as a castle.

Chapter 16: The inn is run by a husband and wife, together with their attractive daughter and an Austurian maid named Maritornes, who is ugly, blind in one eye, and hunchbacked. They prepare a makeshift bed for DQ in an attic stable; nearby is the bed, made of the trappings of mules, of a muleteer also staying in the inn that night. SP lies and states that his master has fallen down a cliff and that he himself is just as badly bruised from seeing this happen, and then explains to those listening that his master is a knight-errant who will one day become an emperor. DQ finally speaks, in his archaic chivalric style, and offers his services to the women. Though they do not understand him very well, they help him to his bed to rest. It seems that the muleteer (who may have been a relative of the Muslim chronicler CHB) has contracted with Maritornes for her services that evening. Once the inn is all quiet, with DQ wide awake thinking of both DT and the beautiful daughter of the lord of the castle, Maritornes enters the room and heads for the muleteer's bed. But as she passes by, DQ, believing she is the love-smitten princess, reaches out and pulls her down beside him. Her coarse hair seems like pure gold to him, the rough cloth of her dress feels like fine silk, and her garlic-laden breath is the aroma of fine perfume. He holds her close, praising her beauty, while affirming his loyalty to DT. The muleteer doesn't like what is going on, gets out of bed, and delivers a furious blow to DQ's jaw. A general melee ensues, involving the muleteer, DQ, SP, Maritornes, and the innkeeper, who has heard the noise and arrived with a candle, searching for Maritornes as the probable source of the confusion. An officer of the Holy Brotherhood militia, who happens to be staying at the inn, also enters the room, finds DQ unconscious, and attempts to impose order. The innkeeper puts out the light, everyone returns to his or her bed or room, and the law officer leaves to search for a light.

Chapter 17: DQ and SP, both lying in pain on their beds, discuss the events that have just taken place. DQ offers the opinion that the castle is enchanted: it must be so, because just a short time before he was engaged in amorous conversation with the beautiful daughter of the lord of the castle when the hand of an outsized giant came out of the dark and delivered such a blow to his jaw that it is all bathed in blood, which leads him to believe that the beautiful maiden is being saved for someone else by an enchanted Muslim. SP is of the opinion that it must have been some 400 Muslims who beat him up and that, not being a knight-errant, he did not deserve it. DQ promises to make the magic balm of Fierabrás. Just then, the officer returns with a candle to see how DQ is but accidentally insults him, calling him 'my good man' rather than 'your grace.' DQ in turn insults the investigator and receives another blow to his head with the candlestick. DQ then tells SP to procure from the lord of the castle the ingredients for the precious balm: olive oil, wine, salt, and rosemary. SP returns with these materials and DQ mixes up a potion while repeating a number of prayers. He takes a big drink of the mixture and immediately begins to vomit and sweat. Exhausted, he falls asleep for some three hours and when he awakens he feels considerably better—because of the magic potion, he believes. SP then drinks some of the

liquid, but, because his stomach is not as delicate as DQ's, does not immediately vomit but experiences such violent pains that he believes he is going to die. DQ offers the opinion that perhaps the medicine does not work for SP because he is not a knight. But at this time, the mixture takes effect and SP is struck with a simultaneous fit of vomiting and diarrhea. DQ, feeling relatively refreshed and anxious to leave in search of adventures, saddles up Rocinante and the ass and helps SP get dressed and mount the ass. As DQ rides out of the inn, the innkeeper stops him and asks for payment for the night's lodging. DQ is surprised to learn that it is an inn rather than a castle, but maintains that knights-errant never pay for lodging and rides out through the gate. SP tries to follow him, insisting that neither will he pay, but a number of other men at the inn pull him off his ass and toss him repeatedly in a blanket, much as pranksters do with dogs during Carnival celebration. DQ hears his squire's cries and returns to the inn, but, unable to climb the wall, merely watches SP's humiliation. He offers SP some of the balm of Fierabrás, but the squire prefers to accept the wine generously offered by Maritornes. SP rides out of the inn satisfied that he got away without paying, not realizing that the innkeeper has kept his saddlebags.

Chapter 18: DQ states that his inability to come to SP's rescue is further proof that the castle is enchanted. SP doubts it, since those who blanketed him were no phantoms but real people with real names like Pedro Martínez and Tenorio Hernández, and the innkeeper was called Juan Palomeque the Left-Handed. Things have been going so badly, suggests SP, that perhaps it would be better if the two of them simply went back home. DQ will have none of it, and the two talk of chivalry as they ride along. Suddenly, DQ sees a large cloud of dust and announces that it is a sign of a great army nearby. SP points out that there must be two armies, as he also sees a second cloud. DQ interprets this as an opportunity for a great adventure, as the two dust clouds are raised by the two armies of a famous pair of mortal enemies: the emperor Alifanfarón, lord of the great isle of Trapobana, and the king of the

Don Quijote I

Garamantas, Pentapolín of the Naked Arm. They are about to go to war because the pagan Alifanfarón is in love with the beautiful Christian daughter of Pentapolín. DQ describes some of the participants in the two armed forces: the valorous Laurcalco, lord of the Silver Bridge; the feared Micocolembo, great duke of Quirocia; and several others. DQ waxes poetic about the famous knights and the geography of their nations and even proclaims that he can hear the whinny of horses, the blowing of trumpets, and the sound of drums. SP, however, can hear nothing but the bleating of many sheep, and in fact the dust clouds have been raised by two herds of sheep passing by. DQ dismisses his squire's fear and charges into battle, his lance lowered against the enemy and manages to kill more than seven sheep. The shepherds of the flocks begin to throw stones at the attacker and when one hits DQ in the ribs, he pulls out the balm of Fierabrás and begins to take a drink. A second stone hits his hand and mouth, knocking out some teeth and bringing the knight to the ground. The shepherds gather up their dead sheep and depart rapidly. SP arrives and reminds DQ that he had warned him that they were nothing but sheep. But no, for DQ they really were two armies, changed into sheep by the envious enchanter who opposes his good deeds. As SP starts to examine DQ's mouth to see how many teeth he has lost, the magic medicine begins to take effect and DQ vomits all over SP. The smell of the mixture is so obnoxious to SP that he, in turn, vomits on his master. He proposes in his heart that he will leave DQ and return home. Then SP discovers that his saddlebags are missing. DQ waxes philosophical over the subject of misfortune, citing holy scripture as they prepare to depart the scene. Again, SP examines DQ's mouth and they determine that he is missing at least three teeth. DQ laments this loss, for he esteems a tooth as highly as a diamond.

Chapter 19: Darkness closes as they ride along, and suddenly they see a number of lights, torches, coming toward them; SP begins to tremble with fear, whereas DQ sees the possibility of another adventure. It turns out to be a number of white-shirted men in a funeral pro-

cession. DQ demands information about the dead man, so that he can take the vengeance that is obviously reserved for him. But the men are in a hurry and do not want to stop and talk. DQ charges, wounds one man, and disperses the rest, causing SP to believe that his master is indeed as valiant as he says he is. DQ talks with the wounded man, a university graduate named Alonso López, who has a broken leg, and learns that the body is that of a man who died of a fever (which exempts DQ from having to avenge his death) and that he was being taken by several priests to Segovia for burial. SP, meanwhile, is gathering up some spoils to take the place of his lost saddlebags. When DQ calls to him to come help the wounded man, SP informs the latter that the one who carried out this great deed is called the Knight of the Mournful Countenance. DQ marvels at this new name, so in keeping with the customs of the heroes of romances of chivalry, but SP says that the name just came to him as he saw the sad figure DQ cuts now that he has lost several teeth. López, who had ridden off, returns and informs DQ that he is now officially excommunicated for having laid hand on something sacred (i.e., the priests). SP insists that they not tarry at this scene but make their way into the hills, for, as they say, 'the dead go to the grave and the living to their daily bread' (the first of his many proverbs). SP takes the lead as they depart. After a short while, they stop to rest in a pleasant meadow.

Chapter 20: Along with the sound made by the brook that runs through the meadow, they also hear an unidentified strong, regular, pounding noise. Although the night is dark and the noise is frightful, DQ informs SP that he will depart to investigate the matter and see what adventure might be involved. SP should wait no more than three days for him and, if he fails to return, go to inform DT that her loyal knight has died. Frightened, SP turns on his rhetoric, in a long and subtle speech, in an attempt to convince DQ not to leave him, but to no avail. So, to keep his master there, SP ties Rocinante's feet so that the horse cannot move. SP decides to tell DQ a story to entertain him: the goatherd Lope Ruiz, loved by the shepherdess

Torralba, takes his flock and flees his pursuer, but has to cross a river where there is but a small boat in which the boatman can ferry only one goat at a time (SP warns DQ that he should keep count of the goats). And so the process begins: one goat, another, another, . . . DQ insists that they have all crossed the river and that SP should get on with the story. When he cannot tell SP exactly how many goats have crossed, SP declares the story over. Near dawn, SP feels the need to do 'that which no one else can do for him.' The noise and foul odor of his act offend DQ, who rebukes him for not respecting the person of a knight-errant. With the arrival of daylight, DQ goes off to find the source of the strange pounding noise, and SP accompanies him. A short distance away, they see that the noise is made by a fulling mill, a device to pound dirt and impurities from cloth. Both of them laugh at the absurdity of the situation, and SP begins to mock DQ's words of the previous night. But SP laughs too much and DQ, offended, strikes him twice with his lance. DQ admits the episode is funny, but insists that they never tell anyone about it. He then cites examples of the respect squires showed their masters in the romances of chivalry and orders SP to be more respectful in the future.

Chapter 21: As they ride along, it begins to rain, and soon they see approaching them a mounted man wearing some shining object on his head. DQ is sure that it is a knight wearing Mambrino's enchanted helmet; SP, however, as he gets a closer look, sees only an ordinary man on an ass wearing something on his head. It turns out that the man is a barber who serves two villages, going from one to the other and wearing his barber's basin as protection from the rain. DQ challenges and charges, causing the man to fall to the ground and flee, leaving both ass and basin to his attacker. Though SP is not sure the object is a magic helmet, he is interested in the ass's trappings, which DQ allows him to keep. As they continue on their way, SP makes the suggestion that they go and serve some emperor or king in order to win a kingdom more quickly. DQ responds by outlining for him a typical trajectory of a knight-errant's career: after winning fame throughout the world, the knight arrives at a court where he is received with honor; there, he meets and falls in love with the princess; the knight leaves to win the war for the king and returns in glory to marry the lady; and the king eventually dies, the knight inherits the realm, and this is where he rewards his faithful squire with an island to govern. SP is sure that, being an Old Christian, he is fit for government.

Chapter 22: Next the knight and squire see approaching them about a dozen men chained together and accompanied by armed men on horseback. SP informs his master that these are criminals on their way to serve in the king's galleys. DQ perceives only that they are being forced to go against their will and sees this as an opportunity for him to help the unfortunate. He inquires of the guards about the status of the prisoners and is invited to hear the specifics of their crimes from each of them personally. He then asks each a series of questions and, in a series of short comic interviews, learns of their wrongdoings. The last man, bearing more chains than any of the others, is by far the most interesting: a hardened criminal named Ginés de Pasamonte, who has been condemned to row in the galleys for ten years (the equivalent of a death sentence). Pasamonte has written the story of his life, which, he claims, is better than *Lazarillo de Tormes* or any other book of its kind. When DQ asks if the book is finished, Pasamonte responds that is it not, because his life is not over yet. DQ pronounces that, after listening to each person, he has determined that they are indeed being taken against their will and it is his duty to set them free. DQ attacks one guard and the other flees, as the prisoners break their chains. DQ asks them to go to El Toboso and inform DT about his efforts on their behalf. When Ginés rejects that idea in no uncertain terms, DQ insults him and orders him to go there alone, carrying his chains. The prisoners gang together and pelt DQ, SP, and their mounts with stones; one smashes Mambrino's helmet; and several take some of their clothing and possessions.

Chapter 23: In large part because of his fear of the Holy Brotherhood's reaction when it is learned that the prisoners have been set free, SP counsels retreat into the nearby Sierra Morena mountains. DQ accedes, but, he insists, not because he is afraid of anyone. As they penetrate the wooded mountains, they come across a dead mule and some decaying saddlebags. Upon investigation, it is learned that the latter contain some papers and a modest amount of gold coins. SP considers the money a just reward for all he has been through recently. DQ is more interested in the writings, and reads a love sonnet and letter addressed to a lady. They see a man, unkempt and dressed in pelts and rags, jumping from one rock to the next, and assume it is the author of the writings. A short distance away, they come across a goatherd who confirms that suspicion and informs them that some six months previously a gentleman had come into these hills in order to do some sort of penance for a lady. He was alternately wild and aggressive and calm and polite. At this time, the wild man appears again and joins them; DQ and the madman confront each other as soul brothers.

Chapter 24: DQ offers his services to the other man and asks to hear his story, which the man agrees to tell after they give him something to eat and so long as they promise not to interrupt him. Cardenio then begins his story: a nobleman from Andalusia, he loved the beautiful Luscinda. But when a powerful duke requested his assistance as friend to his son Don Fernando, Cardenio complied. It turned out that Fernando loved a woman of lower estate, but of a wealthy family. In fact, he had promised to marry her, and once she believed this and surrendered her virginity to him, Fernando lost interest in her. A short while later, Cardenio and Fernando returned to the city where Cardenio lived and Fernando met Luscinda and became interested in her. As a detail in his story, Cardenio mentions that he gave Luscinda a note tucked in a book—*Amadís de Gaula*. DQ interrupts at this moment to talk about the romances of chivalry. Cardenio, pensive for a moment, declares that in *Amadís* the Queen Madásima had carried on an affair with the surgeon Elisabat. DQ disagrees, defending the honor of a (literary) lady. Cardenio throws a stone at him and knocks him down. SP rushes

Cardenio but is knocked to the ground and trampled, and the same fate befalls the goatherd. Cardenio runs off, and SP and the goatherd squabble over whose fault it has been and come to blows. DQ separates them and wants to learn more about Cardenio.

Chapter 25: As DQ leads the pair further into the mountains, SP requests permission to leave and return home to his family. DQ, after defending his actions in defense of the Queen Madásima, promises his squire that he is about to perform a feat that will win him eternal fame: in these hills, he intends to imitate Amadís when he took the name Beltenebros and went to the Peña Pobre to do tearful penance after he believed himself chastised by his beloved Oriana. DQ's theory is that the knight-errant who most closely imitates this greatest of knights most closely approximates chivalric perfection. At the same time, DQ intends to imitate Orlando Furioso who, when he learned of the infidelity of his beloved Angelica, undertook a violent penance. But, SP points out, these knights had reason for their acts, whereas DT has done nothing to provoke such a reaction from DQ. That is the point, says DQ; when she sees what I do without provocation, she will realize what I would do if indeed provoked. DQ asks for Mambrino's helmet, and again SP remarks that it looks like a barber's basin to him. But DQ responds that what seems like a helmet to him and a basin to SP might also seem like something else to another person. That night, while they sleep, Ginés de Pasamonte, who has also entered the Sierra Morena mountains to escape the Holy Brotherhood, comes across the pair and steals SP's ass. (*Note:* This episode was omitted in the first printing and then later erroneously inserted in I, 22, in the second printing. Modern textual criticism most frequently and logically places the event here.) The next day, at a clearing at the foot of a mountain, DQ announces that this is the spot where he will do his penance. He instructs SP to watch his acts of madness so that he can report them accurately, but SP assures him that it is not actually necessary to perform any specific acts, as he will describe them as if they had actually taken place. DQ further informs him that he is about to write a letter to DT that SP should deliver (riding on Rocinante, since the ass is gone) and that, furthermore, DQ will also include an order that SP should be given three of the five ass-colts DQ has at home. While discussing DT, DQ reveals to SP that she is in reality Aldonza Lorenzo, daughter of Lorenzo Corchuelo and Aldonza Nogales of El Toboso. SP, stunned to learn that DT is not really a princess, exclaims that he knows Aldonza quite well and that she is indeed a tough and lusty wench, worthy of a knight's love. DQ calls SP ignorant and tells him an anecdote of a wealthy widow who chooses as a lover a young lay brother. When criticized for choosing such a stupid man, she responds that for her purposes he knows as much philosophy as Aristotle. Similarly, for DQ's purposes, Aldonza-DT is worth as much as any princess on earth. It is enough for DQ to believe that she is beautiful, for he paints her in his imagination as he desires her to be. DQ then writes the letter to DT, imitating the rhetorical and archaic style of the letters of Amadís and other knights, and the order for the three ass-colts. SP mounts Rocinante and is about to leave, when he decides that he really should see a couple examples of DQ's madness. The knight takes off his pants and does a couple of bare-bottomed somersaults that duly impress his squire, who then departs.

Chapter 26: After SP departs, DQ sits down to think about his penance. Since Amadís achieved as much fame as anyone with his relatively calm and tearful penance, there is really no need for DQ to imitate the violent Orlando, which would be harder to do in any case. So he tears the tail of his shirt into strips in order to fashion a makeshift rosary, and spends his time in prayer and writing (inadvertently comic) love poetry, which he carves into the trunk of several trees. Meanwhile, SP arrives at the inn where he had been blanketed. As he hesitates outside the inn, he hears his name and recognizes the priest, Pero Pérez, and the barber, Maese Nicolás, from his village. They have come in search of DQ and ask SP about him. SP explains all about the penance and goes to show them the letters DQ has written, only to realize that he has forgotten to bring them. He

is distraught, but tries to recall the letter to DT. He repeats it in a comic manner, mispronouncing words and distorting the syntax, evoking great laughter from the two men, who have him repeat it twice more. The priest and barber change their plans and decide not to tell SP all about what they want to do but, instead, concoct an elaborate ruse: the priest will dress as a maiden in distress and the barber as her squire; when they get to DQ, the maiden will request his assistance and lead him back to the village.

Chapter 27: The priest and barber enter the inn in order to prepare for their roles as damsel and squire, as SP waits outside, not wanting to return to the scene of his blanketing. They borrow a reddish oxtail from the innkeeper's wife in order to make a fake beard for the barber. The priest, meanwhile, gets dressed up as a woman. No sooner do they leave the inn, however, that the priest has second thoughts. It seems indecorous to him for a man of the cloth to be dressed as a woman, so he proposes exchanging roles with the barber. SP has a good laugh when he sees how the two men are dressed. They decide that they can put on their disguises later, and the three of them set out for the place where DQ is doing his penance. Shortly after SP is sent ahead to tell his master that DT wishes to see him as soon as possible, the two men hear a voice singing songs of lament. It is Cardenio. They join him and he first retells them all that he had told to DQ and SP and then continues his tale. Fernando created an excuse to get Cardenio out of town and then asked Luscinda's father for her hand in marriage, which was granted, as Fernando is far wealthier and of a higher estate than Cardenio. Luscinda managed to get word of her impending marriage to Cardenio, who returned home and talked with her. They agreed that she would refuse to be married during the ceremony and that Cardenio, who would be hidden in the church, would come out and proclaim that she was his. But when the marriage took place, Luscinda said yes and Cardenio remained hidden. He now laments his cowardice at that time and again vows to continue his penance unto death.

Chapter 28: Just then, they hear another voice nearby and when they approach they see what appears to be a beautiful young man bathing his feet in a stream. When the youth takes off his hat, gorgeous long blond hair is revealed, and the men realize that this is one of the most beautiful women they have ever seen. They approach and offer their services, so the woman tells her story: she is the only daughter of a rich peasant with whom the son of a powerful duke fell in love and, promising to marry her, spent a night with her. But then he abandoned her for a woman of higher estate. During her telling of the tale she mentions her name, Dorotea, and that of the deceitful lover, Fernando. Cardenio realizes that this is the woman who has played such an important role in his own tale of woe, but says nothing. Unwilling to accept her role as a deceived woman, Dorotea says, she dressed as a man, took some supplies, and left home accompanied only by a servant, hoping somehow to remedy her situation. She learned of the wedding, Cardenio's disappearance, and the fact that Fernando had taken Luscinda and left town. Along the way, her servant attempted to take advantage of her and she threw him off a cliff. For a while, she served as an assistant to a herder but when he too realized that she was a woman he also tried to take advantage of her and she had to flee. Now she is alone, helpless, and hopeless here in the wilderness.

Chapter 29: Cardenio reveals his identity and swears to avenge Fernando's traitorous deeds against both of them. At this time, SP returns and reports that his master is pining away for DT. When Dorotea learns of the plan devised by the priest and barber she offers to play the role of the maiden in distress, for she has both the natural looks for the job and some appropriate clothing in her knapsack. Furthermore, she has read many romances of chivalry and knows well the conventions and discourse of such ladies in these books. The priest informs SP that this beautiful woman is the Princess Micomicona of the kingdom of Micomicón in Guinea, searching for a knight-errant to avenge a wrong done to her by a giant. SP rejoices at this news and knows that his master

will do all he can to help her, assuming that this can lead to the royal wedding that will result in his becoming governor of an island. Maese Nicolás, wearing the fake beard borrowed from the inn, is to accompany Dorotea as her squire. Meanwhile, Pero Pérez and Cardenio will stay behind and join the group later. SP guides lady and squire to DQ, and Dorotea, now dressed in her beautiful dress, throws herself at his knees and begs a boon, refusing to rise until it is granted. SP assures DQ that it consists in nothing more than killing a giant and restoring her throne in Ethiopia. DQ, of course, agrees, while SP wonders what to do with his future subjects who will all be black, but decides that he can always sell them as slaves. Meanwhile, the priest trims Cardenio's beard and arranges his clothing so that he will not be recognized by DQ. As DQ and the others approach, the priest greets them and makes an excuse for his being there in the mountains. It is decided that they will all travel together, with DQ, Dorotea, and the priest riding the three mounts while the others walk. During the round of mounting and dismounting, the barber is startled by the mule and falls, his fake beard coming off his face. Much to DQ's confusion, the priest replaces it with a magical incantation. As they ride on, the priest comments that he and his friend had a recent encounter with a group of criminals, sentenced to the galleys, set free by some madman.

Chapter 30: SP immediately reveals that it was master who set the criminals free, which provokes an angry response and energetic statement of self-defense from DQ. Dorotea intervenes to tell her 'story': upon the death of her father, Tinacrio the Wise, a wicked giant, Pandafilando de la Fosca Vista, has threatened her kingdom, and so she has come to Spain in search of the famous knight DQ, whom she is to identify by a mole on his back, on the right side, just below the left shoulder. DQ wants to undress to see if he has such a mole, but SP assures everyone that he does. The 'princess' states that she will gladly marry the brave knight who saves her kingdom. DQ gloats in this news and SP jumps with joy. But DQ also realizes that because of his love for DT, he cannot even consider marrying another woman. SP reacts by criticizing DT and arguing for the marriage to the incomparably more beautiful Micomicona. DQ responds by hitting him twice with his lance and calling him a series of insulting names, for DT is the one who infuses him with strength and inspiration and without whom he could do nothing. Again the discreet Dorotea intervenes to reconcile the chivalric pair. Just then SP spots Ginés de Pasamonte approaching on SP's ass. Threatened by SP, Ginés abandons the ass and runs away, leaving SP to be reunited with his beloved companion. (*Note:* Again, this scene is not in the first printing but was included in the second and is normally included here in modern editions.) DQ and SP go off to talk together, and the others comment on the strange case of DQ's madness and SP's simplicity. Meanwhile, DQ asks SP how DT received him when he went to deliver the letter. SP admits that he had forgotten the letter, but then he lies and says that he remembered it well enough to have someone copy it for him.

Chapter 31: SP then describes in some detail his supposed meeting with DT: he discovered her thrashing wheat, with a mannish odor, and other prosaic details based more on a farm lass like Aldonza than on a beautiful princess. DQ consistently transforms her appearance and all her actions into chivalric equivalents. When SP says that she did not read the letter because she is illiterate and that she wants to see her knight-errant as soon as possible, DQ praises her discretion but also recalls that duty requires that he first complete the adventure involving the princess to which he is already committed. SP again brings up the question of marriage, and DQ assures him that even if he does not marry the Princess Micomicona, he will be able to reward SP with his island to govern. When SP notes that knights' love for and obedience to their ladies sounds to him like the sort of love and obedience that should be reserved for God, DQ comments that there are times when the squire appears to be genuinely intelligent. Just then, the group comes across a boy who turns out to be none other than Andrés, whom DQ had 'rescued' from Juan Haldudo (in I, 4). DQ

sees this as an opportunity for everyone to see the sort of contribution knights-errant make to the world and has Andrés tell his story. It turns out that after DQ departed, Haldudo tied and whipped Andrés all the harder and gave him none of his back salary. DQ, embarrassed, wants to take immediate vengeance, but Dorotea reminds him that he is under contract to her and cannot do this. SP offers Andrés a bit of cheese and bread as a consolation. Andrés says that he hopes never to see a knight again and runs off, leaving DQ angry and humiliated.

Chapter 32: The next day, they arrive at the inn of Juan Palomeque and DQ, tired and sore, immediately goes to bed. The innkeeper's wife, speaking in phrases loaded with erotic connotation, is happy to get her tail back from the barber. After dinner, the conversation turns to the romances of chivalry and the innkeeper notes that he has a few of them, left behind some while ago by a traveler, and that at harvest time, when groups assemble at the inn, someone reads from them to the group. He particularly enjoys the battles, but the women tend to like the love scenes best. When Pero Pérez claims that these books are lying fables, Juan Palomeque insists that they cannot be so, for they are printed with permission of royal authorities, and it is not conceivable that lies would be authorized. Meanwhile, the priest notes that the trunk that holds the books also contains some other papers. He takes out one manuscript and begins to glance through it. It is a story entitled *Novela del curioso impertinente* and, out of curiosity, he offers to read it aloud to the assembled group.

Chapter 33: In the city of Florence there are two close friends, the wealthy nobles Anselmo and Lotario, inseparable in their activities and interests. When Anselmo marries the beautiful Camila, he is disappointed that his friend frequents his house less than before. One day he reveals to Lotario an obsession he has: is Camila really as virtuous as she is reputed to be? The only way to find out is to test her and, over the protests of Lotario, Anselmo convinces his friend to be the instrument of this test. Lotario reluctantly agrees but determines in fact to make no effort to seduce his friend's wife. Anselmo, however, comes to realize that he is being deceived by Lotario and pressures him into making a sincere effort. And so Lotario begins a real campaign of seduction.

Chapter 34: Eventually Camila gives in and the two lovers conspire to deceive the husband. But Camila's maid, Leonela, the sole confidant of her mistress's deceit, becomes emboldened and begins to entertain a lover of her own in the house. In a series of misunderstandings, Lotario believes that Camila has another lover and, in a fit of jealousy, reveals to Anselmo that his wife is unfaithful. But in a later conversation with Camila, Lotario learns that she has no lover but him. Camila devises a plan to enact a scene that will convince Anselmo of her fidelity. Anselmo is hidden in a room where Camila, aware of her husband's presence, laments that Lotario is about to compromise her virtue and swears death over dishonor. When Lotario enters, Camila threatens him with a dagger and then stabs herself (a superficial wound near the left arm). The ruse works, and Anselmo believes that his wife is a model of virtue.

Chapter 35: Very little of the story remains to be read when there is an interruption: DQ, still asleep, has taken his sword and, believing he is fighting giants, punctured and cut several wineskins stored in the room where his bed is. Even SP believes that he has seen the blood (the red wine, of course) covering the floor. DQ is finally quieted down and goes back to bed, while the others reassemble to hear the end of the story. A further misunderstanding involving Leonela's lover leads to new suspicions and anxieties, and so Camila takes a cache of jewels and money and flees to Lotario's house. Lotario places her in safe keeping at a convent where a sister of his is prioress. Anselmo, meanwhile, realizes that his wife has been unfaithful and has fled. When he goes to tell this to Lotario, he also learns that his friend has disappeared. Upon returning home, he finds that even his servants have abandoned him. Dishonored and embarrassed, he departs for the estate of another friend who lives outside of town. A chance encounter with another traveler from Florence results in his learning that the whole

city is talking about the scandal involving him, his wife, and his best friend. Distraught, he reaches his friend's home, locks himself in his room, and begins to write a letter in which he accepts all blame for what has happened. When the friend comes to the room, he finds Anselmo slumped dead over his unfinished letter. Upon hearing of her husband's death, Camila enters the convent, and Lotario enlists in the armed services and dies in battle. Upon hearing this news, Camila formally takes the veil and then also dies shortly afterward. Upon finishing the story, the priest states his approval of the style, but doubts the psychological motivation of a married man.

Chapter 36: As the story ends, four men and a woman, all wearing masks to protect themselves from the sun and dust of the road, arrive at the inn. As they enter in silence, Dorotea covers her face and Cardenio hides in DQ's room. There follows a long, confusing, complicated scene of recognition, for the travelers are none other than Fernando, three of his friends, and Luscinda. Eventually, Dorotea confronts the man who wronged her and in a long rhetorical speech affirms her love for him and his obligation toward her; she ends by offering herself as his slave if he will not have her for his wife, reminding him that true nobility consists above all in virtue. Fernando, moved by this emotional appeal, concedes his error and accepts Dorotea as his wife. Cardenio and Luscinda likewise are reunited.

Chapter 37: SP, who had witnessed the previous scene, enters the room where DQ is asleep and informs him that the princess has turned into an ordinary lady and that their future kingdom has evaporated. DQ, inclined to attribute SP's misunderstandings to the enchantment that is characteristic of this place, dresses and prepares to go and clear up the confusion. Meanwhile, Fernando and Luscinda are informed of DQ's madness. Fernando urges Dorotea to continue her ruse, so when DQ confronts her with what SP has said, she cleverly assures him that she is today exactly what she has been and that they should continue as before. DQ begins to berate SP for his criticism of the princess, but just then a new pair of travelers arrives at the inn: a man dressed like someone who has just returned from Muslim lands and a beautiful Muslim woman. The man assures them that they have just arrived from Algiers and plan to be married as soon as the woman, whose name is Zoraida (though she prefers to be called María), is baptized in the Christian religion. Though everyone is desirous of knowing more of the story of the newcomers, nothing is asked of them for the time being. A large dinner table is set up and DQ is given the seat at the head. After eating, he takes the floor and begins a speech about the relative merits of arms over letters, a common theme in the Renaissance.

Chapter 38: DQ finishes his speech, having argued persuasively for arms over letters, and Fernando begs the newcomer to tell his story. He promises to do so, noting that his true story may not have all the appeal of a fictional one.

Chapter 39: His name is Ruy Pérez de Viedma (not actually mentioned until I, 42), native of León, one of three sons in a prominent family. Whereas his brothers chose religion and business as their careers, he opted for military service some 22 years ago. After serving in Italy and Flanders, he took part in the famous battle of Lepanto against the Turks. During the battle he was captured by Uchalí, king of Algiers, a famous and daring pirate. For a few years Ruy Pérez rowed in the Turkish galleys and then found himself present when the fortress of La Goleta fell to the enemy. His mention in passing of another soldier present then sparks the interest of one of Fernando's friends, and it turns out that the man is his brother.

Chapter 40: After reciting two sonnets written by this man, Ruy Pérez continues his story. At Uchalí's death, he became the property of Azán Agá, who eventually became king of Algiers, where he spent time in captivity in the *bagnio, or general prison. Also there in captivity was a Spanish soldier, a certain Saavedra (i.e., MC himself), whose escape attempts were even more marvelous than his own adventures. One day, Pérez and some friends saw that someone was lowering a message to them from a window. It was snatched back up when the others attempted to take it, and he alone was

allowed to receive it. It contained some money and a message written in Arabic, which they had translated by a renegade who was a friend. The message was that a young woman who lived there was a secret Christian, converted by her Christian servant and devoted to the Virgin Mary (whom she calls Lela Marién), who wanted to escape with Pérez to Spain where she could be baptized and marry him. It turned out that this was the home of Agí Morato, a rich and powerful man, who had a beautiful young daughter named Zoraida. An extended exchange of notes and money made it possible for Pérez and his friends to purchase both their freedom and a ship for their escape.

Chapter 41: Before their escape took place, Pérez had one occasion to talk with Zoraida, using the pidgin language of the region, and, in veiled allusions and double entendres, they were able to clarify their plans. The day of the escape arrived, but as they were leaving the house, Zoraida's father discovered them and had to be taken along so that the deed would not be discovered. When Morato realized that his daughter had betrayed him and their religion, he first tried to commit suicide and then heaped curses upon her. The Christians deposited him and some other Muslims on African soil as he continued to damn his daughter, but as they sailed away he tenderly shouted out his forgiveness and begged her to return. They rowed on and within a very short time were attacked by French pirates, who sank their ship and took them all captive. Pérez was worried for Zoraida's virtue, but the pirates were only interested in money and jewels. Eventually the escapees were placed in a small boat and reached Spanish soil near Vélez Málaga. From there Pérez and Zoraida headed north, hoping to learn about and be reunited with his family, and that is how they arrived at the inn.

Chapter 42: As the captive's story is praised by all who are present, yet another party, consisting of a coach carrying a judge and his daughter, and several mounted travelers, arrives at the inn. Although there is no more room for guests, the innkeeper and his wife volunteer their own quarters for the judge. The daughter, a 16-year-old who is nearly as beautiful as Dorotea, Luscinda, and Zoraida, is to stay in a room with these ladies. The judge turns out to be none other than Juan Pérez de Viedma, younger brother of Ruy, the captive, with his daughter Clara. The priest takes control of the situation and tells the judge that the name Pérez de Viedma reminds him of a soldier by that name whom he had known in captivity in Algiers. The judge has heard nothing from his soldier brother for years and is anxious for news about him. The priest summarizes the captive's story and then oversees the tearful reuniting of the two long-lost brothers. As everyone prepares to retire for the night, DQ volunteers to stand guard outside the castle.

Chapter 43: Later that night, a beautiful voice of a muleteer is heard singing love poetry. Clara recognizes the voice as that of Don Luis, a wealthy nobleman of her own age who is in love with her—although the two of them have never actually spoken—and who has followed her here. Meanwhile, as DQ stands guard and pines for DT, the innkeeper's daughter and Maritornes—two 'semi-virgins'—decide to have some fun at his expense. They call him to a window and immediately DQ imagines again that the daughter of the lord of the castle is interested in him. They ask him to extend his hand to their window, which he does (standing on the back of his horse Rocinante in order to reach up to the window), begging them not to kiss it but merely to admire its sinewy texture and imagine its strength. The two young women tie his hand to the window and abandon him there. After a while, he begins to desire the enchanted sword of Amadís, invoke his lady, call his squire, call on wizards from the romances of chivalry, and, as morning approaches, bellow like a bull. With the dawn, four horsemen arrive at the inn and DQ tries to convince them it is a castle, but they pay him no attention. Rocinante, however, does pay attention to one of the mares who sniffs him, and he returns the compliment—moving out from under DQ, who is left dangling by his hand, his feet barely touching the ground.

Chapter 44: Maritornes hastens to untie DQ, who falls to the ground and again affirms that the castle is enchanted. At this time, the four new travelers ask about a youth dressed as a muleboy who is known to be following the coach that is at the inn. The innkeeper does not know if the person they are looking for is there, so they begin to search for him. During all this, DQ is completely ignored by everyone and he grows increasingly frustrated. One of the travelers finds Don Luis asleep with the mules and other servants, and wakes him up to tell him that they have been sent by their master, Don Luis's father, to bring him back home. By this time nearly everyone in the inn has become aware of the situation, as Don Luis insists that he is free and chooses not to return to his father. But elsewhere in the inn, two other guests attempt to leave without paying their bill and the innkeeper has gotten into a fight with them. The innkeeper's wife and daughter, seeing no one else completely unoccupied, beg DQ to help save the innkeeper. DQ replies that he could only do so if granted permission by the Princess Micomicona. He begs such permission and it is granted, but then another problem occurs to him: the people involved are not knights-errant, so he cannot raise his sword against them—better that SP do it. All the while, the innkeeper is getting the worst of the scuffle. At this point, the narrator turns our attention back to Don Luis, who is appealing to the judge to permit him to marry Clara. The judge demurs, considering how advantageous a marriage this would be for his daughter. Meanwhile, back at the dispute between the innkeeper and the guests, DQ has settled the matter by persuasion and the bill is being paid. But just then, another person arrives at the inn—the barber from whom DQ had taken Mambrino's helmet. The barber and SP immediately get into a fight over possession of the barber's saddlebags, which SP had taken as spoils of the battle. DQ, seeing how well his squire defends himself, decides to dub him a knight-errant in the near future. Several persons step in to break up the fight, but this does not settle the matter of identity: regal trappings of a horse or common saddlebags of an ass; helmet or basin. DQ orders SP to bring the helmet and he returns with it, calling it a *baciyelmo* (basin-helmet).

Chapter 45: Maese Nicolás, seeing an opportunity to have some fun, says that, as a barber himself, he can attest to the fact that this is not a basin but a helmet. To the offended barber's astonishment, the priest, Don Fernando, Cardenio, and others (who know of DQ's madness) agree. DQ, affirming once again that it is a helmet (he is not so sure about the saddlebag-trappings issue), reminds everyone that this castle is enchanted and so he finds it not at all remarkable that such mistakes could be made. Don Fernando suggests that to decide the issue there should be a vote—and, of course, the majority opinion is that it is a helmet. Those who are not in on the joke, such as Don Luis's servants and three officers of the Holy Brotherhood who also happen to be there, disagree, DQ calls one of the officers a liar, and a fight breaks out. Confusion reigns as everyone looks out for his or her own interests amidst the blows, cries, blood, and general confusion of the melee. Finally, DQ calls a halt to the activity, reminding everyone again that all things happen here under enchantment and comparing the fight to the scene of the camp of Agramante in *Orlando Furioso*. Calm reigns until one of the officers realizes that DQ is the highwayman wanted for the freeing of the galley slaves, calls upon his comrades for aid, and tries to arrest DQ, who almost chokes the man before they are broken up. By this time, SP is convinced that things truly are enchanted in this place. DQ defends his actions in freeing the galley slaves as consistent with his chivalric mission.

Chapter 46: The priest manages to calm everyone down, and Don Fernando soothes hurt feelings by paying for everything. DQ, meanwhile, begs the Princesa Micomicona to depart in order to bring her adventure to a close. She agrees, but SP bitterly tells his master that nothing is as it seems, that she is no princess or she wouldn't be necking with one of the men (Don Fernando) in the group. DQ is so enraged that he calls his squire a string of insulting names, which shames and frustrates SP. Dorotea, however, cleverly reminds DQ that since enchantment is the norm in this castle, it is possible that SP was made to see things that did not happen. In order to allow everyone to head their own way and tend to their own business, the

priest and others devise a scheme to enchant DQ. That night, they dress as phantoms, enter DQ's room, and tie him up. The barber Maese Nicolás, in a fearful voice, informs the knight that, according to the magician Mentironiana, he is enchanted, but makes the prophesy that the current adventure will be finished when the Manchegan lion and the Tobosan dove are married and sire their brave pups, which will occur within two years. As part of the enchantment, DQ must be transported in a cage mounted on a cart pulled by two oxen.

Chapter 47: DQ marvels at his enchantment, in a common oxcart rather than a flaming chariot pulled by a hippogriff or something comparable. SP, however, tries to convince him that everything is not right, but DQ refuses to listen. Taking leave of the women of the inn, DQ insists that this misfortune is part and parcel of his profession. As they prepare to depart, the innkeeper gives the priest some more manuscripts that had been left there, particularly one entitled *Novela de Rinconete y Cortadillo*, which might be by the same author who wrote the *Curioso impertinente* that had pleased so much. The group sets out, with the oxcart containing the stoic (and bound) DQ leading the way, flanked by two officers of the Holy Brotherhood, with SP following right behind and leading Rocinante, and with the priest and barber, still in disguise, bringing up the rear. The procession is overtaken by a group of travelers led, it turns out, by a fairly important ecclesiastical figure, a canon from Toledo. The canon inquires about the strange procession, and the priest informs him briefly that DQ is an enchanted knight-errant. SP listens to this explanation and then angrily insists that DQ is no more enchanted than SP's mother, that the priest and barber have lied to DQ and done these things to him out of envy. Fearful that SP might give them away, the priest takes the canon and his servants aside for a private talk. After the priest fills him in on DQ's madness and the current situation, the canon launches into a long discourse on the romances of chivalry, criticizing them for lasciviousness and cheap thrills in stead of spiritual enlightenment.

His final comment is that the epic can be written in prose as well as in verse.

Chapter 48: The canon continues his discourse on literature, admitting that he himself has been tempted to write a good romance of chivalry, and in fact has some 100 folios in draft form, but has chosen not to finish the task. He broadens the discussion to include theater, criticizing sharply contemporary Spanish practices, which fail to live up to good classical standards. Though there have been some good plays written and produced in Spain (MC's *La Numancia* is one of those he cites), the majority of them are completely without art. His praise for one dramatist (Lope de Vega) whose innumerable works have gained and deserved particularly great recognition may be ironic. He proposes a national censor for theater (and for the romances of chivalry). Meanwhile, SP again tries to tell DQ that his enchanters are the priest and barber from their village, but DQ again refuses to admit that possibility and insists that he is indeed enchanted. SP then uses another means to convince him that he is not enchanted, asking him if he has to relieve himself. Indeed he does, replies DQ.

Chapter 49: This proves that DQ is not enchanted, says SP, because everyone knows that those under enchantment have their normal bodily functions suspended, so the fact that DQ has such needs means he cannot be enchanted. Normally that is true, DQ replies, but there are all kinds of enchantments and it would be devastating to him if he were to admit that he allowed himself to be humiliated in this way if not as a result of magic. About this time the group stops to rest and have something to eat, so DQ is permitted out of his cage to join them. After taking care of his needs, he engages the canon in a debate over the historical value of the romances of chivalry. In his argument, DQ mixes the romances with legend and history, at one point citing the historical knight Gutierre Quijada (from whom, he says, he descends directly via the male line). In general, DQ upholds his point of view very well and could be considered to have gotten the best of the discussion.

Chapter 50: DQ ends by insisting that the king's agents would not authorize publication of books that contained untruths, as the canon has suggested. And to prove how wonderful the romances of chivalry are, DQ tells the story of the Knight of the Lake, who descends into a dark lake and has a marvelous adventure in a fabulous castle. About this time, a pretty goat comes by, pursued by a goatherd who is insulting the animal by noting that being female she is by definition fickle. The company invites the goatherd to join them in their meal, and he accepts, offering to tell them the story of what has recently happened to him.

Chapter 51: In the goatherd's village, there lived a beautiful young woman named Leandra, the only child of a wealthy peasant. She was pursued by all the local men, but especially by two of them: the narrator (whose name is Eugenio) and his rival Anselmo. But both were upstaged by a new arrival, Vicente de la Rosa, a dandy and a braggart soldier. Leandra was swayed by his looks and rhetoric and ran away with him, after stealing money and jewels from her father's house. The locals pursued the couple and within a few days found Leandra in a cave, abandoned by her lover, who, she insists, took her valuables but not her virginity. Her father placed her in a convent, and Eugenio, Anselmo, and several other men took to the forests and fields as shepherds and goatherds, lamenting Leandra's fickleness and disloyalty.

Chapter 52: DQ offers to help rescue Leandra from the convent if necessary. Eugenio wonders at DQ's looks and speech and suggests that perhaps he has a few vacant rooms in his head. DQ responds by grabbing a nearby loaf of bread and throwing it at his critic, giving him a bloody nose. Eugenio jumps on DQ and begins to strangle him, but SP intervenes and helps his master begin to get by far the better of the scuffle. Eugenio crawls toward a knife with which to defend himself, but the priest and the canon step in to keep things from getting bloodier. Meanwhile, the barber Maese Nicolás trips up DQ so that the goatherd can begin to bloody his face, while one of the canon's servants restrains SP from helping his master. The entire company laughs uproariously and jumps with joy at the scene and they incite goatherd and knight-errant as one does with dogs in a dogfight. Only SP, who cannot break away from the one restraining him, feels sorry for DQ. At this moment, a trumpet sounds and all stop to look at a procession of hooded men—penitents—carrying a figure of the Virgin Mary. DQ extricates himself from the fight and decides to show everyone present how important knights-errant are in the world by rescuing this damsel in distress. Ignoring SP's warnings about the reality of the situation, DQ challenges the evildoers to relinquish their captive. As the penitents begin to laugh at him, DQ draws his sword and attacks, but one of the penitents hits him hard on his right shoulder with a stick and knocks him unconscious to the ground. SP runs to his master's side and the penitents then go on their way. Fearing that DQ is dead, SP sheds tears and laments his loss. But DQ comes to at this time and asks for SP's help. The squire suggests that they go home, and DQ accepts the suggestion, at least until the evil influence of the stars passes. The traveling party breaks up, and the priest and barber take DQ home. The trip lasts six days and they arrive on Sunday, at midday, passing through the town square when many people are there. DQ is received at home by the housekeeper and his niece, who immediately put him to bed. SP goes home to his wife, who berates him, but he condescendingly informs her that he likes traveling around, visiting castles, not paying at inns, and so forth, and that he hopes to set out again soon with DQ. Unfortunately, however, the author has been unable to find any further documentation on the life of DQ in the Annals of La Mancha. The only thing he did locate was a decaying lead box containing some decomposing manuscripts, particularly some poems written by the members of the Academy of Argamasilla del Alba, a town in La Mancha. He promises to keep looking for material with which to write a continuation, but in the meanwhile, 'perhaps someone else will sing with a better pick.'

Don Quijote II: Segunda parte del ingenioso caballero don Quijote de la Mancha. Madrid: Juan de la Cuesta, 1615 (*DQ* I); The Second Part of the Imaginative

Knight Don Quixote de la Mancha. After the success of *DQ* I, MC was slow to work on a sequel, but when *DQA* was published in 1614, he seems to have hurried to finish his own continuation. Avellaneda may have done the world a great favor, as MC finished *DQ* II in the fall of 1615, and died in the spring of 1616. Perhaps without the challenge of his anonymous rival, he might not have completed his masterpiece before his death. Interesting to note is the complete absence of preliminary verses, whether genuinely contributed by other writers or appended in burlesque fashion by the author himself, as MC had done in *DQ* I. This absence may be a reflection of MC's reaction to the comments of the pseudonymous author of *DQA* about the burlesque poems that precede *DQ* I. In the seventeenth century, *DQ* II was only published three times alone in 1615–17 before it was published 14 more times together with *DQ* I.

Preliminaries: The price is set by Hernando de Vallejo on October 21, 1615. The corrector's statement is signed by Licenciado Francisco Murcia de la Llana on the same date. There are three approvals, signed by Doctor Gutierre de Cetina on November 5, 1615; Maestro Josef de Valdivielso on March 17, 1615; and Licenciado *Márquez Torres on February 27, 1615. The statement by Márquez Torres is quite extraordinary for its length, personal tone, and praise for MC. The king's privilege to publish is signed by Pedro de Contreras on March 30, 1615. The dedication and prologue follow, but there are no preliminary verses.

Prologue: MC begins by invoking the reader who, he expects, is waiting for him to call the author of *DQA* published under a pseudonym the previous year an ass, an idiot, and much more. But he has no intention of doing so. What he does feel bad about, however, is that the anonymous author criticized him for being old and crippled. He reminds the reader that it is true that he lost the use of his left hand, but that was during the greatest event of past, present, and future history (i.e., the battle of Lepanto). He also resents that the anonymous author called him envious, because he does not envy, but rather respects and admires, the

Don Quijote II

works and customary virtuous life of that priest who is a familiar of the Holy Inquisition (i.e., Lope de Vega, whom MC did implicitly satirize in the prologue and text of *DQ* I). If the reader should happen to meet up with the other writer, perhaps he should tell him one of two anecdotes about writing books. The first is about a madman in Seville who inflated dogs by thrusting a reed into their anus and blowing air into it, and then let the air come back out again, warning people that it is no easy task to inflate a dog. Nor is it, MC adds, an easy task to write a book. The second anecdote is about a madman in Córdoba who went about with a marble slab on his head, which he dropped on unsuspecting dogs. One day the owner of a dog warned the man not to drop the slab by saying that his dog was a greyhound (*podenco*). After that, the man saw all dogs as greyhounds and no longer dropped marble on them. This, too, should be a warning to people without talent who try to become writers. After briefly praising his patrons, the Count of Lemos and Cardinal Sandoval y Rojas, MC closes by assuring the reader that this *DQ* II is 'cut by the same artisan and from the same cloth' as *DQ* I, and in it DQ dies and is buried, so that no one can bring him back to life. And he promises the forthcoming appearance of *Persiles*, which he is finishing, and the second part of *Galatea*.

Dedication: To Don Pedro Fernández de Castro, count of Lemos. MC relates that he recently received a letter from the great emperor of China who, in Chinese, wrote requesting copies of *DQ*, which he wanted to use as a text to teach Spanish in an academy that he planned to establish. Furthermore, he requested MC to come to China to be rector of the academy. MC writes that he told the bearer of the letter that he could not make such a long trip because his poor health would not allow it; besides, he had such a generous patron in the count that he had no need to travel to far-off countries in order to receive support. He then promises to send a copy of *Persiles*, which he hopes to finish within four months and which he hopes will be either the best book ever written in Spanish or the worst. The dedication is dated in Madrid, October 31, 1615.

Chapter 1: One month after DQ's return home, he is resting comfortably in bed and showing no signs of his former madness. The priest and barber decide to visit him and verify his return to sanity. The conversation with their friend is very pleasant, and the priest decides to test him by mentioning that the Turks are threatening an invasion. DQ (and it is worth noting that the priest address him as DQ, not as Alonso Quijano, or whatever his name might have been) responds that the king should immediately send all knights-errant from throughout Spain to defend the country against the infidels. The barber decides to tell the tale of a madman in Seville who appeared to have recovered during his stay in the madhouse but who inadvertently revealed that he is still delusional. DQ takes this cautionary tale as an affront and insults the barber. He then defends the concept of the knight-errant in comparison with the courtly knight, praises several fictional knights-errant, and describes what Amadís de Gaula must have looked like. When the priest doubts the existence of giants as described in the romances of chivalry, DQ cites both the Bible and archaeology as proof of giants' existence.

Chapter 2: SP arrives, and the housekeeper and niece try to keep him away from DQ, blaming him in large part for all that has happened. The priest and barber insist that he be allowed to see DQ, and they then depart. DQ and SP have a conversation about several aspects of their earlier adventures, and then SP reveals the news that Sansón Carrasco, who has been away studying at the University of Salamanca, has just returned to the village, with his bachelor's degree, and with the news that a book entitled *El ingenioso hidalgo Don Quijote de la Mancha* has been published. The author, says SP, is a Muslim named Cide Hamete Berenjena (Eggplant); Muslims are, SP notes, fond of eggplants. SP departs to bring the bachelor to talk with DQ.

Chapter 3: A pensive DQ thinks about his fame in books, but worries that his author is a Muslim, for all Muslims are natural liars. Sansón arrives: a man whose small stature belies his name, but one who is fond of practical jokes. He informs DQ that over 12,000 copies of the history of his adventures circulate throughout Spain, having been printed in various cities. He also predicts that soon there will be no nation or language into which it has not been translated. They discuss the most popular episodes of the book (mostly the comic scenes from the first half of the book) and the aesthetics of history. Sansón makes the Aristotelian distinction between history, which must recount things as they actually happened, and poetry, in which the poet can sing of how things might be. SP's role in the book is also discussed, as is the interpolated story of *Curioso*, which many have criticized, not as bad, but as inappropriate in the book. DQ fears that his story—like the paintings of Orbaneja, the painter from Úbeda, who had to identify what he painted so that it could be understood and appreciated by others—will be in need of commentary in order to be understand, but Sansón assures him that that is not the case, as it is read and appreciated by people of all ages and from all social classes. After citing the famous dictum that there is no book so bad that it does not contain some good, Sansón also mentions that there has been criticism about the confusion regarding the theft of SP's ass and the failure to mention what SP did with Cardenio's money that he found. SP promises to clarify those matters—after dinner. He leaves, and DQ and Sansón eat together and take a brief siesta.

Chapter 4: SP returns to DQ's house and tells Sansón how Ginés de Pasamonte stole his ass (a version quite different from the one that appears in the second printed edition of the novel) and that he and his wife have spent the money. They talk again about CHB's book, and DQ asks if the author promises a sequel. Sansón informs him that he does indeed make such a promise; SP seconds the idea and urges DQ to be back on the road; and, to top it off, Rocinante whinnies loudly, which is taken by DQ as a good omen for a third sally. DQ proposes going to Zaragoza, where there are plans to celebrate a jousting tourney. SP delivers a long and intelligent speech about the fame he hopes to gain as a squire. The decision is made to set out within about a week.

Chapter 5: The translator begins this chapter complaining that in it SP speaks with a style that is beyond his intellectual capabilities, and so he considers it apocryphal, but he dutifully translates it as his profession requires of him. SP informs his wife Teresa that he intends to make another sally with DQ, hoping this time to achieve his goal and become a governor of an island. Teresa is skeptical, especially when SP tells her of his plans to marry their daughter to someone of noble blood. Teresa insists that Sanchica marry someone her social equal, such as Lope Tocho, a local man who has already expressed interest in her. SP responds that he has always heard his elders say that you should not refuse to open the door to opportunity when it calls and that they should go with the favorable wind (this is one of the passages where the translator feels SP exceeds his limits). Teresa continues to insist that they should not try to rise above their natural social station and that she, for one, does not want to have a title or *don* attached to her name. SP continues to explain his plans to get ahead and cites the sermon preached the previous year during Lent, in which they were reminded that that which is before our eyes now has more reality than that which we remember from the past (this is the second passage the translator criticizes). The conversation ends with Teresa giving her approval for her husband's departure, but reserving judgment about what his accomplishments might be. Throughout the chapter, SP treats his wife in a manner reminiscent of the way DQ treats him—with condescension, calling her insulting names, and correcting her pronunciation of words.

Chapter 6: DQ chats with his niece and housekeeper about romances of chivalry, the differences between knights of the court and knights-errant, the truthful nature of romances of chivalry, different kinds of lines of descent, and arms and letters. The two women are amazed at his erudition and his abilities. DQ tells them that if he weren't so preoccupied with chivalry there would be almost nothing he could not do or make, for example, cages and toothpicks.

Chapter 7: SP talks with DQ in preparation

for their upcoming departure and requests that he be given a specific salary for his services. DQ rejects the idea, stating that there is no precedent for it in the romances of chivalry. He adds that if SP does not want to serve as his squire under the same indefinite terms as before, that is his right, and DQ will find someone else to do the job. At this moment, Sansón Carrasco enters and, on his knees before DQ, offers to serve as his squire. DQ thanks Sansón for the offer, but rejects it, stating that he can get by with almost anyone as a squire, since SP does not want the position. A tearful SP insists that he does, indeed, want to serve again as squire, and drops his demand for a salary. A few days later, at nightfall, DQ and SP set out on their third sally, headed for El Toboso.

Chapter 8: 'Blessed be Allah,' exclaims CHB, and repeats the blessing three times, as DQ and SP are once again on the road in quest of adventures. As they ride along, Rocinante whinnies (again a positive sign for DQ) and SP's *rucio* 'sighs' (perhaps a euphemism for farts); in fact, there are more of the latter than there are of the former, which SP takes as a sign that his fortune is to surpass that of his master. As they continue, DQ and SP talk about aspects of fame and of famous people in history. SP proposes that it might be easier to gain fame as saints than as knights-errant, and that perhaps they should change their profession. DQ responds that chivalry is a religion and can lead to heaven as well as any other path. They travel throughout the day and arrive at El Toboso in the late afternoon. DQ decides to wait until nightfall before entering the village.

Chapter 9: It is exactly midnight, more or less, when they enter El Toboso. The town is wrapped in a marvelous silence; the only sounds to be heard are the barking of dogs, the braying of donkeys, the snorting of pigs, and the meowing of cats. They see a large building and approach it in hopes that it is the princess's castle, but it turns out to be the town church. DQ tells SP that he has never actually seen DT, but is in love with her on the basis of hearsay reports of her beauty. SP thus learns for the first time that his master does not know DT personally, and states that he has never seen her either.

DQ reminds him that he has reported having talked with her, but SP assures him that their conversation also took place by means of hearsay. Just then a mule driver passes by and they ask him for help in locating the palace, but he is a stranger to these parts and cannot help. At this point, SP suggests that they leave town and let the night pass, so that the next day he can return and arrange a meeting between DQ and his lady. DQ gladly accepts this suggestion.

Chapter 10: The chronicler CHB states that he would prefer not to write this chapter because in it DQ's madness reaches new heights, but he decides to fulfill his duty and write it as it happened, not omitting a single atom of truth. The next morning DQ sends SP off to El Toboso, suggesting to him that he note carefully how DT reacts at each moment, in effect giving him a script to follow should he want to invent another interview with her. SP goes off, but pauses to ponder his dilemma of having to visit someone who does not exist. After a comic soliloquy, he devises a clever scheme: he will wait until he sees a local peasant woman come by on the road and tell DQ that this is DT. If DQ doubts it, SP will insist and blame the situation on enchanters. As luck has it, just as SP returns to where DQ awaits him, three peasant women are passing by on the road, riding some kind of donkeys. SP announces to DQ that DT and two ladies-in-waiting have come to see him. DQ looks but can see nothing but three peasant women on three donkeys, or, at least, so it appears to him. SP, now clearly in control, stops the women and, on his knees, introduces himself and his master (in a beautiful chivalric style). DQ, still seeing only an ugly, foul-smelling peasant woman, addresses her as DT. The one designated as DT responds crudely and spurs her donkey, riding off with her companions. But the mount bucks her off, and as DQ rushes to the rescue, she jumps on the animal and rides away. DQ is confused and frustrated as he contemplates the transformation in his lady perpetrated by the enchanters. SP insists that only DQ was enchanted, as he, SP, only saw her great beauty, especially a mole on her left lip, with golden hairs that descended below her chin. Dejected, DQ decides to go on, and he and SP head off for Zaragoza.

Chapter 11: As they ride on, SP tries to cheer his master up, when suddenly they come face-to-face with a cart filled with various fantastic figures. The first one DQ sees is that of Death itself. DQ asks for an explanation, and the driver tells him that they are actors in the company of Angulo el Malo dressed for their roles in the *auto sacramental* (one-act Eucharist drama) entitled *Las Cortes de la Muerte*; they have not bothered to change costumes since their last performance, as they are on their way to a nearby town to repeat the play. DQ accepts this explanation and comments on how difficult it can be to distinguish between reality and appearances. Things would have ended there, but one of the actors, dressed as a clown, jingles some bells in Rocinante's face, causing him to buck and throw his rider. SP goes to help DQ, and the clown rides off on SP's ass and then takes a pratfall in parody of that by DQ. DQ is angry and wants to take revenge on the whole troupe, but the actors jump down, arm themselves with stones, and await his charge. DQ pauses to consider how to attack with least risk to his person, when SP reminds him that no one in the group is actually armed a knight and therefore DQ should not fight them. DQ realizes that SP is correct and approves his squire's taking care of the revenge himself. But SP says that it is not Christian to do so, and DQ praises his Christian resolution. They go on their way.

Chapter 12: That night as they rest, DQ compares the theater with life, reminding SP that after the play is over and the costumes are removed the king is no greater than the clown, and so it is in life itself. SP says that he has heard this comparison before, but one he likes better is that of the game of chess: after the game is over, all the pieces go together in the same box and none is greater than the other. When DQ observes that SP seems smarter every day, SP attributes the change to the company of his master, for although his brain is like dry and infertile land, DQ's conversation is like manure that makes it flourish. The two pass most of the night in comparable conversation. The narrator takes advantage of this interlude

to comment on the growing friendship between Rocinante and SP's *rucio*. Some even say that the author compared their friendship with famous ones from the past like that between Pilades and Orestes. Soon the noise of others dismounting nearby alerts DQ, who awakens SP to tell him that an adventure is at hand. As they listen, a voice recites a love sonnet and then goes on to lament his love for the beautiful Casildea de Vandalia, for whom he has undertaken several successful chivalric adventures, even making all the knights-errant of La Mancha confess her beauty. DQ courteously introduces himself, and as he and the one referred to in narration as the Knight of the Forest begin to engage in chivalric conversation, the two squires go off for their own talk.

Chapter 13: The two squires discuss proper language, their families, their lives as squires, their masters, and wine, a generous amount of which is provided by the squire of the Knight of the Forest. Whereas the latter consistently criticizes his master and calls him names, SP has only praise for DQ: he harms no one, has no malice in him, and has a childish innocence. On four separate occasions, the squire of the Knight of the Forest suggests that they return home to their wives and children, but on each occasion SP either changes the subject or remains silent, until he finally states firmly that until his master goes to Zaragoza he intends to remain in his service; after that, he may reconsider. With this, the conversation comes to a close.

Chapter 14: The chapter begins with a conversation between the two knights. The Knight of the Forest describes his love for the peerless Casildea de Vandalia, for whom he has done many chivalric deeds. He has defeated knights-errant throughout Spain, but his greatest victory was the one over the famous Don Quixote de la Mancha. DQ states that he doubts that DQ has been defeated by anyone, but the other knight insists that he has done so, and even describes DQ in detail. DQ suggests that perhaps the encounter the other knight believes he had with DQ was a matter of enchantment. The two agree that the only way to settle this dispute is to wait for day and to engage in singular combat to see who is right. The other squire also suggests to SP that they fight at the same time, but SP absolutely refuses to do such a thing. When dawn finally comes, the first thing that SP sees is the nose of the other squire, large and purple as an eggplant, which fills him with fear. DQ can now see his opponent, and notes that his armor is covered with mirrors (and from this point on, he is called the Knight of the Mirrors). After helping SP climb a tree to avoid the other squire, DQ squares off with the other knight, who is already charging. But when the Knight of the Mirrors sees DQ busy with SP, he stops his horse. DQ, however, spurs on Rocinante as his best trot and the other knight finds that he cannot restart his own horse (which is no better than Rocinante), and receives DQ's charge motionless. The result is that DQ unhorses his opponent, winning a clear victory. When he goes to the fallen knight, who is unconscious, and removes his visor, he sees . . . the very face of . . . Sansón Carrasco. Stunned, DQ calls for SP to come and see how the enchanters have changed the appearance of his opponent. SP immediately advises DQ to take his sword and kill this apparition. But the other squire arrives and tells them that the defeated knight is indeed Sansón. He then takes off his false nose and reveals his own identity: Tomé Cecial, friend and neighbor of SP. By this time, Sansón revives and DQ orders him to confess that DT is more beautiful than Casildea. He does so, but using highly suggestive, somewhat obscene, language. DQ also has him confess that he is not Sansón Carrasco but only has his appearance and that the other knight he defeated was not the real DQ. After doing this, Sansón and Tomé depart.

Chapter 15: It is explained how Sansón Carrasco had consulted with the priest and barber and then decided to use the trick of pretending to be a knight-errant in order to defeat DQ and make him return home. As they ride home in defeat, Tomé Cecial asks Sansón who is crazier, one who can't help himself or one who pretends to be mad on purpose. Sansón affirms that it is the former, because he will always be mad, whereas the latter (i.e., himself) can cease pretending whenever he wants to. He adds that he

will again ride out to encounter DQ, but not motivated by altruism, as he was this time, but in order to give DQ a good drubbing and avenge his defeat.

Chapter 16: DQ rides away proud of his victory and disdainful of the powers of enchanters. He cannot believe that Sansón would have actually tried to defeat him, so it clearly was someone else made to look like his friend. SP is noncommittal. Soon they are joined by another traveler, a man of about DQ's age, dressed in an elegant green suit. DQ takes note of the way the man is looking at him, and states that his appearance is unusual because he is a knight-errant so famous that there are already in print some 30,000 copies of the book in which his deeds are recounted (an exaggeration; Sansón had mentioned only 12,000 in II, 3). The other man, whose name is Don Diego de Miranda, has some doubt about the reality of knights-errant. He describes his own life: he is a reasonably well-to-do *hidalgo*, married and with one son, is fond of hunting, reads only inspirational books and never romances of chivalry, frequently entertains his friends, never gossips, does not pry into the lives of other people, hears mass every day, shares his wealth with the poor, and is very devoted to the Virgin Mary. SP dismounts, rushes to the man's side, and begins to kiss his feet. When asked why, he responds that it is because this is the first time he has ever seen a real saint on horseback. Don Diego assures him he is no saint but a great sinner. He also explains that his 18-year-old son, a student at Salamanca, is a problem for him because he wastes his time writing poetry rather than studying seriously. DQ offers the opinion that parents should always love their children, no matter what they do. And besides, he adds, poetry is like a young and tender damsel, who should always be treated with great respect; she should be served and adorned by all other sciences. DQ goes on for some while about poetry, and SP, not interested in this speech, wanders off to buy some curds and whey from a nearby group of shepherds. Suddenly, they are interrupted by an approaching cart adorned with royal banners and DQ, assuming it means a new adventure, calls for SP to bring him his helmet.

Chapter 17: When DQ calls him, SP hurriedly places the curds in the only container he has with him—DQ's helmet. SP can only hand over the helmet and when DQ places it on his head, the whey begins to run down over his face. At first DQ thinks it might be sweat, but when he wipes it away he sees what it is and blames SP for putting the curds in his helmet. But the clever SP calmly responds that he has no idea how the curds got to be there, but perhaps it was by enchantment. DQ is suspicious, but lets the matter ride, as he goes off to see about the new adventure. Approaching is a cart, with one man on it, while another rides alongside on a mule. DQ asks what is in the cart and is told that it contains two ferocious African lions that are being transported to the royal court in Madrid. DQ smiles and, recalling the many romances of chivalry in which the hero faces a dangerous lion, asks the driver to open the cage and let the lions out. Don Diego remarks to SP that DQ must be mad, but SP defends his master by saying that he is not mad but brave. When Don Diego tries to convince DQ of the danger in his request, he is brushed aside. DQ prevails and, after the others have all gone some distance off, the lion-keeper prepares to open the cage. DQ decides to dismount and face the lion on foot. At this point, CHB ponders the difficulty of finding words adequate to describe this daring feat. Finally the cage is opened as DQ stands ready to face the beast. But the lion merely yawns, licks his face with his tongue, and sticks his head out of the cage. Paying no attention to DQ, the generous lion turns around, displaying his hind quarters to the knight-errant, and settles back down in the cage. DQ asks the lion-keeper to take a stick and agitate the beast in order to make him come out of the cage. But the man refuses, assuring DQ that the lion made the choice not to confront him, which is a victory for DQ. DQ accepts this interpretation, the cage is closed, and SP and the others are called. When they return, DQ orders SP to give the lion-keeper two gold coins for his efforts. The lion-keeper then recounts what happened, exaggerating DQ's bravery and the lion's fear of confronting him. DQ then gives himself a new name: the Knight of the Lions. Don Diego marvels at DQ's madness and the latter, noting this, delivers a short speech about the difference between knights of the court and brave knights-errant. Don Diego invites DQ and SP to accompany him to his house, and they accept. For DQ, Don Diego is the Knight of the Green Overcoat.

Chapter 18: As they arrive at Don Diego's house, DQ sees several large earthenware containers of the type notoriously manufactured in El Toboso and, of course, this reminds him of DT, whom he evokes in lines reminiscent of the poetry of Garcilaso de la Vega. DQ and SP are generously received by Don Diego's wife Doña Cristina. CHB then went on to describe the house in detail, but this has been left out by the translator, who does not like such digressions from the truth of the matter. After cleaning himself of the remaining curds and whey, DQ meets Don Lorenzo, Don Diego's son, the poet. The discussion turns at once to the art of poetry, which DQ again describes and praises. At DQ's urging, Don Lorenzo reads two of his compositions, a gloss and a sonnet, which DQ praises extravagantly. DQ and SP spend four days visiting with Don Diego and his family and then depart for Zaragoza, heading first, however, for the Cave of Montesinos where DQ hopes to discover something about the origins of the Lagoons of Ruidera in that vicinity. The Miranda family is left with admiration for DQ's wisdom and intelligence in all areas except matters of chivalry, where his madness is apparent.

Chapter 19: DQ and SP soon join a small group consisting of two priests or students, one of whom is carrying two fencing swords, and two peasants. They are on their way to a wedding celebration, and, at DQ's prompting, they explain the situation. The groom, Camacho, is one of the wealthiest peasants in that part of the country, and the bride, Quiteria, is the most beautiful woman around. A problem, however, exists in the person of Basilio, a poor but handsome, charming, and athletic young man whom Quiteria had loved and hoped to marry before her father arranged the more advantageous liaison with Camacho. There is a brief discussion about arranged marriages and the nature of love. SP participates in the debate and expresses a particular fondness for Basilio. Then the subject changes to fencing, and it turns out that the two students have a difference of opinion about the best way to use the sword. One, a bachelor named Corchuelo, believes in a natural method, relying on strength and intuition, whereas the other, a licentiate, endorses the more scientific method, involving the calculation of angles and foot position (a subject much debated in popular treatises of the day). They decide to settle the question right then and there, with DQ acting as judge. After a brief skirmish, the scientific fencer easily bests the natural one. The party continues on its way to the site of the marriage.

Chapter 20: The travelers arrive at the place where the wedding ceremony is to be held. The first thing SP sees is the great abundance of food, and one of the cooks gives him an entire chicken to eat. Meanwhile, DQ has taken note of the entrance of some elegantly dressed dancers who represent allegorical figures, and he carefully watches and listens to their performance. SP, meanwhile, has decided that he has shifted allegiances from Basilio to Camacho, because of the great generosity of the latter.

Chapter 21: As the marriage ceremony itself is about to begin, Quiteria enters and her beauty is apparent to all; for DQ, in fact, she is the most beautiful woman he has ever seen, after DT. But suddenly Basilio arrives, brandishing a sword, and interrupts the proceedings. He proclaims his love for Quiteria, saying that he cannot live without her, stabs himself, and falls to the ground, covered with blood. With his dying breath, he requests that Quiteria marry him so that, as soon as he dies happily, she, as a virgin widow, can then marry Camacho. It is agreed that this is reasonable, and Quiteria states that it is her will that it be done and gives Basilio her hand. The priest pronounces them man and wife—and suddenly Basilio jumps up perfectly healthy. It turns out that his death was a ruse, faked by stabbing a hollow tube filled with blood. Camacho and his friends are about to take action, but DQ and a few others prevent this from happening. Once Camacho is calmed

down, he agrees generously to recognize the marriage and let the celebration continue. But the new bride and groom prefer to leave at once for their own village, and DQ and SP accompany them.

Chapter 22: DQ and SP spend three days with the newlyweds, during which time DQ gives them some good advice. Knight and squire then depart, headed for the Cave of Montesinos, with a cousin of the licentiate swordsman as a guide. The cousin is a humanist scholar who writes books in imitation of classic authors such as Ovid and Polydorus Vergil. SP makes fun of detailed scholarly investigation by proposing that the cousin can add to his notes the fact that the first man to scratch his head in history was Adam, and the first to do somersaults was Lucifer when he was cast out of heaven. They arrive at the Cave of Montesinos, and DQ invokes DT prior to his descent. A large number of crows and blackbirds flies out of the cave, which is taken as a bad omen. DQ ties a rope around his waist in order to maintain contact with those who remain above, and then descends into the cave. After a while, the rope goes slack, and after waiting for about half an hour, SP and the cousin begin to retrieve the rope. Finally, they feel weight and pull DQ to the surface. His eyes are closed and he appears to be asleep. When they awaken him, DQ invokes the names of Montesinos, Durandarte, Belerma, Guadiana, and Ruidera.

Chapter 23: DQ describes what happened to him in the cave: at about some 70 feet into his descent, he noticed a large niche on the right-hand side and decided to stop there and rest a while. He shouted for SP and the cousin to stop lowering rope, but they obviously could not hear him, so he gathered it up and coiled it as they continued to lower it. As he rested, he fell into a deep sleep, but then suddenly awakened and found himself in a great and beautiful meadow. There was a beautiful palace of transparent crystal and from it emerged a venerable old man with a long beard, carrying an outsized rosary. He approached DQ, called him by name, and introduced himself as Montesinos. Montesinos confirmed the details of the legend about his removing the heart of his dead cousin

Durandarte, but he did not, as the ballads have it, use a dagger, but a very sharp burnished knife. SP interrupts to speculate that it might have been one of the famous knives made by Ramón de Hoces, but DQ points out that Hoces did not live during the ancient time of the events described by Montesinos. DQ resumes his story: leading DQ into the palace, Montesinos showed him a knight not of marble or alabaster but of flesh and blood lying on a tomb: Durandarte himself, under a spell cast by the great French enchanter Merlin. Montesinos described how he removed the heart, which weighed some two pounds. Durandarte then interrupted his squire's narrative and began to recite several lines of the famous ballad. Montesinos addressed his cousin and explained that when he took out his heart, he wiped it off with a lace handkerchief, put a little salt on it to cut down on the odor, and took it to his beloved Belerma. She, together with Durandarte, Montesinos, his squire Guadiana, the *dueña* Ruidera and her seven daughters and two nieces, and other friends have all been kept under enchantment in this cave for over 500 years. The only ones not present were Guadiana, the daughters, and the nieces, for, on account of their constant crying, the daughters and nieces were converted by Merlin into the lagoons of Ruidera, and likewise, the weeping squire Guadiana was converted into the river that bears his name. Montesinos then announced to Durandarte that, as Merlin had foretold, DQ had just arrived, perhaps to disenchant them. Durandarte said that maybe that might happen, but, if not, 'patience and shuffle the cards.' And with this, he rolled over on his side and did not utter another word. Then DQ noticed a procession of women, dressed in mourning and wearing turbans. The last one, whose turban was twice the size of the others, was not at all attractive (flat nose, large mouth, missing teeth, and the like), and she carried a mummified heart. Montesinos announced that it was Belerma, for she and her attendants made this procession four times a week, adding that the lady's yellowish color was not due to menstruation (which she did not experience during enchantment), but to grief. She really was quite beautiful, perhaps even the

equal of the famous DT herself. DQ reminded him that all comparison is odious, and Montesinos apologized. At this point SP interrupts and, as they talk, informs DQ that he was in the cave a little more than an hour. But DQ insists that that cannot be, as he spent three days and nights underground. They agree that only enchantment can explain the discrepancy. During his subterranean sojourn, DQ says that he did not eat or drink, which confirms SP's understanding about enchantment (recall *DQ* I, 48–49). All very interesting, says SP, but he does not believe a word of it. But DQ offers proof that it was true: while in the enchanted grotto one day, he saw three peasant women who turned out to be DT and her attendants just as DQ and SP had spoken with them near El Toboso. Montesinos said that he did not know who these three women were, for they had suddenly appeared there a few days earlier, but he assumed them to be noble ladies. One of the women came up to DQ and said that DT needed some money and asked if he could lend her some against a skirt of hers. DQ gave her the few coins he had, and the lady, so pleased by this gesture, jumped a good two yards in the air. SP again states his unbelief, but DQ insists that every detail is true.

Chapter 24: The translator notes that CHB was concerned about the events DQ described in the Cave of Montesinos. The historian wrote that he could not believe that what DQ said took place actually happened, but neither could he believe that DQ lied. If the adventure described by DQ seems apocryphal to the reader, it is not the historian's fault, and so, without affirming that it is true or false, he recorded the scene as DQ narrated it. The prudent reader can judge for himself, for the historian can do no more. One thing, though: it is considered certain that some say that on his deathbed, DQ recanted his story and said that he invented it. The cousin thanks DQ for allowing him to accompany the chivalric pair on this trip to the cave, for he has learned several new things that he can use in his books. As they continue on their way, the cousin notes that nearby is a hermitage inhabited by a hermit reputed to be very devout, discreet, and generous. SP wonders if maybe he keeps some chickens. DQ notes that few hermits these days are without them, for modern hermits do not lead lives as austere as the original hermits of ancient Egypt. At this time, a young man carrying some lances and other supplies approaches them. When DQ asks why he is in such a hurry, he replies that what he is carrying is for a specific use the next day, but that he has no time to explain; if they happen to coincide in an inn a short distance down the road, he will explain, and he hurries on. DQ and the others arrive at the hermitage, but the hermit is not in, according to the female sub-hermit who greets them; neither can she offer them any wine, only water. So they leave the hermitage and head on toward the inn. Along the way, they meet a young man, a page, also headed in their direction. He explains that he is trying to catch up with a company of soldiers so that he can enlist in the army. DQ gives a short speech about the superiority of arms over letters, and invites the page to dine with them that evening. After a while, the travelers arrive at the inn, which DQ perceives for what it is, and not a castle.

Chapter 25: As soon as they arrive at the inn, DQ locates the man with the lances, helps him care for his mount, and then they all (DQ, SP, the cousin, the page, and the innkeeper) sit down to listen to the man's story: recently in a nearby town, an alderman's ass disappeared. After a couple of weeks, another alderman of the village told him that he had recently seen a donkey in the mountains. The two men decided to go out looking for the beast, braying from time to time like an ass in order to attempt to attract the animal. But all they succeeded in doing was to deceive each other with their realistic braying. Finally, they found the animal, dead and devoured by wolves. Word of the episode spread, and the authenticity of the aldermen's braying became locally famous. In particular, whenever the people from another nearby town saw anyone from that town, they brayed at them. Tensions between the two towns became so great that they agreed to meet the upcoming day in order to settle their dispute by arms. Just then, a man dressed in chamois leather and wearing an eye patch, accompanied

by a large ape with no tail, arrives and announces a performance of a puppet show about the legendary Melisendra. The innkeeper immediately recognizes him as the famous Maese Pedro, puppeteer and owner of a fabulous divining ape. When someone asks the ape a question, he hops onto his master's shoulder and chatters in his ear; usually he is right in what he says. Maese Pedro warns that the ape does not prognosticate about the future, but he often knows things about the present and the past. Just then, the ape jumps on Maese Pedro's shoulder and says something to him, and immediately the puppeteer drops on his knees and praises the never-sufficiently-praised knight-errant DQ and his famous squire SP. All are amazed at the ape's knowledge, and DQ muses on the nature of such abilities, concluding that it may involve a pact with the devil. At SP's suggestion, DQ asks about the events of the Cave of Montesinos. The reply from the ape via Maese Pedro is that some of what DQ said was true and some not. Then the puppeteer and his assistant set up the apparatus for the puppet show.

Chapter 26: The show begins as the assistant announces that this is the true history, taken from French chronicles and Spanish ballads, of Don Gaiferos and his wife Melisendra, who was being held captive of the Muslims in Sansueña (Zaragoza), Spain. In Paris, the Emperor Charlemagne advises Gaiferos to put an end to his inactivity and take action to rescue his wife. Meanwhile, in Spain, a Muslim sneaks up behind Melisendra and kisses her on the lips, but this insolent act is punished by the Muslim King Marsilio. After an interruption in which DQ and Maese Pedro both criticize the narrator for a digressive comment, the narrator continues, describing the arrival of Gaiferos in Sansueña and his rescue of his wife, in spite of a minor accident when her skirt gets caught while she is descending to his horse, leaving her dangling in the air for a moment. As the two ride off, the narrator gets caught up in the emotion of the moment and makes some exaggerated rhetorical exclamations. DQ again interrupts, advising the assistant to use a more moderate style and then criticizing him for saying that the bells of the city were ringing, because the Muslims did not use bells but kettledrums and reed instruments. Maese Pedro then complains of DQ's nitpicking, and the narrator again takes up the story, describing how the Muslims come out of the city in pursuit of the escaping lovers. At this point, DQ jumps up, takes out his sword, and comes to the defense of Melisendra, attacking the puppets and wrecking the scene. The destruction is complete, and Maese Pedro complains loudly about his losses. DQ, saying that he thought the figures were real people and that he believed he was rescuing a lady in distress, orders SP to pay for the damage. The price is negotiated and SP hands over the money. Very early the next morning, Maese Pedro and his ape leave the inn, the young man with the lances goes on his way, as does the page-soldier, and DQ and SP take leave of the cousin.

Chapter 27: CHB begins by making a curious oath: 'I swear like a Catholic Christian,' which is interpreted by the translator to mean that the Muslim is stressing the truthfulness of his oath. He then goes on to reveal the true identity of Maese Pedro: he is none other than the galley slave Ginés de Pasamonte from I, 22. After the encounters with DQ and SP, he acquired the performing ape from some Christian captives returning from North Africa. The ruse was that before entering a town, he and his assistant would learn some facts about the residents and then, when the trained ape jumped on his shoulder and chattered his teeth, pretend that the beast told him certain things. Meanwhile, DQ and SP set out and head toward the Ebro River. Three days later, they come across a large squadron of armed men, totaling over 200. When they see a standard bearing the figure of an ass with his mouth open and his tongue sticking out, accompanied by two lines of verse about braying magistrates, they realize that these are the men from the village where the braying episode had taken place. DQ speaks to them and delivers a long lecture about the concept of a just war, arguing that people should not take up arms for trivial reasons. SP gets caught up in the spirit of things and, after praising DQ's discourse, displays his own

prowess at braying like an ass. One of the men nearest him takes this as an insult and strikes the squire, knocking him to the ground. DQ begins to attack the man, but, seeing so many armed men against him, turns and flees, fearing at any moment that he will be shot in the back. A safe distance away, he turns and sees SP being helped to mount on his ass and riding out to where he is. Meanwhile, the townspeople wait until that evening and then decide that since their opponents have not come out to meet them, they should return home and declare victory.

Chapter 28: When SP arrives at the place where DQ is waiting for him, it is the knight who speaks first, criticizing his squire's impertinence in braying. A muted and obviously angry SP acknowledges that he was wrong in braying, but accuses DQ of running away and abandoning him. DQ, in an argument previously used by SP (I, 23), distinguishes between running away and retreating; the latter is what he has done, he says, in imitation of many valiant men in history. SP is not convinced and, after the two of them ride along in silence for a while, he suggests that perhaps it is time for him to return home to his family. Anxious not to be abandoned by his squire, DQ tells him to let out his feelings, go back home if he wants to, and if he feels it necessary, pay himself for the time he has been in DQ's service. At the talk of money, SP is less melancholy and remembers some of the salaries he has received at various times in the past. DQ repeats that SP can pay himself from DQ's funds for the 25 days they have been away from home this time. But SP insists that he is due a salary from the very beginning, when DQ first recruited him and promised an island, some 20 years ago, give or take three days. At first, DQ laughs at his squire's exaggeration, but then becomes increasingly angry, and winds up calling SP an ass. SP, having lost the initiative in the discussion, admits that the only thing he lacks to be a complete ass is the tail. After a brief rest, the two continue on toward the Ebro River.

Chapter 29: Two days later, they reach the river and DQ sees a small boat tied to the shore. This immediately reminds him of a typical sort of chivalric adventure: an enchanter leaves a boat for a chosen knight-errant who, when he enters it, is magically transported, perhaps even to a different continent, to the site of an adventure that has been reserved just for him. He and SP set out in the boat, much to SP's displeasure, and after a very short while, DQ is convinced that they have traveled a great distance. SP is not so sure, as he still can see Rocinante and the *rucio* where they left them tied. In order to prove how far they have traveled, DQ has SP search his person for lice, citing the common belief that when you cross the equator the lice on your body die. SP makes the search and finds proof that they have not yet crossed the equator. Then they spot a large water mill of the type that is moored in the center of the river in order to take advantage of the fact that the water runs fastest there. DQ announces that the structure is a city, castle, or fortress where a princess is being held captive, and it was to rescue her that he has been magically transported to this place. SP points out that the building is simply a water mill, but DQ rejects this understanding, maintaining that although it looks like a mill, it is really a castle. The boat begins to pick up speed as it heads toward the millrace, and some of the millers shout a warning and try to help avoid an accident. Seeing the millers, covered in flour dust and looking like specters, DQ takes them to be his enemies, and he stands up in the boat, shouting at them and brandishing his sword. The boat upsets, and the millers have to retrieve DQ and SP from the water. Safe on shore, DQ states that in this adventure there have been two rival enchanters at work, one who left him the boat and another who turned the castle into a water mill. All the world is machinations, he says, and he can do nothing about it. He has SP pay the fishermen for their boat, and then he and SP return to their beasts.

Chapter 30: As they ride quietly away from the Ebro River, SP decides, without saying anything to DQ, that he will abandon his master and return home. But events take an unexpected turn when, the next day, they come across a hunting party in a lush meadow. Prominent in the party is a regal-looking noble lady dressed in green. DQ sends SP to inform the woman that the Knight of the Lions, DQ, awaits to kiss her hands and put himself at her service. SP carries out the commission impeccably, and the lady responds that she will be most happy to receive the Knight of the Mournful Countenance, of whom she has already heard, for she has already read *DQ* I and recognizes DQ and SP immediately. While SP takes this good word back to his master, the lady, a duchess, calls to her husband the duke and informs him of the situation. DQ arrives and has a mishap, falling from his horse as he goes to dismount, but recovers as best he can and greets the duke and duchess. After a very brief conversation, the duke invites the knight and squire to his country house, or castle, which is nearby. As they head for the castle, the duchess insists on having SP ride at her side so that she can enjoy his conversation.

Chapter 31: Word is sent ahead to the country house about how to receive and treat DQ. When they get there, DQ is greeted by cries of welcome and two damsels who place on his shoulders a large red cape (which recalls his description to SP in I, 21, about how knights-errant were to be received at royal courts). This was, it is suggested, the first time DQ felt himself to be a real knight-errant and not a pretend one. Upon arrival, SP asks a senior *dueña* to take care of his ass, and the woman, Doña Rodríguez, is insulted and calls SP names. After being lavishly served by maidens and pages, DQ and SP retire to a room alone, and DQ admonishes his squire to watch what he says, because if he reveals himself to be a gross peasant, the duke and duchess might deduce that DQ is a false knight. They go to dinner with the duke, the duchess, and the house priest, a man described as a grave ecclesiastic. At first, there is a little scene in which the duke offers DQ to sit at the head of the table, but the latter refuses. This reminds SP of a story about a peasant who invited a *hidalgo* to his house and got into the same sort of argument about seating; finally, the *hidalgo* insisted that they all just sit down, for wherever he sits will be the head of the peasant's table. DQ is, of course, humiliated by SP's story. During the dinner-table talk, the ecclesiastic realizes that DQ and SP are the people from the book the duke and duchess have read and laughed at, and pronounces a severe criticism of DQ: he is crazy, should go home to his family and mind his own business, and should stop going about the world becoming a laughing stock of others. DQ rises to respond—but that deserves a chapter in itself.

Chapter 32: DQ's response is measured and restrained. He states that his only motivation has been to do good in the world, rather than to enrich himself. He believes that he has had some successes and hopes to die as a knight-errant. SP is the first to react, praising his master's statements, quoting a string of proverbs, and stating that he hopes to be successful as a governor of an island. At this, the duke says that, in the name of DQ, he will make SP the governor of an extra island that he has. DQ tells SP to express his gratitude for this gesture, which he does. Angry, the ecclesiastic proclaims that the duke and duchess are as mad as DQ, and leaves the room. DQ makes some subtle distinctions between offenses and insults, noting that women, children, and men of the cloth, who cannot defend themselves, can offend, as this priest has done, but cannot insult. At this point, four damsels enter with soap and water and, without saying a word, lather DQ's beard and wash it, but only after leaving the knight sitting there with his beard lathered for some time, as one of them goes for water. The duke was not in on this practical joke, and, in order not to offend DQ too much, asks the women to wash his beard, also, but not to run out of water. SP expresses a desire to have his beard washed also, and goes off with a steward for this purpose. The conversation continues, and DQ explains to the duke and duchess how DT has been enchanted and pessimistically states that eventually the enchanters will obscure his fame. The duchess continues the conversation about DT, doubting her existence, and DQ equivocates somewhat. He goes on to speak of his love for DT and then about SP who, he says, is somewhat mischievous, sometimes doubtful, and sometimes believing; but DQ would not trade him for any other squire in the

world. Just then, SP bursts into the room, followed by some of the kitchen servants who had been trying to lather and clean SP's beard, but using dirty dishwater and towels. SP's resistance is backed up by the duchess, who defends wholeheartedly her new favorite. DQ retires for a siesta, and the duchess invites SP to talk with her and her attendants.

Chapter 33: The duchess has SP sit at her side and tell her about DQ. SP begins by stating unequivocally that DQ is absolutely mad, except when dealing with matters other than chivalry, where he shows great sanity and eloquence. When asked why he accompanies DQ, SP responds that he has no choice: they are from the same village and have broken bread together, SP is very fond of him, DQ has given SP his ass-colts, and above all SP is faithful, and so nothing but death itself can separate them. The conversation turns to the enchantment of DT, and the duchess surprises SP by telling him that she has it on good authority that the peasant women whom SP presented to DQ really were DT and two maidens, and that the one enchanted was SP, not DQ. SP then acknowledges that such must be the case, and that therefore what DQ saw in the Cave of Montesinos may also have been truthful. The conversation continues for a while longer, much to the duchess's enjoyment.

Chapter 34: Six days later, a hunt is arranged for the duke and duchess, DQ, and SP. When a ferocious wild boar approaches, SP is frightened and climbs a tree, but the other three go to meet it. After the boar has been killed, SP is heard crying out, and they see him hanging from the tree, where his clothes have gotten caught (a little like Melisendra in II, 26), while his patient ass waits for him at the foot of the tree. A short while later, night falls and the sound of horns is heard. A devil appears, searching for DQ in order to tell him that he is about to receive information about DT, including the manner in which she is to be disenchanted. Next comes a procession of four carts bearing the figures of famous enchanters: Lirgandeo, Alquife, Arcaláus, and one more to be described in the next chapter.

Chapter 35: The final cart arrives; it is a

triumphal car two or three times larger than the previous ones and is pulled by six mules, each ridden by a penitent bearing a large wax candle. Seated on the cart are two figures. The first is a beautiful young woman with her face covered. The second is a death figure, who stands and proclaims in verse that he is Merlin, that the woman beside him is the enchanted DT, and that the means of disenchanting her is for SP to whip himself 3,300 times. SP immediately refuses to do such a thing, and DQ says he will administer the whipping himself. But Merlin insists that the lashes are to be self-administered and voluntary. SP again refuses to consider such a deed, but the figure of DT rises and speaks to him (in a slightly masculine voice), criticizing his hardness of heart in refusing to aid her in her misery. SP insists, but the duke says that if SP does not accept this responsibility, he will revoke the governorship he has promised him. After getting reassurances that the lashes are to be administered when and where SP chooses, he accepts. There is great celebration, the cart goes on its way, and dawn arrives.

Chapter 36: The duke's majordomo had played the part of Merlin and a page was DT in the previous evening's entertainment. The majordomo is busy preparing another trick to play on the knight and squire. The duchess asks SP if he has begun to administer his lashes, and SP says that he has—with his hand. She responds that works of charity done weakly and in a lukewarm fashion have no merit and are not worth anything. Changing the subject, SP says that he has written (or has dictated, for he cannot write but he does know how to sign his name) a letter to his wife. The duchess reads the letter, in which SP informs Teresa that he has been named a governor, that he takes DQ to be completely mad, and that he hopes to make much money as a governor. The letter is dated June 20, 1614. Then some strange figures arrive—two men dressed in mourning, a fife player, and a tall man wearing a transparent black veil that covers a very long white beard. On his knees before the duke, the man identifies himself as Trifadín of the White Beard, squire to Countess Trifaldi, otherwise known as the

Dueña Dolorida. He has come from the kingdom of Candaya in search of the valorous and undefeated knight-errant DQ; the countess waits outside for word of DQ's presence. The duke responds that DQ is here and that the countess may enter.

Chapter 37: While they await the countess's entrance, SP refers to her as Countess Three-Skirts or Three-Tails and makes a critical comment about *dueñas*. Doña Rodríguez speaks in defense of *dueñas*. The fife player announces the countess's arrival, and there is a brief conversation about who is to receive her, with SP taking an active role in the deliberations.

Chapter 38: The two drummers and the fife player usher in a procession of 12 *dueñas*, followed by Countess Trifaldi, led by the hand by the squire Trifaldín, with the three points of her train held by three pages. Here CHB comments that her name Trifaldi did mean Countess Three-Skirts, but in fact her name was Countess Lobuna, because of the many wolves (*lobos*) in her land; if they had been foxes (*zorros*), she would have been called Countess Zorruna. The countess falls on her knees to address the illustrious group, which she does in a style characterized by comic linguistic exaggeration. Before anyone else can respond, SP answers back with the same style featuring comic superlatives, but even more exaggerated. DQ offers his assistance, and the countess tells her story. She is from the kingdom of Candaya, in the Southern Sea, near Trapobana. The kingdom was ruled by Queen Doña Maguncia, widow of King Archipiela. The queen had one daughter, the Princess Antonomasia, whom Trifaldi raised as befitted her status as highest ranking of the queen's *dueñas*. In her teenage years, Antonomasia fell in love with Don Clavijo, a private gentleman who seduced her and made her pregnant. The countess admits that she had a role in arranging their affair, including the preparation of a written agreement taken before religious authorities in order to authorize the marriage. As she goes on with the details of the story, SP interrupts and urges her to continue rapidly, as he is getting tired of the narration.

Chapter 39: Countess Trifaldi continues:

three days after Queen Maguncia learned that the church had given its blessing to the union between the two lovers, she died. At her burial, the evil enchanter Malambruno, a first cousin of the queen, appeared on a wooden horse, vowing to avenge Maguncia's death and punish Don Clavijo and Antonomasia. He transformed the princess into a brass ape and her lover into a crocodile made of some unknown metal. He also erected a metallic pillar on which it is inscribed that the two can only regain their original forms when the valiant Manchegan faces Malambruno in single combat. Then the evil enchanter assembled all the *dueñas* of the palace and did to them what is now revealed: Trifaldi and the other *dueñas* lift their veils and reveal that all their faces are covered by beards of various colors.

Chapter 40: The narrator opens this chapter with several exclamations in praise of CHB. Resuming her narrative, Countess Trifaldi reveals that Malambruno has sent a marvelous wooden horse named Clavileño the Swift, the very same horse once ridden by the valiant Pierres and the fair Magalona, which Malambruno stole using his magic arts. The animal can be guided by a large peg on its forehead and will magically transport DQ and SP to Candaya. SP wants no part of such a voyage, but is persuaded to undertake the adventure with his master. DQ, of course, is anxious for the adventure to begin.

Chapter 41: That evening, four savages dressed in green ivy bring in the great wooden horse Clavileño. SP is adamant that he will not make the trip on the horse, but the duke intervenes and again threatens to withdraw his offer of an island to govern if SP does not go. SP sees that he has no choice, so both he and DQ put on blindfolds and mount the horse. The ride begins amidst shouts of encouragement from all who are watching (SP wonders how he and DQ can hear their voices if they are flying so high). The horse is jostled about to give the impression of motion, large bellows are used to simulate the wind, and lighted torches create the effect of heat from the sun. After a while, the horse crashes to the ground amidst fireworks from its tail. In the courtyard the duke, the

duchess, and others of their household are lying on the ground in a faint; Countess Trifaldi and her retinue have all disappeared. There is a lance in the ground, with a large parchment on which it is written that simply by the fact of DQ's having undertaken this adventure, it is successfully completed and the enchanted spells are lifted. As SP talks about his heavenly ride, he says that out of curiosity he lifted his blindfold and saw the earth far below. It was no larger than a mustard seed and the people who walked about on it were the size of hazelnuts. He also says that he took a short break when they passed the constellation of the Pleiades, getting down off Clavileño to romp with the seven goats for a short while. DQ and everyone else accuses SP of lying, but he insists on the truth of his tale. DQ takes SP aside and suggests a deal: he will believe SP's story if SP agrees to believe what DQ says he saw in the Cave of Montesinos.

Chapter 42: SP says that after his vision of heaven, he is willing to renounce his governorship—if only the duke would give him a small piece of heaven in its stead. But the duke assures SP that once he has tasted power he will lust after it always, for it is a sweet thing to give orders and be obeyed. DQ and SP go off alone, and the knight congratulates his squire on receiving the reward of a governorship, even if it is before the proper time. He then begins to give SP advice on how to conduct himself as governor. The first two points he makes are 1) fear God, for in fearing Him is all wisdom; and 2) know yourself, which is the most difficult kind of knowledge there is. DQ goes on for a while about various aspects of comportment and relationships with other people.

Chapter 43: The advice continues, covering a wide variety of subjects, from statecraft, dress, and diet to details about burping and trimming your fingernails. SP, appreciative of these lessons, states that if DQ considers him unworthy of the position of governor, he will renounce the commission on the spot. But DQ responds that merely to make such an offer is proof that SP is clearly up to the job.

Chapter 44: Some say that in the original version of his manuscript, CHB complained that the translator did not translate it accurately. Be that as it may, CHB also noted that whereas in *DQ* I he included embedded narratives such as *Curioso* and *Capitán*, he abandoned that practice for *DQ* II. Returning to the story: the next day, SP notes that the face of the duke's majordomo is strikingly like that of Countess Trifaldi, but DQ brushes off this similarity. Finally, SP is prepared to go take possession of his island. He is dressed like a lawyer and rides a mule, but with his ass, also elegantly decked out, following behind. As soon as he is gone, DQ misses him and if he could revoke the governorship and have him back, he would. The duchess notes DQ's sadness and asks why he appears so sad, saying that if it is because he misses SP, the duchess has several *dueñas* and maidens who might be able to help. DQ says that he is not sad because of SP's absence, but for other reasons, and asks to be alone. The duchess offers four maidens to accompany him to his room, but DQ refuses. Alone in his room, and by the meager light of two candles, DQ begins to get undressed. When he removes his shoes, he sees that one of his stockings has so many holes in it that it looks like latticework. At this point, CHB interjects a long exclamation about the nature of poverty. This is what DQ is thinking about when he hears two voices from outside his window. The voices belong to women named Emerencia and Altisidora, and they are discussing the arrival of the knight-errant at the castle and the fact that Altisidora has fallen in love with him. She then sings a long love song to DQ. DQ muses to himself that no matter how many other women might pursue him, he will remain faithful to DT. He closes the window and goes to bed.

Chapter 45: SP arrives at his island and refuses to be called Don SP. He is placed upon a throne of judgment and three cases are brought before him: in the first, he wisely decides a dispute involving a tailor and a client who both attempted to deceive the other; in the second, he sees through a trick of hiding money in a hollow cane; and in the third, he properly adjudicates a rape case in favor of the male defendant. Everyone is amazed at the intelligence

and fairness of the new governor, at whom they had only expected to laugh.

Chapter 46: DQ has difficulty sleeping that night, and the next day Altisidora again pretends to be in love with him. Plans are made for that evening, when DQ intends to respond in song to the previous night's music. He accompanies himself on a kind of early guitar (*vihuela*) as he answers the woman's plea for love, affirming his loyalty to DT. As he finishes his song, a bag containing cats with bells tied to their tails is lowered in front of DQ's window, frightening him with the noise they make. A few of the cats escape and enter his room, and DQ, calling them enchanters, attacks them with his sword. One of the cats jumps on DQ's face and badly bites and claws his nose before the duke pulls it off. DQ, his nose badly wounded, withdraws to bed. The duke and duchess feel remorse that the joke turned out so badly.

Chapter 47: SP is taken to a great banquet hall and seated before a table spread with a great variety of excellent food. But each time he attempts to partake of a dish, it is taken away by order of a physician who is standing at his side. Finally, SP asks for an explanation. The physician identifies himself as Doctor Pedro Recio de Agüero, a native of Tirteafuera, and it is his responsibility to see that the governor eats only healthy food. Angry, SP orders the doctor to leave, under penalty of death. Just then, a page rushes in with a message from the duke: he has received news that some enemies are planning to attack the island one night soon; the governor should be on high alert. Another page enters to announce the presence of a peasant who requests a favor. The man, obviously a decent person, is ushered in and introduces himself as a resident of the town of Miguel Turra. He requests a favor for his son who wants to marry a woman named Clara Perlerina. He describes the intended bride in great grotesque detail as missing one eye, her face all pockmarked, with very few teeth, hunchbacked, and so forth. SP listens carefully and inquires about exactly what the man wants. What he requests is a large amount of money as a dowry for the marriage. SP becomes enraged, calls the man a series of names, and has him thrown out.

Chapter 48: DQ's wounds from the cat keep him from going out in public for six days. One night he hears someone at his door and, fearing it is the enamored maiden, states aloud his loyalty to DT. The door opens and he stands up in his bed, wrapped in the bedclothes. The person who enters is a venerable *dueña* wearing a floor-length veil, carrying a single candle. When she sees DQ standing in his bed, she lets out a scream, drops the candle, and falls to the floor. DQ addresses the strange figure who is in his room, and she responds that she is Doña Rodríguez and that she has come to DQ to ask him to right a wrong. But first, she leaves briefly in order to go for another candle. She returns, and, though he is aware of the compromising circumstances of this midnight visit, escorts her from the door to the bed so that they can talk. CHB notes parenthetically that he would give the better of his two cloaks to see the two of them cross the room hand-in-hand this way. DQ returns to his bed and Doña Rodríguez sits on a nearby chair. She begins her story: she was of a poor family and in her youth worked as a seamstress. She married and had a daughter, but her husband was killed and she was left a widow. The duchess had heard of her good reputation as a seamstress and took Doña Rodríguez into her service. Her daughter grew up and fell in love with the son of a wealthy peasant who lives in a nearby village under the duke's control. Giving a promise of marriage, the young man had sex with the daughter, but since then has refused to keep his word. Doña Rodríguez has repeatedly asked the duke to intervene and restore her daughter's honor by making the youth marry her, but he refuses to do so because the young man's father often lends him money and he does not want to offend the man. And this is why she is here, to request that DQ, as a knight-errant and righter of wrongs, make the youth marry her daughter. Furthermore, DQ should know that Altisidora is brazen, not very good-looking, and has bad breath. Even the duchess is not as she seems, for she has two running sores, one on each leg, to drain off the evil humors that fill her body. At this moment, the door is suddenly opened and Doña Rodríguez, in her fright, drops the

candle, plunging the room into total darkness again. Silently, some figures enter, paddle Doña Rodríguez, and repeatedly pinch DQ, for the space of nearly half an hour. Then the figures leave the room, as does Doña Rodríguez, leaving DQ alone and in pain.

Chapter 49: The next day, SP makes it clear that he expects only good, peasant food for dinner and no meddling by Doctor Recio. He also discusses his philosophy of government, which involves favoring peasants, respecting *hidalgos*, rewarding the virtuous, and honoring religion. As before, all are amazed by his wisdom. After a satisfying dinner that evening, SP and his retinue go out to make the rounds of the island. They come across two men who are fighting with swords over the size of a tip one of them should give the other after his large winnings at a gambling house. SP sentences the winner of the money to give the man a large quantity and to distribute more among the poor, and he sentences the other to take the money given him and leave the island. Next, a man gets out of a jail sentence with his clever use of language. Then they come across a beautiful young woman dressed as a man. She explains, only to SP and the majordomo, that she is the *daughter of Diego de la Llana and that her father has kept her confined to their home for some ten years (she even hears mass at home in a private chapel), and so, frustrated by her lack of familiarity with and experience in the world, she convinced her brother to exchange clothes with her so that she could see the world. The brother, dressed in his sister's clothing, is also then brought before SP. The youths are lectured by the governor and sent home. The steward is very taken by the young woman's looks and decides to ask for her hand in marriage. SP thinks that the brother might make a suitable husband for his daughter Sanchica.

Chapter 50: When Doña Rodríguez left her room at night to go see DQ, another *dueña* who sleeps in the same room with her heard her leave and went to inform the duchess about what was happening. The duchess and Altisidora followed Doña Rodríguez and listened at DQ's door. When the truth about the duchess's running sores was revealed, they were the ones who burst into the room and mistreated Doña Rodríguez and DQ. When the duchess told the duke about this, he received great pleasure. The duchess writes a letter to Teresa Panza and dispatches it with a page (the one who had played the role of DT in the procession of enchanters). The page arrives at the village and reads the letter to Teresa and her daughter. The letter informs Teresa of SP's governorship, includes a string of coral beads, and requests that Teresa send some of the excellent acorns that are reputed to be found in the area of the village. Teresa is very pleased at the news and the respectful letter from a great lady. The priest, the barber, and Sansón Carrasco are made aware of what has happened and discuss the matter among themselves and with Teresa and the page. Contradicting what she had said in II, 5, Teresa now begins to envision a future of wealth and status for herself and her family. Sansón offers to write a return letter for Teresa, but she does not trust him and prefers not to have him involved in her affairs. She gets a young acolyte to write the response for her.

Chapter 51: The day after the rounds of the island, SP has to judge a case, submitted by someone from outside the island, that is a variant of the liar's paradox: anyone who tells a lie will be hanged; a man says that he goes to be hanged. SP decides in favor of sparing the man's life; and again, his wisdom in praised. Then a letter arrives from DQ: it consists of more advice for the governor plus an update of what is happening at the duke's palace. SP writes in response: he has had problems with a physician who has made dining difficult, he is worried about the forthcoming invasion of the island, and he hopes to hear soon from his wife. Then SP promulgates several excellent laws for the island that, to this day, are respected as *The Constitutions of the Great Governor SP*.

Chapter 52: DQ begins to feel that the comfortable life he is leading at the duke's palace is not consistent with his condition as a knight-errant, and he decides to leave in search of new adventures. One day, as he is having dinner with the duke and duchess, two women enter: Doña Rodríguez and her daughter. In an impassioned and (sometimes comically) rhetorical

speech, Doña Rodríguez again appeals to DQ as a knight-errant, asking him to undo the wrong done to her daughter. DQ agrees to help her, saying that he will challenge the young seducer, but the duke intervenes and says that they can consider the challenge accepted, and that he will arrange everything. This is acceptable to everyone. Two letters from Teresa Panza arrive. The first is for the duchess: Teresa thanks the duchess for the gifts and requests that her husband send her some money, for she wants to go to the capital and be seen riding in a coach; she also sends some of the acorns requested by the duchess. The second letter is for SP: she describes her joy at hearing the news that he is a governor, comments on other people's reactions to the news of his governorship, and brings SP up to date on recent events in their village.

Chapter 53: CHB, Mohammedan philosopher, notes that just as it is inevitable that things change and are cyclical—spring follows summer, summer follows fall, and so forth—it was inevitable that SP's governorship should come to an end. On the seventh night of his reign, SP is awakened in the middle of the night by a call to arms: the invasion of the island is underway. SP's aides place him between two large shields and tie them together, making him look like a tortoise, as the "battle" begins. There is much noise, shouting, and running back and forth. SP is knocked down and trampled by the participants in the battle. Victory is declared, SP is helped to his feet, and he is released from the shields. It becomes clear to everyone involved that the trick was excessive and that poor SP had been mistreated. The governor slowly and quietly dresses himself and goes to the stable, where he embraces his *rucio*, with tears in his eyes. Addressing the majordomo, the secretary, the steward, Dr. Pedro Recio, and others assembled there, SP announces that he is resigning his governorship and returning to his former freedom. Taking only a bit of bread and cheese, SP embraces everyone and departs, leaving them all with admiration for what he had been and done.

Chapter 54: The duke has no intention of calling to task the young man who deceived

Doña Rodríguez's daughter, in part because the youth has gone to Flanders to escape having to face such a future mother-in-law. In his place, the duke decides to place one of his lackeys, named Tosilos, to enter into combat against DQ. Meanwhile, when he leaves his island, SP has a chance encounter with some foreign pilgrims and joins them for food and wine (the pilgrims rather ostentatiously display ham and wine, clear "proof" that they are neither Jewish nor Muslim). By chance, one of the group is a former neighbor of SP's, a *Morisco* named Ricote. Ricote explains that after the decree expelling *Moriscos* from Spain, he left the country. The king and his counselors were wise, he says, to rid the nation of all *Moriscos*, because even though some were true Christians, the majority conspired against the collective interests of the nation. Before Ricote departed, he buried his treasure, and, leaving behind his wife and daughter, he went to France, Italy, and then Germany, a nation he praises for its religious freedom. He is now traveling incognito in Spain in order to recover his buried treasure and learn something of the whereabouts of his wife, Francisca Ricota, and daughter, Ricota, who, he knows, went to Algiers. He then offers SP some 200 *escudos* if he helps recover the buried treasure, an offer that SP refuses because such an act would be tantamount to giving aid to an enemy of the state. The two talk a little while longer, SP explaining how he became a governor and why he gave up that position, and then they go their separate ways.

Chapter 55: Heading home at night, SP and his ass fall into a deep pit or hole in the ground. He explores the space, but there is no way to get out. The next day, DQ rides out to begin to prepare for his upcoming battle in defense of the honor of the daughter of Doña Rodríguez, and comes across the pit from which SP calls out for help. At first DQ is not sure that it is his squire, but SP proves his identity by braying like an ass. DQ returns to the duke's castle, brings help, and SP is rescued. SP talks briefly about his accomplishments as a governor and why he resigned the post.

Chapter 56: The stage is set for the contest between Tosilos, acting as the deceiver of Doña Rodríguez's daughter, and DQ. The duke carefully instructs his lackey on how to defeat DQ without hurting him. As the two combatants face off and are about to begin, the little blind god, Cupid, takes advantage of the opportunity to win a lackey's soul and shoots him through the heart with an arrow. Tosilos looks at the young woman in question and thinks that she is perhaps the most beautiful person he has seen—and here he is supposedly fighting in order not to have to marry her. Rather than charge DQ, Tosilos halts the proceedings and announces that he admits defeat and is willing to marry the woman. There is great rejoicing until he removes his helmet and Doña Rodríguez and her daughter can see that he is not the real seducer but the lackey Tosilos. DQ assures them, however, that it must be the work of enchanters who wanted to deprive him of a great victory, but that this man will turn out to be the real person he is supposed to be. The duke, however, decides that any marriage should be postponed for two weeks while they wait to see if the man recovers his original form, and in the meantime he should be kept under watch. The daughter decides that she would rather be the honest wife of a lackey than the spurned lover of a nobleman. DQ is awarded the victory, Tosilos is locked up, and mother and daughter are content with the situation.

Chapter 57: DQ decides to leave the castle and return to his life as a knight-errant. The majordomo gives SP 200 gold *escudos*. As they take their leave of the duke and duchess, Altisidora appears and, in song, accuses DQ of having stolen three kerchiefs and two garters. DQ turns to SP and asks if he has them, and SP admits to having the kerchiefs but not the garters. The duke commands DQ to return the stolen goods or face him in single combat, with no fear that enchanters will change him into someone else. DQ absolutely refuses to take arms against a man who has hosted him so generously. Just then, Altisidora remembers that she is wearing the garters, which averts any further conflict between DQ and the duke. With that, DQ and SP leave and head for Zaragoza.

Chapter 58: Upon leaving the duke's palace, DQ observes to SP that freedom is one of the most precious gifts that God has given to mankind. Soon they come across about a dozen men with some wooden figures intended for a church altarpiece. DQ and SP uncover and look at the figures, with DQ commenting on each one. The first is Saint George, depicted characteristically slaying a dragon. DQ notes that he was one of the greatest of divine knights-errant. Next is Saint Martin, sharing his cape with an unclothed man. DQ notes that he, too, was one of Christendom's greatest knights and that since he is sharing his cape it must be a winter scene, for if it were summer he would give it outright to the poor man. SP's comment is to cite the proverb that states that you have to be smart to both give and retain something. Third is the chivalric figure of San Diego Matamoros, Saint James the Moorslayer, patron saint of Spain. The last figure is that of Saint Paul, depicted in the scene when he falls from his horse and has his vision of God. This peaceful disciple and spreader of the word of God receives the highest praise from DQ. DQ then contrasts the fact that these great men conquered heaven by force of arms, while he does not know what, if anything, he has achieved. SP asks what the phrase 'Saint James and close in, Spain' means, and DQ explains that it was the slogan used by Christian knights in combat against the Muslims and that Santiago often appeared in person to lead the Christian forces during their ongoing war, slaying right and left and trampling the enemy under the hoofs of his horse. DQ and SP go on their way, but soon DQ finds himself entangled in a web of green netting. Two beautiful young women, dressed as shepherdesses, emerge from the trees and explain the netting to DQ. It is part of an Arcadian setting that they and some friends have set up as a celebration of the pastoral poetry of Garcilaso de la Vega and the Portuguese poet Camões. DQ visits the setting, makes a brief address to those who are participating in the event, and then goes off to stand as a protective guard on the nearby road. Although no one is present, DQ announces aloud his purpose in standing there. But soon after this, a group of men with a herd of bulls approaches, and DQ, SP, Rocinante, and the *rucio* are all trampled

by the bulls. After DQ shouts a few ineffective threats at the departing herders, he and SP go on their way without taking leave of the shepherds of the new Arcadia.

Chapter 59: DQ's dejection and pessimism are obvious, and he observes to SP that although he is famous, has a book written about him, and is solicited by young women, at a time in his life when he should be receiving recognition and reward, he finds himself trampled by lowly bulls; perhaps, he suggests, he should simply let himself die of hunger. SP chastises him, saying that desperation and the contemplation of suicide are the supreme madness. DQ suggests that this might be a good time for SP to give himself a few hundred of the 3,300 lashes required to disenchant DT, but SP is not willing to start that task at this time. The next day they arrive at an inn (not a castle for DQ), and SP and the innkeeper engage in a comic conversation about what there is to eat. DQ overhears two men talking in the next room, and one of them mentions the newly published *DQA*. DQ enters, introduces himself, picks up the book, and looks through it. He finds three things worthy of criticism:

1. Some of the things said by the author in the prologue
2. That the language is Aragonese
3. That the author is mistaken about the name of SP's wife, referring to her as Mari Gutiérrez rather than her real name of Teresa Panza

In the discussion that follows, the two men, whose names are Don Juan and Don Jerónimo, describe features of the new book, compare the presentation of DQ and SP in the text and in real life (in the book, DQ no longer loves DT and SP is stupid and a glutton), and inquire about recent adventures. When they inform DQ that in the book he goes to Zaragoza, DQ decides on the spot not to go to that city, which will prove the lack of historicity of the new text. At the suggestion of Don Jerónimo, DQ decides to go to Barcelona for the jousts celebrated there. Don Juan and Don Jerónimo are amazed at the difference between the real DQ and the one presented in the book. SP pays the innkeeper, and he and DQ go on their way.

Chapter 60: DQ and SP travel for six days without anything of note happening to them. One night, as they rest among some trees, DQ is worried about the fact that SP has done nothing to bring about the disenchantment of DT and decides to take matters into his own hands, administering the required lashes himself. DQ attempts to strip his squire to ready him for the whipping, but SP defends himself and the two get into a fight. SP gets the better of his master, knocks him to the ground, and pins him there. When DQ accuses him of laying hand on his master, SP affirms that he is his own master. After DQ promises not to touch him again, SP wanders off into the woods, only to feel something hanging from the trees—human feet, connected to legs and bodies. Frightened, he calls to DQ, who comes to his rescue and immediately realizes what has happened. There are several men who have been hanged in these trees; they are, as DQ suspects, some of the famous Catalan bandits who are known to operate in that region. And just then, some 40 bandits arrive on horseback, take DQ and SP captive, and begin to relieve them of their money and possessions. They are soon joined by their captain, the famous Roque Guinart, a robust man in his mid-thirties. DQ recognizes Roque's name, praises him for his fame, and introduces himself. Roque has heard of DQ and recognizes his madness, and he orders his men not to take anything from him. But just as the two begin to talk, a young man arrives hurriedly on horseback and speaks to Roque. It is, however, not a man, but a woman dressed as one, and her name is Claudia Jerónima, daughter of Simón Forte, a friend of the bandit's. She tells her story: she fell in love with Vicente Torrellas, son of an enemy of her father's, and surrendered her honor to him under the promise of marriage. The previous day she learned that Vicente was about to marry another woman, so she dressed as a man, followed him on horseback, and, as soon as she saw him, shot him with a shotgun and two pistols. She has come to Roque for assistance in taking her safely to France. DQ offers his help, but he is

ignored. Roque leaves immediately with Claudia and the two of them arrive at the spot where she shot Vicente. The young man is badly wounded, and before he dies has just enough time to explain that he was not marrying someone else, that he loved only Claudia. Even Roque Guinart is moved to tears by this development. Claudia decides that she will retire to a monastery and take the veil, a decision that Roque applauds. Roque returns to where his men, and DQ and SP, were left. DQ suggests that Roque leave the life of a bandit and become a knight-errant, but Roque only laughs at this suggestion. Some of his men arrive with some captives: two noble infantry captains on horseback who are on their way to Barcelona in order to embark for Italy; two pilgrims on foot on their way to Rome; a coach filled with women, the most important of whom is Doña Guiomar, wife of the chief justice of the ecclesiastical court of Naples, and who is accompanied by her young daughter, a maid, a *dueña*, and some servants. Rather than rob them of everything they have, Roque takes only a small amount of their money and sends them on their way. One of his men grumbles about the generosity of the bandit leader, and Roque immediately takes his sword and kills the man. Before DQ and SP depart, Roque sends a messenger to a friend of his in Barcelona in order to inform him that the knight and squire will arrive in a few days.

Chapter 61: DQ and SP spend three exciting days and nights with the bandits. Then Roque and six of his men accompany them to Barcelona, where they arrive on Saint John's Eve, and both DQ and SP see the ocean for the first time. A man arrives and greets them as the authentic DQ and SP, the ones written about by CHB, and not the characters of the false sequel. The man leads them into the city, and, as they pass through the streets, some young boys place thorny furze under the tails of Rocinante and the *rucio*, causing them to buck and toss their riders to the ground. Finally, they arrive at the large, sumptuous home of a nobleman.

Chapter 62: DQ's host is Don Antonio Moreno, a wealthy nobleman who enjoys having fun. He announces that he has a marvelous bronze head that can answer questions put to it, and then takes DQ out to see the city, placing a sign on his back identifying him so that others can also laugh at the knight; DQ believes that it is his fame that brings all the recognition he receives. At one point a man from Castile stops DQ and harangues him, telling him to go home, mind his own business, and not make such a public fool of himself. That evening, Don Antonio's wife invites friends in for a dance. Two women take turns dancing with DQ until he is exhausted and sits down in the middle of the dance floor. The next day, with several friends of Don Antonio and his wife, DQ and SP get to put questions to the talking head. DQ, of course, asks about what happened to him in the Cave of Montesinos and whether DT will be disenchanted. SP asks if he will return home and if he will have another governorship. The head, like the divining ape of Maese Pedro, answers equivocally. The narrator explains how the trick with the head was done: the figure was hollow and had a hollow tube leading to another room where a nephew of Don Antonio's could hear the questions and answer in response through the head. Don Antonio had informed the Inquisition of the device even before it was displayed, and shortly afterward he is ordered to dismantle it. DQ wants to take another walk through the city, and this time visits a print shop where books are made. DQ talks with some of the workmen about their crafts. One of the books being printed is a translation from Italian, and DQ comments on it and observes that reading a translation is like looking at a great Flemish tapestry, but from the back side: the figures can be made out, but with none of the detail of the front. Another book is a devotional entitled *Light of the Soul*, which DQ praises as the type of book that should be printed and read more frequently. Finally, a new printing of *DQA* is being made, and he notes that this book will have its comeuppance.

Chapter 63: The next day, Don Antonio Moreno takes DQ and SP to visit a galley commanded by his friend. The commandant receives his guests with great honor, but then, according to a previously arranged plan, SP is lifted into the air and passed from hand to hand along one side of the rowers and back along the other. Suddenly, there is great noise and commotion, as it is discovered that a foreign vessel has been sighted off shore. Chase is given, and the galley catches up with what turns out to be an Algerian pirate ship. Two Turks open fire, killing two Spanish soldiers, but the galley closes in and captures the enemy ship, taking the enemy captain, a youth of about 20, and crew as prisoners. The viceroy joins the admiral aboard the ship in order to decide what to do with the captives. To everyone's surprise, the captive captain's identity is revealed: not a Muslim or a Turk, but a Christian woman dressed as a man. She explains: born of *Morisco* parents, she left Spain with an aunt and uncle after the expulsion of her people and went to North Africa. A young Christian man, named Don Gaspar Gregorio, who was in love with her, accompanied her. Her father had left a large amount of money and jewels buried in their hometown. After a complicated series of events, Don Gaspar remained in North Africa, dressed as a woman (in order to avoid being sexually abused in a culture that values beautiful young men more than women), while she came back to Spain in order to retrieve her family's wealth. She is resigned to her fate, and is prepared to die as a Christian. Just then, a man in the crowd speaks up, calling her by name—Ana Félix—and identifying himself as her father, Ricote (SP's neighbor and friend from II, 54). He has retrieved his buried treasure and now pleads for clemency for his daughter. SP verifies the identities of Ricote and Ana Félix. The admiral agrees to spare her, but wants to hang the two Turks who killed two of his men, but the viceroy also pardons them. A plan is devised by which a renegade in Ana Félix's crew is to return to North Africa to retrieve Don Gaspar; Ricote is to finance the expedition and pay for the ransom, if necessary, of the young man.

Chapter 64: Don Antonio's wife is pleased to have Ana Félix in her home, and plans are made to rescue Don Gregorio. One day DQ rides out onto the beach, dressed in full armor. He is approached by another knight-errant, dressed in white armor and bearing a shield adorned with a shining moon. He identifies himself as the Knight of the White Moon; challenges DQ by stating that his lady, whoever she may be, is more beautiful than DT; and states that if he is victorious, DQ will have to return home and not practice chivalry for one year. News of this event spreads rapidly through the city, and the viceroy, Don Antonio, and others assemble to see what will happen. The two knights meet and DQ is unhorsed. His adversary points his lance at the fallen knight and states that he will kill him if he does not admit to the conditions of the combat. DQ, without raising his visor and speaking as if from within a tomb, says that DT is the most beautiful woman in the world and he the most unfortunate knight-errant, since he was unable to defend this truth. He invites his opponent to kill him, since he has taken from him his honor. The Knight of the White Moon refuses to kill DQ, insisting only that he retire for a year. Then, acknowledging the viceroy, he rides off into the city. SP is distraught, seeing his master defeated and his own hopes vanished.

Chapter 65: Don Antonio follows and talks with the Knight of the White Moon: it is Sansón Carrasco, who explains that he feels great pity for DQ and has carried out this masquerade in order to help him regain his sanity. Don Antonio is disappointed that Sansón has deprived the world of the joy of laughing at the mad DQ. Sansón rides off, and Don Antonio informs the viceroy of what he has learned. DQ is bedridden and melancholy for six days, during which time SP talks with him and tries to cheer him up. The expedition to Algiers returns with Don Gregorio, who is reunited with Ana Félix. Don Antonio says that, since he must go to Madrid on business matters, while he is there he will attempt to have an exception made (a bribe might also help) to the extradition of the *Moriscos* so that Ricote and his family can remain in Spain. But Ricote says that a man as principled as Don Bernardino de Velasco, who is in charge of the *Morisco* issue, cannot be bribed. In spite of the personal hardship it has caused him, Ricote again praises the heroic resolution of King Felipe III to banish the *Moriscos*. Still, Don Antonio says that he will see

what he can do while he is in Madrid. It is also agreed that Don Gregorio should accompany Don Antonio and visit his parents to assure them of his well-being; in the meanwhile, Ana Félix remains with Don Antonio's wife and her father Ricote stays in the viceroy's home. Don Antonio and Don Gregorio depart and, two days later, DQ and SP leave Barcelona.

Chapter 66: Upon leaving Barcelona, DQ remarks that this is where his fortune fell, never to rise again. SP reminds him that fortune is supposed to be blind, and he who is down one day may be up the next. But DQ insists that in reality things do not happen by sheer chance but by divine providence and that we all make our own fortune; certainly he has determined his own destiny, paying for his presumption and the weakness of Rocinante. They continue to talk as they pursue their journey home. Five days later, they come across a large group of people outside an inn, one of whom suggests asking these two travelers to decide a wager for them. The problem is that two men, one fat and one thin, are to race. But the fat man insists that the thin man be made to carry a heavy weight so that they will be more equal. SP speaks up and, calling upon his experience as a governor and a judge, proposes that the fat man be made to cut off enough weight to make the two men equal. DQ and SP go on their way, and the villagers comment that if the servant is so smart, imagine what the wisdom of the master must be. That night, as they rest, a courier carrying some mail approaches them and addresses DQ by name. DQ does not recognize the man, but it is Tosilos, the lackey of the duke who refused to fight with DQ in hopes of marrying the daughter of Doña Rodríguez. Tosilos goes on to say that after DQ left the castle, the duke gave him 100 lashes for his disobedience and prevented him from marrying Doña Rodríguez's daughter. In fact, the young woman has taken the veil, Doña Rodríguez has left the duke's employ and returned to Castile, and Tosilos is currently acting as courier, taking some mail from the duke to the viceroy in Barcelona. SP and Tosilos share some food and wine before they all go on their way.

Chapter 67: DQ is dejected and pensive,

worried about the disenchantment of DT, and he again tries, unsuccessfully, to convince SP to begin his lashes. When they reach the same place where they had met the women of the feigned Arcadia, the conversation turns to pastoral themes. DQ gets the idea that during the year he is forbidden to engage in chivalric activities they can instead become shepherds. DQ can call himself Quijotiz and SP can be Pancino; they can go out into the hills and forest, playing musical instruments, writing poetry, and lamenting unrequited love. They can even get their friends involved: Sansón can be Sansonino or Carrascón, the barber, Miculoso, and the priest, Curiambro. SP suggests that even his wife can participate, calling herself Teresona, a name that would also reflect her size. As the conversation continues, DQ lectures SP on Arabic words in Spanish, especially those beginning with *al-*. Finally, SP talks about his natural propensity to speak in proverbs.

Chapter 68: That night, as they continue their conversation, DQ and SP hear a strange noise. Before they can move out of the way, they are trampled by a herd of some 600 pigs. SP is offended and wants to take revenge, but a dejected DQ restrains him, seeing this indignity as a proper punishment from heaven. The next day, they suddenly find themselves surrounded by a group of armed men who call them a series of insulting names and then lead them off in silence to the duke's castle.

Chapter 69: DQ and SP are led into a patio in which two figures like kings or judges are seated on thrones and there is a bier on which there lies the dead body of a beautiful young woman holding the palm branch of virginity. Then the duke and duchess, along with several other people, enter and take seats; DQ recognizes that the body is that of Altisidora. An elaborate ceremony is begun, and an official places a cape and pointed hat, reminiscent of the way criminals of the Inquisition are dressed, on SP and warns the squire not to speak. Then the two figures of authority identify themselves as Minos and Rhadamanthys, judges of the underworld. They reveal that for the deceased Altisidora to be restored to life, SP must be smacked, pinched, and jabbed with pins. SP of course refuses to participate, but he is forced to undergo these indignities. Altisidora immediately comes to life, amidst great cries of joy. In reward, she promises to give SP several articles of clothing.

Chapter 70: Before going to sleep that night, DQ and SP discuss the strange events concerning Altisidora. CHB explains how Sansón Carrasco has stopped at the duke's palace and informed them about what he had done in Barcelona and that DQ and SP would be returning home. Desirous of enjoying themselves more with the knight and squire, the duke and duchess sent out the men to make DQ and SP return to their place and set up the farce involving Altisidora. CHB also adds that he considers those who make fun of two madmen to be as mad as the people they are making fun of. The next day, at SP's prompting, Altisidora describes some of what she saw in hell. There were several devils playing tennis, but using a book instead of a ball. The book was *DQA*, and one of the devils remarked that the book is so bad that he himself could not have written one worse. Altisidora again repeats her love for DQ, but the knight steadfastly reiterates his complete devotion to DT. Altisidora, angry at being rejected, abandons the charade and tells DQ that everything was staged, she really did not die of love, and she would never fall for someone like him. SP interjects the opinion that he never did believe that anyone could die of love. After a brief exchange between DQ and the musician from the previous evening, and some further conversation with Altisidora and the duchess, DQ and SP depart and head for home.

Chapter 71: Desperate to see SP complete his task of disenchanting DT, DQ offers to pay him for each lash he gives himself. Now SP is indeed interested in doing his job, and they negotiate a price. SP goes off into the woods to begin the assignment, but after just six or eight lashes he decides that the price is too low. When he complains, DQ doubles the price. And so SP sets himself to the task, but instead of whipping himself, he delivers furious blows to the nearby trees, stripping the bark from some of them; that day he makes good progress in reducing the number of lashes to be given. That evening they stop at an inn, which DQ sees for what it is, because since his defeat he displays much sounder judgment in all matters. In the inn, there are several scenes from classical mythology painted on the walls, and SP offers the opinion that it will not be long before there is hardly a tavern, inn, or barber shop where the adventures of DQ and SP are not represented. DQ responds by telling again (as he had in II, 3) the anecdote of Orbaneja, the painter from Ubeda, who had to identify in writing what he painted, because no one could know just from looking at it.

Chapter 72: DQ hears another guest in the inn referred to by the name of Alvaro Tarfe, and he recognizes this as the name of a character in *DQA*. The two men strike up a conversation and Tarfe confirms that he spent time with DQA, accompanying him to Zaragoza and having a series of adventures with him. In a short time, DQ convinces Tarfe that he is the real DQ and not the person Tarfe knew under that name. Tarfe concludes that the enchanters who pursue DQ must also have made him believe that he was with the real knight when he was in fact with an imposter; he affirms that he has not seen what he has seen nor has he done what he has done while in the company of the other person calling himself DQ. Finally, with the mayor of the town as a witness, Tarfe signs an affidavit confirming that DQ and SP are the real people by that name, and not the ones with whom he spent time previously. That day and night, DQ and SP travel without anything worthy of note happening to them—except for the fact that SP completes the disenchantment of DT. At the top of a hill overlooking their hometown, SP falls to his knees and asks the town to receive its son SP, not very wealthy but well whipped, and her other son DQ, who comes home the victor over himself. DQ tells him to stop the foolishness, and they descend into their village.

Chapter 73: As DQ and SP enter the village, they hear some boys playing, and one says to another 'You will never see it (*la*) again,' which DQ interprets as a prophetic 'You will never see her (*la*, referring to DT) again.' Just then, also, a fleeing rabbit hides under the legs

of SP's *rucio*, and DQ takes that as another sign that DT is escaping him. But SP catches the rabbit and hands it to DQ (who then gives it to the hunters who have been chasing it) as a symbol that he delivers DT to him. SP also asks the boys what they were talking about and they explain that the reference was to a cricket cage, and SP explains this to DQ. The priest and barber greet the returning pair and, as they pass through town, children gather and comment on the ass of SP and the skinny beast of DQ (double meanings intended). SP is greeted by his wife, who asks if he brings money, but SP responds that he brings things of greater value than that. DQ explains to the priest, barber, and Sansón Carrasco about his defeat and his decision to become a shepherd. They take readily to the latter idea, especially Sansón, who suggests new pastoral names they might assume. DQ then tells his housekeeper and niece that he is not feeling well and wants to go to bed.

Chapter 74: DQ begins to run a fever and spends six days in bed, during which time he is visited by his friends, especially SP, who hardly leaves his side. They all talk about the life of shepherds they are going to lead, and Sansón Carrasco even mentions a friend from whom they can purchase a pair of dogs to guard the sheep. One day, after a six-hour sleep, DQ awakens and in a loud voice praises God. He tells his niece, the only one present at the time, that he has recovered his sanity and now despises the romances of chivalry; he is only sorry that such disillusionment has come so late and that he has no time to read books that might be a light of his soul, for he fears that he is dying. He requests that she call his friends the priest, the bachelor Sansón Carrasco, and the barber, as he wants to confess and make his will. When the three friends arrive, DQ announces that he is no longer DQ, but Alonso Quijano the Good. He is now the enemy of Amadís de Gaula and other knights-errant; he recognizes his error and, by the grace of God, hates such books. Sansón, addressing him as DQ (rather than as Alonso Quijano), says he should come to his senses and talk logically. DQ insists that he is dying, wants to stop fooling around, and requests to see a notary, so that he can make his will. The priest remains alone with DQ and confesses him, while Sansón goes for a notary, soon returning with one and with SP. The priest emerges to tell the others that DQ is truly sane and is truly dying. SP, the niece, and the housekeeper all shed copious tears, for throughout his life, whether as DQ or as Alonso Quijano the Good, he was always a gentle and kindly man, well loved by all who knew him. DQ begins to make his will, and the first item is for certain moneys to go to SP, to whom he turns to beg pardon for the occasion he has given him to be as mad as he himself was. The tearful SP tells DQ not to die, to take his advice and continue living, for the greatest madness any man can have is to let himself die without being killed. He suggests that DQ get out of bed and that they go out to the fields as shepherds, for surely he realizes that in the romances of chivalry the knight who is defeated one day will be victorious the next. But DQ is adamant: there are no birds this year in the nests of yesteryear; he was DQ, but he is now Alonso Quijano the Good. He continues with his will, leaving most of his estate to his niece Antonia Quijana (the first time her name has been mentioned), but only on the condition that she never marry a man who has read romances of chivalry. The whole household is quite upset, but life continues for the living, and inheriting something tempers somewhat the feeling of loss. Finally, the end arrives, and DQ surrenders his soul, that is, he dies. Sansón Carrasco composes a comic epitaph for DQ. CHB turns to his pen and hangs it up, advising it that should someone else take it to write a sequel to DQ, the pen should say that DQ was born for it alone and that no other writer should attempt to continue the story of DQ. *Vale.*

Don Quijote de la Manchísima. Comic and ungrammatical exaggeration (the-*ísimo* ending can only be used with adjectives, not with nouns) of DQ's name used by the Countess Trifaldi in her appeal for help in *DQ* II, 38.

Don Quijote el bueno. *Don Quixote the Good.

Don Quixote. An anonymous late-eighteenth-century musical performed at the Theater Royal in Covent Garden. The only scene from *DQ* that is directly involved is DQ's standing vigil over his arms in the courtyard, from *DQ* I, 3. SP, meanwhile, is anxious to be dubbed a knight-errant. Most of the work involves Teresa and Maritornes as wand-wielding fairies, controlling the action of DQ and SP.

Don Quixote and Christ. In some of the most romantic readings of *DQ*, the protagonist is considered a Christ figure. Soren Kierkegaard was the first to explicitly compare DQ to Christ; Turgenev did the same in his essay on DQ and Hamlet; Unamuno calls DQ 'Our Lord DQ' and 'Saint Quixote of La Mancha'; and poet W. H. Auden makes a similar comparison. Novelist A. J. Langguth makes the same point, calling attention to the physical similarity between the two figures in popular depictions. There is, of course, very little or no textual basis for the comparison. But Eric Ziolkowski proposes that in the modern world, to be truly Christian in the sense of being Christlike is by definition to appear to be (or actually to be) quixotic. To the extent that this proposition is accurate, the DQ-Christ fusion is a legitimate concern. Certainly a fair number of modern novelists have made the comparison, the most obvious case being that of Fyodor Dostoevsky, who based his figure Prince Myshkin in *The Idiot* consciously and explicitly on Christ and DQ.

Bibliography: Eric J. Ziolkowski, *The Sanctification of Don Quixote: From Hidalgo to Priest* (University Park: Pennsylvania State University Press, 1991).

Don Quixote and psychology. The works of MC played an interesting role in the formation of Sigmund *Freud's psychoanalytic theories. But, in addition to that, there are some interesting links between the figure of DQ and some modern approaches to cognitive psychology. In fact, there are aspects of quixotism that appear to be part of the universal character of the human species. Theodore Sarbin was one of the first to employ the equivalent of Harry Levin's "Quixotic Principle" (*quixotic novel) as an organizing theme for psychology: "It is clear that the reading of literary works can serve as an antecedent condition for the enactment of roles based on involvement in one's imaginings. Cervantes provides the paradigm case." For Sarbin, this is a common occurrence, always involving "(a) the phenomenology of book reading, and (b) the discovery of empirical correlates." Perhaps one of the main reasons why the character of DQ has had such resonance with people in all cultures, historical periods, and languages is that the basic premise of the novel is an integral part of the human condition. "In a word," concludes Sarbin, "one may find solutions to life's problems by adopting a fictive perspective other than the perspectives of everyday life." More recently, psychiatrist and biographer Jay Martin has continued this line of thought by defining the "fictive personality" as "the disease that so disturbed the man who became known as Don Quixote de la Mancha that he replaced his own personality with the fictions that he derived from extensive readings in the tales of chivalric romance. He lost or suspended his own unsatisfactory self and replaced it with the characters, thoughts, feelings, and actions created by others. Something splendid, as well as something frightening, happened to him as a result." Though Martin finds examples of the fictive personality throughout literature and history, he considers the first "full portrait" as "given in one of the world's enduring literary characters, Don Quixote. In this outstanding character Cervantes gives us a remarkable, full exhibition of the fictive personality, and he helps thereby to enlarge our sense of the way fictions become imbedded. In its most general sense, the theme of the book is the confusion between illusion or fantasy and reality." Interestingly, the French semiotician Roland Barthes seems to agree. According to Barthes, one of the "pleasures of the text" is "derived from a way of imagining oneself as individual, of inventing a final, rarest fiction: the fictive identity. This fiction is no longer the illusion of a unity; on the contrary, it is the theater of society in which we stage our plural." Barthes, like Sarbin and Jay, is simultaneously describing a crucial aspect of the reading process and a universal feature of human psychology. *DQ* is the first work of fiction in which this process is described, which may be part of the reason for its universal appeal: we are all DQs.

Bibliography: Roland Barthes, *The Pleasure of the Text*, trans. Richard Miller (New York: Hill and Wang, 1975); Helene Deutsch, "Don Quixote and Don Quixotism," in *Neuroses and Character Types* (New York: International University Press, 1965), 218–25; Jay Martin, *Who Am I This Time? Uncovering the Fictive Personality* (New York: W. W. Norton, 1988); and Theodore Sarbin, "The Quixotic Principle: A Belletristic Approach to the Psychological Study of Imaginings and Believings," in *The Social Context of Conduct: Psychological Writings of Theodore Sarbin*, ed. Vernon L. Allen and Karl E. Scheibe (New York: Praeger, 1982), 169–86.

Don Quixote de la Mancha. Protagonist of *DQ* I and *DQ* II. See entries throughout this encyclopedia for details about this character.

Don Quixote in art. *Iconography of Don Quixote.

Don Quixote miscellany. There has to be a catchall category for "everything else" relating to DQ in popular culture through the years. DQ has spawned an industry to a degree that no other literary character even remotely approaches; DQ's image is more universally recognized—even among millions who have never read the book—than that of any other literary character ever created (but, alas, probably not as much as Disney cartoon figures), far more than, say, Sherlock Holmes, who may come in a very distant second. Tall, thin DQ; short, fat SP; the skinny nag Rocinante; the windmills; and Mambrino's helmet—individually most of the time and always when two of them are paired—have been a part of popular culture from the very first months following the publication of *DQ* I. DQ as a cultural phenomenon far exceeds the book (*Don Quixote myth). Not just the thousands of novels, stories, plays, operas, songs, poems, films, cartoons, comic strips, paintings, engravings, drawings, ceramic and porcelain tiles, sculptures, statues, and monuments based on *DQ*; but also dolls, puppets, toy figures, computer games, board games, playing cards, cutouts, and trading cards; restaurants, bars, hotels, cafeterias, and miscellaneous other commercial establishments; labels on cheeses, quince, and wines from La Mancha, as well as specific brands of anise liquor, rum, chocolate, and Cuban cigars; figurines and statuettes made of wood, nuts and bolts, wire, plastic, glass, straw, papier-mâché, ceramic, and porcelain; keychains, coffee mugs, children's place settings, fans, matchboxes, and ashtrays; tickets for trolley, bus, sporting events, and theater; T-shirts, sweatshirts, dress shirts, neckties, skirts, and fans; tapestries, embroideries, needlepoint, brocades, curtains, bedspreads, sheets, pillowcases, and wallpaper; mousepads and place mats; bottle openers and corkscrews; bookends, bookmarks, and bookplates; postcards, greeting cards, calendars, stationary, notepads, paperweights, medals, medallions, pins, stamps, coins, bank notes, and cigar bands; political posters, propaganda, and leaflets; newspapers, magazines, and scholarly journals; and much more.

Bibliography: Juan and Gaziel Givanel Mas *Historia gráfica de Cervantes y del "Quijote"* (Madrid: Plus-Ultra, 1946); and E. C. Riley, *"Don Quixote: From Text to Icon," Cervantes* special issue (winter 1988): 103–15.

Don Quixote myth. DQ, Hamlet, Don Juan, and Faust are probably the greatest (modern) literary myths of all time. As such, they join the great mythic figures of ancient mythology and literature (Mars, Venus, Cupid; Helen of Troy, Odysseus, Penelope), and the Old and New Testament (Eve, Noah, Moses; Jesus, Judas, Peter). To them, we can also add the great myths of modern popular culture (Mickey Mouse, King Kong, Barbie) and modern literature (Sherlock Holmes, Tarzan, Wizard of Oz). And, of course, there are also the mythic figures of the movies (Luke Skywalker, Indiana Jones, Rambo) and icons of popular culture (Marilyn Monroe, Elvis Presley, Madonna). What all of these mythic figures have in common is their recognition outside of their original context, the way in which they have transcended their original texts: one need not have

read *Tirso de Molina's *Burlador de Sevilla* in order to know who a Don Juan is, have seen the original cartoon "Steamboat Willie" in order to recognize Mickey Mouse, or have been a teenager in the fifties in order to laugh at an Elvis impersonator. The same is true of DQ: centuries of editions, translations, retellings, adaptations, festivals, cartoons, jokes, advertisements, musical plays, movies, TV programs, and graphic images that include windmills and/or Mambrino's helmet have made it possible for people the world over to know what "quixotic" means, catch the connotations of a windmill, or recognize the gaunt figure on the old nag as DQ. And, like all great myths, DQ is a protean figure: he is equally recognizable as a deluded madman, a visionary, a comic bumbler, an eccentric do-gooder, a serious but failed reformer, a dreamy idealist, a fanatic true believer, a Christlike moral symbol, or an imaginative escapist. We can all recognize a DQ figure, whether the incarnation be in an aging man, a young woman, an imaginative youth, or a cartoon character. DQ has been legitimately recruited by right-wing traditionalists (the glory that was Spain, the true religion, monarchy, or fascist dictatorship), left-wing revolutionaries (the glory that is yet to come, the impossible dream, true democracy, or the spirit of the people), and all sorts of people in between. If, as has been suggested, the genre of the novel has its origins in the *quixotic novel, it is probably more the mythic than the textual DQ that has made MC's novel the prototype of the eighteenth-century comic novel, the nineteenth-century realist novel, and the twentieth-century modernist and postmodern novel. Parson Adams, Emma Bovary, Isidora Rufete, Prince Myshkin, Isabel Archer, Carol Kennicott, and Moses Herzog, different as they may be, are all DQs, all participants in the DQ myth. Lawrence Sterne, Jacinto María Delgado, Jane Austen, Stendhal, Charles Dickens, Herman Melville, Gustave Flaubert, Benito Pérez Galdós, Miguel de Unamuno, Sinclair Lewis, John Barth, Carlos Fuentes, Alejo Carpentier, Robert Coover, and Kathy Acker—a list of novelists about as

disparate as one can imagine—all write quixotic fiction, in its myriad forms.

Bibliography: Donald W. Bleznick, "Don Quijote
as Spanish Myth," in *Studies on "Don Quijote" and
Other Cervantine Works*, ed. Donald W. Bleznick
(York, SC: Spanish Literature Publications, 1984),
1–19; and Ian Watt, *Myths of Modern Individualism:
Faust, Don Quixote, Don Juan, Robinson Crusoe*
(Cambridge: Cambridge University Press, 1996).

**Don Quixote the Bad [Don Quijote el
malo].** In *DQ* II, 72, a phrase used by *Alvaro
Tarfe to distinguish between the imposter DQA
and the real character, DQ.

**Don Quixote the Good [Don Quijote el
bueno].** In *DQ* II, 72, a phrase used by *Alvaro Tarfe to distinguish between the real DQ
and the imposter, DQA.

**Don Quixote's advice to Sancho [Con-
sejos de Don Quijote a Sancho].** In *DQ* II,
42–43, DQ gives SP advice before the squire
departs to assume the governorship of his 'island.' It is both a parody and a good example
of a common Renaissance theme: wise counselor prepares new prince for his rule (see, for
example, Polonius's advice to Laertes in *Hamlet*). DQ's advice begins with two important
and noble precepts: 1) fear God, and 2) know
yourself. Before he is finished, however, the advice relates to such mundane matters as burping
and paring your fingernails. SP is duly impressed by what his master says to him and offers to relinquish the charge if DQ believes him
unworthy of it. DQ's response is that the very
act of making such an offer is ample proof of
SP's worthiness for the job.

Bibliography: Elias L. Rivers, "Don Quixote's
Fatherly Advice, and Olivares's," *Cervantes* 18, no.
2 (1998): 74–84.

Don Quixote's ear. In the battle with the
*Basque squire, DQ's left ear is partially sliced
off. In spite of his earlier statements to SP that
the code of chivalry does not permit a knight
to complain of physical pain, DQ cannot ignore
the fact that his injured ear hurts more than it
should and acknowledges the pain (twice in I,
10, and once more in I, 11). This is one of the
most important early incursions of reality into
DQ's chivalric fantasy: the ear really hurts,
even though the romances of chivalry say that
it should not (the ear is cured by the folk medicine used by the *goatherds in I, 11). Reality
trumps theory, and DQ's implicit acknowledg-
ment of this fact is an important phase in his
accommodation of reality. Throughout the
novel, the cumulative effect of DQ's many
falls, stonings, beatings, scratches, and miscellaneous battle wounds is to inch him closer and
closer to reality.

**Don Quixote's grandmother [Agüela de
Don Quijote].** DQ cites the testimony of his
grandmother in *DQ* I, 49, as a witness to the
historical authenticity of the Dueña *Quintañona.

Don Quixote's library. DQ's library is quite
extraordinary by Renaissance standards. In I, 6,
it is stated that the library contains over 100
books, but in I, 24, DQ makes the claim that
he owns over 300. Even if the first number is
used, this amounts to an extraordinary private
collection of fictional and poetic works. The library seems to be well organized, by genre,
judging from the order in which the books are
reviewed by the priest and the barber. These
two figures, encouraged by the housekeeper and
DQ's niece, then conduct a general auto-da-fé
on the 'heretical' books that have driven a good
man mad. But once they start to look at the
books, the priest and barber decide to save the
best of them for themselves. It has traditionally
been considered that these two men, and especially the priest, are spokespersons for MC's
own aesthetic judgments concerning the books
in question, but it is always dangerous to assume that what any character says represents
the author's personal opinions. There are exactly five romances of chivalry spared from the
flames: 1) the Spanish *Amadís de Gaula* by
*Montalvo; 2) the Italian *Espejo de caballerías*,
a book about *Boiardo's characters in the loose
translation/adaptation by *López de Santa Catalina and Reinoso; 3) the Portuguese *Palmerín
de Inglaterra*, by *Moraes; 4) the Spanish *Belianís de Grecia* by *Fernández; and 5) the Cat-

alan *Tirante el Blanco*, by *Martorell. Eight other romances of chivalry are condemned to the bonfire. Of the other works mentioned, mostly pastoral romances and epic poetry, 11 books are saved and only five burned. Only 29 of the 100-plus books are mentioned by name; presumably all those not mentioned are burned. Overall, DQ's friends take some 16 of DQ's best books (more than half of what they look at) and destroy the rest. It is interesting to note that there is no reference to any nonfiction book—no historical treatise or devotional manual, for example—of any kind in DQ's collection, but then who knows (as indicated at the beginning of I, 7) what might have been included in the more than 70 books not specifically mentioned. The most interesting book in the library is *Galatea* by MC, who is a 'great friend' of the priest, according to the latter. This first entry of the historical MC into the work (unless one also considers the archive-hunting narrator to be a version of MC: *narrative structure of *DQ*) is a surprising metafictional move more reminiscent of a late-twentieth-century postmodern novel than one from the Renaissance. Perhaps less surprising is the later occasion (I, 40) when the captive Ruy Pérez de Viedma praises the exploits of 'a certain Saavedra,' another appearance by the historical author on the same ontological plane as the characters. The narrating MC makes the interesting comment in I, 9, that the books *Desengaño de celos* and *Ninfas y pastores de Henares*, published in 1586 and 1587, respectively, are 'modern' books. Actually, the newest book in the library is *El pastor de Iberia*, published in 1591, nearly a decade and a half before *DQ* I appears in 1605. Either the priest and the barber did not get to some of the truly recent works in the collection or this passage is an indication (not evidence) that at least the early part of *DQ* I was written in the early 1590s (*chronology of MC's works).

Bibliography: Juan Bautista Avalle-Arce, "Libros y charlas; conocimiento y dudas," in *Don Quijote como forma de vida* (Madrid: Fundación Juan March/Castalia, 1976), 261–90; and Edward Baker, *La biblioteca de don Quijote* (Madrid: Marcial Pons, 1997).

Don Quixote's penance [Penitencia de Don Quijote]. The deranged or despairing knight who goes off alone to do penance for his sins, shortcomings, or failures is a frequent topic in the romances and poems of chivalry. In I, 25, in the Sierra Morena mountains, DQ decides to do a penance in imitation of two of his favorite chivalric heroes. The first is Amadís de Gaula, who believes that his beloved Oriana has disdained him, and who goes off to the remote island called Peña Pobre, takes the name Beltenebros, and lives a prayerful and tearful life. The second is Orlando Furioso, when he learns that his beloved Angelica has been unfaithful to him and goes mad, tearing up trees and otherwise destroying life and property. In a significant theoretical passage, DQ explains to SP the importance of the *imitation of models in achieving excellence and describes the actions of Amadís and Orlando. When SP comments that these knights had some legitimate reason for their penance but that DT has said or done nothing to cause DQ to take a similar course of action, DQ responds that that is the very point: if he does this deed without motivation, just imagine what he would do if he had true cause. The metaphor he uses to describe his actions is both comic and graphic: if he does this *en seco* (dry; i.e., without reason), think what he would do *en mojado* (wet; i.e., if he had a reason). The essence of DQ's action is gratuitous (a concept that we tend to associate with twentieth-century existentialism rather than the Renaissance) rather than motivated. After SP departs to deliver a letter to DT, DQ sits down and thinks through his options and decides to imitate the sorrowful and tearful Amadís rather than the angry and violent Orlando. He does this in part because it is easier to pray, sigh, and cry than it is to uproot trees, sully the waters of the stream, and kill animals, but also because *Cardenio has already coopted the Orlando model with his own violent penance in the same Sierra Morena. DQ makes himself a rosary (*Don Quixote's rosary) out of his shirttail in order to recite 'a million prayers' and carves unintentionally comic verses on the trees. This episode represents a turning point in *DQ* I for several reasons: 1) I, 25, is the longest chapter in the novel; 2) DQ and SP are separated for the first time; 3) in I, 26, the priest and barber reenter the plot and take control of the action; and 4) the remainder of the novel features the stories of other characters more than it does the adventures of DQ and SP.

Bibliography: Juan Bautista Avalle-Arce, "Don Quijote, o la vida como obra de arte (A manera de coda)," in *Nuevos deslindes cervantinos* (Barcelona: Ariel, 1975), 335–87; Harold G. Jones, "Grisóstomo and Don Quixote: Death and Imitation," *Revista Canadiense de Estudios Hispánicos* 4 (1979): 85–92; Alberto Sánchez, "El capítulo XXV del primer *Quijote* (1605), clave sinóptica de toda la obra," *Crítica Hispánica* 11 (1989): 95–113; and Alberto Sánchez, "Sobre la penitencia de Don Quijote (I, 26)," in *Actas del Primer Coloquio Internacional de la Asociación de Cervantistas, Alcalá de Henares 29/30 nov.–1/2 dic. 1988* (Barcelona: Anthropos, 1990), 17–33.

Don Quixote's rosary [Rosario de Don Quixote]. In *DQ* I, 26, as he does his penance for DT in Sierra Morena, DQ fashions a rosary from his shirttail, tying knots for the 11 beads. Using this, he recites 'a million prayers.' The detail of the rosary and the prayers is interesting, because the censors eliminated the reference to a million prayers (perhaps because of the tone that could recall Erasmus's criticism of rote repetition of formulaic prayers) but did not react to the fact that DQ makes his makeshift rosary out of his dirty shirttail (which was perhaps in direct contact with the least clean part of his body).

Bibliography: Roberto Véguez, " 'Un millón de avemarías': El rosario en *Don Quijote*," *Cervantes* 21, no. 2 (2001): 87–109.

Don Quixote-Sancho Panza pair. The leader-follower pair long precedes MC's use of it in *DQ*: lord and disciple, master and servant, knight and squire, and others. But since *DQ*, it is impossible not to see any such pair— especially if there is a tall-thin, short-fat, serious-comic, visionary-practical, and/or idealistic-realistic contrast—as evoking the DQ-SP pair. The roots of this matching of opposites can be found in medieval and Renaissance celebrations of Lent (DQ) and Carnival (SP). Among such pairs suggested as having

something in common with, being derived from, and/or otherwise evoking MC's figures are Mr. Pickwick and Sam Weller, Huck Finn and Jim; Sherlock Holmes and Dr. Watson, Laurel and Hardy, Abbott and Costello, the Cisco Kid and Pancho, Roy Rogers and Gabby Hayes (and a host of other cowboy-sidekick pairs), Batman and Robin, George Burns and Gracie Allen, Dean Martin and Jerry Lewis, Frodo and Sam Gamgee, Joe Buck and Ratso Rizzo, R2D2 and C3PO, Johnny Carson and Ed Mcmahon, and even Dick Cheney and George W. Bush.

Bibliography: Ann Cameron, *Sidekicks in American Literature* (Lewiston, NY: Edwin Mellen Press, 2000).

Don Tonto. *Don Demented.

Don vencido y don molido a palos. *Don Defeated and Don Beaten.

Don Whip or Don Chopped Meat [Don Azote o don Gigote]. In *DQ* I, 30, Dorotea (Princess *Micomicona) cannot remember DQ's name and refers to him in this way.

Doña So-and-So; Doña tal. *Marica.

Doncella(s). *Damsel(s), maiden(s), young women.

Doncella de Dinamarca. The confidante of Oriana in *Amadís de Gaula*. See *Fregona*.

Donnelly, Marcos (1962–). American science-fiction writer. Donnelly has written a short story entitled "The Resurrection of Alonso Quijana" (1992), which is presented as a translation from an old manuscript of *DQ* found by the author's brother in Montreal, Canada. The author claims only to be the translator and editor, making no claims for the text's legitimacy. In a brief forward, MC explains why he, now long dead, has decided to write this brief text from the afterlife in order to set straight the record about DQ. The text consists of six supplements to *DQ* II, 74, in which Alonso Quijana el Bueno renounces knight-errantry, and then has a dream. In the dream, DQ finds himself in the Saudi Arabian desert during what is obviously the 1991 Gulf War, where he meets an American soldier named Santiago Rojas (Saint James the Red, for DQ) and has a series of encounters with Iraqi and American troops and with modern military technology. Throughout, there are a number of editorial footnotes in which the author attempts to clarify the sometimes confusing text; for example, what is the exact significance of and translation for the term "Airachiss": is it "Iroquois," or "Iraqis"? In a brief afterword, MC muses over the significance of his supplement. An interesting combination of clever intertextuality, comedy, and social criticism, Donnelly's story of DQ is quite unlike any other.

Donoso. The author (the name means 'witty') of two short poems, one dedicated to SP and the other to Rocinante, that form part of the burlesque prefatory poems to *DQ* I. It has been suggested that this name could refer to MC's friend, the poet Gabriel *Lobo Laso de la Vega, who might actually be the author of these two poems.

Donosor. In *Casa* 3, the shepherd Corinto's rustic version of Nabucodonosor (Nebuchadnezzar), the Babylonian king who destroyed the temple at Jerusalem and brought the Jewish people to their Babylonian captivity. Notorious for his wickedness, Nebuchadnezzar had a golden image erected in Babylon and ordered everyone to worship it or be thrown into a fiery furnace. For his arrogance and wickedness, he was punished by being made insane, living out his life by grazing the field like an animal. At one point he famously dreamed of a great statue with a head of pure gold, chest and arms of silver, stomach and hips of bronze, legs of iron, and feet of clay.

Doody, Margaret Anne. Theorist of the novel. In what she calls *The True Story of the Novel* (1996), Doody reveals "a very well-kept secret: that the Novel as a form of literature in the West has a continuous history of about two thousand years." In revealing this secret, Doody rejects the parochial and chauvinist Anglo-American appropriation of the genre of the novel as something that arises in eighteenth-century England. In doing so, she points out, first of all, that the English-only source for the novel "ignores the very visible Spanish novels of the sixteenth and early seventeenth centuries." But Doody then continues to stretch the origin of the novel back even farther, to the earliest fictional writings of ancient times. Always the careful scholar, Doody acknowledges a second concept of the theory and history of the novel, *Bakhtin's proposal that the novel emerges during the Renaissance. But she rejects this view, too, insisting that it is based on a spurious distinction between novel and *romance. Doody does away with the romance-novel distinction by fiat, declaring (but not adequately justifying the claim) that "Romance and the Novel are one. The separation between them is part of a problem, not part of a solution." She judges a work to be a novel "if it is fictional, if it is in prose, and if it is of a certain length," which clearly means that the ancients wrote novels. The trouble with this position is that if all fiction is always already novel, then we lose a sense of history and blur, perhaps beyond recognition, certain differences that make a difference.

Bibliography: Margaret Anne Doody, *The True Story of the Novel* (New Brunswick, NJ: Rutgers University Press, 1996); and James Tatum, ed., *The Search for the Ancient Novel* (Baltimore: Johns Hopkins University Press, 1994).

Dorador, El. Renegade from Melilla; his name means 'Guilder.' He participated in MC's second escape attempt in Algiers in 1577, in which the prisoners assembled and waited in a preordained spot for a rescue ship sent by Rodrigo, MC's brother. But El Dorador betrayed his comrades and revealed the plot to *Hassan Pasha, MC's owner. MC took all the blame for the escape plot and was placed in chains for five months, but not punished more severely, in spite of Hassan's reputation for cruelty.

Doré, Paul Gustave (1833–83). French illustrator. Doré's famous illustrations for *DQ* were first published in 1863 in the edition of Louis Viardot's translation of *DQ* into French. The illustrations for the text consist of 370 drawings by Doré, engraved by H. Pisan. In preparation for this assignment, Doré traveled throughout Spain in 1862 and made some preliminary sketches, and then elaborated on them once he was back in Paris. Doré's romantic vision of DQ and SP, together with his superb evocation of the legendary world of chivalry, have made this the single most reprinted and imitated set of graphic interpretations of MC's novel. The Doré images have contributed greatly to the popular concept of DQ, among both readers and those who have never read the novel. There are multiple editions, ranging from inexpensive ones to those of great luxury, adorned with the Doré engravings, which are also available on the Internet. For many, Doré's DQ *is* DQ.

Bibliography: Miguel Romera-Navarro, *Interpretación pictórica del "Quijote" por Doré* (Madrid: Blass, 1946); and Rachel Schmidt, "The Romancing of *Don Quixote*: Spatial Innovation and Visual Interpretation in the Imagery of Johannot, Doré and Daumier," *Word and Image* 14 (1998): 354–70.

Doria, Giovanni Andrea [Juan Andrea de Oria] (1539–1606). Italian nobleman and admiral. He was one of the best sea captains of the Renaissance and fought with Don Juan of Austria in the battle of Lepanto. See *DQ* I, 39.

Doria, Pagano (?–1574). Younger brother of Giovanni Andrea *Doria. He fought in the battles of San Quintín and Lepanto, was page to Felipe II, and later died in the battle of La Goleta. When he entered the Order of *Malta, he left his considerable wealth to his brother. See *DQ* I, 39.

Dorotea. 1. The woman first seen by the priest, barber, and Cardenio in I, 27, and who becomes an important character in DQ's story as well as in *Cardenio*. Dorotea was first alluded to, but not by name, in Cardenio's narrative in I, 24. She tells her story in I, 28; takes over for the barber as the maiden in distress, calling herself Princess *Micomicona, in the effort to trick DQ into returning home (I, 29–30); and participates in the events in Juan Palomeque's inn in I, 32–45. She is an effective speaker who cleverly and discreetly improvises

and invents stories in order to manipulate DQ. She argues brilliantly and convinces Fernando to recognize her as his wife. Along with *Marcela, Dorotea is one of the most original and modern literary women of the Renaissance. **2.** In *Entretenida*, the maid to Marcela.

Bibliography: Salvador J. Fajardo, "Unveiling Dorotea, or the Reader as Voyeur," *Cervantes* 4, no. 2 (1984): 89–108; and Myriam Yvonne Jehenson, "The Dorotea-Fernando/Luscinda-Cardenio Episode in *Don Quijote*: A Postmodernist Play," *MLN* 107 (1992): 205–19.

Dorotea's maid. *Damsel(s), maiden(s), young women.

Dos amigos. *Two friends.

Dos doncellas, Las (Doncellas); The Two Damsels. The ninth story in *Novelas*. It is one of the most "Italianate" and contrived of the collection, and one of the least esteemed today among critics and students because of its coincidences, forced action, and conventional use of the device of the woman dressed as a man.

The action begins as a traveler arrives at an inn at Castelblanco in Andalusia. He dismounts and immediately faints. When revived, he demands a room alone and even pays double in order to assure that no one else will share the room with him that evening. Refusing food, he enters the room, locks the door, and blocks entry with chairs. Everyone is astonished by the good looks and gentle bearing of the youth, who appears to be about 16 or 17 years old. Soon there arrives a second youth as attractive as the first but a little older, causing the innkeeper's wife to comment that angels are lodging in the inn this evening. The local constable arrives for a drink and something to eat, and the discussion around the table—in addition to the usual gossip about news from the court, events in Flanders, the action of the Turks, and so forth—is about the mysterious young man locked in his room. They plan a trick to make him admit the second traveler to the room: the constable knocks and arouses the youth, informs him that the local mayor has ordered that a certain person be lodged at the inn, and this is the only room where such accommodation is possible. The youth silently assents to sharing his room. The two roommates bed down in silence, but the newcomer is awakened by the sighs and sobs of the first occupant. The latter begins to lament aloud the problems she faces— for she is in fact a woman dressed as a man. Primarily, she laments the actions of one Marco Antonio who had promised to marry her but reneged. The other traveler offers consolation and invites the first to tell her story, which, of course, she does. Her name is Teodosia, the daughter of a noble and wealthy Andalusian family. She has a brother who is a student at the University of Salamanca. She fell in love with the son of a comparably worthy and wealthy family from a nearby town. With his promise of marriage, she began an intimate relationship with him. But within two days, he disappeared. Desperate to find him, she dressed in men's clothing and set out in search of him in order either to make him fulfill his promise of marriage or to kill him in revenge for his deceit. The other traveler offers to help her in every way. When day dawns, Teodosia recognizes the other traveler as none other than her brother Don Rafael de Villavicencio. She throws herself at his feet offering him a dagger with which to kill her and avenge his family's honor. He refuses and renews his offer of assistance. They will travel together, Teodosia in masculine disguise and calling herself Teodoro. They learn that Marco Antonio has gone to the Puerto de Santa María in order to board a galley headed for Italy. They therefore head immediately for Barcelona, the port where all Spanish galleys en route to Italy make a stop. Their only company is a servant of Rafael's named Calvete. Near the city, just outside the town of Igualada, they happen upon a company of some 30 travelers who have been held up by a group of Catalan bandits, among whom is one youth of about 16 whose stunning good looks endear him to the brother and sister. This young man says that he is the son of Enrique de Cárdenas who lives in a town near theirs. Rafael knows the Cárdenas family and also knows that they have no son. Actually, the other explains, he is the son of Cárdenas's brother Sancho. But, says Rafael, Sancho has no son, only a daughter.

Yes, the other admits, he is really Don Sancho's majordomo, named Francisco, and he has stolen some money in order to go to Italy in search of fame and adventure. From the beginning, Teodosia suspects that this new person is not a man but a woman, the clue being that her ears are pierced. She takes the newcomer aside, expresses this belief, and convinces her to tell her story. The second woman admits now that she really is the daughter of Don Sancho and her name is Leocadia. She is dressed as a man and in this place because she is following the man who promised to marry her, and even wrote a statement to that effect, but disappeared on the very day that he was to come to her bedroom. The lying lover is none other than Marco Antonio Adorno, who, Leocadia believes, has departed for Italy with the beautiful Teodosia. Teodosia does not reveal her own identity, but, after verifying that Marco Antonio has not slept with Leocadia, suggests that Marco Antonio may not be traveling with his other love interest. Leocadia laments that the bandits have stolen everything she had—money, clothing, and even the written promise of marriage signed by Marco Antonio. Teodosia tells her brother all that she has learned, and the two of them offer to help Leocadia as much as they can. Rafael, meanwhile, has been smitten by Leocadia's beauty and has fallen in love with her. Leocadia is once again outfitted in men's clothing, and the three of them head for Barcelona. Just as they get to the city, there is a large skirmish between some local citizens and a number of men from one of the galleys in the port. In the midst of the fight is a valiant young man dressed entirely in green. It is none other than Marco Antonio. The two women, like Italian woman warriors or Amazons, rush to his side to defend him in the skirmish, and Rafael joins them. The fight is broken up by the arrival of a Catalan gentleman who gets the locals to withdraw. But from a distance they continue to throw rocks at the group from the ship, and one of the rocks hits Marco Antonio in the left temple, badly wounding him. They manage to get him into one of the boats returning to the ship, and Leocadia joins him, but Teodosia cannot make it in time. She and her brother join the

Catalan gentleman, whose name is Don Sancho de Cardona, at his elegant home and convince him to have Marco Antonio brought there for medical treatment. This is done, and Leocadia accompanies him from the ship. The wound is thought to be life-threatening, and, in a dramatic gesture, Leocadia reveals her identity and begs Marco Antonio to marry her before he dies. But the wounded man confesses that his true love is Teodosia and his interest in Leocadia was merely sexual. His plan had been to go to Italy for a few years, but now on his death bed he declares himself married to Teodosia. Rafael brings his sister forth, and she and the wounded lover renew their vows. Leocadia, distraught, leaves the house. Rafael follows her, declares his love, states that his social status and wealth are comparable to those of Marco Antonio, and entreats him to marry him. She accepts. Marco Antonio recovers from his wound and recuperates for a couple of weeks. On his supposed deathbed, he had made a vow to undertake a pilgrimage on foot to the shrine at Santiago de Compostela, and the others now agree to join him in the journey. The two couples, still accompanied by Calvete, make the journey and return home. They arrive there just in time to stop a duel, in the form of a joust between knights-errant dressed in armor with shield, lance, and so on, between the fathers of the two women and the father of Marco Antonio. Wedding ceremonies take place and the couples live happily ever after, leaving illustrious descendants in that location even to this day. Even Calvete, in reward for his good services, is given money to go to study at Salamanca. The local poets celebrated this series of events in verse.

Bibliography: Alda M. Beaupied, "Ironía y los actos de comunicación en *Las dos doncellas*," *Anales Cervantinos* 21 (1983): 165–76; Linda Britt, "Teodosia's Dark Shadow? A Study of Women's Roles in Cervantes' *Las dos doncellas*," *Cervantes* 8, no. 1 (1988): 39–46; Marsha Collins, "El poder del discurso confesional en 'Las dos doncellas,' " *Cervantes* 22, no. 2 (2002): 25–46; Barbara Fuchs, "Empire Unmanned: Gender Trouble and Genoese Gold in Cervantes's 'The Two Damsels,' " *PMLA* 116 (2001): 285–99; Eric Kartchner, "Metafiction in *Las dos doncellas*," *RLA: Romance Languages Annual* 7 (1995): 521–26; Isaías Lerner, "Teoría y práctica de la novel: *Las dos doncellas* de Cervantes," *Edad de Oro* 19 (2000): 155–69; Caroline Schmauser, "Dynamism and Spatial Structure in *Las dos doncellas*," in *Cervantes's "Exemplary Novels" and the Adventure of Writing*, ed. Michael Nerlich and Nicholas Spadaccini (Minneapolis, MN: Prisma Institute, 1989), 175–203; Jennifer Thompson, "The Structure of Cervantes's *Las dos doncellas*," *Bulletin of Hispanic Studies* 40 (1963): 144–50; and Stanislav Zimic, "*Las dos doncellas*: Padres y hijos," *Acta Neophilologica* 22 (1989): 23–37.

Dostoevsky, Fyodor Mikhailovich (1821–81). Russian novelist. In 1876, in his *Dnevnik pisatelia* (1873–81; *The Diary of a Writer*), Dostoevsky wrote the following of *DQ*: "In the whole world there is no deeper, no mightier literary work. This is, so far, the last and greatest expression of human thought; this is the bitterest irony which man was capable of conceiving. And if the world were to come to an end, and people were asked there, somewhere: 'Did you understand your life on earth, and what conclusion have you drawn from it?'—man could silently hand over *Don Quixote*: 'Such is my inference from life.—Can you condemn me for it?' " Dostoevsky was much influenced by *Turgenev's famous lecture/essay on DQ and Hamlet, which he may have heard delivered in 1860. Dostoevsky explicitly based the saintly but foolish Prince Myshkin in *Idiot* (1868–69; *The Idiot*) on the (for him) complementary figures of Christ and DQ (and, to a lesser extent, Mr. Pickwick and Jean Valjean), as his aim was to describe "a truly perfect and noble man." He added, "On earth there is only one positively beautiful person—Christ. . . . Of the beautiful characters in Christian literature Don Quixote is the most finished. But he is beautiful only because at the same time he is also comic." In *The Idiot*, Agalya Epanchin, the figure who most parallels DT, hastily places a note from the prince in a book and only later sees that the book is *DQ*, an act that, like the chapter devoted to a discussion of *Pushkin's ballad "Poor Knight" and DQ (where Agalya says that "the 'poor knight' is also a Don Quixote, only serious and not comic"), is an explicit allusion to one source of the protagonist's character.

Myshkin's defense of and offer to marry Nastasya, another variant of DT, is quintessentially quixotic. And surely there is no small amount of DQ in the figure of Raskolnikov in *Prestuplenie i nakazanie* (1866; *Crime and Punishment*), whose defining idea, largely inspired by his reading about Napoleon, is that some people can impose their own will on the world. Like DQ, Raskolnikov ultimately fails when reality turns out to be unlike the desired ideal.

Bibliography: Vsevolod Bagno, "El *Quijote* en los borradores de *El idiota* de Dostoyevski," *Anales Cervantinos* 32 (1994): 265–70; Anthony J. Cascardi, *The Bounds of Reason: Cervantes, Dostoevsky, Flaubert* (New York: Columbia University Press, 1986); Arturo Serrano Plaja, *"Magic" Realism in Cervantes: "Don Quixote" as Seen Through "Tom Sawyer" and "The Idiot,"* trans. Robert S. Rudder (Berkeley: University of California Press, 1970); and Alan Trueblood, "Dostoevski and Cervantes," *Inti* 45 (1997): 85–94.

Dragontina. A character from Boiardo's *Orlando Innamorato*. See *Poesías* 32.

Dragut (?–1565). A Muslim sea captain who was taken prisoner by Andrea Doria, ransomed by Barbarroja, and became a scourge of the Christians along all the Mediterranean coasts. See *Persiles* III, 10.

Dreiser, Theodore (1871–1945). American novelist. In Dreiser's first and best-known novel, *Sister Carrie* (1900), the quixotic description of the protagonist sets the tone of the story to follow: "A half-equipped little knight she was, venturing to reconnoiter the mysterious city and dreaming wild dreams of some vague, far-off supremacy." This innocent quixotism is soon taken advantage of, and Carrie finds that reality does not correspond to her dreams. By the end of the novel, Carrie is a successful actress, and she has become much more of a pragmatic SP than a dreaming DQ.

Dromedaries; Dromedarios. *Benedictine friars.

Dropsy [Hidropsía]. The illness, probably actually diabetes, from which MC died in 1616.

Drummer(s) [Atambor(es)]. 1. In *Coloquio*, the musician in a company of soldiers who takes Berganza into his service and teaches him to do a variety of tricks. He gives him the name of *perro sabio* (Wise Dog) and together they earn fame and money. **2.** In *Laberinto* 3, the musicians who accompany Porcia (in place of Rosamira) when she appears for her public judgment.

Dryads [Driadas]. Wood nymphs. See *DQ* I, 25.

Du Verdier, Gilbert Saulnier (?–1686). French novelist. Du Verdier's *Le Chevalier hypocondiraque* (1632; *The Hypochondriac Knight*) is one of the several seventeenth-century French satires written in imitation of *DQ*. Like DQ, Don Clarazel de Gontarnos sallies forth in imitation of Amadís de Gaula, has a series of comic adventures, and is manipulated for amusement by other characters.

Duarte de Sosa, Don. In *Persiles* III, 6, the young man killed by Ortel Banedre in Lisbon.

Ducado. *Currency.

Duchess [Duquesa]. The wife of the *duke in *DQ* II, 30–57, 69–70. Like her husband, she has read *DQ* I and jumps at the chance to entertain in their luxurious home the comic figures of DQ and SP. She is particularly fond of SP and loves to hear him talk. When she learns from SP that he has presented a peasant woman to DQ as DT and has encouraged DQ to believe that DT has been enchanted to look that way, she cleverly improvises and convinces SP that the woman in question really was DT and that it was SP who was enchanted (II, 32). When she is warned that Doña Rodríguez has gone to talk with DQ by night, she and *Altisidora listen at the door. When Doña Rodríguez reveals to DQ that the duchess has two running sores on her legs, she and her servants burst into the room and spank Doña Rodríguez and pinch DQ (II, 48). The sores on her legs are incisions made by a physician in order to drain off the evil humors of her body and can be understood by the reader as an external manifestation of her inner corruption.

Duchess of Ferrara [Duquesa de Ferrara]. In *Cornelia*, the mother of the duke of Ferrara, who wants him to marry Señora Livia; after her death, the duke marries the beautiful Señora Cornelia, the mother of his son.

Duel. *Council of Trent.

Dueña(s). 1. From the Latin *domina*, this was the most common term for lady or *married woman* in medieval Spanish; from the same root comes the honorific *doña* and, later, *dama*. In many of the romances of chivalry, a distinction is made between a virginal *doncella* and a *dueña* in the sense of an ex-virgin; in *Belianís de Grecia*, for example, after the protagonist first sleeps with Florisbella, it is recorded that 'the most beautiful *doncella* in the world was thus turned into a *dueña*.' A *dueña*, in MC's time, was generally a matron, a woman who was likely to be older, usually either married or a widow, and in the service of a noble lady. Her role as chaperone, companion, and advisor was the female equivalent of the man's squire. *Dueñas* were often the subject of male criticism and slander, a common target of satiric poetry (e.g., in Quevedo) and prose commentary (as in SP's remarks in II, 31). The *dueña*—who, interestingly, is not a stock figure in the *comedia*—was commonly accused of being old, lazy, ill-tempered, ignorant, prone to gossip, and, above all, lascivious, often acting as intermediary in her mistress's illicit amorous affairs. The most important *dueña* in *DQ* is *Doña Rodríguez in *DQ* II, 31–55, 66. Also noteworthy is the *dueña* *Quintañona (*DQ* I, 13, 16, and 49), the go-between in the love affair between Lancelot and Guinevere in Spanish legend. **2**. In *Casa* 1, the person who accompanies Angelica. **3**. In *DQ* II, 38, 12 participants in the Countess Trifaldi hoax. They march in two rows preceding the entrance of the countess. See also *DQ* II, 41. **4**. In *DQ* II, 45, the term SP uses to refer to the woman who claims to have been raped. There is a carefully calculated irony in SP's usage here of the term in the sense

of non virgin. **5**. In *DQ* II, 50, a servant of the duke and duchess who notes that Doña Rodríguez leaves the room where they are sleeping and informs the duchess of what is happening. **6**. In *DQ* II, 69, six women who slap, pinch, and stick pins in SP in order to bring Altisidora back to life. **7**. In *DQ* II, 60, a woman who makes up part of the retinue of Doña Guiomar de Quiñones. **8**. *Damsel(s), maiden(s), young women.

Dueño del mesón o hospedaje. *Owner of the inn or lodging.

Duero. 1. One of the major rivers in Spain. Its source is in the mountains near the city of Soria, and it runs westward until it forms part of the border between Spain and Portugal, finally emptying into the Atlantic Ocean at Oporto. **2**. In *Numancia* 1, an allegorical figure who prophesies the inevitable defeat of the city but also the future greatness of Spain, especially under the reign of *Felipe II.

Duffield, Brainerd. American dramatist. Duffield is the author of a one-act play entitled *Don Quixote de la Mancha* (1973), which begins when MC comes on stage and sits at a table and writes, as he addresses the audience in order to comment on the play from time to time. The action consists of the housekeeper (here called Belisa) and niece Antonia complaining about the books DQ reads, DQ's appropriation of the shaving basin of the barber Nicholas for his helmet, a visit to the inn where the prostitute Maritorna is presented as DT (she is transformed by the treatment she receives from DQ), the dubbing scene, Master Pedro's puppet show (which DQ attacks and ruins), DQ's defeat by Sansom, and the death scene. After DQ's death, MC goes over to him, lifts the sheet covering his face, and identifies himself to DQ as his creator, stating that both have become immortal. The short play might actually stage very well, with the metatheatrical role of MC the crucial feature.

Bibliography: Brainerd Duffield, *Don Quixote de la Mancha* (Elgin, IL: Performance Publishing, 1973).

Dufresny, Charles, Sieur de la Rivière (1657–1724). French dramatist. It is reported that during the performance of Dufresny's comedy *Sancho Pança* (1694), when the character of the Duke exclaimed, "I begin to grow tired of this Sancho!" a member of the audience shouted, "And so do I!" which brought the play to an abrupt end amidst derisive laughter.

Duke [Duque]. The nobleman who has read *DQ* I and takes advantage of the chance encounter with DQ and SP to entertain them at his country house and prepare a series of practical jokes on them. The duke and duchess are fictional characters, but the facts that they are not named and at times seem to be fictional versions of real people have led some scholars to 'identify' the real persons behind the fiction. The names most frequently proposed are those of Don Carlos de *Borja and Doña María de Aragón, duke and duchess of Luna and Villahermosa, who in fact owned the palace named Buenavía near the town of Pedrola in the region of Aragon, the approximate region where this series of scenes might have taken place. The duke is consistently presented as frivolous, callous, and even cruel. Important is the revelation in II, 48, that the duke has repeatedly refused to restore the honor of Doña Rodríguez's daughter, seduced by the son of a wealthy farmer in the service of the duke, because the young man's father lends the duke money. In other words, the duke fails to fulfill the responsibilities of his rank because of personal economic interests. He also prevents the marriage between Tosilos and the daughter of Doña Rodríguez, failing to fulfill his noble obligations and breaking up that family (II, 56, 66). See also *DQ* II, 30–57, 69–70.

Bibliography: Anthony Close, "Seemly Pranks: The Palace Episodes in *Don Quixote* Part II," in *Art and Literature in Spain: 1600–1800: Studies in Honour of Nigel Glendenning*, ed. Charles Davis and Paul Julian Smith (London: Tamesis, 1993), 69–87.

Duke of Alba. *Alvarez de Toledo, Don Fernando.

Dulcinea del Toboso. DT is perhaps the most significant absent character in all of literature. Neither she nor the woman upon whom she is based, Aldonza Lorenzo, ever appears in *DQ*, yet her presence is everywhere and her name is constantly on the lips of the characters; much of the best comedy in the novel takes place in scenes in which DT is involved. DQ believes that all knights-errant must have a lady love who infuses them with strength by means of their virtue and beauty, and who is able to receive the trophies they send them. The reason knights challenge each other in defense of their ladies' beauty is simple: there is a direct correlation between the real beauty of the woman and the strength she inspires in her knight-errant. When two knights fight over their ladies' beauty, the winner is, by definition, the one with the most beautiful lady, because it is her beauty that makes it possible for him to win. As DQ says to SP in I, 30, 'She fights in me, and wins in me, and I live and breathe in her, and in her I have my life and my being.' In *DQ* I, 1, DQ decides that he cannot be a knight-errant without a lady, and so he invents one, based on a peasant woman named *Aldonza who lives nearby and whom he loved from afar for some time. Immediately, in I, 2, DQ invokes her presence (using comic *fabla*) for inspiration as he rides along and then again in I, 3, before his combat with the two muleteers who disturb his armor. Unbeknownst to DQ, DT provides the narrator-editor (MC) with the key to locating the sequel to the manuscripts from the archives of La Mancha in I, 9. He identifies the Arabic manuscript that a boy is selling as the story of *DQ* when the *Morisco* he pays to help him understand what the text is about laughs at a passage in which it is written that DT is the best pig-salter in all of La Mancha. But if DT is a source of strength for DQ, she is also the source of his most serious dilemmas. Vivaldo's sarcastic criticism of DQ as a knight-errant mostly involves DT and the blasphemous relationship knights have with their ladies (I, 13). His sharp comments make DQ describe DT in detail (a parody of Petrarchan conventions), admit inadvertently that her heritage is not a venerable one (and perhaps not even Old Christian), and lie outright, claiming that he knew that Galaor, Amadís's brother, secretly loved just one woman. Because DQ arbitrarily invents his lady love, he is in no position to accept the offer of marriage from a princess in distress when she appears in his life in the form of the Princess Micomicona (I, 29–30)—even though this is exactly what he had predicted to SP would take place in I, 21, when he outlined the trajectory of the prototypical chivalric career. He takes away the mystery of DT for SP in I, 25, when he reveals that she is based on the slightly vulgar peasant Aldonza Lorenzo, and he only makes matters worse in the anecdote (with a sexual connotation) about a widow that he tells SP to justify his love. His decision to send SP to see DT suggests to the priest and barber the idea that one way to get DQ out of his penance in Sierra Morena would be for SP to tell him that DT has summoned him (I, 27). This leads directly to SP's lies about that emissary (I, 31), and then the decision to begin the third sally by finally going to see her (II, 8). When DQ decides to stand guard outside the castle (inn) and invokes DT, he sets himself up for the humiliation of spending the night standing on Rocinante with his hand tied to the window high above his head and, worse, in the morning, of dangling from that hand in front of the newly arrived travelers (I, 43–44). The decision to head directly to El Toboso in II, 8, leads directly to SP's decision to 'enchant' DT in order to get out of the awkward situation after he and DQ have arrived in that town (II, 9). Although the scene in which SP passes off three peasant women as DT and two maids in waiting (II, 10) is one of the finest comic scenes in the novel, it also sets up the spiraling series of events that dominates much of *DQ* II: DQ's dejection because his enemies the enchanters are now taking out their wrath against him by making the woman he loves suffer (II, 11, 67, and others), and his constant questions about her status to the divining ape of Maese Pedro (II, 25) and, later, the enchanted head in the home of Don Antonio Moreno in Barcelona (II, 62); the vision of DT in financial need in DQ's dream in the Cave of Montesinos (II, 23); the duchess's turning of the tables on SP when she convinces him that it really was an enchanted DT whom SP saw in the guise of a peasant

woman (II, 33); the procession of enchanters that culminates in the 3,300 lashes Merlin says that SP must inflict upon himself in order to disenchant DT (II, 35); DQ's attempt to force his squire to act, resulting in a fight between the two (II, 60); SP's ability to get DQ to pay him to lash himself and then, after convincing DQ to double the price per stroke, his deceit in whipping the trees instead of himself (II, 71); the narrator's passing over of SP's completion of his long-awaited task in a brief aside (II, 72); and, finally, the pathetic scene when, upon arriving home, DQ thinks he hears two boys say prophetically that he will never see DT again (II, 73), a scene in which DT is unflatteringly represented by a rabbit (a symbol of sexuality and promiscuity). If DQ had simply done in the first place what he should have—not invent a lady but meet one in the natural course of chivalric events—many of his woes of *DQ* II would have been avoided. But then much of the humor of the novel would also have been lost. But, at the end of his career of a knight-errant, when Sansón Carrasco as the Knight of the White Moon defeats him in Barcelona (II, 64), there is true nobility in DQ's final defense of DT: 'DT is the most beautiful woman in the world, and I the most unfortunate knight on earth, and it is not right that my weakness should defraud this truth. Drive home your lance, sir knight, and take my life, since you have already taken my honor.' In addition to references cited above, see also the following representative examples: *DQ* I, preliminary poems, 4, 16, 20, 22, 26, 46, 52; *DQ* II, 2, 3, 4, 14, 17, 21, 22, 32, 74.

Bibliography: John Jay Allen, "El desarrollo de Dulcinea y la evolución de don Quijote," *Nueva Revista de Filología Hispánica* 38 (1990): 849–56; Anthony J. Close, "Don Quixote's Love for Dulcinea: A Study of Cervantine Irony," *Bulletin of Hispanic Studies* 50 (1973): 237–56; Arthur Efron, *Don Quixote and the Dulcineated World* (Austin: University of Texas Press, 1971); Javier Herrero, "Dulcinea and Her Critics," *Cervantes* 2, no. 1 (1982): 23–42; Javier Herrero, *Who Was Dulcinea?* (New Orleans, LA: Graduate School of Tulane University, 1985; and Karen Lucas, "The Carnivalesque Uncrowning of Dulcinea," *RLA: Romance Languages Annual* 3 (1991): 488–92; Augustin Redondo, "Del personaje de Aldonza Lorenzo al de Dulcinea del Toboso: algunos aspectos de la invención cervantina," *Anales Cervantinos* 21 (1983): 9–22; Gemma Roberts, "Ausencia y presencia de Dulcinea en el *Quijote*." *Revista de Archivos, Bibliotecas y Museos* 82 (1979): 809–26; Charlotte Stern, "Dulcinea, Aldonza, and the Theory of Speech Acts," *Hispania* 67 (1984): 61–73; and Mario J. Valdés, "*Don Quijote de la Mancha* y la verdad de Dulcinea del Toboso," *Revista Canadiense de Estudios Hispánicos* 25 (2000): 29–41.

Dulcinea del Toboso, Doña. Although SP states in II, 3, that he has never heard DT referred to with the title *doña*, DQ did, in fact, use that title at least once: in I, 8, in the conversation with the *Basque lady—but maybe SP was not listening at the time, as he was busy collecting the spoils of DQ's battle with the Benedictine friars.

Dulcinea's mole [Lunar de Dulcinea]. In *DQ* II, 10, the beauty mark imaginatively described by SP. Whereas DQ only saw the crude reality of the peasant woman (*enchantment of Dulcinea), SP claims to have seen DT in all her glory. Particularly impressive was a mole she had on her right lip (!), rather like a moustache, with seven or eight blond hairs, each longer than the palm of your hand.

Dulcinea's shoe and Casildea's beard [Zapato de Dulcinea y barbas de Casildea]. When DQ defeats Sansón Carrasco dressed as the *Knight of the Mirrors in II, 14, he makes him confess that DT is more beautiful than Casildea de Vandalia. Sansón does so by saying that DT's dirty and tattered shoe is better than the clean, if unkempt, beard of Casildea. Both *shoe* and *beard* were often used as euphemisms for the female genitals in the Renaissance. It is quite extraordinary that Sansón would dare to use such language when the mad and easily angered DQ held a sword over his face, and it is equally extraordinary that DQ does not react to the obviously obscene insult.

Duque. *Duke.

Duque de Alba. *Alvarez de Toledo y Pimentel, Fernando.

Duque de Gravina. In *Galatea* 3, the owner of the property where the duel between Timbrio and Pransiles takes place.

Duque de Nemurs. *Nemurs, Duke of.

Duquesa de Ferrara. *Duchess of Ferrara.

Duquesa. *Duchess.

Durán. Apparently the Spanish name of a city in Algiers. See *Tratos* 2.

Durán, Diego. Poet praised in Calliope's song in *Galatea* 6; possibly a reference to Diego González Durán.

Durandarte. Spanish hero of the ballad tradition. The name is derived from Durendal, Roland's sword, but in Spain it became the name of a brave knight in the Carolingian cycle. Durandarte loved the beautiful Belerma and promised to send her his heart if he should be mortally wounded in battle. When he is so wounded at the battle of Roncesvalles, he has his cousin *Montesinos cut out his heart and carry it to Belerma. DQ meets Durandarte, enchanted and asleep on a tomb, in his dream in the Cave of Montesinos. Durandarte first recites some lines from the ballads that tell his story and then seems indifferent to DQ's presence and the possibility of disenchanting him, commenting, 'Patience and shuffle the cards.' See *DQ* II, 22–24.

D'Urfey, Thomas (1653–1723). English dramatist. D'Urfey is the author of a trilogy entitled *The Comical History of Don Quixote* (parts I and II 1694), and part III, with the subtitle *With the Marriage of Mary the Buxome* (1696). The music for parts I and II was composed by Henry Purcell (1658–1695) and John Eccles (1650–1732); and overall, this may be the finest work in which *DQ* is set to music in the same century in which MC's novel was published. Part I, the best of the three, features the *Cardenio* episode, along with the windmills, the helmet of Mambrino, the galley slaves, and other scenes from the novel. Part II takes place primarily at the estate of the duke and duchess and consists mostly of matters relating to SP's governorship. Part III, with more original material by D'Urfey, centers around Camacho's wedding and a miscellany of adventures such as the lions, the enchantment and disenchantment of DT, and the wedding of SP's daughter, Mary the Buxome. Throughout, DQ is a superficial and comic figure of derision; SP is a wise-cracking country bumpkin; and the women (Altisidora, Marcella, and Mary) are crudely suggestive.

Durindana. Like *Durandarte, a variant of Durendal, name of the sword of Roland in French epic literature. See *DQ* II, 26.

Dwarf [Enano]. When DQ arrives at the inn at the end of his first day of travel, in *DQ* I, 2, he expects a dwarf to announce his arrival at the castle.

⇒ E ⇐

Eandra. In *Galatea* 3, the shepherdess loved by the jealous Orfenio; she never appears in the text.

Early editions of *Don Quixote*. In his discussion with DQ in II, 3, Sansón Carrasco mentions that editions of *DQ* I have already appeared in Portugal, Barcelona, and Valencia, and that one is forthcoming in Antwerp. He is partially correct. By 1615 there had been ten editions of *DQ* I: three in Madrid (1605 twice and 1608), two in Lisbon (1605), two in Valencia (1605), two in Brussels (1607 and 1611), and one in Milan (1610). MC probably did not actually know of all of these printings of his novel. In addition, the English translation of Shelton (1612) and the French translation of Oudin (1614) were also in print. The first Barcelona edition, which would be of both parts, did not appear until 1617. And no edition was printed in Antwerp until 1670, although it is possible that MC confused Brussels and Antwerp here. Sansón's estimate that there were already 12,000 copies in print may not be an exaggeration (but DQ's boast to Don Diego de Miranda in II, 16, that 30,000 copies had been published almost certainly was an overstatement). Clearly, this passage represents a fiction (MC was of course perfectly free to invent all the fictional printings he wanted) and probably some wishful thinking. Sansón's further prediction that 'there will be no nation or language into which it has not been translated' has come true to an extent that neither he nor MC could ever have imagined.

Early modern Spain. *Golden Age.

Earthly Paradise [Paraíso Terrenal]. In the Old Testament, the Garden of Eden. See *DQ* I, 33.

East Indies [Indias orientales]. Portuguese possessions in the Orient, colonized after the voyages of Vasco da Gama. See *DQ* II, 29; *Española*.

Easter [Pascua de Flores]. The annual Christian *paschal festival honoring the resurrection of Jesus; it is celebrated on the first Sunday after the first full moon that takes place on or after March 21. In *DQ* I, 31, it is used in the phrase "buenas son mangas después de Pascua" in the sense of 'better late than never.' See also *Cueva*; *Gitanilla*; *Sultana* 3.

Ebreo, Leone. *Hebreo, León.

Ebro (Ibero). The longest river in Spain, with its source in the Cantabrian Mountains in the north-central part of the country. It flows primarily in a southeasterly direction and empties into the Mediterranean Sea at the Ebro Delta, near the city of Tortosa, southwest of Tarragona. DQ's only important water adventure takes place in the episode of the *enchanted boat on the Ebro River in II, 29. See *DQ* II, 27–29; *Galatea* 6.

***Ecclesiastes* [*Eclesiástico*].** A book in the Old Testament, one of the so-called wisdom books, often ascribed to Solomon. In *Vidriera*, the protagonist quotes a long passage in Latin from this book. See also *DQ* II, 3.

Ecclesiastic [Eclesiástico]. The grave and censorious house priest of the duke and duchess. He is impatient with SP's story and then delivers a severe critique of DQ during the latter's first dinner at the duke's palace in *DQ* II, 31. DQ's response (II, 32) is comparatively noble in its restraint and logic. The priest is clearly an object of satire, as a type of the morally righteous cleric who rules in the home of a nobleman. In II, 36, when the Countess Trifaldi comes in search of DQ to right the wrong done to her and others, DQ remarks that he wishes that the priest were present to see how valuable knights-errant are in the world.

Ecclesiastical court of Naples. *Guiomar de Quiñones, Doña.

Echo [Eco]. In Greek myth, a nymph punished by Hera for talking too much at the wrong time. She was deprived of all speech except for the ability to repeat the last words spoken by others. Eventually, she wasted away to a mere voice. See *DQ* I, 26; *Galatea* 1, 6.

Ecija. A Spanish city located east and slightly north of Seville and southwest of Córdoba, about halfway between the two. Located in a valley on the bank of the Genil River, the city has the nickname of 'the frying pan of Andalusia' for its notorious summer heat. Ecija, whose population at the time was about 8,000, was where MC had his first assignment as a commissary in 1587. Because of the trouble he had there with ecclesiastical authorities, he was excommunicated for the first time.

Edad de Oro; Edad dorada. *Golden Age; *Golden Age, Myth of the.

Edipo. *Oedipus.

Editions of *Don Quixote*. The first deluxe critical edition of *DQ* was that of Lord Carteret published in 1738 in England (*Cervantes in England). Particularly interesting is the frontispiece, an engraving by John *Vanderbank, which presents a young, handsome, virile MC as a prototypical classical figure, a sort of modern Hercules. Arguably, this is the moment when MC passes from the ranks of a popular writer to those of a classic: MC enters the *canon. The first truly scholarly edition of the novel was that of the Rev. John Bowle in 1781. The first pretentious Spanish edition was the four-volume work published in 1780 by the Royal Spanish Academy and edited by Vicente de los Ríos (it also includes illustrations by six different artists); it was followed in 1797–98 by the five-volume edition, also with Royal Academy sponsorship, by Juan Pellicer. The greatest edition of the nineteenth century is that of Diego Clemencín (6 vols.; 1833–39), which is still unsurpassed in many aspects, particularly including the relationship between *DQ* and the romances of chivalry. Landmark editions of the twentieth century include the four-volume edition by Rudolfo Schevill and Adolfo Bonilla (1928–41), as a part of their authoritative *Obras completas* of MC; the ten-volume edition by Francisco Rodríguez Marín (1947–48); and the three-volume edition by Vicente Gaos (1987). Good, reliable, affordable editions in popular series of literary texts are also available: for Planeta by Martín de Riquer; for Cátedra by John J. Allen, for Castalia by Luis Murillo, and for Alhambra by Juan Bautista Avalle-Arce, to name but a few of the best. And, finally, the new edition of *DQ* sponsored by the Instituto Cervantes and carried out by a large team of MC scholars led by Francisco Rico (1998) is a monumental achievement. It sets a standard that one can only hope will be applied to the remainder of MC's works.

Bibliography: John J. Allen, "A *Don Quijote* for the New Millennium," *Cervantes* 19, no. 2 (1999): 204–14; Daniel Eisenberg, "Artículo-Reseña: Rico por Cervantes," *Hispanic Review* 69 (2001): 84–88; and Francisco Rico et al., eds., *Don Quijote de la Mancha*, 2 vols. and CD-ROM (Barcelona: Instituto Cervantes, Crítica, 1998).

Efeso. *Ephesus.

Egeo. *Aseo.

Egión. *Ixion.

Egipto; Egito. *Egypt.

Egisto. *Aegisthus.

Egmont, Lamoral, Count [Conde de Eguemón] (1522–68). Dutch nobleman and soldier executed for heresy by the Duke of Alba. See *DQ* I, 39.

Eguía, Pedro Manuel. Argentine writer. Eguía and Fernando Vargas Caba collaborated on a book entitled *Don Quijote en la Pampa* (1948; *Don Quixote in the Pampa*), a retelling of the story of *DQ* I in octosyllabic verse, written in the dialect of the Argentine Pampa (similar to that of José Hernández in *Martín Fierro*). The major stylistic features of the work are some regional vocabulary, verb forms, and phonetics more characteristic of Argentina than Spain.

Bibliography: Pedro Manuel Eguía and Fernando Vargas Caba, *Don Quijote en la Pampa* (Buenos Aires: Mautone y Sosa, 1948).

Egypt [Egipto, Egito]. Country in northeastern Africa, bordering on the Mediterranean and Red Seas. As a civilization that predates even those of ancient Greece and Rome, Egypt was a source of both mystery and awe for people of the sixteenth and seventeenth centuries. See *Baños* 3; *Coloquio*; *DQ* I, 22; *DQ* II, 6, 21, 24; *Fregona*; *Pedro* 1; *Persiles* II, 7.1, III, 11; *Rufián* 2.

Eight Plays and Eight Farces, Never Performed. *Ocho comedias y ocho entremeses, nunca representadas.*

Ejército español. *Army, Spanish.

El [libro] de las libreas. *Book of Liveries.

El que adoró el plátano. *Man who adored a banana tree.

El Rey. *Preliminaries.

El Toboso. *Toboso, El.

Elches. A term used in Fez for the Muslims of Granada. See *Gallardo* 2; *DQ* I, 41.

Elderly Morisco [Anciano morisco]. In *Persiles* III, 11, in a town near Valencia, the man who invites Periandro and the other pilgrims to stay in his house, but, as his daughter Rafala reveals, it is a trap and they are all to be taken away to North Africa as slaves.

Elderly shepherd [Pastor viejo]. In *Persiles* III, 2–4, the man who offers to provide shelter and a place to hide for Feliciana de la Voz, and then has his sister take to Trujillo the baby they had been given by a mysterious horseman.

Elección de los alcaldes de Daganzo, La (Elección); The Election of Magistrates of Daganzo. The third interlude in *Comedias*. Aspects of *Elección* remind the reader of SP in three ways: first, there is a constant correction of language, particularly of Algarroba, as there is of the language used by SP; second, the anecdote told about Berrocal, who was able to note a slight taste of wood, leather, and metal in a wine, is the same as that told by SP in *DQ* I, 13; and third, the wisdom of the candidate Rana is reminiscent of SP during his term as governor of *Barataria.

Bachiller Pesuña, the notary Pedro Estornudo, and the two aldermen Panduro and Alonso Algarroba discuss the four candidates—Juan Berrocal, Francisco de Humillos, Miguel Jarrete, and Pedro de la Rana—for the position of magistrate in the town of Daganzo. Panduro and Estornudo are inclined toward Rana, Algarroba prefers Berrocal, and Pesuña has no preference. They decide to interview all the candidates. Humillos is particularly proud of being an Old Christian and not being able to read. Jarrete can read a little, and is also an Old Christian, but is also a good farmer and blacksmith. Berrocal's strength is his ability to identify wines. Rana wins the day by giving a reasoned speech on the limits of power of a magistrate. A man announces the arrival of the gypsy musicians, and, as they are joined by the subsacristan, the farce ends in the usual song and dance.

Bibliography: Alberto Castilla, "Ironía cervantina y crítica social: Caracterización de los rústicos en *La elección de los alcaldes de Daganzo*," *Cuadernos Hispanoamericanos* 358 (1980): 189–201; and Stanislav Zimic, "Sobre dos entremeses cervantinos: *La elección de los alcaldes de Daganzo* y *El rufián viudo*," *Anales Cervantinos* 19 (1981): 119–60.

Election of Magistrates of Daganzo, The.
*Elección de los alcaldes de Daganzo, La.

Elena. *Helen.

Eleuco. In *Galatea* 2, the elderly shepherd from the banks of the Henares River.

Eleven circles of Heaven [Once cielos]. In the Ptolemaic, geocentric cosmology of antiquity and the Middle Ages, the 11 circles of heaven were Moon, Mercury, Venus, Sun, Mars, Jupiter, Saturn, the Sphere of the Fixed Stars, the crystalline, the Primum Mobile, and heaven. (There are other ways of counting and describing the heavenly spheres.)

Eleven thousand virgins. *Saint Ursula and the 11,000 virgins.

Elicio. 1. In *Galatea*, the shepherd from the banks of the Tajo River, in love with Galatea, good friend of Damón, and the male protagonist. He is often thought to represent MC himself. **2**. In *Coloquio*, a shepherd mentioned by the dog Berganza.

Eliconia. *Heliconia.

Elijah [Elías]. In the Old Testament, one of the prophets. See *Poesías* 12.

Eliot, George (Mary Ann Evans, 1819–1880). English novelist. Eliot's most quixotic novel, by far, is *The Mill on the Floss* (1860). It is Maggie Tulliver's passion for books and fantasies that makes her the DQ of the novel: "In books there were people who were always agreeable or tender. . . . The world outside the books was not a happy one, Maggie felt." When she runs away to live with the gypsies and be their queen (perhaps reminiscent of *Gitanilla*), Maggie characteristically finds little resemblance between reality and her fantasy. In *Middlemarch* (1871–72), the Reverend Casaubon is clearly quixotic (and explicitly identified as such) in his search for the key to the under-

standing of all mythologies, but the idealistic and altruistic Dorothea Brooke is perhaps even more of a DQ figure.

Bibliography: Chester St. H. Mills, "Eliot's Spanish Connection: Casaubon, the Avatar of Quixote," *George Eliot–George Henry Lewes Studies* 26–27 (1994): 1–6.

Elisabat. A *maestro*, or surgeon, in *Amadís de Gaula*. Elisabat is an honorable character and never has an affair with any woman named Madásima, as charged by Cardenio in *DQ* I, 24. Elisabat does, however, have an amorous episode with Princess Grasinda of Bohemia, and perhaps this is what Cardenio had in mind. It is not difficult to confuse names of chivalric characters. See also *DQ* I, 25, 27.

Elíseos Campos. *Elysian Fields.

Elíseos jerezanos. *Elysian meadows of Jerez.

Elisha [Eliseo]. In the Old Testament, one of the prophets, the successor to Elijah. See *Poesías* 12.

Elizabeth I (1533–1603). Queen of England. The daughter of Henry VIII and Anne Boleyn, Elizabeth succeeded her sister Mary Tudor (wife of Felipe II) in 1558. Her policy was consistently anti-Spanish and anti-Catholic. She is a major character in *Española*, where she is never mentioned by name, and where she protects Isabel while Ricaredo is away on adventures. In the story Elizabeth speaks Spanish, but in real life Spanish was not among the languages she spoke.

Elysian Fields, Elysium [Elíseos Campos]. In Greek myth, a blessed and happy land at the end of the world where a few chosen by the gods come to a sort of paradise. In some versions of the legend, Elysium is part of the underworld, ruled over by *Rhadamanthys, judge of the dead. See *DQ* I, 1, 13, 50; *DQ* II, 35; *Fregona*; *Galatea* 6; *Parnaso* 8; *Persiles* I, 21; *Poesías* 5, 27.

Elysian meadows of Jerez [Elíseos jere-zanos]. An open area near *Jerez de la Frontera. See *DQ* I, 18.

Embajador. *Ambassador.

Embajador de Francia. *French ambassador.

Embajador de Persia. *Persian ambassador.

Embedded narratives, interpolated stories [Novelas inercaladas]. The technique of embedding one narrative within another is as old as storytelling itself, as exemplified by the tales-within-tales of the endless narrative of Scheherezade. Like most of his contemporaries, MC sought variety within a work and did not hesitate to include one narrative within another. The pastoral *Galatea* and the Byzantine *Persiles*, as is typical of these genres, consist of one embedded tale after another, usually with the resolution taking place as part of the primary narrative thread. *DQ* I contains the obviously embedded narratives of *Curioso* (I, 32–34), *Capitán* (I, 39–41), and Leandra (I, 51), different as they are in theme, technique, length, and relationship to the primary narrative. The complex story of *Cardenio* (parts of I, 23–36) also qualifies as an embedded story, but it is broken up into so many narrative units, has different narrators, is told to different narratees, and has the dénouement taking place fully within the primary narrative of the adventures of DQ and SP that its status is highly problematic. The situation in *DQ* II is even more complex, as MC explicitly states that he was sensitive to the criticism of such inclusions in the first part of the novel and has chosen not to continue the practice in the sequel (II, 44). In fact, all the episodes that have some trappings of being an embedded story—Camacho's wedding (II, 20–21), the braying aldermen (II, 25), and the Claudia Jerónima story (II, 60), etc.—are very brief and thoroughly integrated in the primary narration. Perhaps the most original and intriguing example of an embedded narrative in all of MC's work is to be found in the last two stories of *Novelas*: *Casamiento* and *Coloquio*, where

the latter consists of a manuscript written and read by characters in the former.

Bibliography: Howard Mancing, "Embedded Narration in *Guzmán de Alfarache*," in *"Ingeniosa Invención"*: Essays on Golden Age Spanish Literature for Geoffrey L. Stagg in Honor of His Eightieth Birthday*, ed. Ellen M. Anderson and Amy R. Williamsen (Newark, DE: Juan de la Cuesta, 1999), 69–99; Hans-Jörg Nueschäfer, *La ética del "Quijote": Función de las novelas intercaladas* (Madrid: Gredos, 1999); Edwin Williamson, "Romance and Realism in the Interpolated Stories of the *Quijote*," *Cervantes*, 2, no. 1 (1982): 43–67; and Stanislav Zimic, *Los cuentos y las novelas del "Quijote"* (Madrid: Iberoamericana, 1998).

Emblem. A symbolic picture, most often accompanied by a motto, exposition in verse, and/or prose commentary. Derived from medieval allegory and bestiary, the emblem book became a recognized literary-pictorial mixed-media genre throughout Europe in the Renaissance. The prototype of the emblem book was the *Emblemata* (1531) of the Italian humanist Andrea Alciato, which was published some 150 times in various languages throughout the sixteenth and seventeenth centuries. In Spain, the translation by El Brocense of 1573 and Diego López's translation entitled *Declaración magistral de los Emblemas de Alciato* (1615; *Magisterial Declaration of Alciato's Emblems*) made Alciato readily available. In addition, there was a series of emblem books by Spanish writers: Francisco de Guzmán's *Triunfos morales* (1557; *Moral Triumphs*), Juan de Borja's *Empresas morales* (1581; *Moral Symbols*), Juan de *Orozco's *Emblemas morales* (1591; *Moral Emblems*), Hernando de Soto's *Emblemas moralizadas* (1599; *Moralized Emblems*), Sebastián de Covarrubias's *Emblemas morales* (1610; *Moral Emblems*), and Francisco de Villava's *Empresas espirituales* (1613; *Spiritual Symbols*). There is no documentation for MC's specific knowledge of any of these works, but there can be no doubt that he was very familiar with the concept of the emblem and made use of it in his own writing, particularly in some of his poetry. *Calliope's song, for example, is one location where he includes the equivalent of verbal emblems and/or refers implicitly to well-known emblems such as Fortune, Desire, and Time.

Bibliography: Ignacio Arellano, "Visiones y símbolos emblemáticos en la poesía de Cervantes," *Anales Cervantinos* 34 (1998): 169–212; John T. Cull, "Heroic Striving and Don Quijote's Emblematic Prudence," *Bulletin of Hispanic Studies* 67 (1990): 265–77; and Fernando Rodríguez de la Flor, *Emblemas: lecturas de la imagen simbólica* (Madrid: Alianza Forma, 1995).

Emerencia. In *DQ* II, 44, the friend of Altisidora who councils her with regard to her love for DQ.

Emergence of the novel. *Theory and history of the novel.

Eminescu, Mihai (1850–89). Rumanian poet. One of Eminescu's lesser known poetic works is a version of *DQ*. First called *Viziunea lui Don Quixotte* (*The Vision of Don Quixote*), it was revised and retitled *Diamantul Nordului* (1873–74; *The Diamond of the North*). Later the author added a subtitle: "Utopia lui don Quixotte y viziunea lui don Quixotte" (1877; "Don Quixote's Utopia and Don Quixote's Vision"). The protagonist of the poem is obviously quixotic as he sets out to conquer the diamond of the north, a precious stone hidden beneath the Northern Sea, in order to disenchant his beloved Inez. Like DQ, he resists the advances of other women, deals with enchantment, and presents the prize to his lady, who tells him it was only a test. At that point, he awakens and realizes that the woman he loves has not paid him any attention. The DQ of this version has been read as an alter ego of the romantic poet, ever disillusioned by reality, in quest of the impossible absolute, an understanding that is consistent with Eminescu's work in general.

Bibliography: Domnica Radulescu, "Eminescu and the Romantic Interpretation of Don Quijote," *Cervantes* 11, no. 1 (1991): 125–33.

Emperador. *Emperor.

Emperador de Alemaña. *Emperor of Germany.

Emperador de la China. *China.

Emperador de Trapisonda. *Trebizond.

Emperante. *Charlemagne.

Emperatrices y reinas del Alcarria y Extremadura. *Empresses and queens of Alcarria and Extremadura.

Emperatriz. *Empress.

Emperatriz de la Mancha. *Empress of La Mancha.

Emperor [Emperador]. One of the members of the cast of *Las *Cortes de la Muerte* in *DQ* II, 11.

Emperor of China. *China.

Emperor of Germany [Emperador de Alemaña]. Used in narration as a comparison when describing the pride and self-importance SP feels when he departs to take possession of his island governorship in *DQ* II, 44.

Emperor of Trebizond. *Trebizond.

Emprenta. *Print shop.

Empress [Emperatriz]. 1. A character in *Tirante el Blanco* (*Martorell, Johanot), mentioned in *DQ* I, 6. She is the wife of the emperor of Constantinople, the mother of Carmesina, and the lover of the page Hipólito. **2**. In *DQ* II, 11, a member of the cast of *Las *Cortes de la Muerte*.

Empress of La Mancha [Emperatriz de la Mancha]. A phrase used by DQ to refer to DT in *DQ* I, 4.

Empresses and queens of Alcarria and Extremadura [Emperatrices y reinas del Alcarria y Extremadura]. A malicious reference by one of the silk merchants to potential rivals of DT as described by DQ in *DQ* I, 4.

Empyrean heaven [Cielo empíreo]. The highest part of heaven, the abode of gods. See *Fregona*.

En un lugar de la Mancha. *In a village of La Mancha.

Enano. *Dwarf.

Encamisados. *White-robed men.

Encantador. *Enchanter.

Encantamiento de Dulcinea. *Enchantment of Dulcinea.

Enceña. A shepherdess mentioned in *Casa* 2.

Enchanted boat [Barco encantado]. When DQ sees a small boat on the shore of the Ebro River in II, 29, he believes that it has been left there for him by an enchanter so that he can carry out a special adventure. This is a common sort of episode in the romances of chivalry (a good example can be found in *Palmerín de Inglaterra*) and there is a certain logic to DQ's interpretation, at least within the context of chivalric adventure. Three things are particularly significant about the events in this episode. First, although it appears that for the first and only time in *DQ* II, DQ has transformed reality as he frequently did in *DQ* I with the windmills, sheep, and so forth, the scene here is not quite so simple. When SP points out that the building is a water mill, DQ admits that although it looks like a mill, it is really a palace. In *DQ* I, DQ never admitted that the giants 'looked like' windmills or the armies 'looked like' sheep, and this admission on his part suggests that he sees reality as it is (as he did in II, 10, when he actually perceived three peasant women and not DT and two other ladies, as SP insisted). Second, DQ has to multiply enchanters and the complexity of the world here, and admits his helplessness. His 'I can do no more' stands in contrast to his 'I am worth a hundred' (I, 15) in the earlier outing. And third, he continues the pattern of paying for the damage he has caused as he did with the lions (II, 17) and Maese Pedro's puppets (II, 26). This episode brings the first phase of *DQ* II to a close, as the chance encounter with the duchess in II, 30, changes radically the course of the plot. DQ's last words in this section of the novel are 'I can do no more'; they are an accurate statement from an increasingly pathetic knight-errant.

Enchanted head (Bronze head) [Cabeza encantada (Cabeza de bronce)]. In *DQ* II, 62–63, the apparently magic speaking device, made of bronze in the form of the head of a Roman emperor. DQ's host in Barcelona, Don *Antonio Moreno, had the head made in imitation of one he had seen in Madrid. Before he puts it on display, he informs the Inquisition of how it works, and afterward he is ordered to disassemble it in order not to deceive people with apparent magic.
  Bibliography: Joseph R. Jones, "Historical Materials for the Study of the *cabeza encantada* Episode in *Don Quijote*, II, 62," *Hispanic Review* 47 (1979): 87–103.

Enchanted Moor [Moro encantado]. In *DQ* I, 17, as he recovers from his wounds received in the lights-out fight over *Maritornes, DQ explains to SP that his enemy was no mortal human but an enchanted Moor.

Enchanter [Encantador, sabio]. Chivalric romance would be impossible without enchanters and enchantment. The great prototype of the wise enchanter who intervenes in the life of kings, queens, knights, and ladies is *Merlin of Arthurian legend (as acknowledged, for example, in *DQ* II, 23, 35, 41). In the Spanish romances of chivalry, the single most famous figure of enchantment is *Urganda la Desconocida, the benevolent promoter of the best interests of Amadís de Gaula. Virtually every Spanish chivalric romance has one or more enchanters, more often good and helpful than evil, and most of the romances are purported to have been written (in an exotic language) by a wise and all-knowing enchanter—CHB's role in *DQ*. Interestingly, it is not DQ himself, but his friends the priest and barber, assisted by DQ's niece and housekeeper, who introduce enchanters into DQ's chivalric world when they blame the disappearance of his library on the work of an enchanter (I, 7). The enchanter device then becomes central to all that DQ does during his chivalric career and, more than anything else, helps sustain it. At first, DQ has a single enchanter-enemy—*Frestón, borrowed from *Belianís de Grecia*. As the novel progresses, however, DQ increasingly speaks of multiple enchanters, reaching the point in II, 29, where there are two enchanters working against each other in a realm beyond DQ's capability to do anything; and in II, 32, where DQ admits to the duchess that enchanters have dogged him and will eventually condemn his great deeds to oblivion. But if the enchanter is a device used by DQ to rationalize his defeats and ineffectiveness, there really are beings who 'enchant' him: his friends the priest and the barber. After the *Micomicona ruse becomes too complicated by reality, the decision is made in I, 46, to make DQ believe he has been enchanted, so that he can be taken home without protest. The priest and barber play the role of enchanters and, on the way home, are accused by SP of having been motivated by envy (I, 47). As control of the action slips from DQ to other characters (primarily the priest, barber, and Dorotea) in the second half of *DQ* I, DQ's chivalric world begins to fall apart. His renunciation of chivalry in I, 52, and inability to sustain a self-motivated chivalric role in *DQ* II, where much of the action is directed by others (especially the duke and duchess) is, at least implicitly, the result of enchantment. Reference to enchanters abound in *DQ*, but, in addition to the chapters cited above, see especially I, 9, 25, 31; II, 10, 17, 23, 33, 41, 43, 46–47, 56, 70, 72.

Bibliography: Bryant L. Creel, "Theoretical Implications in Don Quixote's Idea of Enchantment," *Cervantes* 12, no. 1 (1992): 19–44; Howard Mancing, "Alonso Quijano y sus amigos," in *Cervantes: Su obra y su mundo. Actas del I Congreso Internacional sobre Cervantes*, ed. Manuel Criado de Val (Madrid: Edi-6, 1981), 737–41; Sebastián Neumeister, "Los encantadores y la realidad del mundo de Don Quijote," in *Actas del II Congreso Internacional de la Asociación de Cervantistas*, ed. Giuseppe Grilli (Naples: Instituto Universitario Orientale, 1995), 297–305; and Richard Predmore, *The World of "Don Quixote,"* Cambridge: Harvard University Press, 1967).

Enchantment of Dulcinea [Encantamiento de Dulcinea].

At the beginning of *DQ* II, DQ and SP leave home and head directly for El Toboso in order to see DT. This is unlike all of *DQ* I, where knight and squire rode in search of adventure with no fixed destination. The reason DQ wants to receive his lady's blessing in person has its roots in the events of Sierra Morena (I, 25–31). While DQ does his penance for DT, SP is to deliver a letter to her, but the squire's encounter with the priest and the barber changes the course of events. SP is instructed to inform his master that he has seen and talked with DT and that she wants to see him at once. But the long, complicated series of events involving Dorotea as the Princess *Micomicona keeps the knight's visit to El Toboso from taking place. But at the beginning of the third sally, there is no previous commitment to a damsel in distress to distract him, and DQ is free to heed DT's call. After arriving at the village and being faced with the need to find a palace that does not exist, knight and squire leave town and the next day SP goes to deliver a message to the lady (II, 9). This is where SP decides to deceive DQ by presenting three peasant women as DT and her attendants (II, 10). The roots of SP's deception can also be found in *DQ* I: in the squire's 'enchantment' of Rocinante in I, 20, and in his imaginative description of his supposed interview with DT in I, 32. On the road outside of El Toboso, SP has to convince DQ of a chivalric fantasy, whereas his master sees only reality, a reversal of their traditional roles. The humor of the scene is greatly increased by the narrator's fussy inability to state accurately and consistently what kind of animal the women are riding (so much for the atoms of truth supposedly adhered to in this scene, according to the editorial remarks at the beginning of the chapter). When DQ assumes that his enemy the enchanter has transformed his beloved into something ugly in order to deprive him of the opportunity to see her, he becomes despondent. This enchantment of DT by SP is perhaps the single most significant event in *DQ* II. Here SP sets in motion a series of events that will spiral out of control through one ironic level after another throughout the rest of the novel. The first irony is that SP does not need to do what he does, as DQ had provided him with a script for a scenario he could simply have repeated back to his master, making him believe he had delivered the message. His brilliant deceit, DQ's reluctant acceptance of this version of reality, and the multiple subsequent turns of fate involving the enchanted DT make this one of the pivotal scenes in the novel and one of the most unforgettable. DQ is from this point on obsessed with the thought of disenchanting DT. Her appearance in DQ's dream in the *Cave of Montesinos (II, 23) is the most important manifestation of this obsession. This episode is also a crucial scene in the process of *quixotization and sanchification, the increasing change in the character of SP and DQ brought about by their mutual interaction. See also *DQ* II, 70.

Bibliography: Erich Auerbach, "The Enchanted Dulcinea," in *Mimesis: The Representation of Reality in Western Literature*, trans. Willard R. Trask (Princeton, NJ: Princeton University Press, 1953), 334–58; Carroll B. Johnson, "A Second Look at Dulcinea's Ass: *Don Quijote*, II, 10," *Hispanic Review* 43 (1975): 191–98; and Howard Mancing, "Dulcinea's Ass: A Note on *Don Quijote*, Part II, Ch. 10," *Hispanic Review* 40 (1972): 73–77.

Enchantment theme. *Enchanter.

Encina, Alejandro de la. Spanish novelist. Encina's novel *La amante de Don Quijote* (1997; *Don Quixote's Lover*) takes place in New York City and features a quixotic and utopian televangelist from Spain whose name is Alonso Quijano and who goes by the name of the Caballero de la Alegre Figura (Knight of the Merry Figure). An important second character, also a Spaniard, is a photographer named Sancho P. Anza. The two develop a friendship and relationship that is explicitly modeled on that of DQ and SP and even dress as those characters for a reception held by the Spanish Embassy (also attended by the writers Camilo José Cela and Francisco Umbral, who are severely criticized, and Antonio Gala, who is praised). During the course of the novel, a terrorist bomb explodes in midtown Manhattan and there are acts of deceit and manipulation, a frame-up, two jailbreaks, along with plenty of sex. A se-

quel, to be entitled *La novia de Don Quijote* (*Don Quixote's Bride*), is announced.

Bibliography: Alejandro de la Encina, *La amante de Don Quijote* (Zarautz: Itxaropena, 1997).

Encina, Juan del (ca. 1468–ca. 1529). Spanish poet, musician, and dramatist. Sometimes called the 'father of the Spanish theater,' Encina wrote and staged about 15 eclogues, some quite short, that are the first fairly substantial dramatic works of the Spanish Renaissance theater. The publication of eight of his early works, along with much of his lyric poetry, in his *Cancionero* (1496; *Songbook*) makes him the first Spanish dramatist to have his work printed. Interestingly, his name is absent from MC's review of the history of the Spanish stage in the sixteenth century in the prologue to *Comedias*.

Bibliography: Henry W. Sullivan, *Juan del Encina* (Boston: Twayne, 1976).

Enciso. It is not clear which Enciso MC refers to in *Parnaso* 2. Possibly it is Bartolomé *López de Enciso, author of a pastoral romance *Desengaño de celos* (*The Truth about Jealousy*; 1566).

Enciso Zárate, Francisco de. Spanish romance writer. Enciso is the author of *Crónica del muy valiente y esforzado caballero Platir, hijo del emperador Primaleón* (1533; *Chronicle of the Very Valiant and Brave Knight Platir, Son of the Emperor Primaleón*), the third romance in the *Palmerín* cycle. It is condemned to the flames during the examination of DQ's *library in I, 6. See also *DQ* I, 20.

Eneas. *Aeneas.

Enemies [Enemigos]. In *DQ* II, 47, the men who make up the supposed threat to the island of Barataria.

Enemiga favorable, La. *Tárrega, Francisco Agustín.

Enfermedad. *Sickness.

Engaña bobos y Saca dinero (1790; *Fool Deceiver and Money Extractor*). An anonymous critique of Pedro *Gatell's *Instrucciones económicas y políticas* . . . (1791), in which SP writes advice to his son. In 1876, it was published again, this time with the critique by Ramón Alexo de *Zidra, and Gatell's original work.

Engaño a los ojos, El (Fooled with Open Eyes). The title of a play MC claimed, in the prologue to *Comedias*, to be writing.

England [Inglaterra, Ingalaterra]. The major rival to Spain within Christian Europe in the sixteenth century. England was perceived by the Spanish as the center of heretical (virtually atheistic) Protestantism. MC presents a relatively tolerant view of Queen Elizabeth and England in *Española*, his one story that takes place largely in that country. In *Persiles*, the symbolic characters of Rosamunda (lust) and Clodio (slander) are from England, but the pilgrims do not visit the British Isles. MC's closest personal contact with the English probably took place in 1605 during the state visit of Lord *Howard to Valladolid, then capital of Spain, while MC lived there. See *Coloquio*; *DQ* I, 13 (where it is Ingalaterra); *DQ* II, 57; *Española*; *Persiles* I, 5, 7.1, 11, 14, 16–18, 21; IV, 12.

English gentlemen. *Gentleman, gentlemen.

English Spanish Girl, The. *Española inglesa, La*.

English translations of *Don Quixote*. The first translation of *DQ* into any language was Thomas Shelton's *The History of the Valorous and Wittie Knight-Errant, Don Quixote of the Mancha* in 1612. Shelton followed this with *The Second Part* . . . in 1620. Other important translations include the following: Peter Motteux (1700), Charles Jarvis (1742; edited by E. C. Riley and reissued in 1992), Tobias Smollet (1755; reissued with an introduction by Carlos Fuentes in 1986), and John Ormsby (1885). In the twentieth century, there has also been a number of quality translations. Three from mid-century stand out: those of Samuel Putnam (1949), J. M. Cohen (1950), and Walter Starkie (1957). More recently there are three others of

note: the first is the excellent revision and modernizing of the classic Ormsby translation (1981) by Joseph R. Jones and Kenneth Douglas, who also edited the volume for the respected Norton Critical Edition series, with the accompanying background material and criticism always included in that series. This immediately became established as the standard text for reading and teaching *DQ* in English translation. Burton Raffel's lively version for contemporary American readers came out in 1995, and has since been edited by Diana de Armas Wilson and published (1999) as a replacement for the Ormsby-Jones-Douglas Norton Critical Edition, a controversial move, as some scholars and teachers feel that it is less accurate and less faithful than the Ormsby et al. version, whereas others applaud its vibrant style; the new critical apparatus is also excellent. Most recently, a new translation by John Rutherford (2000) has been published in the Penguin Books series, replacing the Cohen translation. The early twenty-first-century English-language reader has a greater range of fine translations to choose from than has ever been available in the past.

Bibliography: Burton Raffel, "Translating Cervantes: *Una vez más*," *Cervantes* 13, no. 1 (1993): 5–30; Sandra Forbes Gerhard, *"Don Quixote" and the Shelton Translation* (Madrid: José Porrúa Turanzas, 1982); and Roger Gerald Moore, "A Dog Is a Dog Is a Dog!: A Neo-Postmodernist Reading (Cum Grano Salis) of Burton Raffel's New Translation of *Don Quijote*," *International Fiction Review* 25 (1998): 12–28.

Ennius, Quintus [Enio] (239–169 BCE). Roman poet. Ennius was one of the best and most influential of early Roman writers, and has sometimes been called the 'father of Roman literature.' See *Galatea* 6.

Enrique de Cárdenas, Don. In *Doncellas*, the father of Leocadia, who acts as judge during the duel between the fathers of Marco Antonio and Rafael.

Enríquez de Almansa, Don Alvaro Antonio, Marqués de Alcañices. Spanish poet. Enríquez was a grandee, comendador of the Orden of Santiago, and a prominent member of the courts of Felipe III and Felipe IV. He wrote one of the preliminary sonnets in *Novelas*. In *Parnaso* 2 he is referred to as one of five titled poets from Castile.

Enríquez, Fray Feliciano. *Información de Argel*.

Entertaining Story, The. *Entretenida, La*.

Entrée en France de Don Quichot de la Manche, L' (ca. 1620; The Entry of Don Quixote de la Mancha into France). An anonymous early French masquerade based on MC's novel.

Entremés. *Interlude.

***Entremés de las aventuras del caballero don Pascual del Rábano* (*Interlude of the Adventures of the Knight Don Pascual del Rábano*).** An anonymous farce, probably from the first half of the seventeenth century, which consists primarily of comic word play on the names of knights-errant.

Bibliography: Ricardo Senabre Sempere, "Una temprana parodia del *Quijote*: Don Pascual del Rábano," in *Estudios sobre literatura y arte dedicados al Profesor Emilio Orozco Díaz*, ed. A. Gallego Morell, Andrés Soria, and Nicolás Marín (Granada: Universidad de Granada, 1979), vol. 3, 349–61.

***Entremés de los romances* (*Interlude of the Ballads*).** An anonymous farce from the early seventeenth century in which the hero, a peasant named Bartolo, loses his mind from reading *ballads, sallies forth in search of chivalric adventure, recites lines from a number of the poems (including some that DQ also cites), and is beaten for his efforts. It is virtually impossible not to see the work as related to *DQ*, but the question is whether it is something that MC read and used as a model for some of the events of *DQ* I, 1–5 (*Ur-Quijote*), or whether the anonymous author adapted the early chapters of the novel for the short farce. Some have also attributed the work to MC himself, either as a first draft or as a theatrical adaptation of his DQ story. Although consensus leans slightly

to the former alternative, the question cannot be settled definitively.

Bibliography: Ramón Menéndez Pidal, "The Genesis of *Don Quixote*," in *The Anatomy of "Don Quixote": A Symposium*, ed. Angel Flores and M. J. Benardete (New York: Gordian Press, 1947), 32–55; Geoffrey Stagg, "*Don Quijote* and the 'Entremés de los romances': A Retrospective," *Cervantes* 22, no. 2 (2002): 129–50.

***Entretenida, La* (*Entretenida*); *The Entertaining Story*.** Seventh play in MC's *Comedias*. This is MC's only play in the popular *capa y espada* (cape and sword) genre, the most typical subgenre of the Golden Age *comedia*. But even here, MC does not simply present another genre play, with thoroughly predictable characters and situations. The incest theme is not common in the time period, and neither is a play of this type that fails to end in multiple marriages. There is an interlude included within the play and several other scenes are reminiscent of interludes, which—together with the extraordinary role of the servants, who rival the noble characters in importance—suggests the possibility that MC may have cobbled this play together from some of his short, comic works and/or conceived it largely in these terms.

Act I: The play opens with brief scenes involving the amorous conflict between the lackey Ocaña and the page Quiñones for the love of the kitchen maid Cristina. Then the action shifts to the main characters, Don Antonio and Marcela, who are brother and sister. Don Antonio is describing the woman he loves (also named Marcela) by constantly comparing her with Marcela: she has your name, she looks like you, she is as beautiful as you. Don Antonio's friend Don Francisco arrives and tells Don Antonio that the Marcela he loves has been taken out of the city by her father and her exact whereabouts are unknown. Then there is a conversation between Cardenio and his servant Torrente, who are joined by Muñoz, the squire to Marcela. In exchange for valuable gifts, Muñoz explains that Marcela has been promised in marriage to her very wealthy cousin Don Silvestre de Almendárez, who is supposed to be arriving by ship from the Indies fairly soon. The only way to gain access to Marcela would be for Cardenio to pose as Don Silvestre. In order to pull off this deceit, Muñoz suggests, Muñoz must give Cardenio specific details that would make him appear plausible in the role of Don Silvestre. Meanwhile, Marcela talks with her maid Dorotea about her concern that her brother Don Antonio may have an incestuous love for her. Don Ambrosio, another pretender for Marcela's hand, gives Cristina a note to deliver to Marcela, which she does because, like Muñoz, she is hopeful that such favors will win her rich rewards. Torrente arrives dressed as a pilgrim and posing as Don Silvestre's servant; he tells a story about how they were in a shipwreck and all of Don Silvestre's wealth has been lost. Cardenio then arrives, also in pilgrim dress, and is able to convince Don Antonio that he is Don Silvestre.

Act II: Cardenio, in the guise of Don Silvestre, talks with Marcela, who does not take much of a liking to him. At the same time, Torrente begins to court Cristina, but when he talks with Ocaña he promises not to become a rival for Cristina's hand. Don Ambrosio then learns that the Marcela he is interested in is not Don Antonio's sister Marcela, but Marcela Osorio— the second Marcela, the one Don Antonio also loves. Marcela, meanwhile, reveals to Dorotea that she does not particularly like Don Silvestre (i.e., Cardenio). In order to clear up the question of identity, Don Antonio has Ambrosio point out to him if the Marcela he loves is present. Ambrosio indicates that Marcela looks a lot like the woman he loves, but is not the one, which proves to Don Antonio that Ambrosio is indeed his rival for Marcela Osorio. Ocaña hides behind a tapestry and listens to a conversation between Cristina and Torrente in which she promises to love him if he has Ocaña beaten up. After Torrente leaves, Ocaña confronts her with this, but she says she was only joking. The act ends with Ocaña reciting a comic love sonnet.

Act III: Don Francisco tries to explain to Don Antonio that he has spoken with Marcela Osorio's father and that the latter proposes to give his daughter's hand in marriage to Don Antonio. But Don Antonio is so busy acting like the classic overanxious lover that it takes the frustrated Don Francisco some while to get this information across to him. Finally, Don Antonio understands that he has gotten his fondest desire and begins to make plans to retrieve Marcela Osorio from the monastery where she has been sequestered. Cristina and the other servants request permission to celebrate that evening with song, dance, and an interlude of their own composition. Don Antonio, happy with the whole world, readily grants his permission. The play is staged with the assistance of some musicians and the local barber, who is an excellent dancer. At one point in the action, Torrente appears to stab Ocaña and some local lawmen rush in to investigate, but it was all part of the play, and Torrente merely stabbed a wineskin and it was wine, rather than blood, that was shed. The real Don Silvestre arrives with his friend Clavijo and learns that another man (Cardenio) has taken his identity and has been received into the house. Meanwhile, Don Ambrosio has received a handwritten note from Marcela Osorio accepting his marriage proposal. Then Don Pedro Osorio, Marcela Osorio's father, arrives to tell Don Antonio that he wants to marry his daughter to him. But when Don Antonio tells him that Marcela Osorio has already agreed to marry Don Ambrosio, he goes off angry, vowing to block that marriage. Don Silvestre reveals his identity, and Cardenio's masquerade is exposed. Don Antonio's messenger arrives with word that the Pope has not granted the requested dispensation for cousins to marry, so Marcela cannot marry Don Silvestre. Cristina offers to marry Quiñones, but he refuses her offer. She then offers herself to Ocaña, but he does not want someone else's reject. So no one gets married, and on this note the play ends.

Bibliography: Juan Bautista Avalle-Arce, "On *La Entretenida* of Cervantes," *MLN* 84 (1959): 418–21; Edward H. Friedman, "Double Vision: Self and Society in *El laberinto de amor* and *La entretenida*," in *Cervantes and the Renaissance*, ed. Michael D. McGaha (Easton, PA: Juan de la Cuesta, 1980), 157–66; Aurelio González, "Espacio y construcción dramática en *La entretenida* de Cervantes," in *Actas del V Congreso de la Asociación Internacional Siglo de Oro*, ed. Christoph Strosetzki (Madrid: Iberoamericana, 2001); 635–41; Francisco Jose López Alfonso, "*La entretenida*: parodia y teatralidad," *Anales Cervantinos* 24 (1986): 193–205; and George Mariscal, "Woman and the Other Metaphors in Cervantes' *Comedia famosa de la entretenida*," *Theater Journal* 46 (1994): 213–30.

Envy [Envidia]. A vice personified and addressed at the end of *Parnaso* 3, and called the 'monster of nature' (interestingly, the same epithet MC used for Lope de Vega in the prologue to *Comedias*) in *Parnaso* 8. See also *Persiles* IV, 3.

Eolo. *Aeolus.

Ephesus [Efeso]. One of the main Ionian Greek cities, located on the west coast of Asia Minor. See *Viudo*.

Eracio. A Roman soldier mentioned in *Numancia* 4.

Eranio. In *Galatea* 4, one of the Tajo shepherds, praised for his discretion and wisdom; he never appears in the text.

Erasmism. *Erasmus, Desiderius.

Erasmus, Desiderius (1465–1536). Dutch theologian. Though Erasmus never visited Spain, his thought was received there in the early part of the sixteenth century with more sympathy than in any other European nation. Practitioners of concurrent intellectual and spiritual movements, such as *humanism and *mysticism, particularly within *converso circles, found Erasmian thought very consistent with their beliefs. Unlike Martin *Luther, Erasmus never proposed an alternative to the Church, but worked to reform it from within, placing emphasis on spirituality, virtue, peace, and prayer rather than on ritual and public piety. His major work, the *Enchridion* (1518), was published in Spain as the *Enquiridión o manual del caballero cristiano* (1526; *Enchiridion or Manual of the Christian Knight*) and was reprinted a dozen times by 1556. The work was probably more popular and influential in Spain than in any other country. A conservative reaction, however, soon marginalized Erasmus's standing and his works were placed on the *Index of Forbidden Books* in 1559. Erasmism has long been considered an important element in the work of writers such as Fray Luis de *Granada, Juan and Alfonso de *Valdés, Fray Luis de *León, El Brocense (*Sánchez de las Brozas, Francisco), and MC. Because MC is rarely explicit when dealing with religious matters (*religion in Cervantes), it has proven difficult, if not impossible, to demonstrate the precise nature and degree of Erasmian thought in his work, although, on balance, informed scholarly assessment sees strong traces of Erasmism in much of his work. One reason to detect it there is the fact that his early teacher and mentor, Juan *López de Hoyos, was clearly an Erasmian. The ambiguity, implicit anticlericalism, potential satire, and reserved skepticism of certain passages of *DQ* that might suggest the influence of Erasmian thought are counterbalanced by more explicitly traditional and dogmatic Catholic passages in works such as *Persiles*. It is of course possible that MC's religious and spiritual views evolved during the course of his life and that a lack of consistency in his work reflects change in his beliefs and feelings.

Bibliography: Marcel Bataillon, *Erasmo y España. Estudios sobre la historia espiritual de España*, 2nd ed. (Mexico City: Fondo de Cultura Económica, 1966); A. G. Dickens and Whitney R. D. Jones, *Erasmus the Reformer* (London: Methuen, 1994); Manuel Durán, "Erasmo y Cervantes: fervor, ironía, ambigüedad," in *Cervantes, su obra y su mundo. Actas del I Congreso Internacional sobre Cervantes*, ed. Manuel Criado de Val (Madrid: Edi-6, 1981); 969–73; and Antonio Vilanova, *Erasmo y Cervantes* (Barcelona: Lumen, 1989).

Eraso, Antonio de. A member of the Council of the Indies in Lisbon, secretary to Felipe II, and a friend of MC. In February 1582, MC wrote a letter to Eraso concerning his application for a post in the colonies, expressing his concern that the king was not going to grant the application—which is in fact what happened. Eraso signed the king's approval for *Galatea*.

Erastro. In *Galatea*, the rustic shepherd, rival of Elicio for the love of Galatea.

Erato. *Muses.

Ercilla y Zúñiga, Don Alonso de (1533–94). Spanish soldier and epic poet, for a while page to Felipe II. After some eight years of fighting against the Indians in Chile, Ercilla returned to Spain and wrote *La Araucana* (published in three installments in 1569, 1578, and 1590; *The Araucaniad*), probably the most admired epic poem of the Spanish *Golden Age. It is likely that MC knew Ercilla personally (they might have met in 1581 when MC and Ercilla were both in Lisbon) and clearly admired his work. *La Araucana* is among the books praised and saved from the flames in the examination of DQ's library in I, 6. Allusions to Ercilla have been detected in *Galatea*, it has been suggested that the figure of *Lauso in that work is the personification of Ercilla (but others have suggested that Lauso represents MC himself), and there are some interesting parallels between names of characters in *La Araucana* and *Galatea*—where he is praised in Calliope's song in 6. In *DQ* II, 14, Sansón Carrasco paraphrases two lines from *La Araucana*.

Bibliography: Elizabeth B. Davis, "Alonso de Ercilla's Fractured Subjectivity: Internal Contradictions in *La Araucana*," in *Myth and Identity in the Epic of Imperial Spain* (Columbia: University of Missouri Press, 2000), 20–60; and Diana de Armas Wilson, " 'De gracia estraña': Cervantes, Ercilla y el Nuevo mundo," in *En un lugar de La Mancha: Estudios cervantinos en honor de Manuel Durán*, ed. Georgina Dopico Black and Robert González Echevarría (Salamanca, Spain: Ediciones Almar, 1999), 37–55.

Erebus [Herebo]. In Greek myth, one of the primeval deities who came from Chaos (the Void). See *Tratos* 3.

Erichtho [Erito]. A famous sorceress or witch in classical literature. See *Coloquio*.

Ermilio. In *Numancia* 4, Roman soldier who appears briefly.

Ermita. *Hermitage.

Ermita del Compás. *Hermitage of the Compás.

Ermitaño. *Hermit.

Ermitas, Isla de las. *Island of the Hermitages.

Eróstrato. *Herostratus.

Erotic and/or obscene themes and imagery in Cervantes. Those who would idolize MC and his works as representing the finest, purest, and most sublime aspects of Spanish, if not universal, culture, or those who make use of fictional works for doctrinaire purposes, tend not to be aware, or to deny the existence of, the erotic and, at times, obscene connotations of the words and deeds of MC's characters and narrators. Similarly, issues of sexuality and gender, including what is now called *queer theory, often tend to pass unnoticed, particularly among more traditional readers. No work of MC's would ever be classified as pornographic, but it would be a mistake not to recognize that many of his works contain erotic and/or obscene words, phrases, and/or allusions. Part of the problem of nonrecognition is the dated nature of some of the imagery MC uses: what sometimes carried an erotic connotation in the Renaissance is often not recognized as such in our day. An example of the erotic undertones of MC's texts can be seen in *DQ* I, 27, 32, in the passages dealing with the oxtail borrowed from the inn of Juan Palomeque by the priest and barber as they prepare to dress as a damsel in distress and her squire in order to trick DQ into giving up his penance in Sierra Morena and return home. The oxtail is first mentioned when the barber fashions a beard out of 'a reddish-colored oxtail where the barber hung his comb,' apparently an innocent and incidental reference. When DQ and those traveling with him reach the inn, the innkeeper's wife hurries to recover her tail from the barber so that she can again put her husband's comb back in it. Comb (*peine*) in Spanish cannot help but evoke penis (*pene*), and hair and tail have similar connotations in both English and Spanish for women's pubic hair and genitals. Another example can be seen in the confession of Sansón Carrasco (i.e., the Knight of the Mirrors) when he is defeated by DQ in II, 14. Carrasco admits that DT is more beautiful than his own Casildea de Vandalia, but in these terms: DT's tattered and dirty shoe is worth more than Casildea's badly combed, though clean, beard. The foot-shoe (penis-vagina) imagery is common in Renaissance literature, especially in some erotic and pornographic anonymous poetry of the period, and the beard–pubic hair analogy is the same as the one described above (*Dulcinea's shoe and Casildea's beard). The erotic value of all the cross-dressing and undressing scenes in MC's works—especially the strongly implied homoeroticism when three men—the priest, the barber, and Cardenio—spy upon the voluptuous naked feet of the young man who turns out to be Dorotea dressed as a man (I, 28)—is hard to deny.

Bibliography: *Cervantes* 12, no. 2 (1992), Special issue: Selected Papers from the International Colloquium on Eroticism and Witchcraft in Cervantes, ed. José Antonio Cerezo Aranda and Daniel Eisenberg; Arthur Efron, "On Some Central Issues in *Quixote* Criticism: Society and the Sexual Body," *Cervantes* 2, no. 2 (1982): 171–83; Ruth El Saffar, "Sex and the Single Hidalgo: Reflections on Eros in *Don Quijote*," in *Studies in Honor of Elias Rivers*, ed. Bruno M. Damiani and Ruth El Saffar (Potomac, MD: Scripta Humanistica, 1989), 76–93; Barbara Fuchs, "Border Crossings: Transvestism and 'Passing' in *Don Quixote*," *Cervantes* 16, no. 2 (1996): 4–28; and Carroll B. Johnson, "La sexualidad en el *Quijote*," *Edad de Oro* 10 (1990): 125–36.

Escalanta. **1**. In *Rinconete*, one of the prostitutes who comes to the home of Monipodio when Rinconete and Cortadillo are accepted into the thieves' brotherhood. **2**. A prostitute mentioned in *Pedro* 1.

Escarramán. In *Viudo*, the ruffian whose arrival near the end of the play is a cause for great celebration. Escarramán first appeared in a *jácara* (a humorous ballad celebrating low life) by Francisco de *Quevedo (but some scholars have suggested that Escarramán was, or was based on, a historical figure). He immediately became immensely popular as a folkloric character type, the greatest of all ruffians, especially renowned for his dancing. See also *Cueva*.

Escila. *Scylla.

Escipión. *Scipio.

Escita, Escitia. *Scythia.

Esclava(s); Esclava de Lorena; Esclavos cristianos; Esclavos negros. *Slave(s).

Esclavos de Argel, Los (*The Slaves of Algiers*). An anonymous play of about 1598 that is largely taken from *Tratos*.

Escobar, Baltasar de. Spanish humanist poet who was the secretary to the viceroy of Naples. He is praised in Calliope's song in *Galatea* 6.

Escocia. *Scotland.

Escorial. The palace-monastery constructed by Felipe II in the village of San Lorenzo de El Escorial in the Guadarrama Mountains just west of Madrid. The great structure was built to commemorate the victory over the French at San Quintín in France on August 10, 1557, the day of Saint Lawrence (San Lorenzo). The colossal granite building, designed primarily by the architect Juan de Herrera (1530–97), was to serve as royal palace where Felipe would live and royal pantheon where he would be buried. Construction was begun in 1563 and finished just 21 years later in 1584. Felipe's austere private bedroom was built with a view of the altar of the great church contained within the structure. The building serves as well as any other as a symbol of the grandeur of the Spanish *Golden Age. Pedro de Contreras signed the royal privilege to print *Persiles* in San Lorenzo during the court's residence there.

Bibliography: Gabriel Sabau Bergamín, *Historia de San Lorenzo del Escorial* (Aranjuez, Spain: Doce Calles, 2001).

Escotillo. A name used to refer to a number of men associated with magic. One logical candidate is a thirteenth-century Scotsman named Michael Scotus and another is a sixteenth-century Italian by the name of Scotillo. See *DQ* II, 62.

Escribano. *Notary.

Escritor de Numa. *Livy.

Escritor toscano. *Tuscan.

Escuadra de Malta. *Order of Malta.

Escuadrón de bellas ninfas. *Squadron of beautiful nymphs.

Escudero. *Squire.

Escudero de Amadís. *Gandalín.

Escudero del Bosque. *Squire of the [Knight of the] Forest.

Escudero del de los Espejos. *Squire of the Knight of the Mirrors.

Escudo. *Currency.

Escudos de oro. *Gold *escudos*.

Esculapio. *Asclepius.

Esgueva. A notoriously dirty river in Valladolid, cited in *Parnaso* 8 in contrast to the more beautiful Pisuerga.

Eslava Galán, Juan (1948–). Spanish novelist. Eslava Galán's novel *El comedido hidalgo* (1994; *The Moderate Hidalgo*) is an account of two years in the life of Don Alonso de Quesada in Seville in the late 1590s. Don Alonso is a crippled veteran of the battle of Lepanto who will someday write *DQ*; in other words, this is a fictional version of a crucial period in the life of MC, presented under the name of a variant of one of his characters. The author mixes historical figures (e.g., MC's friend Tomás Gutiérrez), characters who will appear in MC's later works (Chiquiznaque, Tomás Rodaja, Aldoncilla), and purely fictional characters (Doña Dulce Castro, her son Moquimber). The protagonist has money problems, spends time in the prison in Seville, meets up with the woman he loved in his youth (Doña Dulce, a name obviously intended to suggest a model for the eventual DT), and schemes to reunite her with her long-lost son. The novel ends with the public reading (by Chiquiznaque, not MC) of Alonso de Quesada's satiric sonnet to the tomb of Felipe II (*Poesías* 25). Overall, this is a vivid historical novel that fictionalizes the life of MC in an original and interesting manner.

Bibliography: Juan Eslava Galán, *El comedido hidalgo* (Barcelona: Planeta, 1994).

Esmirna. *Smyrna.

Esopo. *Aesop.

Esoteric readings of *Don Quixote*. Like any other protean text, DQ lends itself to the widest possible variety of understandings. There has been a long tradition of what are called *esoteric readings*, ways of understanding the text in a special, secret way, with surprising revelations of the "true" meaning of *DQ*. The novel has been seen as a satire on the national politics of Felipe II or the duke of Lerma, and as an allegory criticizing the duke of Medina Sidonia. It has been read as a paean to the Virgin Mary, as a radical statement of a free-thinking atheist, and as a cabalistic Jewish text. In the late eighteenth century, *DQ* became the pretext for a variety of personal, political, and religious satires, as seen in the works of Jacinto María *Delgado, Pedro *Centeno, Pedro *Gatell, and others. The heyday of esotericism was the nineteenth century, and no one was more central to the interpretive polemics surrounding the novel than Nicolás *Díaz de Benjumea. Others of the time who engaged in similar readings were Teodomiro Ibáñez, who held that DQ was not a critique of the romances of chivalry but a monument to Christian literature; Benigno Pallol, writing under the pseudonym of Polinous, and who saw the novel as a critique of both the politics of Felipe II and the Inquisition; Adolfo Salidías, for whom DQ symbolized the politics of the aristocracy, whereas SP was the symbol of the struggle for democracy; Baldomero Villegas, who saw DQ as an allegory in which serious hidden meanings lie beneath the comic surface, and DQ represents MC himself, whereas SP is the Spanish people; and Atanasio *Rivero, who found secret anagrams throughout *DQ*. Lined up against, and consistently criticizing, these writers were more solid scholars and intellectuals such as Juan Valera, José María Asensio y Toledo, and Marcelino Menéndez y Pelayo. Special readings have, not surprisingly, continued into the present age; recent examples include the book in which Guillem Morey Mora argues that El Greco is the secret author of and the main character in *DQ*, Francis Carr's thesis that Francis Bacon wrote not only the plays of Shakespeare but also the works of MC, the thesis of Leandro Rodríguez that MC was Jewish, George Camamis's book proposing that DQ is a satire on the papacy and a vindication of Giordano Bruno, and Fernando *Arrabal's suggestion that MC was homosexual.

Bibliography: Manuel Ferrer-Chivite, "La Interpretación del *Quijote* de D. Benigno Pallol," in *Desviaciones lúdicas en la crítica cervantina: Primer convivio Internacional de "Locos Amenos,"* ed. Antonio Bernat Vistarini and José María Casasayas (Salamanca, Spain: Ediciones Universidad de Salamanca, 2000), 255–64; James Iffland, "Exorcizando la 'prosa satánica' de Cervantes (con una apostilla sobre el delirio hermenéutico)," in *Desviaciones lúdicas en la crítica cervantina: Primer convivio Internacional de "Locos Amenos,"* ed. Antonio Bernat Vistarini and José María Casasayas (Salamanca, Spain: Ediciones Universidad de Salamanca, 2000), 291–304; Ascensión Rivas Hernández, *Lecturas del "Quijote" (Siglos XVII–XIX)* (Salamanca, Spain: Ediciones Colegio de España, 1998): and Carlos Romero Muñoz, "Baldomero Villegas, crítico 'esotérico' del *Quijote* (1897–1899, 1903)," in *Desviaciones lúdicas en la crítica cervantina: Primer convivio Internacional de "Locos Amenos,"* ed. Antonio Bernat Vistarini and José María Casasayas (Salamanca, Spain: Ediciones Universidad de Salamanca, 2000), 443–71.

Espada de Roldán. *Roland's sword.

Espada del perillo. *Sword of the Perillo brand.

Espalder. *Rower.

España. *Spain.

España, Don Juan de. A knight in the Order of Santiago and a minor poet. He is included on the list of good poets in *Parnaso* 2.

Españas, las. The way Dorotea refers to Spain in her story of the Princess Micomicona in *DQ* I, 30. The term is also used occasionally in other contexts as a synonym for España (Spain). The plural form implies the time before all of Spain was united under a single crown, as it refers to all the 'Spains' that made up the peninsula.

Española inglesa, La (Española); The English Spanish Girl. The fourth story in *Novelas*. *Española* is, with *Amante*, one of the most romancelike of MC's short stories, with shipwrecks, brave deeds, lovers who are separated and reunited, and so forth. Its novelty lies in MC's presentation of the court of Elizabeth I of England. The queen is presented as severe, but generous, and fond of speaking Spanish. All the important English characters are Christians (i.e., Catholics, as opposed to Protestants) who practice their religion faithfully, if secretly. This could be read as a commentary on the parallel situation in Spain, where the main task of the *Inquisition was to ferret out those who were secret Jews or Muslims. Overall, the plot of *Española* anticipates that of *Persiles* in general and the story of the tragic Don Manuel de Sosa Coitiño (*Persiles* I, 10) in particular.

In the raid on Cádiz (in 1596), one English gentleman, Clotaldo, takes as a prize a young Spanish girl of about six years of age. Although the count of Essex attempts to have her returned to her parents, Clotaldo is successful in taking her back to England with him. It turns out that Clotaldo's family, which consists of his wife Catalina and their son Ricaredo, is secretly Catholic. The girl's name is Isabel, but in England she is called Isabela, and she is as discreet as she is beautiful. Isabel learns to speak English like a native, but maintains her Spanish by talking with Spaniards brought to the house for this purpose. She is well educated, learns to read and write, and plays musical instruments marvelously. As they grow up together, Ricaredo becomes increasingly aware that he is deeply in love with Isabel, so much so that although he is supposed to marry a wealthy Scottish woman, he falls ill because of his feelings for Isabel. One day he tells her of his feelings and proposes marriage, even it means foregoing the blessing of his parents. Isabel in turn offers her love to Ricaredo. When Ricaredo explains his feelings to his parents, they support him and look for a way out of the previously arranged marriage. But at this time, a messenger informs them that the queen (Elizabeth) has expressed a desire to meet the beautiful young Spanish woman of whom she has heard so much. Catalina is afraid that Isabel might somehow let slip the fact that they are Christians, but Isabel assures her that she can handle the situation. When the day arrives for the presentation of Isabel in the palace, she is dressed in an extremely elegant dress adorned with pearls. Her beauty stuns everyone in the palace (except for one lady-in-waiting who criticizes her dress), including the queen, who is extremely taken with Isabel. When Clotaldo asks permission to marry Isabel to Ricaredo, the queen responds positively, but only after Ricaredo has earned that right by proving his merit. Ricaredo asks what he has to do to prove himself, and the queen replies that within two days two ships are to sail in search of booty. The baron of Lansac is to be the general and command one ship, and Ricaredo is to be captain of the second. In the meantime, the queen herself will be Isabel's guardian. Ricaredo goes to take leave of Isabel, but neither can speak and they both shed copious tears. Two days later the ships set sail, but Ricaredo has a problem: under no circumstance can he take arms against Catholics, and if a situation should present itself where he would be expected to do so, he fears that he would be seen either as a Catholic or a coward. After six days at sea, near the Strait of Gibraltar, they spot three ships, one large and two small. Ricaredo pulls his ship near that of Lansac in order to get instructions, but finds that the general has just died of apoplexy during the night, and Ricaredo, as second in command, assumes the general's responsibilities. As they draw near the three ships, Ricaredo recognizes that they are not Spanish, as he had feared, but Turkish. Since his own two ships are flying Spanish colors, in order to disguise their origins and intentions, the Turks assume that they recently came from the New World and will be

easy prey. In an intense battle, the Turks are routed and the two smaller ships sunk. When Ricaredo and his men board the larger ship, they are told that it is a Portuguese vessel, coming from Portuguese East Indies, laden with valuable spices, pearls, and diamonds. It had arrived at this spot just two days earlier and, crippled by a storm and without cannon fodder, had been easy prey for the Turkish ships, commanded by the corsair Arnaut Mamí. The Turks did not have time to unload the cargo, so it was still full of its treasure. Ricaredo insists that all the Christians be freed, and loads them, plus a few Turks who were not killed, into the smaller of his two ships, while transferring artillery and other goods from this ship to the large Portuguese vessel. Ricaredo makes a brief speech to the freed Christians, gives each one four gold *escudos*, and sends them on their way. The last Christian to board, however, and the one who had provided most of the information about the ship, requests to be taken, along with his wife, who is also with him, to England, rather than be sent back to Spain. The reason for this request is that some 15 years previously, he had lost most of his wealth and his only daughter in the English raid on Cádiz, and he thought that perhaps in England he might learn of his daughter's fate. Ricaredo confirms that these are Isabel's parents, and (without telling them anything about her) agrees to take them with him. Within nine days, they arrive in London. Ricaredo enters the royal palace and informs the queen of the death of Lansac, of his encounter with the Turks, and of the bounty-laden Portuguese ship. The queen is pleased and says that Ricaredo has indeed won the jewel, Isabel, she has kept safe for him during his absence. Ricaredo spends some time with Isabel and other ladies of the court, one of whom, named *Señora* Tansi, teases Ricaredo about coming into the palace fully armed, as though he expected to meet enemies rather than friends. Another, a very young girl, sees her reflection in his armor and observes that war must be a very beautiful thing. Others murmur among themselves that it is impertinent to come into the palace armed as Ricaredo is. The next day, Ricaredo returns to give the queen a more detailed account of his skirmish, but first he introduces the two Spaniards from Cádiz. There is a tearful recognition scene among father, mother, and long-lost daughter (whom her mother identifies by a mole behind her right ear). The queen approves of the way Ricaredo has arranged this reunion, as she is with everything he has done, and promises that he and Isabel will be married in a few days. But then a complication arises. The queen's highest-ranking chambermaid has a son, 22 years old, named Count Arnesto, and he also loves Isabel—so much so that he tells his mother that if he cannot have her, he will kill himself. The chambermaid tries to convince the queen to marry her son to Isabel or, at least, to delay the marriage to Ricaredo for a while. But Elizabeth is true to her word and insists that Ricaredo and Isabel should marry. Arnesto then arms himself, goes to Ricaredo's home, states that Ricaredo is not worthy of Isabel, and issues a challenge for her hand. Ricaredo agrees that neither he nor anyone else is worthy of Isabel, but accepts the challenge to his honor. As he is putting on his arms, word of Arnesto's action gets back to the queen, who sends her captain of the guard to arrest Arnesto. He does so, and Arnesto is sent off to prison in a tower. The chambermaid tries once again to influence the queen, saying that since Isabel is such a source of trouble she should be sent back to Spain, and, furthermore, she is secretly a Catholic. The queen has no intention of exiling her and, as for the religious matter, it merely shows how faithful she has been to her upbringing. Furious, the chambermaid decides to take revenge on Isabel and prepares a poison, which she gives to her that very day. The poison takes effect and Isabel becomes very ill, but the physicians are able to save her life. The queen has the chambermaid, who claims she has done the world a favor in eliminating a Catholic, locked up. Isabel does not die, but loses all her hair and her face is disfigured, making her a monster of ugliness, the diametric opposite of her previous unmatched beauty. Ricaredo remains faithful, however, and, with permission of the queen, takes Isabel to his home. Although within two months she begins to recover a little of her former looks, Ricaredo's parents decide to rees-

tablish contact with the Scottish women first intended as Ricaredo's bride. When the woman arrives, she turns out to be the most beautiful woman in all of Britain, except for Isabel in her prime. But Ricaredo goes to Isabel and, taking her hand in his, promises to marry her. He suggests that if she and her parents return to Spain and wait two years, he will have had a chance to avoid the marriage with the other woman and return to her. Isabel accepts these terms and also promises her undying love. Ricaredo tells his parents that he cannot marry the woman from Scotland, whose name is Clisterna and who is also a Catholic, until he makes a pilgrimage to Rome. The queen gives her blessing for Isabel and her parents to return to Spain, and makes complicated arrangements for their transport and for the transfer of a large amount of money by way of French bankers to them in Spain. Arriving in Cádiz, they transfer to Seville, where they rent a house in Santa Paula, near the convent where a cousin of Isabel's is a nun, and await the arrival of the money from England. When the money arrives, Isabel's father is able to restore his credit and reestablish his business activities. Isabel, meanwhile, completely regains her original beauty. Isabel rarely leaves the house, except to visit her cousin, whose voice is the most beautiful among the nuns in the convent. One day, as the end of the two-year period approaches, they receive a letter from Cristina, Ricaredo's mother, with the news, verified by Ricaredo's servant Guillarte, that Ricaredo has been treacherously murdered in Italy by Count Arnesto. That very day, Isabel vows to take the veil. She prepares to do so on the date of the two-year anniversary of her separation from Ricaredo, wearing the same elaborate dress she had worn when first presented to the queen of England, in a public ceremony attended by many prominent people and two high church officials. But at the last minute, a voice comes from the crowd in attendance, stating that Isabel cannot become a nun as she is his wife. It is Ricaredo, wearing the clothes of a Christian freed from Muslim captivity. Isabel recognizes him and the religious ceremony is halted. A man in the crowd also recognizes him as the English corsair who had given him freedom some two years earlier. After Isabel explains to everyone their story up to the point when she and Ricaredo were separated, Ricaredo takes over the narration: he left England and went to Rome, where he had an audience with the Pope and then arranged for some money transfers to Seville. In the city of Acquapendente, between Florence and Rome, he saw Count Arnesto with four servants. Believing he had not been seen, Ricaredo stayed in his room, rather than go out in public. But that night, four men wielding pistols broke into his room and shot him, leaving him for dead. Ricaredo's page, Guillarte, fled, also sure that his master was dead. Although he had multiple wounds, none was life-threatening. Once cured, he headed for Spain, but was taken captive by Turkish pirates and held in Algiers. He was able to negotiate his ransom by means of Trinitarian friars, and, once free, headed for Spain and arrived in Seville that very day. Ricaredo and Isabel marry and to this day live in a house near Santa Paula; their story is an example of the power of virtue and beauty.

Bibliography: Edward T. Aylward, "Patterns of Symmetrical Design in *La fuerza de la sangre* and *La española inglesa*," *Crítica Hispánica* 16 (1994): 189–203; Marsha S. Collins, "Transgression and Transfiguration in Cervantes's *La española inglesa*," *Cervantes* 16 no. 1 (1996): 54–73; Carroll B. Johnson, "*La española inglesa* and the Practice of Literary Production," *Viator* 19 (1988): 377–416; José Montero Reguera, "La española inglesa y la cuestión de la verosimilitud en la novelística cervantina," in *Actas del IV Congreso Internacional de la Asociación Internacional del Siglo de Oro*, 2 vols. (Alcalá de Henares: Servicio de Publicaciones de la Universidad de Alcalá de Henares, 1998), vol. 2, 1071–77; Thomas A. Pabón, "The Symbolic Significance of Marriage in Cervantes' *La española inglesa*," *Hispanófila* 21 (1978): 59–66; María Caterina Ruta, " 'La española inglesa': El desdoblamiento del héroe," *Anales Cervantinos* 25–26 (1987–88): 371–82; Geoffrey Stagg, "The Composition and Revision of 'La española inglesa,' " *Studies in Honor of Bruce W. Wardropper*, ed. Dian Fox, Harry Sieber, and Robert ter Horst (Newark, DE: Juan de la Cuesta, 1989); 305–21; and Stanislav Zimic, "El *Amadís* cervantino: Apuntes sobre 'La española inglesa,' " *Anales Cervantinos* 25–26 (1987–88): 469–83.

Españoles. *Spaniards.

Espartafilardo del Bosque, duque de Nerbia [Duke of Nerbia]. In *DQ* I, 18, one of the participants in the battle (of sheep) as described by DQ.

Espejo de caballerías. *López de Santa Catalina, Pedro.

Esperanza. *Our Lady of Hope.

Esperia. *Hesperia.

Espérides. *Hesperides.

Espías y centinelas. *Spies and sentinels.

Espina, Concha (1869–1955). Spanish novelist, dramatist, and poet. Espina wrote *Las mujeres del "Quijote"* (1905; *The Women of "Don Quixote"*), one of the earliest and more sensitive (if far from what later feminists would write) surveys of female characters in MC's novel. Her own best novel, *La esfinge maragata* (1914; *The Maragatan Sphinx*, translated as *Mariflor*), presents a basically realistic view of the life of the *Maragatos* (natives of Astorga), and centers on young Mariflor, who conceives of the man she loves, Rogelio Terán, in quixotic and chivalric terms. Rogelio is also described in such terms by the narrator: 'History, fantasy and legend danced madly behind the blond forehead of the dreamy youth.'

Bibliography: Concha Espina, *La esfinge maragata* (Madrid: Renacimiento, 1914).

Espiñeira, Antonio (1855–1907). Chilean dramatist. In his fantasy entitled *Alboroto en el cotarro* (1878 *The Disturbance*), MC, accompanied by DQ and SP, arrives in Parnassus. Espiñeira's play *Cervantes en Argel* (1886) is based on MC's own life, *Casa*, and *Tratos*; and his *Martirios de amores* (1887; *Martyrs for Love*) dramatizes the *Ezpeleta murder and the involvement of MC and his family in the subsequent investigation.

Espinel, Vicente (1550–1624). Spanish musician, poet, and novelist, whose best-known work is *Vida del escudero Marcos de Obregón*

(1618; *Life of the Squire Marcos de Obregón*), a blend of picaresque, courtly, and autobiographical fiction. Espinel is credited with having added the fifth string to the Spanish guitar and with having invented the verse form called the *espinela* (**décima*). Espinel praises MC (along with many other contemporary authors) in his poem "La casa de la memoria" ("The House of Memory"). He, in turn, is praised in Calliope's song in *Galatea* 6 and called 'great' in *Parnaso* 2; later, Apollo sends his regards to Espinel in the letter to MC in *Adjunta*. In *DQ* I, 8, there is a reference to a 'famous poet of our times' who wrote a satire against the ladies of Seville, which is probably an allusion to Espinel's *Sátira contra las damas de Sevilla* (written about 1578; *Satire against the Ladies of Seville*).

Bibliography: George Haley, *Vicente Espinel and "Marcos de Obregón": A Life and Its Literary Representation* (Providence, RI: Brown University Press, 1959).

Espinela. **Décima.

Espinosa, Cardinal Don Diego de (1502–72). Bishop of Sigüenza, president of the Consejo de Castilla, and inquisitor general. After the death of **Isabel de Valois in 1568, during the period of mourning of Felipe II, Espinosa served as regent of Spain. MC, writing on behalf of the academy of Juan **López de Hoyos, addressed *Poesías* 5 to him in the commemorative volume edited by López de Hoyos.

Espinosa, Pedro (1578–1650) Spanish poet, novelist, and anthologist. Espinosa was a decent lyric poet, but he is best remembered for his anthology entitled *Primera parte de las flores de poetas ilustres de España* (1605; *First Part of the Flowers of Illustrious Poets of Spain*). Virtually every poet of some esteem in the early seventeenth century is included in the anthology, but MC is not—a clear indication of his lack of standing as a lyric poet in the eyes of his contemporaries.

Espinosa, Silvestre de. A little-known poet praised in Calliope's song in *Galatea* 6.

Espíritu de Merlín. **Spirit of Merlin.

Espíritu Santo. **Holy Spirit.

Esplá, Oscar (1886–1976). Spanish composer. His symphonic version of *Don Quijote velando las armas* (1929; *Don Quixote Standing Guard over His Arms*) is one of the finer musical interpretations of MC's novel.

Esplandián. Protagonist of the romance of chivalry *Las sergas de Esplandián*, the first sequel to *Amadís de Gaula* (**Montalvo, Garci Rodríguez de). See *DQ* I, 6; *DQ* II, 1, 38.

Espolón. A square overlooking the Pisuerga River in Valladolid and a popular place for a leisurely stroll. It is where Campuzano and Peralta go after the reading of *Coloquio*, in the final, brief, segment of *Casamiento* that closes *Novelas*.

Esportillero. **Carrier.

Esposa seis meses del año. **Prosperina.

Esquerdo, Vicente. Spanish dramatist. A play of his entitled *La ilustre fregona*, presumably an adaptation of *Fregona*, was staged in 1619, but the play is lost. It has also been suggested that *La ilustre fregona y amante al uso*, also attributed to Lope de **Vega, is either this play or one similar to it, or that one play is based on the other.

Esquife. A linguistic error made by DQ's niece in *DQ* I, 5. She means to say Alquife, husband of Urganda la Desconocida and magician from *Amadís de Gaula*, but mistakenly says the word for a small boat (skiff).

Esquilache, Príncipe de. **Borja, Don Francisco de.

Esquivias. A small town northeast of Toledo and south of Madrid, just north of La Mancha. In MC's day, Esquivias was quite famous for its wines. It was also the home of MC's wife, Catalina de **Palacios. The two met there in 1584 when MC went to the town to arrange with Juana de **Gaitán, the widow of his friend

Pedro *Laínez, the posthumous publication of the poet's last book. For nearly two decades following his marriage in December of that year, MC made at least occasional visits to Esquivias, where his wife continued to live while he worked as a commissary and tax collector in Andalusia. Although Esquivias may technically not be part of La Mancha, it is close enough and it is of such crucial importance in MC's life that it has often been proposed as the major rival to *Argamasilla del Alba as the 'village of La Mancha' that was DQ's home. The case for Esquivias rests on two factors: MC's familiarity with the town and the documented presence of a number of people with names identical (or at least very similar) to those of characters in *DQ*. Research has turned up a family of *hidalgos* with the surname Quijada, a deceased relative of MC's wife named Alonso *Quijana, another relative named Gabriel Quijada de Salazar, a parish priest named Pedro Pérez, a Mari Gutiérrez, and others with names like Ricote, Carrasco, and Lorenzo. So perhaps at least some of the fictional characters of *DQ* were based, at least to some degree, on real historical figures. There is the obligatory Casa de Cervantes (Home of Cervantes) in Esquivias, but it is not the building on the site of where MC and his wife actually lived. Perhaps surprisingly, Esquivias does not appear in *DQ*, but its wine is mentioned in *Vidriera*, *Coloquio*, *Elección*, and *Cueva*.

Bibliography: *Homenaje de Esquivias a Cervantes* (Toledo, Spain: Ayuntamiento de Esquivias, 1987).

Essex, Count of. *Devereux, Robert.

Estacio. A Roman soldier mentioned in *Numancia* 4.

Estampero. *Printer.

Estancias polifemas. *Stanzas from Luis de Góngora's poem *Polifemo*.

Este family. This family, with the title of duke of Ferrara, dominated the nobility of the Italian city of Ferrara from the fourteenth century to the sixteenth. In *Cornelia*, the character named Alfonso de Este, duke of Ferrara, is fictional, but there was a real Alfonso II d'Este (1533–1597) who was the fifth and last duke of Ferrara and upon whom the fictional character is based. The reference in *Galatea* 6 to the poet who read to this family is to Ludovico *Ariosto, who read parts of *Orlando Furioso* to Isabella d'Este in Mantua. Ariosto dedicated the first edition of his great poem to Cardinal Ippolito d'Este. See also *DQ* II, 1.

Esteban de Solórzano, Don. In *Vizcaíno*, the name used by Solórzano to make Cristina think he is a nobleman.

Estefanía de Caicedo, Doña. In *Casamiento*, the woman who deceives Campuzano in their marriage, leaves him with a case of syphilis, and takes all his goods, only to learn later that his jewels are all fakes.

Estefanía, Doña. In *Fuerza*, the mother of Rodolfo who arranges the marriage between her son and Leocadia.

Ester. *Esther.

Esteso y López de Haro, Luis (ca. 1880–1928). Spanish humorist, essayist, dramatist, and novelist. Esteso's curious book *El nieto de Don Quijote: Andanzas y correrías por algunos pueblos de España: En colaboración con Cervantes, Antonio de Guevara, el Arcipreste de Hita, Gil Polo, Quevedo, Rojas Villandrando, Enríquez Gómez, José de Acosta y otros ingenios; en el que se demuestra que el "Falso Quijote" lo escribió Lope de Vega. Por el rey del hambre y de la risa* (1918; *The Grandson of Don Quijote: Wanderings and Travels through Some Towns in Spain: In Collaboration with Cervantes, Antonio de Guevara, el Arcipreste de Hita, Gil Polo, Quevedo, Rojas Villandrando, Enríquez Gómez, José de Acosta and Other Wits; in which It Is Demonstrated that Lope de Vega Wrote the "False Quixote." By the King of Hunger and Laughter*) begins with the author's claim to be the grandson of DQ. Before DQ died in the Manchegan town of San Clemente, he and DT had one son, the father of the author. The remainder of the book consists of Esteso's travels throughout Spain, comments on the places he visits, the books he reads during these travels, and passages, some of them quite long, quoted from the authors mentioned in the subtitle and from Esteso himself. The final chapter makes a case for Lope de Vega as the author of *DQA*. The short book is an odd mixture of travelogue, memoir, fictional autobiography, self-justification, and literary criticism. Esteso is also the author of 1) *Viajes por España. Viaje cómico. El nieto de Don Quijote. Viaje de placer* (1914; *Travels through Spain. Comic Trip. The Grandson of Don Quixote. Pleasurable Trip*); 2) *Nuevo Viaje al Parnaso; La Musa Picaresca. Los Poetas, Novelistas, Autores Dramáticos y Críticos que escribían en el año 1917 y varios monólogos más.—De Jacinto Benavente á Luis Esteso. Diferencias literarias. Prólogo de EL LAZARILLO DE TORMES* (1917; *New Voyage to Parnassus; the Picaresque Muse. The Poets, Novelists, Dramatic Authors, and Critics Who Were Writing in the Year 1917 and Various Other Monologues.—From Jacinto Benavente to Luis Esteso. Literary Differences. Prologue of LAZARILLO DE TORMES*); and 3) *Cartas amorosas. Nuevas cartas amorosas. Despertadoras de amantes sufridos. Nuevo formulario para expresar el amor. Con un prólogo de Miguel de Cervantes Saavedra, y una invocación en verso a Don Quijote* (1918; *Love Letters. New Love Letters. Alarms for Suffering Lovers. New Formula to Express Love. With a Prologue by Miguel de Cervantes Saavedra, and an Invocation in Verse to Don Quixote*).

Bibliography: Luis Esteso y López de Haro, *El nieto de Don Quijote: Andanzas y correrías por algunos pueblos de España* (Madrid: J. Pueyo, 1918).

Esther [Ester]. In the Old Testament, the heroine of the book that takes its title from her name. She was the Jewish wife of Persian King Ahasuerus who saved her people from slaughter by Haman. See *Persiles* III, 5.

Estigia, laguna; Estigio. *Stix.

Estoille, Claude de l' (1597–1652). French dramatist. He is the author of *La belle Esclave* (1643; *The Beautiful Slave*), based on *Amante*,

and at least partly derived also from the plays on the same theme by *Guérin de Bouscal and *Scudéry.

Estrada, Alonso de (1540–1610). Spanish poet who emigrated to Peru; he is praised in Calliope's song in *Galatea* 6.

Estrambote. A brief stanza added to another poem with an otherwise invariable form, such as a sonnet, usually for comic effect. An example can be seen in MC's famous sonnet to the tomb of Felipe II (*Poesías* 26).

Estrecho Hercúleo. *Gibraltar, Strait of Gibraltar.

Estrómbalo. *Stromboli.

Estudiante(s). *Student(s).

Estudiante poeta. *Lorenzo, Don.

Estudio de la Villa. *López de Hoyos, Juan.

Ethiopia [Etiopía]. A country in eastern Africa bordering on what today are the Sudan, Kenya, and the Somali Republic. In *DQ* I, 29, SP incorrectly remembers the home of the Princess *Micomicona, calling it Ethiopia rather than Guinea. See also *DQ* I, 47.

Ethiopian [Etiope]. In *Poesías* 15, the dark-skinned Ethiopian is contrasted with the light-skinned Scythian.

Etna. The Sicilian volcano where Vulcan was supposed to have his forge. See *Poesías* 30.

Eugenio. 1. In *Galatea* 1, the shepherd from the Henares, beloved of Lidia. **2.** The goatherd who tells the story of Leandra in *DQ* I, 51, and then gets into a fight with DQ in I, 52. The ill-tempered DQ starts the fight by unchivalrously throwing a loaf of bread at the goatherd, who has just commented that DQ must have some empty rooms in his head. At first, Eugenio tries to strangle DQ but SP rescues his master; then, the goatherd tries to stab DQ, but the priest and the canon of Toledo intervene to prevent bloodshed. Next, the barber trips DQ so that Eugenio can beat him, and at the same time one of the canon's servants restrains SP from helping. The canon, the priest, and the officers all laugh heartily at the scene, and only SP sympathizes with DQ, frustrated that he cannot help. The scene provides an interesting contrast between the laughing and gloating 'friends' of a bloodied and desperate DQ on the one hand, and a faithful but outnumbered and overpowered SP on the other.

Bibliography: John G. Weiger, "The Curious Pertinence of Eugenio's Tale in *Don Quijote*," *MLN* 96 (1981): 261–85.

Euríalo. *Nisus and Euryalus.

Euro. *Euste.

Europa. In Greek myth, the beautiful daughter of the king of Tyre. Europa was so desired by Zeus that he took the form of a handsome bull and swam to the island where she was amusing herself with her companions. Because the animal seemed so tame, Europa climbed on his back, and Zeus was thus able to swim away with her to Crete, where she became his lover and bore him *Minos and *Radamanthys, the judges of the underworld. See *Persiles* III, 15.

Europe [Europa]. For MC, the nations that made up the continent of Europe were important and relevant in the following descending order: Spain, Italy, Portugal, Flanders, England, France, and Germany. His references to Europe in general are relatively few; see, for example, *DQ* I, 18, 48; *Galatea* 4; *Gitanilla*; *Persiles* II, 21; III, 1, 12; *Vidriera*.

Eusebia. 1. In *Persiles* II, 17–21, the French woman who has secluded herself in a hermitage on the Island of the Hermits with Renato, whom she has informally married and with whom she lives virtuously. When news comes that Renato has been cleared of the charges against him, she returns with him to France. **2.** In *Persiles* IV, 12–13, the queen of Frisland and mother of Sigismunda and Eusebia. She encourages Sigismunda to choose Persiles over his brother Maximino and to undertake the trip to Rome. **3.** In *Persiles* IV, 13–14, the younger

daughter of the Queen Eusebia of Frisland and the sister of Sigismunda. After Sigismunda's life-threatening illness in IV, 11, Sigismunda decides to take the veil rather than marry Persiles; but she suggests that he can still marry into her royal family by marrying her beautiful younger sister Eusebia. When Sigismunda regains her senses and marries Persiles, Eusebia is promised to Arnaldo.

Euste. Probably an error for Euro, the western wind. See *Laberinto* 2.

Eustoquia. In *Persiles* IV, 12, the wife of Maximino, king of Thule, and mother of the two princes Maximino and Persiles.

Euterpe; Euterpi. *Muses.

Evangelio. *Gospel.

Evans, Mary Ann. *Eliot, George.

Eve [Eva]. In the Old Testament, the first woman, supposedly formed from one of Adam's ribs. She lived with Adam in the paradise of the Garden of Eden until she was tempted by a serpent to taste of the tree of good and evil, thus bringing sin into the world. See *DQ* I, 33; *Persiles* III, 4.

Evil One [Malo]. A term for the devil. See *DQ* II, 61.

Ex illis. A term meaning 'from there'; in *Retablo*, a reference to having Jewish heritage.

Exarque, Onofre. A Spanish trader who participated in MC's fourth and final escape attempt in 1579 by arranging to buy a frigate to transport MC and some 60 other captives back to Spain.

Exemplary Novels. *Novelas ejemplares.

Eximeno y Pujades, Antonio (1729–1808). Spanish musicologist and writer. Eximeno's posthumous *Don Lazarillo Vizcardi, sus investigaciones músicas con ocasión del concurso a un magisterio de capilla vacante* (2 vols., 1872; *Don Lazarillo Vizcardi, His Mu-*

sical Research on the Occasion of the Competition for a Vacant Directorship of a Chapel) starts out well in the preliminary pages, as a messenger delivers a recently published novel by Antonio Eximeno and written 'in the style of *DQ*.' But it is all downhill after that. The work is a fiction about the musical education of the title character, but it is also, as much as anything, a treatise on music.

Bibliography: Antonio Eximeno y Pujades, *Don Lazarillo Vizcardi*, 2 vols. (Madrid: Sociedad de Bibliófilos, 1872–73).

Extremadura. A region of Spain located west of Madrid and bordering on Portugal, composed of the provinces of Mérida and Badajoz. Along with Alcarria, it is compared to La Mancha by one of the merchants DQ encounters in I, 4. See also *Celoso*; *DQ* I, 20, 32, 49; *Gitanilla*.

Ezino. *Zino.

Ezpeleta, Don Gaspar de (1567–1605). Spanish nobleman, knight in the Order of Santiago. According to a satirical poem by Luis de Góngora, Ezpeleta took an embarrassing fall during a bullfight staged to commemorate the birth of Prince Felipe (later King Felipe IV) and the state visit of Lord *Howard in Valladolid in 1605. On June 27, shortly after the English ambassador's departure, Ezpeleta was murdered in front of the building where MC and his family were living. Ezpeleta had been in trouble with the law on a previous occasion and had a reputation as a womanizer (his wife and child were still in Pamplona while he was in Valladolid). He was known to have been involved with Inés Hernández, wife of a royal clerk named Melchor Galván. MC's sister Magdalena administered first aid to the man as he lay dying. The police officer who investigated, Cristóbal de Villarroel, in a classic case of police cover-up, went out of his way to keep Galván and his wife from becoming implicated in any way. MC and ten others (including his sister Andrea, daughter Isabel, niece Constanza, friend Juana *Gaitán, Mariana *Ramírez, and Diego de *Miranda) were briefly incarcerated (in the same jail where both MC's father and grandfather had also spent time) as a part of the investigation. All were eventually cleared of any involvement. During the investigation, the term "las Cervantas" ("the Cervantes women") was used as a slur to refer to the women of MC's family. In her testimony, his sister Andrea describes her brother as 'a man who writes, conducts his business, and has many friends.' The court records for this case comprise one of the most valuable documents in the personal life of MC.

Bibliography: Jean Canavaggio, "Aproximación al Proceso Ezpeleta," *Cervantes* 17, no. 1 (1997): 25–45.

Fabiana. *Favignana.

Fabio. In *Cornelia*, the servant of the Duke of Ferrara who is to take Cornelia Bentibolli's baby from the servant Sulpicia but by mistake does not receive the child, who is given to Don Juan de Gamboa instead. At the end of the story, Fabio marries Sulpicia.

Fabius, Quintas (Quinto Fabio): Quintas Fabius Maximus Verrucosus (ca. 275–203 BCE). Famous Roman general and politician. In *Numancia*, he is a Roman soldier and brother of Scipio.

Fabla. A term (derived from the archaic form of *habla* [speech] < *fabla*) used to describe an intentionally archaic style of speaking or writing. Since the romances of chivalry were always purported to be translations of old texts, several of them are written in a style that evokes an earlier state of the Spanish language. *Amadís de Gaula*, DQ's favorite reading, really was a rewrite of a medieval text, and Garci Rodríguez de *Montalvo (who states in his prologue that he modernized the language of the old text) deliberately retained an archaic flavor, both in the parts he kept or adapted from the medieval text and in those he himself wrote. In order to imitate his literary heroes, DQ often speaks in *fabla*, especially early in his chivalric career. The major characteristics of DQ's archaic speech are the word initial *f-* whereas the Spanish of MC's day had already evolved to *h-*; the retention of the archaic second-person plural verb ending *-edes*; and a limited archaic vocabulary: *cautivo* (wretched), *afincamiento* (sorrow), *ca* (because), and so on. The effect of such archaic speech by DQ, especially when combined with his archaic armor—it was not his father's, nor even his grandfather's, but his great-grandfather's—is comic, and attention is drawn to the fact that it evokes laughter from several characters in the novel; DQ, in other words, looks and sounds like someone from about a century in the past. DQ's archaic speech generally declines in frequency during the course of the novel; he uses none after II, 32. Other characters, including SP and the priest, quickly learn to use *fabla* in imitation of DQ and in order to manipulate him. Modern readers often fail to recognize *fabla*, seeing the language and style of *DQ* as generally somewhat old-fashioned, and thus miss its comic function. The preliminary sonnet to *DQ* I by Solisdán is also written in *fabla*.

Bibliography: Francisco López Estrada, "La risible *fermosura*: un rasgo de la comicidad inicial del *Quijote*," *Anthropos* 100 (1989): vi–ix; and Howard Mancing, "Cervantes and the Tradition of Chivalric Parody," *Forum for Modern Language Studies* 11 (1975): 177–91.

Fabricio. A member of the Roman camp mentioned in *Numancia* 4.

Fábulas que llaman milesias. *Milesian fables.

Faetonte. *Phaethon.

Falari; Fálaris. *Phalaris.

Falces, Mosén Luis de. A Spanish knight mentioned by DQ in *DQ* I, 49 (*Crónica de Juan II*).

Falcón, César (1892–1970). Peruvian novelist. In the introductory pages of his novel *El buen vecino Sanabria U* (1947; *Good Neighbor*

Sanabria U), Falcón states his aim to write in the tradition of MC, 'the highest authority among our writers,' and states that Sanabria has a 'spiritual relationship' to *Rinconete* and *DQ*. This relationship is mentioned again in the first paragraph of the novel, but not after that. Calixto Sanabria U is a picaresque politician and international businessman who unscrupulously rises to the highest realm of wealth, power, and influence.

Bibliography: César Falcón, *El buen vecino Sanabria U* (México City: Ediciones de Historia Nueva, 1947).

Falcón, Doctor (Jaime). Spanish mathematician and sometimes poet praised in Calliope's song in *Galatea* 6.

Falconí Almeida, Patricio. Ecuadorian poet. Falconí's book *La costilla de Don Quijote* (2000; *Don Quixote's Rib*) is a single long poem (or, depending on how you choose to read it, a sequence of very short poems) of love directed to an unnamed woman. In the opening lines, the poet invokes his beloved and states that she comes, not from Adam's rib, but from that of DQ. There is only a single additional reference to DQ in the poem, but given the title metaphor and the prominent placement of the concept in the text, the suggestion is, perhaps, that the woman is the poet's ideal, an ideal inspired in DQ's love for DT.

Bibliography: Patricio Falconí Almeida, *La costilla de Don Quijote* (Quito, Ecuador: Ediciones La Posada de Borges, 2000).

Falerina. A sorceress in Boiardo's *Orlando Innamorato*. See *Persiles* IV; *Poesías* 32.

Falla, Manuel de (1876–1946). Spanish composer. Falla's *El retablo de Maese Pedro* (1923; *The Puppet-Show of Maese Pedro*) is an adaptation of *DQ* II, 26, in which DQ interrupts the puppet show. There was a strong revival of interest in puppet theater in Spain in the early twentieth century, with Federico García Lorca taking a lead role. Falla combined music and puppetry more brilliantly than any of his contemporaries in this superb rendition of the famous scene from *DQ*. For the most part, the

actual text of the novel is followed in the lyrics of DQ, Maese Pedro, and the boy who interprets the action of the puppets.

Bibliography: Manuel de Falla and Manuel Angeles Ortiz, *El retablo de Maese Pedro: Bocetos y figurines* (Madrid: Pabellón Transatlántico, Residencia de Estudiantes, 1996); and Peter Leister and Angelica Rieger, "La recepción del *Quijote* en *El Retablo de Maese Pedro* de Manuel de Falla (1923)," in *Actas del V Congreso de la Asociación Internacional Siglo de Oro*, ed. Christoph Strosetzki (Madrid: Iberoamericana, 2001), 793–806.

Fame [Fama]. 1. Unlike fortune, fame, in the sense of renown or recognition, was not often personified among the Greeks and Romans. But she sometimes is in MC's works, as in *Numancia* 4, where she speaks the final words of the play, stressing the eternal worldwide fame that the tragic story will have; *Parnaso* 6, where she is the mother of Vainglory in MC's dream; and *Persiles* II, 10, where it is the name of one of the four boats in the fishermen's regatta. See also *DQ* I, 40; *Galatea* 6; *Poesías* 20, 30, 34. **2.** *Castle of Fame. **3.** *Nine Worthies.

Familiar. *Inquisition.

Familiar of the Holy Office [Familiar del Santo Oficio]. In the prologue to *DQ* II, a clear allusion to Lope de *Vega.

Families [Linajes]. In a conversation with his niece and the housekeeper, in *DQ* II, 6, DQ describes four types of family lines: those that begin humbly and rise to greatness; those that start out great and remain that way; those that start out great but peter out; and those that always have been and always will be in between the two extremes, the common people. Later (II, 20), SP reduces all this to two kinds of families: the Haves and the Have Nots.

Famosa (lengua) de la hampa; Famous (language) of the underworld. *Germanía.

Famoso poeta andaluz; Famous Andalusian poet. *Barahona de Soto, Luis.

Famoso poeta destos reinos; Famous poet of these kingdoms. *Argensola, Lupercio Leonardo de.

Famoso poeta destos tiempos; Famous poet of our times. *Espinel, Vicente.

Famoso y único poeta castellano; Famous and singular Castilian poet. *Vega Carpio, Lope Félix de.

Faraones y Tolomeos de Egipto. *Pharaohs and Ptolemys of Egypt.

Fares. A Jewish name mentioned in *Baños* 3.

Faría(s), Don Francisco de. Doctor of theology and priest, as well as translator and poet. He is mentioned as one of the good poets in *Parnaso* 2.

Farnesio, Alejandro, Duke of Parma (1545–92). Spanish general. Farnesio fought with Don Juan of Austria in Lepanto and then, beginning in 1578, was governor of the Netherlands, where he carried out the ongoing military struggle to subdue the stubborn Dutch. His inability to connect with the flotilla of the Invincible Armada was a major factor in the defeat of that expedition. He is alluded to twice in MC's first poem to the Invincible Armada (*Poesías* 20).

Faro de Alejandría. *Lighthouse (Pharos) of Alexandria.

Faro de Micina. *Lighthouse of Messina.

Farquhar, George (1678–1707). English dramatist. Two of Farquhar's plays, the early *Love and a Bottle* (1698) and the later and much better *The Beaux' Stratagem* (1707), whose great popularity the author did not live to see, show some influence of *DQ*. In the latter play, the character of Archer specifically compares the events taking place to DQ's adventures in the inn of Juan Palomeque in *DQ* I.

Farsantes. *Actors.

Fates (Fierce sisters) [Parcas (Fieras hermanas)]. In Greek myth, the three sisters, elderly spinners, whose work represented the birth, life, and death of all humans: Clotho (Cloto) presides at birth, holding the spindle; Lachesis (Láqueda) turns the spinning wheel of life; and Atropos cuts the string, the moment of death. In Roman myth, they were called the Parcae, and their names were Nona, Decuma, and Morta. The canvas by Diego de *Velázquez entitled *Las hilanderas* (*The Spinners*) is probably the most famous painting of the theme. See *DQ* II, 38; *Gallardo* 2; *Numancia* 2; *Persiles* I, 18; *Rufián* 2.

Father [Padre]. Saturn, the father of the gods. See *Fregona*.

Father and mother [Padre y madre]. In *Tratos* 2, the Christians whose two sons are sold into slavery.

Father of Ascanio Colona. *Colonna, Ascanio.

Father of Doña Catalina de Oviedo [Padre de doña Catalina de Oviedo]. *Lamberto de Oviedo.

Fátima. 1. In *Gallardo* 3, the name given to *Margarita in order to deceive her brother. **2.** In *Tratos*, servant to Zahara, who uses magic to conjure up a demon to help her mistress win the love of the Christian slave Aurelio.

Faulkner, William (1897–1962). American novelist and short-story writer. Faulkner claimed that, like Carlos *Fuentes, he reread *DQ* every year, "as some do the Bible." Yet the influence or presence of *DQ* in Faulkner is less obvious than it is in many other writers. It is best seen in a series of heroes who, in their own sometimes subtle ways, are profoundly quixotic. To various degrees, they tend to be highly impractical, plagued by illusion, inspired by literary models, nostalgic for an idealized *Golden Age, with a strong sense of honor, and often on a private quest. Included in this group are Quentin Compson (whom Faulkner himself compared to DQ) in *The Sound and the Fury*

(1929), the entire Bundren family in *As I Lay Dying* (1930); Gail Hightower (with his SP in Byron Bunch) in *Light in August* (1932); Lucas Beauchamp in *Intruder in the Dust* (1948), Gavin Stevens in *The Town* (1957) and *The Mansion* (1959); Lucius Priest in *The Reivers* (1962), the tall convict in "Old Man," Gavin (again compared to DQ by the author himself) in "The Town," and Isaac McCaslin in "The Bear" and "Delta Autumn."

Bibliography: Montserrat Ginés, "Honor for the Sake of Honor: The Windmills of Yoknapatawpha," and "Faulkner and the Quixotic Utopia," in *The Southern Inheritors of Don Quixote* (Baton Rouge: Louisiana State University Press, 2000); 72–123; and George Ann Huck, "The 'Quijotismo' Influence in Faulkner," in *Cervantes, su obra y su mundo: Actas del I Congreso Internacional sobre Cervantes*, ed. Manuel Criado de Val (Madrid: Edi-6, 1981), 1137–49.

Fauns [Faunos]. Mythological creatures who inhabited the plains. See *DQ* I, 26.

Favart, Charles-Simon (1710–94). French actor and dramatist, protégé of Madame de Pompadour. Favart wrote a popular three-act comic ballet entitled *Don Quichotte chez la Duchesse* (1743; *Don Quixote at the Home of the Duchess*), with music by Boismortier, based primarily on the Altisidora episode from *DQ* II, 44, 46. For Favart, Altisidora is truly in love with DQ and not just playing a role. But when the knight rejects her marriage proposals, she turns him into a bear and SP into a monkey, and the enchanter Merlin has to intervene to restore them to their original form. By the end of the play, SP departs for Africa, where he marries an heiress in the Congo, and DQ departs for Japan to search there for DT.

Favignana [Fabiana]. The largest of the Egadean Islands, located to the west of Trapani. See *Amante*.

Favila (or Fávila) (eighth century CE). Son of the legendary Pelayo and king of Asturias, who was killed by a bear. See *DQ* II, 34.

Fe de erratas. *Preliminaries.

Fear [Temor]. In *Casa* 2, an allegorical figure conjured up by Malgesí.

Febo. *Apollo.

Febres Cordero, Tulio (1860–1938). Venezuelan writer. His satiric novel *Don Quijote en América, o sea, la cuarta salida del ingenioso hidalgo de la Mancha* (1905; *Don Quixote in America, or, The Fourth Sally of the Ingenious Hidalgo of La Mancha*) begins with the burial of DQ, when the priest opens the casket one final time. A young African, a descendent of CHB, who is present insists that DQ is not dead and, sure enough, the knight rises and sets out again on Rocinante and accompanied by SP. After a brief trip to Africa, knight and squire return to Spain and descend into the Cave of Montesinos where they spend some 300 years under enchantment. Upon emerging from the cave, DQ dresses as a bullfighter and he and SP, now known as Sanchano, go to Barcelona in order to depart for America, accompanied by a young Venezuelan named Santiago (who is in some ways more quixotic than DQ in this sequel). DQ now calls himself Dr. Quix of Manchester, or the Knight of the Order of Progress. Upon arrival at Mapiche, a city not far from the equator, the bicycle-riding DQ has a series of adventures that include his invention of a machine for catching tigers and a trip in a hot-air balloon so that they can measure the temperature of the sun. DQ's adventures are little more than a pretext for the author's antiprogress, antiliberal beliefs.

Bibliography: Tulio Febres Cordero, *Don Quijote en América, o sea La cuarta salida del ingenioso Hidalgo de la Mancha* (Mérida, Venezuela: Tip. de "El Lápiz," 1905); and Ernestina Salcedo Pizani "El Quijote como permanente posibilidad de recreaciones del tema. Dos ejemplos venezolanos: *Don Quijote en América*, de don Tulio Febres Cordero (1905), y *Leyendas del Quijote*, de Pedro Pablo Paredes (1977)," in *Cervantes, su obra y su mundo: Actas del I Congreso Internacional sobre Cervantes*, ed. Manuel Criado de Val (Madrid: Edi-6, 1981), 933–42.

Fecund Virgin [Virgen fecunda]. In *Poesías* 33, the phrase MC uses in praise of *Saint of Teresa de Jesús.

Federico, Duke of Novara. In *Laberinto*, the father of Rosenda, who orders his daughter jailed until the charges against her can be cleared or verified.

Feigned Aunt, The. *Tía fingida, La.

Feigned (or Mock) Arcadia. *Arcadia.

Felice Arabia. *Arabia Felix.

Felicia. The enchantress who uses her magical water to resolve all the shepherds' romantic problems and sufferings in *La Diana* (*Montemayor, Jorge de); she is mentioned during the examination of DQ's library in *DQ* I, 6. See also *Coloquio*.

Feliciana de la Voz. In *Persiles* 3, the woman (whose legal name is probably Feliciana Tenorio) whose newborn baby is deposited with the group of pilgrims and who then also joins the group and tells the story of how she escaped from her father after giving birth (but she does not recognize the baby as hers). When asked, she explains that she is called *de la Voz* because of her extremely beautiful singing voice. Feliciana joins the group of pilgrims and rivals Constanza as the second most beautiful of the women, after the incomparable Auristela. In III, 5, in the monastery of Guadalupe, she (ironically, an unwed mother) is moved to sing a song in praise of the Virgin, and her voice is immediately recognized by her father and brother, who also happen to be there. The men want to kill her in order to avenge their honor that she has besmirched, but this is prevented, and a happy marriage is arranged with her lover Rosanio. It has been suggested that this character is based on recent events in the life of Doña Feliciana de Cervantes de Gaete, a relative of MC's, who married Don Pedro de Orellana (*Orellana, Don Juan de) in Trujillo in 1615.

Bibliography: Diana de Armas Wilson, "Some Perversions of Pastoral: Feliciana de la Voz," in *Allegories of Love: Cervantes's "Persiles and Sigismunda"* (Princeton, NJ: Princeton University Press, 1991), 200–22.

Felicísimo ingenio destos reinos. *Fertile wit of these kingdoms.

Felipe II (Felipo) [Philip II] (1527–98). King of Spain. Son of Carlos V and Doña Isabel of Portugal, Felipe II assumed the throne in 1556, when his father abdicated. He had married his cousin, Doña María of Portugal, at the age of 16; but she died in 1545 after the birth of their only child, Carlos (who died in mysterious circumstances in 1568). He next married Mary Tudor (11 years his senior), queen of England, in 1554, but she was childless at the time of her death in 1558 (she was succeeded by *Elizabeth I; we can only speculate on the course of history had Catholic Mary and Felipe ruled England in the second half of the sixteenth century instead of Protestant Elizabeth). Felipe's third marriage was to Isabel de *Valois, daughter of Henri II of France, and took place in 1560. The royal couple had two daughters, *Isabel Clara Eugenia and *Catalina Micaela, and the queen's death at the age of 22 in 1568 had a profound effect on Spanish culture (and gave MC the opportunity to write and publish his first poetry, *Poesías* 1–5). Felipe's fourth marriage, in 1570, was to his niece Doña Ana of Austria (20 years his junior), and in 1578 produced his son Felipe (who would become *Felipe III; three other sons died very young); Ana died in an epidemic in 1580. The king outlived all four of his wives and five of his seven children. Felipe inherited the most powerful empire in the history of the world: Spain, the Netherlands, Parma and the kingdom of Naples (including Sardinia and Sicily) in Italy, bits of North Africa, a few possessions in Asia, and most of the Americas; to this was added Portugal in 1580. He was the undisputed leader of the Christian world, in constant struggle with the Turks, the Muslims, and the Protestants (who were not considered Christians). Less striking in looks, less bold in actions, and less successful a statesman than his father, Felipe was a civil servant and a bookkeeper. Nevertheless, he held together a vast and complex political, military, economic, and religious empire for more than four decades. He was honest, devout, diligent, frugal, and generous. He celebrated the great successes of the victory over the French in San Quintín in 1557 and the rout of the Turks at Lepanto in 1571, but he also suffered the disastrous defeat of the Invincible Armada in 1588 and a series of bloody defeats in the Netherlands. MC never praised Felipe II as he did his father Carlos V. His most memorable act with regard to the man who was king during most of his life was to write and then publicly read the satiric sonnet about the king's tomb (*Poesías* 26). See also *DQ* I, 39; *Gitanilla*; *Numancia* 1, 4; *Poesías* 1, 5, 8, 21; *Sultana* 2; *Tratos* 1.

Bibliography: Ferdinand Braudel, *The Mediterranean and the Mediterranean World in the Age of Philip II*, 2 vols., trans. Siàn Reynolds (New York: Harper and Row, 1972): Henry Kamen, *Philip of Spain* (New Haven, CT: Yale University Press, 1997): Geoffrey Parker, *The Grand Strategy of Philip II*. New Haven: Yale UP, 1998; Geoffrey Parker, *Philip II*, 3rd ed. (Chicago: Open Court, 1995); and R. A. Stradling, *The Armada of Flanders: Spanish Maritime Policy and European War, 1568–1668* (Cambridge: Cambridge University Press, 1998).

Felipe III (Filipo Tercero) [Philip III] (1578–1621). King of Spain. Son of Felipe II and Doña Ana of Austria, Philip III assumed the throne in 1598, upon the death of his father. He was weaker than his glorious father and grandfather and turned over much of the affairs of state to his *valido* (favorite), the duke of Lerma, who then turned some things over to Rodrigo Calderón. During Felipe's reign, as the flow of silver from the New World diminished, Spain sank further into debt and bankruptcy, while the king and his court lived in ever greater splendor and degeneracy. Military setbacks continued in the Netherlands and elsewhere, and political hegemony shifted to England, France, and Germany. Perhaps the most significant event of his reign was the expulsion of the *Moriscos* beginning in 1609. By the time of his death, Spain still appeared to be the strongest nation in Europe, but in fact it was a depopulated, corrupt, bankrupt, degenerate country whose shortcomings would soon be visible to everyone. See *DQ* II, 65; *Gitanilla*; *Persiles* III, 6, 11.

Bibliography: Paul C. Allen, *Philip III and the*

Pax Hispanica, 1598–1621: The Failure of Grand Strategy (New Haven, CT: Yale University Press 2000); and Fernando Díaz-Plaja, *La vida y la época de Felipe III* (Barcelona: Planeta, 1998).

Felipe IV (1605–65). King of Spain. Son of Felipe III and Doña Margarita of Austria, Philip IV assumed the throne in 1621, upon the death of his father. Under his reign, Spain's decline continued and became even clearer to the rest of the world. His birth in Valladolid is celebrated in a long allegorical poem sung by Preciosa in *Gitanilla*.

Felipe, León (León Felipe Camino Galicia, 1884–1968). Spanish poet. The quixotic León Felipe is best known for his passionate poetry about the Spanish Civil war and his own subsequent exile. Recurrent themes throughout his work are DQ and MC. In what may be his best-known poem, "Romero solo" ("Romero Alone"), included in his *Versos y oraciones del caminante* (1920; *Verses and Prayers of the Traveler*), there is a brief mention of the justice administered by the peasants SP and Pedro Crespo (from Calderón's *El alcalde de Zalamea*). In the same volume, the prophetic poem "Vencidos" ("Defeated") is about DQ as an example of the noble defenders of lost causes. In the second part of *Versos y oraciones del caminante* (1929), Felipe includes the poem "Pie para el niño de Vallecas, de Velázquez" ("Foot for the Child of Vallecas, by Velázquez"), a meditation on a painting by Diego de *Velázquez, which includes the lines that were to become his signature theme: 'Basin, helmet, halo / This is the order, Sancho.' Felipe also wrote several essays about MC and *DQ*, and during the height of the Spanish Civil War published an article in which he extolled DQ and SP as the essence of the Spanish people—in contrast to the duke and duchess who, like the rebel Fascists, simply used the land and people for their own ends. In his book entitled *El payaso de las bofetadas y el pescador de caña* (1938; *The Buffeted Clown and the Fisherman with the Cane Pole*), Felipe makes DQ into the apocalyptic emblem of the war: sad, defeated, beaten by the mocking crowds, and yet 'the bravest

and most legitimate man born on this rotten and abominable planet.' In his collection entitled *¡Oh, este viejo y roto violín!* (1965; *Oh, This Old and Broken Violin!*), there is a poem entitled "Diálogo perdido (Entre Don Quijote y Sancho Panza)" ("Lost Dialogue [between Don Quixote and Sancho Panza]"), a conversation between knight and squire about the eternal search for peace and spiritual wholeness. Finally, Felipe's posthumous book *Rocinante* (1969) brings together many lines of the poet's work throughout his career. Felipe uses his evocation of Rocinante, DQ, and MC in his metapoetry about the genesis of the book; reprises his Cervantine and quixotic themes of the past (especially the 'Basin, helmet, halo'); and meditates on the Civil War, making Rocinante into the mutely neighing grotesque horse of Pablo Picasso's *Guernica*.

Bibliography: León Felipe, *¡Oh, este viejo y roto violín!* (Mexico City: Tezontle, 1965); León Felipe *Rocinante* (Mexico City: Finisterre, 1969); *Homenaje de Castilla–La Mancha a León Felipe* (n.p.: Junta de Comunidades de Castilla–La Mancha, 1986); and Alberto Sánchez, "Cervantismo y quijotismo de León Felipe," *Anales Cervantinos* 22 (1984): 181–98.

Felipo. *Felipe II.

Felipo de Carrizales. In *Celoso*, the protagonist, who locks his young bride Leonora away to preserve her innocence. At the end of the story, he acknowledges the futility of his efforts and takes responsibility for all that has happened.

Félix Alba, Duchess. In *Pedro* 3, the mother, by Rosamiro (the queen's brother), of Belica.

Felixmarte de Hircania. *Ortega, Melchor.

Féliz Flora. In *Persiles* III, 13, one of the three candidates for the position of wife of the Duke of Nemurs, who soon after (III, 14) is rescued by Antonio the younger, who is wounded in the effort. She helps nurse Antonio back to health, never leaving his side for a month. With Belarmina and Deleasir, she accompanies the pilgrims to Rome, but when they

return to France with the Duke of Nemurs, she remains in Rome with the pilgrims. In IV, 14, she marries Antonio.

Female slaves. *Slave(s).

Female subhermit. *Hermit.

Feminist readings. *Women in Cervantes.

Fencing. There was a major debate in MC's time about the best approach to fencing. One view was that the subject could be studied and performed scientifically, using mathematics and geometry, by carefully measured angles, precise movements, correct placement of the feet, and so forth. Two important treatises on the subject were the *Filosofía de las armas* (1582; *Philosophy of Arms*) by Jerónimo de Carranza and the *Libro de las grandezas de la espada* (1600; *Book on the Greatness of the Sword*) by Luis *Pacheco de Narváez. The opposing camp held that there was nothing scientific about fighting with a sword, and that it was passion and energy that mattered most. In *DQ* II, 19, the licentiate and the bachelor Corchuelo (*priests or students) decide the matter, and the scientific method wins. Francisco de *Quevedo also treats the subject in fiction in *El Buscón*, but the result is exactly the opposite of the one described in this episode.

Fénix. *Our Lady of Saint Llorente.

Fénix de Arabia. *Phoenix of Arabia.

Feo Blas. In *DQ* I, 15, SP's comic deformation of the name of *Fierabrás. It makes a chivalric figure into 'Ugly Blas' (Blas being a common rustic name).

Ferdinand of Aragon. *Fernando of Aragon.

Feria (heria) de Sevilla. *Market of Seville.

Fernández de Avellaneda, Alonso. *Avellaneda, Alonso Fernández de.

Fernández de Castro y Osorio, Don Pedro, Conde de Lemos (1576–1622). Spanish grandee and literary patron. The count of Lemos was the powerful and influential nephew and son-in-law of the duke of Lerma (*privado* of King Felipe III), president of the Council of the Indies, viceroy of Naples, and president of the Supreme Council of Italy. He was MC's most important patron, the person to whom he dedicated *Novelas, Comedias, DQ* II, and *Persiles*. Lemos also considered himself a man of letters; he translated some of the poetry of Claudian and wrote a play entitled *La casa confusa* (*The Confused House*), which has not survived. Among the writers supported, at least to some extent, by the count of Lemos were MC, Lope de Vega, Luis de Góngora, Antonio Mira de Amescua, and Francisco de Quevedo. When he was named viceroy of Naples in 1610 (a position he occupied from 1611 to 1616), Lemos had his secretary, Lupercio Leonardo de *Argensola, arrange for several writers to accompany him to Italy. Argensola was an old friend of MC, and seems to have promised, or at least implied, that MC would be included in the retinue, but in the end he was not chosen for the honor. MC was clearly bitter about having been left out of the group at the last minute (as was Luis de Góngora) and made his feelings clear in *Parnaso* 3. On the return trip from Parnassus, in *Parnaso* 8, MC stops in Naples and while there praises the contribution of the count of Lemos to the celebration of the marriage of Louis XIII of France and Doña Ana of Austria, in Naples in 1612. In *Adjunta*, he is referred to in the letter from Apollo as MC's patron. DQ's remark about 'a prince I know . . .' in II, 24, is usually presumed to be an allusion to the count of Lemos.

Bibliography: Eduardo Pardo de Guevara y Valdés, *Don Pedro Fernández de Castro, VII Conde de Lemos [1576–1622]: Estudio histórico*, (Santiago de Compostela, Spain: Xunta de Galicia, 1997).

Fernández de Córdoba, Don Alonso, Conde de Alcaudete (?–1565).

Spanish nobleman and soldier, member of the Order of Santiago. He was active in the Spanish wars in North Africa; held the position of governor of Oran, which he defended valiantly in the attack of 1563, and other Spanish possessions; and

was named supreme commander of Spanish interests in Africa. In *Gallardo*, he is the general of Oran.

Fernández de Córdoba, Don Diego. Spanish nobleman who lost his son Felipe, godson of King Felipe II, in the battle of the Armada. See *Poesías* 21.

Fernández de Córdoba, Don Gonzalo, Duke of Sessa (?–1578).

Spanish soldier and statesman. He was lord of Cabra (where MC's uncle Andrés lived), served twice as governor of Milan, fought in the civil wars of Granada with Don Juan of Austria, and fought at Lepanto. MC may have met the duke in Cabra in the 1560s, and he knew him a decade later when he was quartered in Palermo, where the duke was viceroy. The duke wrote one of the glowing letters of recommendation for MC that impressed his captors so much that they raised the price of his ransom well above the norm.

Fernández de Córdoba, Gonzalo. *Hernández de Córdoba, Gonzalo.

Fernández de Córdoba y Figueroa, Don Pedro [Marqués de Priego, señor de la casa de Aguilar y de Montilla] (1563–1606).

Spanish nobleman. Fernánadez de Córdoba was the marqués de Priego and lord of the city of Montilla, as mentioned in *Coloquio*.

Fernández de Lizardi, José Joaquín (1776–1827).

Mexican novelist and journalist. Fernández de Lizardi is usually considered the first novelist of Spanish America and is best known for his somewhat picaresque novel *El periquillo sarniento* (1816; *The Itching Parrot*), which also shows the direct influence of *DQ*, which is cited on several occasions. He also wrote *La educación de las mujeres, o la Quijotita y su prima: Historia muy cierta con apariencias de novela* (first part 1818, complete work 1831–32; *The Education of Women, or Little Female Quixote and Her Cousin: A Very True History with the Appearance of a Novel*), whose protagonist, Doña Pomposa, bears some resemblance to DQ, as the character called Sansón Carrasco makes clear in an explicit comparison: 'Don Quijote was mad and so is Doña Pomposa. Don Quijote had lucid intervals in which he spoke beautifully on matters not pertaining to chivalry. Doña Pomposa has hers, in which her conversation is not unpleasant; but she goes off when matters of love and beauty are broached. . . . Don Quijote had his imaginary lady whom he judged to be a princess; Doña Pomposa will soon have in her head a preventative lover whom she will make worthy of her favors, and he will be an ambassador or a general.' A third novel, the posthumous *Don Catrín de la Fachenda* (1832), features a somewhat quixotic nobleman who considers anything but the exercise of arms beneath his dignity. All of Fernández de Lizardi's semiquixotic satires are relatively weak efforts, with more historical then aesthetic interest.

Bibliography: Luis González Cruz, "Influencia cervantina en Lizardi," *Cuadernos Hispanoamericanos* 286 (1974): 188–203; Pedro Lastra, "Don Catrín, Don Quijote y la picaresca," *Revista de Estudios Hispánicos* 23 (1989): 101–12: and John Skirius, "Fernández de Lizardi y Cervantes," *Nueva Revista de Filología Hispánica* 2 (1982): 257–72.

Fernández de Moratín, Leandro. *Moratín, Leandro Fernández de.

Fernández de Moratín, Nicolás. *Moratín, Nicolás Fernández de.

Fernández de Pineda, Rodrigo. Spanish poet praised in Calliope's song in *Galatea* 6.

Fernández de Sotomayor, Gonzalo. A little-known Spanish poet praised in Calliope's song in *Galatea* 6.

Fernández de Torreblanca, Leonor. *Torreblanca, Leonor de.

Fernández de Velasco, Juan (1550–1613). Spanish writer, condestable of Castile and León, and twice governor of Milan. He is best known for his critical commentary on Fernando de Herrera's annotated edition of the poetry of Garcilaso de la Vega. He is cited in *Parnaso* 4 as the patron of Pedro *Mantuano.

Bibliography: Juan Montero, *La controversia so-*bre las "anotaciones" herrerianas (Seville, Spain: Ayuntamiento, 1987).

Fernández, Gonzalo. *Hernández de Córdoba, Gonzalo.

Fernández Guerra y Orbe, Aureliano (1816–91). Spanish literary scholar, journalist, and dramatist. He wrote a successful play entitled *La hija de Cervantes* (1849; *Cervantes's Daughter*), based on the events surrounding the murder of Gaspar de *Ezpeleta in front of the home of MC and his family in Valladolid in 1605.

Fernández, Jerónimo (?–ca. 1579). Spanish romance writer. Fernández is known only as the author of *Historia del magnánimo, valiente e invencible caballero don Belianís de Grecia* (parts I–II, 1547; parts III–IV, 1579; *History of the Magnanimous, Valiant, and Invincible Knight Don Belianís of Greece*). The first installment of this romance was avidly read and praised by the Emperor Carlos V, who personally requested that the author publish the sequel. As the major rival to *Amadís de Gaula* in the second half of the sixteenth century, *Belianís* was the most popular and influential chivalric romance of the second wave of that genre's (declining) popularity. Probably much of the reason the story appealed to the Spanish emperor (and to other readers, including MC) was its culminating battle in Book II, when the modern Christian King Beliano and his three sons, featuring the invincible Belianís, accompanied by the magically disenchanted Greek hero Achilles, gloriously vanquish the disenchanted representatives of the evil pagan emperor, the great Trojan hero Hector, three of his brothers, and his ally Memnon of Ethiopia. Thus there is a battle between five great ancient Trojan heroes representing the non-Christian forces and one great ancient Greek and four great modern Greek heroes representing Christianity: paganism versus Christianity and ancients versus moderns all at the same time. The outcome is hardly in doubt: after several pages of furious blows and hand-to-hand combat described in minute detail, all five of the Trojans are killed, as is Achilles, while the modern Greek Christians survive victorious. The book reinforced the glorious vision of Spanish hegemony: a modern Christian nation that would unite the world under one political and religious banner (*Golden Age). It is only coincidence that *Belianís* was published in the year of MC's birth. But just as its popularity was unrivalled in the royal court of Carlos V, the youthful, optimistic, patriotic MC also treasured the book, or at least so one would judge based on its role in *DQ.* ' Belianís is the second knight-errant, after Amadís, to dedicate a sonnet to DQ in the prefatory verses to *DQ* I. In I, 1, before deciding to become a knight-errant, the protagonist considers writing a sequel to one of his favorite romances—*Belianís* (although he is dismayed by the large number of wounds the protagonist both dishes out and receives; in the notes to his monumental edition of *DQ*, Diego Clemencín claims to have counted 101 serious wounds that Belianís receives in Books I and II). *Belianís* and *Amadís* are the only two Spanish romances of chivalry not burned in the inquisition of the books that make up DQ's library in I, 6; but whereas *Amadís* is praised without reservation, the priest complains that *Belianís* needs some editing and recommends to the barber that he take the book home but let no one read it. DQ's archenemy, responsible for many of his defeats and humiliations, is not Arcaláus from *Amadís* but Fristón (whose name DQ inexplicably cites as *Frestón, the only time he commits an error with a name from his romances) from *Belianís*. In I, 25, when DQ delivers his famous and important disquisition on the theme of *imitation, he specifically rejects Belianís as a model in order to concentrate on that of Amadís. Throughout MC's novel, only *Amadís* is praised more and cited more often than *Belianís*, which is clearly for DQ the second most important exemplar of fictional chivalric characters. The recent publication of a careful modern annotated edition of *Belianís* has made this important book available for the first time to MC specialists. See also *DQ* I, 13, 20, 38, 52; *DQ* II, 1, 38.

Bibliography: Jerónimo Fernández, *Hystoria del magnánimo, valiente e inuencible cauallero Don Be-lianís de Grecia*, ed. Lilia E. F. de Orduna, 2 vols. (Kassel, Germany: Reichenberger, 1997); Howard Mancing, " 'Bendito sea Alá': A New Edition of *Belianís de Grecia*," *Cervantes* 21, no. 2 (2001): 111–15; Lilia E. F. de Orduna, "Héroes troyanos y griegos en la *Hystoria del magnánimo, valiente e inuencible cauallero don Belianís de Grecia* (Burgos, 1547)," in *Actas del IX Congreso de la Asociación Internacional de Hispanistas, 18–23 agosto 1986, Berlín.* ed. Sebastian Neumeister, 2 vols. (Frankfort: Vervuert, 1989), vol. 1, 559–68; and Sylvia Roubaud, "Calas en la narrativa caballeresca renacentista: el *Belianís de Grecia* y el *Clarián de Landanís*," in *La invención de la novela: Seminario hispano-francés organizado por la Casa de Velázquez (noviembre 1992–junio 1993)*, ed. Jean Canavaggio (Madrid: Casa de Velázquez, 1999), 49–84.

Fernández López, Ventura. *Venzel Prouta, F.

Fernández, Marcos. Spanish dramatist. His *Olla podrida a la española* (1655; *Spanish Stew*) includes a character identified as the grandson of SP, Toncho Panza, who compares himself to and comments on the adventures of his grandfather.

Fernández Shaw, Carlos (1865–1911). Spanish poet and librettist. Fernández Shaw was most successful when he teamed with composer Ruperto Chapí on popular *zarzuelas (light musical comedies). Examples of their work are *Las bodas de Camacho* (1902; *Camacho's Wedding*), based on *DQ* II, 20–21, and *La venta de Don Quijote* (1902; *The Inn of Don Quixote*).

Fernández Suárez, Alvaro (Juan de Lara). Uruguayan dramatist. *El retablo de Maese Pedro* (1946; *Maese Pedro's Puppet Show*), a 'devilish farce for men and dolls' in two acts and two preacts, by Fernández Suárez is perhaps the most original and interesting rewriting of the famous scene from *DQ* II, 26. In the scene that precedes the first act of the puppet show, Maese Pedro is accompanied by DQ, SP, and a woman named Doña Marilinda. They come on stage in preparation for the puppet show, and, among other things, DQ looks out and sees the (contemporary, live) audience watching the performance, but the other characters cannot see these people. DQ describes the looks and twentieth-century dress of the audience, singling a few out for specific commentary, metatheatrically turning the actors into spectators and vice versa. In the first act of the puppet show, and in absurdly comic dialogue, Gaiferos argues with Carlomagno about whether or not he should attempt to rescue his wife held prisoner in Spain. Gaiferos is reluctant to risk his life for a woman who is less than a model of virtue and, besides, his chess game with Roldán is not yet over. DQ and Doña Marilinda intervene and talk with Gaiferos, attempting to convince him to act. Carlomagno threatens him with execution and, in exasperation, swears that he will cut off his own manly beard if Gaiferos does not go. Finally, Gaiferos agrees to do as he should, not for his wife's sake, but for the sake of the emperor's beard. In the second preact, Maese Pedro kills time as he describes how long it takes for Gaiferos to make the long journey from France, across the Pyrenees, to Sansueña in Spain. As they discuss the action of the puppet play, SP defends Gaiferos's unwillingness to undertake the deed, and there is a discussion about what a million dollars is worth in Spanish money. In the final act of the puppet show, Gaiferos rescues his lady, and DQ intervenes, cutting the heads off several puppets. The puppets are put back together, but with the heads and bodies mixed up: a Muslim has Melisendra's head, she has that of Gaiferos, King Marsilio has that of his horse, while the horse has that of the king. This, of course, leads to a series of comic exchanges and ironic remarks. The performance ends in song and dance, in which the spectators are invited to participate. The very witty dialogue and the multiple levels of metatheater make this one of the most genuinely quixotic and Cervantine of all rewrites of *DQ*.

Bibliography: Alvaro Fernández Suárez, *El retablo de Maese Pedro* (Montevideo, Uruguay: Letras, 1946).

Fernández y González, Manuel (1821–88).

Spanish poet, dramatist, and historical novelist. Fernández y González was one of the most prolific (he wrote over 300 volumes of literature) and popular novelists of the nineteenth century. Two of his novels are based on the life of MC: *El manco de Lepanto* (1874; *The Cripple from Lepanto*) and *El príncipe de los ingenios, Miguel de Cervantes Saavedra* (1876; *The Prince of Wits, Miguel de Cervantes Saavedra*).

Fernando de Andrada, Don. In *Baños*, the gentleman who sees his beloved Costanza being taken by the Muslims, jumps into the sea in order to be captured also and be with her, and is reunited and eventually escapes with her and the other Christians at the end of the play.

Fernando de Azevedo, Don. In *Gitanilla*, the noble magistrate of Murcia, member of the Order of Calatrava, who turns out to be the father of Preciosa.

Fernando de Saavedra, Don (Juan Lozano). In *Gallardo*, the protagonist, who disguises his identity by taking the name of Juan Lozano and even dressing as a Muslim before marrying Margarita in the final scene.

Fernando, Don. The second son of the wealthy and influential Duke Ricardo, a grandee of Spain, and Cardenio's rival in *Cardenio*. He is first mentioned by the goatherd in *DQ* I, 23, then in Cardenio's narrative in I, 24, is discussed again in Dorotea's narrative in I, 27–28, and enters the story in I, 36, when he arrives at Juan Palomeque's inn and recognizes Dorotea as his wife. He is present from then until the party breaks up, and he and Dorotea return to their home, while DQ is taken home in a cage. Don Fernando is particularly prominent in the dispute over the basin-helmet, in petting with Dorotea, and in paying generously for many of the expenses run up by DQ and the others in I, 45–47.

Fernando [Ferdinand] of Aragon (1452–1516). King of Spain. He married *Isabel of Castile in 1469, ascended to the throne of that kingdom in 1474, and also became king of his native Aragon five years later, thus forming the political union that would unite Spain and make possible the nation's swift rise to the status of the largest empire in the history of the world (*Golden Age). Together Fernando and Isabel were known as the *Reyes Católicos* (*Catholic Monarchs). Although known as a great defender of the faith, Fernando himself had *converso* ancestors. He is mentioned as one of the great kings of Spain to come in the future in the prophecy made by the figure of War in *Numancia* 4.

Ferraguto [Ferragut]. In *Casa*, a Spaniard, originally a character in Boiardo's *Orlando Innamorato*, who kills Argalia by throwing him into a river.

Ferrán, Jaime (1928–). Spanish jurist, translator, and poet. Ferrán's *Canciones para Dulcinea* (1959; *Songs for Dulcinea*) is a book of 52 short poems in free verse addressed to DT. The poems are not the usual retelling of episodes from *DQ* or rhetorical evocations of the characters from the novel, but are simply expressions of a love relationship, with only a few brief allusions to *DQ*.
Bibliography: Jaime Ferrán, *Canciones para Dulcinea* (Madrid: Escuela Gráfica Salesiana, 1959).

Ferrara. City in northern Italy, not far from Bologna. Some of the action in *Cornelia* takes place there. See also *Laberinto* 2; *Vidriera*.

Ferrara, Dukes of. *Ruggiero.

Ferré, Rosario (1938–). Puerto Rican novelist and poet. Ferré's story/essay entitled *El coloquio de las perras* (1990; *The Colloquy of the [Female] Dogs*) begins by recalling MC's *Coloquio* in order to introduce a pair of *perras* (female dogs, bitches) who discuss the image of women in the works of major Spanish American male dogs/novelists: Borges, Fuentes, García Márquez, and others. Then the dogs take on women writers (such as Isabel Allende), literary critics of both genders, and other aspects of Spanish American letters. From time to time there is a phrase or allusion that recalls MC's *novela*, and, like Berganza and Cipión, the two modern dogs occasionally warn each other about gossip and backbiting. The dogs' pene-

trating (and bitchy) comments are both deliciously satiric and very perceptive. Ferré's dialogue is very good satire and literary criticism at the same time.
Bibliography: Rosario Ferré, *El coloquio de las perras* (San Juan, Puerto Rico: Editorial Cultural, 1990).

Ferrer (de Cardona), Don Luis (1574–1641). Spanish poet. Ferrer was a knight in the Order of Santiago and member of the Academy of the Night Revelers. He is praised in *Parnaso* 3.

Ferrer, Eulalio. *Museo Iconográfico del *Quijote*.

Ferrer, Juan. Spanish book publisher in Valencia. Francisco de Robles filed a court action against Ferrer in 1605 to keep him from publishing a pirated edition of *DQ* I.

Ferretis, Jorge (1902–62). Mexican novelist. In Ferretis's *Cuando engorda "El Quijote"* (1937; *When "Don Quixote" Gets Fat* or *Makes You Grow Fat*) it is the Mexican revolution itself that is DQ. What begins as an idealistic attempt to change the world for the better becomes complacent and lazy as self-interest and profit come to the fore. The DQ connection is only in the title and the metaphor of the revolution as DQ.
Bibliography: Jorge Ferretis, *Cuando engorda "El Quijote"* (México City: México Nuevo, 1937).

Ferreyra Videla, Vidal. Argentine writer. In Ferreyra Videla's *Andanzas de Don Quijote y Fierro* (1953; *Adventures of Don Quixote and Fierro*), supposedly based on material retrieved from the Archives of La Mancha, DQ meets Martín Fierro, prototype of the Argentine gaucho and protagonist of José Hernández's epic poem of the Pampas, *Martín Fierro* (1872). The two great literary figures talk at length, often repeating the same words attributed to them in the works by MC and Hernández.
Bibliography: Vidal Ferreyra Videla, *Andanzas de Don Quijote y Fierro* (Buenos Aires: Dolmen, 1953).

Fertile wit of these kingdoms [Felicísimo ingenio destos reinos]. In I, 48, the canon of Toledo refers sarcastically to Lope de *Vega in this way.

Festival of Santa Ana. *Saint Anne.

Fetala. In *Amante*, the Turk who assumes ownership of Ricardo after the raid on Sicily, but who dies soon after.

Fez. Capital city of the kingdom of Morocco. During the Renaissance, many of the *Moriscos* exiled from Spain, particularly Granada and Aragon, went to Fez, where they were often called *elches*. See *Amante*; *Baños* 3; *DQ* I, 41; *Gallardo* 3; *Pedro* 3.

Fidias. *Phedias.

Field, Nathaniel (1587–1620). English dramatist. His *Amends for Ladies* (ca. 1611) is related to *Curioso*, but is either drawn very loosely from that *novela* or is taken from the subplot of *Cardenio* by *Shakespeare and Fletcher.

Fielding, Henry (1707–54). English novelist and dramatist. Fielding considered MC on a par with Lucian and Swift as "that great Triumvirate" of satiric writers. Fielding's first effort in quixotism was his burlesque ballad-opera *Don Quixote in England: A Comedy* (1734), in which DQ and SP are transplanted to English soil. DQ is a proper gentleman except when matters of chivalry are involved: he takes inns for castles, worries about enchanters, and so forth. He is the constant butt of mockery by other characters. SP is lazy and gluttonous, and frequently quotes proverbs. But this relatively weak effort was only a warm-up for what was to come in his novels. After writing *Shamela* (1741), a parody of Samuel Richardson's popular *Pamela* (1740), Fielding's first important novel was *Joseph Andrews* (1742), or, in its full title, *The History of the Adventures of Joseph Andrews, and His Friend Mr. Abraham Adams: Written in Imitation of the Manner of Cervantes*. The subtitle makes explicit the profound conceptual debt the work owes to MC.

Among the narrative techniques Fielding employs that are also characteristic of *DQ* are the 'true history' device, the intrusive narrator, the search for sources, comic character names, comic chapter titles, links from one chapter to the next, and a variety of embedded narrations. Some of the comic inn scenes, with naughty romps in the sack, mistaken identities, and brawls, are directly modeled on DQ's and SP's adventures in the *inn of Juan Palomeque (especially in I, 16–17). Parson Adams is one of the great DQ figures in literature: honorable, impractical, forgetful, gullible, idealistic, bookish (Aeschylus is his *Amadís de Gaula*), and always ready to defend persons and ideals. Adventures, scenes, situations, and several characters from *DQ* are cited throughout the novel. Even though some Fielding scholars have ignored or even denied the importance of MC in Fielding's novel, there can be no question that DQ is of fundamental importance in the conception and execution of *Joseph Andrews*. Many of the same characteristics are also found in Fielding's greatest novel, *The History of Tom Jones, a Foundling* (1749). Although there is no strong DQ character like Parson Adams in *Tom Jones*, young Tom's idealism, naïveté, and good intentions all evoke aspects of DQ, as does his idealization of Molly as a DT figure; and the schoolmaster-barber Partridge recalls aspects of SP. At one point, Fielding invokes MC as one of several satiric and comic muses for his work. Overall, the novel's spirit, techniques, comic tone and devices, characters and character names, allusions, and citations all maintain its place firmly within the quixotic tradition.

Bibliography: Luisa Antón-Pacheco Sánchez, *Sátira y parodia en el "Quijote" y "Joseph Andrews"* (Madrid: Universidad Complutense, 1989); Isolina Ballesteros, "La presencia de *Don Quijote* de Cervantes en *Joseph Andrews*," *Anales Cervantinos* 27 (1989): 215–24; Stephen Gilman, "On Henry Fielding's Reception of *Don Quijote*," in *Medieval and Renaissance Studies in Honour of Robert Brian Tate*, ed. Ian Michael, Richard A. Cardwell, and Ian Macphersen (Oxford: Dolphin, 1986), 27–38; Pedro Javier Pardo García, "Formas de imitación del *Quijote* en la novela inglesa del siglo XVIII: *Joseph Andrews* y *Tristram Shandy*," *Anales Cervantinos* 33 (1995–

97): 133–64; and Alexander A. Parker, "Fielding and the Structure of *Don Quixote*," *Bulletin of Hispanic Studies* 33 (1956): 1–16.

Fields of Alcudia [Campo de Alcudia].
An open area in the southern part of the modern province of Ciudad Real near the Valley of Alcudia. See *Rinconete*; *Sultana* 2.

Fields of Montiel [Campo de Montiel].
A large open area in La Mancha located about midway between Manzanares and Albacete. In *DQ* I, 2, DQ rides through the fields of Montiel the first day he leaves home. See also *DQ* I, prologue, 7, 52; *DQ* II, 8.

Fields of Santa Barbara [Campos de Santa Bárbara].
An open area at the northern end of the Calle de Hortaleza in Madrid, near the gate of Santa Bárbara, where a well-known hermitage was located. See *Gitanilla*.

Fierabrás.
A Saracen giant from Boiardo and Ariosto (*balm of Fierabrás and *Historia del emperador Carlomagno y los doce pares de Francia*).

Fieras hermanas; Fierce sisters.
*Fates.

Fife player [Pífaro].
The servant who accompanies the arrival of Trifaldín in *DQ* II, 36.

Fig [Higa].
A vulgar gesture made by placing the thumb between the index and middle fingers of a closed fist. It is a phallic symbol, used both as an insult and as a symbol of fertility. See *DQ* II, 31.

Figueroa.
*Suárez de Figueroa, Doctor Cristóbal.

Figueroa, Constanza de.
*Ovando, Constanza de.

Figueroa, Cristóbal Suárez de; Figueroa, Doctor Cristóbal de.
*Suárez de Figueroa, Cristóbal.

Figueroa, Don Lope de.
Distinguished Spanish soldier. MC served in the regiment commanded by Figueroa beginning in 1572.

Figueroa, Francisco de (1536–ca. 1617).
Spanish soldier and poet, often referred to as *el Divino* (The Divine One), as he is in *Adjunta*. On his deathbed, Figueroa requested that the poetry to which he had devoted much of his life be burned, but only part of it actually was. To the degree that MC's pastoral romance *Galatea* is a roman à clef, Figueroa has been identified as the character Tirsi. Figuroa, like Juan Rufo and a few others, most likely was included in a small circle of literary friends of MC; he is warmly praised at the very end of Calliope's song in *Galatea* 6.

Bibliography: Sofía Carrizo Rueda, "Cervantes crítico-poeta: el caso de Francisco de Figueroa," in *Cervantes: Actas del Simposio Nacional Letras del Siglo de Oro Español*, ed. Carlos Orlando Nállim et al. (Mendoza, Spain: Instituto de Literaturas Modernas-Facultad de Filosofía, Universidad Nacional de Cuyo, 1994), 317–26.

Figuerola, Francisco José.
Argentine jurist and poet. Figuerola's *Don Quijote ¡Vuelve!* (1992; *Don Quixote, Come Back!*) is a pretentious prose-poetic plea to DQ to return to earth as squire to Christ in His second coming in order to combat the dehumanization characteristic of modern society.

Bibliography: Francisco José Figuerola, *Don Quijote ¡Vuelve!* (Buenos Aires: F. J. Figuerola, 1992).

Figueroa y Córdoba, Don Diego (1619–73).
Spanish poet and dramatist. He was a minor dramatist of the Calderón cycle and often wrote in collaboration with his brother José. His *Hija del mesonero, o La ilustre fregona* (1660; *The Innkeeper's Daughter, or The Illustrious Kitchen Maid*) is an adaptation of *Fregona*.

Filardo.
In *Galatea* 4, a shepherd praised for his erudition and discretion; he never appears in the text.

Fili.
1. In *Galatea* 2, the shepherdess loved by Tirsi; she never appears in the text. 2. In *DQ* I, 23, the woman's poetic name (compare Phyllis) used by Cardenio in a love sonnet (presumably addressed to Luscinda), which DQ and SP find in the saddlebags of the dead mule Cardenio

abandoned in the Sierra Morena. When SP hears DQ read the sonnet, he does not recognize the name for what it is, presumes that the initial *f-* is another example of his master's archaic **fabla*, and interprets the word as *hilo* (thread). Interestingly, the same sonnet, with a change only in line 9 where Fili is mentioned, is also included in *Casa 3. 3*. **Pastoral names.*

Fílida. 1. A shepherdess from Luis **Gálvez de Montalvo's pastoral romance *El pastor de Fílida*. See *Coloquio*; *Galatea 6*. **2**. **Pastoral names.*

Filipo Tercero. **Felipe III.*

Filis. **Argensola, Lupercio Leonardo de.*

Filleau de Saint-Martin, François (?-ca. 1695). French translator and novelist. Filleau's influential translation of *DQ* (4 vols., 1677–79) omitted the final chapter, in which DQ dies, in order to leave the way open for his own continuation, which he published as *Histoire de l'admirable Don Quichotte de la Mancha* (1695; *History of the Admirable Don Quixote de La Mancha*). The sequel begins with an Arabic narrator named Zulema who reports that CHB was incorrect about the death of DQ and who claims to have investigated the activities of DQ and SP after their return home in MC's II, 73. DQ attempts to renounce everything relating to chivalry, SP takes on a more prominent role, Dorotea and a few other characters are reintroduced, and there are some embedded narratives (which actually make up the majority of the text). Filleau's sequel was very popular in France and was translated to German within a year.

Fine china from Pisa. **Pisa.*

Fineo. **Phineus.*

Fingida Arcadia. **Arcadia.*

First Part of La Galatea, Divided into Six Books. **Galatea, La.*

First translations of *Don Quixote*. Some of the most important first translations of *DQ* are the following:

English: 1612, *DQ* I by Thomas Shelton; 1620, *DQ* II also by Shelton

French: 1614, *DQ* I by César Oudin; 1618, *DQ* II by François Rosset (*Note: Curioso* was translated to French separately, with no mention of MC as author, in 1608 with French and Spanish texts on facing pages.)

Italian: 1622, *DQ* I by Lorenzo Franciosini; 1625, *DQ* II also by Franciosini

German: 1683, anonymous, based on the popular French translation of Filleau de Saint-Martin; 1775, directly from Spanish by F. J. Bertuch

Dutch: 1676–77, by Charlotte Dorothy Diehl

Russian: 1769, based on François Filleau de Saint-Martin, by N. Osipov; 1838, directly from Spanish by Konstantin Massal'skii

In addition, the novel has been translated, in whole or in part, into dozens of languages and has often been described as the most frequently translated secular text in the history of the world. Probably the most recent effort as of this writing is the partial translation (2002) by Ilan Stavans of *DQ* I into Spanglish (the mixture of Spanish and English as spoken in large parts of the United States and Puerto Rico): "In un placete de La Mancha of which nombre no quiero remembrarme . . ."

Bibliography: Carmelo Cunchillos Jaime, "La primera traducción inglesa del *Quijote* de Thomas Shelton (1612–1620)," *Cuadernos de Investigación Filológica* 9 (1983): 63–89; and Isolina Sánchez Reguera, "El hispanista francés César Oudin primer traductor de *El Quijote* al francés." *Anales Cervantinos* 23 (1985): 115–31.

Fisherman sailor [Marinero pescador]. In *Persiles* II, 13, Periandro tells of the sailor in his group of fishermen-pirates who becomes so desperate to be with his family that he attempts to hang himself, but Periandro cuts him down and saves him.

Fishermen [Pescadores]. 1. The owners of the boat DQ uses for an adventure in II, 29.

When the boat is sunk, DQ pays them for their loss. **2**. In *Persiles* I, 13, the group of men who receive the fleeing Transila but then sell her to pirates.

Fishermen, Island of the. *Island of the Fishermen.

Fishermen pirates. *Pirate(s).

Fitzgerald, F. Scott (1896–1940). American novelist. In Fitzgerald's *The Great Gatsby* (1925), the protagonist Jay Gatsby is just as much a self-selected and self-created persona modeled on an ideal concept as is DQ: Gatsby "sprang from his Platonic conception of himself. . . . So he invented just the sort of Jay Gatsby that a 17-year-old boy would be likely to invent, and to this conception he was faithful to the end." Gatsby's "quest" for Daisy—a relatively ordinary, but in his eyes ideal, woman—also recalls DQ's devotion to DT.

Fitzroy, Isobel. English novelist. It may only be coincidence that Fitzroy's novel *A Quixotic Woman* was published in 1905, the third centenary of the publication of *DQ* I. The novel tells the story of the beautiful Lady Mildred Buzzwell-Hubbard and her apparently quixotic renunciation of upper-class social values as she heroically struggles through life with her difficult and pretentious mother and forced (but unconsummated) marriage to a rich bigamist, in order in the end to marry the ever-loving (and slightly quixotic) Alec Mackenzie. Only the title and the use of *quixotic* and *quixotism* in two chapter titles make clear the DQ connection.
   Bibliography: Isobel Fitzroy, *A Quixotic Woman* (London: John Murray, 1905).

Flaminia, Via. *Via Flaminia.

Flanders [Flandes]. The North Sea provinces of Belgium, formerly an independent nation. In *Golden Age Spain, the name *Flandes* was used to refer to the Low Countries (Belgium, Luxembourg, and the Netherlands) in general, particularly those parts ruled by Spain. Spanish nobles and educated youths (e.g., Tomás Rodaja in *Vidriera* and Don Antonio de

Isunza and Don Juan de Gamboa in *Cornelia*) often included Flanders along with Italy in their tour of Europe, and the career of many Spanish soldiers (e.g., Ruy Pérez de Viedma in *Capitán*) included duty in Flanders. Andrés in *Gitanilla* and both Don Diego de Carriazo and Don Juan de Avendaño in *Fregona* cover their escape from home by informing their parents that they have decided to go to see Flanders rather than return directly to the University of Salamanca. It has been suggested that MC himself may have served in Flanders at the beginning of his military career, but there is no documentation for this. The ongoing wars in Flanders (Imperial Spain's Vietnam)—which continued for nearly a century, from 1567 to 1659—did as much as anything to sap Spanish wealth and manpower, and it was thus a major contributing factor in the inevitable decline of Spain. Two of the highly esteemed imports from Flanders were fine lace and cheese. See also *Casamiento*, *Celoso*; *Coloquio*; *Doncellas*, *DQ* I, 39; *DQ* II, 34, 54; *Guarda*; *Pedro* 1; *Rinconete*; *Rufián* 1–2; *Persiles* I, 5; III, 10; *Sultana* 2; *Tratos* 3.
   Bibliography: Geoffrey Parker, *The Army of Flanders and the Spanish Road, 1557–1659: The Logistics of Spanish Victory and Defeat in the Low Countries' Wars* (Cambridge: Cambridge University Press, 1972).

Flask, Mr. [Señor Redoma]. In *Vidriera*, a name used once to refer to the protagonist.

Flaubert, Gustave (1821–80). French novelist. The heroine of Flaubert's *Madame Bovary* (1856–57) has often been described as a "DQ in skirts." Indeed, of all the many female reincarnations of DQ, Emma is the most original, profound, and influential. Flaubert's admiration for MC knew no bounds. It has been suggested that it was his reading of *DQ* in his childhood that convinced Flaubert to become a novelist rather than a dramatist. His voluminous correspondence is peppered with references to MC and *DQ*, some of which are particularly relevant. For example, Flaubert recognizes MC's realism, not in terms of superficial, detailed descriptions of external reality, but in terms of the ability to afford the reader the opportunity to evoke a realistic context for the characters and their actions: "How clearly one sees those roads in Spain that are never described." For Flaubert, *DQ* is the book "I knew by heart even before I read it." Like DQ, Emma Bovary is steeped in genre fiction, in her case the popular womens' romances (like *Paul and Virginia*), historical romances (such as those of Walter Scott), womens' magazines, and the novels of Balzac and George Sand; her heroines include Mary Queen of Scots, Joan of Arc, and Heloise: "She was the amorous heroine of all novels and plays, the vague 'she' of all poetry." Disillusioned and bored by her marriage to the prosaic Charles, Emma dreams of true love and adventure. Her literary dispositions incline her to situations that promise to be exciting liaisons but that turn out to be tawdry affairs with cynical and mediocre opportunists. Some French critics put much stock in the originality and influence of *Bovarysm*, but this is less an original concept than an adaptation of the more profound and original *quixotism*. In *L'éducation sentimental* (1869; *Sentimental Education*) there is a complete quixotic cast: Frédéric Moreau is DQ, Madame Arnoux is DT, and Deslauriers is SP. *Bouvard et Pécuchet* (1881) takes quixotic role-playing to dizzying heights, as the two middle-aged friends embrace a series of professions, each one based on their careful study of books. In spite of the setbacks they suffer at every turn, they continue onward to each new adventure. Few great writers are as thoroughly Cervantine and quixotic as Gustave Flaubert.

Bibliography: William J. Berg, and Laurey K. Martin, *Gustave Flaubert* (New York: Twayne, 1997; Anthony J. Cascardi, *The Bounds of Reason: Cervantes, Dostoevsky, Flaubert* (New York: Columbia University Press, 1986); Harry Levin, *The Gates of Horn: A Study of Five French Realist Novelists* (New York: Oxford University Press, 1963); and Laurence M. Porter, "Cervantes Saavedra, Miguel de," in *A Gustave Flaubert Encyclopedia* (Westport, CT: Greenwood Press, 2001), 52–53.

Flemish banks/shores/pinewood [Bancos de Flandes]. An ambiguous phrase used by SP in *DQ* II, 21, with reference to Quiteria the Beautiful on the day of her wedding. It simultaneously suggests images of wealth, navigating treacherous shores, and a nuptial bed made of fine imported wood.

Flérida. *Pastoral names.

Fleshpots of Egypt [Ollas de Egipto]. A reference to the decadent luxury of the Egypt in which the Jews were held in captivity before their exodus. See *DQ* I, 22; *DQ* II, 21.

Fletcher, John (1579–1625). English dramatist. Fletcher was the greatest collaborator in seventeenth-century English theater. In addition to some 15 plays of his own, he collaborated with Francis *Beaumont on about that many more (including *The Knight of the Burning Pestle* and *The Coxcomb*), and wrote other plays with Philip *Massinger (*The Custom of the Country*, *The Double Marriage*, *The Beggar's Bush*, *A Very Woman*), Middleton, Jonson, *Shakespeare (*Cardenio*), and others. Fletcher's *The Scornful Lady* is based on *Amante*; *The Chances* (ca. 1615) is based on *Cornelia*; *The Queen of Corinth* (1619) has its source in *Fuerza*; in *The Pilgrim* (1621), one of the characters tells the story of the madman of Seville told by the barber in *DQ* II, 1; his *Rule a Wife and Have a Wife* (1624) takes its subplot from *Casamiento*; and *The Fair Maid of the Inn* (ca. 1625) is an adaptation of *Fregona*.

Bibliography: R. Patricia Grant, "Cervantes' *El casamiento engañoso* and Fletcher's *Rule a Wife and Have a Wife*," *Hispanic Review* 12 (1944): 330–38; and Diana de Armas Wilson, "Of Piracy and Plackets: Cervantes' *La señora Cornelia* and Fletcher's *The Chances*," in *Cervantes for the 21st Century/Cervantes para el siglo XXI: Studies in Honor of Edward Dudley*, ed. Francisco La Rubia Prado (Newark, DE: Juan de la Cuesta, 2000), 49–60.

Flor de aforismos peregrinos (The Flower of Unusual Aphorisms). In *Persiles* IV, 1, the book of sayings being compiled by a pilgrim. All the members of the group headed by Periandro and Auristela make a contribution to the book.

Flora. In Roman myth, the goddess of flowers and the spring. The annual festival held in her honor, the Floralia (late April to May 1), was generally an opportunity for sexual licentiousness. For this reason, Flora was associated with promiscuity and prostitution. Antonio de *Guevara made Flora into a specific person, an ancient prostitute and a model of that profession, in his *Epístolas familiares* (1539; *Familiar Letters*), and it is to this Flora that MC refers in the prologue to *DQ* I. See also *Galatea* 6; *Parnaso* 8; *Persiles* IV, 7.

Bibliography: Carolyn A. Nadeau, *Women of the Prologue: Imitation, Myth, and Magic in "Don Quixote I"* (Lewiston, PA: Bucknell University Press, 2002).

Florence [Florencia]: Firenze. Italian city, capital of Tuscany, located northwest of Rome. In MC's day, as today, Florence was considered one of the greatest of intellectual and artistic centers in the world. The city was also well-known as a center where cloths (*raja*, *raso*) of various qualities were manufactured. The story of *Curioso* (*DQ* I, 33–35) is set in Florence. See also *DQ* I, 6; *Persiles* III, 8, 19; *Vidriera*.

Florentine cloth; Florentine satin. *Florence.

Florentine merchant. *Merchant(s).

Florian, Jean Pierre Claris de (1755–94). French novelist and writer of fables. Florian wrote a pastoral novel, *Galatée* (1783) in imitation of *Galatea*, which was also popular when translated into Spanish and which was continued by Cándido María *Trigueros. His posthumous translation, *Don Quichotte de la Manche* (6 vols., 1810), was very popular and influential.

Florida. The peninsula in the southeastern part of North America, which was discovered and first explored by the Spanish and where they established cities and colonies. The coast of Florida was considered to be dangerous for navigation. See *Rufián* 2.

Florimorte. An error or misprint for Felixmarte, the protagonist of the romance of chivalry that bears his name (*Ortega, Melchor).

Florimorte de Hircania. *Ortega, Melchor.

Florinda; Florinda la Cava. *Cava, La.

Floripes. A Saracen princess, sister of Fierabrás and in love with Guy de Borgoña (*Historia del emperador Carlomagno y los doce pares de Francia*). See *DQ* I, 49.

Florisa. In *Galatea*, a shepherdess and close friend of Galatea.

Flotir. *Palmerín* cycle.

Flower of Unusual Aphorisms, The. *Flor de aforismos peregrinos.*

Flying carpet [Manto volador]. In *Persiles* I, 8, the magical device used by the witch to fly Rutilio from Italy to Norway.

Foces. An Aragonese family name mentioned in *DQ* I, 13.

Foix, Odet de, Viscount of Lautrec (1485–1528). A French soldier who spent years fighting in Italy. In *DQ* I, 35, it is reported that Lotario, protagonist of *Curioso*, died while fighting in a battle involving Monsiur de Lautrec. The reference is most likely to the battle of Cerignola (1503), in which Lautrec's French forces were opposed by Spanish forces headed by the Gran Capitán (*Hernández de Córdoba, Gonzalo).

Folía. *Chacona.

Folklore and folktales in Cervantes. MC was very familiar with the folklore of his time and incorporated anecdotes and stories from a variety of popular sources—oral culture, the ballad tradition, and published collections of tales from Spanish, Muslim, medieval, and classical sources—into his works. His greatest folkloric creation is SP, the earthy peasant from the tradition of *carnival, the voice of popular wisdom in his proverbs, the teller of popular tales (as in his story about counting goats in I, 20, and in his anecdote of the peasant and the *hidalgo* in II, 31), and the participant in folk anecdotes (as in the scene with the innkeeper in II, 59). SP draws on folk wisdom to resolve the legal dilemmas presented to him as governor (II, 45) and later on the way home (II, 66).

Pedro de Urdemalas, protagonist of MC's play of the same name, is also a popular folkloric figure. In addition, MC's works feature frequent folkloric characters, tales, situations, and references; some of the more prominent examples are Muñatones (*DQ* I, 7), Quintañona (*DQ* I, 13, 16, 14; *DQ* II, 23), the 'two friends' theme (*DQ* I, 33), Orbaneja (*DQ* II, 3, 71), the braying aldermen (*DQ* II, 25), Perogrullo (*DQ* II, 62), Bachellor Pasillas (*Coloquio*), Malmaridada (*Parnaso* 1), Juana la Chasca (*Parnaso* 2), Escarramán (*Viudo*; *Cueva*), Maricastaña (*Casamiento*), Cantimpalos (*Vizcaíno*), and Pero García (*Viejo*).

Bibliography: Mac E. Barrick, "The Form and Function of Folktales in *Don Quijote*," *Journal of Medieval and Renaissance Studies* 6 (1976): 101–38; Maurice Chevalier, "Literatura oral y ficción cervantina," *Prohemio* 5 (1974): 161–96: and Mauricio Molho, *Cervantes: raíces folklóricas* (Madrid: Gredos, 1976).

Follower of the fleeing nymph. *Apollo.

Fonseca. Knight-errant mentioned only one time in *Tirante el Blanco* (*Martorell, Johanot), who is cited in *DQ* I, 6.

Fonseca, Fray Cristóbal de (ca. 1550–1621). Augustinian writer and preacher. His best-known work is the *Tratado del amor de Dios* (1592; *Treatise on God's Love*), a religious essay that borders on mysticism. MC's friend cites the *Tratado* approvingly in the prologue to *DQ* I.

Fooled with Open Eyes. *Engaño a los ojos.

Forastero. *Outsider.

Forest of Love, The. *Bosque amoroso, El.

Forests of Erífile. *Balbuena, Bernardo de.

Forgetfulness [Descuido]. One of the allegorical figures that accompany Morpheus, god of dreams, in *Parnaso* 8.

Forms of address. In the modern Spanish of Spain (things are often very different in areas of Spanish America) there are two basic forms of address, familiar (singular *tú* and plural *vosotros*) and formal (*usted* and *ustedes*). But in MC's day the situation was more complicated, as there were more options and each one carried with it important social connotations. The singular *tú* was used to address equals or inferiors, including children, while the singular *vos* and plural *vosotros* (both of which took the second person plural verb form) were used with superiors. But, perhaps because of overusage, *vos* came to be the form used to address equals, and, later, even inferiors. Meanwhile, *vuestra* (or *vuesa*) *merced* (your grace; the form that eventually evolved into the modern *usted*), with a third-person singular verb (*vuestras mercedes* in the plural), became the term for polite address. The term *vuestra señoría* (your lordship) was used for people with titles such as count or marquis, bishops, ambassadors, and so forth. *Vuestra excelencia* (your excellency) was reserved for dukes, viceroys, and military generals. *Vuestra majestad* (your majesty), of course, was only for royalty. To shift from one form of address to another when speaking with someone was to send a message of respect or lack thereof (see the example provided by Antonio the Barbarian in *Persiles* I, 5). But, to complicate matters, exceptions to the general usage abound in the literature of the Spanish *Golden Age. All forms of address should be understood according to context in every case. *DQ* illustrates both the general rules and some of the exceptions. DQ uses both *tú* and *vos* with SP, whereas the latter consistently refers to his master as *vuestra merced*.

Forsi altro canterà con miglior plectio. The final words of *DQ* I, taken, slightly misquoted, from *Orlando Furioso*: 'perhaps another will sing with a better pick,' meaning that maybe another writer will continue the story better than MC can. In effect, MC grants permission for someone else to write a sequel, but when *Avellaneda did just that, MC was greatly offended.

Förtsch, Johann Philipp. *Hinsch, Heinrich.

Fortunate Ruffian, The. *Rufián dichoso, El.

Fortune (Turning wheel, Wheel of fortune) [Fortuna (Variable rueda, Rodaja de la Fortuna)].

Originally, the Roman goddess Fortuna may have been associated with fertility and then, by extension, good luck in general. References to fortune abound in the writings of MC and his contemporaries. Traditionally, fortune is depicted as blindfolded and accompanied by a wheel, whose continual movement represents the mutable nature of human existence, suggesting that one's luck can turn at any moment and the person who is up today may be down tomorrow. (In modern times, fortune is still associated with the wheel, especially the roulette wheel in gambling casinos.) Fortune, either personified or used as a common noun, is frequent throughout the works of MC, most often in an offhand reference to luck or chance. But occasionally the reference is of interest; for example, MC refers to the fall from fortune of the famous historical figures of Don Alvaro de *Luna, *Hannibal, and King *Francis I of France in the prefatory poem attributed to *Urganda la Desconocida. In *DQ* II, 19 and 66, SP twice cites the belief that fortune is blind, but DQ both times insists that there is no such thing as fortune, that it is a matter of God's providence or that we make our own fortune in the world. Typical of his age, MC tends to convert the old pagan goddess into either mere chance or Christian divine providence. For other selected examples, see also *Coloquio*; *DQ* I, 34, 47; *DQ* II, 10, 19; *Fregona*; *Galatea*; *Gallardo* 3; *Laberinto* 1; *Numancia* 1, 4; *Parnaso* 6; *Pedro* 1; *Persiles* I, 1, 5, 14; II, 10, III, 4, IV, 1, 14; *Poesías* 1, 5, 20; *Sultana* 2–3; *Tratos* 2–4.

Fortunilla, La (1691; *The Little Fortune*).
An anonymous *entremés* based on *Cueva*.

Fortuny, Juan de.
A merchant from Valencia who was involved in ransoming Christian captives held in Algiers. He had some dealings with Leonor de *Cortinas, MC's mother in 1582, in an attempt to pay off debts incurred in raising funds for the ransom of MC.

Fountain of Slate [Fuente de las Pizarras].
A fictional location where some of the action in *Galatea* takes place. See *Galatea* 1, 4–5.

Four prayers [Cuatro oraciones].
The four major prayers of Catholicism: the *Pater Noster* (*Padrenuestro*) (Our Father), the *Ave Maria* (Hail Mary), the *Credo* (I believe), and the *Salve Regina* (Hail Holy Queen). They are mentioned as a group in *Baños* 1 and then cited individually in *Baños* 2–3; *Fregona*.

Four S's [Cuatro S].
In *DQ* I, 34, Leonela refers to the four qualities a lover should possess: *sabio* (wise), *solo* (unattached), *solícito* (persistent), and *secreto* (discreet).

Fourcroy, Bonaventure (ca. 1610–1691).
French dramatist. He wrote a comedy entitled *Sancho Pança* (1659), which has been lost.

Fourth sphere [Cuarta esfera, cuarto cielo].
The heavenly sphere of Apollo, or the sun. See *Fregona*; *Galatea* 6.

Fowles, John (1926–).
English novelist. Sarah Woodruff, heroine of Fowles's *The French Lieutenant's Woman* (1969), is a typical quixotic dreamer; she would "lay awake at nights imagining scenes from the more romantic literature of her adolescence, scenes in which starving heroines lay huddled on snow-covered doorsteps or fevered in some bare, leaking garret. . . . She had read far more fiction and far more poetry, those two sanctuaries of the lonely, than most of her kind. They served as a substitute for experience." Her lover, Charles, is more prosaic and realistic, but he does conceive of his servant, Sam (derived to some extent from Dickens's Sam Weller), as "his Sancho Panza, the low comedy that supported his spiritual worship of Ernestina-Dorothea" (does he mean Dulcinea?). In fact, Sam is not very much like SP, in spite of the explicit connection. What most recalls MC in this novel, however, is the frequent self-conscious metafictional narrative play. Fowles as narrator accompanies Charles on a train ride; he provides multiple endings for the story; he ruminates on the nature of the novel. Typical is a chapter that begins, "I do not know. This

story I am telling is all imagination. These characters I create never existed outside my own mind. . . . But I live in the age of Alain Robbe-Grillet and Roland Barthes; if this is a novel, it cannot be a novel in the modern sense of the word." No, it is a novel in the original, Cervantine sense of the word, a sense that provides the basis for fiction throughout the centuries. Later in the chapter, the author/narrator sums up the original Cervantine insight that has inspired literature throughout the centuries: "We are all in flight from the real reality. That is a basic definition of *Homo sapiens*."

Frailecitos descalzos. *Little barefoot friars.

Frailes cartujos. *Carthusian friars.

Frailes de la Orden de San Benito. *Benedictine friars.

Franca de Rojas, Ana (Ana de Villafranca) (1564–99). Wife of Alonso *Rodríguez and lover of MC. She is the mother of MC's only child, Isabel de *Saavedra, born in November 1584. After her husband's death, she took over the tavern previously run by him.

France [Francia]. The only work by MC in which France plays a prominent role is *Persiles*. First, there is the story of *Renato and Eusebia, in II, 18–21, and then in III, 13–18, the pilgrims pass through France on their way from Spain to Italy and have some adventures there. There is no indication that MC ever visited or traveled through France. His most frequent references to France involve the legendary heroes and heroines of the Carolingian ballad cycle. See *Casa* 1; *Cueva*; *DQ* I, 6, 41, 49; *DQ* II, 11, 23–24, 26, 33, 40–41, 54, 60, 64; *Española*; *Gallardo* 2; *Parnaso* 1, 8; *Persiles* I, 16–17, II, 7.1, III, 10, 12–14, 18–19, IV, 5, 6, 8; *Tratos* 1; *Vidriera*.

Francenia. *Pastoral names.

Francenio. 1. In *Galatea* 3–4, a shepherd and friend of Lauso and Arsenio. **2.** A shepherd mentioned in *Casa* 2.

Franchote. A term used by SP to describe his friend *Ricote whom he meets traveling as a foreign pilgrim. *Franchote* (or *franchute*) was—and still is—a disdainful term used by Spaniards to describe foreigners, particularly French ones. See *DQ* II, 54.

Francia, rey de. *King of France.

Francis I [Francisco I] (1494–1547). King of France and rival to Carlos V of Spain. In the battle of Pavia in 1525, when an entire French army of some 30,000 troops was killed, wounded, or taken prisoner, Francis himself was captured. He was taken to Madrid and imprisoned for nearly a year while terms of surrender and concession were negotiated (he read Spanish romances of chivalry during his captivity). After his release and return to France, however, Francis failed to honor the terms of the treaty. He is mentioned in the poem by Urganda la Desconocida in the preliminary pages to *DQ* I as an example of how fortune can make the powerful fall to obscurity.

Francis, Esteban. *Nicolas Nabokov.

Francisca. *Pastoral names.

Francisca Ricota. The wife of *Ricote and mother of *Ricota.

Francisco. 1. In *Tratos*, the older son sold to a Muslim merchant and who announces the arrival of a Christian rescue ship near the end of the play. In *Tratos* 2, one of the Muslim merchants wants to change the boy's name to Mamí. **2.** In *Doncellas*, the name used by Leocadia during the time she is dressed as a man. **3.** In *Entretenida* 1, the friend of Don Antonio who informs him that his beloved Marcela has been taken out of town to an undisclosed location by her father.

Francisco I. *Francis I.

Francisco de Cárcamo, Don. In *Gitanilla*, a member of the Order of Santiago and the noble father of Don Juan de Cárcamo, his son who takes the name of Andrés Caballero when he becomes a gypsy in order to prove his love for

Preciosa. He may be loosely based on the historical Alonso de Cárcamo, member of the order of Calatrava (not Santiago) who held the office of magistrate in the late sixteenth and early seventeenth centuries.

Francisco de Humillos. In *Elección*, one of the candidates for the position of magistrate.

Francisco de Pizarro, Don. *Pizarro, Don Francisco de.

Francisquilla. In *Pedro* 2, a gypsy who has a minor role in the dance for the king and queen.

Francisquito. In *Baños*, one of the children taken during the raid on Spain, who is later martyred when he refuses to renounce his religion and resists the advances of the lustful cadí.

Francos, Calle de. *Calle de Cervantes.

Frank, Bruno (1887–1945). German poet, dramatist, and novelist. Frank wrote a historical-biographical, and basically very romantic, novel about MC entitled *Cervantes* (1934; translated as *A Man Called Cervantes*). Frank stays within the known chronological and factual outline of MC's life, but invents lively scenes involving purely fictional incidents and a variety of imagined and historical characters, such as Gina, a prostitute in Rome and young MC's lover. Don Juan of Austria is presented as one of the great illusionists of the time. There is throughout the novel a conscious attempt to evoke the spirit of the historical and cultural context within which MC lived. Although a very conventional and relatively unimaginative story, this is probably the best fictional version of MC's life before Stephen *Marlowe's *The Death and Life of MC*.

Frank, Waldo (1889–1967). American writer. Frank's *Virgin Spain: The Drama of a Great People* (1926) is a sympathetic, at times romantic, vision of Spain, not unlike other books of its kind. But the book ends with an interesting fictional dialogue, a sort of parable, entitled "The Port of Columbus," a conversa-

tion between MC and Christopher Columbus in Palos de la Frontera, from which Columbus's ships sailed on his first voyage. The characters gaze alternately west to America and east to Spain and Europe, contemplating the relationships between them and the significance of Columbus's accomplishments. Symbolizing America is a City of White Towers, but, as the two men talk, the towers veer, twist, and fall, making way for a new America. Perhaps the parable takes on new meaning after September 11, 2001.

Bibliography: Waldo David Frank, *Virgin Spain: The Drama of a Great People* (New York: Duell, Sloan and Pearce, 1926).

Frateco. A pseudonym (it is Italian for 'little friar') used by the author of *Der Don Quijote von München* (1934; *The Don Quixote of Munich*), a documentary novel with satiric overtones in which Adolf Hitler is compared to DQ. The novel traces Hitler's career from the end of World War I to his assumption of power in 1933, following historical facts well enough, but rounding out the portrait of the great quixotic character with some imaginative details.

Bibliography: Frateco, *Der don Quijote von München* (Amsterdam: Nederlandsche Keurboekerij, 1934).

Fratín. *Paleazzo, Giacomo.

Fray Candil (Emilio Bobadilla, 1862–1921). Cuban novelist, short-story writer, and poet. Bobadilla traveled and lived in Spain and was very popular there in the early years of the twentieth century. He wrote an "Oda" (1886) and at least six sonnets to various characters in *DQ* (DT, SP, Rocinante, and so on).

Frayn, Michael (1933–). English dramatist and novelist. Frayn's *The Two of Us: Four One-Act Plays* (1970) consists of four short plays, each for two actors. The second is entitled "The New Quixote"; in it, a young man begins to move in with an older woman whom he met the previous evening and with whom he has spent the night. He is ecstatically in love and slowly brings the woman around to accepting him as her lover. Since there is no mention of MC, DQ, or any character, scene, or event from DQ, it is presumably the man's idealization of a somewhat older DT as his ideal love that makes him quixotic.

Bibliography: Michael Frayn, *The Two of Us: Four One-Act Plays* (New York: Samuel French, 1970).

Frazzi, Vito. *Casella, Mario.

Free cities of Germany [Ciudades libres de Alemania]. The Protestant cities that did not belong to the Holy Roman Empire. See *Persiles* II, 19.

Freedom [Libertad]. It has been argued that the single most constant theme in nearly all the works of MC is that of freedom. As one who spent five years in slavery, MC knew personally the value of freedom and what it cost. His plea to Mateo *Vázquez in *Poesías* 8 (the most important part of which also appears in *Tratos* 1) is one of the earliest expressions of the theme. Many of his plays and fictional narratives, particularly those dealing with captivity in Algiers and Constantinople, stress freedom. Ambiguous as it may be, the plea for religious freedom made by the *Morisco* Ricote in II, 54, is consistent with many other passages throughout MC's works. Marcela (I, 14), Zoraida (I, 37, 39–41), and Preciosa (*Gitanilla*), three of MC's most original and compelling women characters, speak in defense of their personal and religious freedom. And SP and DQ both make eloquent statements about freedom, the former when he relinquishes his governorship in order to return to his former freedom (II, 53) and the latter when he leaves the castle of the duke and duchess and states that freedom is 'one of the most precious gifts that heaven has ever given to men' (II, 58).

Bibliography: Luis Rosales, *Cervantes y la libertad*, 2nd ed. corregida, 2 vols. (Madrid: Ediciones Cultura Hispánica del Instituto de Cooperación Iberoamericana, 1985); and Alberto Sánchez, "Libertad, humano tesoro," *Anales Cervantinos* 32 (1994): 9–21.

Fregona ilustre. *Illustrious Kitchen Maid.

French ambassador. *Mayenne, Duke of.

French disease [Morbo gálico]. Syphilis. Although it was long believed to be certain that syphilis was brought to Europe from America by the crew of Christopher Columbus, recent evidence suggests that that may not be the case. Whatever the actual facts, the Spanish attributed the disease to the French. See *DQ* II, 22.

French literature. No great French writer of the middle ages or sixteenth century—Villon, Rabelais, or Montaigne—was known in Spain. In comparison with the profound influence of Italian writers and Italian literature on MC and his contemporaries, the influence of France is virtually negligible. The one exception has to do with the characters of the medieval French chivalric tradition, especially Charlemagne and Roland (*Carolingian cycle), though even here they often come filtered through the work of the Italians Boiardo and Ariosto and/or the medieval Spanish ballad tradition. In addition to frequent allusions to and citations of these heroes by DQ and other characters, they appear prominently in *Maese Pedro's puppet show (*DQ* II, 26). The enigmatic *Casa* is specifically about the great French chivalric heroes, but they are presented in an ambiguously comic light and appear foolish in comparison with the Spanish Bernardo del Carpio and the Saracen Marfisa.

French merchant. *Merchant(s).

French pirates. *Pirate(s).

Frestón. Fristón, the evil enchanter who strives constantly to hinder the work of the great knight-errant Belianís de Grecia (*Fernández, Jerónimo), but then who becomes the chronicler of his heroic deeds. In *DQ* I, 7, the priest and barber hit upon the idea of blaming the disappearance of *DQ's library on the intervention of an evil enchanter. At their instigation, DQ's niece describes the enchanter's deed and says that he was called Muñatón. DQ corrects her, saying that he must have been Frestón, clearly referring to Fristón from *Belianís* but mistaking his name, the only error DQ (not the narrator or other characters) ever makes with a name from the romances of chivalry. From then on, beginning with the adventure of the windmills in I, 8, Frestón is the evil enchanter, not always mentioned by name, who foils DQ's exploits.

Freud, Sigmund (1856–1939). Austrian psychoanalyst.

As a teenager, Freud learned Spanish specifically in order to read MC in the original. He was particularly impressed by MC's short stories, especially *Coloquio* (which he may actually have read only in excerpt in a Spanish primer). For a decade, Freud participated in a kind of "cult" centered around MC, which was called the "Academia Española," and corresponded with his most intimate friend, Eduard Silberstein, on the subject of MC's works; the two of them even signed their letters "Berganza" (Silberstein) and "Cipión" (Freud). It has not passed without comment that in *Coloquio*, Cipión listens to and comments on the narrative of Berganza, a relationship that parallels that of analyst and patient. MC is second only to Goethe as the writer most admired by Freud, and throughout his life he maintained an intense interest in *DQ* and, as his correspondence with his fiancé Martha Bernays makes clear, he 'reveled' in his readings of the novel. He was particularly attracted to the *Cardenio* episodes, *Capitán*, the events at the inn of Juan Palomeque, SP's Barataria episodes, and the Doré engravings that illustrated the edition he read. Freud considered DQ a prototype of the paranoid personality—suspicious of reality, believing that he was pursued by enchanters—the first such described in Western literature. Certainly at least two dream scenes in MC's works—DQ's in the Cave of Montesinos in II, 23; and Periandro's in *Persiles* II, 15—provide the sort of material that invites Freudian interpretation.

Bibliography: John Farrell, *Freud's Paranoid Quest; Psychoanalysis and Modern Suspicion* (New York: New York University Press, 1996); E. C. Riley, "Cervantes, Freud, and Psychoanalytic Narrative Theory," *Modern Language Review* 88 (1993): 1–14; and S. B. Vranich, "Sigmund Freud and 'The Case History of Berganza': Freud's Psychoanalytic Beginnings," *Psychoanalytic Review* 63 (1976): 73–82.

Frías, Damasio de. Spanish author of dialogues and poetry praised in Calliope's song in *Galatea* 6.

Frías, Heriberto (1870–1925).

Mexican novelist. Frías's sensational and influential novel *¡Tomochic! Episodios de campaña* (first published anonymously in 1893; *Tomochic! Episodes in the Campaign*) was later revised and expanded and, with the author's name, finally published in a definitive edition under the title *Tomochic: Novela histórica mexicana* (1906; *Tomochic: A Mexican Historical Novel*). The novel was based on the author's own military experiences in the brutal crushing of the rebellion of the village of Tomochic by federal forces of dictator Porfirio Díaz. Its sequel, *El triunfo de Sancho (Mazatlán): Novela de crítica social mexicana* (1911; *The Triumph of Sancho Panza [Mazatlán]: A Novel of Mexican Social Criticism*), was also based on the author's personal experiences as a journalist in Mazatlán. In it, the quixotic, idealistic Miguel Mercado, hero of the first novel, settles in Mazatlán and becomes a journalist. At one point a friend says to him, 'You're barking at the moon, Quixotedog! . . . Yes, you are a Don Quixote in the body of Sancho Panza!' At the end of the novel, Miguel publishes an article that he intends as a defense of Mazatlán and its inhabitants, but that everyone in power takes as a personal insult and threat. The moneyed interests, and the local pride they enflame with their interpretation of the article, force Miguel to leave town. The moral is that SP—for Frías, the symbol of vulgarity, stupidity, and self-interest—ultimately wins out over DQ—the symbol of idealism, intelligence, and self-sacrifice.

Bibliography: Heriberto Frías, *El triunfo de Sancho (Mazatlán)* (Mexico City: Imprenta de Luis Herrera, 1911).

Friend [Compadre].

In *Viejo*, the friend of Cañizares who commiserates with him about the problems caused by his young wife.

Friend of Anselmo [Amigo de Anselmo].

A minor but important unnamed character in *Curioso* (*DQ* I, 33–35). It is in his friend's house that Anselmo takes refuge and dies after his wife and best friend have deceived him.

Friend of Cervantes [Amigo de Cervantes]. In the prologue to *DQ* I, the fictional personage who counsels MC on how he should write his prologue and compose the preliminary verses himself. He also insists that the whole purpose in writing *DQ* was to criticize the romances of chivalry.

Friend of Don Antonio's wife [Amiga de la mujer de don Antonio]. A person who is present and asks a question during the exhibition of the *enchanted head. See *DQ* II, 62.

Friend of Fernando. *Aguilar, Don Pedro de.

Friends of Basilio [Amigos de Basilio]. Those present at *Camacho's wedding who rush to the aid and defense of Basilio when he interrupts the ceremony with his fake suicide. See *DQ* II, 21.

Friends of Don Antonio Moreno [Amigos de Don Antonio Moreno]. Two friends who are present during the exhibition of the *enchanted head. See *DQ* II, 62.

Friends of Don Fernando [Camaradas de don Fernando]. The men who accompany Fernando when he arrives at the inn of Juan Palomeque in *DQ* I, 36. One of them is the brother of a man who was captive in Algiers with Juan Pérez de Viedma and recites a pair of sonnets his brother wrote (I, 39–40).

Friends of Rodolfo [Amigos de Rodolfo]. In *Fuerza*, the four young men who keep the family at bay while Rodolfo abducts and rapes Leocadia; two of them, who also accompany Rodolfo on his seven-year trip to Italy, confirm their participation in this act to his mother Doña Estefanía.

Friends of the captive [Amigos (camaradas) del cautivo]. In *DQ* I, 40–41, the three friends of Ruy Pérez de Viedma who are with him when Zoraida first contacts him and who eventually escape with him.

Friends of the wounded [Compañeros de los heridos]. In *DQ* I, 3, companions of the muleteers DQ hits when they attempt to disturb his armor during his vigil in the inn before being dubbed a knight-errant.

Friere de Lima, Simón. A merchant in Seville who held some funds for MC, both MC's own and some taxes he had collected, and who then went bankrupt and absconded with the money.

Frisland [Frislanda]. An island that is depicted on maps of northern Europe from the Middle Ages and Renaissance, but that corresponds exactly to no known place. It is not to be confused with Friesland, a region of the Netherlands, or the Frisian islands, located in the North Sea near the Netherlands and Germany. For MC, it is the homeland of Princess Sigismunda. See *Persiles* IV, 12, 14.

Fritón. In *DQ* I, 7, the comic mispronunciation, suggesting *frito* (fried), by the housekeeper of the name of DQ's enemy, the enchanter *Frestón.

Fröding, Gustaf (1860–1911). Swedish poet. In one of Fröding's best books, *Nya dikter* (1894; *New Poems*), there is a poem entitled "Don Quixote." When asked if he is not tired of his travels and adventures, DQ responds that "the windmills still move," suggesting that the quixotic quest is needed in all times and places.

Frontino. The horse ridden by several characters, among them the warrior woman Bradamante, in *Ariosto's *Orlando Furioso*. See *DQ* I, 25; *DQ* II, 40.

Frozen sea [Mar helado]. Probably the Baltic Sea, in MC's ambiguous and fabulous northern geography. It is first mentioned in *Persiles* II, 16, and then in II, 18, when Periandro and his sailors are trapped in the ice, it turns out that they are just off the coast of *Bituania, kingdom of King *Cratilo. If Bituania represents (more or less, again, in MC's geography) Lithuania, then it is logical to assume that the reference here is to the Baltic, which does border that nation.

Fúcar. *Fuggar.

Fuchs, Georg (1868–?). German dramatist. Fuchs wrote the libretto for the opera *Don Quijote, der sinnreiche Junker von der Mancha* (1911; *Don Quixote, Reformed Junker of La Mancha*), with music by Anton Beer-Waldbrunn.

Fuego, isla del. *Island of Fire.

Fuenfrida. A well-traveled pass in the Guadarrama Mountains, near Segovia. In *Rinconete*, it is the birthplace of Rinconete.

Fuente de las Pizarras. *Fountain of Slate.

Fuente del alcornoque. *Spring of the Cork-tree.

Fuente, Doctor (Rodrigo) de la (ca. 1510–ca. 1589). A physician who was also a professor at the University of Toledo. In *Fregona*, he is mentioned as the physician who attends the mother of Costanza.

Fuentes, Carlos (1928–). Mexican novelist. Fuentes has acknowledged that, like William *Faulkner, he rereads *DQ* every year—in Fuentes's case always around Easter time. Fuentes has written an important and original essay on both *DQ* and the act of reading entitled *Cervantes, o la crítica de la lectura* (1976; "*Don Quixote*" or, *the Critique of Reading*); in it he equates the accomplishments of Christopher Columbus and MC—the discoverer of the New World and the creator of the modern novel. He describes *DQ* as the novel "written by everybody, read by everybody." In Fuentes's most ambitious and most highly acclaimed novel, *Terra Nostra* (1975), a companion piece to his critique of reading, MC (who appears as 'the Chronicler'), DQ, and SP join a host of other classic literary and historical figures (Celestina, Don Juan, Christopher Columbus, and Carlos V) in a fantastic evocation of the Spanish heritage of the New World. Specific recollections of scenes and characters from *DQ*—the wind-

mills, the armies of sheep, the galley slaves, SP's governorship, wicked enchanters, DT, and more—integrate MC's novel fully into the fantastic text. In *La cabeza de la hidra* (1978; *The Hydra Head*) Fuentes does to the espionage novel something like what MC did to the romances of chivalry; novels like *The Maltese Falcon* and the spy thrillers of John Le Carré, and films like *Casablanca* and the James Bond movies, are the equivalent of *Amadís de Gaula* in this novel. At one point the protagonist Félix Maldonado attacks a ship with a machete and is called 'an improbable DQ.' Authorial intrusions and ambiguous sources for the story recall MC's technique and the role of CHB in *DQ*. Like other writers of the Spanish American Boom generation and practitioners of 'magical realism,' much of the lucid self-referentiality, ambiguity, and cultural analysis in the novels and stories of Fuentes are at least suggestive of the great cultural icons of MC and DQ who are always acknowledged at least indirectly, if not specifically.

Bibliography: Carlos Fuentes, "*Don Quixote*": or, *The Critique of Reading* (Austin: Institute of Latin American Studies, University of Texas, 1976); Javier Herrero, "Carlos Fuentes y las lecturas modernas del *Quijote*," *Revista Iberoamericana* 45 (1979): 555–62; Julio Ortega, "Carlos Fuentes: para recuperar la tradición de la Mancha," *Revista Iberoamericana* 55 (1989): 637–54; and Philip Swanson, "Writing the Present, Reading the Past: Cervantes, Güiraldes, Fuentes," in *Cervantes and the Modernists: The Question of Influence*, ed. Edwin Williamson (London: Tamesis, 1994), 121–33.

Fuentes de la duquesa. *Running sores of the duchess.

Fuertes, Gloria (1918–). Spanish poet and children's author. Fuertes has a three-line poem "Por La Mancha" in *Historia de Gloria* (1980; *Gloria's Story*) about the quixotization of SP and the sanchification of DQ.

Fuerza de la sangre, La (Fuerza); The Power of Blood. The sixth story in *Novelas* and the most tightly constructed and cohesive of the collection. It consists of an interesting combination of romance plot with the realism of a violent rape. The power of blood is literal when the boy Luis lies bleeding on the ground but is saved by a man who recognizes in the boy's face the image of his own son (who is, in fact, the father of Luis). But the ending of the story also acknowledges both the power of noble blood (and of privileged social status) when Rodolfo marries the beautiful Leocadia and the power of the divine blood shed in Christ's crucifixion. Overall, the *novela* presents an exemplary tale of the redemption of sin by the power of the cross.

One warm summer evening in Toledo, an elderly *hidalgo* takes a stroll with his wife, young son, daughter who is about 16 years old, and maid. They encounter a group of carefree young gentlemen led by one Rodolfo, about 22 years of age, who cover their faces with masks and make fun of the family, eyeing the wife, daughter, and maid. Rodolfo, taken by the beauty of the daughter, whose name is Leocadia, convinces his friends to help him kidnap her. They do, and Rodolfo carries Leocadia, who faints and then is blindfolded, away to his home. There, in the privacy of his bedroom, he rapes her before she regains consciousness. When she does, and when she realizes what has happened, she begs her assailant to do two things: first, take her to a place near the cathedral of the city, from which she can find her way home; and, second, not say anything about this to anyone, for a secret shame is always preferable to public dishonor. Rodolfo tries again to have his way with Leocadia, but, awake, she successfully defends herself as she could not when unconscious. Not sure what to do, Rodolfo goes out to seek the advice of his friends, but changes his mind and returns, planning to tell them that he had let the woman go. While he is gone, Leocadia carefully examines the room, noting the rich bed and other luxurious furnishings, and takes a small silver crucifix from the wall, which she hides in the sleeve of her dress. When Rodolfo returns, he blindfolds Leocadia and takes her to the cathedral, where he leaves her. She makes her way home and tearfully describes to her parents what has happened. They agree that they should keep the matter secret and act as though it had

never happened. Within a few days, Rodolfo leaves with two friends for a previously planned trip to Italy, almost completely forgetting about the episode. Leocadia, however, cannot forget, for she is pregnant. In due time she delivers a boy, whom she names Luis, and takes him to relatives in a village to raise for four years. After this period of time, he is brought back home as Leocadia's nephew and is raised to read and write very well. One day, when Luis is seven years old, while out on an errand, he stops to watch a horse race. One of the horses gets out of control and tramples Luis, leaving him badly hurt and bleeding copiously from a head wound. An elderly gentleman in the crowd rushes to help, and takes the boy to his home. Leocadia and her family are notified, and go to the house, to find Luis well attended by a famous physician, who announces that the wound is not as bad as he had first thought. Leocadia recognizes the room in which Luis is being attended, and specifically the bed in which he is lying, as the scene of her dishonor. To be sure, she even counts the steps as she leaves and remembers that that was the exact number she descended on the night of her rape. Back home, she tells her mother all that she has found out. Her mother checks, and, sure enough, the family that lives in that house has a son named Rodolfo, who has spent the last seven years in Italy with two friends. Leocadia then speaks with Doña Estefanía, wife of the man who took Luis to his house. She explains all that happened seven years ago and produces the silver cross as a witness to the act. Doña Estefanía believes her, as does her husband when he hears the story. That very night, they send a letter to Rodolfo in Naples, informing him that they have arranged a marriage for him with a very beautiful young woman. Within three weeks of receiving the letter, Rodolfo is back home, anxious to meet his future bride. Doña Estefanía takes the two friends aside and persuades them to admit that one night right before their trip to Italy Rodolfo had indeed abducted a young woman, the final proof of the case for Doña Estefanía. To test her son, Doña Estefanía shows him a portrait of a plain-looking woman (not Leocadia), and tells him that this is to be his wife. Rodolfo reacts strongly by insisting that he must marry a woman who is beautiful, since he already has wealth and status. As they sit down to dinner, his parents also invite a 'guest' of theirs, Leocadia, who arrives (with Luis) very stunningly dressed. Rodolfo is smitten by her beauty and wishes that the woman his parents had chosen for him were half as lovely. As the dinner progresses, Leocadia is overcome with emotion and faints in Doña Estefanía's arms. Rodolfo rushes to her side, stumbling twice in his haste. They cannot revive Leocadia and fear that she may be dying. In the ensuing uproar, Leocadia's parents and the parish priest who has been summoned for the occasion and who are waiting in a nearby room enter the scene. The tearful Rodolfo also faints briefly, but revives and is told by his mother that Leocadia is to be his bride. The priest is there specifically to formalize the marriage of the couple. Leocadia finally regains consciousness, in the arms of Rodolfo as on the night of the rape, but this time with honor. Rodolfo recognizes his own image in the face of his son Luis, and everyone celebrates, with Rodolfo especially anxious for the night to come so that he can be alone with Leocadia. The couple lives happily ever after, leaving many descendants in the city of Toledo, where they still live to this day. Theirs is a case that illustrates the power of blood—that spilled by the injured Luis.

Bibliography: John J. Allen, "*El Cristo de la Vega* and *La fuerza de la sangre*," *MLN* 83 (1968): 271–75; R. P. Calcraft, "Structure, Symbol and Meaning in Cervantes's *La fuerza de la sangre*," *Bulletin of Hispanic Studies* 58 (1981): 197–203; María Elisa. Ciavarelli, *El tema de la fuerza de la sangre. Antecedentes europeos: Siglo de Oro español, Juan de la Cueva, Cervantes, Lope, Alarcón* (Madrid: José Porrúa Turanzas, 1980); Dina de Rentis, "Cervantes's *La fuerza de la sangre* and the Force of Negation," in *Cervantes's "Exemplary Novels" and the Advantage of Writing*, ed. Michael Nerlich and Nicholas Spadaccini (Minneapolis, MN: Prisma, 1990), 157–74; Edward H. Friedman, "Cervantes's 'La fuerza de la sangre' and the Rhetoric of Power," in *Cervantes's "Exemplary Novels" and the Advantage of Writing*, ed. Michael Nerlich and Nicholas Spadaccini (Minneapolis, MN: Prisma, 1990), 125–56; Elizabeth Teresa Howe, "The Power of Blood in Cervantes' *La fuerza de la sangre*," *Forum for Modern Language Studies* 30 (1994): 64–76; Paul Lewis-Smith, "Fictionalizing God: Providence, Nature and the Significance of Rape in *La fuerza de la sangre*," *Modern Language Review* 91 (1996): 886–97; Pedro Javier Pardo García, "Formas de imitación del *Quijote* en la novela inglesa del siglo XVIII: *Joseph Andrews* y *Tristram Shandy*," *Anales Cervantinos* 33 (1995–97): 133–64; Adriana Slaniceanu, "The Calculating Woman in Cervantes's *La fuerza de la sangre*," *Bulletin of Hispanic Studies* 64 (1987): 101–10; and Marcia Welles, "Violence Disguised: Representations of Rape in Cervantes' 'La fuerza de la sangre," *Journal of Hispanic Philology* 13 (1989): 240–52.

Fuggar [Fúcar]. The name of a family of famous, wealthy, and powerful German bankers, based in Augsburg, during the Renaissance. The Fuggars financed many of the military and political activities of both Carlos V (whom they helped elect Holy Roman Emperor over his rival Francis I of France) and Felipe II, and as a result were major recipients of the gold and silver brought from the New World. To call someone a Fuggar was to allude to his or her great wealth. See *DQ* II, 23; *Rufián* 2.

Fulano. A term used to refer to someone without mentioning a specific name; an ordinary person; a so-and-so. See *Galatea* 1; *Pedro* 1; *Persiles* I, 5.

Fulling mill [Batán]. A structure for making cloth ready to be used. A fulling mill consists of a waterwheel with wooden hammers used to pound fuller's earth into the cloth in water, a process that cleans the cloth of impurities and makes it easier to work with. In *DQ* I, 20, DQ and SP hear a frightful noise during the dark night. Immediately, DQ delivers a high-sounding speech about his chivalric duty and announces that he will investigate this possible adventure at once. But SP is afraid to be left alone at night and does all he can to make his master remain with him. First he attempts to convince DQ to stay by uttering his longest and most rhetorical speech of the novel, then he ties Rocinante's feet so that the horse cannot move, and next he tells his master a story; finally, so frightened that he refuses to leave DQ's side for any reason, he has to relieve himself, an act that particularly offends DQ. Morning finally comes, and the two go together to investigate the mysterious sounds—only to find that they are made by six hammers of a fulling mill. On the previous night DQ had interpreted the base reality of the percussion of the hammers' pounding as something menacing, and now he is forced to recognize his mistake. He does not compound the problem by insisting that enchanters have changed something dangerous into prosaic machinery (as he had with the windmills, for example), but recognizes the fulling mill for what it is, actually laughing at the absurdity of their fear during the night. But SP laughs even harder and begins to parody DQ's noble speech of the previous evening. DQ displaces his anger and embarrassment onto SP, hitting his squire with his lance because of what he perceives as an insolent mocking of his chivalric mission. SP apologizes for his excessive laughter but suggests that this will be a good story to tell. DQ disagrees, stating that they should never tell anyone about the incident and then upbraiding SP for his inappropriate intimacy. DQ then attempts to establish a new relationship with his squire, one in which SP will show more respect. In order to do this, DQ lies about the exaggerated deference chivalric squires showed toward the knights-errant they served (*Gandalín). This is one of the longest, most obviously comic, and most unexpectedly important chapters in *DQ* I. Here SP comes into his own more than at any time previously. His rhetorical speech has at least three stylistic registers and is brilliantly constructed. When the speech fails, SP turns to his more characteristic *industria* (cleverness or ingenuity) and ties Rocinante's feet. In effect, he 'enchants' DQ's horse so that he cannot move, an act that prefigures the 'enchantment' of DT in II, 10, perhaps the single most significant episode in all of *DQ* II. Some consider the story of Lope Ruiz and Torralba that SP tells DQ as an example of popular, folkloric narrative with the structure of a repetitive bedtime story parents tell their children to put them to sleep, complete with the counting of sheep (actually, goats). Others see

it as a kind of shaggy-dog story, an elaborate joke related by SP. DQ's frequent interruptions and discussion of narrative technique with SP both illustrate the difference between oral and written narrative and are a subtle consideration of aesthetic theory in miniature. SP's need to do 'that which no one can do for him' is perhaps the funniest (and crudest) scene in the novel, and it is one that some subsequent translators and editors, particularly in the eighteenth century, simply omitted. The final scene of laughter, in spite of DQ's anger and violent reaction, places the two characters on equal terms (and further humanizes DQ) to a greater extent than at any time previously. See also *DQ* II, 3, 41.

Bibliography: José María Casasayas, "Sancho Panza a tres horas del alba (Comentario a *DQ* 1, 20, aventura de los batanes)," *Anales Cervantinos* 25–26 (1987–88): 121–36; Edward Dudley, "Ring around the Hermeneutic Circle," *Cervantes* 6, no. 1 (1986): 13–27; Howard Mancing, "La retórica de Sancho Panza," in *Actas del Séptimo Congreso de la Asociación Internacional de Hispanistas*, ed. Giuseppe Bellini (Rome: Bulzoni Editore, 1982), 717–23; George Shipley, "A Prologue and Afterward for an Inquiry into *Don Quixote*, Part I, Chapter 20," in *Studies in Honor of Elias Rivers*, ed. Bruno M. Damiani and Ruth El Saffar (Potomac, MD: Scripta Humanistica, 1989), 169–83; and George Shipley, 'Sancho's Jokework,' in *Quixotic Desire: Psychoanalytic Perspectives on Cervantes*, ed. Ruth El Saffar and Diana de Armas Wilson (Ithaca, NY: Cornell University Press 1993), 135–54.

Furetière, Antoine (1619–88). French satirist, critic, and lexicographer. Furetière's *Le rroman bourgeois* (1666; *The Bourgeois Romance*) is a satirical fiction replete with embedded stories and digressions. The butt of the satire is Parisian bourgeois society, especially lawyers and literary figures. In the second part of the romance, Furetière's specific target is Charles *Sorel, whose *Berger extravagant* is parodied in an urban, rather than rural, setting. Furetière even names his protagonist Charroselles in an obvious allusion to Sorel. In addition to the somewhat quixotic protagonist, Javotte both reflects DQ and Emma Bovary in her obsessive reading, and there is a somewhat

SP-like character in Belastre (who even becomes a judge, rather like SP on his island); there are also some narrative techniques reminiscent of CHB and the narrative structure of *DQ*. It has been suggested the Furetière did not know MC's novel, but that seems highly improbable.

Bibliography: James A. Parr, "Comparataive Anatomy: Cervantes's Don Quixote and Furetière's Le Roman bourgeois," in *Echoes and Inscriptions: Comparative Approaches to Early Modern Spanish Literatures*, ed. Barbara A. Simerka and Christopher B. Weimer (Lewisburg, PA: Bucknell University Press, 2000), 108–24.

Furies. Three spirits—Megaera (Megera), Tisiphone (Tesifón), and Allecto (Alecto)—of punishment who avenged wrongs done to family, and especially murder. See *Galatea* 4.

Furrier. *Quartermaster.

Furst, Peter (1910–). German-American novelist. Furst's novel *Don Quixote in Exile* (1996) is a largely autobiographical account of a Jew's flight from early Nazi Germany, first to Spain, then to other European countries, to the Dominican Republic, and, at the book's end, to the United States. There is nothing explicitly quixotic about either character or plot, but evidently the author conceived of a self-imposed exile motivated by ideological and philosophical concerns as a quintessentially quixotic endeavor.

G

Gabacho. *Belmonte.

Gabriel. *Pérez del Barrio Angulo, Gabriel.

Gaeta. Italian city on the Mediterranean Sea located northwest of Naples. See *DQ* I, 52; *DQ* II, 18; *Galatea* 3, 5; *Guarda*.

Gaete y Cervantes, Don Gaspar de. A resident of Trujillo, apparently related to the Cervantes de Gaete family of that city and thus a relative of MC's. In Madrid in 1608, MC was a witness to a document signed by Don Gaspar.

Gaiferos, Don. A character from the Carolingian cycle of the Spanish ballad tradition. He does not exist in French literature. Gaiferos was supposed to be the nephew of Charlemagne who married the emperor's daughter, Melisendra. But before the marriage took place, Melisendra was abducted by Muslims and taken to Spain, where she languished in captivity for seven years before her betrothed rescued her. It is at this point that *Maese Pedro's puppet show begins. See *DQ* II, 25–26, 64; *Guarda*.

Gaita zamorana. *Zamora bagpipe.

Gaitán, Juana. Widow of MC's friend Diego *Laínez, whom she married late in his life, and neighbor of MC's wife Catalina in *Esquivias. Even after her second marriage to young Diego de Hondaro, Gaitán remained within MC's circle of friends until her death. In Valladolid, she lived with her husband, sister, and niece in the same building as MC and his family.

Galafrón. The father of Angélica in *Casa* 1.

Galalón. *Ganelon.

Galán. *Young lover.

Galaor, Don. The brother of Amadís de Gaula, famous for his practice of rescuing damsels, spending the night with them, but making a commitment to no one. He is the Don Juan of the Spanish romances of chivalry. In *DQ* I, 1, the barber Maese Nicolás actually prefers him to his brother, whom he considers somewhat more of a crybaby. In *DQ* I, 13, Vivaldo suggests that Galaor is an exception to DQ's statement that all knights-errant have a certain lady whom they love. DQ counters with the affirmation that he knows for certain that Galaor did indeed have a specific lady love. In this case Vivaldo is right, and it is likely that DQ, who knows *Amadís* very well, is simply lying in order to save face. See also *DQ* I, 20, 52; *DQ* II, 2; *Pedro* 1.

Galarza, Beltrán de. A Sevillian famous for telling tall tales and funny anecdotes. See *Parnaso* 1.

Galarza, Don Antonio de. Nothing is known about this writer whom MC mentions as a poet in *Parnaso* 2 and as a dramatist in the prologue to *Comedias*.

Galatea. 1. In Greek myth, Galatea was a Nereid loved by the Cyclops Polyphemus. She, however, loved the youthful and handsome Acis. When Polyphemus discovered the two together, he killed his rival with a huge boulder. This is the subject of *Góngora's *Fábula de Polifemo*, one of the most beautiful and famous long poems of the Spanish* Golden Age. 2. But there is also another Galatea in Greek myth. The sculptor Pygmalion scorned all women alive because of their imperfections, vowed to create a perfect woman, and sculpted a statue of unmatched beauty. Angry, the goddess Aphrodite made him fall in love with the statue, but she relented and brought the statue to life as the mortal woman Galatea. **3**. In *Galatea*, the titular protagonist, the shepherdess loved by Elicio and Erastro, universally praised for her beauty and discretion, promised by her father Aurelio in marriage to a shepherd from Portugal. MC's Galatea in *Galatea* draws from or alludes to both of the ancient myths. **4**. *Pastoral names.

Bibliography: Edward Dudley, "Goddess on the Edge: The Galatea Agenda in Raphael, Garcilaso and Cervantes," *Calíope* 1 (1995): 17–45.

Galatea, La: Primera parte de la Galatea, dividida en seis libros. Alcalá de Henares: Juan Gracián, 1585 (*Galatea*); *First Part of La Galatea, Divided into Six Books*.

MC's first book, published at the height of the vogue of the pastoral romance. The novel had two editions in the sixteenth century and four more in the seventeenth, but none after 1618, by which time the pastoral was no longer in vogue in Spain (when it was really just beginning in France). The action takes place in an idealized pastoral setting near Toledo and its famous Tagus River. The shepherds are not realistic rustics who have to work hard to care for their flocks and face inclement weather, but genteel nobles (several of whom are assumed to be based on MC's personal friends and acquaintances) who use the circumstance to lament their lost and/or unrequited loves. The romance has a complicated structure, alternating between prose and poetry and between a primary narration and a number of embedded stories. The result is the least linear of the Spanish pastoral romances, the one with the most complex structure of interwoven stories. No other work in the genre incorporates so much nonpastoral material, as stories of adventure and courtly intrigue are prominent in some of the embedded tales. Neither is any other pastoral romance characterized by so much physical violence and death as this one. Well received in its day (even Lope de *Vega wrote approvingly of it) and very popular in translation, especially in French, *Galatea* is one of the more interesting works in the genre. In *DQ* I, 6, the barber comes across this book during the examination of DQ's library, says that the author of *Galatea* is a good friend of his, and spares the book from the flames. His opinion is that *Galatea* shows some originality but does not finish what it began; it is necessary to wait, he says, for the appearance of the promised second part (which was never published). See also *Novelas*, prologue; and *Parnaso* 4.

Preliminaries: The price is set by Miguel de Ondarza Zavala on March 13, 1585. The corrector's statement is signed by Licenciado Várez de Castro, dated February 28, 1585. The approval for the Royal Council is signed by Lucas Gracián de Antisco (Dantisco) on February 1, 1584. The approval by the king's representative is signed by Antonio de Eraso on February 22, 1854. After the dedication and prologue, there are three laudatory sonnets, one each by Luis *Gálvez de Montalvo, Luis de *Vargas Manrique, and Gabriel *López Maldonado.

Dedication: To Ascanio *Colona, abbot of Santa Sofía. In addition to lavish praise for Colona, under whose protection MC dares to place himself, there is a brief reference to MC's having served in the household of Cardinal *Acquaviva in Rome.

Prologue: Addressed to 'curious readers,' most of the prologue is about the vicissitudes of writing poetry. Suggesting that the novel was written some time earlier, perhaps in the very early 1580s (or, at least partially, even in the late 1560s), MC states that he has not published this work sooner because he did not want to appear to be rash, but neither did he want to be one of those who wrote but never published their work. He assumes some will criticize him for mixing philosophical reasoning with pastoral poetry, but he hopes that this objection will be lessened if the reader understands that many of the characters in the book are real people in pastoral disguise. He ends by begging the reader's pardon, stating that he has written in order to please, and hopes that if this work does not, some of those yet to come will.

Book I: The action begins *in medias res* with a poem being sung by the shepherd Elicio, who is in love with the peerless beauty, the shepherdess Galatea, who is indifferent to his affection. As Elicio continues to sing of his unrequited love, he is joined by the rustic shepherd Erastro with his goats and dogs. Erastro is also in love with Galatea, although there is a note of comedy in the fact that such a lowly and comic figure should aspire to the love of the most beautiful and most highly esteemed of all shepherdesses. The two friendly rivals engage in a song of poetic debate about their love. As they finish their song, they see two shepherds come running out of the forest; one catches up with the other and brutally stabs him to death. Elicio follows the murderer and convinces him to explain what has happened. The assassin-shepherd, whose name is Lisandro, agrees and relates the series of events that led up to his mortal deed. This introduces the first embedded narrative: the story of Lisandro and Leonida. The son of noble and rich Andalusian parents, Lisandro and his family formed one of two rival political bands. One day he met and was smitten by love for the beautiful Leonida, daughter of the chief of the rival band. He befriended Silvia, intimate friend of Leonida, in order to attempt to get closer to the one he loved. Silvia had a relative named Carino, close friend (and secret enemy) of Leonida's brother Crisalvo, who was at the same time in love with Silvia. An exchange of letters began to bring Lisandro and Leonida together, and eventually they planned to marry. But a series of complications, rivalries, and jealousies led Carino to hatch a vicious plot of revenge. Convincing Crisalvo that Silvia had betrayed him, Carino arranged for Crisalvo and four accomplices to intercept her on the way to an illicit rendezvous. In fact, it was Leonida on her way to the union with Lisandro whom Crisalvo and his band attacked and stabbed to death. Lisandro arrived in time to take his beloved in his arms and hear her last words, revealing the mastermind behind her assassination. A six-month pursuit had ended earlier that day when Lisandro finally caught up with and killed Carino. Elicio offers Lisandro his friendship and takes the distraught stranger back to his hut for the night. The next day the shepherds are joined by

Galatea, whose own voice and music are divine, on her way to meet her friend Florisa. The two shepherdesses go their separate way and come across a third shepherdess who is lamenting her misfortune in prose and verse. They hide and listen further in order to know more about this stranger. Finally they reveal themselves, assure the newcomer that they wish her only well, and ask to hear her story. She consents and begins to recount the second embedded tale: the story of the twins of the Henares River, featuring the love of Teolinda and Artidoro. Teolinda's parents, wealthy peasants, permitted her to take up the pastoral life, in which she spent entire days gathering flowers and making wreaths. Never did she experience the effects of love until one day when she saw a new shepherd in the region and fell in love at first sight. The newcomer, named Artidoro, possessed the most beautiful voice, ran faster, and was stronger than anyone else; in general, he demonstrated an all-around superiority in comparison with the other shepherds. Furthermore, it appeared as though Artidoro also felt affection for Teolinda. But at this point, the story is interrupted by the noisy arrival of a large group of local shepherds, among them Elicio, Erastro, Lisandro, and Aurelio, Galatea's father, and their hunting dogs. Among the newcomers is Lenio, a shepherd who has never fallen in love and whose constant theme is the destructive nature of love. He engages both Elicio and Erastro in a debate on the subject and tempers begin to rise. Lisandro decides to take leave of his new friends and supporters and return home to face his sad fate. The group breaks up, Galatea anxious to hear the continuation of Teolinda's story, which will continue in the next book.

Book II: Teolinda continues her story: she and Artidoro made clear their chaste and honest amorous feelings for each other, which they strove to hide from everyone else. But the arrival of Teolinda's sister Leonarda complicated matters. Leonarda is the virtual twin of her sister and, when she met Artidoro she was offended by his amorous statements, which he made in the mistaken belief that he was talking to Teolinda, and she rebuffed his advances. Believing that he had offended his beloved, Artidoro immediately departed and, when Teolinda learned of this, left in search of him. It was while looking for him that she met Galatea and told her story. At this time two new shepherds arrive: Tirsi and Damón. The two new shepherds befriend Elicio and the others and there is a general round of singing of amorous poems. As the shepherds walk toward the village, they pass by a hermitage from within which they hear a harp being tuned. Erastro informs them that for the last couple of weeks, the hermitage has been inhabited by a stranger and suggests that perhaps he is about to sing something that will reveal his status. That is exactly what happens, and the shepherds listen to his sad song of love. When he finishes, they enter the hut and find that he has fainted. They revive him and convince him to tell his tale. Of course, he complies and begins to narrate the third embedded tale, that of 'the two friends' from Jerez de la Frontera: his name is Silerio and his very close friend is named Timbrio; the two of them were inseparable. When Timbrio had to leave town over a point of honor, Silerio followed within a few days. In Catalonia, Silerio caught up with Timbrio only to find that his friend had been condemned to death, having been caught in the company of a well-known Catalan bandit. Silerio created a disturbance allowing Timbrio to escape and take refuge in a church. But then Silerio was jailed and sentenced to death for freeing a prisoner. But fate intervened and there was a Turkish raid on the town in which they were located. Amidst the murder, rape, and pillage carried out by the Turks, both friends escaped, wounded, and headed separately for Naples. This time, when Silerio caught up with Timbrio he found that his friend was stricken by a new malady: love. Timbrio had fallen in love with the divinely beautiful Nísida. Silerio conceived of a plan to help his good friend: he disguised his identity and with his guitar gained entry to noble homes as a traveling entertainer. In the home of Nísida's family, he took one look at the lovely lady and also immediately fell in love with her. But in spite of his own feelings, he managed to promote the cause of his friend on occasions when he was alone with

Nísida and her sister Blanca. Although Silerio tried to cover his true feelings, Timbrio learned that Silerio also loved Nísida and, in an act of self-sacrifice, prepared to leave immediately so that his good friend could pursue his love. But Silerio thwarted Timbrio's plan by convincing him that was really Blanca whom he loved. At this point, his story is interrupted by the arrival of a new group of shepherds who have come for the marriage between Daranio and Silveria scheduled for the following day. As everyone retires for the evening, Silerio is convinced to continue his story—as the next book begins.

Book III: The action opens with the continuation of Silerio's tale: Pransiles, Timbrio's old rival from Jerez, challenged Timbrio to a duel within six months. Before he departed for Spain in order to attend to his honor, Timbrio sent Nísida a letter in verse declaring his eternal love and explaining the situation. Nísida admitted that she, too, adored Timbrio, and she decided to follow him. With her parents, she departed for Spain. At this time the laments of another shepherd, Mireno, again interrupt the story. Mireno had loved the shepherdess Silveria, but Silveria's parents arranged for her to marry the wealthy Daranio. Now, on the eve of that wedding, Mireno is critical of Silveria for abandoning him for a man with more money; poverty, he concludes, is a curse. Silerio again resumes again his story: Nísida could not bear to watch the duel but remained nearby, with the understanding that Silerio would come to her immediately with news of her beloved, wearing a white signal on his arm if Timbrio was victorious and unadorned if he lost. Timbrio of course vanquished his rival and then generously spared his life. Silerio rushed to tell Nísida the news but forgot the white signal. When Nísida saw him coming, she believed that Timbrio had been killed and fainted dead away. Timbrio heard what happened and mistakenly believed that Nísida was dead, so he immediately departed for Naples. Silerio again set out to follow his good friend. Meanwhile, Nísida's swoon had lasted a full 24 hours, and when she recovered she and her parents also set out to return home. Upon arrival in Naples, Silerio learned that Timbrio had already left again, this time on a ship destined for Spain. The tireless Silerio thus again returned to Spain and searched for Timbrio without finding him. He even went to Toledo, the original home of Nísida's family, but no one there had news of either Timbrio or Nísida. Tired and dejected, Silerio decided to withdraw from the world, and that is how he came to occupy this hermitage apart from the cares of the world. His newfound friends assure him that he should take heart and that all will work out well in the end. The next day dawns in splendor and with great joy on the part of everyone except Mireno, who again begins to complain that it is unfair for parents to determine whom their children should marry. Elicio consoles him with the reminder that, after all, he can still carry on a chaste, platonic love affair with the married Silveria. In order not to add a negative note to the marriage celebration, Mireno departs, leaving Elicio with a song of goodbye to give to Silveria, and which Elicio immediately reads to the other shepherds. Then the wedding ceremony begins, with the protagonists Daranio and Silveria richly dressed in pastoral style. The marriage and sumptuous banquet take place, with the only discordant note being a song against love sung by Lenio. Then, as a special treat, a long 'eclogue' is staged/sung by four distinguished guests: Orompo, who represents sadness because of the early death of his beloved Listea; Orfenio, who represents jealousy because of his love for the beautiful shepherdess Eandra; Crisio, who represents absence because the beautiful Claraura has left him; and Marsilio, who represents lack of love since Belisa no longer loves him. After the performance, much admired by all, Damón gives a long speech in which he maintains that the performance of the jealous Orfenio was the most impressive because of the destructive power of jealousy, the emotion from which he himself also suffers. At this point, the elderly shepherd Arsindo arrives with Francenio and Lauso and requests Tirsi to be the judge in a dispute between the two over which has written the best poetic gloss on a statement about love. After listening to the two poems, Tirsi praises both and suggests that the woman who inspired them should be the judge.

As evening approaches, Galatea and Florisa are anxious to hear the continuation of the story of Teolinda.

Book IV: Teolinda prepares to take her leave when the shepherdesses see four mounted hunters who are accosted by two shepherdesses with their faces covered. They stop the hunters and call one aside in order to talk with him. The other hunters go on their way, and Galatea and her friends decide to follow the masked women and the remaining hunter in order to listen to their conversation. This is the fourth embedded tale: that of Rosaura, Grisaldo, and other nobles from the kingdoms of Castile and Aragon. As the shepherdesses listen, Rosaura is accusing Grisaldo of inconstancy and deceit: he had promised to marry her but was now engaged to Leopersia. In his defense, Grisaldo maintains that Rosaura had become so jealous and had feigned love for another man, Artandro, that he had given in to his parents' wishes and consented to marry Leopersia. Rosaura threatens suicide if Grisaldo does not accept her, and, of course, he does. They embrace in love. At this point, the other woman accompanying Rosaura removes her mask and is immediately recognized by Teolinda as her sister Leonarda. The listeners join the reunited lovers and all comment on how much like identical twins Teolinda and Leonarda are. Rosaura fills in some of the background of the story: Artandro's arrival on the scene gave her a chance to attempt to pressure Grisaldo into loving her but it backfired and he had departed with plans to marry Leopersia. Rosaura told her parents that she wanted to visit an aunt and received permission to depart. At the aunt's home, she explained her plan to dress as a shepherdess and follow Grisaldo, hoping to intercept him engaged in his favorite pastime, hunting. The aunt gave her permission to do this, but with the stipulation that she go accompanied by the discreet Leonarda; Rosaura agreed and the two women set out. The plan obviously worked, and that is how the scene that was witnessed came about. Meanwhile, Leonarda brings Teolinda up to date on their own situation: after Teolinda had left their village, a shepherd arrived whom everyone took to be Artidoro but who turned out to be his brother Galercio, virtually his identical twin. By the time he left town, Leonarda had fallen in love with him. It was at this time that Rosaura's aunt requested her to accompany Rosaura on her quest. But now a new shepherd emerges from the trees and, believing himself to be alone, prepares to sing. It is Lauso, well-known to the local shepherdesses who are curious to learn the identity of the woman he loves. They listen as he sings of his love for the shepherdess Silena (an unknown person for them). They continue toward the village and encounter a large group of shepherds who are interested in finding out the identity of the new (and now masked) shepherdesses. But the women continue on their way and the men proceed to a nearby fountain for the siesta hour. But first, Silerio takes leave of the rest in order to return to his hermitage and his misery. By chance, at the fountain there are already three gentlemen and two beautiful women. These noble travelers invite the shepherds to join them there. One of the women is so beautiful that only Galatea herself surpasses her in beauty. One of the gentlemen, Darinto by name, praises the simple and virtuous pastoral life in comparison with the intrigue and confusion of their own courtly life. Damón notes that his good friend, the shepherd Lauso, has recently composed a poem on the same theme, and he recites it from memory. As usual, the loveless Lenio takes advantage of the situation presented by the conversation to rail against love. Tirsi begins to question him on the subject and the two agree to a debate. As they are about to begin, Galatea and the other shepherdesses arrive just in time to hear the famous dispute. Lenio begins and delivers a long speech in criticism of love: he is particularly critical of love as a desire for bodily beauty; he cites all the evils committed in the name of love; he recalls famous cases of ill-fated love from myth, the Bible, and history; and he ends with a poem against the effects of love. Tirsi replies: he distinguishes between love and desire; he enumerates the positive effects of three kinds of love: honest, useful, and enjoyable; he praises the effects of corporal beauty, especially the beauty of a woman's face; he notes that love makes

everyone equal; and he ends with a poem in praise of the effects of love. Darinto notes that the superiority of the pastoral life is illustrated by the brilliance and subtlety of this debate—which has taken place not in the learned halls of a university but in a sylvan grove. He is reminded by Elicio that, after all, Tirsi had studied long and with distinction at the University of Salamanca. At this point, one of the noblewomen makes a comment to the other and calls her Nísida. In short order, it is determined that the until-now-unnamed travelers are none other Timbrio, his beloved Nísida, and her sister Blanca. They are delighted to learn that Timbrio's good friend Silerio is nearby and are anxious to see him. When Darinto hears the news, however, he immediately mounts his horse and departs. Timbrio follows and talks with Darinto before he continues on his way and then Timbrio returns to the group. But then a young shepherd girl, Maurisa, arrives and asks for help for her brother who is in danger because of the disdain of another shepherdess. The shepherd is on his knees before a shepherdess named Gelasia and he is threatening to commit suicide because of her hard heart. Lenio and the elderly shepherd Arsindo intervene, and Gelasia explains that she has never loved anyone, does not believe in love, and has given this man no reason to believe she will return his love. Lenio recognizes a soul sister here and offers her his services; the two of them depart. Meanwhile, the suicide-threatening shepherd turns out to be none other than Galercio, the virtual twin of Artidoro, who is loved by Leonarda—who is now upset at this demonstration of his love for another woman. Maurisa takes Rosaura and Galatea aside and explains that Grisaldo plans to have Rosaura brought to his aunt's house two days hence and marry her; in the meantime, she is to stay with Galatea. Galercio and Maurisa depart, and Teolinda and Leonarda follow them. Timbrio, Nísida, Blanca, and most of the shepherds head for Silerio's hermitage. Elicio and Erastro accompany Galatea, Florisa, and others, and sing a duet in praise of Galatea's beauty. As night falls, everyone is anxious to learn how the various plots will turn out.

Book V: Timbrio is about to resume his narrative, but first the assembled shepherds hear the voice of Lauso singing of his love. Lauso joins them and they all head toward the hermitage, which gives Lauso a chance to talk with his good friend Damón whom he has not seen for years. Lauso sings two more poems before they arrive at the hermitage, but when they arrive it is empty. Silenio, however, is nearby, singing of his sadness. He is stunned to hear the voices of his beloved Nísida and Timbrio, and many tears are shed as they are reunited. Finally, Timbrio is able to renew his tale: he arrived in Naples, where everything reminded him of his presumed-dead Nísida. So he went to the port of Gaeta and took a ship headed for Spain. But a storm disabled the ship and after some days the travelers were able to return to Gaeta, repair the ship, and set out again. They arrived in Genoa, and then continued on their voyage. One night, Timbrio went on deck and sang a song of his sadness, fainting at the end of it. But he awakened to find himself with his head in the lap of a beautiful woman dressed as a pilgrim. The pilgrim was none other than Nísida herself who, together with her sister Blanca, had set out in that dress as cover for women traveling alone, but of course their real purpose was to locate Timbrio. They had followed him to Gaeta and arrived there in time to board, by good fortune, the same ship he was on because of the storm delay and damage repair. But no sooner had this wonderful reunion taken place than the alarm was sounded: the ship was about to be attacked by Turkish pirates. Fifteen armed galleys surrounded the Christian ship and demanded its surrender. They resisted, sank one pirate vessel, and fought in hand-to-hand combat for 16 hours before being taken. The badly wounded Timbrio and the two beautiful captives were transferred to the ship of the pirate leader, the feared Arnaut Mamí. But soon after that, a storm arose and scattered the pirate ships, completely disabling Mamí's. Some days later, the galley drifted aground in Catalonia—in fact, in the same town the Turks had raided earlier when Timbrio and Silenio were believed to be criminals. The locals took revenge, killing virtually all the pirates and sacking the ship. During this

activity, Timbrio, the two women, and a man they had met on the ship, named Darinto, proceeded on to Barcelona. After Timbrio recovered from his wounds, they continued toward Toledo in order to be reunited with Nísida's family, and that is how they came to be in this spot at this time. The reason Darinto had departed was that on the ship he had fallen in love with Blanca and now he realizes that she loves Silerio and that Silerio is nearby. The voice of Lauso reaches their ears and they listen to his song. He joins them, but just then Aurelio, Galatea's father, arrives and informs them that he, together with Elicio and Erastro, had found Darinto face-down in the grass, sighing, and lamenting his love. The two shepherds stayed with Darinto while Aurelio came to inform the rest. But when the group returns to the spot, Darinto is gone, Elicio lies fainted on the ground, and Erastro sits crying. They revive Elicio and he tells them that he simply fainted away for no known reason, which Erastro confirms. Before leaving, Elicio takes his friend Damón aside and explains to him the reason for his faint: he has just learned that Aurelio has arranged for his daughter Galatea to marry a shepherd from Portugal. Elicio knows that he will not be able to live without the company of the woman he adores. They go on and soon hear the lovely voice of Galatea, who, in the company of several of her friends, is singing a song in which she makes clear that her father's decision is against her will and she does not want this marriage. In the discussion that follows, Galatea impresses Damón with the profundity of her philosophical position as she argues against arranged marriages. Just then a group of men arrive who subject the shepherds and capture and carry off the beautiful Rosaura. The leader of the men is Artandro, angry that Rosaura had promised to marry him but is now preparing to marry his rival Grisaldo. Galatea states that since his motive was love, she can understand this abduction. Next, Erastro also sings of his fate should his beloved Galatea be taken away from this area. Then the four courtly adventurers, Timbrio, Sileno, Nísida, and Blanca, all in turn sing sonnets about their love, surprising the shepherds at how well they perform. Next, Lauso reappears and informs the rest that he is now free of his love for Silena. He sings the praise of disdain, his prior object of criticism. The next to arrive are the elderly shepherd Arsindo and the teenage Maurisa, with whom Arsindo has clearly been smitten in spite of the great difference in their ages. They tell the group that Lenio has fallen in love with the frigid Gelasia, and that Leopersia's family is angry that Grisaldo no longer wants to marry her but has renewed his commitment to Rosaura. Then they ask where Rosaura is so that they can inform her of Grisaldo's plans. After the shepherds tell Maurisa of the abduction of Rosaura, she briefly informs them that Leonarda is engaged to her brother Artidoro and Teolinda is hopelessly in love with her other brother Galercio, who still has eyes only for the disdainful Gelasia. Then she departs to deliver the news about Rosaura. A horn sounds; it is the venerable Telesio calling for a meeting of the assembled group of shepherds the next day at the site of the tomb of the shepherd Meliso in order to remember and acknowledge him. Lenio sings once more the praises of love, and all retire for the night.

Book VI: At dawn, the various shepherds and shepherdesses assemble for Telesio's convocation. They proceed to the Valley of the Cypress Trees, a natural navelike place of beauty, made even more wonderful by the artful additions made to it. There are buried famous shepherd-poets, among whom the most prominent is Meliso. Telesio carries out some semipagan, semi-Christian rites, and then the music begins. The natural music of the singing birds combines with the instruments and voices of the shepherds to form an effect that surpasses both. Next, Tirsi, Damón, Elicio, and Lauso sing a long song in praise of the revered poet Meliso. The long ceremony over, the participants dine and prepare to spend the night there. But in the midst of the darkness, a flame ignites at Meliso's tomb and the figure of the muse Calliope appears in its midst. She announces that she has come to sing the praises of the great living Spanish poets and then begins her long song, a panegyric of just over 100 poets. Her song occupies the entire night, and the next

morning the company breaks up, groups of shepherds and shepherdesses going their various ways. A number of them, and of the non-shepherd travelers, sing songs. Then there is a poetic riddle game to pass the time. Shouts of help are heard, and several shepherds arrive in time to see Galercio being pulled from the river by two strangers. Galercio had attempted to commit suicide since his beloved Gelasia only disdains him. Gelasia appears at the top of a rock overlooking the river and sings a sonnet defending her desire to remain independent. She departs, and Lenio ascends to the very same spot in order to sing of his love also for the cold Gelasia. Teolinda then tells Galatea and Florisa how her sister Leonarda, seeing Galercio in love with Gelasia, shifted her attention to Artidoro and, pretending she was Teolinda, tricked him into promising to marry her. Even when the deceit became known, Artidoro decided to remain true to his word and renew his vow to marry Leonarda. Tirsi takes out a paper that had been retrieved from Galercio and reads it. It is, of course, a complaint about Gelasia's hardness, which Tirsi finds more reasonable than the shepherdess's position. Next it is learned that the two strangers who had rescued Galercio are friends of the Portuguese shepherd who is to marry Galatea, and they inform the rest that this shepherd will arrive in three days to finalize the marriage plans. Day ends and the company breaks up, individuals and small groups going their different ways, the Timbrio et al. group finally proceeding to Toledo. Galatea sends a note to Elicio reiterating her desire not to marry the man from Portugal and suggesting that perhaps Elicio can find a way to prevent it. Elicio writes back saying that he will do all he can. The plan is for Tirsi and Damón to try to convince Aurelio to cancel the arranged marriage. But, if this should fail, the others have agreed to assemble a large group of shepherds from the Tajo and Henares communities prepared to fight in defense of Galatea if necessary. At this point the story is brought to a close, with the promise that in the second part all the unfinished stories will be resolved.

Bibliography: Juan Bautista Avalle-Arce, ed., *La "Galatea" de Cervantes: Cuatrocientos años des-*

pués (Newark, DE: Juan de la Cuesta, 1985); *A Celebration of Cervantes on the Fourth Centenary of
"La Galatea," 1585–1985: Selected Papers*, ed.
John J. Allen, Elias Rivers, and Harry Sieber, special
issue of *Cervantes* (Winter 1988); Bruno M. Damiani, "Death in Cervantes' *Galatea*," *Cervantes*, 4
no.1 (1984): 53–78; Frederick A. de Armas, "Ek-
phrasis and Eros in Cervantes' *La Galatea*: The Case
of the Blushing Nymphs," in *Cervantes for the 21st
Century/Cervantes para el siglo XXI: Studies in
Honor of Edward Dudley*, ed. Francisco La Rubia
Prado (Newark, DE: Juan de la Cuesta, 2000), 33–
47; Edward Dudley, "Goddess on the Edge: The *Galatea* Agenda in Raphael, Garcilaso and Cervantes*,"
Calíope 1 (1995): 27–45; Aurora Egido, *Estudios sobre "La Galatea," "El Quijote" y "El Persiles"*
(Barcelona: PPU, 1994); Alban Forcione, "Cervantes
en busca de una pastoral auténtica," *Nueva Revista
de Filología Hispánica* 36 (1988): 1011–43; Rosalie
Hernández-Pecorano, "Cervantes's *La Galatea*:
Feminine Spaces, Subjects, and Communities," *Pa-
cific Coast Philology* 33 (1998): 15–30; Carroll B.
Johnson, "Cervantes' *Galatea*: The Portuguese Connection," *Iberoromania* 23 (1986): 91–105; Francisco López Estrada, " 'Dissoluble nudo': Una
compleja lección de *La Galatea*," in *"Ingeniosa invención": Essays on Golden Age Spanish Literature
for Geoffrey L. Stagg in Honor of His Eighty-Fifth
Birthday*, ed. Ellen M. Anderson and Amy R. Williamsen (Newark, DE: Juan de la Cuesta, 1999),
123–36; Francisco Márquez Villanueva, "Sobre el
contexto religioso de La Galatea," in *Actas del II
Congreso Internacional de la Asociación de Cervantistas*, ed. Giuseppe Grilli (Naples: Instituto Universitario Orientale, 1995), 181–96; Mary Gaylord
Randel, "The Language of Limits and the Limits of
Language: The Crisis of Poetry in La Galatea," *MLN*
97 (1982): 254–71; Elizabeth Rhodes, "Sixteenth-
Century Pastoral Books, Narrative Structure, and *La
Galatea* of Cervantes," *Bulletin of Hispanic Studies*
66 (1989): 351–60; José Manuel Trabado Cabado,
*Poética y pragmática del discurso lírico: El canci-
onero pastoril de "La Galatea"* (Madrid: CSIC,
2000); and Mirta R. Zidovec, "La idea del tiempo en
La Galatea de Cervantes: Una expresión del pensamiento renacentista," *Hispania* 73 (1990): 8–15.

Galatea, La, Part II. MC never published,
and probably never even began to write, the
second part of his 1585 pastoral novel *Galatea*.
He did, however, mention the sequel in *DQ* I,
6, where the priest comments that the evalua-
tion of *Galatea* will depend on its completion

in the second part; the dedication to *Comedias*;
the prologue to *DQ* II; and even the dedication
to *Persiles*, the last thing he wrote, on his
deathbed.

Galba, Martí Joan de. *Martorell, Joanot.

Galeano, Eduardo (1940–). Uruguayan
writer. Galeano's trilogy, *Memoria del fuego*
(1982–86; *The Memory of Fire*) is an ambitious, if oblique, effort to narrate the history of
America, especially Spanish America. His technique is to evoke key events and people in a
series of brief, telling moments. The first volume is entitled *Los nacimientos* (1982; *Births*)
and concentrates on the formative periods of
American history, including European origins.
There are two brief entries that deal with MC.
The first takes place in Seville in 1597 and is
entitled "En un lugar de la cárcel" ("In a place
in jail"), an evocation of the first line of *DQ* I.
An aging ex-soldier who has been through captivity and humiliation in Spain sits in jail still
feeling the sting of official rejection of his petition for an administrative job in the colonies.
Now he begins to sketch out 'the misadventures
of a poet-errant' and writes the opening lines
of *DQ* I. The second takes place in 1616 in
Madrid and is entitled simply "Cervantes." SP
brings DQ news that their 'father' is on his
deathbed and, over the squire's reluctance, the
knight vows to 'cleanse the honor of the one
who gave us birth as free men while in jail' by
going in quest of adventure in America.

Bibliography: Eduardo Galeano, *Memoria del
fuego (I): Los nacimientos* (Madrid: Siglo XXI de
España, 1982).

Galeotes. *Galley slaves.

Galercio. In *Galatea* 4–6, the shepherd who
is the virtual twin brother of Artidoro and who
first loves the cold Gelasia and then Leonarda.

Galgo. *Greyhound.

Galiana. In Muslim legend, a princess whose
palace, located near the Tagus River, became a
proverbial symbol of great riches. See *DQ* II,
55.

Galicia. The area in northwestern Spain, on the Atlantic Ocean, north of Portugal, where the language is about halfway between Spanish and Portuguese. The Cervantes family may have had its remotest origins in this part of the country. Galicia's capital is La Coruña, but the most important city in the region is *Santiago de Compostela, which in the Middle Ages was a major shrine visited by Christian pilgrims from all over, as it is by the characters in *Doncellas*. See also *Galatea* 5.

Galician muleteers. *Yangüeses.

Galíndez, Bartolomé (1896–?). Argentine poet, critic, and short-story writer. Galíndez's book *El amor de Sancho* (1931; *Sancho's Love*) opens with three critical essays on *DQ* and ends with a short story that has the same title as the book. The story consists of a three-chapter section that may have taken place after either the episode in Puerto Lápice (*DQ* I, 8) or that of the enchanted inn (I, 16–17)—CHB does not confirm either option. DQ and SP encounter the beautiful duchess of Torre Blanca, and SP falls in love with her. In an inn that DQ takes to be a castle, SP requests that DQ arm him a knight-errant so that he can pursue his love as an equal. They proceed to the duchess's nearby castle (which DQ sees as an inn), are admitted, and SP is dubbed a knight with the name of Don Sancho de Argamasilla. But that night DQ and SP are whipped by *dueñas* and thrown out of the castle. Back at the inn, DQ upbraids SP for having fallen in love with an innkeeper, while SP merely sheds a tear. The author's attempt at replicating an archaic style is not very successful, and his display of chivalric wisdom (DQ's utterances are filled with names and events from chivalric romances and legends) is tiresome.

Bibliography: Bartolomé Galíndez, *El amor de Sancho* (Buenos Aires: Araujo Hnos., 1931).

Galindo, Gregorio. A grammar teacher who also wrote some poetry. See *Parnaso* 7.

Gallarda. An elegant, courtly dance. See *Parnaso* 8; *Viudo*.

Gallardo español, El (Gallardo); The Valiant Spaniard. The first play in *Comedias*. The play presents a version of the siege of the Spanish fortress of Oran in 1563. The writing of this play may well be related to MC's emissary to Oran in 1581, and there are some autobiographical elements in the character of Fernando de Saavedra (as the name suggests). Like all of MC's early works, there is a disjointed structure, an overabundance of characters, and the plot is sometimes difficult to follow.

Act I: The Muslim Arlaxa is curious to see the famous Spaniard Fernando de Saavedra, of whom she has heard so much, and tells Alimuzel that if he brings Saavedra to her as a captive she will marry Alimuzel. Although the magnitude of the task daunts Alimuzel, he accepts. Meanwhile, in Oran, Alonso de Córdoba, the general of the city, is preparing his defenses for the forthcoming expected Turkish assault. Alimuzel arrives and issues a public challenge to Saavedra, but Córdoba refuses to permit Saavedra to accept the challenge, on the grounds that he is too valuable a soldier to risk losing at a time like this. Guzmán is to inform Alimuzel of this decision, but Saavedra tells Guzmán to let Alimuzel know that if he can wait until Monday night, Saavedra will meet him. As Alimuzel waits for an answer, Nacor, a *jarife* (kind of priest) and rival for Arlaxa's hand, is considering killing Alimuzel in a cowardly manner when Guzmán arrives. Alimuzel accepts Saavedra's proposal, but after Guzmán leaves, Nacor convinces Alimuzel that it is a trick and promises that he will confirm to Arlaxa that Saavedra refuses to fight Alimuzel. Back in Oran, Córdoba receives a petition from the women and children of the city requesting that they not be evacuated to safety before the upcoming battle, as has been ordered, but that they be allowed to help. Recognizing the generosity and nobility of the gesture, Córdoba accepts the proposal. Guzmán returns and informs Córdoba that Alimuzel has departed, but secretly tells Saavedra that he will be there on Monday. Buitrago, the comic relief in the play, comes around begging, in his usual aggressive manner, for money in exchange for prayers for the souls of the departed. Buitrago has a famously enormous appetite, but he is also a brave soldier. Meanwhile, Arlaxa talks with her captive slave Oropesa, whose extravagant praise of Saavedra is what originally sparked her curiosity. Alimuzel and Nacor arrive, and Nacor betrays Alimuzel, saying that he would not wait for Saavedra. Alimuzel is enraged but cannot touch Nacor because of his *jarife* status. Several Muslims arrive with a Christian who has surrendered in order to be brought to Arlaxa as a captive. The Christian—none other than Saavedra—does not reveal his identity, nor does Oropesa, but promises to help Alimuzel meet Saavedra. Back in Oran, Robledo accuses Saavedra of becoming a renegade, but Guzmán defends him. The two are about to duel, but the skirmish is broken up by Córdoba and his brother.

Act II: When Arlaxa inquires about the identity of the newly arrived Christian, Saavedra calls himself Juan Lozano and says he is a good friend of Saavedra's. Oropesa describes the heroic deeds of Saavedra. In order to impress Arlaxa, Nacor promises to bring Saavedra to her. Meanwhile, Doña Margarita de Valderrama, accompanied by the elderly Vozmediano, arrives in Oran dressed as a man, searching for Saavedra. She has a short encounter with Buitrago and is offended by his aggressive begging. Nacor comes to Oran and offers to betray his people and allow Córdoba an easy victory if he can have Arlaxa as a reward. Doña Margarita, having heard the gossip that Saavedra has renounced his faith, wants to be taken captive by the Muslims in order to find out the truth. Arlaxa tells of a dream she had in which Nacor is a traitor and invites a Christian attack. The attack comes, Nacor tries to abduct Arlaxa, but Buitrago kills him. Saavedra helps Doña Margarita become a captive. She begins to tell her story, revealing that she is a woman. The Turkish squadron approaches Oran.

Act III: Doña Margarita finishes her story: with no inheritance, she left her convent to follow Saavedra, with whom she fell in love based solely on what she had heard of him. Meanwhile, a Christian prisoner is brought before Arlaxa. He is none other than Don Juan de Valderrama, brother of Doña Margarita. He recognizes Doña Margarita as his sister, even though she is now dressed in Muslim garb, but she insists that he is mistaken, and Arlaxa says that she is her sister Fátima. In a Muslim attack on Oran, Saavedra is exceptionally valiant, killing several Muslims (including one king) and wounding many others. Don Juan also recognizes Vozmediano, who claims that his name is Pedro Alvarez. The Turkish assault takes place and the Turks are beaten back. Saavedra reveals his identity to all, and offers to marry Doña Margarita, who accepts. Don Juan blesses the marriage and offers half the family inheritance. Arlaxa and Alimuzel also marry.

Bibliography: María Soledad Carrasco Urgoiti, "*El gallardo español* como héroe fronterizo," in *Actas del Tercer Congreso Internacional de Cervantistas, Gala Galdana, Menorca, 20–25 de octubre de 1997* (Palma, Spain: Unversitat de Islas Baleares, 1998), 571–81; Frederick A. de Armas, "Los excesos de Venus y Marte en *El gallardo español*," in *Cervantes, su obra y su mundo: Actas del I Congreso Internacional sobre Cervantes*, ed. Manuel Criado de Val (Madrid: Edi-6, 1981), 249–59; E. Michael Gerli, "Aristotle in Africa: History, Fiction, and Truth in *El gallardo español*," *Cervantes* 15, no. 2 (1995): 43–57; Gethin Hughes, "*El gallardo español*: A Case of Misplaced Honour," *Cervantes* 13, no. 1 (1993): 65–75; Eric J. Kartchner, "Dramatic Diegesis: Truth and Fiction in Cervantes's *El Gallardo Español*," *Yearbook of Comparative and General Literature* 47 (1999): 25–35; and William Stapp, "*El gallardo español*: La fama como arbitrio de la realidad," *Anales Cervantinos* 17 (1978): 123–36.

Gallega, La. In *Fregona*, the employee at the inn who loves and propositions Lope Asturiano.

Galley slaves [Galeotes]. About a dozen criminals condemned to row in the royal galleys as punishment for their crimes, whom DQ and SP come across in *DQ* I, 22. DQ interviews several of them, decides that they are being taken away against their will, sets them free, instructs them to go to DT and tell her who gave them their freedom, and is stoned for his efforts. Interestingly, DQ chooses to follow the letter of the order of chivalry—free those being taken against their will—and ignores the spirit—

punish those who harm the innocent. DQ's interviews with the criminals offers MC a chance for some formulaic humor and to display his knowledge of thieves' jargon. The first criminal is punished because he is a lover (of others' goods); the second, for singing (i.e., ratting on others); the third, for being short of funds (with which to bribe someone); the fourth, as a procurer or go-between, a profession DQ somewhat incongruously praises; the fifth, a student whose crime is not mentioned; and the sixth, the master criminal and autobiographer *Ginés de Pasamonte. DQ's attack on the guards is a clear criminal act, and SP's fear that they well be the targets of an investigation by the Holy Brotherhood is well-founded (see I, 45). This is the last of the great quixotic adventures (that begin in I, 15) that make up the most comic and most admired part of *DQ* I. From the next chapter on, other characters (the priest and the barber, Dorotea, et al.) will control the action, and much attention will be focused on the stories read or told to the group. See also *DQ* I, 25, 29–30; *DQ* II, 3.

Bibliography: Miguel García Posada, "El episodio quijotesco de los galeotes: ambigüedad lingüística y significación," *Hispanic Review* 49 (1981): 195–208; José F. Martín, "Diálogo y poder en la liberación de los galeotes," *Cervantes* 11, no. 2 (1991): 35–42; and Augustin Redondo, "De las terceras al alcahuete del episodio de los galeotes en el *Quijote* (I, 22): Algunos rasgos de la parodia cervantina," *Journal of Hispanic Philology* 13 (1989): 135–148.

Gallo de Andrada, Juan. Spanish civil servant who set the price for *DQ* I.

Galtenor. **Platir.*

Galván, Melchor. *Ezpeleta, Don Gaspar de.

Gálvez de Montalvo, Luis (ca. 1546–ca. 1591). Spanish poet and novelist, whose *El Pastor de Fílida* (1582; *Filida's Shepherd*) combines pastoral and courtly elements and was one of the more popular and widely read and praised books of its time. The priest describes it as a 'precious jewel' and saves it from the flames during the scrutiny of DQ's library

in I, 6. Gálvez also translated Luigi *Tansilo's *Lagrime di San Pietro* as *Las lágrimas de San Pedro* (1587; *The Tears of Saint Peter*), which is quoted in *Curioso* (*DQ* I, 34). MC first met Gálvez in Madrid in the 1560s and the two were probably friends thereafter. Gálvez wrote one of the laudatory sonnets for *Galatea*. He is praised (as Luis de Montalvo) in Calliope's song in *Galatea* 6. See also *Coloquio*.

Bibliography: José María Alonso Gamo, *Luis Gálvez de Montalvo. Vida y obra de ese gran ignorado* (Guadalajara Spain: Institución Provincial de Cultura "Marqués de Santillana," 1987).

Gambetas. A popular dance. See *Viudo*.

Gambling. MC proves consistently throughout his works that he had an intimate familiarity with various forms of gambling; see, for example, *Rinconete*, *Persiles* III, 13. It has been suggested that several documents and references in his personal life also point to both gambling debts and winnings, but there is no absolutely clear documentation for any of this. Anyone who spent several years as a soldier and several more associating with all sorts of marginal and criminal types in places like Seville (where there were a reputed 300 gambling houses), as did MC, could hardly have avoided gaining first hand experience with the world of cards and dice.

Bibliography: Jean-Pierre Etienvre, "Paciencia y barajar. Cervantes, los naipes, y la burla," in *Figures du jeu: études lexico-sémantiques sur le jeu de cartes en Espagne: XVIe–XVIIIIe siècle* (Madrid: Casa de Velázquez, 1987), 33–53.

Gamboa. One of two powerful factions in the Basque country through the time of the *Catholic Monarchs. See *Gitanilla*.

Ganadero. *Herdsman.

Ganadero del Quintanar. *Barcino.

Gananciosa. In *Rinconete*, one of the prostitutes who comes to the home of Monipodio when Rinconete and Cortadillo are accepted into the thieves' brotherhood.

Ganapán. *Porter.

Ganchoso. 1. In *Rinconete*, a *pícaro* in Monipodio's house (perhaps the same character as Ganchuelo). **2**. In *Rufián* 1–2, a ruffian friend of Cristóbal de Lugo in Seville.

Ganchuelo. In *Rinconete*, the carrier (perhaps the same character as Ganchoso) who guides Rinconete and Cortadillo to Monipodio's house and explains to them some terms in thieves' slang (**germanía*).

Gandalín. Amadís de Gaula's squire who eventually marries Oriana's confidante, the Doncella de Dinamarca, and becomes lord (not count, as DQ says) of the Insula Firme. He is the author of a sonnet dedicated to SP as one of the preliminary poems to *DQ* I. In *DQ* I, 20, DQ cites the example of Gandalín, who, DQ says, only spoke to his master with hat in hand and head bowed, in order to illustrate to SP how much more respectful he should be. Gandalín is a loyal servant and counselor to Amadís and never assumes the subservient pose DQ attributes to him. In fact, what DQ tells SP is a lie—or, at least, a willful distortion of the truth—spoken with the authority of one who knows the text in order to make a point to someone who has no means of calling the claim into question. See also *DQ* I, 50.

Bibliography: Eduardo Urbina, "Sancho Panza y Gandalín, escuderos," in *Cervantes and the Renaissance*, ed. Michael D. McGaha (Easton, PA: Juan de la Cuesta, 1980), 113–24.

Gandul(-Marchenilla). A town located just southeast of Seville and southwest of Córdoba; it was known for producing good bread. See *Rinconete*.

Gandulandín. An infernal deity (invented by MC) evoked by Fátima in *Tratos* 2.

Ganelon [Galalón (de Maganza)]: Guenelon. One of the Twelve Peers of France and lord of the Maganza clan. He is known (in Spain, not in France) as the famous traitor responsible for the defeat of the French and the death of Roland at the battle of Roncesvalles. He is a popular villain in the Spanish **romancero*, chivalric legends, and tales in general. His cowardly role is featured in *Casa*, where he is a significant character. See also *Casa* 3; *DQ* I, 1, 27–28; *Parnaso* 4.

Gange(s). The holy river of India. See *Galatea* 6; *Gitanilla*.

Ganimedes. *Ganymede.

Ganivet, Angel (1865–98). Spanish essayist, novelist, and journalist. Ganivet's most famous work is *El idearium español* (1896; *Spain, an Interpretation*), in which he frequently refers to DQ in order to understand Spain. For example, he writes that MC 'was the greatest of all conquistadors, for he conquered Spain while locked in a prison.' Pío Cid, protagonist of Ganivet's two novels *La conquista del reino de Maya por el último conquistador español, Pío Cid* (1895; *The Conquest of the Kingdom of Maya by the Last Spanish Conquistador, Pío Cid*) and *Los trabajos del infatigable creador, Pío Cid* (1898; *The Labors of the Tireless Creator, Pío Cid*), is one of the most clearly quixotic characters in Spanish literature at the end of the nineteenth century. Cid consistently sees beauty where there is squalor, is idealistic in his belief in concepts such as love and justice, and is conscious of the fact that he creates his life as he lives it.

Bibliography: Judith Ginsberg, *Angel Ganivet* (London: Tamesis, 1985); and Herbert Ramsden, *Angel Ganivet's "Idearium español": A Critical Study* (Manchester, UK: University of Manchester, 1967).

Gante. *Ghent.

Gante and Luna [Gante y Luna]. Enigmatic citations in *DQ* I, 51. Some editors change the names to Garci Lasso (or *Garcilaso), the soldier associated in I, 49, with Diego Pérez de Vargas, who is mentioned immediately following these names. Others have preferred to identify the first as Juan de Gante, a soldier mentioned in the *Carlo Famoso* (1566) of Luis de *Zapata, and the second as Marco Antonio Lunel, who is mentioned in Pedro Vallés's *Historia del capitán Don Hernando de Auolos, Marqués de Pescara* (1561; *History of*

Captain Don Hernando de Auolos, Marqués of Pescara).

Bibliography: María Soledad Carrasco Urgoiti, "Nota a una alusión del *Quijote*," in *Estudios sobre literatura y arte dedicados al Profesor Emilio Orozco Díaz* (Granada, Spain Universidad: University of Granada, 1979), I, 241–49.

Ganymede [Ganimedes]. In Greek myth, the son of the king of Troy who was carried off to become the cupbearer of Zeus. Because of his legendary beauty, Ganymede came in the Middle Ages to represent homosexual love. See *Amante*; *Gitanilla*; *Parnaso* 2; *Persiles* II, 5; III, 1, 21.

Garamantas; Garamants. *Pentapolín del Arremangado Brazo [of the Rolled-up Sleeve].

Garay, Maestro (Francisco de). Spanish poet highly esteemed in his time. He is praised in Calliope's song in *Galatea* 6.

Garay, Nuño. *Tablante de Ricamonte.

Garaya. *Geraya.

Garcerán (de Borja, Don Pedro) Luis (ca. 1538–1592). Spanish nobleman and poet praised in Calliope's song in *Galatea* 6.

Garcés, Enrique (ca. 1530–?). Portuguese poet who traveled to Peru and then returned to Spain. He is the author of *Los sonetos y canciones del poeta Francisco Petrarcha* (1591; *Sonnets and Songs of the Poet Francesco Petrarcha*), a work that MC may have known in manuscript, since he refers to Petrarch in *Galatea* 6 (1585), although he could also have known Petrarch's work directly in Italian.

García, Antonio. Mexican writer. García wrote the libretto for a three-act *zarzuela* entitled *Don Quijote en la venta encantada* (1871; *Don Quixote in the Enchanted Inn*), with music by Miguel Planas. The action primarily involves aspects of *Cardenio,* the 'enchantment' of DQ, and the knight's encounter with the white-robed men on the way home. This probably was the first theatrical work related to MC written by a Spanish American.

García Cuevas, Francisco. Spanish dramatist. García Cuevas collaborated with composer Antonio de Reparaz (1833–1886) on three *zarzuelas* based on works by MC: *Las bodas de Camacho* (1866; *Camacho's Wedding*), *La venta encantada* (*The Enchanted Inn*), and *La Gitanilla*.

García de Paredes, Diego (1466–1530). Spanish soldier who fought with the Gran Capitán Gonzalo Hernández de Córdoba against the Muslims in Granada and later in Sicily. A man of great physical strength, sometimes referred to as 'the Samson of Extremadura' (the region from which he came), García de Paredes became a popular legendary figure in literature. His (somewhat novelized) biography was written by Hernán *Pérez de Pulgar. See *DQ* I, 32, 49, 51; *Rufián* 1.

García Lorca, Federico (1898–1936). Spanish poet and dramatist. García Lorca is generally recognized as the greatest poet of the twentieth century in Spain, and his tragic assassination at the beginning of the Spanish Civil War cut short a brilliant career at a very young age. The book that established his reputation as a poet was the *Romancero gitano* (1928; *Gypsy Ballads*). One of the fine poems in the collection is entitled "Preciosa y el aire" ("Preciosa and the Air"), a lyrical evocation of a beautiful young gypsy woman, either parallel to or a reincarnation of Preciosa from MC's *Gitanilla*. In the summer of 1932, Lorca and Eduardo Ugarte headed a traveling troupe called La Barraca (The Cabin), made up of university students, that went throughout Spain, staging a variety of dramatic pieces from the *Golden Age for the populace; among the works they presented were versions of *Guarda* and *Retablo*.

Bibliography: Rupert C. Allen, *The Symbolic World of Federico García Lorca* (Albuquerque: University of New Mexico Press, 1972); and Carl W. Cobb, *Federico García Lorca* (New York: Twayne, 1967).

García Luna, Luis. *Bécquer, Gustavo Adolfo.

García Márquez, Gabriel (1928–).

Colombian novelist. García Márquez is the author of the most acclaimed novel yet written in Spanish America: *Cien años de soledad* (1967; *One Hundred Years of Solitude*), a work sometimes anachronistically called a modern classic and/or the *DQ* of Spanish America. *Cien años* is the defining novel of the movement called "magic realism," a blend of romance/fantasy (in theme and character) and novel/realism (in style and technique), often with *postmodern pretense. It is the story of the Buendía family, the city of Macondo, an endless revolution, cyclical time, an allegory of Colombian history, the invention of ice, and Melquíades, a sage historian (but also a gypsy and a charlatan; he is similar to CHB, the truthful historian of *DQ* and a lying Muslim at the same time) and his manuscript about the events of the novel. There is a strong romance quality to the story and a nostalgia for a remote *Golden Age of innocent beginnings. Founding father of Macondo, José Arcadio Buendía, is quixotic in his attempts to bring the advances of modern civilization to his people. Colonel Aureliano Buendía's endless series of rebellions against the conservative powers that rule also has a strong quixotic element. The last of the Buendías, Aureliano Babilonia, winds up a recluse, surrounded by books and manuscripts that he uses as his only access to reality. Just as MC introduces himself into *DQ* as the author of *Galatea* (*DQ* I, 6) and as a captive soldier named Saavedra in Algiers (I, 40), there is a character named Gabriel Márquez who shows up in Macondo and becomes a friend of Aureliano's. After a whirlwind destroys the city, Gabriel tells the tale of what happened, as he seems ultimately to be writing Melquíades's manuscript. Few novelists have ever captured the spirit of MC as thoroughly and in such an original way as García Márquez.

Bibliography: Chester S. Halka, "Perspectivismo en *Don Quijote* y *Cien años de soledad*: Una comparación," *Hispanófila* 30 (1987): 21–38; Bernard McGuirk and Richard Cardwell, eds., *Gabriel García Márquez: New Readings* (Cambridge: Cambridge University Press, 1987; and Edwin Williamson, "The Quixotic Roots of Magic Realism: History and Fiction from Alejo Carpentier to Gabriel García Márquez," in *Cervantes and the Modernists: The Question of Influence*, ed. Edwin Williamson (London: Tamesis, 1994), 103–20.

García Martí, Victoriano (1881–1966).

Spanish essayist. García Martí's *La voz de los mitos, grandeza y servidumbre del hombre* (1941; *The Voice of Myth: Man's Grandeur and Servitude*) is a somewhat pretentious two-act dialogue involving the great mythic characters of DQ, Don Juan, Faust, and Hamlet, with (in comparatively minor roles) the women they love: DT, Doña Inés, Margarita, and Ophelia. Each male character articulates his version of his own myth, and, at the end, they decide they are not really of this world.

Bibliography: Victoriano García Martí, *La voz de los mitos, grandeza y servidumbre del hombre* (Madrid: Espasa-Calpe, 1941).

García Mora, José (1829–?).

Spanish writer. His *Don Integro o el nuevo Quijote de Barcelona* (1885; *Don Integro or the New Quixote from Barcelona*) is a thin satiric fiction whose protagonist is a virulently reactionary Catholic and Carlist absolutist.

García Pavón, Francisco (1919–).

Spanish novelist, short-story writer, and drama critic. Best known as a prominent writer of detective fiction, García Pavón is also an accomplished writer of short stories. His book *La guerra de los dos mil años* (1967; *The Two-Thousand-Year War*) contains one story entitled "La Cueva de Montesinos." In it, the narrator takes the woman he loves to the Cave of Montesinos in La Mancha, hoping that it might help rekindle their deteriorating relationship. Two extraordinary things happen in the cave: she removes all her clothing and covers herself with mud, but leaves the cave when he fails to respond to her attempt at seduction; he, meanwhile, discovers a way to see a whole new world of tiny people in the cave. At the end, she goes off, while he returns to the cave and speculates that perhaps, at a certain time in the autumn of our life, we all return to our own Cave of Montesinos.

Bibliography: Francisco García Pavón, *La guerra de los dos mil años* (Barcelona: Destino, 1967).

García Romero. A little-known Spanish poet praised in Calliope's song in *Galatea* 6.

Garciasol, Ramón de (1913–94). Spanish poet, biographer, and book editor. Garciasol is the author of a good biography of MC entitled *Vida heroica de Miguel de Cervantes* (1944; *The Heroic Life of Miguel de Cervantes*) and has written critical essays on MC. His book entitled *Hombres de España: Cervantes* (1968; *Men of Spain: Cervantes*) consists of a sequence of 59 sonnets mostly addressed to MC, evoking scenes from his life: as a child, in Naples, as the author of *DQ*, at the time of his death, and so forth. The sonnets are vigorous, tense, and passionate, at times with a genuine note of tenderness. It is Garciasol's homage to the writer he most admired and to whom he dedicated a significant part of his intellectual and creative efforts.

Bibliography: Ramón de Garciasol, *Hombres de España: Cervantes* (Málaga, Spain: Librería Anticuaria el Guadalhorca, 1968; and Alberto Sánchez, "Ramón de Garciasol, poeta y cervantista (1913–1994)," *Anales Cervantinos* 32 (1994): 303–7.

Garcilasan or Timoneda [Garcilasista o timoneda]. In *Parnaso* 7, MC sets up an opposition between two kinds of poetry based on the names of *Garcilaso de la Vega and Juan de *Timoneda. The former suggests both quality in verse, as Garcilaso was considered the greatest poet of the Spanish Renaissance, and the "new" Italianate verse form of 11-syllable lines, whereas the latter suggests both mediocrity in verse and the more traditional eight-syllable line.

Garcilaso de la Vega. Spanish soldier; not to be confused with the poet of the same name. Garcilaso distinguished himself in the conquest of Granada. See *DQ* I, 49.

Garcilaso de la Vega (Our great Spanish poet, Our poet, Our . . . ingenious poet) [Gran poeta castellano nuestro, Nuestro poeta, Nuestro . . . ingenioso poeta] (ca. 1501–1536). Poet, courtier, and soldier. At the urging of his friend Juan *Boscán, Garcilaso became the first great writer of poetry in the Italianate meter in Spanish; he was the most famous and adored poet of the sixteenth century. His small oeuvre, about three dozen sonnets, five *canciones* (songs), three eclogues, and a handful of other poems, was considered a modern classic. His work was first published by Boscán's widow together with that of her husband: *Las obras de Boscán y algunas de Garcilaso* (1543; *The Works of Boscán and Some by Garcilaso*). Within a decade, the book was published over a dozen times in Spain and throughout the Spanish-speaking world in Europe. Later, Garcilaso's work was published alone (1569) and twice in annotated editions (1574 by El Brocense and 1580 by Fernando de *Herrera). A prototypical Renaissance man, Garcilaso exercised both *arms and letters, and died as a soldier in the war in Provence. Garcilaso was clearly MC's most beloved poet, and he evokes Garcilaso frequently throughout his writings. For example, in *Poesías* 4, on the occasion of the death of the queen Doña Isabel de Valois, he alludes to Garcilaso's Sonnet X, 'Oh sweet souvenirs, found now to my misfortune,' by evoking the famous vocabulary and images of that poem. When DQ and SP arrive at the home of Diego de Miranda (II, 18) they see several *tinajas*, or large storage jars (representing wealth and abundant food) of the type traditionally manufactured in El Toboso, and the reminder of her home town brings DT to DQ's mind. He remembers her by citing the same lines of Garcilaso's poetry and then paraphrasing them, 'Oh Tobosan jars, how you bring back to my memory the sweet object of my bitter regrets!' (Another interesting recollection of this famous line can be found in *Persiles* II, 15.) When DQ and SP come across the Feigned *Arcadia in II, 58, the two poets whose work is being enacted are Garcilaso and Luis de *Camões. There are well over a dozen allusions to and citations of Garcilaso in *DQ* alone. When Tomás Rodaja, the protagonist of *Vidriera*, travels to Italy, the only books he takes along on the trip are an unannotated edition of the works of Garcilaso and a book of prayers. See also *Adjunta*; *Baños* 2; *DQ* I, 14; *DQ* II, 6, 8, 32, 49, 58, 69–70; *Galatea* 2–3, 6; *Guarda*;

Parnaso 3, 5, 7; *Persiles* I, 4; II, 15; III, 8; *Poesías* 4, 5, 8; *Rufián* 1; *Tratos* 2.

Bibliography: Jorge Aladro-Font, and Ricardo Ramos Tremolada, "Ausencia y presencia de Garcilaso en el *Quijote*," *Cervantes* 16, no. 2 (1996): 89–104; Anne J. Cruz, *Imitación y transformación: El petrarquismo en la poesía de Boscán y Garcilaso de la Vega* (Amsterdam: Johns Benjamins, 1988); Sharon Ghertman, *Petrarch and Garcilaso: A Linguistic Approach to Style* (London: Tamesis, 1985); Daniel L. Heiple, *Garcilaso de la Vega and the Italian Renaissance* (University Park: Pennsylvania State University Press, 1994); and Elias L. Rivers, "Cervantes y Garcilaso," in *Homenaje a José Manuel Blecua* (Madrid: Gredos, 1983); 565–70.

Garcilaso de la Vega, El Inca (1539–1616).

Soldier, translator, and historian of the Incas. El Inca Garcilaso was the son of an Incan mother and Spanish father, a relative of the poet *Garcilaso de la Vega. After living for 20 years in Peru, where he learned the language and culture of his mother's people, he moved to Spain where he had his military and literary career. His most important work was the *Comentarios reales de los Incas* (1609, 1617; *Royal Commentaries of the Incas*), an invaluable history of the Incan civilization before and during the Spanish conquest. He was also the translator of León *Hebreo's *Dialogues of Love* (1590; *Díalogos de amor*), the great Platonic treatise on love, an important influence on Cervantes, especially in his *Galatea*. It is not known to what extent, if any, MC might have known directly the *Comentarios reales*, but there are a number of parallels and possible echoes in *Persiles* that suggest that MC did indeed know Inca Garcilaso's work. It is also possible that the two men had personal contact, perhaps during MC's work as a comissary in the late 1580s.

Bibliography: Raúl Porras Barrenechea, *El Inca Garcilaso en Montilla (1561–1614)* (Lima, Peru: San Marcos, 1955); and John Varner, *El Inca: The Life and Times of Garcilaso de la Vega* (Austin: University of Texas Press, 1968).

Garcilaso without commentary.

In *Vidriera*, one of the two books Tomás Rodaja takes with him on his trip to Italy. The poet *Garcilaso de la Vega was recognized early in the sixteenth century as a modern classic. His work was published a number of times, twice in annotated editions. Garcilaso is the poet most often mentioned and cited in MC's works, and Rodaja's preference for his works without commentary may well mirror that of the author.

Garcitoral, Alicio (1902–).

Argentine novelist. Garcitoral's novel *Alonso Quijano el Bueno* (1938) chronicles the life of Alonso Quijano before he becomes DQ. The pivotal event is when the woman he loves, Aldonza Lorenzo, marries someone else. The *hidalgo* then meets MC, who entertains him with his stories of his adventures as a soldier and a captive in Algiers. He finally takes refuge in the romances of chivalry that lead to his madness.

Garden(s) of Hesperides. *Hesperides.

Gardner, Rev. S. A. *Berkeley, August.

Garrett, Almeida (1799–1854).

Portuguese dramatist, poet, and novelist. Garrett is probably the most important romantic writer of Portugal and was an ardent defender of freedom and progress. Probably his best work is the play *Frei Luis de Sousa* (1843), a tragedy based on the life of Manuel de *Sousa Coutinho. His best prose work is *Viagens na Minha Terra* (1846; *Voyages in My Land*), rambling autobiographical recollections within a thin fictional plot. In a famous passage in that book, which sums up the author's most basic philosophy, Garrett writes that the world is one vast Barataria, dominated by SP (symbol of materialism), and that only in the future will come DQ (symbol of spiritualism). Garrett's long, unfinished and unpublished (until 1978) poem *Magriço, ou, os doze de Inglaterra* (*Magriço, or, The Twelve from England*), a chivalric epic, features some of the narrative techniques seen in DQ and also frequently discusses both MC and DQ, again a romantic and symbolic figure. Garrett may be the Portuguese writer who most identified with MC and was most influenced by him.

Bibliography: Maria Fernanda de Abreu, "Almeida Garrett: Os caminhos de Cervantes—Modos de criticar," in *Cervantes no romantismo português: Cavaleiros andantes, manuscritos encontrados e* *gargalhadas moralíssimas* (Lisbon: Estampa, 1997), 185–239.

Garrido de Villena, Francisco. Spanish poet, the author of *El verdadero suceso de la famosa batalla de Roncesvalles con la muerte de los doce Pares de Francia* (1555; *The True Event of the Famous Battle of Roncesvalles, with the Death of the Twelve Peers of France*), a long heroic poem in octaves, a book not found in the examination of DQ's library in I, 6, but that, according to the inquisitorial priest, would be condemned to the flames if it were to be located.

Garzones. *Boys.

Gasabal. Squire to Galaor, brother of Amadís de Gaula. As DQ says in *DQ* I, 20, he is mentioned only once in the book.

Gascon spoken in Gaul [Gascona de la Galia]. A dialect listed among the languages described by Madrigal in *Sultana* 2.

Gascons [Gascones]. Inhabitants, often Huguenots, of the province of Gascony in France. A high percentage of the Catalonian bandits of the sort who appear in *DQ* II, 60, were Gascon Huguenot refugees from France.

Gaskell, Elizabeth (1810–65). English novelist. Gaskell's best-known novel is *Cranford* (1953), which features a bookish character named Mr. Holbrook who is introduced as "a tall, thin, don Quixote–looking old man" and who is repeatedly described in these terms. In *Ruth* (1853), both the protagonist and the minister Benson are described as quixotic.

Gaspar Gregorio, Don (Pedro Gregorio, Don Gregorio, Don Gaspar). The wealthy young Christian nobleman who is the lover of *Ana Félix (also known as Ricota). He is first mentioned, as Pedro Gregorio, by SP in his conversation with *Ricote in *DQ* II, 54. When he is again discussed in II, 63–65, we learn that Gregorio followed his love to North Africa and was left there, dressed as a woman in order to preserve his virtue, while Ana returned to Spain, dressed as a man and in command of a ship, in search of her family's wealth. His rescue is arranged while DQ recovers from his defeat by the Knight of the White Moon. Throughout these later chapters, the name Pedro is forgotten or ignored, and his name is authoritatively given as Don Gaspar Gregorio (and twice he is properly called Don Gaspar); most of the time he is called Don Gregorio, technically incorrect if his surname is Gregorio (at one point, Ana Félix refers to him as Don Gaspar Gregorio and Don Gregorio in the same sentence). This might be some sort of playfulness on MC's part, but if so it is rather pointless; more likely, it is an example of carelessness or confusion.

Gasparo Corso, Andrea. One of five brothers from Corsica who were prominently engaged in commerce and diplomacy in the Mediterranean Sea in the sixteenth century. Andrea, probably also a spy, ran the family office in Algiers during part of the period of MC's captivity. He was the model for the figure of Andrea in *Sultana*.

Gassol, Francisco. He signed the permission to print in Aragon for *Novelas*.

Gate of el Campo [Puerta del Campo]. One of the four gates of the city of Valladolid, close to which MC lived during his residence in that city. See *Casamiento*; *Coloquio*; *Fregona*.

Gate of Guadalajara [Puerta de Guadalajara]. A gate located in the heart of Madrid, near the Plaza Mayor. The area was a commercial center and a city landmark, famous for its colossal statues. The site was the location of one of the *mentideros* of the city and was also much frequented by prostitutes and vagabonds. It was destroyed in a fire in 1582. See *DQ* II, 48; *Juez*; *Vizcaíno*.

Gate of Jerez [Puerta de Jerez]. A gate in Seville located near the Torre de Oro through which carts loaded with silver delivered by ship from the Indies entered the city on their way to the House of Trade. See *Coloquio*; *Española*.

Gate of la Carne [Puerta de la Carne].
The graphic name of this entrance to Seville, 'Gate of Meat,' came about because it was by means of this entry that cattle on the way to the slaughterhouse came into the city. See *Coloquio*.

Gate of la Sagra [Puerta de la Sagra].
One of the principal gates in the walls of the city of Toledo. See *Persiles* III, 7.

Gate of the Aduana [Puerta de la Aduana]. An entryway into Seville where the customhouse [*aduana*] was located. See *Rinconete*.

Gate of the Arenal [Puerta del Arenal].
An entryway into the Arenal district of Seville by the Guadalquivir River, a district frequented by *pícaros* and other marginal types. See *Rinconete*.

Gatell, Pedro. Spanish writer. Gatell was a critic and rival of Jacinto María *Delgado and the most active satirist using *DQ* as a springboard/pretext for his opinions in the late eighteenth century in Spain. He is the author of 1) *La moral de Don Quixote deducida de la historia que de sus gloriosas hazañas escribió Cide-Hamete Benengeli. Por su grande Amigo el Cura. Dala a luz el Br. D. P. Gatell* (2 vols. 1789, 1792; *The Moral of Don Quixote Deduced from the History about his Glorious Deeds that Cide Hamete Benengeli Wrote. By His Great Friend the Priest. It is Given Birth by Br. D. P. Gatell*), a text supposedly written by Pero Pérez, the priest from *DQ*, which the author-editor acquired from a pharmacist; 2) *Instrucciones ecónomicas y políticas, dadas por el famoso Sancho Panza, Gobernador de la Insula Barataria, á un hijo suyo, apoyándolas con refranes castellanos, en que le prescribe el método de governarse en todas las edades y empleos. Segunda impresión aumentada con otra instruccion. Las da á luz D. A. A. P. y G.* (1791; *Economic and Political Instructions Given by the Famous Sancho Panza, Governor of the Island Barataria, to One of His Sons, Supporting Them with Spanish Proverbs, in which He Prescribes the Method of Governing Oneself in All Ages and Walks of Life. Second Impression Augmented with Other Instruction. They Are Published by D. A. A. P. y G*); 3) *La moral del mas famoso escudero Sancho Panza, con arreglo á la historia que del mas hidalgo manchego Don Quixote de la Mancha escribió Cide Hamete Benengeli* (1793; *The Moral of the Most Famous Squire Sancho Panza, in Accord with the History which Was Written about the Most Hidalgo Manchegan Don Quixote de la Mancha by Cide Hamete Benengeli*), this time with no pretext of a discovered manuscript; and 4) *Historia del mas famoso escudero Sancho Panza, desde la gloriosa muerte de Don Quixote de la Mancha hasta el último dia y postrera hora de su vida* (two parts, 1793, 1798; *History of the Most Famous Squire Sancho Panza, from the Time of the Glorious Death of Don Quixote de la Mancha until the Last Day and Final Hour of His Life*). By far the most interesting is the last of these, the only one that is a true fiction, as opposed to a polemical work with the merest guise of fictionality. In this work, SP becomes the mayor of his village and is a model governor.

Bibliography: Howard Mancing, "Jacinto María Delgado and Cide Hamete Benengeli: A Semi-Classic Recovered and A Bibliographical Labyrinth Explored," *Cervantes* 7, no. 1 (1987): 13–43; and Juana Toledano Molina, "Una novela cervantina del siglo XVIII: *La historia del más famoso escudero Sancho Panza, después de la muerte de Don Quijote de la Mancha*," in *Actas del II Coloquio Internacional de la Asociación de Cervantistas* (Barcelona: Anthropos, 1991), 227–32.

Gatos. *Cats.

Gautier, Théophile (1811–72). French poet and novelist. Gautier's novel *Mademoiselle de Maupin* (1835) illustrates his aesthetic of art for art's sake. The protagonist talks frequently about chivalry and characteristically attempts to remake reality in the image of romance and fantasy, with herself as heroine. One of the characters specifically says to her that she should "perceive that what had seemed so beautiful to you through the prism of love was really very ugly, and that what you had taken for a real hero from a novel was, when all was said, only a prosaic bourgeois in dressing-gown and slippers." And near the end of the novel, the protagonist herself admits her quixotism: "I imagined that the world was full of admirable young men, and that on the roads you would encounter populations of Esplandians, Amadises and Lancelots of the Lake in search of their Dulcineas."

Gavilán. **1**. In *Galatea* 1, one of the dogs accompanying Erastro when he first appears. **2**. In *Coloquio*, the name by which Berganza is known when he is in the service of Nicolás el Romo.

Gayos. A Roman family name mentioned in *DQ* I, 13.

Gayton, Edmund (1608–66). English writer. Gayton is the author of the curious *Pleasant Notes upon Don Quixot* (1654), in which the author (anticipating *Unamuno, but in a radically different spirit) comments on *DQ* I, chapter by chapter, choosing short passages (from the Shelton translation) and making facetious comments, puns, and jokes about them. Gayton's comments are often obscure and/or irrelevant, may sometimes be funny, frequently involve capricious associations, and are occasionally slightly obscene or, at least, indelicate; certainly they are often extraordinarily insensitive. For example, knights-errant, he says, suggest wandering Jews; SP sees windmills where DQ sees giants because he cleans out his eyes everyday, but DQ does not. MC's story is merely a pretext for weak, whimsical, and farcical humor.

Bibliography: Edward M. Wilson, "Edmund Gayton on Don Quixote, Andrés, and Juan Haldudo," *Comparative Literature* 2 (1950): 64–72.

Gelasia. In *Galatea* 4–6, the disdainful shepherdess, who refuses to love anyone and prizes her freedom; she is loved by Galercio and Lenio. In many ways, Gelasia is similar to and anticipates *Marcela in *DQ* I, 14.

Generación agarena. *Descendants of Hagar.

General. *Commandant.

General of Oran [General de Orán]. *Lions.

Generosity [Liberalidad]. In *DQ* II, 20, one of the eight nymphs who participates in the celebration of *Camacho's wedding.

***Generous Lover, The.** **Amante Liberal, El.*

Geneva [Ginebra]. A city in Switzerland, on Lake Geneva. See *Guarda*.

Genil. A river that rises in the Sierra Nevada Mountains east of Granada, flows through that city, and then west and northwest until it empties into the Guadalquivir, midway between Córdoba and Seville. See *DQ* I, 18.

Genís, Alonso. A criminal (whose name actually was Gonzalo Genís) executed not, as stated by a character in *Fregona*, by the count of Puñonrostro (*Arias de Bobadilla, Don Francisco, Count of Puñonrostro), but by his predecessor, the count of Priego (*Carrillo de Mendoza, Don Pedro).

Genízaros. *Janissaries.

Genoa [Genova]. Italian port city north of Rome on the Mediterranean Sea; the birthplace of Christopher Columbus. Genoa was an important commercial and banking center in the Renaissance and there were many Genoese bankers and wealthy merchants in Spain, particularly Seville. The Genoese are often figures of satire and criticism, frequently fleeced by scheming women and *pícaros*. See *Doncellas*; *DQ* I, 39; *Española*; *Fuerza*; *Galatea* 5; *Gitanilla*; *Parnaso* 3; *Persiles* II, 2; III, 10, 12; *Tratos* 2; *Vidriera*.

Bibliography: Ruth Pike, *Enterprise and Adventure: The Genoese in Seville and the Opening of the New World* (Ithaca, NY: Cornell University Press, 1966).

Genoese [Ginoveses]. Residents or inhabitants of *Genoa. See *Vizcaíno*.

Gente de barrio. *Neighborhood people.

Gente más lucida. *Most distinguished people.

Gentil de Vargas, Antonio. *Vargas Gentil, Don Antonio de.

Gentiles hombres de a caballo. *Gentlemen on horseback.

Gentility [Hidalguía]. The official legal term for all categories of *nobility in Spain. The idea was that nobility descends to individuals by way of their heritage; one was the 'son of someone' (*hidalgo) of worth or merit. Related to the idea of gentility was that of *purity of blood, but the two concepts are not exact equivalents. Proof of gentility could be obtained by an official patent of nobility. This privileged and honorific status (passed on in the male line to all children, male and female, legitimate and illegitimate) was recognized throughout society; perhaps most significantly, it carried with it an exemption from taxation and imprisonment for debt.

Gentleman, gentlemen [Caballero(s)]. **1.** In *Galatea* 2, the Catalan bandit captain who befriends Timbrio. **2.** In *DQ* I, 41, the 50 armed and mounted men who meet Ruy Pérez de Viedma, Zoraida, and the other escaped captives when they come ashore in Spain. At first, the men fear that the group is part of a Muslim raiding party, but one of the men is none other than *Pedro de Bustamante, uncle of one of the captives, which makes recognition easier for all involved. **3.** In *Gitanilla*, a man wearing the emblem of the Order of Calatrava who invites Preciosa in to sing for a group of men. **4.** In *Gitanilla*, a friend of Francisco de Cárcamo who is critical of gypsies and reads the sonnet that begins 'When Preciosa plays the tambourine' written for her by the page-poet. **5.** In *Rinconete*, the young nobleman who comes to Monipodio's house to complain that his commission was not adequately carried out by Chiquiznaque. **6.** In *Vidriera*, the noble young students who take on Tomás Rueda as their servant during their stay in Salamanca. **7.** In *Fuerza*, the elderly man who rushes to the aid of the injured Luis because the boy reminds

him so much of his own son Rodolfo (who is in fact Luis's father). **8.** In *Pedro* 3, the man with the king when he learns that Belisa is his niece. **9.** In *DQ* II, 8, the nobleman who thought of gaining eternal fame by killing *Carlos V in what was once the Pantheon and now is the Temple of Santa Maria della Rotonda in Rome, in the anecdote told by DQ. The anecdote is well-known, and the emperor visited the site in 1536, but no other text confirms the details described here. **10.** In *DQ* II, 61, the man who greets DQ and SP on the beach outside Barcelona and then guides them to the home of Don *Antonio Moreno. **11.** In *Persiles* I, 5, the second son of a titled nobleman who offends Antonio the Barbarian, causing his exile from Spain and beginning his adventures. **12.** In *Persiles* I, 5, a group of English gentlemen are returning to England after a tour of Spain, when Antonio the Barbarian offends and slaps one, causing them to put him to sea in a small boat. **13.** In *Persiles* II, 2, an elderly man who has seen in Genoa a ship overturned on shore just like the one on Policarpo's island.

Gentlemen on horseback [Gentiles hombres de a caballo]. Two men who attend the funeral of *Grisóstomo. One of them *Vivaldo, engages DQ in extended conversation on the subject of knight-errantry. See *DQ* I, 13.

Georgics. *Virgil.

Geraya. A character, whose name actually is Garaya, in *Rogel de Grecia* (by Feliciano de *Silva) mentioned in *DQ* I, 24.

Gerchunoff, Alberto (1883–1949). Argentinean critic and short-story writer. Gerchunoff is the author of the interesting collection of fictions entitled *Los gauchos judíos* (1919; *The Jewish Gauchos*), which includes the story "Las bodas de Camacho" ("Camacho's Wedding"), based on *DQ* II, 20–21. He is also the author of one of the more personal and sensitive—and unique—books on MC in *La jofaina maravillosa: Agenda cervantina* (1922; *The Marvelous Basin: A Cervantine Agenda*). In the introductory section, Gerchunoff discusses how he first read *DQ* as a youth and how he has returned to it throughout his life. The main part of the book consists of 18 brief essays/fictions on MC, his works, and his characters. These short pieces are both a personal critical commentary and a fictional evocation. Some, especially those devoted to some of MC's women characters (Preciosa, Luscinda, Zoraida), are more like straightforward commentary. Others are more obviously creative, such as the conversation between Rocinante and the priest and barber, or the presentation of La Tolosa and La Molinera, prostitutes at the first inn (I, 2–4), the day after DQ leaves.

Bibliography: Alberto Gerchunoff, *La jofaina maravillosa: agenda cervantina* (Buenos Aires, Biblioteca Argentina de Buenas Ediciones Literarias, 1922); and Carlos Orlando Nállim, "Un apasionado divulgador del *Quijote*: Alberto Gerchunoff," in *Cervantes en las letras argentinas* (Buenos Aires: Academia Argentina de Letras, 1998), 81–96.

Gerhardi(e), William (1895–1977). English novelist and dramatist. Gerhardi's satiric play entitled *Perfectly Scandalous* (1927) was released two years later with the revised title of *Donna Quixote, or Perfectly Scandalous*. The action all takes place in the Pension Villa Tirol in the Austrian Alps and centers around the aristocratic Mrs. Brandon, other guests, and the owners and staff of the pension. The protagonist is described as "an exceedingly thin, bony lady past middle-age," a physique that matches her supposedly quixotic nature. She is, however, one of the most obnoxious and acid-tongued DQs of all time. Early in the first act, after she has already twice uttered her trademark "perfectly scandalous" (and variants "perfectly awful" and "perfectly dreadful"), criticized the League of Nations and the "yellow races" (who should be stamped out), and explained how she loathed her family (father, mother, husband, and daughter), another character notes that she is an "embittered woman," but nonetheless "Donna Quixote. . . . You must needs do things, silly things, useless things; still you must do them." The remainder of the play continues in the same vein until this least likeable of female DQs dies in the last act.

Bibliography: William Gerhardi, *Donna Quixote, or Perfectly Scandalous* (London: Duckworth, 1929).

German guards. *Papal guards.

Germanía (Germanesca). The argot of professional thieves and other marginal types, the people of the *hampa* (underworld). MC demonstrates in his works that he knew this linguistic register very well. The best examples of it are seen in the discussion between DQ and the galley slaves (I, 22) and in the talk of the people who assemble in Monipodio's house in *Rinconete*. See also *Sultana* 2.

Germany [Alemania]. Germany is the least important major European nation in MC's work. In the sixteenth century, Carlos V was first allied with Germany against France, but later he became engaged in armed struggle with the Protestant rulers of country who were in rebellion against Hapsburg rule. In *DQ* II, 54, the *Morisco* Ricote praises Germany for its religious freedom. Since MC had no direct familiarity with the political and religious situation there, however, this assessment can be read variously as wishful thinking, subtle satire, or a false impression. See also *DQ* I, 49; *DQ* II, 44, 54, 63; *Persiles* I, 5; *Rufián* 1–2.

Getino de Guzmán, Alsono. Musician and dancer, member of Lope de Rueda's acting troupe, who the Cervantes family knew in Seville and who later moved to Madrid and lived in the same building as they. In 1567 Getino received the commission to celebrate the birth of Catalina Micaela, second daughter of Felipe II and Isabel de Valois. He ordered the construction of some triumphal arches and decorated them with poetry, including one by the 20-year-old MC, his first "literary" effort (*Poesías* 1). Later Getino held a position as royal bailiff and took an active role in arranging money for MC's ransom from captivity in Algiers. He was involved in the opening of the *Corral de la Cruz and may also have helped MC's entry into the theatrical world in Madrid.

Ghent [Gante]. A city in eastern Flanders, today Belgium. See *Rufián* 2; *Vidriera*.

Giants [Jayanes, Gigantes]. 1. The ten enemies with whom DQ says he was fighting when he explains his wounds after he is brought home in *DQ* I, 5. **2**. *Windmills.

Gibraltar, Strait of Gibraltar (Straits of Hercules) [Gibraltar, Estrecho de Gibraltar (Estrecho Hercúleo)]. The promontory in southwestern Spain that overlooks the narrow strait connecting the Atlantic Ocean and the Mediterranean Sea. In *Española*, it is at the Strait of Gibraltar (also known as the *Pillars of Hercules) where Ricaredo successfully commands his ships in action against Turkish ships. See *Casa* 3; *DQ* I, 41; *Persiles* IV, 12.

Gide, André (1869–1951). French critic, playwright, diarist, and novelist. Gide's landmark novel, *Les faux-monnayeurs* (1926; *The Counterfeiters*), one of the founding texts of *postmodernism, is thematically linked to *DQ* in two ways. First, the self-consciousness and self-referentiality of the narrative structure in which the narrator Edouard is writing a novel to be called *Les faux-monnayeurs* recalls CHB and the narrative self-consciousness of *DQ*. Second, the theme of the novel is precisely that of reality and appearances: "I am beginning to catch sight of what I might call the 'deep-lying subject' of my book. It is—it will be—no doubt, the rivalry between the real world and the representation of it which we make to ourselves. The manner in which the world of appearances imposes itself upon us, and the manner in which we try to impose on the outside world our own interpretation—this is the drama of our lives. The resistance of facts invites us to transport our ideal construction into the realm of dreams, of hope, of belief in a future life, which is fed by all the disappointments and disillusions of our present one." Though less explicitly, the same literary self-consciousness and narrative technique and the same theme run throughout Gide's *Les caves du Vatican* (1914; *The Vatican Cellars*, translated as *Lafcadio's Adventures*): "What a gulf between the imagination and the deed."

Gigantes benitos. *Benedictine giants.

Gigli, Girolamo (1660–1722). Italian dramatist. His *Il Don Chisciotte, ovvero Un pazzo guarisce l'altro* (1698; *Don Quixote, or One Madman Cures Another*) is a musical comedy. Interestingly, at the end of the play, when DQ recovers his sanity, it is not as a prelude to death but in order to live out a normal life.
   Bibliography: Giusepe Carlo Rossi, "Una 'fantasia' italiana su *Don Chisciotte*," *Hispano-Italic Studies* 2 (1979): 87–92.

Gigote, Don. *Don Whip or Don Chopped Meat.

Gil. A generic pastoral name mentioned in *Pedro* 1.

Gil Berrueco. In *Persiles* III, 10, the town crier and executioner in the community where the two students try to pass themselves off as former captives in Algiers.

Gil el Peraile. In *Pedro* 2, a peasant only mentioned in the play who is to participate in the dance for the king and queen.

Gil, Fray Juan. Spanish priest. He was the procurer general of the Trinitarians and redeemer for the crown of Castile, and in this capacity delivered the necessary ransom money to buy MC's freedom on September 19, 1580. The rescue was quite dramatic, as MC's owner, Hassan Pasha, was about to depart for Constantinople at that very time, and his slaves, including MC, were already on board the ship, in chains and shackles, to row it. Had MC not been freed at that time, it is probable that he never would have been heard from again. See *Tratos* 4.
   Bibliography: Constancio Rodero Saez, *El gran libertador de Miguel de Cervantes: Fr. Juan Gil* (n.p.: Ayuntamiento de Arévalo con la colaboración del Excmo, Ayuntamiento de Alcalá de Henares, 1988).

Gil Polo, Gaspar. *Polo, Gaspar Gil.

Gilbert, Sir W(illiam) S(chwenk) (1836–1911). English dramatist and humorist, known primarily for a series of 14 comic operas on which he collaborated with the composer Sir

Arthur Sullivan (1842–1900): *H.M.S. Pinafore* (1878), *The Pirates of Penzance* (1879), *The Mikado* (1885), and others. The last work on which the team collaborated before their estrangement was *The Gondoliers; or, The King of Barataria* (1889). The plot revolves around a group of gondoliers in Venice, one of whom is revealed to be the heir to the throne of the imaginary kingdom of Barataria (the name of SP's island in *DQ* II). There is no explicit reference to *DQ* in this typical Gilbert and Sullivan comedy, but the inclusion of a character named Casilda (recall Sansón Carrasco's Casilda, or *Casildea), as well as the presence of a duke (here named Duke of Plaza-Toro, a grandee of Spain) and duchess might suggest that *DQ* did in fact provide some of the direct inspiration for the work.

Bibliography: W. S. Gilbert and Arthur Sullivan, *The Gondoliers; or, The King of Barataria* (London: Chappell, 1889).

Gilberto. In *Rufián* 1, the student who loses a large sum of money in a card game with the protagonist Cristóbal de Lugo.

Gilliam, Terry (1940–). American film director. There is at least a mild quixotic element in almost all of Gilliam's work: for example, *The Fisher King* (1991, a retelling of the grail story with Robin Williams as a quixotic street person who lives in a world of his own creation, a world populated by castles, knights, and damsels in distress) and *The Adventures of Baron Munchauson* (1989, based on the novel of Karl *Immermann). In 1999–2001 Gilliam worked on a project he had had in mind for a decade: a film entitled *The Man who Killed Don Quixote*, starring Johnny Depp as a modern advertising executive who goes back in time and becomes SP (with Jean Rochefort as DQ and Vanessa Paradis as DT). But after only a few days of filming, with disastrous weather—a flood in La Mancha, of all places—and a major illness to Rochefort, work was halted and the project was abandoned (shades of Orson *Welles). Gilliam's film was never made, but a film about his unmade film was made: *Lost in La Mancha*.

Gilliland, Alexis A. (1931–). American science-fiction writer. Gilliland has written a trilogy with the following titles *The Revolution from Rosinante* (1981), *Long Shot for Rosinante* (1981), and *The Pirates of Rosinante* (1982). A space colony (called a *mundito*), led by intelligent computers (who are quixotically adorned with images of twentieth-century movie stars), rebels and wins its political independence from a despotic North American Union. The banner of the Mundito Rosinante is "a rickety green horse on a white field"; its anthem is "The Impossible Dream"; there is a Taverna Cervantes; and a nearby *mundito* named Don Quixote is trashed and used as a shield for Rosinante.

Giménez Caballero, Ernesto (1899–?). Spanish essayist. Giménez Caballero's *"Don Quijote" ante el mundo (y ante mí)* (1979; *"Don Quixote" before the World [and before Me]*) is a chaotic presentation of the influence of *DQ* in world literature. Included also in the book is the author's own filmscript entitled *El príncipe manco* (*The Crippled Prince*), a dramatization of the life of MC and his characters. Giménez Caballero traces his unsuccessful efforts, beginning in the 1940s, to get the work filmed in Spain, Italy, and Argentina. He even insists that he preceded Dale *Wasserman in writing a crucial scene that takes place in the prison of Seville.

Bibliography: Ernesto Giménez Caballero, *"Don Quijote" ante el mundo (y ante mí)*, prologue by Gladys Crescioni Neggers (San Juan, Puerto Rico: Inter American University Press, 1979).

Giménez Pastor, Arturo (1872–?). Uruguayan poet. Giménez Pastor includes a long poem, "Convocatoria a la Apoteosis de Cervantes" ("Convocation to the Apotheosis of Cervantes"), in his book *Estela lírica* (1938; *Lyrical Wake*). The title is accurate: the poem consists of a call to characters—first a brief evocation of many of the minor characters, and then, in more detail, DT, SP, and DQ—from *DQ* to come together in praise of MC.

Bibliography: Arturo Giménez Pastor, *Estela lírica* (Buenos Aires: Albatros, 1938).

Giménez y de Ancisco, Diego. *Jiménez de Enciso, Diego.

Ginebra. *Geneva; *Guinevere.

Ginés de Pasamonte (Ginesillo de Parapilla, Don hijo de la puta, Don Ginesillo de Paropillo). In *DQ* I, 22, the last and most important of the *galley slaves interviewed by DQ. A repeat criminal, he has been condemned to ten years in the galleys, probably a life sentence. He is insultingly called *Ginesillo de Parapilla* by one of the guards and then, after DQ sets him free and he refuses to go to see DT, DQ also calls him *Don hijo de la puta* (son of a whore) and *Don Ginesillo de Paropillo*. Ginés informs DQ that he is also the author of his own autobiography, entitled *La vida de Ginés de Pasamonte* (*The Life of Ginés de Pasamonte*). When DQ asks if it is good, Ginés responds that it is better than *Lazarillo de Tormes* and all others of that genre. This is a valuable passage for literary history, as it demonstrates that MC, surely like many of his time, was aware of the picaresque novel as a fictional life-writing genre. Although it is not directly alluded to here, the obvious model of a galley slave who writes the story of his life is Mateo *Alemán's extraordinarily popular *Guzmán de Alfarache* (1599, 1604). It was only in the wake of *Guzmán* that the picaresque novel began to gain ascendancy in the literary world: *Lazarillo* had been published in 1554, but there was no significant published successor until *Guzmán*, and then a flurry of activity in the first years of the seventeenth century: *López de Ubeda's *Justina*, Gregorio González's unpublished *El guitón Honofre* dated 1605, and *Quevedo's *Buscón*. When DQ also asks Ginés if his work is finished, the response goes straight to the heart of the dilemma of all autobiographers: 'How can it be finished when my life is not yet finished?' MC, the great technical experimenter in prose fiction, never wrote a novel or story narrated entirely in the first person (although there are long first-person narratives in several of his works). Ginés de Pasamonte may well have been based to some degree on the historical figure of Gerónimo de *Pasamonte, a sol-

dier whom MC knew in Italy, and who fought at Lepanto, was a captive in Algiers for many years, and wrote an autobiography. It has been proposed that Gerónimo is the author of *DQA*, and that he wrote the sequel as a means of getting revenge for the insult of being converted into a character in *DQ* I. Ginés returns later in the book when he is responsible for the *theft of SP's ass, and then again later in *DQ* II as the figure of *Maese Pedro. Overall, Ginés de Pasamonte is one of the great secondary characters created by MC. See also *DQ* II, 4, 27.

Bibliography: Juan Manuel de Prada, "Tres versiones de Ginés de Pasamonte," in *Nuevas visiones del "Quijote,"* ed. José Luis García Martín (Oviedo, Spain: Ediciones Nobel, 1999), 115–58; Augustin Redondo, "De Ginés de Pasamonte a Maese Pedro. Algunos datos nuevos sobre este personaje cervantino y su actuación," in *Texte. Kontexte. Strukturen. Homenaje a Karl Alfred Bülher* (Tübingen, Germany: G. Nar, 1987), 221–29; Martín de Riquer, *Cervantes, Passamonte y Avellaneda* (Barcelona: Sirmio, 1988); and Ann E. Wiltrout, "Ginés de Pasamonte: The *pícaro* and His Art," *Anales Cervantinos* 17 (1978): 11–17.

Ginesa. In *Pedro* 2, a gypsy who has a minor role in the dance for the king and queen.

Ginosofistas de la Etiopía. *Gymnosophists from Ethiopia.

Giralda. The bell tower of the cathedral of Seville, originally constructed in the twelfth century as a minaret and finished off by the Christians with a bronze weathervane (*giraldillo*) at the top. In *DQ* II, 14, when Sansón Carrasco is boasting of his achievements as the Knight of the Mirrors, he tells DQ that one of his victories was over the great giantess of Seville named Giralda who is as strong as if she were made of bronze. See also *DQ* II, 22.

Giraldi Cinzio, Giambattista (1504–73). Italian poet, dramatist, and short-story writer. His *Ecatommiti* (1565; *Hecatommithi*) is a collection of 112 novelas in the manner of Boccaccio. It was published in Spanish in 1590 and was widely read in Spain, undoubtedly including by MC, whose *Ortel Banedre, for example, seems to be derived at least in part from Giraldi.

Girón de Rebolledo, Alonso. A religious poet praised in Calliope's song in *Galatea* 6, where he is called simply Alonso Rebolledo.

Girón, Licenciado. A renegade from Granada known in Algiers as Abdaharramán. He assisted MC in his fourth and final escape attempt in 1579 by making arrangements with Onofre *Exarque to provide a ship for the escape.

Gissing, George (1857–1903). English novelist. In Gissing's novel *The Private Papers of Henry Ryecroft* (1903), the quixotic diary-writing protagonist muses about history and injustice and appends the following comment: "Come, once more before I die I will read *Don Quixote*."

Gitana vieja. *Old gypsy woman.

Gitanilla, La (Gitanilla); The Little Gypsy Girl. The first story in *Novelas*. The action takes place in the year 1610 and, since *Novelas* was finished and ready for publication in 1612, it is very possible that it was the last, or one of the last, stories written. It is the longest story in the collection and is generally considered one of the best. Its position at the beginning of the collection is, perhaps, an indication of the author's own confidence in the story, the opening showpiece of the book. The protagonist is the living incarnation of poetry, described in the same terms used by both Vidriera and DQ in *DQ* II, 16 (*poetry). Like *Fregona* later in the book, this story blends novel and romance, mixes social and ethnic classes and values, and contains some of MC's better poetry. Preciosa is the embodiment of poetry itself, as well as the personification of all that is, as her name suggests, precious. Her own equation of virtue with virginity, and her description of her virginity as the most precious jewel she possesses, links the images and makes her the nexus of poetry, beauty, value, and virtue. Certainly the choice of a gypsy as a romantic heroine in the mold of beautiful noble ladies (which she turns

out in the end to be) must have struck contemporary readers as a bold and surprising move. Interestingly, the lively, talkative, active agent that Preciosa is as a gypsy disappears completely when it is revealed that she is a noble lady. The impression with which the reader is left is that rank and privilege also carry with them, at least for women, very severe restraints. Whether MC himself perceives what is lost when a woman moves from the margin to the center, from novel to romance, is not clear.

A wily old gypsy woman has raised as her niece a beautiful young girl whom she calls Preciosa, teaching her to read and write, sing and dance, and instructing her in the ways of the world. When the girl is 15 years old, the old woman decides to let her appear and perform in public. From the start, Preciosa is a success and draws much attention and praise. She becomes known as *La Gitanilla*, the Little Gypsy Girl. Her performance in Madrid is so spectacularly successful that a lieutenant in the crowd invites her to his home to perform for his wife Doña Clara. In a rapid succession of events, Preciosa receives a ballad written specifically for her and the promise of a regular supply of new material—which, in accord with her demand, will always be in good taste—then accepts an offer to perform for a group of men (reassuring her friend Cristina that there is more to fear from one man alone then from several together) and display her wit and wisdom as well as her musical talents. Then, at Doña Clara's house, she again impresses everyone with her performances, but also with her ability as a fortune teller. A few days later, just outside of Madrid, the gypsy troupe is stopped by a richly dressed young man, who reveals that he is the only son of a rich nobleman, and who proposes marriage to Preciosa. Preciosa responds that, since she has one precious jewel—her virginity—that she values so highly that she is prepared to take it to the grave rather than lose it before she is absolutely sure about the man involved, she imposes two conditions before accepting the proposal: 1) she must investigate and verify that the youth is who he claims to be, and 2) he must agree to a two-year trial as a gypsy before they can be married. He accepts these conditions and they agree that, if everything checks out all right, a week later they will meet in the same place and he will become one of the troupe under the name of Andrés Caballero. In the city, Preciosa again meets the man who gave her the first poem. He claims not to be a poet, but a fan of poetry, which he reveres as a most precious jewel; for him, poetry is an extremely beautiful maiden—chaste, honest, discreet, intelligent, and modest—in which are contained the limits of the highest discretion. This time he gives her a sonnet he has written especially for her. Then, following Andrés's information about his family, she sees on a balcony an elderly man of about 50 dressed in the prestigious habit of the Order of Santiago. They accept his invitation to enter and find there several men, including Andrés (whose real name is Juan, or Juanillo, as his father calls him), with whom she engages in a brief exchange of double entendres that appears innocent to the rest of the group. While she is dancing, the sonnet falls from her pocket and one of the men, who had earlier made cynically critical remarks about gypsies, picks it up and reads it ('When Preciosa plays the tambourine') and praises the poet who wrote it. Preciosa corrects him, saying that the author is not a poet but a page and a decent man. At this juncture, the narrator interrupts and admonishes Preciosa that such a gratuitous comment about another man can only pierce the heart of Andrés: just look at him there in a cold sweat; be more careful. Meanwhile, the old gypsy woman has verified the nobility and wealth of the family. The next week, at the appointed time, Andrés meets with the gypsy troupe. He has told his parents that he is going to Flanders, and then he slipped away from his accompanying servant. After an initiation ceremony for Andrés, a wise old gypsy, holding Preciosa's hand, explains to Andrés the ways of gypsy life. Among them: Preciosa can be either his wife or his lover, it does not matter, for gypsies are not much fond of official legal status; they regard the law of friendship as inviolable; they have no jealousy; they may practice incest, but never adultery; men decide how their women are to be treated and can leave an aging woman; they live happy and free and are the lords of the countryside; they have no concern for the concept of honor; and they live by their wits. Preciosa reminds him of the two-year probationary period—her personal rule, not a usual gypsy custom—in which they are to live as brother and sister. Andrés accepts all the terms. A problem arises with the concept of theft—a gypsy staple but an anathema to Andrés. He solves the problem by insisting on performing all his thefts entirely alone, and then buys things, presenting them as stolen. In everything else he is a great success, always winning the prize in running, jumping, bowling, throwing the bar, and so forth. His fame begins to rival that of Preciosa herself. One night, the dogs raise a ruckus and the gypsies discover that the animals have cornered and bitten a man approaching the camp. The gypsies bring him back to their camp, cure him, and hear his suspicious story. It turns out to be the poet-page from Madrid escaping a complicated honor situation in which he was involved in a killing, and he is also interested in seeing Preciosa again. Although his real name is Don Sancho, he introduces himself as Alonso Hurtado, but it is decided that he will be called Clemente and can accompany the gypsies to southern Spain, where he can then catch a ship bound for Italy. Clemente and Andrés become good friends, composing poetry and music in honor of Preciosa. Clemente nearly matches Andrés as the strongest, fastest, and cleverest of the males in the troupe in every informal contest. In a town just outside of the city of Murcia, there occurs the near-tragic event that leads to the dénouement. A wealthy young woman named Juana Castrucha falls in love with Andrés and offers to marry him. He, of course, rejects this offer and, in a jealous rage, Juana places some items in his saddlebags and accuses him of theft. The police and a crowd of people arrive and Andrés is arrested. One young soldier, nephew of the local mayor, insults and slaps Andrés. Responding more as the noble Don Juan with wounded pride and offended honor, Andrés fights back, taking the soldier's own sword and killing him with it. Although the mayor is ready to hang him on the spot, Andrés is placed in jail in chains and the whole gypsy troupe is detained (all but Clemente, who continues on toward Italy). The wife of the local magistrate, curious to see the beautiful gypsy girl everyone is talking about, has Preciosa brought to her. The magistrate's wife is moved, in large part because Preciosa reminds her so much of the young woman her own lost Constanza would have been. Preciosa tearfully proclaims Andrés's innocence and begs for mercy. The old gypsy woman then comes forth and solves everything. Taking the magistrate's wife aside, she explains and proves that 15 years earlier, in 1595 in Madrid, she had stolen a newly born baby named Doña Constanza de Azevedo y de Meneses, daughter of Doña Guiomar de Meneses and Don Fernando de Azevedo. Birthmarks confirm Preciosa's identity as Doña Guiomar's stolen daughter. Andrés's noble status is also revealed. The old gypsy is forgiven; Juana Castrucha admits her lie; the local mayor is bought off. The noble youth's families accept their children's choices, and Don Juan de Cárcamo marries Doña Constanza de Azevedo y de Meneses amidst great festivities. The poets of the city, including the famous *Licenciado* Pozo, celebrate the event in verse.

Bibliography: Jonathan Burgoyne, "*La gitanilla*: A Model of Cervanates's Subversion of Romance," *Revista Canadiense de Estudios Hispánicos* 25 (2000): 373–95; Gerard Flynn, "*La gitanilla*: Accidents and Occasions," *Hispanic Journal* 11 (1990): 29–44; María Antonia Garcés, "Poetic Language and the Dissolution of the Subject in *La Gitanilla* and *El licenciado Vidriera*," *Caliope* 2 (1996): 85–104; Michael E. Gerli, "Romance and Novel: Idealism and Irony in *La Gitanilla*," *Cervantes* 6, no.1 (1986): 29–38; Ana Eva Guasch Melis, "Gitanos viejos y gitanos nuevos: los grupos sociales en La Gitanilla," in *Actas del VIII Coloquio Internacional de la Asociación de Cervantistas*, ed. José Ramón Fernández de Cano y Martín (El Toboso, Spain: Exmo, Ayuntamiento de El Toboso, 1999); 327–40; Francisco Márquez Villanueva, "La buenaventura de Preciosa," *Nueva Revista de Filología Hispánica* 34 (1985–86): 741–68; Charles D. Presberg, "Precious Exchanges: The Poetics of Desire, Power, and Reciprocity in Cervantes's *La gitanilla*," *Cervantes* 18, no. 2 (1998): 53–73; Joan Resina, "Laissez faire y reflexividad erótica en *La gitanilla*," *MLN* 106 (1991): 257–78; Robert ter Horst, "Une Saison en enfer: *La gitanilla*," *Cervantes* 5, no.2 (1985): 87–127; and Alison Weber, "Pentimento: The Parodic Text of *La Gitanilla*," *Hispanic Review* 62 (1994): 59–75.

Gitano viejo. *Old gypsy.

Gitanos. *Gypsies.

Glass Graduate, The. *Licenciado Vidriera, El.*

Glaucus [Glauco]. In Greek myth, a fisherman who ate a magical herb and became immortal, turning into an oracular god of the sea. See *Galatea* 6.

Gloria Vana. *Vainglory.

Glosa [Gloss]. A poetic commentary on a theme announced in an opening refrain, which may be written in any of a variety of meters, and which traditionally incorporates the refrain as the last line of each stanza. See *Poesías* 23.

Glowacki, Aleksander. *Prus, Boleslaw.

Gnatho [Gnatón]. A comic character from Terence's play *Eunuchus* (*The Eunuch*). See *Parnaso* 2.

Gnido. *Cnossus.

Goa. A Portuguese colony on the southwestern coast of India. See *Parnaso* 4.

Goat [Cabrón]. A name for the devil, who sometimes appears in this form. See *Coloquio.*

Goatherd(s) [Cabrero(s)]. 1. In *DQ* I, 10–12, the men who receive and host DQ and SP, giving them food and shelter for the night. They listen politely to DQ's speech on the *Golden Age, which they do not understand, and then one of them cures DQ's ear wounded in the battle with the *Basque squire (I, 9) with a folk remedy consisting of rosemary leaves, saliva, and salt (which will become the basis for DQ's recipe for the *balm de Fierabrás in I, 17). One of the goatherds also sings for DQ's entertainment, and another, named Pedro, tells the story of Grisóstomo's death for his beloved Marcela. The next day, the goatherds take DQ and SP to the site of Grisóstomo's funeral and participate in that event (I, 13–14). These simple and generous men are among the most decent and respectful people DQ ever meets on his travels; they are gentle, kind folk who, unlike most members of higher social status, do not make fun of or laugh at DQ in any way. **2.** In *DQ* I, 23, 27, the person who tells DQ what he knows about *Cardenio: when he arrived in the Sierra Moreno mountains and how he acted.

God Is Christ [Dios es Cristo]. The expression "a lo de Dios es Cristo" is not merely a tautology, but means 'haphazardly' or 'as I please.' See *Gallardo* 2; *Parnaso* II; *Rufián*; *Vidriera*.

God of Battles. *Mars.

God of the blacksmiths; God of the forge. *Vulcan.

God of the horrendous face. *Pluto.

God of the winged shoe. *Mercury.

Goddess of the crops. *Ceres.

Godfrey of Bouillon [Godofre de Bullón] (ca. 1060–1100). French soldier. He was one of the leaders of the First Crusade. See *DQ* I, 48.

Godínez, Felipe (1588–ca. 1659). Spanish *converso* priest and dramatist. Godínez, a doctor of theology and well-known priest and orator, was accused of being Jewish in 1624 and had to repent in an auto-da-fe. He is praised as a poet in *Parnaso* 2, even though the majority of his writings were produced after MC's death.
    Bibliography: Piedad Bolaños Donoso, *La obra dramática de Felipe Godínez* (Seville: Diputación Provincial de Sevilla, 1983).

Godos. *Goths.

Godoy, Armand. French poet and literary critic. Godoy's *Dulcinée* (1957) consists of 14 sonnets on the theme of DQ's love for DT.
    Bibliography: Armand Godoy, *Dulcinée* (Paris: Grasset, 1957).

Godwin, William (1756–1836). English philosopher and novelist, father of Mary *Shelley. Godwin abandoned traditional Christianity for a fervent belief in enlightenment values based on reason, which he expressed most famously in *An Enquiry Concerning Political Justice* (2 vols., 1793). He was the theoretical leader of what became known as "English Jacobinism." Godwin was particularly fond of *DQ*, which he described as the "most admirable book in the world," and at least some reflection of DQ can be seen in the protagonist of his best-known novel, *Things as They Are; or, The Adventures of Caleb Williams* (1794, revised several times through 1831). Godwin admired *DQ*, saw the world in terms of chivalry and romance, and sometimes explicitly saw himself as a quixotic in his controversial defense of enlightenment idealism. It was as a perceived fanatic that he was excoriated in Charles *Lucas's *The Infernal Quixote* (1801).

Goethe, Johann Wolfgang von (1749–1832). German poet, dramatist, novelist, theoretician, and scientist. Goethe was the greatest figure of German classicism and the most important European writer of the period. His celebrated and influential novel *Die Leiden des jungen Werthers* (1774; *The Sorrows of Young Werther*) deals, among other things, with the quixotic theme of books: the power of reading, the influence of books on readers, and the relationship between literature and life. Perhaps as much as any novel ever written (even more than *Amadís de Gaula*), this one inspired widespread imitation of the tragic romantic hero, to the point of becoming the pretext for a number of suicides. *Wilhelm Meisters Lehrjahre* (1795–96; *Wilhelm Meister's Apprenticeship*) contains frequent references to MC and DQ and makes extensive use of the sort of metafictional play, mock-historical concerns with textual accuracy, and literary self-consciousness that originates with MC. The figure of Mignon from that novel bears considerable resemblance to Preciosa from *Gitanilla*, a similarity not unexpected, given Goethe's admiration of the *Novelas*. Ludwig *Tieck specifically derived his concept of romantic irony from MC's *DQ*, *Sterne's *Tris-

tram Shandy, and Goethe's *Wilhelm Meister*. And, of course, there are those who would find similarities between DQ and Goethe's *Faust*: both men, nearing 50 years of age, devote themselves to a particular kind of reading, which has the effect of transforming their lives. One can even point out similarities between SP and Mephistopheles as reality instructors for DQ and Faust. Goethe's play *Der Triumph der Empfindsamkeit* (*The Triumph of Sentimentalism*) is about a sentimental (and quixotic) prince named Oronaro who is in love with an unusual DT: a life-size doll made in the image of the woman he loves and that he cherishes more than the beloved herself. Further, the doll is stuffed with popular sentimental books, including the author's own *Werther*. In a scene clearly based on the inquisition of books in *DQ* I, 6, King Andrason, whose role is comparable to that of the priest Pero Pérez in *DQ*, examines, discusses, and condemns to the flames the books taken from the doll.

Bibliography: J. A. Bertrand, *Cervantes en el país de Fausto* (Madrid: Ediciones Cultura Hispánica, 1950); and Joseph Bickermann, *Don Quijote y Fausto, los héroes y las obras*, trans. Félix García (Barcelona: Ediciones Araluce, 1932).

Gogol, Nikolay Vasilievich (1809–52). Russian novelist, short-story writer, and dramatist. It has long been affirmed that Gogol traveled in Spain and spoke Spanish, but actual proof for these assertions is lacking. Gogol's *Mertvye dushi* (1842; *Dead Souls*) was, according to its author, specifically conceived, at least in part, after Pushkin's suggestion that he write a novel in the style of *DQ*, and it was written as a Russian parallel to MC's ridicule of knight-errantry. The protagonist, Chichikov, buys and sells the 'souls' of dead serfs; he is only marginally quixotic in comparison with other literary figures (or even with the explicitly quixotic Kostanzoglo in the same novel), but the novel has a certain ironic tone, sense of humor, and episodic structure reminiscent of *DQ*. It is also clear that *Coloquio* was part of the inspiration for Gogol's *Zapiski sumasshedshego* (1835; *Diary of a Madman*) in which a mad office clerk (who imagines himself to be the king of Spain) overhears two dogs talking and learns that they also write letters to one another. He manages to locate and read the satiric letters, which recall the spirit of MC's critical dogs.

Bibliography: Bruce T. Holl, "Gogol's Captain Kopeikin and Cervantes Captive Captain: A Case of Metaparody," *The Russian Review* 55 (1996): 681–91.

Golandia. Possibly Gotland, but perhaps a purely imaginary island. In *Persiles* I, 11, it is the island in the Baltic Sea sparsely inhabited by Christians, where there is an inn in which Periandro and company take refuge.

Gold escudos [Escudos de oro], 200. The amount of money promised to SP by Ricote in *DQ* II, 54, if he helps him retrieve his buried treasure. SP refuses the offer. It is also the same amount of money given to SP by the duke's majordomo in II, 57–58, as DQ and SP prepare to leave the castle.

Gold from the Tiber. *Tiber.

Goldaraz Campo, Fermín. Spanish poet. Goldaraz Campo's unusual *Peleas quijotescas* (1964; *Quixotic Battles*) is a book of just over 100 verse passages ranging in length from a few lines to several pages. Almost all of the lines are octosyllabic, and the *redondilla* is the most frequent verse form. The subjects of the passages include specific episodes of *DQ*, *DQ*-related matters from the press that have caught the author's attention, and items of pure whimsy. So we have, for example, passages that describe DQ's freeing of the galley slaves and his battle with the Knight of the Mirrors; but there are also passages that consist of a conversation between two wild boars and a televised interview with SP. The tone throughout is very lighthearted.

Bibliography: Fermín Goldaraz Campo, *Peleas quijotescas* (Barcelona: Tipografía Emporium, 1964).

Golden Age [Siglo de Oro; Edad de Oro]. The Golden Age of Spanish culture and history in general, and literature in particular, is an ill-defined period of nearly two centuries including most of the sixteenth and seventeenth centuries. Its beginning might be designated by the landmark year of 1492, when the two most important Christian kingdoms of the Iberian peninsula, Castile and Aragon, united by the 1479 marriage of Fernando and Isabel, conquered Granada, the last stronghold of the Muslims in Spain, in January, thus successfully bringing to a close the seven-century reconquest of the peninsula. This political union made it possible, really for the first time in history, to talk and write of a single political entity—Spain—instead of the various kingdoms of the peninsula. In the same year, the expulsion of the Jews in March emblematically represented the preoccupation with religious and cultural purity that would be characteristic of the age. And, finally, with these major steps out of the way, in April the *Catholic Monarchs acceded to the requests of the Genoese navigator, Christopher Columbus, to undertake an unprecedented voyage west in search of the fabulous Indies. This cluster of events marks the beginning of the century-long hegemony of Spain in Europe and the western world. Spain was propelled with unprecedented swiftness from a vague idea to the political reality that was at the heart of an empire that exercised global power to an extent never before seen in Western history, far exceeding the empires of ancient Rome or modern Britain. From its small home base, and with but a rudimentary technology, the Spanish monarchs maintained sovereignty over their far-flung but surprisingly coherent collection of colonies for nearly three centuries. Former Spanish colonies throughout the world still feature churches, civic buildings, and parks of great beauty and grandeur that remain from the age of Spain's control—municipal structures that have no counterparts in the former English, French, or Dutch colonies. The nation-building project, the self-defining enterprise, and the acquisition of a consciousness of who they were and what they were called to do became the implicit concern of all Spaniards in the Renaissance. In the sixteenth century, under the reigns of Carlos V (1517–56) and Felipe II (1556–98), Spain—with its estimated ten mil-

lion inhabitants—dominated European politics, warfare, the economy, and the arts as had no other country before it. The shipments of gold and silver from the New World seemed to bring a constant flow of riches (about 20 percent of the bullion from the colonies went directly to the crown). The crowning achievement in the arenas of both politics and religion was the great victory over the Turks in the battle of Lepanto (in which MC served valiantly) in 1571. The Spanish military forces had a well-deserved reputation of invincibility. The Spanish *army, was honed into a great fighting force during the wars of Granada and in Italy by Gonzalo *Hernández de Córdoba, known as *el Gran Capitán* (the Great Captain), early in the sixteenth century; it was undefeated for a century and a half until the battle of Rocroi in 1643. There was a strong sense of patriotism and manifest destiny as God's chosen people. The spirit of the age is reflected in a famous sonnet by Hernando de *Acuña, addressed to the Spanish monarch (probably Carlos V, but, since its date of composition is uncertain, perhaps to Felipe II), in which a glorious universal Spanish rule is envisioned in the line 'one monarch, one empire, and one sword.' Spaniards were convinced that Spain was the logical successor to ancient Greece and Rome and was literally destined to rule the world (after forcing the demonic Protestants to return to the fold and conquering the Islamic infidels in Africa and the Middle East). In literature, the great poetry of Garcilaso de la Vega, Fray Luis de León, and Saint Juan de la Cruz in the sixteenth century, followed by the equally great lyrics of Lope de Vega, Góngora, and Quevedo in the seventeenth, do indeed mark this period as the most outstanding flowering of poetic achievement in Spain's history. The achievements of the Spanish theater of the late-sixteenth and the seventeenth century, by far the most vigorous and influential in Europe, and led by the works of Lope de Vega, Tirso de Molina, and Calderón de la Barca, have never been equaled. And in prose fiction, the Spanish Renaissance and Baroque periods represent the most original period of experimentation and achievement in the history of Europe, with the writing of many of the greatest sentimental, chivalric, pastoral, historical, and adventure romances of all time, together with the stunning achievement of the novel in dialogue (*Celestina*), the picaresque novel (*Lazarillo*), *DQ*, and *Novelas*. No other European nation of the time matches the literary achievements of Spain in its Golden Age. Works of Spanish literature (*Cárcel de amor*, *Celestina*, *Amadís*, *Lazarillo*, *Diana*, *Guzmán*, *DQ*, *Novelas*, *Persiles*, and many more) were translated into other European languages and were much admired and imitated, but virtually no European literature except Italian (Petrarch, Boccaccio, Ariosto, Castiglione, and so on) was translated into Spanish. The center of painting gradually shifted from Italy to Spain, particularly in the work of El Greco and Velázquez (but also including the notable achievements of Ribera, Zurbarán, Murillo, and others). Velázquez is arguably the single most original and influential European painter before the twentieth century. Spanish was the dominant language throughout Europe, much as English is in the world today; for example, it is estimated that in seventeenth-century France, there were published some 400 Spanish grammar books, dictionaries, original language texts, and bilingual editions (see MC's remarks on the universality of Spanish in France in *Persiles* III, 13). Most of the rest of Europe affected the fashions, manners, and values of Spain, even as they criticized Spanish arrogance, pride, and barbarity. But things started to fall apart toward the end of the sixteenth century. The disastrous defeat of the Invincible *Armada in 1588 was followed by other military and political setbacks; there was a steep decline in the supply of precious metals from the Indies; and by the time Felipe II died in 1598, to be succeeded by his weak, frivolous, and ineffective son Felipe III, there was a widespread feeling of *desengaño, or disillusionment. Though most of the vigor of Spain's greatest period was long gone by the middle of the seventeenth century (a convenient date to cite is 1659, the year of the Peace of the Pyrenees between Spain and France, in which Spain made major concessions), it is customary to date the end of the Spanish Golden Age in 1681, when Pedro

*Calderón de la Barca, the last great writer of the period, died. Today, instead of terms like Renaissance, Baroque, and Golden Age, many scholars prefer to write of the "Early Modern Period." Terminology is important, as any word or phrase used to describe a historical era carries with it implicit connotations of power and authority.

Bibliography: Anthony J. Cascardi, *Ideologies of History in the Spanish Golden Age* (University Park: Pennsylvania State University Press, 1998); R. Trevor Davies, *The Golden Century of Spain: 1501–1621* (London: Macmillan, 1937); Marcellin Defourneaux, *La vida cotidiana en la España del Siglo de Oro*, trans. Ricardo Cano Gavina and Aurora Bel Gaya (Barcelona: Argos Vergara, 1983); Antonio Domínguez Ortiz, *The Golden Age of Spain, 1516–1659*, trans. James Casey (New York: Basic Books, 1971); John H. Elliott, *Imperial Spain: 1469–1716* (New York: St. Martin's Press, 1963); John H. Elliott, *Spain and Its World, 1500–1700: Selected Essays* (New Haven, CT: Yale University Press, 1989); Víctor Infantes, "La narrativa del Renacimiento: estado de las cuestiones," in *La invención de la novela: Seminario hispano-francés organizado por la Casa de Velázquez (noviembre 1992–junio 1993)*, ed. Jean Canavaggio (Madrid: Casa de Velázquez, 1999), 13–48; Tom Lewis and Francisco J. Sánchez, eds., *Culture and the State in Spain, 1550–1850* (New York: Garland, 1999); John Lynch, *Spain 1516–1598: From Nation State to World Empire* (Oxford: Oxford University Press, 1991); and Anthony Pagden, *Lords of All the World: Ideologies of Empire in Spain, Britain, and France, 1492–1830* (New Haven, CT: Yale University Press, 1995).

Golden Age, Myth of the. The myth of an Edenic past, popular in Greek and Roman culture where it has its greatest expression in Ovid, Hesiod, and Virgil. According to Hesiod, history was divided into four ages, those of gold, silver, bronze, and iron. The age of gold was always identified as being some ill-defined time in the distant past. Every historical period has a vision of a long-gone golden age of peace and harmony. The idyllic pastoral world of poetry and prose romance, as in *Galatea*, is a fundamental expression of the values of the age of gold. The topic was a popular one in the Renaissance, and DQ's speech on the subject when he is with the goatherds (I, 11) is one of the finest expressions of the myth. In the ancient time of abundance and harmony, says DQ, women feared no threat to their virtue, but with the passing of time and as we approached our current age of iron, the order of chivalry was introduced to provide necessary defense for innocent people, especially women. Thus it is that DQ links his own chosen profession with one of the great cultural myths of all time. An irony of the presentation of this topic in *DQ* is that the illiterate goatherds understand little of DQ's elegant speech, and so the effect is lost on his audience, even if it is not on the reader. See also Aurelio's substantial speech on the same subject in *Tratos* 2, Fray Antonio's brief comment with reference to his previous life as a *pícaro* in *Rufián* 2, and Clemente's evocation of the Golden Age in *Pedro* 1.

Bibliography: Henry Kamen, "Golden Age, Iron Age: A Conflict of Concepts in the Renaissance," *Journal of Medieval and Renaissance Studies* 4 (1974): 135–55; Harry Levin, *The Myth of the Golden Age in the Renaissance*, (New York: Oxford University Press, 1969); and Geoffrey L. Stagg, "*Illo tempore*: Don Quixote's Discourse on the Golden Age and Its Antecedents," in "*La Galatea,*" de Cervantes—cuatrocientos años después (Cervantes y lo pastoril), ed. Juan Bautista Avalle-Arce (Newark, DE: Juan de la Cuesta, 1985), 71–90.

Golden apples [Manzanas de oro]. In Greek myth, the golden apples that grew in the garden of *Hesperides and were guarded by the dragon Ladon, and were stolen by Heracles as one of his 12 *labors. See *Celoso*.

Golden Ass, The. *Apuleius.

Goldknopf, David. Theorist of the novel. In *The Life of the Novel* (1972), Goldknopf makes the usual "rise of the novel" assumption that the novel was something new that appeared for the first time in England in the eighteenth century. For Goldknopf, what was truly original and innovative about this new genre was "a dynamic, responsive *internal node* of organization: the 'I.'" Although Goldknopf recognizes that the "I" was discovered in the Renaissance, he believes that it was not until the eighteenth century that this discovery was manifest in the

writing of fiction: "A quite special set of conditions had to assemble before the novel could come into being. The central condition has been, it seems to me, the modern state of consciousness created by the entwining of the mind's inward and outward searchings. Time entered this process as biography: units of potentiality stretched between birth and death. The unique conjunction of social circumstances which catalyzed the emergence of the novel early in the eighteenth century was in itself, in part, the outgrowth of the modern state of consciousness." Although some of the ideas expressed here resonate with concepts and vocabulary central to M. M. *Bakhtin's theory of the novel, it never occurs to Goldknopf that the very conditions he describes are more characteristic of the sixteenth than the eighteenth century. Goldknopf's "discovery" that the I-narrator is of such importance in the novel is presented in complete ignorance of the Spanish *picaresque novel, which, beginning with *Lazarillo de Tormes* (1554) and lasting for about a century, featured exactly the sort of first-person narrator Goldknopf finds so new in the English eighteenth century. There is nothing in Goldknopf's concept of the novel that is not fully present in the dual Spanish novel tradition of the picaresque and *DQ* (neither of which is even mentioned in Goldknopf's book): realistic fictions that present themselves as history, with a narrating *I* that reveals a modern state of consciousness. The novel was alive and well in Spain long before David Goldknopf suspects.

Bibliography: David Goldknopf, *The Life of the Novel* (Chicago: University of Chicago Press, 1972).

Goldsmith, Oliver (1730–74). Irish essayist, novelist, and dramatist. Goldsmith's once very popular and influential novel *The Vicar of Wakefield* (written in 1761–62, published in 1766) features the quixotic Dr. Primrose, who is a link between *Fielding's Parson Adams and *Dickens's Mister Pickwick. The idealistic cleric lives imaginatively dedicated to his ideals. His defense of the innocent in opposition to the powerful local squire lands him in jail, where he believes his fellow inmates to be as innocent as he is himself (a recollection of

DQ's encounter with the galley slaves in I, 22), but never dampens his spirit.

Goleta, La. A fortress situated strategically at the entrance of the Lake of Tunis and thus a natural defensive position for that city. In 1535 Carlos V, with the assistance of the naval forces of Andrea Doria, led an expedition against La Goleta, captured it, and then went on to take *Tunis. Some 20,000 Christian prisoners were released. Even though La Goleta was strengthened by Don Juan of Austria in 1573, the fortress, together with the city of Tunis, fell to the Turks in 1574 after a long siege. Don Juan's attempt to retake Tunis and La Goleta later that same year was unsuccessful. See *Amante*; *DQ* I, 39–40, 42; *Tratos* 4.

Golfo de las Yeguas. *Horse Latitudes.

Goliath [Golías, Goliat]. The legendary Old Testament giant killed by David. See *DQ* I, prologue; *DQ* II, 1; *Poesías* 25.

Gomecillos, Licenciado. In *Retablo*, the governor of the town where the marvelous show is produced; in a series of asides, he admits that he can see nothing of the show being described.

Gomes Leal, António Duarte (1848–1921). Portuguese poet. Gomes Leal is perhaps the most extravagant, inconsistent, and enigmatic figure in turn-of-the-century Portuguese literature. In his book *Claridades do Sul* (1875; *Southern Lights*), Gomes Leal included a poem entitled "D. Quichote" and later, in 1902, he published a poem entitled "Sam Francisco d'Assiz e D. Quixote." Gomes Leal's DQ is a romantic and noble figure.

Gómez Arias (fourteenth century). A knight who became famous in a poem about a young woman who was seduced and then abandoned by him. The maid Cristina cites the song as she teases her mistress in *Viejo*.

Gómez de la Serna, Ramón (1888–1963). Spanish novelist, essayist, and writer of *greguerías* (pig-squeals), a series of thousands of unique and unclassifiable aphoristic metaphors, the work for which he is best known. An active and flamboyant figure in Spanish intellectual life in the early part of the twentieth century, Gómez de la Serna founded a famous *tertulia* (informal literary discussion group) at the Café Pombo in Madrid. His novel *El caballero del hongo gris* (1928; *The Knight of the Derby Hat*) is a loosely structured tale of a man named Leonardo who buys a new derby, and sallies forth 'into the street converted into what he was to be for the rest of his life: the Knight of the Derby Hat.' In Paris, he founded a DQ society to further Spanish-French cultural relations.

Bibliography: Rodolfo Cardona, *Ramón: A Study of Gómez de la Serna and His Works* (New York: Eliseo Torres, 1957); and Rita Mazzetti Gardiol, *Ramón Gómez de la Serna* (New York: Twayne, 1974).

Gómez (de Luque), Gonzalo. Spanish poet, author of *Libro primero de los famosos hechos del príncipe Celidón de Iberia* (1583; *First Book of the Famous Deeds of Prince Celidón de Iberia*), a long (40 cantos) chivalric romance in verse, for which he is praised in Calliope's song in *Galatea* 6.

Gómez de Sandoval y Rojas, Don Diego, Conde de Saldaña (ca. 1584–1632). Spanish nobleman; the son of the Duke of Lerma and *privado* to Felipe III. He ran an academy of poets in his home in Madrid, which was attended by MC. He is praised in *Parnaso* 2.

Gómez, Licenciado Don Gabriel. A lawyer who became a judge in Lima. He is listed among the good poets in *Parnaso* 2.

Gómez Valderrama, Pedro (1923–92). Colombian diplomat, poet, novelist, and essayist. Gómez Valderrama frequently expressed interest in and admiration for MC, whom he referred to as 'our maestro,' and he invoked the figure of the *pícaro*-puppeteer Maese Pedro in his short-story collection entitled *El retablo de maese Pedro* (1967), although none of the nine stories is explicitly related to *DQ*. One of Gómez Valderrama's best-known fictions, however, is the lead story in his collection *La procesión de los ardientes* (1973; *The Proces-*

sion of the Ardent), "En un lugar de las Indias" (first published separately in 1970; "In a Place in the Indies"), whose very title evokes the first line of *DQ* I. Don Alonso (Quijano) writes a story about the life of Don Miguel (de Cervantes) in America. Central to the story is MC's request to be appointed to a position in America, which in real life was denied, but in the story is granted at the same time that a similar petition by Don Alonso is denied. Doña Catalina chooses not to accompany her husband to the colonies, and so MC arrives alone in America. Over time, he takes as his lover a mulatta named Piedad and sinks into alcoholism and depression. On his deathbed, it is revealed that he has been writing a long manuscript, but Piedad has used the pages for kindling. This clever rewriting of history, reversal of roles between author and character, and displacement of the action of the original story to a different continent make this one of the most original and interesting short quixotic fictions ever written.

Bibliography: Luis Correa-Díaz, "América como Dulcinea: La *salida* transatlántica de Cervantes," *Hispanic Journal* 21 (2000): 459–80; and Luis Correa-Díaz, "El Quijote Indiano/Caribeño novela de caballería y crónica de Indias," *Anales Cervantinos* 34 (1998): 85–123.

Gonella, Pietro [Gonela]. The buffoon of the duke of Ferrara in the fifteenth century. Gonella became a popular figure in Renaissance culture, as a skinny clown accompanied by an equally skinny horse. In *DQ* I, 1, Rocinante is compared to Gonella's horse.

Góngora y Argote, Don Luis de (1561–1627) (Magno cordobés, Poeta que haya hecho alguna sátira a esa señora Angélica [Great Cordoban, Poet who wrote a satire about that Señora Angélica]). Considered by many as the greatest poet ever to write in the Spanish language, Góngora's cultured, cultivated, artificial style was both highly praised and viciously attacked during his lifetime. Góngora's most characteristic poetry is characterized by abundant neologisms, a Latinized vocabulary, an intricate syntax, difficult and original metaphors and images, frequent mythological and historical allusions, and con-

ceptual subtlety. The term *culterano* (perhaps maliciously intended to suggest *luterano*, Lutheran) was often applied to his work in recognition of the cultured and learned background needed to understand it (the term *gongorismo* means obscure and hermetic poetry written in imitation of the style of Góngora and as such is a virtual synonym for *culteranismo*). His *Soledades* (*Solitudes*) and *Fábula de Polifemo and Galatea* (*Fable of Polyphemus and Galatea*), both written about 1613, are long poems that best represent his characteristic style. Vilified by his rivals and critics such as Francisco de *Quevedo, who wrote brilliant and deadly satiric sonnets in parody and criticism of his work, Góngora never failed to respond in kind. A multifaceted writer, Góngora wrote hundreds of short, simple lyric poems and *ballads in the traditional Spanish meters (especially the octosyllabic line), about 200 sonnets, and the two long poems mentioned above. MC may be counted among Góngora's admirers; in Calliope's song in *Galatea* 6, he refers to the poet's 'rare, bright and matchless wit.' No poet receives lengthier or higher praise than Góngora in *Parnaso* 2 and again in *Parnaso* 7 where he is referred to as the "magno cordobés" ('the great Cordovan'). Góngora's famous ballad *Angélica y Medoro* (1602) is alluded to as a satire (not really an accurate description) by the barber in the discussion with DQ in II, 1.

Bibliography: Marsha Suzan Collins, *The "Soledades," Góngora's Masque of the Imagination* (Columbia: University of Missouri Press, 2002); David William Foster and Virginia Ramos Foster, *Luis de Góngora* (New York: Twayne, 1973); María Cristina Quintero, "The Cervantine Subtext in Góngora's *Las firmezas de Isabela*," *Cervantes* 11, no. 2 (1991): 59–67; and Mary Gaylord Randel, "Reading the Pastoral Palimpsest: *La Galatea* in Góngora's *Soledad Primera*," *Symposium* (1982): 71–91.

Gongorismo. *Culteranismo.

González de Bobadilla, Bernardo. Spanish poet and romance writer. His pastoral romance entitled *Primera parte de las ninfas y pastores de Henares* (1587; *First Part of the Nymphs and Shepherds of Henares*), or simply *Ninfas de Henares*, as it appears in *DQ*, is condemned to the flames in the scrutiny of books in *DQ* I, 6. Like Bernardo de la *Vega, the author of *Ninfas de Henares y pastores* is cited in *Parnaso* 4 by a poet from the ship of those not chosen to make the trip to Parnassus as an example of one unjustly ignored. See also *DQ* I, 9.

González (de Salazar), Doña Alfonsa. Spanish nun and perhaps a relative of Catalina de *Palacios, MC's wife. Miguel Toledano dedicated a book entitled *Minerva sacra* (1616; *Sacred Minerva*) to her and MC contributed one of the prefatory sonnets (*Poesías* 35).

González Durán, Diego. *Durán, Diego.

González, Fernán (915–970). Spanish military leader who united forces to form a unified kingdom of Castile and became one of the legendary figures in the reconquest of the Iberian Peninsula. He is the subject of the anonymous thirteenth-century poem entitled *Poema de Fernán González*, where his victories over Muslims are described in terms of miracles. See *DQ* I, 49.

González, Genaro (1949–). Mexican-American novelist. González's semiautobiographical novel *The Quixote Cult* (1998) tells the story of a Chicano named De la O, who gets idealistically involved in the Mexican American National Organization (MANO) and tries to organize migrant workers. The *DQ* connection comes in when De la O and other students read and discuss the novel in class and then take it as a constant point of reference in their work. With chapter titles that include "The Unbeatable Foe," "Kid Quixote," "Working within the Windmills," and "Adios, Dulce Nena," together with a car named Roci (for Rocinante), and a variety of plays on words and allusions, MC's novel is evoked throughout the text. When De la O is accused of being part of a cult (MANO), he muses, "Afterwards I give his comments more thought, and they don't seem that farfetched. After all, I decide, Christianity started as a cult, one that caught on. It's the same with Quixote: Most people who admire his ideals would never dream of actually putting them into practice." The idealized character of Nena (= DT) comments late in the novel, "Some say Cervantes saw Quixote as ridiculous and out of touch, which is how people in his time saw him too. All that stuff about noble causes and fighting against all odds, all that's what we want to believe now. . . . Isn't that the most unromantic thing you ever heard?" Recontextualizing the characters and theme of *DQ* in the socially active world of marginalized Chicanos in late-twentieth-century America, González demonstrates again the universality of MC's novel.

Bibliography: Genaro González, *The Quixote Cult* (Houston, TX: Arte Público Press, 1998).

González, Miguel (1918–). Cuban-American poet. González's *Don Quijote en America* (1988; *Don Quixote in America*) begins with a poem with the identical title as the volume. In it, the poet evokes MC, compares him with many great Spanish American heroes (Bolívar, Hidalgo, Sarmiento, Martí, and others), and places himself in the same tradition. Later in the book, his pair of sonnets to DQ and Christ continues the same line of thought.

Bibliography: Miguel González, *Don Quijote en America* (Madrid: Betania, 1988).

González Perera, Mario. Uruguayan writer. The lead story in González Perera's *Del Quijote a Gardel* (2000; *From Don Quixote to Gardel*) is "La peña de los viernes" ("The Thursday Meeting Group"), a brief story in which the narrator is initiated into the 'Order of the Knights of the Round Table' in a group of intellectuals who meet on Thursdays. His initiation is to answer two questions: 1) why even hungry polar bears do not eat penguins and 2) who said the famous words 'They are barking, Sancho, the sign for us to ride.' He is stumped by the first, but knows that DQ is the answer to the second. It turns out that the first is easy: polar bears inhabit the Arctic and penguins the Antarctic. He refuses to believe that he is wrong about the second and is frustrated to learn, after much study, that the second, a fairly common phrase, is found nowhere in MC's works.

Bibliography: Mario González Perera, *Del Quijote a Gardel* (n.p.: Contexto, 2000).

González, Señora. In *DQ* II, 31, the name that SP first uses when speaking to Doña *Rodríguez upon arrival at the duke's country home.

Good Fame [Buena Fama]. In *Casa* 2, allegorical figure conjured up by Malgesí.

Good Fortune [Buena Fortuna]. In *Persiles* II, 10, one of the four boats in the fishermen's regatta, the one that wins the race.

Good Lineage [Buen Linaje]. In *DQ* II, 20, one of the eight nymphs who participates in the celebration of *Camacho's wedding.

Gorbea Lemmi, Eusebio de (1881–1945). Spanish novelist, essayist, and dramatist. Gorbea's *Don Quijote de Vivar* (1928) begins with an introduction by the author/editor in which he describes how archival research brought to light a manuscript written by Per Abbat, the fourteenth-century copyist of the manuscript of the *Poema de Mío Cid*. The work consists of an autobiographical account by an elderly monk who in his youth had been associated with Ruy Díaz de Vivar, El Cid. At one point, El Cid makes a suggestive remark about a knight-errant who might live and fight for an ideal, rather than for booty and conquest. This fascinating concept, together with the narrator's haunting recollection of a beautiful young woman he had once seen (and whom he later sees in the figure of a young girl, a friend of his daughter's, named Dulce but called Dulcinea), gives him the idea of a different kind of knight-errant. He begins to write of this imaginary figure, starting with the phrase, 'In a village . . . ' But the remainder of his story could not be found.
    Bibliography: Eusebio de Gorbea Lemmi, *Don Quijote de Vivar* (Madrid: Prensa Moderna, 1928).

Gordian knot [Nudo gordiano]. In Greek legend, a knot tied by King Gordius of Phrygia that, according to an oracle, could only be untied by the person who would become the ruler of Asia. When Alexander the Great went to Gordium, he attempted to untie the knot, could not, and so drew out his sword and simply cut it. The phrase 'to cut the Gordian knot' therefore means to find a quick, efficient solution to a difficult problem. See *DQ* II, 19; *Entretenida* 3; *Gallardo* 1.

Gorky, Maksim (Aleksey Maksimovich Peshkov 1858–1936). Russian short-story writer, novelist, and dramatist. In 1910, an article on "The Quixotism of Russian Intellectuals" was published anonymously under the initials A. M. Since Gorky often wrote under pseudonyms, and since the initials correspond to those of his own first two names, it has often been suggested that he is the author of the essay. The thesis of the essay is that Russian intellectuals virtually personify the quixotic motivation of defending the downtrodden and abused; Russian intellectuals are ever ready to take on powerful enemies no matter who they may be.

Gorra milanesa. *Milanese cap.

Gospel(s) [Evangelio(s)]. The New Testament Christian Gospels (books relating to the life and teachings of Jesus) in general, rather than any particular book of the bible. See *DQ* I, prologue; *Gitanilla*; *Persiles* III, 20.

Gothic letters [Letras góticas]. Presumably medieval manuscript writing (*old physician).

Goths [Godos]. The Visigoths, one of the Christianized Germanic tribes—barbarians, in Roman eyes—that brought about the final destruction of the Roman Empire and overran Europe. The Visigoths settled in the Iberian Peninsula in the fifth century and dominated the area until the Muslim invasion in 711. The civic and religious capital of the Visigoths was Toledo. It was traditional for Spaniards who claimed *purity of blood to trace their ancestry back to the Goths as proof that there was no trace of Jewish or Islamic inheritance in their lineage. See *Persiles* III, 8.

Governor [Gobernador]. 1. The Florentine official who arrests the escaping Leonela in *Curioso* (*DQ* I, 35). **2.** In *Persiles* I, 3, the leader of the barbarians, who buys Periandro from Arnaldo. **3.** In *Persiles* III, 1, the official in Lisbon (he is also the archbishop of the city of Braga) who welcomes Periandro and the other travelers to the city. **4.** In *Persiles* IV, 6, the administrator in Rome who intervenes in the bidding war between Prince Arnaldo and the duke of Nemurs for a painting of Auristela. He receives the painting as a gift from Periandro, who purchases it to settle the dispute (IV, 7). In IV, 13, he has Pirro Calabrés arrested and, within four days, executed.

Goya, Francisco de (1746–1828). Spanish artist. Goya submitted an illustration (of the braying aldermen episode, *DQ* II, 25) for the great 1780 edition of DQ published by the Royal Spanish Academy, but it was rejected (William *Hogarth had suffered a similar fate earlier in England). Years later, a more mature Goya included among his *Caprichos* (*Caprices*) a brilliant scene of DQ reading his romances of chivalry with fantastic figures (representing his thoughts and fantasies) in the background.
Bibliography: John J. Ciofalo, "Goya's Enlightenment Protagonist—A Quixotic Dreamer of Reason," *Eighteenth-Century Studies* 30 (1997): 421–36.

Goytisolo, Juan (1931–). Spanish novelist, short-story writer, and essayist. Goytisolo calls MC 'the precursor to whom I feel myself the closest' and frequently cites MC in his writings about fiction. According to Goytisolo, he and all other novelists 'Cervantize' even when not aware of it. Goytisolo's *Las semanas del jardín* (1997; *Weeks in the Garden*) takes its title from MC's often promised but never written book of that name (*Semanas del jardín*). The metafictional work is presented as the collaborative effort of 28 storytellers—one for each letter of the Arabic alphabet—who get together in a Cervantine garden to tell the story of an apocryphal poet named Eusebio. One of the purposes of the collaborators is to 'put an end to the oppressive notion of the Author'; "Juan Goytisolo" is merely a name invented for the purpose of publishing the book. (*Note:* Spanish novelist Rafael Sánchez Ferlosio also published a book entitled *Las semanas del jardín*, 1974, but it is a collection of journalistic essays, not a fiction.)

Bibliography: Juan Goytisolo, *Disidencias* (Barcelona: Seix Barral, 1989): and Pina Rosa Piras, "El cervantismo de Juan Goytisolo," *Cervantes* 19, no. 2 (1999): 167–79.

Graces [Gracias]. In Greek myth, three minor goddesses who personified grace and beauty, enhancing the enjoyment of life. Called Euphrosyne (Eufrosine), Aglaia (Aglae), and Thalia (Talía), they accompanied both Aphrodite, Eros, and the Muses, gave wisdom its charm, and moderated the influence of wine and spirits. See *Galatea* 1.

Gracián Dantisco (de Antisco), Lucas (1543–87). Scholar, writer, and censor, brother of Tomás. His best-known work was the popular and frequently reprinted manual of courtly behavior entitled *El Galateo español* (1586; *The Spanish Gallant*), an adaptation of Giovanni della Casa's *Galateo* (1558). He granted the approval to print for MC's *Galatea*. Gracián Dantisco probably formed part of the circle of personal friends of MC.

Gracián (Dantisco), Tomás de (1558–1621). Spanish poet and book censor, brother of Lucas. He is praised in Calliope's song in *Galatea* 6 and again in *Parnaso* 7.

Gracián, Juan. The printer who published MC's first book, *Galatea*.

Gracián y Morales, Baltasar (1601–57). Spanish moralist and novelist. In addition to being the author of a number of nonfiction treatises, Gracián is best remembered for his long, moralistic, and allegorical fiction entitled *El Criticón* (published in three parts, 1651, 1653, 1657; *The Critic*). It is the story of the journey-quest of a father and son through Europe in search of their wife and mother. The fiction is largely a pretext for a long series of moral, philosophic, and social commentaries. Although he makes comments on a number of writers of the Golden Age, Gracián never mentions MC. But he does express his opinion about fictions in general, calling them trash for the ignorant; the romances of chivalry come in for particular invective, and, in what is often considered an indirect remark about *DQ*, he states that some have tried to criticize this foolish genre but have only wound up writing things even more foolish. Earlier, in *El discreto* (1646; *The Discreet Man*) Gracián expressed his disdain for *DQ* in an offhand comment that not all crazy knights come from La Mancha.

Bibliography: Alban K. Forcione, "El desposeimiento del ser en la literatura renacentista: Cervantes, Gracián y los desafíos de *Nemo*," *Nueva Revista de Filología Hispánica* 34 (1985–86): 654–90; and Roberto Mansberger Amorós, "El *Quijote* y *el Criticón* como antiquijote a la luz de la doctrina del juicio del ingenio: Apuntes para una interpretación," *Anales Cervantinos* 33 (1995–97): 337–46.

Gracias. *Graces.

Gradas. *Steps.

Gradaso. A pagan king in Ariosto's *Orlando Furioso*. See *Viejo*.

Graham, Kenneth. American novelist. Graham's *Don Quijote en Yanquilandia* (1955; *Don Quixote in Yankeeland*) is translated from English, but the original seems never to have been published. It is the story of how DQ, in his tomb, reads that George Washington has been proclaimed first president of the United States and comes back to life in order to go, with SP, to the new nation in order to meet Washington. The famous Spanish pair become celebrity tourists. SP becomes mayor of Harlem, with millions of *micomicones* (African Americans) as his subjects. DQ becomes an advisor to President True-man (Truman). The novel gets ever more extravagant: DQ and SP meet Al Capone in Chicago, have a powwow with an Indian tribe, participate in a cattle roundup in Texas, make a film about themselves in Hollywood, and fly themselves back east in a small plane, and DQ delivers a pompous speech to Congress. The extravagant silliness is only occasionally made palatable with a modicum of real humor. Perhaps the funniest moment in the book is when the cast for the film is listed: DQ and SP as themselves, a couple of fictional male actors, and Marilyn Monroe as DT, Bette Davis as Marcela, Greer Garson as Luscinda, Lana Turner as Dorotea, Rita Hayworth as the duchess, and Carmen Miranda as Teresa Panza.

Bibliography: Kenneth Graham, *Don Quijote en Yanquilandia*, trans. Ignacio Dived (Madrid: Ediciones Ensayos, 1955).

Grajales. In *Guarda*, a friend of the sacristan Lorenzo Pasillas.

Gran Bastardo de Salerno, El (*The Great Bastard of Salerno*). A play supposedly written by an aspiring young poet who talks with MC in *Parnaso* 8.

Gran Bretaña. *Great Britain.

Gran Canaria. One of the Canary Islands, an archipelago of seven islands off the western coast of Africa. The islands were explored and settled by the Spanish primarily in the fifteenth century and have been part of Spain since then. The name *Canaria* is derived from *can* (dog), for a breed of dog native to the islands; the bird, *canary*, was later named after the islands. See *Galatea* 6.

Gran capilludo. *Great hooded one.

Gran Capitán. *Hernández de Córdoba, Gonzalo.

Gran Consejo. *Great Council.

Gran Mameluco de Persia. *Great Mameluke of Persia.

Gran marqués. *Great Marquis.

Gran músico de Tracia. *Orpheus.

Gran Panza, el. *Great Panza, The.

Gran pastor del ancho suelo hispano. *Carlos V.

Gran poeta castellano nuestro. *Garcilaso de la Vega.

Gran Señor. *Great Lord; *Great Turk.

Gran señor de Delo. *Apollo.

Gran Sultana doña Catalina de Oviedo

Gran Sultana doña Catalina de Oviedo, La (Sultana); The Wife of the Great Sultan, Doña Catalina de Oviedo. Fifth play in *Comedias*. It may be a reworking of MC's earlier (lost) play entitled *La gran turquesa* (*The Great Turkish Woman*). The protagonist is based on a historical figure (who may have been Venetian rather than Spanish) who was taken as a captive to Constantinople, where she married the Sultan Murad III. The psychological dilemma faced by Doña Catalina, how to marry a man she loves but who is of a different religion, is treated with delicacy. Less delicate is the virulent anti-Semitic comedy involving the captive Madrigal. The play was staged for the first time in 1992 (*Cuenca, Alberto de).

Act I: As the play opens, two renegades, the Christian Roberto and the Turk Salec, are discussing Turkish customs in Constantinople. An example is provided as the Great Turk Amurates himself passes by and dispenses justice as is his practice. Roberto explains that he is in the city searching for a young man, named Lamberto, who was his pupil and disciple in Prague. Lamberto was about to marry the beautiful Clara, when she was taken captive by the Turks. Roberto believes that Lamberto may have come here in search of Clara. In a change of scene, Mamí and Rustán, two eunuchs, are engaged in conversation. Mamí accuses Rustán of having shielded a beautiful captive Spanish woman in Amurates's harem for some six years. But he, Mamí, is going to denounce Rustán to Amurates. Rustán then talks with Doña Catalina de Oviedo, the captive he has been protecting, and the two of them worry about what may happen when Amurates learns the truth. Mamí tells Amurates about Rustán's betrayal, and Amurates insists on seeing this supposedly great beauty. The captive Madrigal, in a conversation with another Christian, Andrea (a spy who has already been able to gain the freedom of five Christians), tells how he played a trick on a Jew by placing bacon in his cooking pot. The two Christians agree that Jews are an infamous and dirty race, while the Jews rail at Madrigal, their scourge. Meanwhile, Amurates goes to the harem and insists on seeing

Doña Catalina, while Rustán tells him that he has waited until Doña Catalina had regained her health and beauty, which has just been in the last three days, before presenting her to him. Doña Catalina is summoned, and Amurates is immediately awed by her beauty, offering to marry her, name her the Gran Sultana, and turn over to her control of not only him but all of his empire. Although Amurates's first instinct is to execute Rustán for his treachery, he does not do it because Doña Catalina asks him to spare the eunuch. Doña Catalina asks for, and is granted, three days to consider the situation.

Act II: Madrigal is brought before the Gran Cadí, accused of illicit sexual relations with a Muslim woman. He is sentenced to death, but talks his way out of execution by claiming the ability to understand the language of the birds and teach an elephant to speak Turkish within ten days. The ambassador from Persia has an audience with four pashas, who throw him out when he speaks well of Felipe II and Spain. Rustán talks with Doña Catalina about her dilemma, as she insists that she will never give up her religion, even if it costs her life. They are joined by Amurates, who wants to call her Catalina la Otomana, a name that she rejects. As they negotiate the terms of their relationship, Amurates concedes that she can maintain her Christian faith and continue to dress as a Spanish Christian. With this, the marriage is agreed upon. This is followed by a scene between Clara, dressed in Turkish style and calling herself Zaida, and Lamberto, dressed as a Turkish woman and calling himself Zelinda. They worry that they will be caught, she pregnant, and he a man dressed as a woman in Amurates's harem. Madrigal then appears as the elephant instructor, and assures the cadí that the lessons are going well. In response to the cadí's questions about what the birds are saying, he tells him a series of made-up stories. Rustán comes along searching for a Christian tailor who might make dresses for the new Gran Sultana. The cadí cannot believe that a Christian slave has become the wife of Amurates and goes off to verify the fact. Madrigal offers himself as a tailor, but so does an elderly Christian who has overheard the conversation. Madrigal's claim is easily dismissed, and the elderly man begins to take Doña Catalina's measurements. It turns out that this is Doña Catalina's father, and he reproaches her for her decision. She faints, and Amurates, outraged by the effect these two men have had on his beloved, orders them put to death. The act ends with Doña Catalina, unconscious, in the arms of Amurates.

Act III: Mamí tells Rustán that if Doña Catalina had not recovered so quickly, her father and Madrigal would have been killed, but at her request Amurates spared their lives. Doña Catalina again talks with her father and tries to persuade him that her marriage is not an impediment to her maintaining her religion, but he insists that she is committing a mortal sin. Musicians are brought in for a festival, with the music to be Spanish style, rather than Turkish. During the celebration, Madrigal summarizes the life of Doña Catalina in a ballad, placing the action in the year 1600. Madrigal again teases the cadí, promising that for 30 *escudos* he can purchase for him a wonderful parrot just brought from the Indies that can tell marvels, that Madrigal will interpret, of course. The cadí's concern is for heirs to continue the royal line. To that end, Amurates is encouraged to choose a partner (or more than one) from his harem, but after seeing Doña Catalina, no woman is attractive to him. Finally, he is urged to look at two more women from his harem: Zaida (Clara) and Zelinda (Lamberto dressed as a woman). He chooses Lamberto as a mate. Desperate, Zaida-Clara goes to Doña Catalina and tells her of her situation and that of Zelinda-Lamberto, and Doña Catalina promises to help. In a change of scene, Lamberto's sex has been discovered and Amurates orders him killed. But Lamberto invents a tale of having been born a woman, but, admiring everything about men, prayed to become a man, and, sure enough, the Prophet suddenly and miraculously turned her into a man. Amurates is skeptical, but the cadí assures him that such a thing is possible. Doña Catalina then convinces Amurates to eject Clara and Lamberto from the harem, rather than kill anyone, which he does, leaving them to Doña Catalina's disposition. Doña Catalina immediately proposes naming

Lamberto the pasha of Chius, but Amurates goes her one better, naming him pasha of Rhodes. Doña Catalina also promises that if it is heirs Amurates wants, she will gladly provide them for him. Madrigal talks with Roberto and fills him in on what has happened with Doña Catalina, Lamberto and Clara, and so forth. Rustán ends the play addressing the audience and calling the performance a 'new and true story.'

Bibliography: Jean Canavaggio, "Sobre lo cómico en el teatro cervantino: Tristán y Madrigal, bufones *in partibus*," *Nueva Revista de Filología Hispánica* 34 (1985–86): 538–47; Luciano García Lorenzo, "Cervantes, Constantinopla y La Gran Sultana," *Anales Cervantinos* 31 (1993): 201–13; Luciano García Lorenzo, "*La Gran Sultana* de Miguel de Cervantes: adaptación del texto y puesta en escena," *Anales Cervantinos* 32 (1994): 117–36; Ottmar Hegyi, *Cervantes and the Turks: Historical Reality versus Literary Fiction in "La gran sultana" and "El amante liberal"* (Newark, PE: Juan de la Cuesta, 1992); Susana Hernández Araico, "Estreno de *La gran sultana*: teatro de lo otro, amor y humor," *Cervantes* 14, no. 2 (1994): 155–65; Paul Lewis-Smith, "*La gran sultana Doña Catalina de Oviedo*: A Cervantes Practical Joke," *Forum for Modern Language Studies* 17 (1981): 68–82; George Mariscal, "*La Gran Sultana* and the Issue of Cervantes' Modernity," *Revista de Estudios Hispánicos* 28 (1994): 185–211; and Maryrica Ortiz Lottman, "*La gran sultana*: Transformations in Secret Speech." *Cervantes* 16, no. 1 (1996): 74–90.

Gran Turco. *Great Turk; *Amurates.

Gran Turco Selín. *Selim II.

Gran turquesca, La (The Great Turkish Lady). One of MC's early plays from the 1580s, which has been lost. It is included in the list of his plays in MC's conversation with Pancracio de Roncesvalles in *Adjunta*. Perhaps *Sultana* is a reworking of this early play.

Granada (Kingdom of Granada) [Reino de Granada]. After Seville, the second most important city in Andalusia; it is located directly south of Madrid and east and slightly south of Seville. In the Middle Ages, Granada was second only to Córdoba in Muslim-dominated Spain. The kingdom of Granada was the last Muslim stronghold in the Iberian Peninsula, and its fall in 1492 set into motion the chain of events that led to the discovery of the New World and the rise of Spain to the status of a great world empire. By the mid-sixteenth century, its population was about 50,000, including many *Moriscos*. See *Casa* 1; *Coloquio*; *DQ* I, 41; *DQ* II, 57; *Parnaso* 2; *Persiles* II, 8; *Tratos* 2, 4; *Viudo*.

Grande; Grandee. *Nobility.

Grande governador da ilha dos lagartos, O (1774; The Great Governor of the Island of the Lizards). An anonymous Portuguese interlude, derived from Antonio José da *Silva's *Vida do grande D. Quixote*, which is a parody of SP's governorship.

Granolleques. A well-known Catalan family. See *Doncellas*.

Grass, Günter (1927–). German poet, dramatist, and novelist. His most famous novel, *Die Blechtrommel* (1959; *The Tin Drum*), features prominently a scene in which the Polish cavalry rides into combat against the German army. The Poles are compared to Pan Kichot (DQ in Polish) as they are presented as being absurdly, tragically out of contact with the horrors of modern warfare.

Grau, Jacinto (1877–1958). Spanish dramatist and novelist. Grau collaborated with Adrià Gual on an adaptation of *Las bodas de Camacho* (1903; *Camacho's Wedding*) from *DQ* II, 20–21. Quiteria makes her unhappiness at having to marry the rich Camacho known from the beginning, and she is clearly relieved when Basilio stages his fake suicide in order to marry her. DQ and SP are little more than ornaments during the action, as considerable stress is placed on the cooks and servants who prepare the wedding feast and on the songs and dances. Grau is also the author of *El curioso impertinente*, based on *Curioso*.

Bibliography: Luciano García Lorenzo, ed. "Jacinto Grau: *Las bodas de Camacho* y *El Rey Candaules*," *Anales Cervantinos* 11 (1972): 217–72.

Grave embajador. *Mercury.

Graves, Richard (1715–1804). English writer. Graves's anti-Methodism satire *The Spiritual Quixote; or, The Summer's Ramble of Mr Geoffry Wildgoose; a Comic Romance* (3 vols., 1773) is inspired by MC and Henry Fielding. Geoffrey Wildgoose is a spiritual version of DQ and his is a "Spiritual Quixotism." Included in the novel is an "Essay on Quixotism," in which the term is defined as "a desire of imitating any great personage, whom we read of in history"; Wildgoose's models are church reformers. His SP is a cobbler named Jeremiah Tugwell, and together they set out in "Quest of Spiritual Adventures." The play with Tugwell's name (Tagwell, Tackwell, Tugwool, and Tugmutton) is reminiscent of some the play with names, particularly that of DQ, in MC's novel. References and allusions to DQ are frequent throughout this truly uninspired adaptation of the DQ myth that was extraordinarily popular in its time.

Great Britain [Gran Bretaña, Bretaña]. England, Wales, and Scotland, together with several smaller islands, such as the Hebrides, the Orkney Islands, and Shetland Islands. For DQ Great Britain was, above all, the location for the story of King Arthur. See *DQ* I, 13, 49; *DQ* II, 23; 31.

Great Council [Gran Consejo]. In *Amante*, the Turkish administrative body described by Ricardo as more or less equivalent to the Spanish Royal Council.

Great hooded one [Gran capilludo]. In *Gallardo* 3, a reference to Cardinal Francisco Jiménez de Cisneros, who conquered Oran in 1309.

Great Lord. *Great Turk.

Great lord of Delos. *Apollo.

Great Mameluke of Persia [Gran Mameluco de Persia]. The mamelukes were members of an army, originally composed of slaves, that took power in Egypt in the thirteenth century, ruled there for some two and a half centuries, and remained as an important factor in Egyptian society until early in the nineteenth century. In Arabic, the word means *slave* and is often used in a figurative sense. DQ's mention of the Great Mameluke of Persia in I, 21, involves two errors: there was never a title of Great Mameluke (as there is Great Turk, for instance), and the setting could not have been Persia. The word *mameluco* also refers to an ignorant person, a dolt, a chump.

Great Marquis [Gran marqués]. In *Poesías* 24, a reference to Don Alvaro de *Bazán, first Marquis of Santa Cruz de Mudela.

Great musician of Thrace. *Orpheus.

Great Panza, The [Gran Panza, el]. In *DQ* II, 51, the way the majordomo once refers to SP.

Great shepherd of the spacious Spanish land. *Carlos V.

Great time. This is one of the important concepts of M. M. *Bakhtin. The term refers both to the fact that all significant works of art have roots that go far back in time and that all such works continue to have importance beyond their immediate context: "Works break through the boundaries of their own time, they live in centuries, that is, in *great time* and frequently (with great works, always) their lives there are more intense and fuller than are their lives within their own time." Writers like Rabelais, Shakespeare, MC, and Goethe all live in great time (*Cervantes and the canon). The opposite of great time is what Bakhtin calls "small time": "The present day, the recent past, and the foreseeable (desired) future." Consideration of works only in small time is not profitable: "Trying to understand and explain a work solely in terms of the conditions of its epoch alone, solely in terms of the conditions of the most immediate time, will never enable us to penetrate into its semantic depths. . . . Everything that belongs only to the present dies along with the present." A modern critical term that applies here is *presentism*: the tendency to value only recent works of literature (often done in the name of multiculturalism or gender equity) and relegate the past to the dustbin of history. What lives in great time, for Bakhtin, is the *novelistic image*, particularly the image the reader creates of the novelistic hero: "Every age re-accentuates in its own way the works of its most immediate past. The historical life of classic works is in fact the uninterrupted process of their social and ideological reaccentuation." No work illustrates the re-accentuation of the novelistic image as does *DQ*: "In any objective stylistic study of novels from distant epochs it is necessary to take this process continually into consideration, and to rigorously coordinate the style under consideration with the background of heteroglossia, appropriate to the era, that dialogizes it. When this is done, the list of all subsequent re-accentuations of images in a given novel—say, the image of Don Quixote—takes on an enormous heuristic significance, deepening and broadening our artistic and ideological understanding of them. For, we repeat, great novelistic images continue to grow and develop even after the moment of their creation; they are capable of being creatively transformed in different eras, far distant from the day and hour of their original birth."

Bibliography: M. M. Bakhtin, *Speech Genres and Other Late Essays*, trans. Vern W. McGee, ed. Caryl Emerson and Michael Holquist (Austin: University of Texas Press, 1986).

Great Turk [Gran Turco]. The generic name given to the sultan of the Ottoman empire. In MC's time, the position was held by *Suleiman the Magnificent until his death in 1566, *Selim II from 1566 to 1574, and *Murad III from 1574 to 1795. See *Amante*; *Coloquio*; *DQ* I, 40; *DQ* II, 36, 63; *Española*; *Gitanilla*; *Retablo*.

Great Turkish Lady, The. **Gran Turquesca, La.

Greece [Grecia]. The country that occupies the southern part of the Balkan Peninsula on the Mediterranean Sea. Ancient Greece was considered the cradle of Western civilization. See *DQ* I, 6, 49, 52; *DQ* II, 74; *Galatea* 4; *Parnaso* 3; *Pedro* 1; *Poesías* 24.

Greek Commander. *Núñez de Guzmán, Hernán.

Greek romance. *Adventure romance.

Greene, (Henry) Graham (1904–91). English novelist, short-story writer, and dramatist. In his very popular *Travels with my Aunt* (1970), the narrator, Henry Pulling, makes a remark that resembles the position of Miguel de *Unamuno: "Hamlet is no less real then Winston Churchill, and Jo Pulling [his aunt] no less historical than Don Quixote." As he travels with his Aunt Augusta, Pulling calls upon DQ to understand his situation: "I felt as though I were being dragged at her heels on an absurd knight errantry, like Sancho Panza at the heels of Don Quixote, but in the cause of what she called fun instead of chivalry." On a very different note, the whisky priest of *The Power and the Glory* (1940) is quixotic in his belief that he is the last remaining Christian force in a godless world. Late in his career, Greene abandoned the relatively clear distinction between his serious novels (dealing with weighty questions of faith, politics, and psychological crises) and "entertainments" (lighter fictions, mostly stories of crime detection and international intrigue) to write the hybrid *Monsignor Quixote* (1982), which seems to fit in neither category, even as it partakes of both. Important in Greene's concept of DQ, as he himself has stated, was *Unamuno's extensive (and prototypically romantic) writings on the subject. Father Quixote, parish priest in El Toboso, who claims to be a direct descendant of DQ, suddenly finds himself promoted to monsignor and, in the company of the town's atheist Marxist ex-mayor, named Sancho Zancas, sets out in his old automobile (which, not surprisingly, he has named Rocinante) on a journey to Madrid. The sometimes doubting priest and the sometimes believing atheist consume large quantities of wine as they engage in long conversations about theology, political theory, and, of course, MC and *DQ*; each one influences the other increasingly as the novel progresses. Some of the adventures they have during the course of the trip recall specific characters and scenes from

DQ: windmills–Holy Brotherhood/Guardia Civil; Sansón Carrasco/Father Herrera; Don Diego de Miranda/Señor Diego; and penitents/church procession. When priest and politician visit the city of Salamanca, they pay homage to Greene's own admired friend, Miguel de Unamuno, as they contemplate his monument in that city, and Sancho remarks to Father Quixote, "You know how he loved your ancestor and studied his life." This is not the most profound retelling of the story of DQ, but it is an intelligent and entertaining one, worthy of respect and attention. *Monsignor Quixote* was also made into a film in 1988 directed by Rodney Bennett, with Alec Guiness as DQ and Leo McKern as SP.

Bibliography: Jean Canavaggio, "*Monseñor Quijote*, de Graham Greene, o el penúltimo avatar del quijotismo," in *Actas del coloquio cervantino, Würzburg 1983*, ed. Theodor Berchem and Hugo Laitenberger (Münster, Germany: Aschendorffsche Verlagsbuchhandlund, 1987), 1–10; Isabel Castells, "*Monseñor Quijote*, de Graham Greene, o la crucifixión del texto cervantino según el Evangelio de Unamuno," in *Desviaciones lúdicas en la crítica cervantina: Primer Convivio Internacional de "Locos Amenos*," ed. Antonio Bernat Vistarini and José María Casasayas (Salamanca, Spain: Ediciones Universidad de Salamanca, 2000), 173–88; Patrick Henry, "Cervantes, Unamuno, and Graham Greene's *Monsignor Quixote*," *Comparative Literature Studies* 23 (1986): 12–25; and Jae-Suck Choi, *Greene and Unamuno: Two Pilgrims to La Mancha* (New York: Peter Lang, 1990).

Greenland [Groenlanda]. The largest island in the world, located in the North Atlantic. It was discovered in 983 by Eric the Red. For MC, it was a mysterious, exotic, snow-covered, legendary place. See *Persiles* IV, 13.

Gregorian calendar. *Julian calendar.

Gregorio, Don. *Gaspar Gregorio, Don.

Gregory, Lady Isabella (1859–1939). English dramatist. In Gregory's play *Sancho's Master* (1927), SP appears first as a local peasant who helps the housekeeper and the notary Sampson Carasco burn DQ's books. It is only after he learns that an enchanter has carried off his books that DQ decides to become a knight-errant and recruits SP to be his squire. After a few adventures (at the inn, with the galley slaves), DQ and SP meet the duke and duchess, but continue to have adventures from other parts of the original novel, most notably the defeat of Carasco disguised as a knight-errant. The final act takes place at the duke's castle and includes the Clavileño episode and a few others before SP becomes a governor, with the usual scenes from that part of the novel (Pedro Recio, SP's resignation from office). At the end of the play, DQ becomes weak and ill and wants to return home; his (and the play's) last words, however, are "Dulcinea del Toboso is the most beautiful woman in the world."

Bibliography: Lady Gregory, *Three Last Plays* (London: G. P. Putnam's Sons, 1929).

Greyhound [Galgo]. In *DQ* I, 1, it is stated that DQ owns a greyhound, but the dog is never mentioned again in the novel.

Griboyedov, Aleksandr Sergeyevich (1795–1829). Russian dramatist. Griboyedov's *Gore ot uma* (written in 1822–24 but not published, in censored form, until 1833; *Woe from Wit*) features a character called Chatski, who has been suggested as a model for *Dostoevsky's Prince Myshkin. Chatski, explicitly compared to DQ by his author, has many of the qualities considered quixotic in the romantic age: he is idealistic, impractical, and ineffective. He even has a DT in Sofia Pavlovna, whom he sees as he imagines her rather than as she is.

Griegos. *Greeks.

Griffin (Gryphon) [Grifo]. In Greek myth, a fabulous animal with the body of a lion and the head and wings of an eagle. See *DQ* II, 58.

Grijalba. A very small town located slightly northwest of Burgos and south of Santander. It is mentioned only in the name of Doña *Rodríguez de Grijalba.

Grisaldo. In *Galatea* 4–5, the noble son (not a shepherd) of the rich Laurencio, promised to Leopersia, but in fact in love with Rosaura.

Grisóstomo. The nobleman and university student who dresses as a shepherd in order to follow and pursue his love for the beautiful *Marcela. DQ and SP hear his story in *DQ* I, 12, and then attend his funeral in I, 13–14, where they also listen to a reading of his final poem, his *Song of Despair. Grisóstomo (the name is a rustic variant of Crisóstomo) provides an interesting early contrast to DQ. Both are inspired by their reading to imitate literary models—chivalric in one case, pastoral in the other—but Grisóstomo plays his role to the hilt, actually dying for his beloved Marcela. References to a rope and knife in his poem suggest that his death was probably suicide (but there is some ambiguity in the presentation here, as it is also suggested that Grisóstomo simply died of love), an understanding reinforced by the use of the word *desesperarse* (to despair, often specifically in the sense of 'to commit suicide'; see SP's use of the word in this way in *DQ* II, 59).

Bibliography: Herman Iventosch, "Cervantes and Courtly Love: The Grisóstomo-Marcela Episode," *PMLA* 89 (1974): 64–76; and Harold G. Jones, "Grisóstomo and Don Quixote: Death and Imitation," *Revista Canadiense de Estudios Hispánicos* 4 (1979): 85–92.

Grisóstomo's song. *Song of Despair.

Groenlanda. *Greenland.

Grumete. *Cabin boy.

Gryphius, Andreas (1616–64). German poet and dramatist. Best-known as a poet, Gryphius's comedies are nowadays at least as appreciated as his tragedies, more interesting as historico-literary documents than as works of art. Among the tragedies, the one entitled *Cardenio und Celinde* (1657), based only very loosely on the Cardenio episodes of *DQ* I, is often considered the first bourgeois drama in German literature.

Guadalajara. A city located northeast of Madrid and northwest of Cuenca; it is the capital of the province of the same name. See *DQ* I, 39.

Guadalajara, Gate of. *Gate of Guadalajara.

Guadalcanal. A town located west and slightly north of Córdoba and north and slightly east of Seville. It was well-known for its wines, particularly its whites. See *Entretenida* 3; *Pedro* 1; *Rinconete*; *Vidriera*.

Guadalquivir. The most important river in Andalusia, also known by its Roman name of *Betis. It rises in the Sierra de Cazorla mountains, northeast of Granada and west of Alicante. It travels mostly southwesterly, passing through Córdoba and Seville, before turning more toward the south and emptying into the Atlantic Ocean at Sanlúcar de Barrameda. All ships coming from America sailed up the Guadalquivir some 87 kilometers (nearly 40 miles) to Seville in order to unload their cargoes. The dock area of the city was one of the most animated and exciting places in all of Spain on the days when the fleet arrived. See *Pedro* 1.

Guadalupe, Virgen de. *Our Lady of Guadalupe.

Guadarrama. Spanish mountain range located just west of Madrid. See *DQ* I, 4; *Parnaso* 8.

Guadiana. The river that flows from La Mancha, where it originates in the Lagoons of *Ruidera, then runs underground for a while, before coming again to the surface in a series of springs (the Ojos de Guadiana); from there, it flows west to Badajoz and then south to form the border between Spain and Portugal before emptying into the Atlantic Ocean. In his dream-vision in the Cave of Montesinos, DQ hears the legend of how Guadiana, the squire of Durandarte, wept so copiously at the time of the knight's death that he was turned into a river. See *DQ* I, 18, 20; *DQ* II, 22–24.

Gual, Adrià. *Grau, Jacinto.

Guánuco. A river in northern Venezuela. See *Galatea* 6.

Guard [Guardián]. A character who appears briefly in *Laberinto* 1.

Guarda cuidadosa, La (Guarda); Sir Vigilant. The fourth interlude in *Comedias*. *Guarda* is one of the better works in this group, with a coherent action and interesting characters. The protagonist, a prototypical example of the poor but proud soldier, is one of MC's best theatrical creations. It is generally assumed that since the date of May 6, 1611, is mentioned in the work, it was probably written at that time.

The farce begins with a conversation between two rivals for the hand of the maid Cristina de Parrazes: Lorenzo Pasillas, a sub-sacristan, and an unnamed poor soldier, dressed in picaresque style. Cristina has often shown a preference for Pasillas, but has never done anything but criticize and reject the soldier. Nevertheless, the soldier drives Pasillas off and remains outside Cristina's house, a jealous but faithful guardian. A boy named Andrés comes along begging, and the soldier gives him a coin so that he will not call at the house where Cristina lives. Another youth, named Manuel, arrives selling cloth. Cristina calls to him, but the soldier chases him away, and then does the same with a shoemaker named Juan Juncos who has brought shoes Cristina has ordered. Cristina's master arrives and the soldier informs him that he plans to marry Cristina. Just then Pasillas returns with a friend named Grajales, both with comic arms, including a rusty sword and a shield adorned with the tail of a fox. As they begin to skirmish, Cristina calls to her mistress, who joins the scene. The mistress asks Cristina what is going on and she admits that the men are fighting over her. When her master asks her if one of these men has dishonored her, she responds that, yes, Pasillas dishonored her the other day in the middle of the street—by calling her dirty and dishonest. Her master is relieved by this revelation of her innocence and naïveté. She shows him and he reads the note (dated May 6, 1611) that Pasillas has given her, in which he proposes marriage. Her master tells her to choose between the two, and after each makes a final pitch, she chooses Pasillas. Musicians enter, and the farce ends with the usual song and dance.

Bibliography: Luciano García Lorenzo, "Experiencia vital y testimonio literario: Cervantes y La guarda cuidadosa," *Anales Cervantinos* 15 (1976): 171–80: and Francisco Márquez, "Tradición y actualidad literaria en *La guarda cuidadosa*," *Hispanic Review* 33 (1965): 152–56.

Guarda del Pontificado; Guarda del Pontífice. *Papal guards.

Guardián Bají. In *Baños*, the Muslim who decides the fate of many of the captives taken in the raid on Spain.

Guards [Guardas]. In *DQ* I, 22, the two royal guards who are taking the galley slaves off to serve their sentences. They permit DQ to interview the criminals and then refuse his request that they be set free. DQ attacks and unhorses the one with the gun, while the other flees.

Guarini, Giambattista (1538–1612). Italian poet and dramatist. He is best known for his pastoral drama *Il pastor fido* (1590; *The Faithful Shepherd*), written in emulation of Torquato *Tasso's *Aminta*. The play was extremely popular and influential throughout the Renaissance in Europe. It was translated into Spanish by Cristóbal Suárez de Figueroa as *El Pastor Fido* (1602, revised ed. 1609), a work praised by DQ, in II, 62, as a model translation.

Guarino Mezquino. The protagonist of *Crónica del muy noble caballero Guarino Mezquino*.

Guarnacha. An Italian wine mentioned in *Vidriera*.

Guatimala; Guatemala. Country in Central America, located to the south and east of Mexico. See *Parnaso* 7.

Guedí. A site in the city of Constantinople. See *Sultana* 3.

Guenelon. *Galalón.

Guerard, Albert J. (1914–2000). American novelist. In Guerard's *The Bystander* (1958), the protagonist and narrator, Antony, is clearly quixotic in his perception of the woman he loves, his DT, Christiane Mondor: she "has been, for me, the one person whose image could not be scarred; who could not, whatever she chanced to do or not do, be contaminated or harmed or even changed. She was to be mine in at least that particular way! It was she who filled my daydreams of that spring, and who would be waiting for me when I came out of it at last—out of school and dependency, out of my fumblings and uncertainties and the long dark tunnel of adolescence." When a reality-instructor friend tells him of Christiane's affair with another man, he rejects reality: "For it was still true that Christiane Mondor was not 'like that' at all; and that she could be, in time, whatever I wanted her to be."

Guérin de Bouscal, Guyon (ca. 1613–75). French dramatist. Guérin's first dramatic effort derived from one of MC's works was *L'Amant libéral* (1637; *The Generous Lover*), an adaptation of *Amante*. About a year later he staged a version of *Dom Quixote de la Manche* (published 1639), derived in part from *Pichou's dramatized version of the Cardenio story. In 1640 he published a sequel, *Dom Quichot de la Manche* (1638), and two years later followed with *Le Gouvernement de Sanche Pansa* (1642; *The Government of Sancho Panza*), which also includes an episode taken from *Rinconete*. The second and third plays in the series are more original and interesting; they are based largely on certain events of *DQ* II, particularly involving the duke and duchess and the scenes and masquerades they organize for DQ and SP. A highlight of the play about SP's governorship is the scene where the physician impedes the hungry squire's eating. Guérin is the most original and innovative French dramatic adapter of MC in the seventeenth century and arguably as good as, if not better than, the Spaniards and Englishmen whose work is most comparable.

Bibliography: C. E. J. Caldicott, "The Trilogy of Guérin de Bouscal: A Phase in the Progression from *Don Quixote* to Molière's *Don Juan*," *Modern Language Review* 74 (1979): 553–71.

Guerra. *War.

Guerra justa. *Just war.

Güerta del Rey. *King's Garden.

Guests [Huéspedes]. In *DQ* I, 44, two men who have spent the night in Juan Palomeque's inn attempt to sneak out without paying. When Palomeque stops them, a fight breaks out. The innkeeper's wife and daughter turn to DQ (as the only one not busy at the time) and ask for help, but he hesitates, first until he secures permission from the Princess Micomicona to undertake an adventure while under contract to her, and then again when he notes that the men are not armed knights-errant and therefore not worthy opponents for him. While the narrator directs the reader's attention to other events in the inn, however, DQ talks to the two men and convinces them to pay their bill. This is an excellent example of how DQ is more effective when he talks than when he attacks. It is also an ironic recollection of the fact that DQ himself left the same inn without paying in I, 17.

Guevara, Antonio de. Quartermaster general to the Invincible Armada and in command of the operation to requisition supplies for the expedition. He set up the bureaucratic structure for which MC worked as a commissary beginning in 1587. It was his deputy Diego de *Valdivia who actually hired MC. In 1590, in a scandal of national proportions, Guevara and his main officials based in the city of Puerto de Santa María on the Bay of Cádiz were charged with corruption and jailed, and Guevara was removed from office. MC was not implicated in any direct way in this affair.

Guevara, Bishop Antonio de (1480–1545). Preacher, chronicler, advisor to Carlos V, and author. Two of Guevara's books were among the most read in the sixteenth century. The first is the *Libro áureo de Marco Aurelio* (1529; *Golden Book of Marco Aurelio*), a manual for leadership, which he later expanded and published under the more popular title of *Reloj de príncipes* (1539; *Dial of Princes*). The second is *Menosprecio de corte y alabanza de aldea* (1539; *Disdain for the Court and Praise for the Village*), a long essay in praise of the rustic life away from the intrigue and pomp of the Court. Guevara's mannered style in the *Reloj* became, after the book was translated and widely read in England, an early model for Euphuism, the elegant and affected style so popular in the English Renaissance. In the prologue to *DQ* I, MC cites Guevara, the famous bishop of Mondoñedo, as a quintessential example (Lope de *Vega is implicated, also) of those who disregard mere accuracy and relevance in their ostentatious displays of erudition. MC also mentions there the famous prostitutes Lamia, Laida, and *Flora from Guevara's *Epístolas familiares*. Other aspects of the prologue, along with features of CHB, may also reveal MC's debt to Guevara.

Bibliography: Pilar Concejo, "Huellas del obispo de Mondoñedo en *El Quijote*," in *Cervantes, su obra y su mundo. Actas del I Congreso Internacional sobre Cervantes*, ed. Manuel Criado de Val (Madrid: Edi-6, 1981), 901–7; Ernest Grey, *Guevara, a Forgotten Renaissance Author* (The Hague: Nijhoff, 1973); and Carolyn A. Nadeau, "Recovering the Hetairae: Prostitution in *Don Quijote* I," *Cervantes* 17, no. 2 (1979): 4–24.

Guevara, Don Fernando de. A Spanish knight mentioned by DQ in *DQ* I, 49 (*Crónica de Juan II*).

Guevara, Eduardo ("Che") (1928–67). Argentine revolutionary. The legendary Che Guevara was a follower of Fidel Castro who took on the mission of spreading the Marxist revolution throughout Spanish America; he died in the mountains of Bolivia. At one point, as he prepared to depart for Africa to study revolutionary techniques, he wrote a farewell letter to his parents, beginning thus: 'I can feel Rocinante's ribs beneath my heels again; I am beginning my travels again with my shield on my arm.' *DQ* was a favorite of Guevara's, and he read passages from the novel to his troops in

Bolivia. Virtually every biography of Guevara includes a comparison of him with DQ (*real-life Don Quixotes*).

Guillarte. In *Española*, Ricaredo's page, who inaccurately reports that Ricaredo has been killed.

Guillén Barrios Gómez, Virginia. Mexican writer. Guillén's *Don Quijote, caballero de las causas nobles (desde Guanajuato)* (1975; *Don Quixote, Knight of Noble Causes [from Guanajuato]*) is a weak romantic musical by a writer who claims always to have loved *DQ*. The play brings together and interweaves local Guanajuato legend, national patriotism, and a noble DQ. The author wrote both the libretto and the music for the work.
　Bibliography: Virginia Guillén Barrios Gómez, *Don Quijote, caballero de las causas nobles (desde Guanajuato)* (México City: n.p., 1975).

Guillén, Jorge (1893–1986). Spanish poet. A member of the so-called Generation of 1927 and exile after the Civil War, Guillén is one of the most distinguished Spanish poets of the twentieth century. In *Aire nuestro* (1968; *Our Air*), a major compendium of Guillén's verse, there are two long poems inspired by *DQ*. The first is "Noche del caballero" ("The Knight's Night") and recreates the scene of *DQ* I, 20, when DQ and SP hear the frightening noises of the fulling mills during a dark night. The second, "Dimisión de Sancho" ("Sancho's Resignation") is a moving evocation of the end of SP's reign as governor of Barataria (*DQ* II, 53), perhaps a more sensitive rendering of that scene than any of the dozens of theatrical versions of SP's governorship.
　Bibliography: Javier Yagüe Bosch, "Dos episodios del *Quijote* en *Aire nuestro* de Jorge Guillén," *Criticón* 53 (1991): 7–55.

Guillermo. A shepherd who appears briefly in *Baños* 3.

Guillermo the Rich [Guillermo el rico]. In *DQ* I, 12, the father of Marcela.

Guinarde, Roque. A variant of the name of the famous Catalan bandit Perot *Roca Guinarda. See *Cueva*.

Guinea. The traditional name for the west African coast near the equator; essentially, it is where Equitorial Guinea is today. It is cited by the priest in *DQ* I, 29, as the home of the princess (Dorotea) who has come to Spain in search of DQ to right a wrong. The phrase "nacer in Guinea" ("to be born in Guinea") is either a variant of "nacer en las malvas" ("to be born among the mallows; i.e., 'in the sticks' "), an allusion to a humble birth; or a reference to the chickens (*gallinas*) of Guinea, and thus a statement disavowing cowardice; it is used in *Rufián* 1. See also *Coloquio*; *Rufián* 2.

Guinevere [Ginebra]. In Arthurian legend, the wife of King Arthur and lover of Lancelot, who is frequently mentioned in the romances and ballads of the Arthurian tradition. See *DQ* I, 13, 16, 49; *DQ* II, 19, 23; *Fregona*.

Guiomar. 1. In *Celoso*, one of the black slaves who serves Leonora and who speaks broken Spanish. **2.** In *Juez*, the woman who wants to divorce her useless soldier husband.

Guiomar de Meneses, Doña. In *Gitanilla*, the wife of the magistrate of Murcia, who is taken by the beauty of Preciosa and who turns out to be her mother.

Guiomar de Quiñones, Doña. In *DQ* II, 60, the noble woman, wife of the chief justice of the ecclesiastical court of Naples, traveling with the Spanish infantry captains taken prisoner but then released by *Roque Guinart.

Guiomar de Sosa, Doña. In *Persiles* III, 6, the woman who protects Ortel Banedre after he has killed her son Don Duarte.

Guisando. *Bulls of Guisando.

Guisopete. In *DQ* I, 25, SP mispronounces in this way the name of *Aesop (Esopo or Isopete).

Gulf of the Lion [Golfo de León]. A bay in the Mediterranean Sea, located off the southern coast of France, from Toulon to Spain. See *Vidriera*.

Gunpowder Mill [Molina de la Pólvora]. A mill in the Triana district of Seville. See *Coloquio*.

Gurreas. An Aragonese family name mentioned in *DQ* I, 13.

Gutiérrez de Castro, Tomás (?–1604). Spanish actor and innkeeper. A childhood friend of MC's in Córdoba, Gutiérrez was associated with the Cervantes family for many years. After abandoning his career as an actor, he opened an inn on the Calle de Bayona, near the cathedral in Seville. MC must have stayed at his friend's inn during at least some of his visits to Seville.

Gutiérrez Rufo, Juan. *Rufo Gutiérrez, Juan.

Guy de Borgoña: Gui de Bourgogne. A French knight, usually considered one of the *Twelve Peers of France, mentioned by DQ in *DQ* I, 49 (*Crónica de Juan II*; *Historia del emperador Carlomagno y los doce pares de Francia*).

Guzmán. In *Gallardo*, a Spanish captain in Oran and friend of Fernando de Saavedra.

Guzmán, Alonso Pérez de. *Pérez de Guzmán, Alonso.

Guzmán de Alfarache; *Guzmán de Alfarache*. *Alemán, Mateo.

Guzmán, don Gonzalo. A Spanish knight mentioned by DQ in *DQ* I, 49 (*Crónica de Juan II*).

Guzmán, Francisco de. Spanish poet and soldier known for his religious and moralizing works. He is praised in Calliope's song in *Galatea* 6.

Guzmanes. A Castilian family name mentioned in *DQ* I, 13.

Gymnosophists from Ethiopia [Ginosofistas de la Etiopía]. An ancient priestly caste. See *DQ* I, 47.

Gypsies [Gitanos]. 1. A wandering people who exist throughout the world, especially in Europe, and who are believed to have originated in Egypt. The gypsies first entered Spain in the fifteenth century, largely as a result of Turkish advances in the Balkans, and immediately became one of the most marginalized and hated ethnic groups in the country. Gypsies were considered pernicious to the nation because they were perceived to be anarchical, lazy, incestuous, promiscuous, and ungodly; they were vagabonds, thieves, prostitutes, heretics, and witches. In spite of a series of legal attempts to eliminate or integrate them, they maintained their unique status on the margins of society and never settled down in any single location. Although the first appearances of gypsies in Spanish literature are from the early sixteenth century, it is really only late in the century and early in the seventeenth that they become a significant topic in literary texts; in fact, MC's *Gitanilla* may be the single most substantial work of literature concerning gypsy life in the Spanish *Golden Age. It is not clear to what extent MC actually had firsthand knowledge of gypsy life, but he must have had at least some contact with them during his years of traveling in Andalusia. He seems ambivalent on their role in Spanish society. The opening line of *Gitanilla* captures the official and most widely held view of gypsies: 'It seems as though all gypsies, both male and female, are born into this world to be thieves.' The story itself, however, often paints a much more sympathetic vision of gypsies— but then this sympathy itself is undercut when the best athletes among them and the only truly virtuous "gypsies" are the nobles in disguise (or, like the protagonist, noble without knowing it). The comments about the gypsies made by the talking dog Berganza in *Coloquio* are negative in every respect. **2**. In *Gitanilla*, the group of about ten or 12 that receives Andrés Caballero into their band and becomes his companions during the time he lives with them. **3**. In *Coloquio*, they take Berganza into their company for some three weeks. He is very critical of their way of life.

Bibliography: Jan Yoors, *The Gypsies of Spain* (New York: Macmillan, 1974).

Gypsy musicians. *Musicians.

❧ H ❧

Habacuc [Abacú]. In the Old Testament, the prophet sent by God to bring food to Daniel in the lion's den. See *Baños* 1.

Habela Patiño, Eugenio. **Centeno, Pedro.

Habit of Saint Peter [Hábito de San Pedro]. The traditional garb of the university student, consisting of a cassock, long cloak, and student cap, all black. It is the dress worn by Sansón Carrasco in *DQ* II, 3.

Hadji Murad [Agi Morato, Agimorato]. A Slovenian renegade living in Algiers during the time of MC's captivity there. He was a man of prestige (a *hadji* is one who has made the pilgrimage to Mecca), serving as a major administrative official in Algiers, one of the wealthiest men in the city, and well connected to the Great Turk himself, for whom he sometimes carried out diplomatic duties. MC uses him and his daughter *Zahara as models in *Capitán* (*DQ* I, 40–41) where he is called Agi Morato and is a loving father abandoned by his escaping daughter. In *Baños*, he is called Agimorato and is only mentioned as the father of Zahara.
  Bibliography: Jaime Oliver Asín, "La hija de Agí Morato en la obra de Cervantes," *Boletín de la Real Academia Española* 27 (1947): 245–339.

Hadrian [Adriano]: Publius Aclius Hadrianus (117–138). Roman emperor known especially for his intelligence, culture, and generosity, and for the buildings he had constructed. See *DQ* II, 8.

Haedo, Fray Diego de. Spanish priest and sociologist/historian. Haedo published the *To-pografía e historia general de Argel* (1612; *Topography and General History of Algiers*), a description of the life and times of Christian captives in Algiers. Haedo states that he did not actually write the book himself, merely to have edited and completed an unfinished work by his uncle. The uncle, an inquisitor recognized for his work for prisoners released from North Africa and also named Diego de Haedo, was supposed to have compiled the account from reports made by former captives in Algiers. In fact, the work was almost certainly written by Antonio de *Sosa, a companion of MC in Algiers. More recently, it has been proposed that the actual author of the entire *Topografía* is none other than MC himself, but this suggestion has not received much support and is not likely to convince many.
  Bibliography: Daniel Eisenberg, "Cervantes, autor de la *Topografía e historia general de Argel* publicada por Diego de Haedo," *Cervantes* 16, no. 1 (1996): 32–53.

Hagar. *Descendants of Hagar.

Halcón noruego. *Norwegian falcon.

Halima. 1. In *Amante*, the renegade wife of the cadí; she is in love with the Christian captive Ricardo, but at the end of the story reconverts to Christianity and marries Mahamut. **2.** In *Baños*, the wife of Cauralí, who is in love with the Christian captive Don Francisco.

Halm, Friedrich (1806–71). German dramatist and prose writer. The influence of *Curioso* is evident in his short story "Das Haus an der Veronabrücke" ("The House by the Verona

Bridge") and in a play he planned to write to be entitled *Freund und Frau* (*Wife and Friend*).

Hambre. *Hunger.

Hanging gardens [Pensiles]. The Hanging Gardens of Babylon, one of the Seven Wonders of the Ancient World. See *Parnaso* 3; *Persiles* IV, 7.

Hanley, James (1901–85). Irish sailor and novelist. Hanley's *Don Quixote Drowned* (1953) consists of a series of essays about people he knew during his life, particularly during his seafaring days. The first chapter, which also serves as the title of the book, is about a sailor named Crawley who drowns at sea. Crawley is not a quixotic comrade whose life is chronicled here, but a mean-spirited man who takes the author's most beloved book, *DQ*, and throws it overboard (DQ drowned). In response, Hanley strikes the sailor and the next day is punished by having to cast all the rest of his books into the sea. Crawley's later drowning is more an act of poetic justice than anything.

Hannibal [Aníbal] (247–182 BCE). Son of Hamilcar Barca and the leader of the Carthaginians against Rome in the Second Punic War. He won important victories over the Romans in the Iberian Peninsula, but his most famous feat was the invasion of Italy itself, which he accomplished by crossing the Alps with a large army that included elephants. He is mentioned as an example of how fortune can make the powerful fall to obscurity in the poem by Urganda la Desconocida in the preliminary pages to *DQ* I. See also *DQ* I, 49; *Persiles* II, 19.

Hapsburgs. *Austria, House of.

Hard versus soft readings of *Don Quixote*. The distinction between "hard" and "soft" readings of *DQ* has its origins in a classic essay by Oscar Mandel in 1958. A prototypical hard critic is one who refuses to sympathize or identify with DQ. The hard critic reads *DQ* as a satire, a funny book, and nothing else; he or she considers that this is the only "right" way

to understand the novel, and disdains those soft-headed readers who mistakenly understand the novel in terms of tragedy or nobility. Erich Auerbach, author of a famous essay on the enchanted DT, can be taken as a prototypical hard critic when he writes: "The whole book is a comedy in which well-founded reality holds madness up to ridicule." The soft critic is one who very much sympathizes and/or identifies with DQ. The soft critic reads *DQ* as a serious psychological study and/or a profound philosophical statement of human nature, asserts his or her right to react sympathetically to the text, and pities those hard-hearted readers who cannot see beyond the superficial comedy. The English Hispanophile Gerald Brenan, in his history of Spanish literature, can serve as a prototype of the soft position: "The significant thing about this novel—its claim to be twice over a tragedy—is that it not only shows us the defeat of the man of noble feelings by the second-rate and vulgar, but that it convinces us that that defeat was right." When the soft position is taken to its logical conclusion, DQ's nobility and idealism make him into a Christ-like hero (*Don Quixote and Christ). Miguel de *Unamuno, in his *Vida de Don Quijote y Sancho*, is perhaps the ultimate soft reader of *DQ*. The *reception history of *DQ* has been a vacillation between these two extremes. As is usually the case, most readings fall somewhere between the two extremes, but often closer to one than the other. It is worth noting that in the prologue to *Persiles*, MC recounts a meeting with a student who, among other things, refers to him as "el regocijo de las Musas" ("the delight of the Muses"), that is, a famous comic writer, but he insists that the title is not appropriate. Apparently, then, MC saw himself and his work (especially *DQ*) as something more than mere burlesque and satire.

Bibliography: John J. Allen, *Don Quixote: Hero or Fool? A Study in Narrative Technique*, 2 vols. (Gainesville: University Presses of Florida, 1969, 1979); Anthony Close, *The Romantic Approach to "Don Quixote": A Critical History of the Romantic Tradition in "Quixote" Criticism* (Cambridge: Cambridge University Press, 1978); Oscar Mandel, "The

Function of the Norm in *Don Quixote*," *Modern Philology* 55 (1958): 154–63; and John G. Weiger, *The Substance of Cervantes* (Cambridge: Cambridge University Press, 1985).

Hardy, Alexandre (ca. 1570–1631). French dramatist. Hardy was a prolific early dramatist, important in the development of the French theater of the seventeenth century. Perhaps his best-known play is the tragicomedy entitled *La Force du sang* (*The Power of Blood*), based on MC's *Fuerza. Novelas* was translated into French in 1615, and Hardy's play was published in 1626, which means that it was probably written in the late 1610s or early 1620s, but Hardy may have read Spanish and may not have depended on the translation. It is generally assumed to be the first foreign theatrical adaptation of one of MC's short stories. One of the more interesting modifications in the original story made by Hardy is the changing of the crucifix Leocadia takes from Rodolfo's room into a small statue of the Greek hero Hercules. Hardy's *Cornélie* (1625) is derived from *Cornelia*. His *La belle Egyptienne* (1615; *The Beautiful Gypsy*) has its origins in *Gitanilla* (the title is the one used for *Gitanilla* by Rosset in his translation of MC's *Novelas*); the play transforms the theme of Preciosa's freedom and self-reliance to one of a straightforward desire to achieve the life of an aristocrat. Hardy's *L'ilustre fregonne* is not based on MC's *Fregona*, but on a story by Diego de *Agreda y Vargas. Finally, *Eusébie et René* is based on the French characters of Eusebia and Renato in *Persiles* II, 17–21.

Bibliography: Theodore Braun, "Cervantes and Hardy: From *La fuerza de la sangre* to *La Force du sang*," *Anales Cervantinos* 17 (1978): 167–82.

Harpía; Harpy. *Phineus.

Harquebus [Arcabuz]. The most popular firearm used in the Spanish army during the years MC served in the military. It weighed over ten pounds and was almost five feet in length. Clumsy and ineffective as the weapon was, the harquebus represented the latest in military technology in the late sixteenth century.

Harquebusiers [Arcabuceros]. 1. In *Española*, some 50 soldiers who accompany Ricaredo as he takes command of the Portuguese ship freed from the Turks. **2.** In *Baños* 1, two Christians who attempt to defend against the Muslim raid on Spain.

Harriero(s). *Muleteer(s).

Harrieros gallegos. *Yangüeses.

Hartley, L. P. (1895–1972). English novelist. Hartley's *The Love-Adept* (1969) is a self-conscious novel about novel-writing in the tradition of *DQ*. As the novel begins, James Golightly is struggling with the ending of his novel entitled *The Love-Adept*. After he manages to finish it, he sends prepublication copies to four friends, all named Elizabeth (the novel is dedicated to 'Elizabeth'). Most of the novel consists of correspondence between James and the Elizabeths about the novel, especially the ending (which three of the Elizabeths never manage to read). In a letter to Elizabeth II, James cites MC, "the wisest and the most humane of novelists," and his "extraordinary" ending for *DQ*. Later, in a letter to Elizabeth IV, James praises Homer, in the *Iliad* and the *Odyssey*, and then adds: "Of all the novelists comparable to Homer in stature, only Cervantes, I think, *improvises* the ending. *Don Quixote* is not constructed, according to any canons of art; it doesn't work up to anything; it hasn't a dénouement or a climax, the logical issue of what has gone before, unless Don Quixote's disillusion with Dulcinea (which no doubt was always in the author's mind) could be counted as an anti-climax." Finally, in the last chapter, James writes to Elizabeth IV, discusses his theory of an ending, and cites her as his DT. Then, in a closing epilogue, the four Elizabeths meet at a cocktail party and it is revealed that James is marrying Elizabeth IV. The whole point of *The Love-Adept*, whose ending is discussed down to the very last lines of the novel, is the nature of novelistic endings, and the model throughout is *DQ*.

Hassan Pasha (Azán Agá; Hazán Bajá) (1545–91). A Venetian (original name: Andreta; also known as Hassan Veneciano) who converted to Islam. Known as a man of considerable culture, Hassan served under Dragut and Uluj Alí, and later became king of Algiers from 1577 to 1580, and again from 1582 to 1583, at which time he moved definitively to Constantinople. He was MC's owner during the years 1577–80, a period during which he had as many as 2,000 slaves. In 1580 he married the daughter of *Hadji Murad, the historical model for *Zoraida in *Capitán*. In spite of his reputation for cruelty, he pardoned MC after his escape attempts. Hassan Pasha apparently provided the historical model for several of MC's characters: the king of Algiers in *Tratos*, *Capitán*, *Gallardo*, and *Baños*; and the viceroy of Cyprus in *Amante*. Confusing the issue somewhat, however, is the fact that there was also a king of Algiers with the same name in the 1560s (when the action of *Gallardo*, for example, takes place), so it is possible that this second historical figure was also a model for MC. For MC, the name of Hassan Pasha may have come to represent generically the stock character of the renegade Muslim ruler.

Bibliography: Jaime Oliver Asín, "La hija de Agí Morato en la obra de Cervantes," *Boletín de la Real Academia Española* 27 (1947): 245–339.

Have Nots; Haves. *Families.

Hawthorne, Nathaniel (1804–64). American novelist and short-story writer. Hawthorne was intimately involved in the ongoing nineteenth-century debate involving the concepts of romance and novel, and, as part of his awareness of the literary traditions and genres within which he wrote, he had his own personal but very clear vision of the role of MC and *DQ* in the aesthetics of fiction. Further, almost all of Hawthorne's work—his sketches, stories, and tales, as well as his novels—includes direct and indirect references and allusions to the themes and techniques of *DQ*. This is particularly evident in the famous 'Custom House' introduction to *The Scarlet Letter* (1850), where the author/narrator claims to be little more than the editor of an authentic story for which he discovered the manuscript. The fiction itself

also includes a variant on the quixotic theme of the influence of reading, as seen, for example, when the doctor warns the intellectual minister: "Aha! see now, how they trouble the brain,— these books!—You should study less, good Sir, and take a little pastime; or these night-whimsies will grow upon you!" The same author-editor-sources discourse also runs through *The House of the Seven Gables* (1851), a novel in which Hepzibah's fantasies also recall those of DQ: "Thus did Hepzibah bewilder herself with these fantasies of the old time. She had dwelt too much alone—too long in the Pyncheon House—until her very brain was impregnated with the dry rot of its timbers. She needed a walk along the noonday street to keep her sane."

Bibliography: G. R. Thompson, *The Art of Authorial Presence: Hawthorne's Provincial Tales* (Durham, NC: Duke University Press, 1993); and G. R. Thompson, and Eric Carl Link, *Neutral Ground: New Traditionalism and the American Romance Controversy* (Baton Rouge: Louisiana State University Press, 1999).

Hazán Bajá. *Hassan Pasha.

Hazén. In *Baños* 1, the Spanish renegade who wants to reconvert to Christianity; he kills Yzuf and is taken away to be executed.

Hebreo, León [Leone Ebreo] (Judas Abravanel or Abarbanel, 1460–1521). Jewish philosopher and writer of Portuguese origin, who lived primarily in Spain and Italy. He was the personal physician to Fernando and Isabel, and he chose to leave Spain in 1492, the year of the expulsion of the Jews, rather than convert to Christianity. His Platonism is evident in his treatise entitled *Dialoghi d'amore (Dialogues of Love)* in the work's idealization of beauty and love, their spiritualization, and their redemptive powers. The book may have been written as early as 1502, either in Italian or Spanish, but was commonly known through its 1590 translation by *Garcilaso de la Vega, El Inca, and it was very popular in Spain for years before it was banned. Hebreo was the most authoritative Platonic voice in the Spanish *Renaissance, and, as such, directly influenced all who wrote on *pastoral themes and dealt with love, including *Garcilaso de la Vega, Fray Luis de *León, Jorge de *Montemayor, Lope de *Vega, and MC. MC cites Hebreo as an authority on the subject of love in the prologue to *DQ* I, and his influence is pervasive in *Galatea*.

Bibliography: Seymour Feldman, *Philosophy in a Time of Crisis: Don Isaac Abravanel, Defender of the Faith* (New York: Routledge, 2002).

Hechicera. *Witch.

Hechos del Emperador, Los. *Avila y Zúñiga, Don Luis de.

Hecht, Ben (1894–1964). American journalist, novelist, dramatist, and film writer. In the collection *A Thousand and One Afternoons in Chicago* (1922), the final story is entitled "Don Quixote and His Last Windmill." In it, Hecht relates a dinner he had with writer Sherwood Anderson, which was interrupted by a diner at a nearby table who bought drinks and cigars for them and eventually for the entire restaurant. Invited to join them, the man, a Russian Jewish émigré named Sam Sklarz, explains that he has grown rich as owner of a box factory, is about to open a dance hall, and he wants to celebrate. The next day, there is an item in the newspaper: a Sam Sklarz, owner of a box factory who had just gone bankrupt, committed suicide after spending the last of his remaining money in a final restaurant spree.

Bibliography: Ben Hecht, *A Thousand and One Afternoons in Chicago* (Chicago: Covici-McGee, 1922).

Hector [Héctor, Hétor]. In Greek myth, the oldest son of King Priam of Troy. He was the leader and the bravest warrior of the Trojans in the war with Greece, killing 31 Greeks during the conflict. Hector was killed by Achilles, and his body was dragged behind a chariot to the Trojan camp. See *DQ* I, 32, 47, 49; *DQ* II, 40; *Entretenida* 3; *Rinconete* (where he is cited as a great musician).

Helen [Elena]. In Greek myth, the wife of Menelaus and the most beautiful woman in the world. When she was kidnapped by *Paris, the events of the Trojan War were set in to motion. After the war, she returned to her husband in Sparta. Her name suggests the power of a woman's beauty to change the course of history. See *DQ* I, 21, 25; *DQ* II, 32, 71; *Laberinto* 2.

Helicon [Helicón]. A mountain in southern Greece considered to be the home of the Muses. See *Poesías* 28, 29.

Heliconan [Helicona]. An adjective based on Helicon and used to refer to the famous fountains (Hippocrene and Aganippe) of that mountain, which were reputed to inspire those who drank from them. See *Galatea* 6; *Parnaso* 3.

Heliodorus [Heliodoro] (third century CE). Greek fiction writer. Heliodorus's *Ethiopian History* (or *History of Theogenes and Chariclea*) is the tale of Princess Chariclea of Ethiopia and Prince Theogenes of Thessaly who set out for Egypt after swearing eternal love and chastity until their marriage. The fantastic tale of their adventures (separations, abductions, shipwrecks, voyages, pirates, and the like) forms the prototype of the romance of adventure. The first translation into Spanish (from Jacques Amyot's French version) was by Francisco de Vergara with the title of *Historia etiópica* (1554; reprinted in 1581). A second, superior version, entitled *Historia etiópica de los amores de Teágenes y Cariclea* (1587; *Ethiopian History of the Love of Theogenes and Chariclea*), was made by Fernando de Mena. MC almost certainly knew the latter version and may also have read the earlier one; clearly, he knew and admired the work, and in the prologue claims it as his explicit model for *Persiles*: 'a book that dares to compete with Heliodorus.'

Bibliography: Alban K. Forcione, "Heliodorus and Literary Theory," in *Cervantes Aristotle and the Persiles* (Princeton, NJ: Princeton University Press, 1970), 49–87; and Heliodorus, *Historia etiópica de los amores de Teágenes y Cariclea*, trans. Fernando de Mena, ed. Francisco López Estrada (Madrid: Aldus, 1954).

Hemstreet, Charles (1866–?). American writer. Hemstreet's novel *The Don Quixote of America* (1921) is the story of John Eagle, whose physical appearance—short and fat—is more like that of SP than DQ, but who has some of the knight's book-inspired concept of the world and his own idealistic and crusading qualities. Eagle, accompanied by a tall, thin Van Dawson, makes a trip across America, exploring lands and surveying forests, planning to build great cities. At one point late in the novel, Eagle realizes that he should reward his faithful companion's services by dubbing him a knight. This reference is, after the title itself, the closest thing in the text to an allusion to DQ.

Bibliography: Charles Hemstreet, *The Don Quixote of America* (New York: Dodd, Mead, 1921).

Henares. A Spanish river that rises in the Guadarrama Mountains north of Alcalá de Henares, flows through that city (birthplace of MC), and empties into the Jarama east of Madrid. See *DQ* II, 44; *Galatea* 1–3; *Persiles* III, 8.

Hera. In Greek myth, the wife of Zeus (Juno, wife of Jupiter, is her counterpart in Roman myth). She was the goddess of marriage and married women; ironically, she was also the jealous wife of a frequently philandering husband. When Heracles (Hercules in Roman myth) was born of Zeus and Alcmena, his stepmother Hera sent two snakes to kill the infant, but Heracles strangled them in his cradle. According to some versions, and as cited by Sansón Carrasco in *DQ* II, 14, she also commanded Heracles to perform the 12 extraordinarily dangerous acts of bravery known as the Labors of Heracles.

Heraclius [Heraclio] (575–641). Emperor of the Eastern Roman (or Byzantine) Empire. He was reputed to have entered Jerusalem bearing the Holy Cross (on which Christ was crucified), and won the Holy Sepulcher (*Santa Casa*): (where Christ was buried). See *DQ* I, 48.

Hercules [Hércules]. 1. The Roman name for the greatest hero of Greek myth, Heracles. He was a semidivine, the son of Zeus and Alcmena, and was especially renowned for his great strength. The phrase "the labors of Hercules" refers to the deeds he was to accomplish in his 12 years of probation before becoming a god (*Pillars of Hercules). See *Adjunta*; *DQ* I, 1; *DQ* II, 2, 14, 32; *Galatea* 4; *Gallardo* 1–2; *Novelas*, dedication; *Persiles* III, 15; *Retablo*. **2.** In *Persiles* II, 12, Periandro, during his long narration, is compared to Hercules. The reference here is to a Celtic Hercules, described by Lucian, and not to the legendary Greek and Roman hero. This Hercules kept his many captives in tow by delicate golden chains linking his tongue and their ears, causing them not to flee but to stay near and praise him. He is thus a symbol of eloquence.

Hercules's stepmother. *Hera.

Herder, Johann Gottfried (1744–1803). German romantic critic and popular philosopher. Herder was attracted to *DQ* throughout his life, and his changing understanding of the protagonist parallels the evolution of his philosophy and aesthetic theory. At first, Herder was uncomfortable with the ridicule DQ receives and preferred the earthy, good-natured SP. Later he conceived of DQ as a prototype of the *Schwärmer* (person who becomes overly enthusiastic about an idea), a victim of the reading of imaginative literature, and a warning for a type that was to become all too common in the eighteenth century. In his criticism of his former mentor and friend Immanuel Kant, Herder likens Kant to DQ riding Clavileño—blindfolded so as not to see reality; both are *Schwärmer*. Throughout his life, Herder maintained SP, particularly in his role as governor, as a positive model.

Herdsman [Ganadero]. In *DQ* I, 28, the person for whom Dorotea works for a few months during her quest to find Don Fernando.

Herdsman from Quintanar. *Barcino.

Herdsmen. *Men on horseback.

Herebo. *Erebus.

Herfiel, Andrés. Spanish novelist. Herfiel's novel *Los nietos de Sancho Panza* (1978; *The Grandchildren of Sancho Panza*) is a tale of several generations and bears little noteworthy resemblance to *DQ* except for the final pages, where the title and organizing concept are explained. The bachelor and idealist DQ left no descendants, but the fecund SP clearly did. Today no one fights to undo evil or conquer islands, except for money: 'Quixotes then, are an extinct species, while the line of his squire Sancho is multiplied by the myriad throughout the wide world.' In effect, we are all 'the direct descendents, the grandchildren of the legendary Sancho Panza.'
   Bibliography: Andrés Herfiel, *Los nietos de Sancho Panza* (Madrid: Vassalo de Mumbert, 1978).

Heria (feria) de Sevilla. *Market of Seville.

Hermana del anciano ganadero. *Sister of the elderly shepherd.

Hermanas que trabajan tanto. *Danaids.

Hermano de la hija de Diego de la Llana. *Daughter of Diego de la Llana.

Hermano de Lira. *Lira's brother.

Hermanos de la Capacha. *Brothers of la Capacha.

Hermit [Ermitaño]. 1. In *DQ* I, 26, DQ refers to, but does not name, Andalod, the hermit who ministered to Amadís during his penance on the Peña Pobre. **2**. In *DQ* II, 24, the humanist cousin who accompanies DQ and SP to the Cave of Montesinos tells them of a nearby hermit with a reputation for piety and generosity. After DQ makes some satirical remarks about the relative luxury in which modern hermits live, they decide to stop by the hermitage and request something to drink. But the hermit is not there, and they are received by a female subhermit (*una sotahermitaño*), who can only offer them some water. The presence of a female "assistant," especially after DQ's remarks, makes this episode clearly satiric.
   Bibliography: Ernest A. Siciliano, "The Absent Hermit of the *Quijote*," *Romance Notes* 12 (1971): 404–6.

Hermitage of the Compás [Ermita del Compás]. The ironic name of a well-known house of prostitution in Seville in the *Compás district of the city. See *Rufián* 1.

Hermitages, Island of the. *Island of the Hermitages.

Hernández (Fernández) de Córdoba, Gonzalo (1453–1515). Spanish soldier known as the *Gran Capitán* (Great Captain). Hernández de Córdoba gained great fame in service to the *Catholic Monarchs during the wars against the Muslims leading up to and including the fall of Granada and then later in Italy. See *DQ* I, 32, 49.

Hernández, Inés. *Ezpeleta, Don Gaspar de.

Hernández, José (1834–86). Argentine poet. It has frequently been remarked that Hernández's poem *Martín Fierro* does for the myth of the gaucho what *DQ* did for the myth of the knight-errant. The comparison is made explicit in the novel featuring these two characters by Vidal *Ferreyra Videla.

Hernández Verdeseca, Catalina. *Catalina.

Hernando. In *Baños* 3, the name once used by Halima to refer to Don Fernando.

Hernando de Cifuentes. In *Española*, the person who sells Ricaredo the house near the convent of Santa Paula in which he and Isabel live.

Hero. *Leandro.

Herodias [Herodes, Herodías]. In the Old Testament, the wife of King Herod. She convinced her daughter Salomé to request the head of John the Baptist on a platter as a reward for her dance. In *Retablo*, it is Herodias herself, rather than her daughter, who is the dancer. See also *Galatea* 4.

Herostratus [Eróstrato]. The man who burned down the Temple of Diana (Artemis for the Greeks) in Ephesus, one of the Seven Wonders of the ancient world, in order to gain fame. See *DQ* II, 8.

Herradura, La. A small Mediterranean port city south of Granada, between Málaga and Almería. In 1562 there was a strong storm there, in which more than 20 ships sank and 4,000 men died. See *DQ* II, 31; *Gallardo* 3.

Herrera, Antonio de (1549–1625). Spanish historian. Herrera is the most likely candidate for the authorship of the **Relación de lo sucedido en la ciudad de Valladolid . . .*, (1605; *Account of What Happened in the City of Valladolid*) often attributed to MC.

Herrera, Capitán Pedro de. Spanish poet and soldier. In *Casamiento*, he is mentioned as a friend of Campuzano's in Valladolid.

Herrera de Gamboa, Juan, el Maganto. In *Persiles* III, 2, the author of a play about Cephalus and Procris, which is attended in Badajoz by Periandro and the pilgrims. This seems quite clearly to be a historical name, but it has not been identified by any editor or scholar.

Herrera, Fernando de (1534–97). Poet, priest, historian, and literary scholar, called *el Divino* (the Divine) for the technical and conceptual perfection of his lyric poetry. Herrera's heroic odes and songs (such as those dedicated to the battle of Lepanto and the Invincible Armada), little read or appreciated today, were written to extol the greatness of his nation and its manifest destiny. His lyric poetry, and especially the sonnets dedicated to Doña Leonor de Milán, Countess of Gelves, his idealized love, whom he called *Luz* (Light); are much finer and more readable, though sometimes cold and lifeless. Herrera conceived of himself as one of Spain's truly great writers, but few today would place him in that category. His scholarly, annotated edition (1580) of the already classic lyric poetry of **Garcilaso de la Vega amounts to a coherent poetic theory and defense of an ornate literary style—and at the same time seems to have a subtext of illustrating how much better is his own approach to poetry than was that of the supposedly greatest of Spanish poets (perhaps a case of anxiety of influence). It was the dedication to this book that MC plagiarized for his own dedication of *DQ* I to the duke of Béjar. Herrera also carefully oversaw the meticulous preparation of the 1582 published version of his own works. Little or no direct contact is known to have taken place between Herrera and MC, but both shared a patriotic attitude and both wrote poetry to celebrate the victory at Lepanto, a battle in which MC served and about which Herrera wrote an important history. MC wrote a sonnet (*Poesías* 29) on the occasion of Herrera's death, and he praises him as one of the deceased poets in *Parnaso* 2. Herrera is cited again with other poets called 'Divine' in *Adjunta* and is praised in Calliope's song in *Galatea* 6.

Bibliography: Fernando de Herrera, *Anotaciones a la poesía de Garcilaso*, ed. Inoria Pepe and José María Reyes (Madrid: Cátedra, 2001); Oreste Macrí, *Fernando de Herrera* (Madrid: Gredos, 1972); Mary Gaylord Randel, *The Historical Prose of Fernando de Herrera* (London: Tamesis, 1971); and Pedro Ruiz Pérez, *Libros y lecturas de un poeta humanista: Fernando de Herrera, 1534–1597* (Córdoba: Servicio de Publicaciones, Universidad de Córdoba, 1997).

Herrera, Licenciado Don Pedro de. An ecclesiastical figure and minor poet praised in *Parnaso* 2.

Herrera (Temiño), Juan Antonio de (ca. 1583–1634). A lawyer in Madrid and contributor to anthologies of poetry. See *Parnaso* 4.

Herrera (y Ribera), Don Rodrigo de (1578–1641). A respected nobleman, knight in the Order of Santiago, and an occasional dramatist. He is listed among the good poets in *Parnaso* 2.

Herreros, Enrique G. (1903–77). Spanish artist. Herreros's illustrations for an edition of *DQ* published in 1964 are cartoons in which physical traits are exaggerated: SP is extraordinarily short and fat, DQ is extremely tall and thin, Maritornes is particularly ugly and grotesque, and so forth. But the illustrations capture the comic connotations of the text perhaps better than any other graphic interpretation of MC's novel.

Bibliography: Miguel de Cervantes, *El ingenioso hidalgo don Quijote de la Mancha*, illus. Enrique G. Herreros (Madrid: Editora Nacional, 1964).

Herreruelos de Holanda. *Holland.

Herron, Shaun (1912–). Irish-Canadian novelist. Herron's thriller *The Bird in Last Year's Nest* (1974) is set in the context of political and guerrilla resistance in the post–Civil War Spain of Francisco Franco. The title comes from the Spanish proverb quoted by DQ in II, 74, as he is dying (ironically, it is the last proverb in the novel and comes from DQ, rather than SP). There are also Spanish proverbs throughout Herron's novel, both in the epigraphs at the head of every chapter and in words spoken by characters, especially Don Ugalde, in the text. A number of these proverbs are also spoken by SP at various times in *DQ*, and it is clear that MC's novel is the source for many of them. The proverbs contribute to the tone and flavor of the book, and they cannot fail to ring familiar to the reader of *DQ*, but Herron's novel is quixotic only to the extent that resistance to a powerful totalitarian government is necessarily so to some extent.

Hesperia [Esperia]. A Greek word meaning *western land,* used for Italy by the Greeks and for Spain by the Romans. MC refers to Spain by this name in *Parnaso* 7.

Hesperides [Hespérides, Espérides]. In Greek myth, the daughters of Nyx and Erebus (Night and Darkness), who tended a garden in which grew the tree that gave the *golden apples. See *Parnaso* 3; *Persiles* IV, 7.

Hesse, Hermann (1877–1962). German novelist and poet. Hesse's most popular novel *Steppenwolf* (1927) features a quixotic protagonist—Harry Haller, also known as Steppenwolf. Haller's revolt against reality and escape into fantasy and madness are consistently and

explicitly described as being like DQ's: "I had played Don Quixote often enough in my difficult, crazed life, had put honor before comfort, and heroism before reason. There was an end of it! . . . Yes, I understood the invitation to madness and the jettison of reason and the escape from the clogs of convention in surrender to the unbridled surge of spirit and fantasy." Hesse's last and best novel, *Das Glasperlenspiel* (1943; *The Glass Bead Game*, but translated as *Magister Ludi*), has a narrative structure that parallels that of MC in *DQ*. The title page reads, "The Glass Bead Game: A tentative sketch of the life of Magister Ludi Joseph Knecht, together with Knecht's posthumous writings, edited by Herman Hesse." The text begins as follows: "It is our intention to preserve in these pages what scant biographical material we have been able to collect concerning Joseph Knecht, or Ludi Magister Josephus III, as he is called in the Archives of the Glass Bead Game." From time to time in the novel, there is reference to how this "history" came to be written, and the various written and oral sources for the text. The formal similarity with MC, who writes the life of DQ drawing from materials in the Archives of La Mancha and other sources, is obvious.

Hétor. *Hector.

Hiacinto. *Hyacinth.

Hibernia. *Hybernia.

Hibla. A mountain in Sicily famous for its honey. See *Parnaso* 4.

Hidalgo. 1. In *Fuerza*, the father of Leocadia. **2.** In *DQ* II, 31, a character in an anecdote narrated by SP upon arrival at the castle of the duke and duchess. **3.** In *Persiles* I, 5, a friend of Antonio the Barbarian who advises him on forms of address. **4.** *Nobility.

Hidalgo, Gaspar Lucas. Spanish writer. He is the author of *Diálogos de apacible entretenimiento* (1609; *Dialogues of Pleasant Entertainment*), by far the most popular book of the age on manners and decorum, set forth in a series of witty, occasionally scatological, and often entertaining anecdotes and examples. There is no direct evidence that MC knew the book, but it is more likely than not that he was indeed familiar with this very popular and influential work.

Hidalguía. *Gentility.

Hidaspe. A river in India that marked the extent of the land conquered by Alexander the Great, and therefore a term for something very far distant. See *Galatea* 6.

Hidra de Lernea. *Hydra of Lernea.

Hidropsía. *Dropsy.

Hieronymite Order. *Saint Jerome.

Higa. *Fig.

Highwaymen [Salteadores]. In *DQ* I, 29, according to the priest, four criminals freed by some madman (i.e., DQ), who robbed him and the barber.

Hija de [Spanish name]. *Daughter of [same name].

Hija de Peneo. *Daphne.

Hija de un caballero rico. *Daughter of a rich nobleman.

Hija del corregidor. *Daughter of the magistrate.

Hija del ventero. *Innkeeper's daughter.

Hija pequeña. *Young daughter.

Hijas de Dánao. *Danaids.

Hijo. *Son.

Hijo de [Spanish name]. *Son of [same name].

Hijo de la puta. *Son of a whore.

Hijo de la Tierra. *Anteus.

Hijo de Latona. *Apollo.

Hijo de Pedro de Lobo. *Pedro de Lobo.

Hijo de Sancho Panza. *Sanchico.

Hijo de un labrador. *Peasant's son.

Hijos de Teógenes. *Teógenes's children.

Hijos del mercader. *Merchant's children.

Hill of Carmen [Cuesta del Carmen]. A hill, street, and plaza in Toledo, where the monastery of *Our Lady of Carmen was located. See *Fregona*.

Hill of Zambra [Cuesta de Zambra]. A high spot on the road in the mountains between Málaga and Antequera. In *Vidriera*, it is where Tomás Rodaja meets the infantry captain who will take him to Italy.

Hill of Zulema [Cuesta Zulema]. A large hill southwest of Alcalá de Henares and supposedly the burial place of the "famous" (but unidentified) *Muzaraque, as mentioned in *DQ* I, 29.

Hilo. *Fili.

Hilo portugués. *Portuguese thread.

Himavo. *Limabo.

Himeneo. *Hymen.

Hinsch, Heinrich. German dramatist. Hinsch wrote the text for *Der irrende Ritter Don Quixotte de la Mancia* (1690; *The Knight-Errant Don Quixote de la Mancha*), with music by Johann Philipp Förtsch. It is the first German opera based on *DQ* directly from Spanish rather than from the more popular French translations widely read in late-seventeenth-century Germany. Most of the action is taken from the adventures of DQ with the duke and duchess in II, 30–57 (DQ's battle with the cats, the bearded *dueñas*, and so forth). In the prologue DQ is presented as a wise fool, someone who, in his madness, can state the truth with impunity. In the opera itself, however, DQ is much more serious than comic, inspiring pity as much as comic derision, anticipating the eighteenth-century romantic understanding of his character.

Bibliography: Barbara P. Esquival-Heinemann, "Some Forgotten Don Quijote(s)," *Cervantes* 12, no.1 (1992): 45–57.

Hipócrates. *Hippocrates.

Hipocrene. *Hippocrene.

Hipogrifo. *Hippogriff.

Hipólita. *Hippolyte.

Hipólita la Ferraresa. In *Persiles* IV, 7, the beautiful Roman courtesan, from the northern Italian city of Ferrara, who attempts unsuccessfully to seduce Periandro. Then, jealous, she enlists the aid of Julia, the wife of the Jew Zabulón, who is reputed to be the greatest witch in Rome, to poison Auristela. But when she sees that Periandro is dying along with Auristela (IV, 10), she has the spell lifted. Later (IV, 13), she repents and offers her wealth in support of Persiles and Auristela. When her lover Pirro Calabrés sees this, he wounds Periandro and is executed for his crime.

Hipólito. *Hippolytus.

Hipólito (Ipólito). Squire and lover of the empress of Constantinople in *Tirante el Blanco* (*Martorell, Johanot), mentioned in *DQ* I, 6.

Hippocrates [Hipócrates] (fourth century BCE). Ancient Greek physician who became the prototype of a medical healer and ethicist, whose work gave rise to what is known as the Hippocratic Oath. See *DQ* II, 49.

Hippocrene [Hipocrene, Ipocrene]. A fountain sacred to the muses on Mount Helicon in Boeotia, supposedly created by the stamping of the winged horse Pegasus. Anyone who drank from the fountain was supposed to acquire the inspiration to write poetry. See *Galatea* 6; *Parnaso* 2–3.

Hippogriff [Hipogrifo]. A winged horse with the head of an eagle, the spawn of a griffin and a mare. In *Ariosto's *Orlando Furioso*, Astolfo rides the hippogriff as he searches for information about Orlando. The ride on Clavileño (*DQ* II, 41) is a parody of this famous fabulous animal. See *DQ* I, 25; *Novelas*, dedication.

Hippolyte [Hipólita]. In Greek myth, the queen of the Amazons, who married Theseus. See *Doncellas*.

Hippolytus [Hipólito]. In Greek myth, the son of Theseus and Hippolyte, queen of the Amazons. Theseus's second wife, Phaedra, fell in love with Hippolytus but he rejected her advances. She committed suicide, leaving a note accusing her stepson of having raped her. Hippolytus was banned from the kingdom by Theseus and died in an accident upon leaving. See *Galatea* 4.

Hiqueznaque (Chiquiznaque). River in North Africa, today called the Ain Sefra, near Mostaganem. See *Tratos* 3.

Hired gunmen [Pistoletes]. In *Española*, four men employed by Count Arnesto to kill Ricaredo; in Acquapendente, they fire upon him and leave him for dead, but of course he recovers.

Historia [history]. The term MC uses to refer to the genre of *DQ*. He could not use the modern term *novela* (novel), because in the Renaissance, largely under the influence of the Italian writers of *novelle* (short fictions), that word was used for what today would be called a *cuento* (short story). But MC capitalizes on the polysemy of the word, which means both *history* and *story*, in his constant metafictional treatment of the genesis and status of the work. *DQ* is a "true" (hi)story; that is, it is a true account and a fiction at the same time. Further, this true history is presented as having been written by CHB, a Muslim and therefore, by definition, a liar. Throughout *DQ* (and *Persiles* and other works, to varying degrees), MC plays with the ambiguous and shifting relationships between history and fiction. Given the classic distinction between the poet and the historian (the latter must write things as they were, whereas the former can write them as they might have been) cited by Sansón Carrasco in *DQ* II, 3, one might say that in *DQ*, MC writes poetry (i.e., fiction) with the technique of history; that is to say, he writes a novel.

Bibliography: William Nelson, *Fact or Fiction: The Dilemma of the Renaissance Storyteller* (Cambridge: Harvard University Press, 1973); and Bruce W. Wardropper, "*Don Quixote*: Story or History?" *Modern Philology* 63 (1965): 1–11.

Historia de don Quijote de la Mancha, escrita por Cide Hamete Benengeli, historiador arábigo [History of Don Quixote de La Mancha, Written by Cide Hamete Benengeli, Arabic Historian]. In *DQ* I, 9, MC buys a manuscript with this title from a boy in Toledo and then pays a bilingual *Morisco* to translate it for him. His edition of this translation became the text of *DQ* that we read, but under a modified title.

Historia de la demanda del Santo Brial (History of the Quest for the Holy Skirt). The substitution of the word *brial* (skirt) for *grail* gives a comic connotation to this popular Arthurian romance published in Spanish in 1515. See *Coloquio*.

Historia de la linda Magalona, hija del rey de Nápoles, y de Pierres, hijo del conde de Provenza (1519; History of the Lovely Magalona, Daughter of the King of Naples, and of Pierre, Son of the Count of Provence). An anonymous translation of a medieval Provençal romance of chivalry that had six editions in the sixteenth century. See *DQ* I, 49, DQ also discusses a flying horse episode (antecedent of the Clavileño episode in II, 41), but there is no such scene in this romance.

Historia del emperador Carlomagno y los doce pares de Francia (History of the Emperor Charlemagne and the Twelve Peers of France). An anonymous French romance translated into Spanish in 1525. It enjoyed great popularity, with ten printings in the sixteenth

century. It tells the story of the Saracen admiral Balán, who held court in the Castillo de Aguas Muertas (Castle of Dead Waters) with his son *Fierabrás and his daughter Floripes. The only way to reach the castle was by means of the marble bridge of Mantible, which was defended by the giant Galafre and an army of pagans. Those who wanted to cross the bridge were required to pay a tribute of 100 maidens, horses, falcons, and dogs. Floripes fell in love with Guy de Borgoña, one of the Twelve Peers of France; helped save him; and then converted to Christianity and married him. DQ refers to several of these characters in his conversation with the Canon of Toledo in I, 49. See also *Celoso*.

Historia del famoso caballero Tirante el Blanco. *Martorell, Johanot.

Historia del Gran Capitán Gonzalo Hernández de Córdoba, con la vida de Diego García de Paredes. *Pérez del Pulgar, Hernán.

Historia peregrina sacada de diversos autores (Strange Story Taken from Several Authors). In *Persiles* IV, 2, an alternate title suggested for the book of aphorisms compiled by a pilgrim whom Periandro and the rest of the group meet near Rome.

History. *Historia.

Hoces, Ramón de. According to SP and DQ, a famous maker of knives and swords who lived and worked in Seville. The name is probably historical, but it is also possible that it is an invention of MC's. See *DQ* II, 23.

Hoffman, Lee (1932–). American science-fiction writer. In her novel *Always the Black Knight* (1970), set in the far future, the protagonist, Kyning, plays the evil knight (riding a robot horse) dressed in black in a show staged on various planets, always scripted for him to lose to his hated rival. In his spare time Kyning reads and quotes from *DQ*, he constantly compares himself to DQ, and he dubs the woman he loves DT. Throughout the novel the themes of books versus life, reality versus fantasy, the nature of true chivalry, and so forth are prominent. In the final scene, Kyning defends his beloved DT and rights a wrong done by his rival, whom he kills in the process. Mortally wounded himself, however, he dies happily for the love of a beautiful woman.

Hoffmann, E(rnst) T(heodor) A(madeus) (1776–1822). German novelist and composer. Hoffmann's most famous novel is the unfinished two-volume story of a cat: *Lebensansichten des Katers Murr nebst fragmentarischer Biographie des Kapellmeisters Johannes Kreisler* (1819–21; *The Opinions of the Cat Murr, with a Fragmentary Biography of Conductor Johannes Kreisler*). But Hoffmann also turned to MC for a story about a dog: "Nachrichent von den neuesten Schicksalen des Hundes Berganza" (1814; "Report on the New Adventures of the Dog Berganza"). In this sequel to *Coloquio*, Berganza is alone (Cipión having died; taking his place in the dialogue is the author-narrator) and in Bamberg, Germany, where he serves only two masters, a musician and a young woman.

Bibliography: Blanca Ruiz, "Recepción de las *Novelas ejemplares* en los románticos alemanes," *Anales Cervantinos* 29 (1991): 217–28; and Galo Yagüe Marinas, "Reflexiones sobre el *Coloquio de los perros*, de Cervantes, y las *Nuevas aventuras del perro Berganza*, de E.T.A. Hoffmann," *Anales Cervantinos* 24 (1986): 163–77.

Hogarth, William (1697–1764). English painter and engraver. Hogarth was one of a number of artists invited to submit illustrations for the famous 1738 edition of *DQ*, the first annotated edition of the novel (*iconography of Don Quixote). He prepared a series of six engravings, but his work was not accepted (although one was used in the book), and those done by John *Vanderbank were chosen to illustrate the book. The Hogarth illustrations were finally published in 1791.

Holland [Holanda]. The Netherlands. Holland was especially famous in Spain as a source of many types of the fine cloth: Cambray linen (*Holanda Cambray*), capes (*herreruelos*), and sheets (*sábanas*). See *DQ* II, 44, 51, 53; *Guarda*.

Holofernes. In the Old Testament, one of Nebuchadnezzar's generals who laid siege to Bethulia until he was killed by *Judith.

Holy Brotherhood [Santa Hermandad]. Both a militia or armed body of policemen called *cuadrilleros* (because of the type of arrows, *cuadrillos*, they used in their crossbows when the institution was first created) and a tribunal first organized by Fernando and Isabel in 1476. The Holy Brotherhood could thus apprehend criminals and try them, without the intervention of any other civil authority; it had a reputation for efficiency; and it often inspired fear in the hearts of wrongdoers. The Holy Brotherhood underwent some modification from time to time, but it remained an important law enforcement and legal institution in Spain until 1835. In many ways, it was the forerunner of modern Spain's fabled Guardia Civil (Civil Guard), so prominent during the years of the Franco dictatorship (1939–75), and still active throughout the country. The Holy Brotherhood is mentioned frequently in *DQ*, beginning with SP's worry that the episode with the *Basque squire might be called to the attention of the police (I, 10). It becomes more prominent in the encounter with members of this organization in the first stay in the *inn of Juan Palomeque (I, 17), SP's insistence that he and DQ leave the scene where they freed the *galley slaves (I, 22–23), and especially in the brawl and attempt to arrest DQ during the second stay at Palomeque's inn (I, 45). See also *DQ* I, 29; *DQ* II, 4; *Persiles* III, 4.

Holy Crucifix of Saint Augustine [Santo Crucifijo de Santo Agustín]. An object of veneration in the church of San Agustín (today San Roque) in Seville. See *Rinconete*.

Holy Father. *Pope.

Holy images [Imágenes de relieve]. In *DQ* II, 58, the four large wooden figures of Christian saints being taken to form part of the altarpiece of a village church. DQ and SP look at each of the figures, and DQ describes each one in terms of knight-errantry. Particularly interesting is the contrast between the bellicose Saint James and the peaceful Saint Paul, with the latter coming across as a much greater figure.

Bibliography: Edward Sarmiento, "Don Quixote and the Holy Images," *Dublin Review* 44 (1947): 38–47.

Holy League [Santa Liga]. The alliance forged in 1571 by Pope Pius V and Felipe II that combined the forces of Spain, Venice, and the papacy against the Turks. The major accomplishment of the alliance was to assemble the forces led by Don Juan of Austria in the decisive victory over the Turkish forces in the battle of *Lepanto. The League was dissolved in 1573 when Venice signed a peace treaty with Turkey.

Holy monastery. *Monastery of Belem.

Holy Office. *Inquisition.

Holy Sacrament [Santísimo Sacramento]. The consecrated bread used in the Eucharist (Communion), representing the body of Christ. In *Persiles* III, 11, when the Turks raid the city being visited by Periandro and the pilgrims, the band of Christians locks itself in the church, and the local priest takes with them the Holy Sacrament so that Christ cannot be defiled by the infidel invaders.

Holy Sepulcher. *Heraclius.

Holy Thursday [Jueves Santo]. The day before Good Friday in Holy Week; also known as Maundy Thursday. See *Cueva*; *Rinconete*.

Holy Week [Semana Santa]. The week before Easter. See *Poesías* 25.

Holy Year [Año Santo]. A year of plenary indulgence or remission of punishment for sins, on certain conditions. A regular Holy Year (also known as a Jubilee) is held every 25 years (e.g., in 1550, 1575, and 1600 in MC's lifetime), but they are also proclaimed on special occasions (e.g., in 1560 and 1606). It is not clear if the Holy Year mentioned in *Persiles* III,

9, was intended to refer to any particular year or is simply a special occasion in fictional time.

Hombre a caballo. *Rosanio.

Hombre a pie. *Man on foot.

Hombre de muy buen talle. *Impressive-looking man.

Hombre español. *Spaniard.

Hombre portugués. *Portuguese man.

Hombre sentado en la delantera. *Man sitting up front.

Hombre vestido de ganadero rico. *Man dressed as a wealthy cattle dealer.

Hombre vestido de un gabán verde. *Knight of the Green Overcoat.

Hombres. *Men.

Hombres de a caballo. *Horsemen.

Hombres vestidos de luto. *Men dressed in mourning.

Homer [Homero] (probably eighth century BCE). Greek epic poet, author of the *Iliad* and the *Odyssey*. Whether there was actually a single individual who went by this name, whether there were two or three historic individuals to whom the name Homer refers, or whether the name just became a catchall for authorship of all ancient oral epic poetry is the subject of much debate. At any rate, Homer stands for the best of the great oral narrative tradition of antiquity. See *DQ* I, prologue, 6, 25; *DQ* II, 3, 16, 74; *Galatea* 6; *Parnaso* 2.

Homicidio de la Fidelidad y la Defensa del Honor. Le Muerte de la Fidélité, et la Defense de l'Honneur, Où est racontée la triste et pitoyable avanture du Berger Philidon, et les raisons de la belle et chaste Marcelle. Avec un Discours de Don Quixote De l'Excellence des Armes sur les Lettres (1609; The Murder of Faithfulness and Defense of Honor,

Hondaro, Diego de (?–1605)

Where the Sad and Pityable Adventure of the Shepherd Philidon Is Told, along with the Speech of the Beautiful and Chaste Marcella. With a Discourse by Don Quixote on the Excellence of Arms over Letters). An anonymous bilingual text published in Paris. It adapts and expands on the story of Grisóstomo and Marcela from *DQ* I, 12–14, and adds on DQ's speech on arms and letters from I, 37–38.

Hondaro, Diego de (?–1605). The second husband of Juana Gaitán, widow of MC's friend Pedro *Laínez. He lived with Juana in the same house as MC and his family, but died before the events relating to the murder of Gaspar de Ezpeleta there on June 27, 1605.

Honor (Honra). Spain's exaggerated code of honor that played such an important part in Spanish life and literature can be traced back at least as far as the legal treatise of Alfonso X called the *Siete Partidas* (1256; *Seven Divisions*), where it was stated that a defamed man, even if innocent, was considered dishonored. Most often, *honor* and *honra* are used interchangeably, but at times *honor* is employed to suggest the abstract quality itself, whereas *honra* tends to refer to the "honorable" opinion (i.e., *fama* or reputation) one held in the eyes of others. A man's honor could be sullied by a mere rumor, and it was his duty to defend his reputation as a good Christian, a nobleman, a man above any sort of menial labor, a man of his word, a faithful husband, a protective father, and the proud possessor of a recognized virtuous wife and/or virginal daughter. A stain on one's honor often led to a swordfight and bloodshed. There was a spectacular (if rare) case of honor and revenge in Seville in 1555, in which a man proved his wife's adultery in court and received permission to punish both her and her lover. In a public act, he stabbed them to death and then removed his hat to show to all in attendance that he had no horns (the metaphorical symbol of cuckoldry). Lope de *Vega wrote in his *ars poetica* entitled *Arte nuevo de hacer comedias* (1609; *The New Art of Play Writing*) that cases of honor always moved the public, and he made the theme of honor a cornerstone of his theater. The theme also runs through most fiction of the time, especially short fiction, so popular in Spain in the wake of MC's *Novelas*. Though a woman's honor was sometimes referred to, women were seen primarily as the (naturally weak) vessel of their husbands' (or fathers') honor. Honor was valued more than life itself—as reflected, for example, in the long discussion between Lotario and Anselmo (*DQ* I, 33) in which the former says that to take away his friend's honor would be the same as killing him; in DQ's willingness to accept death since he was unable to defend his honor in the encounter with the Knight of the White Moon (*DQ* II, 64); and in the decision by Eusebio (*Persiles* II, 19) to accept death rather than dishonor when he loses a duel. The preoccupation with honor is at the heart of the personal misfortunes of characters such as *Antonio the Barbarian and *Ortel Banedre in *Persiles*. See also *Doncellas*; *Persiles* I, 14; II, 2.

Bibliography: David R. Castillo, "A 'Symptomatic' View of the Honor System in Cervantes's Theater," in *(A)wry Views: Anamorphosis, Cervantes, and the Early Picaresque* (West Lafayette, IN: Purdue University Press, 2001), 113–30; José Manuel Losada Goya, "Honor y pureza de sangre en *El Quijote*," in *Actas del II Congreso Internacional de la Asociación de Cervantistas*, ed. Giuseppe Grilli (Naples: Instituto Universitario Orientale, 1995); 395–404; José Antonio Maravall, *Poder, honor y élites en el siglo XVII* (Madrid: Siglo XXI, 1979); and Julian Pitt-Rivers, "Honour and Social Status," in *Honour and Shame: The Values of Mediterranean Society*, ed. Jean G. Peristiany (Chicago: University of Chicago Press, 1966), 19–77.

Hoorne, Count of. *Montmorency-Nivelle, Philipe.

Horace [Horacio]: Quintus Horatius Flaccus (65–8 BCE). Roman poet. Horace's best-known works are his *Odes*, distinguished by their stylistic polish and perfect form. Horace's famous dictum that at times even Homer nods off is quoted without attribution by Sansón Carrasco in *DQ* II, 3. See also *Coloquio* (where his *Poetics* is mentioned); *DQ* I, prologue; *DQ* II, 16; *Galatea* 6.

Horacio. 1. *Cocles, Publius Horatius. **2**. *Horace.

Horae [Horas]. In Greek myth, the daughters of Zeus and Themis, goddesses of the three seasons (spring, summer, and winter; fall was not considered a separate season). See *Parnaso* 3.

Horas. 1. *Horae. **2**. *Hours.

Horas de Nuestra Señora (*Hours of Our Lady*). A book of prayers. In *Vidriera*, it is one of the two books Tomás Rodaja takes with him on his trip to Italy.

Hornachuelos. In *Pedro* 1, a local farmer who tries to swindle Lagartija, but is made to pay what he owes him.

Hornets [Abispones]. In *Rinconete*, two old men, members of Monipodio's brotherhood of thieves, who circulate throughout Seville and take note of places where there is much money and/or material goods.

Hornos, Conde de. *Montmorency-Nivelle, Philipe.

Horror. In *Casa* 2, the identity taken by Malgesí as he introduces the procession of allegorical figures.

Horse latitudes [Golfo de las yeguas]. A gulf located between Spain and the Canary Islands, so-called because of some mares (*yeguas*) that were supposedly drowned in the vicinity. See *Entretenida* 3.

Horsemen [Hombres de a caballo]. 1. In *DQ* I, 8, four or five people who accompany the Basque lady in the coach. **2**. In *DQ* I, 43, four men who arrive at the inn of Juan Palomeque and find DQ is standing on Rocinante with his hand tied, as Maritornes and the innkeeper's daughter left him the previous evening. When one of the men's mares sniffs at Rocinante, the latter returns the compliment and moves out from under his master, leaving DQ dangling in the air.

Horses of the Sun [Caballos del Sol]. In Greek myth, the four horses who pull Helios's chariot (*Sun) across the heavens every day: Pyoeis, Eous, Aeton, and Phlegon. See *DQ* II, 40.

Hortigosa. 1. In *Casamiento*, the *dueña* of Doña Clementa. **2**. In *Viejo*, the neighbor who brings the young lover to Doña Lorenza's house.

Hortigosa, Fray Diego de. The man who signed one of the four approvals of *Novelas*. Hortigosa, not a very common name, is also the name of two of MC's female characters (see *Casamiento*, *Viejo*).

Hospital of the Resurrection [Hospital de la Resurrección]. Hospital in Valladolid erected in the year 1579 and torn down in 1890. Both the hospital and the home in which MC lived were located on the same street very near the Puerta del Campo. It is in this hospital that Campuzano of *Casamiento* overhears the two dogs talking and writes down what they say: the text of *Coloquio*.

Hours [Horas]. A generic term for a book containing prayers for certain hours of the day. See *Entretenida* 3; *Fregona*; *Rufián* 1.

Hours of Our Lady. *Horas de Nuestra Señora.

House of Austria. *Austria, House of.

House of Jealousy and Forest of Ardenia, The. *Casa de los celos y selva de Ardenia, La.

House of Trade [Casa de Contratación, or La Lonja]. The name of the famous Seville Exchange building that began operation in 1598; it was designed by Juan de Herrera, architect also of El Escorial. La Lonja was the clearinghouse for all financial dealings with the Spanish colonial possessions in America, a commission created by royal ordinance in 1503, the year Seville became the port with exclusive rights to carry on trade with the Indies. MC was clearly familiar with its operations. Today it is the site of the valuable historical Archivo de Indias (Archive of the Indies), the major depository of documents relating to Spanish exploration and colonization of America. See *Coloquio*; *Rinconete*.

Housekeeper [Ama]. In *DQ*, the unnamed woman in her forties who works in DQ's employ, first mentioned in I, 1. She worries constantly for his well-being, willingly participates in the burning of his books (I, 6), and always takes care of him when he returns home. She is leery of SP and tries to keep him from DQ, and SP responds by calling her Satan's housekeeper (*ama de satanás*) (*DQ*, II, 2). See also *DQ* I, 5; *DQ* II, 4, 6–7, 73–74.

Howard, Lord Charles, Earl of Nottingham (1536–1624). English admiral and statesman. Howard led the expedition that raided *Cádiz in 1596, and he headed English forces defending the country against the attack of the Invincible *Armada in 1588. In 1605, he led the English delegation to the Spanish court in Valladolid in order to ratify the peace treaty of 1604, negotiated after the death of Queen Elizabeth (it has been speculated, with no evidence, that William Shakespeare may have formed part of the retinue—which could conceivably have led to a meeting between Shakespeare and MC; see the fictional version of such a meeting in a short story by Anthony *Burgess). Howard is a leading figure in the *Relación de lo sucedido en la ciudad de Valladolid . . . , attributed by some to MC. Luis de *Góngora wrote a stinging satiric sonnet about the presence of the Lutheran heretics in Spain and suggested that MC was commissioned to write up the account of the events: 'We stayed poor; Luther went away rich. / They commanded Don Quixote, Sancho Panza, and his ass / to write an account of these accomplishments.' Whether MC was an official chronicler of these events or not, the recent publication of *DQ* I was known to all involved (*Pinheiro da Veiga), and it may well have been that when Howard and the others in his party returned to London (perhaps with copies of the sensational and popular *DQ* in their pos-

session) knowledge about and popularity of *DQ* began to spread in England.

Howells, William Dean (1837–1920). American novelist, critic, and dramatist. As a boy growing up on a farm in Ohio, Howells was profoundly influenced by his reading of *DQ*; later, he praised MC's design of *DQ* as "the supreme form of fiction" and added that "if we ever have a great American novel, it must be built upon such large and noble lines." Howells's best-known novel is *The Rise of Silas Lapham* (1885), a strong tale about the social and moral dilemmas of a family with newly acquired wealth. The title character's daughter, Penelope, is described by her mother as a DQ in the making: "She reads a great deal. . . . She seems to be at it the whole while. I don't want she should injure her health, and sometimes I feel like snatchin' the books away from her. I don't know as its good for a girl to read so much, anyway, especially novels. I don't want she should get notions." The theme of the influence of novel reading runs throughout the novel. Another character has "read a great many novels with a keen sense of their inaccuracy as representations of life, and had seen a great deal of life with a sad regret for its difference from fiction."

Bibliography: Edwin S. Morby, "Willliam Dean Howells and Spain," *Hispanic Review* 14 (1946): 188–92.

Huarte de San Juan, Juan (ca. 1530–ca. 1588). The most important Spanish physician of the Renaissance. Huarte is best known for his *Examen de ingenios para las ciencias* (1575; *Scientific Examination of Men's Wits*). His work was translated into French, Italian, and English in the sixteenth century, and it was one of the most important and influential medical treatises of the Renaissance in all of Europe. Huarte's medical theory was an important statement of what was perhaps the reigning theory of human biology and psychology in the Renaissance. The human body was considered to consist of four humors: blood, cholera, bile, and melancholy. ("Humor" then stood for temperament; to be "humorous" often meant to be mad; thus the link between medical theory and comedy.) Health and psychological status were determined by the relationships among these elements, and these relationships, in turn, were influenced by heat, humidity, and other conditions. People were often described in terms of their dominant humor; they were melancholic, phlegmatic, sanguine, or choleric. Sleep was considered one of the best means of restoring the proper balance among the humors. Like most of his contemporaries, MC apparently knew Huarte's theories, as it has been shown how his vocabulary and imagery informs the description of the madness and pathology of DQ, Anselmo of *Curioso*, the protagonist of *Vidriera*, Antonio the Barbarian (*Persiles* I, 5), and other characters. DQ's brain, for example, is hot and dry from his excessive reading and lack of sleep, which leads to an imbalance and a predominantly choleric personality, together with an imaginative and inventive intelligence. But if choler is dominant early in the novel, by the time of DQ's death melancholy becomes more prominent. In II, 48, it is revealed that the duchess has two running sores, incisions made by a physician, to drain off the evil humors from her body.

Bibliography: Otis H. Green, "El *ingenioso hidalgo*," *Hispanic Review* 25 (1957): 175–93; Chester S. Halka, "*Don Quijote* in the Light of Huarte's *Examen de ingenios*: A Reexamination," *Anales Cervantinos* 19 (1981): 3–13; Daniel L. Heiple, "Renaissance Medical Psychology in *Don Quijote*," *Ideologies and Literature* 2, no. 9 (1979): 65–72; and Teresa Scott Soufas, *Melancholy and the Secular Mind in Spanish Golden Age Literature* (Columbia: University of Missouri Press, 1990).

Huerta del Rey. *King's Garden.

Huertas, Calle de. *Calle de Huertas.

Huésped. *Innkeeper.

Huéspeda. *Landlady.

Huéspedes. *Guests.

Huete, Fray Pedro de. Priest and occasional poet praised in Calliope's song in *Galatea* 6.

Hugo, Victor (1802–85). French poet, dramatist, and novelist. Hugo's Esmeralda in *Notre-Dame de Paris* (1831) is based on the gypsy Preciosa in *Gitanilla*. The protagonist of Hugo's *Les Misérables* (1862), Jean Valjean, is simultaneously quixotic and very pragmatic in his struggle against injustice. The character of Monseigneur Bienvenu in the same novel also has some characteristics of DQ.

Humanism [Humanismo]. One of the characteristics of the Renaissance is the intensely renewed interest in things human, as opposed to things divine. In Europe during the centuries-long period now known as the Middle Ages, emphasis was generally centered on the spirit and the afterlife more than on the body and the here-and-now. Although there was no bipolar reversal of this attitude at any point, there was a gradual increase in matters concerning the history, nobility, dignity, and potential of humankind itself. Although it is often asserted that Roman Catholic dogmatism prevented any "rebirth" of the secular human spirit in Spain, that is simply not the case. Of course the Renaissance was more glorious and illustrious in Italy than anywhere else on the continent. Of course certain central aspects of humanist thought, such as scientific inquiry and religious renovation, were more prominent in other countries at the time. And of course the Inquisition and the Council of Trent did all they could to impede independent thought and heterodox belief. It was only natural that new ideas and new challenges to tradition should find particularly enthusiastic reception in heterodox quarters, which meant that the *converso* community was often the locus of humanistic activity in Spain. By the same note, it was the *converso* subgroup that was most suspect as a fertile ground for ideas and activities most objectionable to the reigning ideology. Censorship and repression led to the forced or voluntary exile and prolonged foreign residence of some of the finest original humanist scholars of the period: Benito Arias Montano, Alfonso and Juan de Valdes, and Luis Vives. Yet it is undeniable that a new spirit and a new attitude characterized the Spain in which MC was born and lived. Humanism was distinguished by an intense interest in history, classical erudition, and intellectual and literary scholarship. Important works of foreign humanists—especially the Italians Pietro Bembo, Baldassar Castiglione, Lorenzo Valla; the Portuguese-Spanish-Italian León *Hebreo; and the Dutch *Erasmus of Rotterdam—were translated into Spanish and received much admiration, attention, and imitation. The study of the Greek and Latin languages; the reading, translating, and commentary on classical authors; and the renewed interest in Platonism and Aristotelianism all flourished to a notable degree. The universities at Salamanca and, especially, Alcalá de Henares were by all standards major centers of humanist thought. Among the most important humanists of the period were Antonio de Nebrija (classical philology and grammar), Juan de Mal Lara (proverbs), Juan de Valdés (linguistics), Pero Mexía (classical rhetoric), Alonso de López Pinciano (aesthetics) Juan *Huarte de San Juan (medicine), Bartolomé de Las Casas (medicine), Fernán Pérez de Oliva (philosophy), Alonso de Proaza (rhetoric and translation), and many more. Humanist thought thoroughly informed the poetry of *Garcilaso de la Vega, Fray Luis de *León, Fernando de Hererra, and others. MC's formal education was limited at best, but his early teacher and mentor was the humanist/Erasmian Juan López de Hoyos. Furthermore, MC traveled and lived abroad, especially in Italy, and may well have gained much of his familiarity with humanist thought by reading some works directly in Italian. Clearly he had the sort of natural intellectual curiosity that aligned him sympathetically with humanism and humanistic concerns, as reflected in characters such as the protagonist of *Vidriera*. In addition, MC had a considerable knowledge of Greek, Roman, Italian, and Spanish literature, history, and culture in general. But at the same time he could be skeptical and critical. The portrait of the unnamed pedantic humanist scholar who accompanies DQ and SP to the Cave of Montesinos in II, 22, is typical. Although not a humanist himself, MC as we know him would not have been possible without the humanism of the Spanish Renaissance.

Bibliography: Anthony Goodman, and Angus MacKay, eds., *The Impact of Humanism on Western Europe* (London: Longman, 1990); Donald R. Kelley, *Renaissance Humanism* (Boston: Twayne, 1991); Charles G. Nauert, *Humanism and the Culture of Renaissance Europe* (Cambridge: Cambridge University Press, 1995); Alexander A. Parker, "An Age of Gold: Expansion and Scholarship in Spain," in *The Age of the Renaissance*, ed. Denis Hay (New York: McGraw-Hill, 1967), 221–48; and Domingo Ynduráin, *Humanismo y renacimiento en España* (Madrid: Cátedra, 1994).

Humid god; Húmido dios. *Neptune.

Humors, theory of bodily. *Huarte de San Juan, Juan.

Hunger [Hambre]. In *Numancia* 4, an allegorical figure who appears during the destruction of the city.

Hunt, Edward Eyre (1885–1953). American writer. Hunt's *Tales from a Famished Land* (1918) is a collection of fictionalized, semiautobiographical pieces of reportage concerning Belgium after World War I. The shortest story in the collection is entitled "Doña Quixote" and concerns the Baroness Virginie, whose rebellious nature ("I am going to England to be a suf-fer-a-gette. I will burn churches and bite people. I hate men!") and who prefers to be called *madame*, rather than *mademoiselle*. The narrator, however, noting her more Mediterranean than Viking appearance, decides to call her neither of these titles, preferring the Spanish *Doña*, and dubs her Doña Quixote.

Bibliography: Edward Eyre Hunt, *Tales from a Famished Land* (Garden City, NY: Doubleday, Page, & Company, 1918).

Hunter, J. Paul. Theorist of the novel. Early in the first chapter of his book *Before Novels*, Hunter writes, "Ever since the serious study of English literary history began, the early eighteenth century has seemed the time when a distinct new form of prose fiction emerged, and the only questions have been why and exactly when." Not one to question this assumption, Hunter proposes to examine the cultural and literary contexts that led up to this great English achievement. But he laments that he cannot devote more attention to, for example, the relationships between early French prose fiction and that of England, and then he adds: "In the best of possible worlds, I would like to go further, saying for example something useful about the Spanish tradition, especially Cervantes, for the English novel (let alone the larger novel species) could hardly be what it became without him. But interested as I am in what happens when Cervantic imitation and reaction comes into the novel in England, this is the only place that I mention *Don Quixote*—partly because others have interpreted Cervantes's influence extensively already, but mostly because I feel unqualified in the present context of knowledge about different cultural traditions to speak comprehensively and authoritatively." Thus is MC (who is not even mentioned in the book's index; neither is the Spanish picaresque novel ever discussed in the book) dismissed in a single reference, even though one might think that a book about what was read before novels as they are known in the Anglo-American tradition might feature MC and *DQ* more prominently than any other writer or book.

Bibliography: J. Paul Hunter, *Before Novels: The Cultural Contexts of Eighteenth Century English Fiction* (New York: W. W. Norton, 1990).

Hunters, huntsmen [Cazadores, monteros]. 1. In *Laberinto* 1, two men who accompany Manfredo on his hunt. **2.** In *DQ* II, 30, the men who accompany the duke and duchess on their hunt when DQ and SP meet them. **3.** The servants of the duke who arrange and assist in the boar hunt in *DQ* II, 34. **4.** In *DQ* II, 73, the men chasing the *rabbit that hides under the legs of SP's *rucio*. DQ hands the rabbit over to them.

Hurgada. In *DQ* I, 5, when the beaten DQ is returned home after his first brief sally, he requests that a call be sent out to the enchantress *Urganda la Desconocida to cure his wounds. The housekeeper, who does not recognize the name, huffs that no *hurgada* (meddling woman; the word also has a sexual connotation, suggestion something like 'poked') is called for at this time.

Hurtado, Antonio (1825–78). Spanish poet, novelist, and dramatist. Perhaps Hurtado's best work is *Madrid dramático: cuadros de costumbres de los siglos XVI y XVII* (1870; *Dramatic Madrid: Scenes of Everyday Life from the Sixteenth and Seventeenth Centuries*), a series of evocations, in dramatic verse and actual drama, of the life and times of figures such as Lope de *Vega, *Quevedo, and MC. The section entitled "El facedor de un entuerto y el desfacedor de agravios: Historia breve de un muerto relatada por sus labios" ("The Doer of a Wrong and the Undoer of Offences: A Short History of a Dead Man Told by Himself") was first published separately in 1869. It is set in Madrid in 1615, at the famous *mentidero de comediantes*, where men gathered to talk about literary matters, particularly those involving the contemporary theater. The extravagant braggart Gil Zapata, for his looks sometimes called DQ (and who even claims to have been the model for DQ), tells how he personally knew MC very well, gives a slanderous version of his life, and suggests that he is probably dead. A quiet man who listens to all this then speaks and makes it clear that Gil Zapata is a liar, and he presents a very different picture of MC. After the unknown man leaves, the reader realizes that he actually is MC, a fact also suspected by some of those who are present. Hurtado also collaborated with Adelardo López de Ayala (1829–79) on a four-act theatrical adaptation of *Curioso*.

Bibliography: Antonio Hurtado, *Madrid dramático*, ed. Angel González Palencia (Madrid: Saeta, 1942).

Hurtado de Mendoza, Diego, Duke of El Infantado. *Cervantes, Licenciado Juan de.

Hurtado de Mendoza, Don Antonio (1586–1644). An important figure in the royal court, secretary of Felipe IV, and a knight in the Order of Calatrava. He wrote extensively: poetry of various kinds and theatrical works. MC undoubtedly knew him in Madrid in the 1580s when they both were writing and staging plays. He is praised among the good poets in *Parnaso* 2.

Hurtado de Mendoza, Don Diego (1503–75)

Bibliography: Gareth A. Davis, *A Poet at Court: Antonio Hurtado de Mendoza* (Oxford: Dolphin Press, 1971).

Hurtado de Mendoza, Don Diego (1503–75). Spanish soldier, diplomat, military historian, poet, and humanist. He was the son of the famous poet Iñígo López de Mendoza, Marqués de Santillana, and the close friend of Luis de Granada. Formerly often identified as the author of *Lazarillo de Tormes*, a most unlikely possibility, Hurtado was one of the more admired and influential figures of his time. MC certainly knew Hurtado's poetry, both his restrained, classical lyrics and his more erotic and scatological verse, and must have admired it. In *Galatea* 6, the venerable figure of *Meliso is generally considered to represent Hurtado de Mendoza. In 1610, MC contributed a laudatory sonnet (*Poesías* 30) to a publication of Hurtado's poetry.

Bibliography: David H. Darst, *Diego Hurtado de Mendoza* (Boston: Twayne, 1987); and Helen Nader, *The Mendoza Family in the Spanish Renaissance: 1350–1550* (New Brunswick, NJ: Rutgers University Press, 1979).

Hurtado de Toledo, Luis. *Moraes, Francisco de.

Husband [Marido]. In *Rufián* 1, the man whose wife propositions and is rejected by Cristóbal de Lugo and whom he places under close surveillance.

Hussey, Eyre. English novelist. Hussey's novel entitled *Dulcinea* (1902) is set in the horse-oriented society of the fox hunt and the steeplechase and features a great mare named Dulcinea. The horse is the primary factor in the growing love affair between the beautiful young seamstress, skillful rider, and mesmerist named Kitty Henderson and society gentleman Frank Donaldson, Dulcinea's owner. The novel ends after the tragic death of the horse in a riding accident with the marriage between the two and erection of a polished granite obelisk inscribed with a single word: "Dulcinea." When Kitty first meets the mare, she remarks that the name sounds familiar, and Donaldson responds, "You are thinking of Don Quixote, perhaps." In addition to the heroine's mesmerism, she has accurate "presentiments" of what is to come, and there is another character (a blind woman) who can read thoughts and see the future.

Bibliography: Eyre Hussey, *Dulcinea* (London: Edward Arnold, 1902).

Hyacinth [Jacinto, hiacinto]. Both a flower and the name of a saint: Jacinto. See *Poesías* 23.

Hybernia [Hibernia, Ibernia]. In *Persiles*, the home to Mauricio and his daughter Transila. Often associated with Ireland (though not by MC), this is a mythical kingdom of the northern regions. See *Persiles* I, 12, 21–22.

Hyde, Dayton O. (1925–). American rancher and naturalist. Hyde's *Don Coyote: The Good Times and the Bad Times of a Maligned American Original* (1986) is an account of how a coyote came into the author's life and changed it radically. The coyote begins to follow him, especially as he works with his large, old tractor. One day, he sees the coyote in a special way: "His head sparkled in sunlight, as though it were a silver object emblazoned with blue. Don Quixote wearing a silver baptismal basin for a helmet. A spectacle right out of Cervantes!" He names him Don Coyote on the spot and their relationship begins. Hyde begins to buck the local tide, where common knowledge has it that the only good coyote is a dead one. One day, a hunter shoots and apparently kills Don Coyote, leaving a gap in Hyde's life. He begins to raise coyotes, study them, and learn how to live with them—a process that raises his consciousness in general and makes him a better and more environmentally and ecologically sound rancher. Then, one day, Don Coyote himself reappears, missing one leg and his tail from the hunting incident. From then on he is always around, like a guiding spirit, as Hyde raises his litter of coyotes. Often, such namesakes and concepts are forced, but in this case it works well.

Bibliography: Dayton O. Hyde, *Don Coyote* (New York: Arbor House, 1986).

Hydra (of Lernea) [Serpiente, Hidra de Lernea]. In Greek myth, a serpent with nine heads (the number varies), one of which was immortal and the rest of which were always re- placed by two new ones when cut off. The hy- dra was killed by *Hercules as the second of his 12 labors. See *Casa* 2; *Fregona*.

Hymen [Himeneo]. In Greek myth, the god of marriage. See *Galatea* 3.

Hyrcania. *Tiger from Ocaña.

I

I narrator. *Narrative structure of *Don Quixote*.

Ibernia. *Hybernia.

Ibero. *Ebro.

Ibert, Jacques (1890–1962). French composer. Ibert composed a ballet in four scenes entitled *Le Chevalier errant* (*The Knight-Errant*) and directly inspired in *DQ*. He also wrote the score for the 1933 film of *DQ* directed by Georg Wilhelm Pabst and starring the great Russian tenor Feodor Chaliapin (*Cervantes in film).

Icarus [Icaro]. In Greek myth, the son of Daedalus who used artificial wings to escape the labyrinth of Crete. But he flew too close to the sun, which melted the wax that held the wings together, causing him to fall into the sea and die. He represents high aspirations but faulty planning; he is a symbol of pride or haughtiness. See *Entretenida* 1.

Iceland [Islanda]. An island nation in the northern Atlantic Ocean, located between Greenland and Norway. It is the modern name of *Thule, the homeland of Periandro. See *Persiles* IV, 13.

Iciar, Juan de. A well-known calligrapher who in 1555 published a treatise on writing well. MC mentions him in *Parnaso* 7.

Iconographic Museum of *Don Quixote* [Museo Iconográfico del *Quijote*]. A museum devoted to works of art relating to *DQ* in Guanajuato, Mexico. Over the years, Eulalio Ferrer amassed a large, high-quality collection of over 600 works of art related to *DQ*, and in 1987 he established the museum that houses his unique collection of paintings, engravings, drawings, and sculptures. It is the only museum of its type in the world. The collection features the work of such distinguished artists as the Spaniards Salvador *Dalí, Pablo *Picasso, and José Moreno Carbonero; the Mexicans José Guadalupe *Posada, Mario Orozco Rivers, and Pedro Coronel; and the French Gustave *Doré and Honoré *Daumier.

Bibliography: Antonio Rodríguez, *Museo iconográfico del "Quijote"* (Mexico City: Fundación Cervantina Eulalio Ferrer, 1987).

Iconography of Don Quixote. *DQ* is the most frequently illustrated book in history; no literary figure has been represented in art—paintings, engravings, drawings, and sculpture—as often as DQ. No comprehensive attempt will be made here to cite the literally hundreds of artists who have rendered artistically characters and/or scenes from the novel. The first illustration of *DQ* appeared in a 1618 English edition and depicted DQ, wearing Mambrino's helmet, followed by SP, and with a windmill in the background. The first illustrated edition of the novel was printed in Holland in 1657, with illustrations by Jacobo Savry. The first paintings done outside the book were the 34 scenes by the French artist Jean Mosnier, commissioned by Queen Maria de Medici, for the palace of Cheverny. The romantic engravings of Gustave *Doré, in 1863, are by far the most famous graphic interpretations of the novel. Among other famous illustrators of *DQ* are Tony *Johannot, Salvador *Dalí, Daniel *Urrabieta Vierge, Enrique *Herreros, and Pilar *Coomonte (the first woman to do an illustrated edition of the novel). In addition to graphic interpretations done for the book, artists such as Charles-Antoine *Coypel, Francisco de *Goya, Honoré *Daumier, Pablo *Picasso, and José Guadalupe *Posada have made unforgettable interpretations of the figures of DQ, SP, Rocinante, the windmills, and so forth. The graphic image of DQ has entered into world culture as has that of no other literary figure. There is hardly any modestly educated person (in the Western world, at least) who does not immediately recognize the figure of DQ, even without ever having read the novel. Whether it be Pablo Picasso's ubiquitous black-and-white sketch, the wooden figurines on sale in tourist and souvenir shops throughout the Hispanic world, the popular *Lladró porcelains, or cartoons, the figure of DQ is everywhere. Certainly the other great mythic figures of modern literature—Don Juan, Hamlet, Faust—enjoy no such status (*Don Quixote myth). SP is not far off the mark when, in *DQ* II, 71, he predicts that soon there will hardly be a tavern, inn, or barber shop without scenes depicting the adventures of him and his master.

Bibliography: Francisco Calvo Serraller, ed., *Ilustraciones al "Quijote" de la Academia por varios dibujantes y grabadores, en la imprenta de Joaquín Ibarra, Madrid, 1780* (Madrid: Turner, 1978); Juan Givanel Mas and Gaziel, *Historia gráfica de Cervantes y del "Quijote"* (Madrid: Plus-Ultra, 1946); Carlos Reyero, ed., *Cervantes y el mundo cervantino en la imaginación romántica* (Madrid: Comunidad de Madrid, Consejería de Educación y Cultura, Dirección General de Patrimonio Cultural, 1997); and Rachel Schmidt, *Critical Images: The Canonization of Don Quixote through Illustrated Editions of the Eighteenth Century* (Montreal, Canada: McGill-Queen's University Press, 1999).

Iglesia Católica Romana; Iglesia de Dios Nuestro Señor. *Roman Catholic Church.

Iglesia de Santa María. *Our Lady of Almudena.

Iglesia mayor. *Cloister of the cathedral.

Iglesia, o mar, o casa real. *Pérez de Viedma family.

Igualada. A town located northwest of Barcelona and east of Zaragoza. See *Doncellas*.

Iliad; Ilíada. *Homer.

Ilium. Another name from *Troy, after the name of the legendary founder, Ilus. See *Galatea* 4.

Illescas. A town located between Madrid and Toledo. The sanctuary of Our Lady of Illescas, with its image of the Virgin, became an important site of pilgrimage in the seventeenth century (it had not been such in the sixteenth century). See *Entretenida* 1; *Fregona*; *Persiles* III, 21.

Ilustre fregona, La (Fregona); The Illustrious Kitchen-Maid. The eighth story in *Novelas*. Like *Gitanilla*, this tale is an attempt to combine two worlds and two literary traditions. Here, it is the world of the *pícaro* that is joined with that of the courtly novel. The rapturous description of picaresque life, with its interesting emphasis here on the tuna fisheries of southern Spain, is one of the most interesting and valuable of such set pieces (others are found in Mateo *Alemán's *Guzmán de Alfarache* and Juan de Luna's continuation of *Lazarillo de Tormes*).

Burgos is the home of two noble families, that of Don Diego de Carriazo and that of Don Juan de Avendaño. Each has a son, the first named Diego like his father, the second named Tomás. At the age of 13, Diego de Carriazo leaves home and lives for three carefree years as a *pícaro* in various cities—Madrid, Toledo, and Seville—and especially in the context of the tuna fisheries of Andalusia. He is so good at this way of life that he could give lessons to the great Guzmán de Alfarache himself. After this time, he returns home and becomes close friends with Tomás, who is enthralled by Diego's stories of the picaresque life. The two boys decide to set out again as *pícaros*, and, lying to their parents by saying that they want to go to Salamanca to study, and tricking the servants who are sent to accompany them, they set off for Seville. But along the way they hear a couple of muleteer assistants talking about how the count of Puñonrostro has driven marginal types like *pícaros* out of Seville. The youths continue their discussion, and the topic turns to the Inn of the Sevillano in Toledo, where there is a singularly beautiful kitchen maid. Even a local nobleman's son is reputed to be in love with her. Tomás becomes very interested in seeing this young woman, and persuades Diego to go with him to Toledo for this purpose. When they get there, Tomás sees Costanza, the famous kitchen maid, and is stunned by her beauty. He convinces his friend to stay for a couple of days. After Tomás sees Costanza again, this time in a very rich dress, he is completely in love with her. He gets the innkeeper to take him on as a stableboy and convinces Diego to take work as a water carrier. Careful not to reveal their real identities, Tomás takes the name of Tomás Pedro and Diego takes that of Lope Asturiano. Two women who work at the inn, no longer young and far from attractive, immediately take a romantic interest in the two youths: La Argüello in Tomás Pedro and La Gallega in Lope Asturiano. On his first day on the job, Lope Asturiano gets into an altercation with another water carrier, whom he badly injures. He, in turn, is beaten by a group of others until the law comes and puts him in jail. Tomás Pedro pretends to send for money to get Lope released, actually using some of that which the two had brought with them from home, and within three weeks the injured boy recovers and Lope is set free. During all this time, Tomás has not been able to speak a single word to Costanza, but he is convinced that she is no common kitchen worker, for he has never seen her do anything more demanding than embroidery and keep watch over the silverware; he is convinced that destiny has brought him and Costanza together and that she is in reality more than what appears on the surface. That night, there is a song and dance celebration in the inn; Lope plays the guitar and sings popular songs, improvising as he goes, until a more refined voice (that of the magistrate's son) is heard singing a more sophisticated love song to Costanza. One of the celebrants, a muleteer named Barrabás, makes a sarcastic comment about poets who write things that no one can

understand. Afterward, La Argüello and La Gallega come to the room of Lope and Tomás and beg to be admitted, but the two youths refuse to open the door to them. The next day, as Tomás is taking care of the animals in the stable, the innkeeper comes across the ledger where information on the feedings is kept, and also finds there a love poem Tomás has written to Costanza. He and his wife discuss the matter, Costanza assures them that she has had nothing to do with anyone, and they decide to wait and see what might develop before taking any action. Later that day, Costanza complains of a toothache, and Tomás offers to write out for her a prayer that is a surefire toothache remedy. The note that he gives her, however, is one in which he reveals his identity and his love, and offers to marry her. She returns the 'prayer' to him, but does not tell anyone else about the incident. While all this is taking place at the inn, Lope is out looking to buy an ass so that he can resume his work as a water carrier. He finally buys one from a young man and then gets into a card game with this man and two others. Within a short time, he loses all his money and begins to bet the ass, a quarter at a time. He continues to lose until he has nothing left, but then he comes up with an idea. He has yet to bet the fifth quarter of the ass—the tail. After some wrangling, he is allowed to return to the game with the ass tail as his stake. He begins to win and eventually wipes out the man who sold him the ass, but, compassionate, he returns to him the money he has won. In no time, the story of the ass tail spreads; wherever Lope Asturiano goes, someone refers to it, and the boys of the city begin to taunt him with the refrain, 'Asturiano, hand over the tail.' Because of this, Lope decides to stay in his room for several days. Then late one night the magistrate of Toledo, accompanied by some law officers, enters the inn and demands to speak to the owner. He wants to know more about this serving wench his son Periquito seems to be so in love with. When he sees Costanza, he admits that his son has good reason to be in love. He inquires more about Costanza, and the innkeeper takes him aside to tell him the story behind her being in the inn: just over 15 years ago, a beautiful women of about 40 and dressed as a pilgrim arrived at the inn, accompanied by several servants. Since she was ill, she summoned a physician, but only as a ruse to deceive her servants. She told the innkeeper the truth, that she was pregnant and on her way to the Monastery of Our Lady of Guadalupe, but she was about to give birth. She gave the innkeeper a large sum of money and asked him to care for the child until she returned from her pilgrimage. She gave birth that night to a beautiful daughter, who never even cried. When she recovered, she continued on her pilgrimage and then returned to the inn, with her strength nearly restored, but clearly suffering from dropsy. She then gave the innkeeper a gold chain with some parts missing and a parchment that contained a code, as well as more money, and asked him to keep the child until she called for her or someone else with the countersigns showed up. The innkeeper had Costanza, who was baptized with this name as the lady had requested, raised in a nearby village for two years, and then had her brought to the inn where he and his wife raised her almost as their own daughter. He has waited until this day for more information about Costanza, who is very devout, can read and write, and sings beautifully. He then shows the magistrate the chain and the parchment, which reads 'T I I T E R E I N.' The magistrate takes the chain and the parchment and departs. The very next day, two elderly gentlemen, with four servants, arrive at the inn. They turn out to be Don Diego de Carriazo and Don Juan de Avendaño, the fathers of Lope Asturiano and Tomás Pedro. The former announces that he has come to claim Costanza, and shows the proofs of the missing parts of the chain and the other half of the parchment. The magistrate is summoned with his halves of the proofs, and upon arrival immediately recognizes his cousin Don Juan. The second piece of parchment reads 'H S S H T U S G.' When the two are matched up the message reads 'THIS IS THE TRUE SIGN.' Don Diego reveals that he is Costanza's father and tells his story: Costanza's mother was a widow, retired to a small village. One day when he was hunting, he stopped to see her and found

her asleep. Unable to resist the temptation, he raped her, and never saw her again; two years later, he heard that she had died. Then, just 20 days previously, he was summoned to the deathbed of a man who had been the lady's majordomo. The dying man told him about the birth of Costanza and gave him a very large sum of money and the countersigns. At this point they are interrupted by a group who bring in Lope Asturiano, with his face all bloodied. He had gotten into a scrape with some of the boys who were teasing him, had beaten one, and was injured while resisting arrest. Tomás Pedro is also brought in, and the fathers and sons are reconciled. Costanza is introduced to her father, and all repair to the home of the magistrate for dinner. That night the marriages are arranged: Don Juan's son (Tomás Pedro) is to marry Costanza; Don Diego's son (Lope Asturiano) is to marry a daughter of the magistrate; and the magistrate's son Don Pedro is to marry the daughter of Don Juan. Everyone lived happily ever after, with the poets of the Tagus River (in Toledo) celebrating the events of the Illustrious Kitchen Maid in verse. Diego and his wife have three children, all of whom are students in Salamanca, but to this day he never sees a water carrier without recalling his days in Toledo and fearing that someday, when he least expects it, someone will call out, 'Hand over the tail, Asturiano.'

Bibliography: William H. Clamurro, "Identity, Discourse, and Social Order in *La ilustre fregona*," *Cervantes* 7, no. 2 (1987): 39–56; Eleodoro J. Febres, "*La ilustre fregona*: configuración de la balanza en su forma y contenido," *Anales Cervantinos* 32 (1994): 137–55; Laura Gorfkle and Amy R. Williamsen, "Mimetic Desire and the Narcissistic (Wo)man in *La ilustre fregona* and the *Persiles*: Strategies for Reinterpretation," *Hispania* 77 (1994): 11–22; Javier Herrero, "Emerging Realism: Love and Cash in *La ilustre fregona*," in *From Dante to García Márquez: Studies in Romance Literature and Linguistics Presented to Anson Conant Piper*, ed. Gene H. Bell-Villada, Antonio Giménez, and George Pistorius (Williamstown, MA: Williams College, 1987), 47–59; Robert M. Johnston, "Picaresque and Pastoral in *La ilustre fregona*," in *Cervantes and the Renaissance*, ed. Michael D. McGaha (Easton, PA: Juan de la Cuesta, 1980), 167–77; Monique Joly, "En torno a las antologías poéticas de *La gitanilla* y *La ilustre fregona*," *Cervantes* 13, no. 2 (1993): 5–15; Eric Kartchner, "Metafiction in *La ilustre fregona*: The Search for Meaning in Semiotic Carnival," *RLA: Romance Languages Annual* 10 (1988): 646–52; and Tomás Pabón Corominas, "Ansias de amor: Tomás de Avendaño en *La ilustre fregona*," in *Actas del VIII Coloquio Internacional de la Asociación de Cervantistas*, ed. José Ramón Fernández de Cano y Martín (El Toboso, Spain: Exmo, Ayuntamiento de El Toboso, 1999), 239–46.

Illustrious Kitchen Maid [Ilustre fregona, Fregona ilustre]. In *Fregona*, the name by which Costanza, maid at the Inn of the Sevillano, is known far and wide.

Illustrious Kitchen-Maid, The. *Ilustre fregona, La.*

Image of the Virgin. *Penitents.

Imágenes de relieve. *Holy images.

Imitation (Imitatio) [Imitación]. An important theme in MC's works. In the prologue to *DQ* I, MC's 'friend' insists that as long as a writer imitates good models, his work can be successful. In an important passage in I, 25, DQ discusses the significance of imitation at length as he prepares to imitate the models of Amadís de Gaula and Orlando Furioso in his *penance in Sierra Morena. Mimesis, imitation, and verisimilitude all address aspects of *imitatio* in the sense of reproducing a kind of literary realism (not in the stricter sense in which that term is used in later centuries, particularly the nineteenth).

Bibliography: David H. Darst, *Imitatio: Polémicas sobre la imitación en el Siglo de Oro* (Madrid: Orígenes, 1985); and E. C. Riley, "Don Quixote and the Imitation of Models," *Bulletin of Hispanic Studies* 31 (1954): 3–16.

Imitative Academy (Academy of the Imitators) [Academia Imitatoria (Academia de los Imitadores)]. The first *literary academy established in Madrid in the 1580s. MC was probably one of the original members, along with others such as *Calderón de la Barca, Lope de *Vega, *Quevedo, *Ruiz de

Alarcón, *Tirso de Molina, *Vélez de Guevara, and many, many more. See *Coloquio*.

Immermann, Karl Leberecht (1796–1840). German novelist and dramatist. Immermann's most important novel is *Münchhausen* (1838–39; *The Adventures of Baron Munchausen*), a satire on decadent nobility and toadyism. In it, the quixotic Baron von Münchhausen is filled with impractical projects of a political bent. The novel has been made into a movie by Terry *Gilliam (1989).

Impregnable island, the. *Malta.

Impressive-looking man [Hombre de muy buen talle]. In *DQ* II, 62, the translator of a book from Italian to Spanish whom DQ meets and with whom he talks in a printshop in Barcelona.

In a village of La Mancha [En un lugar de la Mancha]. In *DQ* I, 1, the famous opening line of the novel. It is a citation of an octosyllabic line in a popular ballad, and as such probably was immediately familiar to most of MC's contemporary readers. MC undoubtedly chose not to identify the village (perhaps for some reason based on personal experience, perhaps to begin with the first words of the text his program of ambiguity and uncertainty, or perhaps out of mere whim), and the claim of *Argamasilla del Alba to be that village is not consistent with the deliberate imprecision of the text. It is worth noting that the phrase "en un lugar de" also appears at the beginning of *Celoso* and *Capitán*.

Bibliography: Juan Bautista Avalle-Arce, "Tres comienzos de novela (Cervantes y la tradición literaria. Segunda perspectiva)," in *Nuevos deslindes cervantinos* (Barcelona: Ariel, 1975), 213–43.

Inclán, Federico Schroeder (1910–). Mexican dramatist. In his play *Don Quijote murió del corazón* (1985; *Don Quixote Died of a Heart Attack*), DQ awakens in a twentieth-century mental hospital. He begins a series of conversations with a psychiatrist named Dr. Huerta, who also takes on the role of SP. In this case, DQ suffers from multiple personality disorder and frequently slips into and out of the roles of his other two identities: Alonso Quijano el Bueno and Miguel de Cervantes. The effect of having all three of these personalities comment on the other two is at times quite interesting, even if the overall concept of DQ is a fairly standard romantic one. From time to time, scenes from *DQ* are projected onto a background screen as the two characters discuss the novel. At the end of the play, as DQ prepares to sally forth again, Dr. Huerta-SP struggles with him and defeats him. DQ refuses to surrender and repeats the same words he spoke in *DQ* II, 64, in defense of DT's beauty. In MC's novel, Sansón Carrasco extracts from the defeated knight the promise to return home for a year; in Inclán's play, Huerta-SP extracts from him a promise to remain in the mental hospital until he returns with a specialist. But while the squire-doctor is gone, DQ has a heart attack and, after commending himself to God, dies.

Bibliography: Federico Schroeder Inclán, *Don Quijote murió del corazón* (Mexico City: Universidad Autónoma Metropolitana, 1985).

Index of Forbidden Books [*Indice de libros prohibidos*].

Beginning in 1551, the Inquisition began periodically to publish lists of banned books. The most famous such list was that of 1559, which included the works of *Erasmus, the Valdés brothers, Fray Luis de Granada, the anonymous *Lazarillo de Tormes*, and others. Such public *censorship is, of course, a powerful direct means of curtailing the reading and thought of the populace. But the practice also can be counterproductive when forbidden fruit becomes more attractive and more actively sought out than it might otherwise have been. The circulation of works in manuscript and the passing of copies of older editions from one person to another were common practices (compare the popularity and circulation of the novels of Henry Miller and D. H. Lawrence in first half of the twentieth century in America—not to mention the lurid paperbacks by writers like Mickey Spillane among teenagers in the 1950s). It is hard not to read the examination of DQ's library in I, 6, as a parody of book censorship in Spain.

Bibliography: Angel Alcalá, *Literatura y ciencia ante la Inquisición española* (Madrid and Berkeley: Ediciones del Laberinto, 2001, and University of California Press, 1991); and Virgilio Pinto Crespo, *Inquisición y control ideológico en la España del siglo XVI* (Madrid: Taurus, 1983).

India. In MC's day, a distant, mysterious, exotic land, associated with the Portuguese (who had colonies there, such as Goa), wealth in jewels and spices, and exotic religious practices (*East Indies). See *DQ* I, 47; *Parnaso* 4.

India de Portugal. *Portuguese India.

Indiana amulatada. *Dark-skinned Indian girl.

Indiano. *Peru.

Indias orientales. *East Indies.

Indice de libros prohibidos. *Index of Forbidden Books*.

Indies [Indias]. In MC's day, the term most commonly used by Spaniards to refer the New World, or the Americas, was *Indias*. Many Spaniards went to the Indies in hopes of returning home wealthy and respected (recall MC's applications for administrative posts in the New World), and those who did were called *Indianos*. In *Celoso*, Carrizales is MC's best example of an *Indiano*. See also *Casa* 2; *DQ* I, 8, 29, 39, 42; *DQ* II, 54, 66; *Galatea* 6; *Gitanilla*; *Entretenida* 1–3; *Pedro* 1; *Persiles* II, 15; III, 6, 11; *Poesías* 21; *Sultana* 3; *Viudo*.

Bibliography: Diana de Armas Wilson, *Cervantes, the Novel, and the New World* (Oxford: Oxford University Press, 2000).

Indus [Indo]. A river in northwestern India that flows into the Arabian Sea. See *Galatea* 6.

Inés. In *Pedro* 1, a young gypsy woman, a friend of Belica.

Infantado, Duque de. *Cervantes, Licenciado Juan de.

Infernal doorman; Infernal Three-Headed Guardian of the Gate. *Cerberus.

Información de Argel (Information Relating to Algiers). On October 10, 1580, after his release from slavery in Algiers, MC arranged for the preparation of a notarized document relating to his activities during the period of his captivity. A large part of the motivation was the fact that the man who had betrayed MC's final escape attempt, Juan *Blanco de Paz, had been attempting to impugn MC's character, even to the extent of bribing witnesses. Using quarters provided by his friend Diego de Benavides as the site for the occasion, MC had a dozen witnesses make sworn depositions in the presence of his rescuer, Fray Juan *Gil, and Pedro de Rivera, apostolic notary in Algiers. In the document, MC puts forth exactly 25 items to which each witness is to respond. The items affirm that MC is an Old Christian *hidalgo*, describe his valiant escape attempts during his years of captivity, and detail the cowardly betrayal of the final escape plan by Blanco de Paz. The witnesses called by MC made their depositions in support of all or most of the items enumerated by MC. The list of witnesses includes the following names: Alonso Aragonés, Diego Castellano, Rodrigo de Chaves, Hernando de Vega, Juan de Balcázar, Domingo Lopino, Fernando de Vega, Cristóbal de Villalón, Diego de Benavides, Luis de Pedrosa, Feliciano Enríquez, and Antonio de *Sosa, MC's good friend and chronicler of life in Algiers. The document is one of the more valuable proofs of MC's activities during his years of captivity and reveals a man of courage, loyalty, and character. MC finally set sail for Spain on October 24, 1580.

Bibliography: *Información de Miguel de Cervantes de lo que ha servido a S. M. y de lo que ha hecho estando captivo en Argel, y por la certificación que aquí presenta del duque de Sesa se verá como cuando le captivaron se le perdieron otras muchas informaciones, fees y recados que tenía de lo que había servido a S. M*, ed. Pedro Torres Lanzas (Madrid: Sosé Esteban, 1981); and Emilio Sola and José F. de la Peña, *Cervantes y la Berbería: Cervantes, mundo turco-berberisco y servicios secretos en la época de Felipe II* (México City: Fondo de Cultura Económica, 1995).

Ingenios de la Mancha. *Wits of La Mancha.

Ingenioso hidalgo don Quijote de la Mancha, El. *Don Quijote I.

Inglaterra. *England.

Inglis, H(enry) D(avid) (1795–1835). English travel writer. Inglis's *Rambles in the Footsteps of Don Quixote* (1937) is an interesting and original mixture of travelogue, fiction, and literary criticism. The account of a trip through La Mancha introduces characters from *DQ* and the picaresque novel, and features an ongoing discussion of the novel by the author and his fictional traveling companion, the barber Lázaro, who has his own lengthy story to tell. Along the way they meet bandits, muleteers, innkeepers, and peasants, and the author comments on daily aspects of life as he observes it (one interesting detail: he notes that is it customary for peasant women in La Mancha to cover their heads with the tail of their skirts, rather than with a mantilla, a custom SP's wife Teresa mentions in II, 5). Although the author treats *DQ* as a funny book and a satire, his fictional companion considers it to be more serious.

Bibliography: H. D. Inglis, *Rambles in the Footsteps of Don Quixote* (London: Whittaker and Co., 1837); and W. U. McDonald, "Inglis' *Rambles*: A Romantic Tribute to *Don Quixote*," *Comparative Literature* 12 (1960): 33–41.

Ingratitud vengada, La. *Vega, Lope de.

Inhabitants of Golandia, two. In *Persiles* I, 11, the men who guide the boats containing Periandro, Auristela, and their group to the harbor on the island.

Inn [Venta]. Wayside inns dotted all major and some minor roads connecting urban centers in Spain. Because this was a nation in which there was constant travel of soldiers, nobles, churchmen, merchants, muleteers (the truck drivers of the day), rogues, and *pícaros* from one place to another, a network of overnight stopping places was essential. These inns were occasionally fairly comfortable places to take meals and spend the night, but more often they were spare, minimally furnished, and noisy places, enlivened at night by the drinking, carousing, and gambling of the muleteers and other low-life types. Most of the time, it was expected that travelers themselves would provide their own bedclothing and food; exceptions could always be made for guests wealthy enough to pay for such extra services. Colorful inns provide the locale for many memorable scenes in MC's works; see especially the famous scenes in the *inn of Juan Palomeque in the first part of *Don Quixote*.

Bibliography: Moisés García de la Torre, "Cervantes y el mundo de los caminos: las mulas. Realidad histórica y ficción literaria," in *Cervantes, su obra y su mundo: Actas del I Congreso Internacional sobre Cervantes*, ed. Manuel Criado de Val (Madrid: Edi-6, 1981), 213–25.

Inn of Juan Palomeque. The inn that is prominent in *DQ* I, 16–17, 26–27, and 32–47. Typical of many roadside inns of the period, the one run by Juan Palomeque and his family also becomes the scene of marvelous events: the reading of the tragic love story of *Curioso* (I, 33–35); the reunion of the four lovers of the *Cardenio* story in I, 36; the appearance of the captive Ruy Pérez de Viedma and his renegade lover Zoraida (I, 37) and the telling of their adventures in *Capitán* (I, 39–41), together with the reunion of the Pérez de Viedma brothers (I, 42); and the partial telling of the story of the Clara-Luis romance (I, 42–44). In this series of chapters, there is an extraordinary amount of coincidence, presence of stunningly beautiful women (Dorotea, first of all, followed by Luscinda, Zoraida, and Clara), shedding of tears, and happy endings that all take place within a matter of a few days. Here a simple roadside inn is converted into a sort of prosaic 'palace of Venus,' an enchanted site where all the lovers' problems are solved. The classic example of such a palace is that of the magician Felicia in *Montemayor's *La Diana*, where all the lovers' problems are solved by means of the magic

water Felicia gives everyone to drink. MC seems to be suggesting both that the line between literature and life is easy to blur and that no magic drinks are required to work out personal problems.

Inn of la Barbuda [Venta de la Barbuda]. An inn mentioned in *Entretenida* 3. The word *barbuda*, which means 'bearded woman,' is involved in some comic wordplay involving the names of the two Caribbean islands Barbuda and Bermuda.

Inn of la Solana [Posada de la Solana]. An inn in Valladolid, probably located on the street of the same name. In *Casamiento*, it is where Campuzano is staying.

Inn of la Zarza [Venta de la Zarza]. The phrase "a la venta de la Zarza" does not refer to a specific inn, but rather means to shout and make a great confusion. It is used in *Vizcaíno*.

Inn of Molinillo. In the Golden Age, the name of a well-known inn on the road from Madrid to Andalusia, almost equidistant between Toledo and Córdoba, very near Almodóvar del Campo. In *Rinconete*, it is where Rinconete and Cortadillo meet.

Inn of the Alcalde. In the Renaissance, an inn on the road from Castile to Andalusia. It was located very near the *Inn of Molinillo. See *Rinconete*.

Inn of the Sevillano [Posada del Sevillano]. One of the best and most frequented inns in Toledo. In *Fregona*, it is where Costanza lives, supposedly as a kitchen maid, and where most of the action takes place.

Innkeeper [Ventero, huésped, mesonero, patrón del hospedaje, dueño del mesón o hospedaje]. 1. In *DQ* I, 2–3, the owner of the first inn DQ visits, who greets him upon his arrival, humors him in his chivalric madness, puts him on display for the entertainment of his clients when DQ stands guard over his arms, and dubs him a knight in a burlesque ceremony. He is described as a sort of retired *pícaro* who spent his youth in a variety of well-known haunts of criminals, vagabonds, gamblers, prostitutes, and *pícaros* (*picaresque geography). **2.** In *Fregona*, the man who raises Costanza from infancy, and who employs Avendaño as stable-boy and Carriazo as water carrier. **3.** In *DQ* II, 25–26, the owner-operator of the inn visited by DQ and SP. It is in this inn that *Maese Pedro puts on his puppet show **4.** In *DQ* II, 59, the owner of the establishment where DQ meets Don Juan and Don Jerónimo, readers of *DQA*. The innkeeper and SP engage in a comic conversation about what there is to eat. **5.** In *Persiles* I, 12–16, the owner-operator of the inn on the otherwise deserted island where Periandro and company meet Mauricio and his group and then are later joined by Arnaldo. **6.** In *Persiles* III, 4, the man who provides the evidence that clears the pilgrims in the death of Don Diego de Parraces.

Innkeeper's daughter [Hija del ventero]. The unnamed attractive young daughter of *Juan Palomeque, the owner of the inn that is the scene of much of the action in the second half of *DQ* I. She receives and ministers to DQ in I, 16–17, his first visit to the inn, when he believes she is a princess, the daughter of the lord of the castle, who is in love with him, which leads directly to the melee involving Maritornes in I, 16. On the second, extended visit DQ makes to the inn (I, 32–47), she remains mostly in the background, except for when she describes how she enjoys the love scenes in the romances of chivalry (I, 32), when she and Maritornes trick DQ and tie his hand to a window as he stands on Rocinante's back (I, 43), and when she and her mother enlist DQ's help when two men try to sneak out of the inn without paying and get into a fight with her father (I, 44). Overall, she comes across as a charming, polite, and decent young woman.

Innkeeper's wife [Ventera]. The unnamed wife of Juan Palomeque who participates in the events in the inn in *DQ* I, 16–17, 26–27, 32–47. Her two most interesting moments come when she suggestively evokes the erotic connotations of her husband's comb and her own

oxtail in I, 27, 32 (*erotic and/or obscene themes and imagery in Cervantes), and when she begs DQ in his capacity as a knight-errant (and because he is the only one not already preoccupied) to help her husband, who is having difficulty with two guests who are attempting to leave the inn without paying (I, 44).

Inquisition: Holy Roman and Universal Inquisition (Holy Office) [Santa Inquisición Romana y Universal (Santo Oficio)]. Probably the most famous official institution of religious and political suppression in European history. Medieval Spain under Muslim rule—the Spain of the three religions (Judaism, Christianity, and Islam)—was for centuries a truly pluralistic and multicultural society. But as political and military power shifted definitively to the Christian forces during the Reconquest, religious intolerance became the norm. There had been purges and massacres of Jews in the thirteenth and fourteenth centuries, but in the politically divided Christian kingdoms there was no official mechanism to carry out religious purification. From the beginning of their joint reign, however, the *Catholic Monarchs, Fernando and Isabel, made evident their unwillingness to rule over a multicultural nation. The Inquisition (an institution that had existed, in much milder versions, in France and Italy since the thirteenth century) was instituted in 1478 as an integral part of Spain's nationalistic political ideology. It was governed by the Consejo Supremo de la Inquisición (Supreme Council of the Inquisition), a board whose chair held the title of inquisitor general. The fact that the Inquisition, like other royal councils, was a governmental and secular, rather than an ecclesiastical, institution is often ignored when mistakenly attributing its activities to the Catholic Church. Collaborating with the Inquisition was a large number (over 20,000 in the seventeenth century) of *familiares*, sort of informal and voluntary (but sometimes quite fanatical) secular watchdogs or informers (Lope de *Vega, like other nobles and well-known writers who considered the title an honor, was a familiar near the end of his life). The first inquisitor general was the infamous Tomás de Torquemada, who in fact was no worse than others in his position, although his name has become synonymous with fanaticism, torture, and repression (*Black Legend). After the conquest of Granada in 1492, one of the first acts of the Catholic Monarchs was to expel the Jews from the newly united kingdom; the Muslims suffered the same fate in 1502. The first generation of *converso* (i.e., those living immediately after the expulsion decree of 1492) were among those most severely persecuted. Subsequently, the Inquisition grew steadily in power and influence, persecuting especially the *converso* community and, to a lesser extent, converted Muslims, Protestants, and a variety of witches and sorcerers. Lack of *purity of blood, any hint of secret Jewish or Islamic practices (*Marranos* or *Moriscos*), or participation in Protestant, Erasmian, or other heterodox activity made one susceptible to Inquisitorial investigation, where anonymous testimony and torture (which encouraged victims to reveal God's truth) were common practices; and, when all else failed, burning at the stake in an *auto-da-fé was an option (although one used less frequently than in other countries—such as England). In fact, one of the most serious penalties that the Inquisition prescribed was the wearing of a *sambenito (a distinctive yellow robe) for a period of time, or for one's natural life (after which it was hung in the parish church as a damnation of the wearer's descendants). In spite of the Inquisition's legendary reputation for secrecy, fanaticism, and cruelty, it was by contemporary standards no worse than other European tribunals. It was not formally abolished until 1843. Among the more famous Spaniards of the time who were officially investigated by the Inquisition were Saint Ignacio de *Loyola and Fray Luis de *León. MC is not known to have had direct personal contact with the Inquisition, but there is no question that his life was affected by its policies (*censorship). When MC applied in 1582 for a civil service job in the New World he was turned down, perhaps on the basis of suspected *converso* heritage. Had he in fact emigrated, there is very little chance that he would have written anything resembling *DQ* as we

know it. It is difficult not to see a parody of the Inquisition in the auto-da-fé of DQ's books in I, 6–7. Concern for the Inquisition also shows up in the quick explanations of the tricks behind the apparently magical divining monkey (*DQ* II, 25) and talking head (II, 42). Cenotia, sorceress from *Persiles* II, 8–17, explains how the Inquisition caused her to leave Spain. When DQ and SP are searching in the faint moonlight for the home of DT in El Toboso (II, 9), they detect the form of a large building that DQ assumes must be her palace. On coming closer, however, they find that it is nothing more than the village church, and DQ says, 'It's the church we have come upon [run into, come up against], Sancho.' Whether meant as nothing more than a simple statement of fact in that context or also with some second sense of caution when dealing with matters of the Church, the statement has become proverbial in Spanish in the second sense. See also *Cueva*; *DQ* I, 41; *DQ* II, 69; *Fregona*; *Persiles* II, 8; *Tratos 2*.

Bibliography: Angel Alcalá, *Litertura y ciencia ante la Inquisición española* (Madrid: Ediciones del Laberinto, 2001); James M. Anderson, *Daily Life during the Spanish Inquisition* (Westport, CT: Greenwood Press, 2002); Ricard García Cárcel, and Doris Moreno Martínez, *Inquisición: Historia crítica* (Madrid: Teams de Hoy, 2001); Henry Kamen, *Inquisition and Society in Spain in the Sixteenth and Seventeenth Centuries* (Bloomington: Indiana University Press, 1985); H. C. Lea, *A History of the Inquisition of Spain* (New York: AMS, 1966); Antonio Márquez, "La Inquisición y Cervantes," *Anthropos* 98–99 (1989): 56–58; Antonio Márquez, *Literatura e inquisición en España (1478–1834)* (Madrid: Taurus, 1980); B. Netanyahu, *The Origins of the Spanish Inquisition in Fifteenth-Century Spain* (New York: Random House, 1995); and Mary Elizabeth Perry, and Anne J. Cruz, eds., *Cultural Encounters: The Impact of the Inquisition in Spain and the New World* (Berkeley: University of California Press, 1991).

Inquisitors [Señores inquisidores]. Officials of the Inquisition who order Don *Antonio Moreno to disassemble the enchanted bronze head so as not to deceive people with apparent magic. See *DQ* II, 62.

Insula [Island]. A Latinate and archaic form of the word for *isla* (island) used regularly in the romances of chivalry and also throughout *DQ* by the protagonist. It is one of the keys in the archaic (*fabla) and otherwise rhetorical and affected style of discourse DQ characteristically uses, and it is turned to comic use by SP and others who want to humor or manipulate DQ. In *DQ* I, 7, when DQ recruits SP as his squire, he promises him an *ínsula* to govern. Although he may not know what the term means, SP is attracted to the possibility of a governorship, and it is the very first thing he mentions the first time he speaks in the novel. The niece and housekeeper seem not to understand the term in II, 2. The enigmatic promise of the *ínsula* is a constant source of comedy throughout the novel until the duke bestows an 'extra' one he has upon SP in II, 32. SP's exemplary conduct as governor of the landlocked *ínsula* *Barataria is one of the most surprising and gratifying features of *DQ* II. Interestingly, *ínsula* alternates with *isla* in *Persiles*, especially in Books I–II where it carries none of the parodic and comic connotations seen in *DQ*. This usage could be a reflection of the possibility that MC was composing both *DQ* I and the first two books of *Persiles* at the same time in the 1590s. It also reflects the stylistic usage of these terms in Fernando de Mena's 1587 translation of Heliodorus's *Ethiopian History*, the obvious and explicit model for *Persiles*.

Insula Firme. Island in *Amadís de Gaula*, won and first governed by the protagonist and later by his squire Gandalín. See *DQ* I, 20, 50.

Interés. *Wealth.

Interlude [Entremés]. A popular one-act comic dramatic form that was a standard feature of Spanish *comedia performances. The purpose of the interlude was to vary the pace and entertain the audience between the acts of full-length plays. The word suggests an appetizer or tasty morsel (and still has that use in Spanish bars and restaurants today). Its characters are stereotypes, its situations farcical, its language bawdy and comic; it almost inevitably ends in song and dance. The form has its origins in the sixteenth century, and is especially associated

with the important itinerant theatrical impresario Lope de *Rueda. MC's eight interludes in *Comedias* are among the finest examples of the genre (*MC the dramatist). There is an *entremés* included within *Entretenida* 3. See also *Coloquio*; *Pedro* 3.

Bibliography: Eugenio Asensio, *Itinerario del entremés desde Lope de Rueda a Quiñones de Benavente, con cinco entremeses inéditos de D. Francisco de Quevedo*, 2nd rev. ed. (Madrid: Gredos, 1971); and Cory A. Reed, *The Novelist as Playwright: Cervantes and the "Entremés nuevo"* (New York: Lang, 1993).

Interpolated stories. *Embedded narratives.

Interpreter [Intérprete]. In *DQ* II, 44, a term used to refer to the *Morisco* translator of CHB's manuscript.

Invincible Armada. *Armada, The Invincible.

Ipólito. *Hipólito.

Iranzo (Liranzo), Lázaro Luis. Soldier and poet praised in Calliope's song in *Galatea* 6.

Ireland [Irlanda]. One of the northern British Isles and, with Northern Ireland, the modern nation of the same name. In *Persiles* I, 12, it is mentioned along with Hybernia as a kingdom of the northern regions. See also *Persiles* I, 17, 21; II, 10.

Iriarte, Tomás de (1750–91). Spanish poet, dramatist, and literary theoretician. Iriarte is best known for his *Fábulas literarias* (1782; *Literary Fables*), a series of typically neoclassical beast tales in verse, always with a moral lesson. He was also a critic and polemicist, active in many of the ongoing literary and intellectual disputes of his century. In *Los literatos en cuaresma* (1773; *Writers in Lent*), he introduces MC as a critic of contemporary theater, thus giving a very light fictional guise to his literary criticism.

Iris. In Greek myth, the goddess of the rainbow. See *Gitanilla* I; *Pedro* 1.

Irisarri, Antonio José de. *Altagumea, Hilarión de.

Irlanda. *Ireland.

Irving, John (1942–). American novelist. In Irving's novel *Setting Free the Bears* (1968), the two main characters are the motorcycle-riding Siggy (DQ) and Graff (SP), who set out on the quixotic mission of setting free the animals living in captivity in the zoo. All their careful plans go awry, however, when the reality of the situation imposes itself on their project. By the end of the story, with Siggy dead, Graff manages to carry out at least a partial "zoo-bust," and the final scene of the novel is one in which a pair of bears are seen heading for the wilds. Irving's more popular novel, *The World According to Garp* (1978), is less obviously quixotic but in its exuberance, loose structure, and use of embedded fictions, is in some ways more Cervantine in spirit.

Irving, Washington (1783–1859). American short-story writer and historian. Irving loved Spain, traveled throughout the country, and wrote extensively about it; his *Tales of the Alhambra* (1832) captures much of the spirit of Muslim Spain and can be read today with almost as much interest as it had in the nineteenth century. Irving admits to having "studied for years in the chivalric library of Don Quixote" (he gathered documents for a biography of MC, but never completed the project) and once called *DQ* the profane Bible. Peter Stuyvesant, narrator of the Knickerbocker *History of New York* (1809), has much of the quixotic about him.

Isabel (Isabela). In *Española*, the title character, a beautiful young Spanish woman raised in England who eventually marries the brave Ricaredo. It is probably not mere coincidence that Isabel is the Spanish equivalent of Elizabeth, the name of the queen of England (whose name is never mentioned in the story).

Isabel Castrucho (Isabela Castrucha), Señora. In *Persiles* III, 19–20, the young woman being taken by her uncle Alejandro to Italy to be married. She pretends to be possessed by demons until the man she loves, Andrea Marulo, can arrive. He does arrive in III, 21, and the two are married.

Bibliography: Diana de Armas Wilson, "The Histrionics of Exorcism: Isabela Castrucha," in *Allegories of Love: Cervantes's "Persiles and Sigismunda"* Princeton, NJ: Princeton University Press, 1991), 223–47.

Isabel Clara Eugenia (1566–1633). *Isabela Clara Eugenia.

Isabel de Avellaneda, Doña. In *Gallardo* 1, the woman who signs the petition sent to Alonso de *Fernández de Córdoba, general of Oran, asking that the women and children of the city not be evacuated.

Isabel de Valois, Doña (1546–68). The daughter of Henry II of France and Catherine de Medici. She was the third wife of King *Felipe II of Spain. Her death at the age of 22 provided the theme of MC's earliest surviving works, five short poems in commemoration of the queen's passing. One (*Poesías* 1) was not published until the nineteenth century, but the other four (*Poesías* 2–5) were all published in a 1569 homage volume in honor of the queen, edited by MC's Erasmian mentor, Juan *López de Hoyos.

Isabel [Isabella] of Castile (1451–1504). Queen of Spain. She married Fernando of Aragon in 1469, ascended to the throne of her native Castile in 1474, and also became queen of Aragon five years later, thus forming the political union that would unite Spain and make possible the nation's swift rise to the status of the largest empire in the history of the world (*Golden Age). Together, Fernando and Isabel were known as the Reyes Católicos (*Catholic Monarchs).

Bibliography: David A. Boruchoff, ed., *Isabel la Católica, Queen of Castile* (New York: Palgrave, 2002); and Peggy K. Liss, *Isabel the Queen: Life and Times* New York: Oxford University Press, 1992).

Isabela (Isabela la española). In *Española*, the name by which *Isabel is known while she lives in England.

Isabela

Isabela. *Argensola, Lupercio Leonardo de.

Isabela Clara Eugenia (1566–1633). Daughter of Felipe II and Isabel de Valois. She was the king's favorite daughter and the only one who lived to maturity. She was active in politics and held the position of governor of Flanders. MC refers to her at the end of *Poesías* 4.

Isabella of Castile. *Isabel de Castilla.

Isabel's parents [Padres de Isabel]. In *Española*, they are among the Christian captives freed by Ricaredo, who then takes them to London where they are reunited with their daughter.

Iseo; Iseult. *Tristan and Iseult.

Isla de [Spanish phrase]. *Island of [English equivalent].

Isla de Cádiz. *Cádiz.

Isla inexpugnable, la. *Malta.

Isla, Padre José Francisco de (1703–82). Spanish preacher and prose writer. Isla wrote a single novel, *Historia del famoso predicador fray Gerundio de Campazas, alias Zotes* (published in two installments, 1757–68; *History of the Famous Preacher Fray Gerundio de Campazas, alias Zotes*), with the first part banned by the Inquisition and the second circulating for years in manuscript before seeing print. It is the best-known, even if not the best, Spanish fiction of the entire eighteenth century. The novel is a (very dated) satire on the rhetorical excesses of preachers, with the protagonist quixotically attempting to restore traditional values. Along the way, Fray Gerundio is accompanied by Bastián Borrego, his SP, who is characterized above all by his comic language. Immensely popular in its time, it is rarely read today.
Bibliography: José Francisco de Isla, *Historia del famoso predicador fray Gerundio de Campazas, alias Zotes*, ed. Russell P. Sebold, 4 vols. (Madrid: Espasa-Calpe, 1960).

Island. *Insula.

Island of Fire [Isla del fuego]. In *Persiles* II, 13, the place where King Leopoldio catches up with his unfaithful wife and her lover.

Island of the Barbarians [Isla de los bárbaros]. In *Persiles* I, 1–6, the place where the action begins and where Periandro and Auristela are first reunited. Society on the island is characterized by patriarchy, anarchy, superstition, slavery, human sacrifice, and cannibalism. The tribe of barbarians lives in a primitive, uncivilized culture, purchasing women for their future king who will lead them in world conquest. Uncontrollable passions—lust and violence—lead to the destruction of the island by fire in I, 4. Periandro and Auristela, together with a few others, are saved from the holocaust on the island by the Christian Antonio the Barbarian and his family. See also *Persiles* III, 19.
Bibliography: Eduardo González, "Del *Persiles* y la isla bárbara: Fábulas y reconocimientos," *MLN* 94 (1979): 222–57.

Island of the Fishermen [Isla de los pescadores]. The island in *Persiles* II, 10–12, populated by fisherfolk who, when Periandro and Auristela arrive fleeing from a pirate, are about to celebrate a double marriage. The elaborate ceremony is interrupted by pirates who carry off Auristela and the two brides. They are pursued on the high seas by Periandro and his own pirate ship manned by the fishermen. See also *Persiles* III, 8.

Island of the Hermitages [Isla de las Ermitas]. In *Persiles* II, 17–21, the island where Renato and Eusebia have their pious hermitages. Periandro and company visit the island, learn the story of the occupants, and learn news of European politics before departing. When word comes that Renato and Eusebia can return with honor to France, *Rutilio takes over the hermitage in order to do penance for his sins. See also *Persiles* IV, 8.

Island of wolves [Isla de los lobos]. In *Persiles* I, 5, the island populated only by wolves, where Antonio the Barbarian hears one wolf tell him to go on his way.

Islanda. *Iceland.

Islands of Lizards [Islas de los Lagartos]. A generic name used for uninhabited islands, perhaps where prisoners would be exiled. Some place these islands to the west of Jamaica. It is possible that the reference is to the Cayman (from *caimán*, a kind of alligator native to American rivers) Islands of Jamaica. See *DQ* II, 38.

Islas de Riarán. An area of the city of Málaga made up of blocks of houses called *islas* (islands) because each building stands independently, rather than being connected as was (and is) usual in urban construction. They were built in the fifteenth century by Garci López de Arriarán, after whom they were named. Because of the labyrinth created by the spaces between the buildings, the area became a favorite haunt of criminals and *pícaros* (*picaresque geography).

Isopo. *Aesop.

Isunza, Pedro de (?–1593). The successor to Antonio de *Guevara as quartermaster general, in charge of the commissaries, of whom MC was one, who requisitioned supplies for the crown.

Italia. *Italy.

Italian [Italiano]. Given his extended residence in Italy (1569–75), it is likely that MC spoke and read Italian quite well. Italian words and phrases occur more frequently than those of any other foreign language in his works.

Italian literature. Italy is the nation whose literature had the most profound impact on Spanish Renaissance literature in general and on MC in particular. There is hardly an English, French, German, Dutch (with the exception of Erasmus), or Portuguese (exceptions were Gil Vicente and Camões, who also wrote in Spanish) creative writer whose work in a modern language was even known in sixteenth- and early seventeenth-century Spain. But the Spanish always revered Italian letters and avidly read translations of Italian poets, short-story writers, and writers of humanistic, political, and aesthetic works. Major Italian writers who had an important influence on Spanish Renaissance literature include Pietro *Aretino, Ludovico *Ariosto, Matteo *Bandello, Pietro Bembo, Matteo Maria *Boiardo, Giovanni *Boccaccio, Baldassar Castiglione, Giambattista Giraldi *Cinthio, *Dante Alighieri, Giovanni Della Casa, Leone *Ebreo, Marsilio Ficino, Giambattista Guarini, Niccolò Machiavelli, Pedro Mártir, Andrea Navaggiero, Francesco *Petrarca, Jacopo *Sannazaro, Torquato *Tasso, and Lorenzo Valla.

Bibliography: Joaquín Arce, *Literaturas italiana y española frente a frente* (Madrid: Espasa-Calpe, 1982); and Frederick A. de Armas, "Cervantes and the Italian Renaissance," In *The Cambridge Companion to Cervantes*, ed. Anthony J. Cascardi (Cambridge: Cambridge University Press, 2002), 32–57.

Italy [Italia]. By far the most significant European country, after Spain itself, for MC. Italy was the birthplace of the Renaissance and Rome was the heart of Christendom; Italian literature flourished with originality and brilliance far earlier than did that of any other European country. The Italians were literally the only people whom the Spanish respected as having produced a culture comparable (if not superior) to their own. The tour of, or extended residence in, Italy was *de rigor* for most Spanish noblemen, intellectuals, and writers, including MC. The protagonist of *Vidriera* visits and travels in Italy as an essential part of his humanist education. In *Persiles*, the lovers Persiles and Sigismunda travel from the barbaric northern lands to Rome in order to reveal their identities and marry. In the sixteenth century, more than half of Italy was under Spanish domination: Parma, Naples, Sardinia, Sicily, and Milan. Many educated Italians spoke Spanish, literary works from Spain were often read in the original language, and a number of books were printed in Spanish in Italy. In many Italian writings of the time—correspondence, travelogues, and social commentary—Spaniards were generally regarded as arrogant, intolerant, rapacious, pompous, crude, abusive, and prone to arguing and fighting; Spanish literature was perceived as primitive, forced, and mannered; and Spain itself was seen as a land mongrelized by Jews and Muslims, thoroughly lacking all the refinements so typical of Italy. In Spanish eyes, however, even as its past accomplishments were revered, contemporary Italy (and especially Rome) was a den of intrigue, corruption, and sin, where the men were dandies, the women were whores, and the clergy was corrupt and degenerate. MC first went to Rome late in 1569, immediately after a warrant for his arrest was published in Madrid; there he worked for a while in the household of Cardinal Acquaviva. He remained as a soldier based in Italy, primarily Naples (which he calls the greatest city in Europe, if not the entire world, in *Vidriera*),

until 1575. His cherished hopes of returning to Naples as part of the retinue of the count of Lemos in were not fulfilled, leaving him bitter and resentful toward the *Argensola brothers. See *Amante*; *Celoso*; *Coloquio*; *Cornelia*; *Doncellas*; *DQ* I, 6, 33, 39, 51; *DQ* II, 25, 54; *Española*; *Fuerza*; *Galatea* 2; *Gallardo* 3; *Gitanilla*; *Parnaso* 1, 8; *Persiles* I, 5; II, 7.1; III, 10, 12, 16; *Sultana* 2; *Tratos* 3; *Vidriera*.

Ixion [Egión, Ixión]. In Greek myth, a king of Thessaly, known as the first Greek to murder one of his kinsmen, the father of the centaurs, and a ruler who attempted to seduce Hera, the wife of Zeus. His punishment by Zeus was to be bound to a constantly revolving wheel of fire in the underworld. See *DQ* I, 14; *Galatea* 4.

J

Jabalí. *Wild boar.

Jabón napolitano. *Naples soap.

Jaca. A medium-sized city in the foothills of the Pyrenees Mountains, located southeast of Pamplona and north and slightly east of Zaragoza. See *DQ* II, 44.

Jaccaci, August F. (1857–1930). English travel writer. Jaccaci planned to make a trip to La Mancha with the artist Daniel *Urrabieta Vierge so that they could work together on a book about the land and people of the region. They did not actually make the trip together, but they traveled the same route separately and then collaborated on a book entitled *On the Trail of Don Quixote, Being a Record of Rambles in the Ancient Province of La Mancha* (1897). Jaccaci's account of the trip, with a wealth of detail about the countryside, buildings, people, dress, customs, and more, is abundantly illustrated by Urrabieta Vierge's superb drawings. The result is one of the best evocations ever of La Mancha, which in the late nineteenth century was still more like it was in the Renaissance than like it is today.
   Bibliography: August F. Jaccaci, *On the Trail of Don Quixote, Being a Record of Rambles in the Ancient Province of La Mancha*, illus. Daniel Vierge (London: Lawrence and Bullen, 1897).

Jacinta. In *Pedro* 1, a friend of Clemencia and Benita, who is merely mentioned.

Jacinto. 1. *Hyacinth. **2.** *Pastoral names.

Jacinto, Fray. *Fray Diego.

Jacob. In the Old Testament, one of the Jewish patriarchs. See *Coloquio*.

Jadraque. An unusual term, perhaps invented by MC, and used in *Persiles* III, 11, to refer to a kind of subdeacon or assistant sacristan in a *Morisco* context.

Jailer [Carcelero]. In *Laberinto*, the keeper of the tower where Rosamira is incarcerated while awaiting her trial.

James, Henry (1843–1916). American novelist, dramatist, critic, and aesthetician. Along with Jane Austen, James stands at the head of what R. F. Leavis calls "the great tradition" of the novel: tightly structured, serious, subtly ironic, realistic fictions. These are the novels least likely to remind one of *DQ*, as they lack the overt comedy and laughter, the exuberance, the reality-fantasy theme, and/or the self-reflexive narrative technique typical of *DQ*. Yet one of James's novels is *The Portrait of a Lady* (1881), whose protagonist, Isabel Archer, is in every way a quixotic character whose youthful reading and flights of imagination are her most important characteristics: "To say that she had a book is to say that her solitude did not press upon her; for her love of knowledge had a fertilizing quality and her imagination was strong. . . . Her reputation of reading a great deal hung about her like the cloudy envelope of a goddess in an epic. . . . The girl had a certain nobleness of imagination which rendered her a good many services and played her a great many tricks. She spent half her time in thinking of beauty, and bravery, and magnanimity."

Jamestad. In *Elección*, Panduro's comic mispronunciation of *Majestad* (Majesty).

Jándula. A river in Andalusia that rises in the Sierra Morena mountains and flows south until

399

it empties into the Guadalquivir River near Andújar. See *Persiles* III, 6.

Janissaries [Genízaros, Jenízaros]. Turkish infantry, made up primarily of tributary children of Christians who served as the sultan's personal guard and constituted a large part of the regular army. A large number of janissaries also fought in the battle of Lepanto. The category was abolished in the nineteenth century. See *Amante*; *Baños* 2; *Tratos* 2.

Janus [Jano]. In Roman myth, the god of doorways, gates, and beginnings. His symbol was a double-faced head, simultaneously looking in two opposite directions, both backward and forward. See *Parnaso* 3.

Jarama. A Spanish river that rises in the Guadarrama Mountains north of Madrid, flows southward, and empties into the Tagus near Aranjuez. See *DQ* II, 44, 58; *Parnaso* 8.

Jaramilla. In *DQ* I, 30, the queen of Micomicón and mother of the Princess *Micomicona.

Jardín de flores. *Torquemada, Antonio de.

Jardines de Hespérides. *Hesperides.

Jarife. An honorific name given to Muslims believed to be descendants of Mohammed. In *Persiles* III, 11, the *jadraque* who helps Periandro and the others avoid being taken captive to Africa and who longs for the day when the *Moriscos* will be banished from Spain is a *jarife*. In *Gallardo* 1, Nacor is a *jarife* and claims that this gives him special 'untouchable' status. Attempting to take advantage of this special privilege, Nacor publicly slanders Alimuzel, knowing that nothing will be done to him. It does not, however, save him from being killed by the Christian soldier Buitrago.

Jarnés, Benjamín (1888–1949). Spanish novelist, dramatist, and biographer. Jarnés is the author of a one-act "monodrama" for a single actor entitled *Cardenio* (1939). In his monologue, Cardenio, dressed as described in *DQ* I, 23, awakens in the Sierra Morena mountains and talks with a chirping bird, recites his poetry from the novel, talks with DQ and SP (present, but mute) about Luscinda and Fernando, and finally, in the most interesting and original part of the play, talks with MC as if he were present. Cardenio does not want to return to the novel and have to go to the inn and be reunited with Luscinda, Fernando, and Dorotea. Rather like Marcela in *DQ* I, 14, he wants his freedom in the wilds. If he does return to the book, he says, it will be to kill Sansón Carrasco. Apparently left alone by MC, the play ends as Cardenio ambiguously evokes Luscinda.

Bibliography: J. S. Bernstein, *Benjamín Jarnés* (New York: Twayne, 1972); and Benjamín Jarnés, *Cardenio* (México City: Miguel N. Lira, 1940).

Jason [Jasón]. In Greek myth, the son of Aeson and leader of the Argonauts, who recovered the Golden Fleece. See *DQ* I, 52.

Jaula de palos enrejados. *Cage of wooden bars.

Jáuregui, Juan de (1583–1641). Poet, translator, and artist. Jáuregui is allegedly the painter of MC's portrait, as described in the prologue to *Novelas*. This description more or less matches two extant Jáuregui portraits, although there is no proof whatsoever that either portrait is of MC. Controversy was stirred when the Royal Spanish Academy pronounced one of the portraits authentic (it still hangs in the Academy headquarters in Madrid). The second portrait, more often accepted as authentic, is in the possession of the Marqués of Casa Torres. Prudence suggests a skeptical attitude in both cases. Jáuregui was a decent poet and theorist of poetry, criticizing (while imitating) the poetic style of Góngora. Jáuregui's translation of Tasso's *L'Aminta* (1607) is praised by DQ in the bookstore in Barcelona (II, 62) as being worthy of the original text, and his poetry is lauded extravagantly in *Parnaso* 2.

Bibliography: Enrique Lafuente Ferrari, *La novela ejemplar de los retratos de Cervantes* (Madrid: Dossat, 1948).

Jayanes. *Giants.

Jealous Old Man from Extremadura, The. *Celoso extremeño, El.*

Jealous Old Man, The. *Viejo celoso, El.*

Jealousy [Celos]. A constant theme in MC's works. Examples of the destructive power of intense jealousy can be seen in *Galatea* 3, in the figure of Orfenio; in the obsessively jealous figures of Carrizales in *Celoso* and Cañizares in *Viejo*; in *Persiles*, the two cases of Auristela's jealousy of Sinforosa (I, 23; II, 1–6) and Policarpo's jealousy of Periandro (II, 11); and in *Poesías* 22, MC's ballad on the cave that is the abode of jealousy. The theme is treated somewhat more lightheartedly in *Casa*; see especially the procession of allegorical figures conjured up by Malgesí in *Casa* 2 (which features the same cave imagery as *Poesías* 22).

Jean Paul (Johann Paul Friedrich Richter, 1763–1825). German novelist. Almost all of Jean Paul's novels deal to some degree or other with the quixotic conflict between the ideal and the real, and the specific expression of this is found in *DQ*: MC "carried to its full conclusion the humoristic parallel between realism and idealism, between body and soul; his twin stars of folly shine over the face of humanity as a whole." Jean Paul's last important novel, *Der Comet* (1820; *The Comet, or Nikolaus Markgraf*), which he wrote thinking specifically of Rabelais and MC, has as a protagonist a man who, like DQ, imitates the books he reads. But there is an important difference between them: whereas DQ reads many romances of chivalry in order to assume one identity, Nikolaus, a religious and political fanatic, switches his identity with each book he reads.

Jeanmaire, Federico (1957–). Argentine novelist. Jeanmaire's *Miguel: Phantasmata Speculari* (1990) is a fictional autobiography of MC, addressed to his beloved daughter Isabel. Jeanmaire follows chronology and known facts quite faithfully, but adds imaginative details to fill in the gaps. In addition, there are interpolated sections consisting of a short story, a pair of recipes, and the author's digressive comments and observations. Perhaps the most interesting is that in the novel MC explains that the reason for his sudden departure for Italy in 1569 was a deadly matter of honor involving a prostitute and a (partially blind) man named Jorge de Borges, a professional *chulo* (rogue, usually loud in manner and dress): MC kills Borges!

Bibliography: Federico Jeanmaire, *Miguel: Phantasmata Speculari* (Barcelona: Anagrama, 1990).

Jenízaros. *Janissaries.

Jerez de la Frontera. City in southwestern Spain, located just northwest of Cádiz and south and slightly west of Seville. The city's most important industry is the production of sherry, but it is also famous as the location of the Real Escuela Andaluza de Arte Ecuestre (Royal Andalusian School of Equestrian Art), the Spanish riding school. See *DQ* I, 49; *Entretenida* 3; *Galatea* 2–3; *Gallardo* 2–3.

Jerez, Puerta de. *Gate of Jerez.

Jericho [Jericó]. A town in Jordan, located north of the Dead Sea. One of the oldest cities in the world, its founding goes back to some 6000 years BCE. In the Old Testament, the city's walls were miraculously destroyed when Joshua ordered the trumpets to be sounded. See *Persiles* III, 5.

Jerigonza de ciegos. *Blind men's jargon.

Jerjes. *Xerxes.

Jerónimo, Don. In *DQ* II, 59, one of the two men DQ meets in an inn on the way to Zaragoza. He and his friend Don Juan are talking about the newly published *DQA*. The two men discuss the book with DQ and SP and become convinced that the people with whom they are talking are the real men, and that the book is false.

Jerusalem [Jerusalén]. The most important Hebrew city and the scene of many significant events of early Christianity, especially the crucifixion of Christ. In its long and contentious history, Jerusalem has been under the control of the Hebrews, Romans, Persians, Arabs, Crusaders, Turks, and British. See *Galatea* 4; *DQ* I, 48; *Viejo*.

Jerusalem Delivered; Jerusalén libertada. *Tasso, Torquato.

Jerusalén, La. *Conquista de Jerusalén, La.

Jesuits [Jesuitas]. The Society of Jesus, a religious order founded by the Spaniard Ignacio de *Loyola in 1534. The Jesuits set up a school in Seville in the mid-sixteenth century. In *Coloquio*, the children of the merchant whom Berganza serves attend the Jesuit school; as a group, the Jesuits are highly praised by both Berganza and Cipión as excellent teachers.
Bibliography: Ernest A. Siciliano, *The Jesuits in the "Quijote" and Other Essays* (Barcelona: Hispam, 1974).

Jesus Christ [Jesucristo, Cristo] (ca. 4 BCE–ca. CE 29). Hebrew prophet and teacher, believed by Christians to be the Messiah, upon whose life and teachings Christianity was founded. There are references, direct and indirect, to Christ throughout MC's works, often in the form of oaths and other formulaic expressions. Examples can be found in *Baños* 1; *Casa* 3; *Cueva*; *Elección*; *Poesías* 14, 26; *Sultana* 2; *Tratos* 2, 4; *Viejo*.

Jew [Judío]. 1. In *Amante*, a merchant who sells the slave Leonisa to the cadí. **2.** In *Rinconete*, a character only mentioned briefly. **3.** In *Baños* 2, the man who is made fun of by Tristán. **4.** In *Sultana* 1, the man who discusses with the Jew Zabulón the way in which they are tormented by Madrigal. **5.** *Abiud.

Jewers, Caroline A. Theorist of the novel. Jewers stakes out a position between those who believe that all fiction, from the earliest days of the Greek romance to the present, can be legitimately called a novel, and those who believe that the novel is a modern genre that emerged in the Renaissance. Her aim is to promote medieval French chivalric romances as already possessing those characteristics—especially parody—that we associate with the novel. Her assessment of *DQ* is blatantly self-contradictory. On one hand, she affirms that it is beyond question that "Cervantes is the first and greatest practitioner of the novel," and, on the other (and in the very same passage), she endorses Edwin *Williamson's position that *DQ* occupies a halfway house of fiction: "while it is undoubtedly a parody of chivalric romance, it nevertheless remains one." That there was some degree of parody in medieval French romance is undeniable, but that does not mean that those romances were novels. The difference in tone, structure, character, narrative technique, and much more between medieval romance and *DQ* is enormous. *Bakhtin's position that medieval parody (along with carnival and other aspects of culture and literature) was part of "novelistic discourse" and one of the factors that made possible the eventual emergence of the novel in the Renaissance is far more convincing than Jewers's effort. This is an original and valuable contribution to the history and theory of the novel, but overall it is both inconsistent and unconvincing.
Bibliography: Caroline A. Jewers, *Chivalric Fiction and the History of the Novel* (Gainesville: University Presses of Florida, 2000).

Jews [Judíos]. People descended from the ancient Hebrews and/or whose religion is Judaism; after 1492, there were none, officially, in Spain. Having successfully completed the seven-century reconquest of Spain from the Muslims, Fernando and Isabel, on March 30, 1492, issued the edict ordering the expulsion of all professed Jews from the country (*Sephardic Jews, Sephardim). Some 50,000 Jews chose to leave Spain at that time; thus the nation that was about to become the most powerful in the world lost many of its best theologians, jurists, financiers, and physicians—at a time when this intellectual elite would have been invaluable. Those who remained accepted (often under duress and sometimes in name only) the Christian faith. This group was known as *conversos* or New Christians, and it is often to them that one is referring when using the term *Jew* in the context of Renaissance Spain. Cervantes himself, it has been suggested, had a *converso* family background (*Cervantes family). One of the greatest insults to a person of the sixteenth or seventeenth centuries in Spain was to be called a Jew. Jews appear as characters in several of MC's plays and *novelas* in settings outside of Spain, particularly Algiers. One gains a strong sense of anti-Semitism in these works; in none of them is a Jew presented sympathetically or even ambiguously as is, for example, the *Morisco* Ricote in *DQ* II, 54.

Bibliography: Manuel Aguilar and Ian Robertson, *Jewish Spain: A Guide* (Madrid: Altalena, 1984); Yitzhak Baer, *A History of the Jews in Christian Spain*, trans. Louis Schoffman et al., 2 vols. (Philadelphia: Jewish Publication Society of America, 1961); and Haim Beinart, *The Expulsion of the Jews from Spain*, trans. Jeffrey M. Green (Portland, OR: Littman Library of Jewish Civilization, 2002).

Jew's harp (or trump) [Trompa de París]. An ancient musical instrument (*birimbao*, in modern Spanish) made of an elastic steel tongue attached to a lyre-shaped metal frame played by holding the frame between the teeth and plucking the projecting tongue with the finger. Loaysa plays one in *Celoso.*

Jiménez de Cisneros, Cardinal Francisco. *Cisneros, Cardinal Francisco Jiménez de.

Jiménez de Enciso, Don Diego (1585–ca. 1634). A poet and dramatist mentioned in *Parnaso* 4.

Jimia de bronce. *Brass ape.

Jimios. *Apes.

Job. In the Old Testament, a Hebrew patriarch who endured long suffering but whose faith did not waver. To have the "patience of Job" is a proverbial expression of the willingness to withstand seemingly undeserved trials and tribulations. See *Rufián* 3.

Johannot, Tony (1803–52). French artist. Johannot's illustrations for a 1836–37 French edition of *DQ* are the first to depart from the more mechanical and stereotyped seventeenth- and eighteenth-century illustrations of the novel. He is also the first illustrator of the novel to have his name printed on the title page. Johannot's romantic view of DQ and his context prepared the way for Gustave *Doré and subsequent great illustrators of MC's work.

Bibliography: Rachel Schmidt, "The Romancing of *Don Quixote*: Spatial Innovation and Visual Interpretation in the Imagery of Johannot, Doré and Daumier," *Word and Image* 14 (1998): 354–70.

John of Austria, Don. *Austria, Don Juan of.

John of the Cross, Saint. *Saint Juan de la Cruz.

John of the Indies, Prester. *Prester John of the Indies.

John the Baptist. *Saint John the Baptist.

Johnson, Charles (1679–1748). English dramatist. Johnson's comedy *The Generous Husband* (1713) is based on *Celoso.*

Johnson, Samuel (1709–84). English poet, lexicographer, and essayist. Johnson once stated that, after Homer's *Iliad*, *DQ* was "the greatest [book of entertainment] in the world." His opinion of the character DQ as expressed in the *Rambler* is one of the best expressions of the shift in the *reception history of the novel from purely comic and burlesque to something more universal and profound: "Very few readers, amidst their mirth or pity, can deny that they have admitted visions of the same kind; though they have not, perhaps, expected events equally strange, or by means equally inadequate. When we pity him we reflect on our own disappointments; and when we laugh, our hearts inform us that he is not more ridiculous than ourselves, except that he tells what we have only thought." The slow realization over time that *DQ* is the expression of a basic aspect of the universal human condition has become increasingly recognized in psychology (*Don Quixote and psychology). Johnson was also particularly fond of the Spanish romances of chivalry, most notably including *Belianís de Grecia.*

Bibliography: Eithne Henson, *"The Fictions of Romantick Chivalry." Samuel Johnson and Romance

Jong, Erica (1942–)

(Cranbury, NJ: Associated University Press, for Rutherford University Press, 1992).

Jong, Erica (1942–). American novelist. Jong's reputation and popularity soared with the publication of *Fear of Flying* (1973), a novel about the quixotic Isadora Wing's quest for her "platonic ideal," which she dubs the "zipless fuck." Wing searches restlessly, gives herself over to literature and fantasy, imaginatively playing roles in which she is a glamorous heroine. She searches "for the impossible man . . . it was a kind of quest"; she refers to herself as "Isadora Wing, fighter of windmills, professional mourner, failed adventuress." She relates her own life to that of ordinary women and housewives, who also live in fantasies: "They constantly dreamed of escape. They constantly seethed with resentment. Their lives were pickled in fantasy." She begins to see herself as "a fictional character invented by me." Finally, at the end of the novel, her fantasy of the zipless fuck becomes a real possibility, but she rejects it and the stranger on the train. Wing's is a typical quixotic quest, where the only victory is over herself, with a circular return to the beginning, but now disillusioned. Jong's novel is a good example of the pervasiveness of the quixotic theme in popular, middlebrow literature.

Jordan River [Río Jordán]. The river of supposedly miraculous waters where John the Baptist baptized Jesus Christ. Specifically, the river's water was alleged to have magical curative and restorative powers. According to popular belief in the Hispanic world, on *Saint John's Eve, June 24, all bodies of water in the world are supposed to carry within them at least a drop of water from the Jordan and therefore also acquire some degree of that river's powers. See *Retablo; Vidriera*.

Jorge, Micer. *Vourapag, George.

Joyce, James (1882–1941). Irish novelist and short-story writer. For all that *Ulysses* (1922) is directly inspired by Homer's epic poem, its protagonist Leopold Bloom is arguably more quixotic than Homeric, frequently getting himself and others into difficult situations, and living largely in his dreams. And it has been proposed that the earthy Molly Bloom displays certain elements of DT.

Bibliography: Mary Powers, "Myth and the Absent Heroine: Dulcinea del Toboso and Molly Bloom," *Indiana Journal of Hispanic Literatures* 5 (1994): 251–61.

Juan (Juanico). In *Tratos*, the younger son sold to a Muslim merchant and who renounces his religion and takes the name of Solimán.

Juan Bautista Marulo. In *Persiles* III, 20–21, the father of Andrea who gives approval for his son to marry Isabela Castrucha.

Juan Berrocal. In *Elección*, one of the candidates for the position of magistrate.

Juan Castrado. In *Retablo*, the alderman of the town where the marvelous show is produced.

Juan Claros. In *Viudo*, the ruffian who accompanies the prostitutes who vie to replace the late Pericona as Trampagos's 'wife.'

Juan de Almendárez, Don. In *Entretenida* 3, the supposed brother of Don Silvestre, but an error by the servant Torrente helps expose his and Cardenio's attempted fraud.

Juan de Austria, Don. *Austria, Don Juan of.

Juan de Avendaño, Don. In *Fregona*, the father of Tomás de Avendaño, one of the story's protagonists.

Juan de Cárcamo, Don (Don Juanico). In *Gitanilla*, the real name of *Andrés Caballero, which he reassumes at the end of the story in order to marry Doña Constanza de Azevedo y de Meneses, formerly known as Preciosa. There was a nobleman and member of the Order of Santiago of this name who might have been the model for the fictional character. The historical Don Juan was the son of Alonso de *Cárcamo, not Francisco as in *Gitanilla*. The identity of names in a case such as this, however, may be completely coincidental (Cárcamo is not that uncommon a surname), and the relationship between the historical figure and the literary character is tenuous at best.

Juan de Gamboa, Don. In *Cornelia*, the Spanish student who receives the newborn baby of Cornelia Bentibolli and then helps her resolve her honor conflict.

Juan de las Indias, Preste. *Prester John of the Indies.

Juan de Orellana, Don. *Orellana, Don Juan de.

Juan de Ubeda. A name cited by SP in *DQ* I, 29, to illustrate the practice of taking one's surname from the place in which one was born.

Juan de Valderrama, Don. In *Gallardo* 3, the brother of Margarita, who arrives in Algiers and approves of his sister's marriage to Fernando de Saavedra.

Juan, Don. In *DQ* II, 59, one of the two men DQ meets in an inn on the way to Zaragoza. He and his friend Don Jerónimo are talking about the newly published *DQA*. The two men discuss the book with DQ and SP and become convinced that the people with whom they are talking are the real men, and that the book is false.

Juan Espera en Dios. The name of the Wandering Jew in Spanish, who, according to this version of the legend, always had a few coins in his pocket. See *Galatea* 2.

Juan Gaycoa. A variant or corruption (printing error?) of *Jaungoikoa* (Lord on High), a Basque name for God, used by the Basque squire in *Casa* 1.

Juan Haldudo. Known as 'the Rich,' a well-to-do peasant who is a native of the village of Quintanar de la Orden. In *DQ* I, 4, he mocks and parodies DQ's archaic language and chivalric mission when he reneges on his promise to free and pay the boy *Andrés.

Bibliography: Charles Oriel, "Dialogue in/of Ad-

ventures: *Don Quijote*, Part One, Chapter Four," *RLA: Romance Languages Annual* 3 (1991): 545–49.

Juan Juncos. In *Guarda*, a shoemaker driven away from Cristina's house by the soldier.

Juan Latino (ca. 1518–ca. 1573). A black slave who was self-taught and also educated and supported by the duke and duchess of Sessa. He obtained his freedom and acquired considerable celebrity as a Latinist and humanist, holding the position of professor of rhetoric and Latin in Granada. See the preliminary poem by Urganda la Desconocida in *DQ* I.

Juan Lozano. In *Gallardo*, the name taken by *Fernando de Saavedra in order to hide his identity.

Juan, Mase. *Mase Juan.

Juan Palomeque, el Zurdo [the Left-handed]. The innkeeper who first receives DQ in I, 16, and attempts unsuccessfully to collect for his night's stay in I, 17 (his name is first mentioned by SP in I, 18). After briefly dealing with the priest and barber upon their return to the novel (I, 26–27), Palomeque again hosts DQ and SP, this time along with the priest and barber, Dorotea and Cardenio, and then a multitude of others in I, 32–47. His insistence on the literal truth of the romances of chivalry (I, 32) makes him comparable to DQ, but with the difference that he clearly perceives that knights-errant represent a historical era long over and that chivalry is no longer applicable to the present day. His argument that the romances must tell the truth since they receive the imprimatur of the religious and legal censors anticipates DQ's own argument along the same lines later (I, 50). He is also an officer in the Holy Brotherhood, as were many innkeepers of the period, and as such acts in support of his colleagues in I, 45. He clearly is fond of reading and listening to literary texts, enjoys the reading of *Curioso* by the priest, and generously gives the priest the remaining manuscripts that have been left in the inn (I, 47). Overall, he appears to be a decent and honest family man and businessman, qualities that distinguish him from the first innkeeper DQ encounters (I, 2–4) and from many others in that profession throughout Spain.

Juan Paulín (San Paulín). Apparently Saint (or Juan) Paulín was invoked as an allusion to poverty. See *Pedro* 1–2.

Juan Pérez de Viedma, Licenciado. The brother of Ruy Pérez de Viedma, the captive who tells his story in *Capitán*. He has studied law at Salamanca and is an judge (*oidor*) who has recently been appointed to a position on the tribunal (*audiencia*) of Mexico. Juan arrives, coincidentally, at the *inn of Juan Palomeque, where he is reunited with his long-lost brother in *DQ* I, 42.

Juan Tiopieyo. The brother-in-law of Ricote who, according to SP, helped his sister and niece (*Ricota) leave Spain after the expulsion of the *Moriscos*. See *DQ* II, 54.

Juan Tocho. In *DQ* II, 5, a neighbor of SP whose son Lope is interested in Sanchica.

Juana Carducha. In *Gitanilla*, the wealthy young woman who falls in love with Andrés Caballero, apparently a gypsy, and is stung by his rejection of her offer to marry him. She frames him in a theft, causing his arrest and thus putting into motion the train of events that ends in the revelation of the true identities of Andrés and Preciosa and their marriage.

Juana Castrada. In *Retablo*, the wife of the alderman Juan Castrado.

Juana de Rentería. In *Baños* 1, a character mentioned as a captive Christian who, years before, raised Zahara in her home in Algiers.

Juana Gutiérrez. *Name of Sancho's wife.

Juana la Chasca. Either a folkloric character or a historical person, a butcher's wife who lived in Madrid and whose name acquired folkloric status. See *Parnaso* 2.

Juana Marcha. In *Retablo*, the name of the mother of Juan Castrado.

Juana Panza. One of the names for Teresa Panza. This is how she is referred to in the final scene of *DQ* I, 52, when SP returns home (*name of Sancho's wife).

Juana Téllez. Probably just a common woman's name intended as a contrast to the list of poetic ideal women's names mentioned in *Adjunta* (*pastoral names). It may be, however, that it is an allusion to Magdalena Girón, the daughter of Juan Téllez Girón, who is generally assumed to be the Fílida of Luis *Gálvez de Montalvo's pastoral romance *El pastor de Fílida*.

Juanelo. *Turriano, Giovanni.

Juanica. A name from a popular song cited in *Coloquio*.

Juanico, Don. In *Gitanilla*, name used by Don Francisco de Cárcamo to refer to his son Don Juan (who becomes Andrés Caballero while he lives among the gypsies). Preciosa then uses the name to tease Don Juan.

Juanito. In *Baños*, one of the children taken during the raid on Spain.

Judas. **1**. Judas Iscariot, in the New Testament, the apostle who betrayed Christ for 30 pieces of silver. See *DQ* I, 27; *DQ* II, 19, 70; *Fregona*; *Sultana* 2–3. **2**. The legendary Wandering Jew, who is condemned to wander the earth until the second coming of Christ because of his scornful behavior at the time of the crucifixion. DQ refers to Judas in II, 19, as the only person who would have the patience (and time) to hear out all of SP's proverbs.

Judas Macabeo. *Nine Worthies.

Judas Macarelo. In *Rinconete*, Juliana la Cariharta's error for Judas Macabeo (Maccabean).

Judge [Juez]. **1**. In *Laberinto* 3, the official who is to decide the fate of Rosamira. **2**. In *Juez*, the divorce court judge who prefers reconciliation to divorce. **3**. *Juan Pérez de Viedma.

Judges [Jueces]. A book in the Old Testament, dealing with the early history of the Jews in Israel (*Bible). DQ cites this book in I, 49, as part of his argument that documentation for the existence of knights-errant has existed throughout all time.

Judgment Day [Día del Juicio]. In Christian myth, the end of the world; the day on which God makes his final judgment on all people. See *DQ* I, 45.

Judío. *Jew.

Judith [Judic, *sic* for Judit]. In the Old Testament, the heroine of the book named for her. Most famously, Judith saved the city of Bethulia when it was under attack by Holofernes, one of Nebuchadnezzar's generals. During the siege, Judith, a beautiful and pious Jewish widow, left the city, went to Holofernes's camp, seduced the general, and then decapitated him as he lay sleeping. She returned to the city with his severed head and her actions inspired the Jews to rout the enemy. Lope de *Vega wrote a particularly beautiful sonnet on this subject entitled "Al triunfo de Judit" ("To Judith's Triumph"). See *Persiles* III, 17.

Jueces. *Judges.

Juegos olímpicos. *Olympic games.

Jueves Santo. *Holy Thursday.

Juez. *Judge.

Juez de los divorcios, El (Juez); The Divorce Court Judge. The first interlude in *Comedias*. One of the stock formats for an interlude is that of a series of characters brought on stage, one after another, to be questioned, given a chance to appear foolish, and be made fun of; it is a static format, with little or no action and no particular resolution. The series of comic types who appear in this work—the harpy, the old man, the soldier, the porter— were all well-known to MC's readers. Many MC scholars have been unable to resist the temptation to see in this work a reflection of the writer's own marriage, often assumed (not always with justification) to have been unhappy, based on the long separations between MC and his wife and the lack of children from the union. But any relationship of this sort is tenuous at best, for the situation is of the type that writers in the period often ridiculed and satirized.

The scene is the court of the divorce judge, with an attorney and a scribe also present. The first case is that of Mariana and the old man who is her husband. Mariana complains that her husband is impertinent, always sick, and has bad breath. The old man replies that for some 22 years she has mistreated him more than she has cared for him. The judge finds no grounds for divorce. Next, Doña Guiomar comes to complain about her husband, a soldier. Her complaint is that her husband is more a stick of wood than a man; he is never home, he is always out with his friends, and when he actually is at home he does nothing at all. He admits that much of what she says is true, but adds that she is jealous, bitchy, and much more. Before a decision is rendered, the next case is presented. The plaintiffs are Aldonza de Minijaca and her husband, a surgeon. The husband has four complaints against his wife, but all are vague and imprecise. Aldonza, however, has 400 against her husband, and she begins to list them: he is a second Lucifer, he is jealous, he is not the professional physician she had thought he was, she can't stand him . . . The judge cuts her off here and dismisses the case. Next, a porter arrives, alone, and complains about his wife, whom he married while drunk. The judge is about to announce a sentence when several musicians arrive and bring the farce to a close with the customary song and dance. The refrain in the song is that 'the worst reconciliation is better than the best divorce.'

Bibliography: I. Arellano, "Un pasaje cervantino dificultoso en *El juez de los divorcios*," *Romance Notes* 26 (1985): 54–58; Mary Gaylord Randel, "The Order in the Court: Cervantes' *Entremés del juez de los divorcios*," *Bulletin of the Comediantes* 34 (1982): 83–95; Pablo Restrepo-Gautier, " 'Y así, a todos os recibo a prueba': Risa e ideología en *El juez de los divorcios* de Cervantes," *Anales Cervantinos* 32 (1994): 221–39; and W. Rozenblat, "¿Por qué escribió Cervantes *El juez de los divorcios?" Anales Cervantinos* 12 (1973): 129–34.

Jugador. *Dice player.

Jugurta. In *Numancia*, a Roman officer under Scipio.

Juicios de Sancho. *Sancho's judgments.

Julia. 1. In *Laberinto*, daughter of the duke of Rosena and sister of Manfredo, who dresses first as a shepherd, then as a student, and then as a peasant woman. While dressed as a man, she uses the name Camilo. At the end of the play, she marries Anastasio. **2**. In *Persiles* IV, 8, the wife of the Jew Zabulón and the witch whom Hipólita enlists to help eliminate Auristela so that she will have a better chance of seducing Periandro. In IV, 10, Hipólita has her lift her spell and Auristela recovers.

Julia, Via. *Via Julia.

Julian calendar. In effect in Spain until the Gregorian correction of March 1582 (which was not adopted so quickly throughout Europe; e.g., it was not endorsed by Britain until 1751). All dates cited prior to 1582 are according to the Julian calendar; all those cited after that date are according to the Gregorian calendar.

Julián, Count Don. Governor of Ceuta who, according to legend and the ballad tradition, made possible the Muslim invasion of Spain in 711 to avenge the rape of his daughter, Florinda la *Cava, by the Visigothic King Rodrigo. See *DQ* I, 27.

Juliana la Cariharta. In *Rinconete*, the prostitute who has been beaten by her boyfriend Repolido, but who makes up with him at Monipodio's house.

Julianilla. In *Entretenida* 3, the engraver's wife, who is just mentioned once.

Julio. In *Baños* 2, a Christian captive.

Julys [Julios]. In *DQ* II, 8, SP takes DQ's references to Julius Caesar to be a reference to the month named after him.

Juno. In Roman myth, the wife of Jupiter (in Greek myth, Hera, wife of Zeus). She was the goddess of marriage and protectress of married women. See *Casa* 2; *Galatea* 4; *Parnaso* 1.

Junquillos. In *Pedro* 2, the town in which the action of the play takes place. There is no location in Spain with this exact name, but there is a Yunclillos located north of Toledo and west of Aranjuez. It is very likely, however, that MC intended his work to take place in a fictional location.

Jupiter [Júpiter]. 1. In Roman myth, the highest and most powerful of the gods, equivalent to Zeus in Greek myth. Among other things, he was the god of weather and rain, responsible for thunder and lightning. See *Casa* 2; *DQ* II, 1; *Gitanilla*; *Numancia* 2, 4; *Parnaso* 1; *Poesías* 28. **2**. An allusion to the Duke of Lerma in a ballad sung by Preciosa in *Gitanilla*.

Just war [Guerra justa]. A concept that has attracted philosophers and politicians for centuries. Under what circumstances is it justified to go to war? Answers have varied through the centuries and are often contaminated by political expediency. When DQ addresses the townspeople during the episode of the *braying aldermen in II, 27, he suggests that there are four reasons when war is justified: to defend the Catholic faith; to defend your own life; to defend your honor, family, and property; and to serve your king in a just war. Going to war because you have been insulted certainly does not quality.

Justinian [Justiniano]: Flavius Petrus Sabbatius Justinianus (ca. 482–565). Roman emperor at Constantinople. He coordinated and codified Roman law throughout the empire and also authored many new laws; he also had hundreds of churches, aqueducts, and other municipal buildings constructed. See *Pedro* 1.

Justiniano, Licenciado Lucas. A priest and author of dramatic works; MC meets him upon his return to Madrid in *Parnaso* 8.

Justo. *Saint Justo and Saint Pastor.

Juvenal; Decimus Junius Juvenalis (second century CE**).** Roman poet. His brilliant satires are characterized by a bitter tone, ironic humor, and pessimism. See *DQ* II, 16.

Kafka, Franz (1883–1924). German novelist and short-story writer. The majority of Kafka's work was left unfinished at the time of his death and he had requested that it be destroyed. But his friend Max Brod saved, edited, and published it, thus making available some of the most profound, original, and influential works of the twentieth century. Most famous for his dark, existentialist, absurd novels *Der Prozess* (1925; *The Trial*) and *Das Schloss* (1926; *The Castle*), Kafka also wrote a brilliant short parable entitled "Die Wahrheit über Sancho Pansa" ("The Truth about Sancho Panza") published in *Beim bau der chinesischen mauer* (1931; *The Great Wall of China*). In it, SP dreams up and names DQ and then follows him enthusiastically. Kafka also prepared an outline for, but did not actually write, a sequel to *DQ* in which the knight was to visit southern France and northern Italy.

Bibliography: Manuel Durán, "Franz Kafka interpreta el *Quijote*," in *Homenaje al Profesor Antonio Vilanova*, 2 vols., eds. Adolf Sotelo and Marta C. Carbonell (Barcelona: Universidad de Barcelona, 1989), vol. 1, 217–28.

Karr, Phyllis Ann (1944–). American fantasy and romance writer. Karr's *My Lady Quixote* (1980) is a formulaic romance that features a protagonist who is compared to DQ by her lover Sir Rodric: "My Lady Quixote! Could you not have found a likelier Sancho Panza than such a hardened criminal as myself?" To this Cassandra responds, "Quixote, if you will, but, unlike the good don, I am going into action with my eyes open to reality and my plans well laid in advance." But these plans include a staged romantic kidnapping and other comparable adventures. Typical of the romance formula, the story has a happy ending with the traditional marriage of the heroine to her handsome and wealthy lover.

Kashner, Sam. American poet. Kashner's book of poems entitled *Don Quixote in America* (1997) includes just one poem, with the same title as the book, in which brief mention is made of SP.

Bibliography: Sam Kashner, *Don Quixote in America* (Brooklyn: Hanging Loose Press, 1997).

Kaüstrios [Caístro]. A river in Lydia (an ancient country in western Asia Minor) that empties into the Aegean Sea. It was famous for its swans and was much celebrated by poets. See *Parnaso* 8.

Kazantzakis, Nikos (1885–1957). Greek poet, novelist, and dramatist. Kazantzakis made three visits to Spain in the 1920s and 1930s, was a friend of Unamuno, and described MC as his favorite author. In the midst of these visits, Kazantzakis wrote a dramatic scenario with the title *Don Quixote* (1932), but the work was neither staged nor filmed. In his novel *Toda Raba* (1929), the character Genaros writes to his son: "As you know, Panteli, my own guide is none of the three great guides of the human soul: neither Faust nor Hamlet nor Don Quixote, but Don Ulysses!" Then in *Taxideuontas* (1933; *Spain*), which is filled with references to MC and DQ, Kazantzakis repeats the idea from his novel, that Ulysses, Faust, Hamlet, and DQ are "the four ruling princes of human souls" but later adds, "For perhaps of all the princes, Don Quixote most faithfully mirrors the fate of man." One of Kazantzakis's series of poetic cantos on the theme of his 'saviors of God' is

"Don Quixote" (1934), which presents a lonely, majestic, saintly DQ, or 'Captain Sole,' as he is called. In his monumental epic *Odysseia* (1938; *The Odyssey*), Homer's original hero has a new series of adventures in search of a 'newer world.' Along the way he encounters descendants of great figures such as Buddha, Christ, Faust, and DQ. Near the end of the poem, Odysseus encounters Captain Sole, who again dons his rusty armor and sallies forth on an old camel named Lightning (another reincarnation of Rocinante) in defense of humanity. After he is taken prisoner by cannibals and is about to be eaten, Captain Sole is rescued by Odysseus, who admires his idealistic determination before he goes on his way. Kazantzakis's best-known novel (and the subject of a famous film starring Anthony Quinn) is *Vios Kai Politeia Tau Alexi Zorba* (1946; *Zorba the Greek*), a work dedicated to SP. Zorba is an exuberant, SP-like lover of life in all its sensual pleasures, whereas the narrator is more DQ-like in his inhibitions and erudition. But each character has his own moral-philosophic idealism that he imparts to the other in an unusual symbiotic relationship that recalls (but does not simply replicate) that between DQ and SP. And finally, Kazantzakis's novel *Ho phtochoules tou Theou* (1956; *Saint Francis*) is yet another variation on the theme of religious quixotism. Here the intense, yet gentle and quixotic, Saint Francis is accompanied by Brother Leo, his practical and not very bright SP.

Bibliography: Jo Anne Englebert, "A Sancho for Saint Francis," *Hispania* 46 (1963): 287–89; Emmanuel Hatzantonis, "Captain Sole: Don Quijote's After-Image in Kazantzakis' Odyssey," *Hispania* 46 (1963): 283–86; Carlos Miralles Sola, "Casantsakis y España." *Arbor* 66, no. 256 (1967): 92–104; and Manuel Orgaz, "Don Quijote en Grecia," *Cuadernos Hispanoamericanos* 34 (1958): 368–70.

Kemble, Charles. *Dieulafoy, Michel.

Kern, Alfred (1919–). French novelist. Kern's *Le Clown* (1957; *The Clown*) features Hans, the clown of the title, who reads *DQ* and compares its main characters to himself: "I was fat, I was thin, servant and knight, figure of fun

and cynic, turn and turn about, and in my adventures Elise [his DT] played a part. . . . Did I not see our display windows, the nickel-plated handrails of our stairs, as so many windmills, as so many ships' gangways?" Near the end of the novel, when another character, Hermann, says of Hans that he is "ever tilting at windmills," Hans responds, "As simple-minded as that? Well, perhaps I am. But don't forget that I am also Sancho Panza. It is you, I should say, who are Don Quixote, with your thin arms and your grubby cuffs." The combination of SP and DQ in a single character here recalls *Daudet's Tartarin, but in fact, in spite of Hans's statements, he is only a marginally quixotic (or sanchesque) figure.

Kesey, Ken (1935–2001). American novelist. The novel that brought wide recognition to Kesey (and which was made into a popular film starring Jack Nicholson) is *One Flew over the Cuckoo's Nest* (1962). As the hero, R. P. McMurphy, gets increasingly caught up in his quixotic quest of defeating Big Nurse et al. in the mental institution, he brings increasing self-awareness and self-reliance to the other mental patients, especially to the narrator, Chief Broom. By the time he is lobotomized at the end of the novel, the others (like SP by the time of DQ's renunciation of chivalry and his death) have matured to the point where they are individually and collectively able to carry on his quest.

Khios [Xío]. An island in the Aegean Sea, off the west coast of Turkey and south of the island of Lesbos. See *Amante*.

Kienzel, Wilhelm. Austrian musician. Kienzel wrote both the libretto and the music for the opera *Don Quixote* (1898), which ambitiously attempts to present aspects of the entire novel and not just certain scenes, such as the *Cardenio* story or SP's governorship.

Kierkegaard, Søren (1813–55). Danish philosopher. Kierkegaard was apparently the first person to compare DQ to Christ. He wrote that in an increasingly secular world, "The only remaining conception of what it is to be Christian will be the portrayal of Christ, the disciples, and others as comic figures. They will be counterparts of Don Quixote, a man who had a firm notion that the world is evil." Kierkegaard's 'knight of the faith' had to be an essentially quixotic figure. He also compared the biblical Abraham to DQ (recalling Fielding's quixotic Abraham Adams).

King [Rey]. In *Pedro* 2, the monarch who visits Junquillos for a celebration and attempts to arrange a tryst with Belica but is thwarted by his jealous wife.

King Midas's reeds. *Midas.

King of Alpujarras [Rey de las Alpujarras]. Probably a reference to a leader of the *Morisco* rebellion, in reaction to increased efforts to make the *Moriscos* conform to Christianity and integrate more fully into mainstream Spanish society, centered in the *Alpujarras mountains near Granada in 1568.

King of France [Rey de Francia]. Dogs were sometimes trained to jump when they were commanded to do so for the 'king of France' but not for the 'innkeeper's bad wife.' The term is thus often used to refer to blind obedience. See *Celoso, Coloquio.*

King Perico's Dance. *Perico.

Kingdom of Granada. *Granada.

Kings, Book of [Libro de los reyes]. In the Old Testament, two books that describe the reigns of the Hebrew kings after David. See *DQ* I, prologue.

King's Garden [Huerta del Rey, Güerta del Rey]. **1**. In *Fregona*, the abundantly irrigated royal gardens of Toledo. **2**. In *Rinconete*, a royal garden on the outskirts of Seville.

Kissing a Fool. A film (1998) that reproduces the basic plot of *Curioso*, but (as suggested by the priest in *DQ* I, 36) in the context of an engagement, rather than a marriage. Max (David Schwimmer, the Anselmo figure) convinces his best friend Jay (Jason Lee, the equivalent of

Lotario) to test the faithfulness of Samantha (Mili Avital, Camila). Jay resists but is convinced, falls in love with Sam, and winds up marrying her. There is no indication that the rewrite of MC's story is intentional, but the parallels are obvious.

Kitchen-boys [Pícaros de cocina]. In *DQ* II, 32, the servants at the duke's palace who try to wash SP's beard with dirty dishwater.

Knight [Caballero]. One of the members of the cast of *Las *Cortes de la Muerte* in *DQ* II, 11.

Knight of Death [Caballero de la Muerte]. A name used by Amadís de Grecia. In *DQ* I, 19, it is mentioned by DQ as a name parallel to his own Caballero de la Triste Figura.

Knight of the Burning Sword [Caballero de la Ardiente Espada]. A name taken by Amadís de Grecia, hero of Feliciano de *Silva's romance of that name, because of a red birthmark in the shape of a sword on his chest. In *DQ* I, 1, DQ considers him a better knight-errant than the great (historical) chivalric hero Cid Ruy *Díaz de Vivar. In I, 18, DQ seems to confuse the enchanted sword won by Amadís de Gaula, who is at one point known as the Knight of the Green Sword (Caballero de la Verde Espada), with the name of his grandson Amadís de Grecia, as described above. In *DQ* I, 19, the name is mentioned by DQ as one parallel to his own Caballero de la Triste Figura.

Knight of the Forest [Caballero del Bosque]. **1**. In *DQ* I, 24, a name used in narration to refer to Cardenio. **2**. In *DQ* II, 12, the first name by which the narrator refers, during the night, to *Sansón Carrasco when he goes out in disguise to encounter DQ. The next day, after the sun rises and DQ can see that his opponent is dressed in armor covered with small mirrors, the narrator calls him the Knight of the Mirrors (Caballero de los Espejos) (II, 14). Neither DQ nor any other character ever uses either of these names. See also *DQ* II, 16, 56, 65, 67, 70.

Knight of the Green Overcoat [Caballero del Verde Gabán]. In *DQ* II, 16–17, the name that, according to the narrator, DQ uses for Don *Diego de Miranda; however, no utterance by DQ or any other character includes the name.

Knight of the Griffin [Caballero del Grifo]. A name used by the protagonist of *Filesbián de Candaria* (1542), a romance of chivalry only recently discovered. In *DQ* I, 19, it is mentioned by DQ as a name parallel to his own Caballero de la Triste Figura. For many years, commentators of *DQ* identified the name as that taken by the count of Aremberg in a historical joust in 1549, but it is not very likely that MC would have known of this precedent.

Knight of the Lake [Caballero del Lago]. In I, 50, DQ illustrates the stylistic and thematic excellence of the romances of chivalry by telling the canon of Toledo and others traveling with them the adventure of a knight who dives into a lake of boiling pitch and finds an enchanted palace at the bottom of the lake. In some ways, this episode anticipates some of the events of the Cave of Montesinos in II, 23.

Knight of the Lions [Caballero de los Leones]. The new name DQ takes for himself after the adventure of the *lion in II, 17. In this, DQ imitates the knights-errant of the romances of chivalry who frequently adopted a new name after a significant event in their lives. Amadís de Gaula is one of those who specifically takes the name Knight of the Lions, as do other knights in *Palmerín de Olivia*, *Primaleón*, and *Belianís de Grecia*. See also *DQ* II, 19, 27, 34.

Knight of the Maidens [Caballero de las Doncellas]. A name used by Florandino de Macedonia in *El Caballero de la Cruz*. In *DQ* I, 19, it is mentioned by DQ as a name parallel to his own Caballero de la Triste Figura.

Knight of the Mournful Countenance [Caballero de la Triste Figura]. In *DQ* I, 19, the name given to DQ by SP after the successful adventure of the dead body. For SP, the name reflects the sad-looking visage DQ presents, with its lean and bony configuration accentuated by the recent loss of teeth in the stoning following the adventure of the armies of sheep. For DQ, it reflects, as he explains at some length, the practice of knights-errant of taking a new and significant name after an important adventure. The name is also one used by Prince Deocliano, whose shield is adorned with the figure of a beautiful but tearful maiden, in the anonymous romance, of chivalry entitled *Clarián de Landanís* (whose first part was published in 1518). MC never mentions this romance and it is possible that his use of the name is coincidental. What is certain is that SP does not know the romance (although he may well be familiar with such chivalric renaming in general) and invents the name as appropriate to DQ's looks. Since *triste figura* literally means 'sad- (or sorry- or miserable-) looking face,' Shelton's original translation of the phrase as 'Knight of the Ill-Favoured Face' is quite accurate. More recent English translations like 'Mournful Countenance' or 'Sorrowful Figure' are less successful in capturing the humor and tend to reinforce the romantic reading of the novel. See also *DQ* II, 27.

    Bibliography: A. F. Michael Atlee, "En torno a una frase del *Quijote*: El Caballero de la Triste Figura," *Anales Cervantinos* 20 (1982): 49–57.

Knight of the Phoenix [Caballero del Ave Fénix]. A name used by Florarlán de Tracia in *Florisel de Niquea*. In *DQ* I, 19, it is mentioned by DQ as a name parallel to his own Caballero de la Triste Figura.

Knight of the Red Cross. *Saint James the Great.

Knight of the Serpent [Caballero de la Sierpe]. A name used by Palmerín de Olivia. Esplandián, son of Amadís, was also called the Caballero de la Serpiente. See *DQ* I, 21.

Knight of the Sun [Caballero del Sol]. A name assumed by the Caballero del Febo (*Ordóñez de Calahorra, Diego de). See *DQ* I, 21.

Knight of the Unicorn [Caballero del Unicornio]. One of the names assumed by both Belianís de Grecia and Ruggiero in *Orlando Furioso*. In *DQ* I, 19, it is mentioned by DQ as a name parallel to his own Caballero de la Triste Figura.

Knight of the White Moon. *Sansón Carrasco.

Knights of La Mancha; Knights of Navarra. *Spanish knights.

Knights who remain at court. *Courtly knights and knights-errant.

Knowles, John (1926–). American novelist. Knowles's *A Separate Peace* (1959) tells the story of the relationship between two boys and the private reality they create for themselves. The imaginative and rhetorically convincing Phineas is DQ to the more intellectual Gene's SP. Phineas convinces his friend that there is no such thing as World War II: "That's what this whole war story is. A medicinal drug . . . the preachers and the old ladies and all the stuffed shirts . . . tried Prohibition and everybody just got drunker, so then they really got desperate and arranged the Depression. They kept the people who were young in the thirties in their places. But they couldn't use that trick forever, so for us in the forties they've cooked up this war fake." Later in life, Gene looks nostalgically back upon the "liberation we had torn from the gray encroachments of 1943, the escape we had concocted, this afternoon of momentary, illusory, special and separate peace."

Komroff, Manuel (1890–?). American dramatist. Komroff's play *Don Quixote and Sancho* (1942) brings to the stage an extraordinarily high number of characters, scenes, incidents, and quotations or paraphrases from MC's text. The play's 13 scenes are jammed with rapid action and dialogue. Most of the scenes from the novel are presented in what amounts to outline form, cutting away all nuance and much detail; others are curious and sometimes quite interesting syncretic versions in which elements from (sometimes radically) different parts of the novel are juxtaposed. In a climactic scene, for example, the Bachelor Carrasco (fiancé of DQ's niece) enlists the aid of DQ's household, his friends the curate and the barber, and the duke and duchess to stage the defeat of DQ. Overall, this romantic version of *DQ* is one of the more ambitious attempts literally to transform the novel to the stage.

Bibliography: Manuel Komroff, *Don Quixote and Sancho* (New York: John Day, 1942).

Konigsberg, Ira. Theorist of the novel. Konigsberg's opening words in his book *Narrative Technique in the English Novel* (1985) are "Defoe, Richardson, and Fielding, the first major novelists . . ." It is thus clear that Konigsberg never calls into question the assumption that the novel is a new genre that rises for the first time in eighteenth-century England. Although Konigsberg distinguishes perceptively between the cognitive acts of watching a play or film and reading a novel, he errs in affirming that such reading experiences "were not possible with earlier fiction" for three reasons: "such works did not (1) deal with concerns and a fictional world realistic and credible enough to relate to the reader's own life, (2) depict events and characters with sufficient specificity to allow the reader an internal visual experience, or (3) describe psychological states in a credible way that permitted the reader to internalize the thought processes of the character." Since all of these aspects of the experience of fiction were abundantly present in the Spanish picaresque and quixotic fiction of the sixteenth- and seventeenth-centuries, Konigsberg's thesis that "the novel was a response to a new awareness of individual perception and to the growing sense that this was the domain of art" becomes untenable. In his brief, passing comments on DQ, Konigsberg consistently groups it with Scarron's *Roman comique* and refers to it as a "comic romance."

Bibliography: Ira Konigsberg, *Narrative Technique in the English Novel* (Hamden, CT: Archon Books, 1985).

Konrad Korzeniowski, Teodor Jozef. *Conrad, Joseph.

Korneichukov, N. I. *Chukovsky, Kornei.

Kosinski, Jerzy (1933–91). Polish émigré to the United States; novelist and essayist. If books are the source of DQ's fantasy, television provides material of life for the autistic Chance, protagonist of Kosinski's slim novel (made into a brilliant film starring Peter Sellers) *Being There* (1971). In all his spare time the illiterate Chance, who works as a gardener, watches television: "By turning the dial, Chance could bring others inside his eyelids. Thus he came to believe that it was he, Chance, and no one else, who made himself be." When his employer dies, Chance has to go out into the world for the first time and has difficulty dealing with reality until he is "adopted" by a powerful business magnate and is incongruously and absurdly perceived as a genius named Chauncy Gardner: "Chance noticed that she had changed his name. He assumed that, as on TV, he must use his new name from now on." His simplistic utterances are perceived as profound, oracular pronouncements, and he gains national prominence as an advisor to entrepreneurs and politicians. Although he does not understand what is happening to him, Chance "did not have to be afraid, for everything that happened had its sequel, and the best that he could do was to wait patiently for his own forthcoming appearance." Kosinski's hero is one of the more original and compelling of all twentieth-century DQs.

Kotzwinkle, William (1938–). American novelist. Kotzwinkle's *Jack in the Box* (1980) is about Jack Twiller, a teenage boy who lives constantly in the worlds of radio drama, the comics, and the movies. As the Masked Rider astride his invisible horse, he struggles constantly to keep the reality of what his mother and others says from spoiling his fantasy. Moving in and out of roles, struggling with the mysteries of sex, and growing up in an often cruel world, Jack is a perfect young DQ.

Krohn, Leena (1947–). Finnish poet, critic, and writer of fiction. Krohn is one of the most respected poets of late-twentieth-century Finland. Her book entitled *Donna Quijote ja muita kaupunkilaisia* (1983; *Doña Quijote and Other Citizens*) consists of 30 brief sections in which the ethereal figure of a woman known only as Doña Quijote is evoked. The unidentified narrator and the tall, straw-thin, fragile Doña Quijote meet and talk frequently, commenting on other people, places, events, and abstract subjects such as the nature of time. The work is fragmented, evoking and/or describing a number of other characters—some schoolgirls, the Looking-Glass Boy, a watchseller—buildings, and places.

Bibliography: Leena Krohn, *Donna Quijote and Other Citizens: Gold of Ophir*, trans. Heidi Hawkins (London: Carcanet, 1995).